French
Fairy Tales

Essays on a Major Literary Tradition

Edited by
Denyse Delcourt

cognella
San Diego, CA

First published in the United States of America in 2011 by Cognella, a division of University Readers, Inc.

15 14 13 12 11   1 2 3 4 5

Printed in the United States of America

ISBN: 978–1–60927–975–2

www.cognella.com 800.200.3908

Contents

Chapter IV: Walt Disney and French Fairy Tales

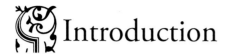 Introduction

This collection of essays is an exploration of a major French literary tradition still greatly influential in modern life, literature and films. The study of fairy tales has benefited from a wide variety of approaches. Sociologists, anthropologists, literary critics, psychologists, and historians have all shown in their own informed ways the importance of fairy tales as a genre as well as their complexities. Choosing which essays to include in this anthology was not an easy task, and omissions are to be expected. I have given preference to the most recent and at times, most provocative scholarship on French fairy tales. One of my goals has been to introduce American readers to previously unknown or lesser known French fairy tales.

Fairy tales have a long history. In classical Antiquity,"old wives tales" already played an important role in children's lives. Passed on from one generation to the next, they were meant to entertain and to educate. In Book III of the *Republic* Plato conceded that stories told to children may contain some truth and, as such, be included in education. For Plato, fictions directed at children should be closely monitored; anything gloomy or blatantly untrue such as ghosts, corpses, and spirits should be eliminated; and lies have no place in tales told to the "too easily molded" children.

It is dubious that what Plato considered as lies were perceived as such by the generation of women who recounted these tales. As many of the authors included in this anthology will attest,"old wives tales," folktales, and/or fairy tales reveal something profoundly true about human nature. If children are so fascinated by fairy tales, it is in part because they are able to recognize themselves in them. The unloved child, the princess, the clever cat, and even the terrible ogre, are all manifestations of who children at times may feel themselves to be. In that sense, fairy tales act as children's mirrors, or to quote Horace's famous definition of literature, *De te fabula narratur* [the story applies to you], fairy tales children hear or read are always about them.

Because storytelling is so closely associated with women and domesticity, it is not surprising that tales meant for children came to be linked to the traditional feminine activities of weaving, knitting, and spinning. This is well exemplified in everyday language in expressions such as "spinning a tale," "weaving a plot," and "losing or finding one's thread," to name a few. Through the figures of the weaving Fates, the close connection between storytelling and human lives is made very clear. In Greek and Latin mythology, the three Fates weave the thread of life until the time comes for one of them to cut it. It is worth recalling here the etymological root of the word "fate" from the past participle of the Latin verb "fari," which means to speak. The Fates are those who have the power to "speak" men and women's stories. For a long time, female storytellers will also "speak" their stories, using their voice to transmit the tales that they themselves once heard.

During the reign of Louis XIV, several of these orally transmitted "old wives tales" were put into writing. As Jack Zipes and others have shown, the bourgeois and highly educated Charles Perrault played a major role in "civilizing" the oral folktales. One of the most prominent authors of fairy tales of that period, Charles Perrault, respectfully acknowledged his debt to the nannies, mothers, and grandmothers who had kept these stories alive. This said, Perrault made sure readers understood that his tales were not exactly the same as those in Mother Goose. Both were meant to please, but his contain a more serious component. Following each of Perrault's tales, a "Moralité" written in verse extracts and expresses the lessons one should have learned from the reading. Not surprisingly, these lessons reflect the social values of the Christian upper class for which Perrault was writing.

Written in a period of absolutism when France was setting standards of *civilité* for the rest of Europe, fairy tales became vehicles for the dissemination of the male-oriented Christian definition of civil order that permeated all aspects of social life at the time.[1] How the France of Louis XIV informed the representation of nobility, religion, marriage, and family in 17th century literary fairy tales is the topic of Dorothy Thelander's fine article reproduced in this anthology.

Most of the essays herein argue for a contextual reading of French fairy tales. However, the particular aspect of 17th century France deemed significant varies from one author to the next. For the historian Robert Darnton, for example, fairy tales reflect not so much the values of the French upper class as those of the peasants'. Intended for peasants, Darnton writes, French oral tales, upon which many 17th century literary fairy tales are based, are not simply works of imagination, but are expressions of the peasants' hopes and struggles in France's Old Regime. While supporting Darnton's historical reading, Catherine Orenstein advocates for a broader approach. She revisits the "The Grandmother's Tale," a folktale version of "Little Red Riding Hood" analyzed by Darnton in his essay. Whereas Darnton focuses on the unsavory details contained in this version (cannibalism; defecation; promiscuity) to support his theory, Orenstein stresses the importance of examining the tale's broader folkloric patterns, contending that only by looking at oral and literary tales' global pattern can we account for their broader, older, and deeper meanings.

In a recent book on the history of French fairy tales, Ruth Bottingheimer questions the belief that Charles Perrault and many of his contemporaries obtained their stories from peasant women.[2] Instead of looking for oral antecedents for French 17th century fairy tales, Bottingheimer argues that scholars should focus on their literary antecedents, most particularly on Giambattista Basile and Giovan Francesco Straparola's influential books of fairy tales published in Italy during the 16th and 17th centuries.

The French fairy tales considered in this anthology were all written between 1690 and 1715 – except Madame Leprince de Beaumont's *Beauty and the Beast* published in 1757. It is worth mentioning that it was women who wrote the vast majority of French fairy tales during 17th century making Charles Perrault an exception. French aristocratic women, and sometimes men, met in "salons littéraires" to exchange ideas and to discuss the tales they had written. In an era of absolutism, the salons were a woman's arena, distinct and separate from the royal court, where they could more freely express their ideas and question social values. Lewis Seifert was one of the first scholars to consider 17th century women's attraction to fairy tales within the historical and literary context of the time.[3] Elizabeth Wanning Harries's essay selected here uses Seifert's scholarship to further examine French women's contribution to the genre with a special emphasis on the differences between their and Perrault's fairy tales. In her article on the prolific fairy tale writer, Madame d'Aulnoy, Marcy Farrell explores the various strategies and compromises the female characters in her tales have to make in order to survive in a male-dominated world. Discussing Madame d'Aulnoy's tales as well as those of other 17th century French women writers, Anne Duggan gives special consideration to the utopian elements often present in their fairy tales.

For many women writers of the time, fairy tales were a means to criticize the role society expected them to play, and to create visions of a better world. How marriage trapped or enslaved women was an issue often addressed in their stories. Contrary to Perrault, many women writers expressed their doubts concerning the heroines' hasty marriages, proposing instead a long period of courtship during which men and women got to know each other. In their views, good marriages are based on mutual respect and understanding, and need to be nurtured. In several of the fairy tales written by women, the traditional ending "they lived happily ever after"

---

1   Jack Zipes. Fairy Tales and the Art of Subversion: The Classical Genre for Children and the Process of Civilization. New York: Routledge, 2006. 9.

2   Ruth Bottingheimer, Fairy Tales: A New History. New York: State University, 2009.

3   Lewis C. Seifert. *Fairy Tales. Sexuality and Gender in France*, 1690–1715: *Nostalgic Utopias*. Cambridge: Cambridge University, 1996.

is either absent or else qualified. In *The Discreet Princess* written by Mlle L'Héritier, for example, the prince and princess after their marriage retain the "greatest tenderness for each other and spent a long succession of beautiful days in happiness."[4] In *The Blue Bird* by Madame d'Aulnoy, the happy marriage is the result of the couple together overcoming many years of hardship. And in Madame de Murat's *Palace of Revenge*, the prince and princess who are at first extremely happy together come to realize that "even of bliss human hearts could tire,"[5] and that marriage is far from being idyllic.

Close reading of several of the most famous French fairy tales is well represented in this collection of essays. Carolyn Fay analyses Charles Perrault's *Sleeping Beauty* from a literary perspective whereas Bettina Knapp uses a Jungian approach. Marina Warner shares her usual brilliant insights on the wicked stepmother figuring in Perrault's version of the tale. Louis Marin and Jack Zipes consider respectively the signs of power and the civilizing process in *The Master Cat, or Puss in Boots*. Catherine Orenstein focuses on the folktale version of *Little Red Riding Hood* while Graham Anderson examines the tale's disturbing message to young girls; and Jerry Griswold and Joan Gould each reveal from their individual perspectives the many meanings of *Beauty and the Beast*.

Even though Europeans have known Charles Perrault's *Donkey Skin* and *Bluebeard* since childhood, American have for the most part never heard of these fairy tales. One could explain this discrepancy by the fact that their storyline involves respectively a father's incestuous desire for his daughter and a male character who happens to be a serial killer of women. In 17th century, *Donkey Skin* epitomized the genre of the fairy tale. The expression "un Peau d'Âne" like in "entendre ou écrire un 'Peau d'Âne'" [to listen to or write a 'Donkey Skin'] was synonymous to "fairy tale." I have chosen two essays to introduce Perrault's *Donkey Skin*. Philip Lewis's long article stresses the importance of food and consumption in *Donkey Skin* while outlining the larger historical context in which Perrault's writing of fairy tales took root, and Maria Tatar's essay proposes new ways of looking at the role played by the tyrannical family in both *Donkey Skin* and *Cinderella*.

In "Butchering Girls," "Monstrous Wives," and "Bluebeard and the Destructive Animus," the scholars Graham Anderson, Maria Tatar, and Verena Kast each write in depth analysis of Perrault's *Bluebeard*. During the 20th and 21st centuries, this disturbing tale has been made into films (the most recent one appeared in France in 2009), music (Béla Bartok's 1911 opera, *Bluebeard's Castle*), and novels. Mary Kaiser acknowledges the special place occupied by Bluebeard in the European imagination in her reading of Angela Carter's 1979 version of this tale entitled *The Bloody Chamber*.

In addition to critical essays, this anthology contains Jack Zipes's beautiful English translations of several 17th century French fairy tales. The fairy tales selected are either lesser known to American readers or known only in later versions such as those of the Brothers Grimm. Charles Perrault's *Donkey Skin* and *Bluebeard* are reproduced here in full. Perrault's original versions of *Little Red Riding Hood* and *Sleeping Beauty* included herein will surprise, and perhaps even shock, many readers. Finally, translations of Madame d'Aulnoy's *The Green Serpent* and Catherine Bernard's *Riquet with the Tuft* will give readers a chance to acquaint themselves with fairy tales written by French women during the 17th century.

It would be a mistake to overlook the fact that Walt Disney's animated movies based on French fairy tales have shaped the way most American think about these tales.[6] As a teacher of fairy tales, I have had not only to come to terms with this fact, but also to try to find ways to utilize students' beliefs that Disney's versions of fairy tales were, indeed, the "original" ones. As a point of reference, Disney's movies have proven to be very useful. Although at first shocked by the differences between Perrault and Disney's versions of *Sleeping Beauty*,

---

4   Marie-Jeanne l'Héritier, *The Discreet Princess, or The Adventures of Finette*. Jack Zipes, trans. *Beauty and the Beast, and Other Classic French Fairy Tales*. Crescent Moon Publishing: 2009. 92.

5   Henriette Julie de Murat, *The Palace of Revenge*. Zipes, trans. 123.

6   On this topic, see Naomi Wood, "Domesticating Dreams in Walt Disney's *Cinderella*." *The Lion and the Unicorn* 20.1 (1996): 25–49.

students came to realize that fairy tales are a very adaptive genre. They discovered that to make sense of fairy tales, one has to consider the time and place in which they were created as well as the audience for which they were intended. This is exactly what Robert Darnton prescribed for the study of fairy tales in his essay mentioned above. Numerous books and articles have recently been published on Walt Disney's rendering of French fairy tales. Critics from film, literary, and cultural studies have analyzed Disney's movies and their effects on global culture using different, and at time complementary, perspectives. The pioneer fairy tale scholar, Jack Zipes, was one of the first to discuss the "spell" casted by Disney on our understanding of fairy tales, and how to break it. Because of its importance in the field of fairy tale studies, I have chosen to include Zipes' essay in this anthology. Included also is Mark Axelrod's excellent article on Walt Disney's *Beauty and the Beast* and other French fairy tales with a special emphasis on the motherless heroines.

I offer this anthology as an invitation to discover new fairy tales and to revisit and reevaluate the fairy tales readers may have heard or read in childhood. May the reader experience them anew with a deeper and richer sense of wonder.

# Selected Bibliography

Anderson, Graham. *Fairy Tale in the Ancient World.* New York: Routledge, 2000

Axelrod, Mark,"Beauties and their Beasts & Other Motherless Tales from the Wonderful World of Walt Disney." *The Emperor's Old Groove: Decolonizing Disney's Magic Kingdom.* Ed. Brenda Hines. New York: Peter Lang, 2003. 29–38.

Barcher, Suzanne,"Beyond Disney: Reading and Writing Traditional and Alternative Fairy Tales." *The Lion and the Unicorn*, vol.12, number 2 (December 1988): 135–150.

Barchilon, Jacques, *Le Conte merveilleux français: de 1690 à 170, cent ans de féerie et de poésie ignorées de l'histoire littéraire.* Paris: Champion, 1975.

Beale, Hazel,"Framing the Fairy Tale: French Fairy Tales and Frame Narratives 1690–1700." *Framed! Essays in French Studies.* Ed. Lucy Bolton. New York: Peter Lang, 2007. 73–90.

Bell, Elizabeth, Lynda Haas, and Laura Sells, eds. *From Mouse to Mermaid: the Politics of Film, Gender, and Culture.* Indiana University Press, 1995.

Belmont, Nicole,"Poétique du conte. Essai sur le conte de tradition orale." *Annales. Histoires, Sciences Sociales.* Vol. 56 (4–5), 2001: 1022–23.

Bettelheim, Bruno. *The Uses of Enchantment: The Meaning and Importance of Fairy Tales.* New York: Vintage Books, 1989.

Bohn, Roswitha,"La participation des *fées modernes* à la création d'une mémoire féminine." *Les femmes au grand siècle, le baroque : musique et littérature, musique et liturgie.* Actes du Colloque de la Seventeenth-Century French Literature, tome II, Arizona State University, Tempe, May 2001, vol.2

Bottigheimer, Ruth. *Fairy Tales. A New History.* New York: State University Press, 2009.
Brocklebank, Lisa. "Rebellious Voices: The Unofficial Discourse of Cross-dressing in d'Aulnoy, de Murat, and Perrault." *Children's Literature Association Quarterly*, 25 (2000) : 127–36.

Butor, Michel,"On Fairy Tales." *European Literary Theory and Practice.* Ed. Vernon W. Gras. New York: Delta, 1973: 174–180.

Cadars, Pierre,"La Barbe Bleue: Secrets et mensonges." *L'Esprit et la lettre.* Ed. François-Charles Gaudard. Toulouse: Presses Universitaires du Mirail, 1999. 59–66.

Carter, Angela. *Little Red Riding Hood, Cinderella, and other Fairy Tales of Charles Perrault*. New York: Penguin Books, 2008.

Cashdan, Sheldon. *The Witch Must Die: The Hidden Meaning of Fairy Tales*. New York: Basic Books, 1999.

Constantinescu, M.,"Les lieux dans les contes de Perrault et dans certaines de leurs réécritures." In Pascale Auraix-Jonchière et Alain Maintenon, eds. Poétique des lieux. *Cahiers de Recherches sur les Littératures Modernes et Contemporaines*. Eds. Pascale Auraix-Jonchière et Alain Maintenon. Université Blaise-Pascal, 2004.

Darnton, Robert. "Peasants Tell Tales. The Meaning of Mother Goose." *The Great Cat Massacre and Other Episodes in French Cultural History*. New York: Basic Books,1984. 9–72.

Defrance, Anne. *Les Contes de fées et les nouvelles de Mme d'Aulnoy (1690–1698): L'Imaginaire féminin à rebours de la tradition*. Genève: Droz, 1998.

Defrance, Anne,"La réfraction des sciences dans les contes de fées." *Féeries* 6 (2009).

DeGraff, Amy Vanderlyn. *The Tower and the Well: A Psychological Interpretation of the Fairy Tales of Madame d'Aulnoy*. Birmingham: Summa Publications, 1984.

Delarue, Paul,"Les contes merveilleux de Perrault et la tradition populaire.» *Bulletin folklorique de l'Île-de-France*, 1951–1953.

Do Rozario, Rebecca-Anne,"The Princess and the Magic Kingdom: Beyond Nostalgia, the Function of the Disney Princess." *Women's Studies in Communication* vol.27, number 1 (Spring 2004): 34–59.

Duggan, Anne E.,"Feminine Genealogy, Matriarchy, and Utopia in the Fairy Tales of Marie-Catherine d'Aulnoy." *Neophilologus* (1998): 199–208.

Duggan, Anne E.,"Nature et Culture in the Fairy Tale of Marie-Catherine d'Aulnoy." *Marvels & Tales* 15:2 (2001): 149–67.

Duggan, Anne E., *Salonnières, Furies and Fairies: the Politics of Gender and Cultural Change in Absolutist France*. Newark: University of Delaware Press, 2005.

Duggan, Anne E.,"Women Subdued: The Abjectification and Purification of Female Characters in Perrault's Tales." *Romanic Review* 99, number 3–4 (2008): 211–226.

Dundes, Alan, ed. *Cinderella: A Casebook*. Madison: University of Wisconsin Press, 1982.

Dundes, Alan, ed. *Little Red Riding Hood: A Casebook*. Madison: University of Wisconsin Press, 1989.

Farrell, Marcy,"The Heroine Violent Compromise: Two Fairy Tales by Madame d'Aulnoy." *Violence in French and Francophone Literature and Film*. Ed. James Day. Rodopi: 2008. 27–38.

Fay, Carolyn,"Sleeping Beauty Must Die: The Plots of Perrault's 'La Belle au bois dormant.'" *Marvels & Tales*, vol.22, number 2 (2008): 260–276.

Franz, Marie-Luise, von. *The Feminine in Fairy Tales*. Revised Ed. Boston: Shambhala, 1993.

Franz, Marie-Luise, von. *The Interpretation of Fairy Tales*. Boston: Shambhala, 1996.

Fumaroli, Marc,"Les Enchantements de l'éloquence. Les Fées de Charles Perrault." *Le Statut de la littérature. Mélanges offerts à Paul Bénichou.* Ed. Marc Fumaroli. Genève: Droz, 1982. 152–186.

Griswold, Jerry. *The Meanings of 'Beauty and the Beast': A Handbook*. Peterborough: Broadway Press, 2004.

Haase, Donald. *Fairy Tales and Feminism: New Approaches*. Detroit: Wayne University Press: 2004.

Hannon, Patricia,"Antithesis and Ideology in Perrault's 'Riquet à la Houppe'." *Cahiers du Dix-septième Siècle* vol. 4, numéro 2 (1990): 105–118.

Hannon, Patricia. *Fabulous Identities: Women's Fairy Tales in Seventeenth-century France*. Atlanta: Rodopi, 1998.

Harf-Lancner, Laurence. *Les Fées au moyen-âge: Morgane et Mélusine; la naissance des fées*. Genève: Slatkine, 1984.

Harries, Elizabeth Wanning. *Twice upon a Time: Women Writers and the History of the Fairy Tale*. Princeton: Princeton University Press, 2001.

Harries, Elizabeth Wanning. "The Violence of the Lambs." *Marvels & Tales*, 19 (2005): 54–66.

Hearne, Betsy,"Beauty and the Beast: Visions and Revisions of an Old Tale." *The Lion and the Unicorn*, vol.12, number 2 (December 1988): 74–111.

Hermansson, Casie. *Bluebeard: A Reader's Guide to the English Tradition*. Jackson: University Press of Mississippi, 2009.

Hoffman, Kathryn,"Of Monkey Girls and Hog-Faced Gentlewomen: Marvels in Fairy Tales." *Journal of Fairy Tales Studies*, vol. 19 (2005): 67–85.

Jasmin, Nadine. *Naissance du conte féminin: Mots et merveilles: Les contes de fées de Madame d'Aulnoy, 1690–1698*. Paris: H. Champion, 2002.

Jacoby, Mario, Verena Kast, and Ingrid Riedel, eds. *Witches, Ogres, and the Devil's Daughter : Encounters with Evil in Fairy Tales.* Boston : Shambhala , 1992.

Jones, Christine,"The Poetics of Enchantment." *Marvels & Tales*, vol.17, number 1 (2003): 55–74.

Jones, Steven Swann. *The Fairy Tale: The Magic Mirror of the Imagination*. New York: Routledge, 2002.

Keeling, Kara K. and Scott T. Pollard, eds. *Critical Approaches to Food in Children's Literature*. New York: Routledge, 2009.

Keyser, Elizabeth. "Feminist Revisions: Frauds on the Fairies?" *Children's Literature*, vol. 17, (1989): 156–170.

Le Marchand, Berenice Virginie. "Reframing the Early French Fairy Tale: A Selected Bibliography." *Marvels & Tales*, Volume 19, Number 1 (2005) : 86–122

Lewis, Philip E. *Seeing through the Mother Goose Tales: Visual Turns in the Writing of Charles Perrault*. Stanford: Stanford U. Press, 1996.

Loskoutoff, Yvan. *La sainte et la fée. Dévotion de l'Enfant Jésus et mode des contes merveilleux à la fin du règne de Louis XIV*. Genève: Droz, 1987.

Mainil, Jean. *Madame d'Aulnoy et le rire des fées: Essais sur la subversion féerique et le merveilleux comique sous l'Ancien Régime*. Paris: Kime, 2001.

Mansau, Andrée, ed. *Enfance et littérature au XVIIe siècle*. Paris: Klincksieck, 1991.

Monjaret, Anne, "De l'épingle à l'aiguille: L'éducation des jeunes filles au fil des contes." *L'Homme* 2005/1 (no 173)

Marin, Louis. "Puss-in Boots: Power of Signs. Signs of Power." *Diacritics* vol.7, no 2 (Summer 1977): 54–63.

Marin, Louis, "Les Enjeux d'un frontispice." *L'Esprit Créateur*, vol. 27, no 3 (1987): 49–57.

Marin, Louis. *Food for Thought*. Mette Hjort, trans. Baltimore: The Johns Hopkins University Press, 1997.

Méchoulan, Eric, "The Embodiment of Culture: Fairy Tales of the Body in the 17th and 18th Centuries." *Romanic Review* (Nov. 1992): 427–36.

Neeman, Harold. *Piercing the Magic Veil: Toward a Theory of the Conte*. Tubingen: Gunter Narr, 1999.

Neeman, Harold, "Marvelous Heroines in Seventeeth-Century French Fairy Tales." *The Image of the Hero in Literature, Media, and Society*. Eds. Will Wright and Steven Kaplan. Pueblo, CO: Colorado State University, 2004. 99–102.

Neefs, Jacques, and Jean M. Goulemot, eds. "Imaginaires de L'Enfance : *MLN: Modern Language Notes*, 117, no. 4 (Sept. 2002).

Nouilhan, Michele, "De Midas à Peau d'Ane ou de l'or à l'ordure." *Pallas: Revue d'Etudes Antiques* 59 (2002): 395–401.

Patard, Geneviève,"Madame de Murat et les fées modernes." *The Romanic Review* vol. 99, numero 3–4 (May 2008): pp.271–80.

Purkiss, Diane. *Troublesome Things: A History of Fairies and Fairy Stories*. London: Allen Lane, 2000.

Raymard, Sophie. *La Seconde préciosité: floraison des conteuses de 1690 à 1756*. Gunter Narr Verlag 2002.

Randall, Catharine,"*Bluebeard's* Curiosity Cabinet: The Sacred Hearth of Textual Materialism." *Romance Notes*, vol. 45, no. 1 (Fall 2004): 89–97.

Ringham, Felizitas,"Riquet à la Houppe: Conteur, conteuse." *French Studies: A Quaterly Review* 52:3 (July 1998): 291–304.

Robert, Raymonde, Nadine Jasmin, et Claire Debru, eds. *Le conte de fées littéraire en France: De la fin du XVIIe à la fin du XVIIIe siècle*. Paris: Champion, 2002.

Seifert, Lewis C. *Fairy Tales, Sexuality and Gender in France, 1690–1715: Nostalgic Utopias*. Cambridge: Cambridge University Press, 1996.

Sermain, Jean-Paul,"Les Contes de fées du XVIIe siècle: lecture en amont ou en aval?" *La littérature, le XVIIe siècle et nous: dialogue transatlantique*. Ed. Hélène Merlin-Kajman. Paris: Presses Sorbonne Nouvelle, 2008.

Sous la cendre: Figures de Cendrillon. Anthologie établie par Niclole Belmont et Elizabeth Lemire. Paris: José Corti, 2007.

Stone, Kay F.. *Some Day your Witch Will Come*. Detroit: Wayne State University, 2008.

Surhone, Lambert M., Miriam T. Timpledon, and Susan F. Marseken. *Ogres: Fairy Tales, Geoffrey of Monmouth, Charles Perrault, Fantasy Fiction, Princess Fiona, Lum Invader*. Betascript Publishing, 2010.

Sweeney, Susan E.,"Female Strategies of Self-Representation in Variants, Versions, and Revisions of 'Bluebeard'."*Interfaces: Image Texte Language* 18 (2000): 147–154.

Thelander, Dorothy,"Mother Goose and her Goslings: The France of Louis XIV as Seen through the Fairy Tale." *The Journal of Modern History*, vol.54, no.3 (Sept. 1982)

Thirard, Marie-Agnès. "Le féminisme dans les contes de Mme d'Aulnoy." *XVIIe siècle*, 52 (2000): 501–14.

Thirard, Marie-Agnès. "Prévisible et imprévisible dans l'oeuvre de Madame d'Aulnoy ou une nouvelle esthétique du conte." *Papers on French Seventeenth Century Literature*, 62 (2005): 181–96.

Thompson, Stih. *Motifs Index of Folk Literature*. 6 vols. Bloomington: IU Press, 1932–36. Reprinted, Copenhagen: Rosenkilde & Bagger, 1955–58.

Tucker, Holly,"Like Mother. Like Daughter: Maternal Cravings and Birthmarks in the Fairy Tales of Madame d'Aulnoy." *The Mother in/and French Literature.* Ed. Buford Norman. Amsterdam: Rodopi, 2000. 33–50.

Tucker, Holly. *Pregnant Fictions: Childbirth and the Fairy Tale in Early-Modern France.* Detroit: Wayne State University, 2003.

Tucker, Holly and Melanie Siemens,"Perrault's Preface to Griselda and Murat's 'To Modern Fairies'." *Marvels & Tales,* vol.19, number 1 (2005): 126–130

Ulanov, Ann. *Cinderella and Her Sisters: The Envied and the Envying.* Daimon, 2008

Vallois, Marie-Claire,"Des *Contes de ma Mère* L'*Oye* ou des 'caquets' de Madame d'Aulnoy: nouvelle querelle chez les Modernes?" Ed. Hélène Merlin-Kajman. *La littérature, le XVIIe siècle et nous: dialogue transatlantique.* Paris: Presses Sorbonne Nouvelle, 2008

Van Elslande, Jean-Pierre," Parole d'enfant: Perrault et le déclin du Grand Siècle." *Papers on French Seventeeth Century Literature* (1999): 439–54.

Van Elslande, Jean-Pierre,"Corps éloquents et morale dans les contes en prose de Charles Perrault." *Classical Unities: Place, Time, Action.* Ed. Erec R. Koch. Actes du 32e Colloque de la North American Society for Seventeenth-Century French Literature. Tulane, 13–15 avril, 2000.

Warner, Marina. *From the Beast to the Blonde. On Fairy Tales and their Tellers.* New York: Farrar, Straus and Giroux, 1994.

Warner, Marina. *No Go the Bogeyman: Scaring, Lulling, and Making Mock.* New York: Farrar, Straud and Giroux, 1999.

Wasco, Janet. *Understanding Disney: The Manufacture of Fantasy.* Cambridge: Polity, 2001.

Ziolkowski, Jan M. *Fairy Tales from before Fairy Tales: The Medieval Latin Past of Wonderful Lies.* Ann Harbor: University of Michigan Press, 2007.

Zipes, Jack (ed.). *When Dreams Came True: Classical Fairy Tales and Their Tradition.* New York: Routledge, 1999.

Zipes, Jack. *Breaking the Magic Spell: Radical Theories of Folk and Fairy Tales.* Lexington: University Press of Kentucky, 2002.

Zipes, Jack. *Fairy Tales and the Art of Subversion: The Classical Genre for Children and the Process of Civilization.* New York: Routledge, 2006.

Zipes, Jack. *Why Fairy Tales Stick: The Evolution and Relevance of a Genre.* New York: Routledge, 2006.

# Selected Filmography

La Barbe Bleue. Catherine Breillat, 2009.

Beauty and the Beast. Walt Disney, 1991.

La Belle et la Bête. Jean Cocteau, 1946.

Cinderella. Walt Disney, 1950.

Little Red Riding Hood. David Kaplan, 1997.

Peau d'Âne. Jacques Demy, 1970.

Sleeping Beauty. Walt Disney, 1959.

La Véritable histoire du Petit Chaperon Rouge. Todd Edwards, 2004.

La Véritable histoire du Chat Botté. Pascal Hérold, 2008.

 # Biography

Charles Perrault (1628–1703) was born in Paris into a wealthy bourgeois family. Until 1683, he worked as Jean-Batiste Colbert's secretary who appointed him Controller-general of Royal buildings, a very important position under Louis XIV. Perrault sided with the Moderns in the so-called Quarrel of the Ancients and the Moderns. The Ancients found their inspiration in the literature of Antiquity whereas the Moderns found theirs in the literature originated from France. An accomplished writer, he was elected to the prestigious French Academy in 1663. Perrault published his first tale, *Grisélidis,* in 1691. A collection of his fairy tales appeared in 1697 under the name of his youngest son, Pierre d'Armancourt.

Catherine Bernard (1692–1712) was born in Rouen. Related to Racine and Fontenelle, she was introduced to the Parisian most important literary salons of the time. Bernard published several tragedies, novels, and poems. Her tragedies were very successful. Her first play written in 1689**,** *Léodamie,* was performed twenty times in Paris. Not wealthy, Bernard depended on patrons to support her. She never married. The fairy tale included in this Anthology, *Riquet à la Houppe*, appeared in 1696 as part of her novel, *Ines de Cordoue.*

Marie-Catherine d'Aulnoy (1650–1705) was born in Normandy into an aristocratic family. At the age of sixteen, she married the baron d'Aulnoy who was forty-six years old. By all accounts, the marriage was a disaster. After two unsuccessful attempts to have her husband killed, she took briefly refuge in a convent. Later, she supposedly traveled to England, Holland, and Spain at times accompanied by one of her lovers. In 1685 she moved back to Paris where she hosted one of the most influential literary salons. Madame d'Aulnoy was a prolific writer. In 1690, she published *L'Ile de la Félicité,* a fairy tale included in her novel, *l'Histoire d'Hippolyte, Comte de Douglas.* Her most famous fairy tales include *The White Cat, The Blue Bird, and the Green Serpent.*

Jeanne-Marie Leprince de Beaumont (1711–1780) was born in Rouen. She married M. de Beaumont who turned out to be a gambler and a philanderer. The marriage was annulled three years later. To support herself, she worked as a governess for British aristocratic families. While in England, she began her remarkable career as a writer. Highly educated, Madame Leprince de Beaumont wrote several pedagogical essays, novels, and stories in which she stressed the importance of education especially for young girls and women. She published more than seventy books in her lifetime. Madame Leprince de Beaumont's most famous fairy tale is *The Beauty and the Beast* published in 1757.

Chapter I

History of French Fairy Tales

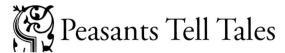

Peasants Tell Tales

The Meaning of Mother Goose

Robert Darnton

THE MENTAL WORLD of the unenlightened during the Enlightenment seems to be irretrievably lost. It is so difficult, if not impossible, to locate the common man in the eighteenth century that it seems foolish to search for his cosmology. But before abandoning the attempt, it might be useful to suspend one's disbelief and to consider a story—a story everyone knows, though not in the following version, which is the tale more or less as it was told around firesides in peasant cottages during long winter evenings in eighteenth-century France.[1]

Once a little girl was told by her mother to bring some bread and milk to her grandmother. As the girl was walking through the forest, a wolf came up to her and asked where she was going.

"To grandmother's house," she replied.

"Which path are you taking, the path of the pins or the path of the needles?" "The path of the needles."

So the wolf took the path of the pins and arrived first at the house. He killed grandmother, poured her blood into a bottle, and sliced her flesh onto a platter. Then he got into her nightclothes and waited in bed.

"Knock, knock."

"Come in, my dear."

"Hello, grandmother. I've brought you some bread and milk."

"Have something yourself, my dear. There is meat and wine in the pantry."

So the little girl ate what was offered; and as she did, a little cat said, "Slut! To eat the flesh and drink the blood of your grandmother!"

Then the wolf said, "Undress and get into bed with me."

"Where shall I put my apron?"

"Throw it on the fire; you won't need it any more."

For each garment—bodice, skirt, petticoat, and stockings^-the girl asked the same question; and each time the wolf answered, "Throw it on the fire; you won't need it any more."

When the girl got in bed, she said, "Oh, grandmother! How hairy you are!"

"It's to keep me warmer, my dear."

"Oh, grandmother! What big shoulders you have!"

"It's for better carrying firewood, my dear."

"Oh, grandmother! What long nails you have!"

"It's for scratching myself better, my dear."

"Oh, grandmother! What big teeth you have!"
"It's for eating you better, my dear."
And he ate her.

What is the moral of this story? For little girls, clearly: stay away from wolves. For historians, it seems to be saying something about the mental world of the early modern peasantry. But what? How can one begin to interpret such a text? One way leads through psychoanalysis. The analysts have given folktales a thorough going-over, picking out hidden symbols, unconscious motifs, and psychic mechanisms. Consider, for example, the exegesis of "Little Red Riding Hood" by two of the best known psychoanalysts, Erich Fromm and Bruno Bettelheim.

Fromm interpreted the tale as a riddle about the collective unconscious in primitive society, and he solved it "without difficulty" by decoding its "symbolic language." The story concerns an adolescent's confrontation with adult sexuality, he explained. Its hidden meaning shows through its symbolism—but the symbols he saw in his version of the text were based on details that did not exist in the versions known to peasants in the seventeenth and eighteenth centuries. Thus he makes a great deal of the (nonexistent) red riding hood as a symbol of menstruation and of the (nonexistent) bottle carried by the girl as a symbol of virginity: hence the mother's (nonexistent) admonition not to stray from the path into wild terrain where she might break it. The wolf is the ravishing male. And the two (nonexistent) stones that are placed in the wolf's belly after the (nonexistent) hunter extricates the girl and her grandmother, stand for sterility, the punishment for breaking a sexual taboo. So, with an uncanny sensitivity to detail that did not occur in the original folktale, the psychoanalyst takes us into a mental universe that never existed, at least not before the advent of psychoanalysis.[2]

How could anyone get a text so wrong? The difficulty does not derive from professional dogmatism—for psychoanalysts need not be more rigid than poets in their manipulation of symbols—but rather from blindness to the historical dimension of folktales.

Fromm did not bother to mention his source, but apparently he took his text from the brothers Grimm. The Grimms got it, along with "Puss 'n Boots," "Bluebeard," and a few other stories, from Jeannette Hassenpflug, a neighbor and close friend of theirs in Cassel; and she learned it from her mother, who came from a French Huguenot family. The Huguenots brought their own repertory of tales into Germany when they fled from the persecution of Louis XIV. But they did not draw them directly from popular oral tradition. They read them in books written by Charles Perrault, Marie Catherine d'Aulnoy, and others during the vogue for fairy tales in fashionable Parisian circles at the end of the seventeenth century. Perrault, the master of the genre, did indeed take his material from the oral tradition of the common people (his principal source probably was his son's nurse). But he touched it up so that it would suit the taste of the salon sophisticates, *précieuses,* and courtiers to whom he directed the first printed version of Mother Goose, his *Contes de ma mère l'oye* of 1697. Thus the tales that reached the Grimms through the Hassenpflugs were neither very German nor very representative of folk tradition. Indeed, the Grimms recognized their literary and Frenchified character and therefore eliminated them from the second edition of the *Kinderund Hausmärchen*—all but "Little Red Riding Hood." It remained in the collection, evidently, because Jeannette Hassenpflug had grafted on to it a happy ending derived from "The Wolf and the Kids" (tale type 123 according to the standard classification scheme developed by Antti Aarne and Stith Thompson), which was one of the most popular in Germany. So Little Red Riding Hood slipped into the German and later the English literary tradition with her French origins undetected. She changed character considerably as she passed from the French peasantry to Perrault's nursery, into print, across the Rhine, back into an oral tradition but this time as part of the Huguenot diaspora, and back into book form but now as a product of the Teutonic forest rather than the village hearths of the Old Regime in France.[3]

Fromm and a host of other psychoanalytical exegetes did not worry about the transformations of the text—indeed, they did not know about them;—because they got the tale they wanted. It begins with pubertal sex (the red hood, which does not exist in the French oral tradition) and ends with the triumph of the ego (the rescued girl, who is usually eaten in the French tales) over the id (the wolf, who is never killed in the traditional versions). All's well that ends well.

The ending is particularly important for Bruno Bettelheim, the ^latest in the line of psychoanalysts who have had a go at "Little Red Riding Hood." For him, the key to the story, and to all such stories, is the affirmative message of its denouement. By ending happily, he maintains, folktales permit children to confront their unconscious desires and fears and to emerge unscathed, id subdued and ego triumphant. The id is the villain of "Little Red Riding Hood" in Bettelheim's version. It is the pleasure principle, which leads the girl astray when she is too old for oral fixation (the stage represented by "Hansel and Gretel") and too young for adult sex. The id is also the wolf, who is also the father, who is also the hunter, who is also the ego and, somehow, the superego as well. By directing the wolf to her grandmother, Little Red Riding Hood manages in oedipal fashion to do away with her mother, because mothers can also be grandmothers in the moral economy of the soul and the houses on either side of the woods are actually the same house, as in "Hansel and Gretel," where they are also the mother's body. This adroit mixing of symbols gives Little Red Riding Hood an opportunity to get into bed with her father, the wolf, thereby giving vent to her oedipal fantasies. She survives in the end because she is reborn on a higher level of existence when her father reappears as ego-superego-hunter and cuts her out of the belly of her father as wolf-id, so that everyone lives happily ever after.[4]

Bettelheim's generous view of symbolism makes for a less mechanistic interpretation of the tale than does Fromm's notion of a secret code, but it, too, proceeds from some unquestioned assumptions about the text. Although he cites enough commentators on Grimm and Perrault to indicate some awareness of folklore as an academic discipline, Bettelheim reads "Little Red Riding Hood" and the other tales as if they had no history. He treats them, so to speak, flattened out, like patients on a couch, in a timeless contemporaneity. He does not question their origins or worry over other meanings that they might have had in other contexts because he knows how the soul works and how it has always worked. In fact, however, folktales are historical documents. They have evolved over many centuries and have taken different turns in different cultural traditions. Far from expressing the unchanging operations of man's inner being, they suggest that *mentalités* themselves have changed. We can appreciate the distance between our mental world and that of our ancestors if we imagine lulling a child of our own to sleep with the primitive peasant version of "Little Red Riding Hood." Perhaps, then, the moral of the story should be: beware of psychoanalysts—and be careful in your use of sources. We seem to be back at historicism.[5]

Not quite, however, for "Little Red Riding Hood" has a terrifying irrationality that seems out of place in the Age of Reason. In fact, the peasants' version outdoes the psychoanalysts' in violence and sex. (Following the Grimms and Perrault, Fromm and Bettelheim do hot mention the cannibalizing of grandmother and the striptease prelude to the devouring of the girl.) Evidently the peasants did not need a secret code to talk about taboos.

The other stories in the French peasant Mother Goose have the same nightmare quality. In one early version of "Sleeping Beauty" (tale type 410), for example, Prince Charming, who is already married, ravishes the princess, and she bears him several children, without waking up. The infants finally break the spell by biting her while nursing, and the tale then takes up its second theme: the attempts of the prince's mother-in-law, an ogress, to eat his illicit offspring. The original "Bluebeard" (tale type 312) is the story of a bride who cannot resist the temptation to open a forbidden door in the house of her husband, a strange man who has already gone through six wives. She enters a dark room and discovers the corpses of the previous wives, hanging on the wall. Horrified, she lets the forbidden key drop from her hand into a pool of blood on the floor. She cannot wipe it clean; so Bluebeard discovers her disobedience, when he inspects the keys. As he sharpens his knife in preparation for making her his seventh victim, she withdraws to her bedroom and puts on her wedding costume. But she delays her toilette long enough to be saved by her brothers, who gallop to the rescue after receiving a warning from her pet dove. In one early tale from the Cinderella cycle (tale type 510B), the heroine becomes a domestic servant in order to prevent her father from forcing her to marry him. In another, the wicked stepmother tries to push her in an oven but incinerates one of the mean stepsisters by mistake. In the French peasant's "Hansel and Gretel" (tale type 327), the hero tricks an ogre into slitting the throats of his own children. A husband eats a succession of brides in the wedding bed in "La Belle et le monstre" (tale type 433), one of the hundreds of tales that never made it into the printed versions of Mother Goose. In a nastier tale,"Les Trois Chiens" (tale type 315), a sister kills her brother by hiding spikes in the mattress of his wedding bed. In the nastiest of all,"Ma mère m'a tué, mon père m'a mangé" (tale type 720), a mother chops her son up into a Lyonnais-style casserole, which her daughter serves to the father. And so it goes, from rape and sodomy to incest and cannibalism. Far from veiling their message with symbols, the storytellers of eighteenth-century France portrayed a world of raw and naked brutality.

How can the historian make sense of this world? One way for him to keep his footing in the psychic undertow of early Mother Goose is to hold fast to two disciplines: anthropology and folklore. When they discuss theory, anthropologists disagree about the fundamentals of their science. But when they go into the bush, they use techniques for understanding oral traditions that can, with discretion, be applied to Western folklore. Except for some structuralists, they relate tales to the art of tale telling and to the context in which it takes place. They look for the way a raconteur adapts an inherited theme to his audience so that the specificity of time and place shows through the universality of the topos. They do not expect to find direct social comment or metaphysical allegories so much as a tone of discourse or a cultural style, which communicates a particular ethos and world view.[6] "Scientific" folklore, as the French call it (American specialists often distinguish between folklore and "fakelore"), involves the compilation and comparison of tales according to the standardized schemata of tale types developed by Antti Aarne and Stith Thompson. It does not necessarily exclude formalistic analysis such as that of Vladimir Propp, but it stresses rigorous documentation—the occasion of the telling, the background of the teller, and the degree of contamination from written sources.[7]

French folklorists have recorded about ten thousand tales, in many different dialects and in every corner of France and of French-speaking territories. For example, while on an expedition in Berry for the Musée des arts et traditions populaires in 1945, Ariane de Félice recorded a version of "Le Petit Poucet" ("Tom Thumb" or "Thumbling," tale type 327) by a peasant woman, Euphrasie Pichon, who had been born in 1862 in the village of Eguzon (Indre). In 1879 Jean Drouillet wrote down another version as he listened to his mother Eugenie, who had learned it from her mother, Octavie Riffet, in the village of Teillay (Cher). The two versions are nearly identical and owe nothing to the first printed account of the tale, which Charles Perrault published in 1697. They and eighty other "Petits Poucets," which folklorists have compiled and compared, motif by motif, belong to an oral tradition that survived with remarkably little contamination from print culture until late in the nineteenth century. Most of the tales in the French repertory were recorded between 1870 and 1914 during "the Golden Age of folktale research in France," and they were Recounted by peasants who had learned them as children, long before literacy had spread throughout the countryside. Thus in 1874 Nannette Levesque, an illiterate peasant woman born in 1794, dictated a version of "Little Red Riding Hood" that went back to the eighteenth century; and in 1865 Louis Grolleau, a domestic servant born in 1803, dictated a rendition of "Le Pou" (tale type 621) that he had first heard under the Empire. Like all tellers of tales, the peasant raconteurs adjusted the setting of their stories to their own milieux; but they kept the main elements intact, using repetitions, rhymes, and other mnemonic devices. Although the "performance" element, which is central to the study of contemporary folklore, does not show through the old texts, folklorists argue that the recordings of the Third Republic provide enough evidence for them to reconstruct the rough outlines of an oral tradition that existed two centuries ago.[8]

That claim may seem extravagant, but comparative studies have revealed striking similarities in different recordings of the same tale, even though they were made in remote villages, far removed from one another and from the circulation of books. In a study of "Little Red Riding Hood," for example, Paul Delarue compared thirty-five versions recorded throughout a vast zone of the *langue d'oïl* Twenty versions correspond exactly to the primitive "Conte de la mère grand" quoted above, except for a few details (some- times the girl is eaten, sometimes she escapes by a ruse). Two versions follow Perrault's tale (the first to mention the red hood). And the rest contain a mixture of the oral and written accounts, whose elements stand out as distinctly as the garlic and mustard in a French salad dressing.[9]

Written evidence proves that the tales existed long before any- one conceived of "folklore," a nineteenth-century neologism.[10] Medieval preachers drew on the oral tradition in order to illustrate moral arguments. Their sermons, transcribed in collections of "Exempla" from the twelfth to the fifteenth century, refer to the same stories as those taken down in peasant cottages by folklorists in the nineteenth century. Despite the obscurity surrounding the origins of chivalric romances, *chansons de geste,* and *fabliaux,* it seems that a good deal of medieval literature drew on popular oral tradition, rather than vice versa. "Sleeping Beauty" appeared in an Arthurian romance of the fourteenth century, and "Cinderella" surfaced in Noel du Fail's *Propos rustiques* of 1547, a book that traced the tales to peasant lore and that showed how they were transmitted; for du Fail wrote the first account of an important French institution, the *veillée* an evening fireside gathering, where men repaired tools and women sewed while listening to stories that would be recorded by folklorists three hundred years later and that were already centuries old.[11] Whether they were meant to amuse adults or to frighten children, as in the case of cautionary tales like "Little Red Riding Hood," the stories belonged to a fund of popular culture, which peasants hoarded over the centuries with remarkably little loss. The great collections of folktales made in the late nineteenth and early twentieth centuries therefore provide a rare opportunity to make contact with the illiterate masses who have disappeared into the past without leaving a trace. To reject folktales because they cannot be dated and situated with precision like other historical documents is to turn one's back on one of the few points of entry into the mental world of peasants under the Old Regime. But to attempt to penetrate that world is to face a set of obstacles as daunting as those confronted by Jean de l'Ours (tale type 301) when he tried to rescue the three Spanish princesses from the underworld or by little Parle (tale type 328) when he set out to capture the ogre's treasure.

The greatest obstacle is the impossibility of listening in on the story tellers. No matter how accurate they may be, the recorded versions of the tales cannot convey the effects that must have brought the stories to life in the eighteenth century: the dramatic pauses, the sly glances, the use of gestures to set scenes—a Snow White at a spinning wheel, a Cinderella delousing a stepsister—and the use of sounds to punctuate actions—a knock on the door (often done by rapping on a listener's forehead) or a cudgeling or a fart. All of those devices shaped the meaning of the tales, and all of them elude the historian. He cannot be sure that the limp and lifeless text that he holds between the covers of a book provides an accurate account of the performance that took place in the eighteenth century. He cannot even be certain that the text corresponds to the unrecorded versions that existed a century earlier. Although he may turn up plenty of evidence to prove that the tale itself existed, he cannot quiet his suspicions that it could have changed a great deal before it reached the folklorists of the Third Republic.

Given those uncertainties, it seems unwise to build an interpretation on a single version of a single tale, and more hazardous still to base symbolic analysis on details—riding hoods and hunters—that may not have occurred in the peasant versions. But there are enough recordings of those versions—35 "Little Red Riding Hoods," 90 "Tom Thumbs," 105 "Cinderellas"—for one to picture the general outline of a tale as it existed in the oral tradition. One can study it on the level of structure, noting the way the narrative is framed and the motifs are combined, instead of concentrating on fine points of detail. Then one can compare it with other stories. And finally, by working through the entire body of French folktales, one can distinguish general characteristics, overarching themes, and pervasive elements of style and tone.[12]

One can also seek aid and comfort from specialists in the study of oral literature. Mil man Parry and Albert Lord have shown how folk epics as long as *The Iliad* are passed on faithfully from bard to bard among the illiterate peasants of Yugoslavia. These "singers of tales" do not possess the fabulous powers of memorization sometimes attributed to "primitive" peoples. They do not memorize very much at all. Instead, they combine stock phrases, formulas, and narrative segments in patterns improvised according to the response of their audience. Recordings of the same epic by the same singer demonstrate that each performance is unique. Yet recordings made in 1950 do not differ in essentials from those made in 1934. In each case, the singer proceeds as if he were walking down a well-known path. He may branch off here to take a shortcut or pause there to enjoy a panorama, but he always remains on familiar ground—so familiar, in fact, that he will say that he repeated every step exactly as he has done before. He does not conceive of repetition in the same way as a literate person, for he has no notion of words, lines, and verses. Texts are not rigidly fixed for him as they are for readers of the printed page. He creates his text as he goes, picking new routes through old themes. He can even work in material derived from printed sources, for the epic as a whole is so much greater than the sum of its parts that modifications of detail barely disturb the general configuration.[13]

Lord's investigation confirms conclusions that Vladimir Propp reached by a different mode of analysis, one that showed how variations of detail remain subordinate to stable structures in Russian folktales.[14] Field workers among illiterate peoples in Polynesia, Africa, and North and South America have also found that oral traditions have enormous staying power. Opinions divide on the separate question of whether or not oral sources can provide a reliable account of past events. Robert Lowie, who collected narratives from the Crow Indians in the early twentieth century, took up a position of extreme skepticism: "I cannot attach to oral traditions any historical value whatsoever under any conditions whatsoever."[15] By historical value, however, Lowie meant factual accuracy. (In 1910 he recorded a Crow account of a battle against the Dakota; in 1931 the same informant described the battle to him, but claimed that it had taken place against the Cheyenne.) Lowie conceded that the stories, taken as stories, remained quite consistent; they forked and branched in the standard patterns of Crow narrative. So his findings actually support the view that in traditional story telling continuities in form and style outweigh variations in detail, among North American Indians as well as Yugoslav peasants.[16] Frank Hamilton Cushing noted a spectacular example of this tendency among the Zuni almost a century ago. In 1886 he served as interpreter to a Zuni delegation in the eastern United States. During a round robin of story telling one evening, he recounted as his contribution the tale of "The Cock and the Mouse," which he had picked up from a book of Italian folktales. About a year later, he was astonished to hear the same tale from one of the Indians back at Zuni. The Italian motifs remained recognizable enough for one to be able to classify the tale in the Aarne-Thompson scheme (it is tale type 2032). But everything else about the story—its frame, figures of speech, allusions, style, and general feel—had become intensely Zuni. Instead of Italianizing the native lore, the story had been Zunified.[17]

No doubt the transmission process affects stories differently in different cultures. Some bodies of folklore can resist "contamination" while absorbing new material more effectively than can others. But oral traditions seem to be tenacious and long-lived nearly everywhere among illiterate peoples. Nor do they collapse at their first exposure to the printed word. Despite Jack Goody's contention that a literacy line cuts through all history, dividing oral from "written" or "print" cultures, it seems that traditional tale telling can flourish long after the onset of literacy. To anthropologists and folklorists who have tracked tales through the bush, there is nothing extravagant about the idea that peasant raconteurs in late nineteenth-century France told stories to one another pretty much as their ancestors had done a century or more earlier.[18]

Comforting as this expert testimony may be, it does not clear all the difficulties in the way of interpreting the French tales. The texts are accessible enough, for they lie unexploited in treasure houses like the Musee des arts et traditions populaires in Paris and in scholarly collections like *Le Conte populaire franqais* by Paul De- larue and Marie-Louise Tenèze. But one cannot lift them from such sources and hold them up to inspection as if they were so many photographs of the Old Regime, taken with the innocent eye of an extinct peasantry. They are stories.

As in most kinds of narration, they develop standardized plots from conventional motifs, picked up here, there, and everywhere. They have a distressing lack of specificity for anyone who wants to pin them down to precise points in time and place. Raymond Jameson has studied the case of a Chinese Cinderella from the ninth century. She gets her slippers from a magic fish instead of a fairy godmother and loses one of them at a village fete instead of a royal ball, but she bears an unmistakable resemblance to Perrault›s heroine.¹⁹ Folklorists have recognized their tales in Herodotus and Homer, on ancient Egyptian papyruses and Chaldean stone tablets; and they have recorded them all over the world, in Scandinavia and Africa, among Indians on the banks of the Bengal and Indians along the Missouri. The dispersion is so striking that some have come to believe in Ur-stories and a basic Indo-European repertory of myths, legends, and tales. This tendency feeds into the cosmic theories of Frazer and Jung and Lévi-Strauss, but it does not help anyone attempting to penetrate the peasant mentalities of early modern France.

Fortunately, a more down-to-earth tendency in folklore makes it possible to isolate the peculiar characteristics of traditional French tales. *Le Conte populaire franqais* arranges them according to the Aarne-Thompson classification scheme, which covers all varieties of Indo-European folktales. It therefore provides the basis for comparative study, and the comparisons suggest the way general themes took root and grew in French soil. "Tom Thumb" ("Le Petit Poucet," tale type 327), for example, has a strong French flavor, in Perrault as well as the peasant versions, if one compares it with its German cousin,"Hansel and Gretel." The Grimms' tale emphasizes the mysterious forest and the naïveté of the children in the face of inscrutable evil, and it has more fanciful and poetic touches, as in the details about the bread-and-cake house and the magic birds. The French children confront an ogre, but in a very real house. Monsieur and Madame Ogre discuss their plans for a dinner party as if they were any married couple, and they carp at each other just as Tom Thumb's parents did. In fact, it is hard to tell the two couples apart. Both simple-minded wives throw away their family's fortunes; and their husbands berate them in the same manner, except that the ogre tells his wife that she deserves to be eaten and that he would do the job himself if she were not such an unappetizing *vieille bête* (old beast).²⁰ Unlike their German relatives, the French ogres appear in the role of *le bourgeois de la maison* (burgher head of household),²¹ as if they were rich local landowners. They play fiddles, visit friends, snore contentedly in bed beside fat ogress wives;²² and for all their boorishness, they never fail to be good family men and good providers. Hence the joy of the ogre in "Pitchin-Pitchot" as he bounds into the house, a sack on his back: "Catherine, put on the big kettle. I've caught Pitchin- Pitchot."²³

Where the German tales maintain a tone of terror and fantasy, the French strike a note of humor and domesticity. Firebirds settle down into hen yards. Elves, genii, forest spirits, the whole Indo-European panoply of magical beings become reduced in France to two species, ogres and fairies. And those vestigial creatures acquire human foibles and generally let humans solve their problems by their own devices, that is, by cunning and "Cartesianism"—a term that the French apply vulgarly to their propensity for craftiness and intrigue. The Gallic touch is clear in many of the tales that Perrault did not rework for his own Gallicized Mother Goose of 1697: the *panache* of the young blacksmith in "Le Petit Forgeron" (tale type 317), for example, who kills giants on a classic *tour de France;* or the provincialism of the Breton peasant in "Jean Bête" (tale type 675), who is given anything he wishes and asks for *un bon péche de piquette et une écuelle de patates du lait* ("crude wine and a bowl of potatoes in milk"); or the professional jealousy of the master gardener, who fails to prune vines as well as his apprentice in "Jean le Teigneux" (tale type 314); or the cleverness of the devil's daughter in "La Belle Eulalie" (tale type 313), who escapes with her lover by leaving two talking pâtés in their beds. Just as one cannot attach the French tales to specific events, one should not dilute them in a timeless universal mythology. They really belong to a middle ground: *la France moderne* or the France that existed from the fifteenth through the eighteenth century.

That time span may look distressingly vague to anyone who expects history to be precise. But precision may be inappropriate as well as impossible in the history of *mentalités*, a genre that requires different methods from those used in conventional genres, like political history. World views can not be chronicled in the manner of political events, but they are no less "real." Politics could not take place without the preliminary mental ordering that goes into the common-sense notion of the real world. Common sense itself is a social construction of reality, which varies from culture to culture. Far from being the arbitrary figment of some collective imagination, it expresses the common basis of experience in a given social order. To reconstruct the way peasants saw the world Under the Old Regime, therefore, one should begin by asking what they had in common, what experiences they shared in the everyday life of their villages.

Thanks to several generations of research by social historians, that question can be answered. The answer must be hedged with qualifications and restricted to a high level of generalization because conditions varied so much in the kingdom, which remained a patchwork of regions rather than a unified nation until the Revolution and perhaps even well into the nineteenth century. Pierre Goubert, Emmanuel Le Roy Ladurie, Pierre Saint-Jacob, Paul Bois, and many others have uncovered the particularities of peasant life region by region and have explicated them monograph by monograph, The density of monographs can make French social history look like a conspiracy of exceptions trying to disprove rules. Yet here, too, there exists a danger of misplaced professionalism; for if one stands at a safe enough distance from the details, a general picture begins to emerge. In fact, it has already reached the stage of assimilation in textbooks like *Histoire économique et sociale de la France* (Paris, 1970) and syntheses like *Histoire de la France rurale* (Paris, 1975/76). It goes roughly as follows.[24]

Despite war, plague, and famine, the social order that existed at village level remained remarkably stable during the early modern period in France. The peasants were relatively free—less so than the yeomen who were turning into landless laborers in England, more so than the serfs who were sinking into a kind of slavery east of the Elbe. But they could not escape from a seigneurial system that denied them sufficient land to achieve economic independence and that siphoned off whatever surplus they produced. Men labored from dawn to dusk, scratching the soil on scattered strips of land with plows like those of the Romans and hacking at their grain with primitive sickles, in order to leave enough stubble for communal grazing. Women married late—at age twenty-five to twenty-seven—and gave birth to only five or six children, of whom only two or three survived to adulthood. Great masses of people lived in a state of chronic malnutrition, subsisting mainly on porridge made of bread and water with some occasional, homegrown vegetables thrown in. They ate meat only a few times a year, on feast days or after autumn slaughtering if they did not have enough silage to feed the livestock over the winter. They often failed to get the two pounds of bread (2,000 calories) a day that they needed to keep up their health, and so they had little protection against the combined effects of grain shortage and disease. The population fluctuated between fifteen and twenty million, expanding to the limits of its productive capacity (an average density of forty souls per square kilometer, an average annual rate of forty births per thousand inhabitants), only to be devastated by demographic crises. For four centuries—from the first ravages of the Black Death in 1347 to the first great leap in population and productivity in the 1730s—French society remained trapped in rigid institutions and Malthusian conditions. It went through a period of stagnation, which Fernand Braudel and Emmanuel Le Roy Ladurie have described as *l'histoire immobile* (unmoving history).[25]

That phrase now seems exaggerated, for it hardly does justice to the religious conflict, grain riots, and rebellions against the extension of state power that disrupted the late medieval pattern of village life. But when first used in the 1950s, the notion of immobile history—a history of structural continuity over a long time span, *la longue durée*—served as a corrective to the tendency to see history as a succession of political events. Event history, *histoire événementielle,* generally took place over the heads of the peasantry, in the remote world of Paris and Versailles. While ministers came and went and battles raged, life in the village continued unperturbed, much as it had always been since times beyond the reach of memory.

History looked "immobile" at the village level, because seigneurialism and the subsistence economy kept villagers bent over the soil, and primitive techniques of farming gave them no opportunity to unbend. Grain yields remained at a ratio of about 5–to–1, a primitive return in contrast to modern farming, which produces fifteen or even thirty grains for every seed planted. Farmers could not raise enough grain to feed large numbers of animals, and they did not have enough livestock to produce the manure to fertilize the fields to increase the yield. This vicious circle kept them enclosed within a system of triennial or biennial crop rotation, which left a huge proportion of their land lying fallow. They could not convert the fallow to the cultivation of crops like clover, which return nitrogen to the soil, because they lived too close to penury to risk the experiment, aside from the fact that no one had any notion of nitrogen. Collective methods of cultivation also reduced the margin for experimentation. Except in a few regions with enclosures, like the *bocage* district of the west, peasants farmed scattered strips in open fields. They sowed and harvested collectively, so that common gleaning and common grazing could take place. They depended on common lands and forests beyond the fields for pasture, firewood, and chestnuts or berries. The only area where they could attempt to get ahead by individual initiative was the *basse-cour* or backyard attached to their household plots, or *manses*. Here they struggled to build up manure heaps, to raise flax for spinning, to produce vegetables and chickens for their home brews and local markets.

The backyard garden often provided the margin of survival for families that lacked the twenty, thirty, or forty acres that were necessary for economic independence. They needed so much land because so much of their harvest was drained from them by seigneurial dues, tithes, ground rents, and taxes. In most of central and northern France, the wealthier peasants rigged the collection of the main royal tax, the *taille,* in accordance with an old French principle: soak the poor. So tax collecting opened up fissures within the village, and indebtedness compounded the damage. The poorer peasants frequently borrowed from the rich—that is, the few relatively wealthy *coqs du village* (cocks of the walk), who owned enough land to sell surplus grain on the market, to build up herds, and to hire the poor as laborers. Debt peonage may have made the wealthy peasants hated as much as the seigneur and the ecclesiastical *décimateur* (tithe collector). Hatred, jealousy, and conflicts of interest ran through peasant society. The village was no happy and harmonious *Gemeinschaft.*

For most peasants village life was a struggle for survival, and survival meant keeping above the line that divided the poor from the indigent. The poverty line varied from place to place, according to the amount of land necessary to pay taxes, tithes, and seigneurial dues; to put aside enough grain for planting next year; and to feed the family. In times of scarcity, poor families had to buy their food. They suffered as consumers, while prices shot up and the wealthier peasants made a killing. So a succession of bad harvests could polarize the village, driving the marginal families into indigence as the rich got richer. In the face of such difficulties, the "little people" *(petites gens)* survived by their wits. They hired themselves out as farm hands, spun and wove cloth in their cottages, did odd jobs, and took to the road, picking up work wherever they could find it.

Many of them went under. Then they took to the road for good, drifting about with the flotsam and jetsam of France's *population flottante* ("floating population"), which included several million desperate souls by the 1780s. Except for the happy few on an artisanal *tour de France* and the occasional troupes of actors and mountebanks, life on the road meant ceaseless scavenging for food. The drifters raided chicken coops, milked untended cows, stole laundry drying on hedges, snipped off horses' tails (good for selling to upholsterers), and lacerated and disguised their bodies in order to pass as invalids wherever alms were being given out. They joined and deserted regiment after regiment and served as false recruits. They became smugglers, highwaymen, pickpockets, prostitutes. And in the end they surrendered in *hôpitaux,* pestilential poor houses, or else crawled under a bush or a hay loft and died—*croquants* who had "croaked."[26]

Death came just as inexorably to families that remained in their villages and kept above the poverty line. As Pierre Goubert, Louis Henry, Jacques Dupâquier, and other historical demographers have shown, life was an inexorable struggle against death everywhere in early modern France. In Crulai, Normandy, 236 of every 1,000 babies died before their first birthdays during the seventeenth century, as opposed to twenty today. About 45 per cent of the Frenchmen born in the eighteenth century died before the age of ten. Few of the survivors reached adulthood before the death of at least one of their parents. And few parents reached the end of their procreative years, because death interrupted them. Terminated by death, not divorce, marriages lasted an average of fifteen years, half as long as they do in France today. In Crulai, one in five husbands lost his wife and then remarried. Stepmothers proliferated everywhere—far more so than stepfathers, as the remarriage rate among widows was one in ten. Stepchildren may not have been treated like Cinderella, but relations between siblings probably were harsh. A new child often meant the difference between poverty and indigence. Even if it did not overtax the family's larder, it could bring penury down upon the next generation by swelling the number of claimants when the parents' land was divided among their heirs.[27]

Whenever the population expanded, landholding fragmented and pauperization set in. Primogeniture slowed the process in some areas, but the best defense everywhere was delayed marriage, a tendency that must have taken its toll in the emotional life of the family. The peasants of the Old Regime, unlike those in contemporary India, generally did not marry until they could occupy a cottage, and they rarely had children out of wedlock or after they reached their forties. In Port-en-Bessin, for example, women married at twenty-seven and stopped bearing children at forty on the average. Demographers have found no evidence of birth control or widespread illegitimacy before the late eighteenth century. Early modern man did not understand life in a way that enabled him to control it. Early modern woman could not conceive of mastering nature, so she conceived as God willed it—and as Thumbkin's mother did in "Le Petit Poucet." But late marriage, a short period of fertility, and long stretches of breast-feeding, which reduces the likelihood of conception, limited the size of her family. The harshest and most effective limit was imposed by death, her own and those of her babies during childbirth and infancy. Stillborn children, called *chrissons,* were sometimes buried casually, in anonymous collective graves. Infants were sometimes smothered by their parents in bed—a rather common accident, judging by episcopal edicts forbidding parents to sleep with children who had not reached their first birthdays. Whole families crowded into one or two beds and surrounded themselves with livestock in order to keep warm. So children became participant observers of their parents' sexual activities. No one thought of them as innocent creatures or of childhood itself as a distinct phase of life, clearly distinguishable from adolescence, youth, and adulthood by special styles of dress and behavior. Children labored alongside their parents almost as soon as they could walk, and they joined the adult labor force as farm hands, servants, and apprentices as soon as they reached their teens.

The peasants of early modern France inhabited a world of stepmothers and orphans, of inexorable, unending toil, and of brutal emotions, both raw and repressed. The human condition has changed so much since then that we can hardly imagine the way it appeared to people whose lives really were nasty, brutish, and short. That is why we need to reread Mother Goose.

Consider four of the best-known stories from Perrault's Mother Goose—"Puss 'n Boots," "Tom Thumb," "Cinderella," and "The Ridiculous Wishes"—in comparison with some of the peasant tales that treat the same themes.

In "Puss 'n Boots," a poor miller dies, leaving the mill to his eldest son, an ass to the second, and only a cat to the third. "Neither a notary nor a lawyer were called in," Perrault observes "They would have eaten up the poor patrimony." We are clearly in France, although other versions of this theme exist in Asia, Africa, and South America. The inheritance customs of French peasants, as well as noblemen, often prevented the fragmentation of the patrimony by favoring the eldest son. The youngest son of the miller, however, inherits a cat who has a genius for domestic intrigue. Everywhere around him, this Cartesian cat sees vanity, stupidity, and unsatisfied appetite; and he exploits it all by a series of tricks, which lead to a rich marriage for his master and a fine estate for himself, although in some of the pre-Perrault versions the master ultimately dupes the cat, who is actually a fox and does not wear boots.

A tale from the oral tradition,"La Renarde" (tale type 460), begins in a similar way: "Once there were two brothers, who took up the inheritances left to them by their father. The older, Joseph,, kept the farm. The younger, Baptiste, received only a handful of coins; and as he had five children and very little to feed them with, he fell into destitution."[28] In desperation, Baptiste begs for grain from his brother. Joseph tells him to strip off his rags, stand naked in the rain, and roll in the granary. He can keep as much grain as adheres to his body. Baptiste submits to this exercise in brotherly love, but he fails to pick up enough food to keep his family alive, so he takes to the road. Eventually he meets a good fairy, La Renarde, who helps him solve a string of riddles, which lead to a pot of buried gold and the fulfillment of a peasant's dream: a house, fields, pasture, woodland,"and his children had a cake apiece every day."[29]

"Tom Thumb" ("Le Petit Poucet," tale type 327) is a French version of "Hansel and Gretel," although Perrault took his title from a tale that belongs to type 700. It provides a glimpse of the Malthusian world, even in Perrault's watered-down version: "Once upon a time there was a woodsman and his wife, who had seven children, all boys. … They were very poor, and their seven children were a great inconvenience, because none was old enough to support himself. … A very difficult year came, and the famine was so great that these poor folk resolved to get rid of their children." The matter-of-fact tone suggests how commonplace the death of children had become in early modern France. Perrault wrote his tale in the mid-1690s, at the height of the worst demographic crisis in the seventeenth century—a time when plague and famine decimated the population of northern France, when the poor ate offal thrown in the street by tanners, when corpses were found with grass in their mouths and mothers "exposed" the infants they could not feed so that they got sick and died. By abandoning their children in the forest, Tom Thumb's parents were trying to cope with a problem that overwhelmed the peasantry many times in the seventeenth and eighteenth centuries—the problem of survival during a period of demographic disaster.

The same motif exists in the peasant versions of the tale and in other tales, along with other forms of infanticide and child abuse. Sometimes the parents turn their children out on the road as beggars and thieves. Sometimes they run away themselves, leaving the children to beg at home. And sometimes they sell the children to the devil. In the French version of "The Sorcerer's Apprentice" ("La Pomme d'orange," tale type 325), a father is overwhelmed by "as many children as there are holes in a sieve,"[30] a phrase that occurs in several tales and that should be taken as hyperbole about Malthusian pressure rather than as evidence about family size. When a new baby arrives, the father sells it to the devil (a sorcerer in some versions) in exchange for receiving a full larder for twelve years. At the end of that time, he gets the boy back, thanks to a ruse that the boy devises, for the little rogue has picked up a repertory of tricks, including the power to transform himself into animals, during his apprenticeship. Before long, the cupboard is bare and the family is facing starvation again. The boy then changes himself into a hunting dog, so that his father can sell him once more to the devil, who reappears as a hunter. After the father has collected the money, the dog runs away and returns home as a boy. They try the same trick again, with the boy transformed into a horse. This time the devil keeps hold of a magic collar, which prevents the horse from changing back into a boy. But a farm hand leads the horse to drink at a pond, thereby, giving it a chance to escape in the form of a frog. The devil turns into a fish and is about to devour it, when the frog changes into a bird. The devil becomes a hawk and pursues the bird, which flies into the bedroom of a dying king and takes the form of an orange. Then the devil appears as a doctor and demands the orange in exchange for curing the king. The orange spills onto the floor, transformed into grains of millet. The devil turns into a chicken and starts to gobble up the grains. But the last grain turns into a fox, which finally wins the transformation contest by devouring the hen. The tale did not merely provide amusement. It dramatized the struggle over scarce resources, which pitted the poor against the rich, the "little people" *(menu peuple, petites gens)* against "the big" *(les gros, les grands)*. Some versions make the social comment explicit by casting the devil in the role of a "seigneur" and concluding at the end: "And thus did the servant eat the master."[31]

To eat or not to eat, that was the question peasants confronted in their folklore as well as in their daily lives. It appears in a great many of the tales, often in connection with the theme of the wicked stepmother, which must have had special resonance around Old Regime hearths because Old Regime demography made stepmothers such important figures in village society. Perrault did justice to the theme in "Cinderella," but he neglected the related motif of malnutrition, which stands out in the peasant versions of the tale. In one common version ("La Petite Annette," tale type 511), the wicked stepmother gives poor Annette only a crust of bread a day and makes her keep the sheep, while her fat and indolent stepsisters lounge around the house and dine on mutton, leaving their dishes for Annette to wash upon her return from the fields. Annette is about to die of starvation, when the

Virgin Mary appears and gives her a magic wand, which produces a magnificent feast whenever Annette touches it to a black sheep. Before long the girl is plumper than her stepsisters. But her new beauty—-and fatness made for beauty under the Old Regime as in many primitive societies—arouses the stepmother's suspicions. By a ruse, the stepmother discovers the magic sheep, kills it, and serves its liver to Annette. Annette manages to bury the liver secretly and it grows into a tree, which is so high that no one can pick its fruit, except Annette; for it bends its branches down to her whenever she approaches. A passing prince (who is as gluttonous as everyone else in the country) wants the fruit so badly that he promises to marry the maiden who can pick some for him. Hoping to make a match for one of her daughters, the stepmother builds a huge ladder. But * when she tries it out, she falls and breaks her neck. Annette then gathers the fruit, marries the prince, and lives happily ever after.

Malnutrition and parental neglect go together in several tales, notably "La Sirène et l'épervier" (tale type 316) and "Brigitte, la maman qui m'a pas fait, mais m'a nourri" (tale type 713). The quest for food can be found in nearly all of them, even in Perrault, where it appears in burlesque form in "The Ridiculous Wishes," A poor woodsman is promised the fulfillment of any three wishes as a reward for a good deed. While he ruminates, his appetite overcomes him; and he wishes for a sausage. After it appears on his plate, his wife, an insufferable scold, quarrels so violently over the wasting of the wish that he wishes the sausage would grow on her nose. Then, confronted with a disfigured spouse, he wishes her back to her normal state; and they return to their former miserable existence.

Wishing usually takes the form of food in peasant tales, and it is never ridiculous. The discharged, down-and-out soldier, La Ramée, a stock character like the abused stepdaughter, is reduced to beggary in "Le Diable et le marechal ferrant" (tale type 330). He shares his last pennies with other beggars, one of whom turns out to be Saint Peter in disguise, and as a reward he is granted any wish he wants. Instead of taking paradise, he asks for "a square meal"—or, in other versions,"white bread and a chicken," "a bun, a sausage, and as much wine as he can drink," "tobacco and the food he saw in the inn," or "to always have a crust of bread."[32] Once supplied with magic wands, rings, or supernatural helpers, the first thought of the peasant hero is always for food. He never shows any imagination in his ordering. He merely takes the *plat du jour,* and it is always the same: solid peasant fare, though it may vary with the region, as in the case of the "cakes, fried bread, and pieces of cheese" *(canistrelli e fritelli, pezzi di broccio)* served up in a Corsican feast.[33] Usually the peasant raconteur does not describe the food in detail. Lacking any notion of gastronomy, he simply loads up his hero's plate; and if he wants to supply an extravagant touch, he adds,"There were even napkins."[34]

One extravagance clearly stands out: meat. In a society of de facto vegetarians, the luxury of luxuries was to sink one's teeth into a side of mutton, pork, or beef. The wedding feast in "Royaume des Valdars" (tale type 400) includes roast pigs who run around with forks sticking out of their flanks so that the guests can help themselves to ready-carved mouthfuls. The French version of a common ghost story,"La Goulue" (tale type 366), concerns a peasant girl who insists on eating meat every day. Unable to satisfy this extraordinary craving, her parents serve her a leg they have cut off a newly buried corpse. On the next day, the corpse appears before the girl in the kitchen. It orders her to wash its right leg, then its left leg. When she sees that the left leg is missing, it screams,"You ate it." Then it carries her back to the grave and devours her. The later, English versions of the tale, notably "The Golden Arm" made famous by Mark Twain, have the same plot without the carnivorousness—the very element that seems to have made the story fascinating for the peasants of the Old Regime. But whether they filled up on meat or porridge, the full belly came first among the wishes of the French peasant heroes. It was all the peasant Cinderella aspired to, even though she got a prince. "She touched the black sheep with the magic wand. Immediately a fully decked table appeared before her. She could eat what she wanted, and she ate a bellyful."[35] To eat one's fill, eat until the exhaustion of the appetite (*manger à sa faim*),[36] was the principal pleasure that the peasants dangled before their imaginations, and one that they rarely realized in their lives.

They also imagined other dreams coming true, including the standard run of castles and princesses. But their wishes usually remained fixed on common objects in the everyday world. One hero gets "a cow and some chickens"; another, an armoire full of linens. A third settles for light work, regular meals, and a pipe full of tobacco. And when gold rains into the fireplace of a fourth, he uses it to buy "food, clothes, a horse, land/"[37] In most of the tales, wish fulfillment turns into a program for survival, not a fantasy of escape.

NOTES

1. This text and those of the other French folktales discussed in this essay come from Paul Delarue and Marie-Louise Tenèze, *Le Conte populaire franqais* (Paris, 1976), 3 vols., which is the best of the French folktale collections because it provides all the recorded versions of each tale along with background information about how they were gathered from oral sources, Delarue and Tenèze also arrange the tales according to the standard Aarne-Thompson classification scheme, so they can be compared with versions of the same "tale type" in other oral traditions. Sec Antti Aarne and Stith Thompson, *The Types of the Folktale: A Classification and Bibliography* (2nd rev.; Helsinki, 1973). References hereafter are to the Aarne-Thompson designations, which can be used to locate the texts in Delarue- Tenèze. In this case, for example, the talc belongs to tale type 333,"The Glutton," and thirty-five versions of it appear in *Le Conte populaire franqais,* I, 373–81. I have chosen the most common version for my translation. For more information on folktales as a historical source, see Stith Thompson, *The Folktale* (Berkeley and Los Angeles, 1977; 1st ed. 1946) and the references in note 7 and 8 to this chapter.

2. *Erich Fromm,* The Forgotten Language: An Introduction to the Understanding of Dreams, Fairy Tales and Myths *(New York, 1951), pp. 235–41, quotation from p. 240.*

3. On the sources and transmission of "Little Red Riding Hood," see Johannes Bolte and Georg Polivka, *Anmerkungen zu den Kinder- und Hausm'drchen der Brüder Grimm,* 5 vols. (Leipzig, 1913–32), I, 234–37 and IV, 431–34 and, for more recent work, Wilhelm Schoof, *Zur Entstehungsgeschichte der Grimmschen Màrchen* (Hamburg, 1959), pp. 59–61 and 74–77. My reading of the evidence supports the interpretations of H. V. Velten,"The Influence of Charles Perrauk's *Contes de ma mère l'Oie," The Germanic Review* V (1930), 4–18 and Paul Delarue,"Les Contes merveilleux de Perrault et la tradition populaire," *Bulletin folklorique d'Ile-de-France,* new series, July-Oct., 1951), 221–28 and 251–60. The Grimms also published a second version of the tale, which ends like the tale known as "The Three Little Pigs" in English (tale type 124). They got it from Dorothea Wild, the future wife of Wilhelm Grimm. She in turn learned it from her housemaid,"die alte Marie," whom Schoof has identified as Marie Müller, the widow of a blacksmith killed in the American Revolutionary War: Schoof, *Zur Entstehungsgeschichte, pp.* 59–61. Although the Grimms took pains to make accurate transcriptions of the tales told to them, they rewrote the texts considerably as they proceeded from edition to edition. For their rewriting of "Little Red Riding Hood," see Bolte and Polívka, *Anmerkungen,* IV, 455.

4. Bruno Bettelheim, *The Uses of Enchantment: The Meaning and Importance of Fairy Tales* (New York, 1977), pp. 166–83.

5. Bettelheim's interpretation of folktales can be reduced to four false propositions: that the tales have usually been intended for children (ibid., p. 15), that they must always have a happy ending (ibid., p. 37), that they are "timeless" (ibid., p. 97), and that they can be applied, in the versions familiar to modern Americans, to "any society" (ibid., p. 5). In criticizing the psychoanalytic reading of folktales, I do not mean to imply that the tales contain no subconscious or irrational elements. I mean to take issue with the anachronistic and reductionistic use of Freudian ideas. For further examples, see the interpretations of "The Frog King" (a phallic fantasy),"Aladdin" (a masturbation fantasy),"Jack and the Beanstalk" (an oedipal fantasy, although there is some confusion as to who is castrated, the father or the son, when Jack

chops down the beanstalk), and other tales in Ernest Jones,"Psychoanalysis and Folklore" and William H. Dcsrnonde,"Jack and the Beanstalk" in *The Study of Folklore,* ed. Alan Dundes (Englewood Cliffs, 1965), pp. 88–102 and 107–9 and Sigmund Freud and D. E. Oppenheim, *Dreams in Folklore* (New York, 1958).

6. For examples of work that combines sensitivity to linguistics, narrative modes, and cultural context, see Melville Herskovits and Frances Herskovits, *Dahomean Narrative: a Cross-cultural Analysis* (Evanston, 111., 1958); Linda Dégh, *Folktales and Society: Story-telling in a Hungarian Peasant Community* (Bloomington, Ind., 1969); *The Social Use of Metaphor: Essays on the Anthropology of Rhetoric,* ed. J. David Sapir and J, Christopher Crocker (Philadelphia, 1977); and Keith H. Basso, *Portraits of "the Whiteman": Linguistic Play and Cultural Symbols among the Western Apache* (New York, 1979). An exemplary study of narrative in an oral tradition that has died out is Dell H. Hymes,"The 'Wife' Who 'Goes Out' Like a Man: Reinterpretation of a Clackamas Chinook Myth," in *Structural Analysis of Oral Tradition,* ed. Pierre Maranda and Elii Köngàs Maranda (Philadelphia, 1971).

7. See Aarne and Thompson, *Types of the Folktale;* Thompson, *Folktale*; and Vladimir Propp, *Morphology of the Folktale,* trans. Laurence Scott (Austin, 1968). Aarne and Thompson used the "historical-geographical" or "Finnish" method, developed by Kaarle Krohn, to produce a world-wide survey and classification of folktales. Other scholars working in the same vein have done monographs on individual tales or cycles of tales. See, for example, Marian R. Cox, *Cinderella: Three Hundred and Forty-five Variants* (London, 1893) and Kurt Ranke, *Die Zwei Brüder: eine Studie zur Vergleichenden Märchenforschung,* FF (Folklore Fellows) Communications No. 114 (Helsinki, 1934). The most important general study of European folktales is still the *Anmerkungen* of Bolte and Polivka. More recent work, especially in the United States, tends to emphasize the linguistic and ethnographic aspects of folktales, to relate them to other forms of folklore, and to interpret them as performances rather than as written texts. See Dundes, *Study of Folklore;* Alan Dundes, *Interpreting Folklore* (Bloomington, Ind., 1980); Richard M. Dorson, *Folklore: Selected Essays* (Bloomington, Ind., 1972); and *Toward New Perspectives in Folklore,* ed. Americo Paredes and Richard Bauman (Austin, 1972).

8. This information comes from Paul Delarue's introduction to *Le Conte populaire franqais,* I, 7–99, which is the best general account of folklore research in France and which also contains a thorough bibliography. The most important collections of French folktales, aside from that of Delarue and Tenèze, are Emmanuel *Cosqu'm, Contes populaires de Lorraine* (Paris, 1886), 2 vols.; Paul Sébillot, *Contes populaires de la Haute Bretagne (*Paris, 1880–82), 3 vols.; and J. F. Bladé, *Contes populaires de la Gascogne* (Paris, 1886), 3 vols. Texts and studies of tales have also appeared in journals devoted to French folklore, notably *Arts et traditions populaires, Melusine,* and *Bulletin Jolklorique d'lle-de-F ranee.* I have drawn on all these sources but have relied primarily on Delarue and Tenèze, *Le Conte populaire fran^ais.*

9. Delarue,"Les contes merveilleux de Perrault."

10. William Thorns launched the term "folklore" in 1846, two decades before Edward Tylor introduced a similar term,"culture," among English-speaking anthropologists. See Thorns,"Folklore" and William R. Bascom,"Folklore and Anthropology" in Dundes, *Study of Folklore,* pp. 4–6 and 25–33.

11. Noël du Fail, *Propos rustiques de Maistre Leon Ladulfi Champenois,* chap. 5, in *Conteurs français du XVIe siècle,* ed, Pierre Jourda (Paris, 1956), pp. 620–21.

12. French folklore could be subjected to a structuralist or formalist analysis of the sort used by Claude Lévi-Strauss and Vladimir Propp. I have tried out those methods on several tales but abandoned them for the looser study of structure that is presented in the last part of this essay. For an example of structuralist analysis applied successfully to tales that could only be known through written texts long after they were recorded, see Hymes,"The 'Wife' Who 'Goes Out' Like a Man."

13. Albert B. Lord, *The Singer of Tales* (Cambridge, Mass., 1960).

14. Propp, *Morphology of the Folktale.*

15. Lowie's remark is quoted in Richard Dorson,"The Debate over the Trustworthiness of Oral Traditional History" in Dorson, *Folklore: Selected Essays,* p. 202.

16. On the different issues of historicity and continuity in oral narratives, see Dorson,"The Debate over the Trustworthiness of Oral Traditional History"; Robert Lowie,"Some Cases of Repeated Reproduction" in Dundes, *Study of Folklore,* pp. 259–64; Jan Vansina, *Oral Tradition: A Study in Historical Methodology* (Chicago, 1965); and Herbert T. Hoover,"Oral History in the United States," in *The Past Before Us: Contemporary Historical Writing in the United States,* ed. Michael Kàmmen (Ithaca and London, 1980), pp. 391–407.

17. Frank Hamilton Cushing, *Zuni Folk Tales* (New York and London, 1901), pp. 411–22. Although Cushing was one of the first researchers to master the Zuni language and record Zuni tales, his translations should be read with some reservations as to their accuracy; they contain an admixture of Victorian religiosity. See Dennis Tedlock,"On the Translation of Style in Oral Narrative," in *Toward New Perspectives in Folklore,* ed. Americo Paredes and Richard Bauman, pp. 115–18.

18. Jack Goody, *The Domestication of the Savage Mind* (Cambridge, 1977). See also the studies published by Goody as *Literacy in Traditional Societies* (Cambridge, 1968). Although he claims not to hold a "great divide" view of history, Goody distinguishes all societies that have acquired writing from all those that have not. Most folklorists and anthropologists reject such an either-or, before-and-after dichotomy, and attribute considerable stability to oral traditions, even after the spread of literacy. See, for example, Thompson, *The Folktale,* p. 437; Francis Lee Utley,"Folk Literature: An Operational Definition," in Dundes, *Study of Folklore,* p. 15; and Alan Dundes,"The Transmission of Folklore," ibid., p.-217.

19. Raymond D. Jameson, *Three Lectures on Chinese Folklore* (Peking, 1932).

20. This remark occurs in Perrault's version, which contains a sophisticated reworking of the dialogue in the peasant versions. See Delarue and Tenèze, *Le Conte populaire francais,* I, 306–24.

21. "Jean de l'Ours," tale type 301B.

22. See "Le Conte de Parle," tale type 328 and "La Belle Eulalie," tale type 313.

23. "Pitchin-Pitchot," tale type 327C.

24. Among the other general works that treat the Old Regime as a peculiar social order that existed in France between the Renaissance and the Revolution, see Pierre Goubert, *L'Aticieti Régime* (Paris, 1969 and 1973), 2 vols, and Roland Mousnier, *Les Institutions de la France sous la monarchic absolue, 1598–1789* (Paris, 1974). These books contain adequate bibliographical guides to the vast literature on French social history during this period.

25. Le Roy Ladurie,"L'Histoire immobile," *Annales: Economies, sociétés, civilisations,* XXIX (1974), 673–92. See also Fernand Braudel's remarks on "une histoire quasi immobile." in the preface to *La Méditerranée et le monde méditerranéen à l'époque de Philippe II, ;* reprinted in Braudel, *Ecrits sur l'histoire* (Paris, 1969), p. 11. The notion of an "unmoving" early modern France owed a great deal to the Malthusian interpretation of social history j developed by Jean Meuvret in the 1940s and 1950s. See especially his influential article,"Les Crises de subsistances et la demographie de la France d'Ancien Regime," *Population,* II (1947), 643–47. Historical demographers have now begun to undercut that view. See, for example, Jacques Dupàquier,"Revolution fran^aise et revolution demographique" in *Vom Ancien Régime zur Französischen Revolution: Forschungen and Perspektiven,* ed. Ernst Hinrichs, Eberhard Schmitt, and Rudolf Vierhaus (Göttingen, 1978), pp. 233–60.

26. For examples of the vast literature on the peasantry and the rural and urban poor, see Pierre Goubert, *Beauvais et le Beauvaisis de 1600 à 1730*: Contribution a l'histoire sociale de la France du XVIIe

siècle (Paris, 1960) and Olwen H. Hufton, The Poor of Eighteenth-Century France, 1750–1789 (Oxford, 1974).

27. For surveys of demographic history, see Dupàquier,"Révolution française et révolution démographique;" Pierre Guillaume and Jean-Pierre Poussou, *Démographie historique* (Paris, 1970); and Pierre Goubert,"Le Poids du monde rural" in *Histoire économique et sociale de la France,* ed. Ernest Labrousse and Fernand Braudel (Paris, 1970), pp. 3–158.

28. Delarue and Tenèze, *Le Conte populaire français,* II, 143.

29. Ibid., II, 145.

30. Ibid., I, 279.

31. Ibid., I, 289.

32. Quotations from ibid., I, 353, 357, 358, and 360.

33. Ibid., II, 398:

34. Ibid., II, 394.

35. 35.. Ibid., II, 269.

36. Ibid., I, 275.

37. Ibid., II, 480; II, 53; II, 182; and I, 270.

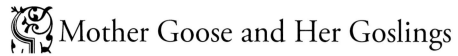

Mother Goose and Her Goslings

The France of Louis XIV as Seen through the Fairy Tale

Dorothy Thelander

When we were very young, we read "Cinderella," "Ali Baba," and "The Little Tin Soldier" with delight and wonder. Then we grew up and left the literature of our childhood to the folklorists and the psychiatrists. In this article, I propose examining fairy tales that received their traditional form in late seventeenth-century France to see what they tell us about the specific culture that produced them.[1] Section 1 discusses the question of whose culture these tales may be said to reflect. Although fairy tales have been studied most systematically by the folklorists, this does not mean that the tales that have come down to us from late seventeenth-century France reflect peasant or folk culture. Rather they reflect, or also reflect, the sophisticated, aristocratic milieu that gave them the form which they have retained ever since. Section 2 discusses the fairy tales' treatment of fundamental social institutions like the monarchy, the family, and the aristocracy. Section 3 tries to elucidate what the supernatural elements in these stories tell us about the attitudes of their authors towards the world around them. The conclusion suggests that the interest in fairy tales in late seventeenth- century France was not unconnected with that "Crise de la conscience européenne" which Paul Hazard ascribed to the period.

I The Literary Fairy Tale and its Folk Sources

The 100 or so fairy tales published in France between about 1690 and 1710 form a remarkable group of stories. Most of them are forgotten, but not "Sleeping Beauty," "Cinderella," "Little Red Riding Hood," "Bluebeard," "Puss 'n Boots," and perhaps a half dozen others. For most of us, they define that group of folktales known as fairy tales: one has only to glance at so basic a source as Stith Thompson's *The Folktale* to realize that even folklorists use them as touchstones.[2] Yet, contrary to the usual definition of folktale—that it is a story of uncertain origin, transmitted orally—these stories all had authors, and not authors who were illiterate or

---

1 I will use the more common term "fairy tale" rather than the technically correct but less familiar *Märchen*. I have also used the English titles for the French tales where this does not create confusion (e.g.,"L'Oiseau bleu" is not "The Blue Bird" of Maeterlinck, so I have not translated it), taking the titles and some of the translated quotations from Iona and Peter Opie, *The Classic Fairy Tales* (London; Oxford University Press, 1974). The chief studies are Mary Elizabeth Storer, *La Mode des contes de fées (1685–1700)* (Paris: Champion, 1928), and Jacques Barchillon, *Le Conte merveilleux français de 1690 a 1790* (Paris: Champion, 1975).
2 *The Folktale* (New York: Holt, Rinehart, and Winston, 1946), pp. 4–5, 7–8.

peasants, but members of the upper classes, usually allied to the literary group called the *précieux*.[3] The stories were not designed for children—their authors tell us that they wrote for adult audiences.[4] Even the seeming exception—the central group written probably by Charles Perrault[5] which was known from an inscription on the frontispiece as the "Contes de ma mère l'oye" and dedicated to a girl (or young woman) of fifteen—was meant to appeal to youths and young adults, not to children.

Although the French authors wrote (or rewrote) fairy tales for sophisticated adult audiences, their audience changed when their works crossed the Channel. Contemporary translations into English of the tales of Charles Perrault, Mme d'Aulnoy, and Fénelon seem to have been Aiméd at children and young adolescents. But in France, many of the tales first appeared in the *Mercure galant* (including Perrault's "Sleeping Beauty"), a serial publication whose title suggests its audience. A few first appeared as chapters in novels.[6]

Most of the fairy tales first published in the *Mercure galant* were subsequently collected by their authors and reprinted in separate (and not inexpensive) volumes. After about 1710, however, the oriental tale and the openly erotic tale replaced the fairy tale as fashionable literature. By the time the tales were reprinted in the *Cabinet des fées* in 1785–89, most of the original volumes were hard to obtain. The tales of Perrault and some of Mme d'Aulnoy, however, had by then reached a larger, if less prosperous and less sophisticated, audience than that of the *Mercure galant*. These fairy tales were the only fiction, other than a few translations of obscure *chansons de geste*, to be circulated repeatedly in the *Bibliothéque bleue*, the famous booklets covered in plain blue wrappers with which peddlars stuffed their sacks. And so the oral transmission of these tales was contaminated and in some cases even supplanted by the written text.

As originally published at the turn of the eighteenth century, the fairy tales form a distinct socioliterary *genre*. Their roots lay in stories that peasant nursemaids and servants told children left in their charge, yet in their written form they were shaped by highly sophisticated writers for an adult and relatively sophisticated audience. Indeed, both the authors and the initial audiences for these tales were associated with, or at least shared the ideals of, the Paris salons, particularly those which cultivated the refinement of language and manners associated with the *précieux*. To indicate this relationship, I shall refer to the tales as Salon tales, without, however, intending by this term to exaggerate the homogeneity of their authorship or of their readers.[7]

---

3 A *précieux* is, of course, more than a person who spoke or wrote in a particular style. Though the *précieux* movement is usually remembered for its excesses in the purification of language and manners, it included serious men and particularly women who wanted legal reforms to give women the right to marry or remain single, to refuse to have children, and to look after their own affairs. Marie-Jeanne L' Héritier de Villandon, niece of Charles Perrault, a *précieuse* and intimate of Mile de Scudéry, wrote four fairy tales. Current studies of *préciosité* include: Dorothy Backer, *Precious Women* (New York: Basic Books, 1974); Carolyn C. Lou *gee, Le Paradis des Femmes: Women, Salons, and Social Stratification in Seventeenth-Century France* (Princeton: Princeton University Press, 1976), and Roger Lathulliere, *La Préciosite: Etude historique et linguistique* (Geneva: Droz, 1966).

4 "Sleeping Beauty" appeared in the *Mercure galant* of February, 1696, with this comment: "Quoyque les Contes des Fées et des Ogres semblent n'estre bons que pour les enfans, je suis persuadé que la lecture de celuy que je vous envoye vous fera plaisir." Marie-Catherine Le Jumel de Barneville de la Motte d'Aulnoy, author of eleven volumes of fairy tales, imagined one group to have been told by some women during a short carriage trip.

5 There is some dispute as to whether Charles Perrault or his adolescent son known as Darmancour or both together wrote the *Contes*. Perrault was the author of the *Paralléle des anciens et des modernes*, a member of the Académie, closely associated with Colbert and interested in almost every facet of art and literature. See Marc Soriano, *Le Dossier Charles Perrault* (Paris: Hachette, 1972) and *Les Contes de Perrault, culture savante et traditions populaires* (Paris: Gallimard, 1968).

6 Catherine Bernard included a version of "Riquet à la houppe in her novel Inés de Cordoue, as did Antoine Hamilton in Le Bélier, and Themisseul de Saint-Hyacinthe in Prince Titi

7 Authors of worldly fairy tales include le Sieur de Préchac, *Contes moins contes que les autres* Louise de Bossigny, comtesse d'Auneuil, *La Tyrannic des fées détruite* and *Les Chevaliers errans* and Catherine Durand Bédacier, *La Comtesse*

The Salon tales share characteristics of folk literature and high literature. They show their folk origins and are distinguished from the high literature of their day by their relative brevity; their use of formulas ("Once upon a time"—"and they lived happily ever after"); the simplicity of their characters; the omnipresence of plots, characters, and motifs borrowed from peasant culture; and the comparative absence of eroticism. They do not take place in an easily recognizable place or time. Above all, the fairy tales are not concerned with the great themes of classical French literature: the tragic conflicts between duties and between love and duty, or the comic consequences of disregarding or exaggerating the norms by which society regulates itself.

But these stories also show the artful hand of their authors. Some of them are considerably more complex than folk tales are likely to be. They pay more attention to detail, particularly in their description of their characters' clothing and appearance. Their wit is more sophisticated, their attitude to their heroes and heroines more ambivalent. Magical elements are less important in the French tales than in fairy tales that have come to us directly from the oral tradition. While the great classical themes may be little more than echoes, the tales still reflect a concern with love, marriage, and advancement in social terms that are foreign to the folk fairy tale.

This is true even of the tales of Perrault, which are sometimes seen as close to the peasant originals because they have relatively unified plots, they seldom elaborate unnecessarily, and they sometimes include rhymes and incantations. There is little real evidence for this view, which assumes that peasant tale-tellers in seventeenth-century France were as concerned about plot structure and the significant detail as were the aristocratic classicists. Furthermore, the complications added to the tales of Mme d'Aulnoy and the other Salon writers are often motifs or engrafted tale-types that themselves appear to derive from oral traditions. Finally, we must always remember that simplicity can conceal quite as much skill and craftsmanship as complexity.

All one can say is that, on the one hand, even the most literary of these stories seems to have been made from bits and pieces of folktale, transformed by the magic wand of literary skill at best and mère upper-class taste at worst. On the other hand, there is no reason to believe that any of the authors accurately reproduced peasant sources. Systematic collecting of folktales did not begin in France until the nineteenth century; during the seventeenth century, no one sat down with a peasant informant on the one hand and a quill pen in the other to take down the speaker's exact words. While most of the fairy tale authors claim to have heard the stories from servants during their own childhood, nothing in the canon of late seventeenth-century literary tradition demanded faithful transcription. In a society where some believed that the cruder passages in Homer ought to be removed, why should our authors refuse to improve on lesser sources?[8]

There are additional reasons for doubting that any of the tales reached their public as they had been told in peasant circles. First, the authors may have remembered only part of what they had heard as children. Indeed, the literary model for many of these fairy tales seems to have been the romances favored by the earlier *précieux*, long tales of improbable adventures in the quest for true love. Second, the peasant informants may have been unreliable—they may have exercised a kind of censorship over the stories that they told their aristocratic charges. Why should the nursemaid not use self-censorship about class or arrange cruel and pleasant elements according to her assessment of both the child's needs and his parents' expectations? This is what present-day storytellers do.

It is difficult to establish the relationship between these literary recensions and their oral peasant sources because we do not have enough alternate versions from which to derive an "Ur-text" for any of these tales, and because we have little solid knowledge of the repertoire from which these tales were drawn or the canons

---

de Mortane and *Les Pet its Soupers de l'été de l'année 1699.* … Charlotte-Rose Caumont de La Force and Henriette-Julie de Castelnau de Mu rat each wrote tales which were somewhat more free in their use of erotic material than the others.

8   The poetic translation of *The Iliad* by Houdar de la Motte in 1713 is half the length of the prose translation of Mme Dacier. This is almost the last battle in France of the Quarrel of the Ancients and the Moderns.

of selection their authors employed.[9] By the nineteenth century, the literary versions of these tales had clearly influenced, and often replaced, the versions that had earlier formed part of the Francophone oral tradition.

The first reliable repertoire of oral tales, Paul Delarue's *Le Conte populaire en France*, was compiled in the middle of the twentieth century.[10] Of the 100 tale types it lists, forty had received literary treatment in the seventeenth century, mostly in the Salon tales. But this does not mean that the Salon tales used 40 percent of the oral repertoire of their day, because it is likely that seventeenth-century France had more than one hundred tale types, many of which have been lost—as in other cultures when oral transmission fades before the printed page. Like other west- ern, industrialized nations, present-day France does not have a lively oral tradition. The *veillées* of the nineteenth and early twentieth centuries, when peasants sat around the fire telling stories, seem to have largely disappeared by the time Delarue began his work. The preservation in Canada and Louisiana (two regions where an oral tradition re- mains alive in small communities) of tale types that had completely disappeared from twentieth-century France suggests that there were others of which we have no record whatsoever.

In any case, I am not concerned with what the fairy tales, restored to their "Ur-text" (if that were possible), might tell us about the peasant culture of seventeenth-century France. In the tales as we have them, peasant and aristocratic elements cannot be rigorously distinguished. Every teller of tales (literate or nonliterate) changes his material to suit his audience and himself. The tales cannot be used to prove the high culture of the noble French peasant or the greater culture of the elite who adopted them for their own purposes. The fairy tales are what they are; they seem to survive national politics and cultural jingoism.

II Social Institutions

A. Government

Although we remember that *Télémaque* and the other stories of Fénelon were composed to educate the Due de Bourgogne in his duties and obligations as heir apparent to Louis XIV, we do not usually think about the political morality of fairy tales. Yet the compiler of the *Cabinet des fées* referred to them as "l'école des rois" (XXXVII, p. 42) with no apparent sarcasm. For him, the purpose of these tales was to teach those who govern the sublime lessons of truth and virtue. Thus, kings, princes, and the merely literate all received the same lessons about government.

Indeed, in these tales, the government is invariably monarchical, if it is mentioned at all. The lack of alterna- tives suggests a real consensus—in the late seventeenth century, the normative government for the French was of course a monarchy. However, the institution of monarchy as described in the Salon tales is slightly different from what we might expect from a "School for Kings." The tales do not talk about the nature of kingship or impose limits on royal power. They do insist that a distinction be made between the good king, the bad king, and the well-intentioned but weak king; this distinction is often crucial to the working out of the plot. The good king is marked by his equity, his spiritual uprightness, and his love for his subjects, as Mile L' Héritier explains in "Ricdan-Ricdon." He may have been killed before the tale begins, but he died a noble death, mourned all the more by his subjects and his family because his killer, who always succeeds him, invariably becomes a bad king and comes to a bad end. The good kings who appear in the tales usually live happily along with the prince-heroes who will someday succeed them.

---

9   In order to understand the tales chosen by our authors, we need to know about those which they did not find worthy of treatment (the "wily peasant" is, for example, absent from the Salon tales)

10   Paul Delarue and M. L. Tenéze, *Le Conte populaire frangais,* 1 (Paris: Erasme, 1957) and 2 (Paris: Maisonneuve et Larose, 1965).

The king must appear kinglike—about this there is no question; even weak kings must have a regal appearance. Bad kings are sometimes ugly. If the good king is ugly, he invariably becomes handsome and tall before the end of the story. Should he have the misfortune to be turned into a bluebird, his minister tells him that it will be impossible for him to continue to reign since no one would obey a bluebird, who might be eaten by a cat; to remain a king, he must be freed from his metamorphosis. This is an extreme situation; but it is generally assumed that good kings will look the part.

The favored style of government combines autocracy with consultation. All well-intentioned rulers are portrayed as consulting others before making major decisions, and these consultations take two forms: with the wise man (or woman or fairy), or with regular advisors, ministers, or other nobles. Unlike the well-intentioned but weak king, however, the good king knows which advice to take and which to ignore. He is always possessed of enough insight to recognize the truth of the wise man or fairy's advice, but his consultations with ministers or nobles have a formalistic quality: these advisors are not treated as men of consequence, functioning rather as an echo or a foil to the strong, autocratic ruler. The weak king, on the other hand, is presented as incapable of making up his own mind and often doing what his advisor of the moment tells him to do (and being punished in consequence). Since he means well, a first mistaken action may be forgiven the weak king: when the king in Mme d'Aulnoy's "La Belle aux cheveux d'or" wrongfully imprisons the hero Avenant, he realizes his error and releases him. When the king again listens to his ministers and imprisons Avenant, he must die. Since he is not evil, merely misguided, he dies painlessly by swallowing his own magic potion. This is a different fate from the one that awaits the evil ruler.

The evil king may inherit his realm, although he often acquires it by conquering and killing a good king. He rules cruelly and capriciously, without love for his subjects. He enforces his will by fear. He usually rules without advice, but if he does consult, it is with men who are as evil as he.

The seeking of advice is not in itself a virtue because the bad king will seek (and get) bad advice. A reign is not virtuous because the advice is good; the virtuous king alone seeks wisdom in his advisors. But to say that a good king receives good advice and an evil king is reinforced in his bad behavior is to say that what nobles do does not matter since they do not change the fundamental character of any king's reign. Yet, at the same time, seeking advice is the proper behavior for a king when the matter to be decided is difficult.

If the good king is sometimes killed before the Salon tale begins, the fate of the evil king within the tale is certain. Wicked regents are treated just as summarily. The ogre king Galifron in "La Belle aux cheveux d'or" and the tyrant usurper in "Ricdan-Ricdon" are both killed. In "L'Oiseau bleu," the people storm the palace when the well-intentioned but weak king dies and they stone the wicked queen to death (with neither leadership nor support from the nobles). The number of queen regents and their generally evil natures remind us of the unpopular queens who had ruled France during the minorities of their sons during the sixteenth and seventeenth centuries: Catherine de Medicis, Marie de Medicis, Anne of Austria. More generally, the frequency with which the evil ruler is punished by death suggests that he has the usufruct of his kingdom only as long as he looks and acts his role and is just to his subjects.

With the exception of the usually evil queen regents, women do not rule alone. If the kingdom descends to a daughter, as it does fairly often, she is married to the king of a neighboring country or to his son at the conclusion of the tale. The marriage serves many purposes: it preserves the tradition that women may not rule, except as regents for their sons; it underscores the idea of royalty as a separate class; and it provides a happy ending.

The marriage would also appear to unite two kingdoms into a greater whole, but the tales do not emphasize the fact that *kingdoms* a re being merged. Indeed, it is significant that the boundaries of the kingdoms which we meet in the Salon tales are never made clear—the reader has no way of knowing where the "neighboring kingdom" begins or ends, The lack of maps is particularly surprising because the *précieux* movement to which these tales can be linked is always presented to us by the *Carte de Tendre*, a cartographic representation of the paths to various kinds of love. Nor is the *Carte de Tendre* unique in the work of the *précieux* and their enemies: there are maps, both verbal and pictorial, for all sorts of imaginary kingdoms in contemporary books—except in these fairy tales. "Ricdan-Ricdon" by Mile L' Héritier provides an excellent example. There are two kingdoms in this tale. The Amsterdam edition includes music for the songs, printed on fold- out pages. Both the expense of this format and the admixture of *précieux* themes would lead us to expect a map of one or both kingdoms, yet there is none.[11]

Indeed, the word "kingdom" is not associated with fixed boundaries or a particular spoken language or a sense of political nationality. Kingdoms are united through marriage and occasionally expanded by conquest. Kingship is, in a sense, a vocation. One may be born in one kingdom and rule another through marriage to the heiress or queen. Two generations later, in the *Encyclopédie* of D'Alembert and Diderot, nation is defined as a "collective word which is used to represent a considerable number of people who inhabit a specific area of land, contained in specific limits *[limites]*, and who obey the same government."[12] *Limites* are not the same thing as boundaries. According to Lucien Febvre: "Before the Revolution, people walked straight across the *limites*: aristocrats, scholars, traders crossed with no surprise. Frontiers existed only for the military and the prince—and only in times of war."[13] Those little dots and dashes which mark the end of one country on present-day maps represent true boundaries; Febvre argues that it took a revolution to give such boundaries to France. If we look at the maps of the *précieux* again, we notice that countries fade into one another, except where rivers, oceans, and mountains serve as barriers—and even these fictional maps are not found in collections of Salon tales.

Nor do these tales present us with any institutions of government that may be indentified with the kingdom and not the king. There is no elaborate apparatus for government—indeed, when the king and his brother leave the kingdom in the hands of their sister while they go off on a quest, she can join them, entrusting the realm to the wisest man, or so it happens in "Princess Rosette." There are no real problems of succession—if the heir is a daughter, a husband who will be king is part of the ending. There are no bitter quarrels over inheritance. The apparatus of government has been reduced to a bare minimum: the monarch, the royal family, a few courtiers. This pattern persists even in the most complicated tales, suggesting that our authors were not simplifying to conform to the needs of a simple story. Rather, the stories reflect what we know from other sources: the nostalgia that gripped so many well-placed persons in France for the idealized monarchy of an earlier age, not necessarily feudal times (in the tales the nobles play too small and often too evil a role for that) but for strong personal kingship without the governmental apparatus of Louis XIV.

B. Religion

If politics in fairyland is reduced to a few moral precepts about the nature and function of kingship, religion is almost entirely absent. Judging from present-day French tales,[14] there ought to have been an occasional reference to Christianity in the peasant sources of our tales.

Modern tales include angels, the devil, and the Virgin: they are totally absent from the Salon tales/Priests are relegated to walk-on roles in marriage and baptismal ceremonies. The characters die without benefit of clergy. Furthermore, there is no indication of a revolt against enforced vocations. No one thinks of entering a convent or seeking the advice of a priest or even going to confession. Of all the children established at the end of the

---

11   La Tour ténébreuse et les jours lumineux, contes anglois *(Amsterdam: Desbordes, 1706), p. 30.*

12   S. *V.* Nation.

13   13   Lucien Febvre,"Frontière: le mot et la notion," in *Pour me histoire à part entière* (Paris: S.E.V.P.E.N., 1962), p.

14   *The Borzoi Book of French Fairy Tales*, Paul Delarue, ed., trans. Austin E. Fife (New York: Knopf, 1956) includes tales from the nineteenth and twentieth centuries with overt Christian elements.

Salon tales, not one enters the Church. Prayer, which one might expect to be a solace to hero and heroine in their tribulations, appears only infrequently and then as a means of gaining time until earthly forces can intervene to set things right. The characters do not go to heaven or hell; they fall into snake pits or live happily on earth ever after. *[handwritten margin notes: Bluebeard / Sleeping Beauty]*

It has been suggested that an admixture of fairies and angels, of magical and Christian elements, was felt to be irreligious, and that our writers deleted references to Christianity from their peasant sources.[15] Perhaps, though it is also possible that the peasant sources did not contain significant Christian elements in the late seventeenth century. Still, several versions of "Little Red Riding Hood" current in France today have the wolf force the girl to eat her grandmother's flesh and drink her blood, thus evoking the Eucharist as well as suggesting cannibalism.[16] Marc Soriano believes that Perrault reworked "Sleeping Beauty" to avoid an ambiguity in some versions which might have been unacceptable to the pious.[17] In earlier redactions, the heroine gives birth to her children before awakening; Soriano thinks that Sleeping Beauty's immediate awakening at the kiss of Prince Charming avoids any comparison with the Virgin Mary. In any case, in the tales as they were published, the Catholic church as an institution is almost entirely absent.

Indeed, the Salon tales contain little or no description of anything that could be called religious behavior. Pagan religiosity is almost as absent from them as Christian. Our writers did not introduce (or substitute) the kind of learned paganism found in all the arts of the seventeenth century, whose popularity led that arbiter of taste, Chapelain, to warn that it was not proper for Christian inhabitants of a Christian kingdom to invoke Jupiter.[18] It is notable that pagan gods and goddesses frequently appear in the moralizing fairy tales of Fenelon, the famous and pious archbishop of Cambrai and tutor to Louis XIV's grandson and heir apparent. The one writer of fairy tales at that time whose religious commitment cannot be questioned seems to have been unable to imagine a world without divine beings. For the others, fairyland is a very secular place.[19]

C. The Family

The family is the central social unit in the Salon tales. The protagonist is usually a member of a nuclear family, and a small one at that. The rich and royal as well as the poor are often presented as childless. Then, through miraculous/fairy intervention, they have one child—the protagonist—who will, at the end of the story, form another family. There are exceptions; Perrault's "Le Petit Poucet" (a kind of French "Hansel and Gretel" with an ogre in place of a witch) does have six brothers, and the ogre has seven daughters, but one or two siblings is the norm. If there are more siblings, they have often left home.

The family is small but the relationship between parents and children is complex. On the surface, the children obey their parents without questioning or complaining. There are exceptions, such as "Peau d'Âne," about a princess who runs away from her father, and "Ricdan- Ricdon," where Rosanie complains about her peasant mother's harsh treatment. But these stories are exceptional in other ways, too. Peau d'Âne is escaping from a father who wants to seduce her—the only open mention of incest in these tales. As for Rosanie, it is later revealed that her true mother is a queen and not the peasant who had nurtured her and about whom she had complained.

---

15   See Soriano, *Le Dossier*, p. 98.

16   *The Borzoi Book of French Fairy Tales*, p. 232.

17   *Les Contes de Perrault*, pp. 125–134.

18   Jean Chapelain, *De la Lecture des vieux romans*, ed. Alphonse Feillet (Paris: Aubry, 1870), p. 9.

19   This does not mean that the authors were irreligious or even just unambivalently secular in their outlook. See below, "Conclusions."

Most commonly, children behave like Gracieuse, who refuses to run away and marry Percinet without her father's consent, even though her father allows her stepmother to torture her and Percinet must intervene repeatedly to save her. Le Petit Poucet does not defy his parents and refuse to go into the woods, though he has overheard his parents planning to abandon the children. The tales would seem to reward obedience, since this virtue ultimately leads to the happiness of the protagonists.

Yet, when we look more carefully, we find that often it is outward obedience (to unjust commands) rather than real obedience which is rewarded. Gracieuse does eventually marry Percinet without her father's consent. Le Petit Poucet intends to outwit his parents and leave a trail to guide him and his brothers back home. Bluebeard's wife disobeys her husband by opening the door of the forbidden room; her punishment is a short period of fear, but, in the end, she is married to a good man and her whole family is enriched. In the politics of the family, the protagonist appears to obey, while doing what he or she wants—not a bad description of how Frenchmen obeyed Louis XIV.

The natural parents of the hero or heroine are supposed to be loving and kind, though they can be induced to act cruelly by someone else or driven to do so by circumstances beyond their control. Some of Perrault's stories are more ambiguous, presenting evil parents, but the stories are so constructed that the reader is almost unaware of the situation. Prince Charming's mother is an ogress who plans to eat Sleeping Beauty and her two children. However, we forget that the ogress is the Prince's mother because he is away at war when she tries to carry out her plan. We are also distracted by her battle of wits with a good huntsman who substitutes animals for the intended victims, even trying to find one whose flesh is as tough as that of a young woman who is supposed to be over one hundred years old. In Perrault's "Diamonds and Toads," the mother who mistreats her good daughter refers to her as "ma fille" only once, when jewels drop out of her mouth. Perrault allows the mother to call the nasty daughter "ma fille" more often, thus emphasizing the relationship here. Interestingly, both Mile L' Héritier's version of the tale and Perrault's manuscript avoid the problem of a woman mistreating her natural daughter by portraying the good girl as the widow's stepdaughter.

Father-son conflicts are almost unknown in the Salon tales. The woodchopper in "Le Petit Poucet" abandons his children in the woods, but this is rare. Rather, all parent-child conflicts are pushed off onto the mother and she is then distanced from the child by being turned into a stepmother. For there is one villain in our tales whose very title suggests fairyland—the wicked stepmother.[20] Invariably, she has been married for her money. All sibling rivalries are dealt with by the same device, but while the wicked stepmother is often killed in a horrible way at the end, the nasty half-siblings usually share in the good fortune of the protagonist. Cinderella's half-sisters are married off well. Only a few of the worst half-siblings like Truitonne in "L'Oiseau Bleu" (who turns into a handsome pig) meet a condign fate. While many children in the late seventeenth century must have had stepparents, and the presence of stepparents and half-siblings undoubtedly complicated family life, the insistent use of these devices in all fairy tales suggests that they are not the product of anything specific to seventeenth-century French culture.

D. Marriage

While the Salon tales, like so many others, offer marriage as the proper resolution for the plot, the picture of marriage which emerges from within them often seems to contradict the promise of that ending. The happy-ending marriage is ideally one in which equally young, rich, handsome, and loving people are united. The marriages within the tales often break with this formula: the couple is not necessarily young; the woman is often married specifically for her money; one of the partners may be ugly or of a lower social status; and love does not

---

20   Snow White's beautiful stepmother who consulted the mirror belongs to the Germanic, not French, tradition.

always unite the partners. Many widows and widowers choose their mates only for money, bringing misery to at least one of their children and, ultimately, some unhappiness to themselves.

One example which illustrates the complexities of this theme is that of Prince Charming's parents. Prince Charming does not tell them about his own marriage to Sleeping Beauty, but covers his absences by claiming to be hunting game. His mother suspects that he has a mistress and questions her son:

> … but he never dared to trust her with his secret, he feared her though he loved her, for she was of the race of *Ogres*, and the King would never have married her, had it not been for her vast riches; it was even whispered about the court that she had Ogrish inclinations; and that when she saw little children passing by, she had all the difficulty in the world to refrain from falling upon them. … (Opie, p. 90)

If the marriage of the Prince's parents had been a good one, we would not have been told that the king had married his wife only for her vast riches. Perrault's "Sleeping Beauty" may have substituted a mother for the jealous wife of Basile's Pentamerone, Day 5, tale 5 (1636), in order to avoid turning a philandering husband into a hero (which would have been odious both to the *dévots* and the *précieuses)*. But Perrault then had to find a new motivation for the attempted murders of Sleeping Beauty and her children. He did that by turning the prince's mother into an ogress. Thus, even the marriage where the child is loved by both parents and where there is no apparent disharmony between the parents is ultimately a misalliance based on money and leading to near tragedy.

In seventeenth-century France, there were many critics of the family- arranged marriage if it involved great disparity of social status, wealth, and especially age and attractiveness. Within the *précieux* movement, there were at least two different attitudes towards marriage. The simpler saw love and marriage in Neoplatonic terms as inherently incompatible. The more complex sought to assure the woman of a degree of freedom within marriage and the right to refuse marriage. The latter view tended to accept marriage, but only if it was based on mutual love.[21]

If the Salon tales can be seen as a product of the *précieux* salons, then some of their anomalies become more explicable. The essential triad for the successful marriage would then be love, looks, and youth. Equality of wealth or social status ought not to be important. And, although very few true misalliances occur in these tales, the reader may perceive them as happening quite frequently since the betrothal usually takes place before we learn that the peasant bride is really a princess. It has been said that these events show the magic power of love to restore the protagonist to his or her lost birthright, and that is true. It is equally true that the prince who asks the ragged girl to marry him is, from his point of view, entering into a misalliance. When, however, the prince enters into it for love alone, the fairy tale makes us forget that it is a misalliance.

Occasionally, crasser motives are suggested, but as long as there is love, they do not matter. In "Diamonds and Toads," the prince estimates that the jewels which drop from the girl's mouth provide a worthy dowry; he is being calculating (even though he loves the girl) because she is not a princess, no matter how many rubies drop from her lips. Indeed, this girl resembles some of the *précieuses*—she is pretty and well-mannered and she is married for love and money. She would only have to learn to be witty to find herself at home in a salon as did Françoise Mignot, of whose parents nothing is known, but who married, first a treasurer of France, then the *Maréchal* Francois de Vitry du Hallier, and finally Jean Casimir, former King of Poland. Misalliances occurred in real life and in fiction; money could make them acceptable to many, but only the transforming power of love could make them fully acceptable to the *précieuses.*

In any case, the Salon tales seem to accept misalliances for the protagonists since they are often an integral part of the plot. The poor (or seemingly poor) heroine is sure to be married to a king or prince. The poor lad will become rich and marry according to his new station. But are we sure that the authors really believe that

---

21 Lougee, pp. 34–40.

the marriage of the hero and heroine will bring them happiness? "And they lived happily ever after" is as much a formula as "once upon a time"; it does not necessarily express a real expectation. Furthermore, some of the tales eschew the formula ending. In the "Yellow Dwarf," at each turn of the plot which would suggest this ending, Mme d'Aulnoy somehow rejects it. The princess is allowed to join her lover only in death, when they are transformed into palm trees, much like the roses growing together from the graves of Tristan and Iseult.[22] Love and marriage just do not go together; the lovers, symbolized by the palms, can be permanently united only outside of marriage because marriage destroys true love. Or as Mme de Murat put it at the end of "L'Heureuse peine," "… quoique se promette l'amour heureux, une noce est presque tou- jours une triste fête."

High literature used the same formula as the fairy story and with the same ambivalence. Most of Molière's plays end with the wedding of the same conventional, handsome couple. Yet marriage is not necessarily happy within the plays. Since love is a passing emotion, even marriage for love becomes no guarantee of happiness. In 1678, Mme de Lafayette had stated this openly: her Princesse de Cleves rejects the handsome, rich young suitor whom she truly loves because she is convinced that his passion will not last. Mme de Lafayette is concerned with the impossibility of combining love and marriage in any permanent and satisfactory way. She has the artistic courage to try unorthodox fictional solutions. Our Salon writers accept the formula endings which tradition has given them, but they do so without the inner conviction that the formula represents reality or the emotional distance from the formula to treat it lightly, so they pervert it by the rest of the tale.

While the newly-married couple may not live happily ever after, their marriage is often a happy ending for their relatives, since the good fortune of hero and heroine often spills over onto their families. In Mlle L' Héritier's "Les Enchantements de l'èloquence," the good daughter brings her father to court. Bluebeard's widow buys captaincies for her brothers and gives Soeur Anne a dowry. Cinderella marries her sisters to two *grands seigneurs*. Le Petit Poucet buys "des Offices de nouvelle création" for his father and brothers. The family group is seen united at such moments, no matter what conflicts have occurred previously (or may occur again). The characters do not have to be Cinderella, or even particularly good, to succeed. They can make it simply by having the right sibling or giving birth to the right child.

E. Aristocracy

As the discussion of marriage and misalliance indicates, these tales present a simple caste structure. In Perrault's works, there are really only two social groups: peasants (who abandon children and wish sausages onto the ends of people's noses) and the aristocracy (who go to balls and have elaborate christening parties). For other writers, society is more complex, but not much more. Mlle L' Héritier separates the financiers and their families from the aristocracy. The financiers are rude, crude, and overly ambitious. For her, serving in the army retains some of its old connotations and gives peasants a moral education which orients them to aristocratic virtues, but it does not and cannot turn them into aristocrats.

Status is first a function of birth, correlated with certain moral and physical characteristics. The peasant is generally lacking in intelligence, moral goodness, and pleasing appearance. These tales consistently ignore the "wily peasant" of oral tradition. They show us a peasant who uses up his three wishes stupidly, a peasant couple who abandon their children because they cannot feed them, and a peasant who fails to warn her daughter about the danger of wolves. The association of negative characteristics with peasants is so marked that highly valued qualities signal immediately to the reader that either the class assigned to the character is a mistake or that the peasant-born will rise to the aristocracy. While the English Tom Thumb tales involve a hero of diminutive size, the Perrault story of "Le Petit Poucet" is vague about the stature of the hero once the tale begins, since no dwarf,

---

22   Compare John Webster, "The Duchess of Malfi" (I, ii): "That we may imitate the loving palms, best emblem of a peaceful marriage/ That nev'r bore fruit divided!"

no matter how cute, could rise in class. Le Petit Poucet is born small, but the story opens when he is seven and there is no indication that he is other than a normal-sized seven-year-old. This is usually attributed to the contamination of one tale tradition by another,[23] but it also allows Le Petit Poucet to fit into the adult world which his good fortune opens to him. The future Marquis de Carabas in "Puss 'n Boots" is handsome and has a good figure. If a miller's son is to marry a princess, he must be able to look the part, as the cat well knows when he hides his peasant clothing.

The moral contrast between castes is depicted unmistakably in Mme d'Aulnoy's "Fortunée." The titular heroine and her brother are both supposedly the orphan children of a poor laborer. Fortunee offers her only possessions to the Queen of the Woods, while her brother Bédou refuses to give his starving sister any food except egg shells. Ultimately, the Queen of the Woods reveals to Fortunée that she is a princess and that Bedou is not her brother. Acting with the generosity of a true aristocrat, Fortunée begs the Queen to help Bédou. The Queen transforms the cottage into a palace. But more than one transformation must take place, for Bédou is truly a peasant; since those who dwell in palaces ought not to act like peasants, Bédou is transformed and becomes gentle, polite, and grateful. These noble virtues cannot be learned, and they can only be acquired by magic.

It should be noted that at no point do our Salon authors suggest that any of the upwardly mobile need to learn new skills. Although the trials of these heroes and heroines are perfectly real, like the Count Almaviva in *The Marriage of Figaro*, they do not have to learn—they only have to take the trouble to be born and perhaps, at the worst, to pass certain tests. There are no lessons in dancing or fencing or the art of conversation. A magic wand alone can convert the truly non-noble like Bédou into noble status, but those born truly noble (even if their father is a miller) never need to learn anything: the only tests that daunt them are those that can be accomplished solely by magic.

Not least important, in the Salon tales external beauty is a sign of inward virtue and nobility. If there is a lapse from this Platonic ideal, it is usually the result of a magic spell. Even then, the aristocrat is usually transformed into a beautiful bird or animal or a wonderful pot of pinks. Soldiers and peasants may become cabbages and chickens, but the noble would never suffer such a fate. An interesting exception that proves the rule occurs in the "Histoire de Pertharité et de Ferandine," inserted in Hamilton's "Le Bélier." The ugly king of Lombardy remarries. The new queen is beautiful, but evil. This situation cannot last. The equilibrium is partially restored early in the tale when the queen is transformed into a good person. At the end of the story, the king becomes handsome. Both are now beautiful and good. Once the tales reach their end (if not before), the hero and heroine are seen in all their glory.

The parade of good looks and beautiful clothes is as important in the Salon tales as it was in courtly French society. The description of the magnificence at the court of Henri II with which *La Princesse de Clèves* opens could serve as an ending for these Salon tales. Although Mme de Lafayette depicts a seriously flawed society, she never suggests that ugliness is allied to virtue any more than the fairy tale writers do. There seems to be, rather, a consensus that true nobility is an innate characteristic, conferring personality traits as well as exemption from the *taille*. It is usually found among aristocrats, though some apparent aristocrats are in reality ogres, and occasionally a child of the people will be revealed as truly noble. This is a society which accepts upward mobility, indeed seems to present upward mobility as a sign of worldly salvation, yet in actuality does not believe that worldly salvation is likely any more than a Jansenist would think that most people reach heaven.

---

23   Opie, pp. 128–129.

III. The Supernatural

The implications which I have just discussed are not deeply hidden; if we were able to ask the writers about them, they would probably agree that these elements are present in their tales. But, like any cultural arti- fact, the Salon tales bear other, less apparent, messages. I do not in- tend to treat the meanings of the tales for the human psyche; however, I would like to explore briefly the nature of the ogres, fairies, and magic which are so essential to these tales.

The unreality of the fairy tale is not limited to magic. "Il était une fois"[24] opens a story that, no matter how real to our subconscious, no matter how accurate in detail of clothing or food, does not describe life as it is experienced. Famine is mentioned only twice in well over a hundred different tales. There are almost no epidemics. Wars occur, but usually only as an explanation for the absence of a character or as a source of revenue. While there are many widowers and a few widows, children seldom die in the tales, although we know that infant mortality was very high. Child abandonment occurs infrequently, and when it does, it is made to sound like an extraordinary event. In "Le Petit Poucet," the woodcutters must abandon their children because there is a general famine. There are seven children (rather than the customary small family), the youngest of whom is seven years old, yet none of his brothers is old enough to leave home or to earn any money. Thus, the abandonment is surrounded by extenuating and extraordinary circumstances, so that the reader may be convinced that such actions never really happen outside of books.

On the other hand, fairies or other magical beings are essential for the fairy tale. Our tales are peopled by fairies, ogres, witches, sorcerers, and even an occasional siren or druid. Each of the main groups has fairly distinctive characteristics and each may reveal different aspects of the social and emotional climate in which the tales were written.

A. Ogres

Ogres (and the female ogresses) are a race whose distinctive characteristic is supposed to be the eating of hu- man flesh. In the Salon tales, ogres marry humans; the offspring are not necessarily cannibals unlike the progeny of marriage between ogres. However, even the purebred French ogre, unlike his English counterpart, does not say: "Fee, fie, foe, fum, / I smell the blood of a Frenchman, / Be he alive or be he dead, / I'll grind his bones to make my bread!" The seventeenth-century French ogre is not a giant like his English counterpart, and he only becomes one in the hands of nineteenth-century illustrators, per- haps through contamination by the British tradition. Equally important, even the pure-bred French ogre is usually shown as eating not the taboo human flesh, but roasts of lamb or beef—the food of the upper classes. Whatever the latent meanings of cannibalism, and they are in- deed profound, our ogres almost never practice it, either because their prey escapes or because they are tricked out of their meal. The French ogre is merely a meat eater in a society where the most important source of calories was bread and where the peasant would consume only a small amount of meat, ever.

---

24   Dictionaries say "Il était une fois" or "Il y avait une fois" are the standard openings for fairy tales. Many, but not all, of the Salon tales begin this way. The French formulas were codified during the seventeenth century and seem to be literary devices ("Once upon a time" is first recorded as late as 1732). The impersonality of "il" puts the authenticity of the story beyond the reach of the author. The imperfect tense emphasizes the lack of a specific past time, while "une fois" insists that the story did happen—once. The use of formulas, in both oral and written tales, denies the reality of the story for which it acts as guarantor. For the twentieth-century reader, it signals that this is a fairy story, which no adult believes in the literal sense and which has been retold often. But we have had almost three hundred years to get used to the formula. Our Salon writers and their readers did not, and I am not sure that we can suppose that they reacted as we do.

Although the oedipal elements in the ogre figure are often quite evident, the ogre also corresponds to a social type. He not only eats the food of the aristocracy, he gorges while others starve. He is depicted as living in a large house in the country, like a rich and powerful land- lord. Since we have no oral peasant versions of the tales prior to the nineteenth century, we cannot know to what class the ogre was as- signed by them or whether the almost complete disappearance of actual cannibalism was a characteristic of all French tales. The depiction of cannibalism may have been removed to make the identification with rich landlords less odious, but the fact that the ogres are not often shown eating human beings makes it easier to ascribe to them the characteristics of a specific social class.

But if the ogre lives like a noble, he neither looks nor acts like one. The ogre thus seems to represent the bad landowner who lacks the Christian virtue of charity and who fails to fulfill his noble function of caring for his peasants. The ogre has no sympathy for them, no sense of obligation to them. Just as we occasionally find that a miller's son is truly noble, so, occasionally, someone living like a noble lacks the inner qualities of true nobility. He must be eliminated since he can never be reformed. In "Le Petit Poucet," the ogre just disappears after losing his seven-league boots (and perhaps his wealth), while the protagonist, who has been starving, becomes rich. The false noble is removed by the true noble, who then adopts the noble life-style.

B. Fairies

Ogres can be a mere convenience for the Salon writer; Perrault chose an ogress mother rather than a blood-thirsty human wife for the prince in "Sleeping Beauty." Fairies, however, are usually an essential part of the fairy tale. There are exceptions such as "Little Red Riding Hood," but although it has been popular ever since Perrault wrote it down, it is really a cautionary tale, not a fairy tale at all. It lacks not only fairies, but in the Perrault version a happy ending—no fairy or woodsman appears to save the girl and she stays eaten. In general, both the English and the French demand fairies in their fairy tales.

To ask of the Salon tale what constitutes a fairy is to ask an unanswerable question. An ogre (or ogress) can be counted on to want to eat any human child he or she encounters, but a fairy cannot be counted on to do or to be anything. (English fairies flit about, displaying their wings and tiny size even for the camera, but the French fairy rarely even has wings and seems never to have been photographed.[25] French fairies may marry mortals. Mélusine, who appears twice in our tales, is reputed to have been an ancestor of the counts of Toulouse. The only two prerequisites for the French fairy are that she be a woman and that she work magic. (Any male character who works magic is called a sorcerer or a magician.) Although the fairy can perform magical feats, she is limited in her power. She cannot break the spell of another fairy, though she may modify its results. Fairy magic serves two literary purposes: first, it allows the introduction of magic into the tale, and, second, it allows the fairy to perform several plot functions, to serve, as it were, as the *dea ex machina* of the author.

The fairy in "Diamonds and Toads" belongs to a group which I will call touchstone fairies. It is their function to allow one or more of the characters to act in such a way that they may reward those displaying the noble virtues of charity and kindness and punish those who are selfish and cruel. In "Diamonds and Toads," the good daughter is rewarded for her kindness to a fairy disguised as a crone. The bad daughter, meeting the fairy disguised this time as a noblewoman but given the same opportunity for charity, fails. The unpleasant characters (like the bad daughter) act in a haughty and unacceptable manner towards the fairy, whether she appears in noble or peasant guise, while the truly noble always act with kindness. Thus the touchstone fairy adjusts the world so that the innately noble can assume their rightful place and enjoy a life of money and ease.

---

25 *Beyond the Looking Glass,* ed. Jonathan Cort (New York: Pocket Books, 1973), pp. xviii-xix reproduces two of the Cottingly photographs of two young girls together with fairies.

The second group of fairies I will call birth fairies.[26] These fairies are capable of good and evil. The birth fairies favor conception, ensure that the noble characteristics are present (congenitally, if not by inheritance), and either directly or indirectly determine the future of the child. At the same time, the fairy curse is essential to the plot. The two motifs are highlighted in the christening feast. Though the fairies are ostensibly invited in order to be thanked, to ensure fairy gifts for the infant, or to foretell the child's fate, the episode of the feast also serves quite different purposes. In the simpler form, one of the invited fairies predicts that the child will bring harm to the family and suggests ways of averting the evil. In the more usual form, one of the fairies is accidentally not invited. Since even the smallest slight to a fairy results in evil, the fairy dooms the child. Her curse is mitigated by one of the other fairies present, and thus we have a Sleeping Beauty or a princess who turns into a white deer because she sees daylight before she comes of age. The constellation around the birth fairy consists of the magical conception, the feast, and the curse on the child, and it is this constellation which requires explanation.

We know that newly-married couples in late seventeenth-century France truly feared the *noueuse d'aiguillette*—the woman whose magic spell could make the husband impotent.[27] Furthermore, at least as early as the fourteenth century, there were two important feasts in French family life: the marriage feast and the one given to celebrate the birth of a child. If the *noueuse* was not invited to the marriage feast, she would cast the dreaded spell. A child would then be born only if the *noueuse* could be forced or induced to lift the spell. In the Salon tales, there is only one feast, the christening feast. However, since the couple has been childless for a long period and the birth is often linked to a fairy's magical intervention, it is as if the spell of the *noueuse* had been lifted. In the fairy tales, as with the *noueuse*, it is the accidentally uninvited guest who casts the spell. If the child dies (or is transformed into an animal), the child might as well never have been born and the spell of impotence never have been lifted. Black magic in the person of a *noueuse* disguised as a fairy fights with white magic, and a real fear which is never mentioned directly in these tales is dealt with in what seems like a very complex fashion. Yet, considering the way we deal with real fears in everyday life, it is not all that complex.

Perhaps the fairy dearest to the hearts of us all is the fairy godmother. This third type of fairy appears unbidden to reward a protagonist who does not pass any test but who already appears worthy of elevation to nobility and/or riches. Cinderella's fairy godmother enables her to get to the ball and furnishes the talismanic piece of clothing that will make it possible for the king's messengers to recognize her. The fairy godmother does not judge the sisters, nor does she punish them. Furthermore, she appears as if by magic to use her magic wand. This kind of fairy seems to occupy an intermediate place between the touchstone fairy and the birth fairy. Even the term used to refer to her is an amalgam of the pagan fairy and the Christian godmother. The godmother's duty in real life is to ensure the child's religious upbringing; her duty within the tale is to look after its secular interests.

All three types of good fairies are used by the authors to arrange the world as it ought to be, or, for the pessimists among us, to stress the degree to which the world is not as it should be. But some of the fairies in the tales are not good, and rather act like witches. The Desert Fairy in "The Yellow Dwarf" turns herself into a beautiful young woman, but she cannot disguise her feet. Misshapen or cloven feet are marks of the devil which cannot be hidden. The birth fairy who condemns a child because she was not invited to the christening is also akin to a witch. Unlike the ogre, whose ineffectualness reduces him to the role of bogeyman and whose alter ego, the selfish landlord, is merely a fact of life, the birth fairy who utters a witch's curse hides real fears.

Witchcraft has apparently been removed from the tales, but in actuality, the name of the spellcaster has merely been changed to suit the society. In the real world of seventeenth-century France, belief in witchcraft was no longer acceptable in those circles that determined the judicial fate of the accused witch. The new science was also

---

26   As Katherine Briggs in *An Encyclopedia of Fairies* (New York: Pantheon, 1976), p. xi, reminds us, *fée* is derived from "the Italian *fatae*, the fairy ladies who visited the household of births and pronounced on the future of the baby.

27   See Roger Vaultier, *Le Folklore pendant la guerre de cent ans d'après les lettres de rémission du thrésor des chartes* (Paris: Guénégaud, 1965), pp. 39–40 for a discussion of these issues.

making inroads on previously held beliefs in magic, although there were many aristocrats who clearly believed in ghosts, spells, potions, and, indeed, all the manifestations of magic and witchcraft that one can imagine.[28] If our writers were sophisticated enough to feel that the traditional witch ought to be replaced by a fairy, what did they do with the other kinds of magic involved in the stories that they were circulating among their friends?

C. Magic Potions and Talismanic Gifts

When we think of magic and magical happenings, we associate them with talismanic gifts and magic potions. The Salon tales treat both of these forms of magic in surprising ways. The magic potion is almost totally absent. Perhaps the particular tales chosen to be recounted never had magic potions in them to begin with. Perhaps the aura of ideal love, which the ending is supposed to convey, seemed to the Salon writers incompatible with love potions. One thing is certain: potions are not absent because people in late seventeenth-century France no longer believed in them. *L'affaire des poisons*, with 226 people accused and thirty-six condemned to death, reached from those who merely used magic potions (or poison) on members of their own families to the Marquise de Montespan who allegedly employed potions and black masses to assure the love of Louis XIV. Whether or not the accusations were true is less important than that quite sophisticated people believed that they might be.

Perhaps, as the *affaire des poisons* suggests, potions were too closely identified with poisons and black magic, like that drink which allows the King to die conveniently and painlessly in "La Belle aux cheveux d'or." Good people do not need potions, just as they do not need black magic. The heroine never needed a potion to retain her beauty and when her husband, the king, drinks what he believes to be a beauty potion, it is really his own secret poison. "Drink me" is a label unknown to our writers and drinking from mysterious small bottles makes one neither bigger or smaller, but simply dead.

The talisman or talismanic gift identifies the recipient as playing a specific role in the tale. In the peasant oral tales of which we have transcriptions, these talismans are magical. Although talismans are often preserved in many of the French tales, they have almost totally lost their magic. The magical glass slipper, which is so skillfully placed with Cinderella's finery for the ball that its importance will be realized only later, can fit only the girl whom the prince will marry (and he will marry whomever the slipper fits). In Perrault's account, the slipper is no more wonderful than Cinderella's ball gowns. The nineteenth century regarded it as so prosaic that it was turned into an ordinary fur slipper, on the grounds that Perrault must have meant to write "vair," not "verre."[29] The red hair that the Yellow Dwarf makes into a ring for his betrothed is another talisman. Yet, within the tale it only reminds the Princess from time to time that she has promised to marry the Dwarf. For Mme d'Aulnoy, the promise is the important thing, not the magic red hair.

Thus, magic gifts and talismans are retained in the Salon tale, but the focus is not on their magic. Wonderful objects are not absent, but the reader is to express amazement at the craftsmanship required to produce them rather than at their truly magical properties. Even the jewels dropping from the mouth of the good daughter are reduced to a handsome dowry. Whatever real magic the writers believed in, it did not reside in the talisman.

D. Talking Animals and Plants

Along with fairies, animals that talk and vegetables that turn into means of transportation are such staples of fairy stories that we do not question them. When reading "Puss 'n Boots," we do not speculate about linguistic theory or about apes communicating in American sign language, although transmutation of matter and language

---

28   See V. Delaporte, *Du Merveilleux dans la littérature française sous le règne de Louis XIV* (Paris, Retaux-Bray, 1891).

29   That discussion is closed by the manuscript copy, where Cinderella has shoes of glass.

acquisition by animals may be compatible with the scientific theories of today. It is not insignificant, however, that when the tales were first published, the first would have been contrary to science and the second to philosophy.

Talking animals have been standard literary elements since before Aesop. Fables depend on the convention of animals and plants being able to give voice to human reactions and emotions. To be sure, such creatures do not inhabit the more elevated literary genres—there is no epic poem in which Henri IV discusses the worth of Paris with his horse. As talking animals appear only in the less serious literature, so actual belief in their existence was usually to be found only among those who thought that barnyard animals talked on Christmas Eve.

Except in the tales of Perrault, the talking animals are likely to be human beings who have been transformed, though with due deference to their social rank. These talking animals are self-conscious; they bewail their fate and try to preserve their normal lives, despite their inappropriate form, as if their authors were assuring us that they, too, found such altered states the least bit improbable.

In his treatment of talking animals, Perrault is quite different from the other writers—much closer to both peasant[30] and literary tradition. Perrault's animals talk because some animals are endowed with the power of speech, and he treats the convention without condescension or apology. Puss never speaks "cattish," yet his rewards are suitable for a feline: a satin pillow and a saucer of cream. Puss may act like a clever valet, but he is a cat down to his last whisker. While presumably neither Perrault nor Mme d'Aulnoy believed that people could be transformed into animals or vegetables, Perrault's matter-of-factness makes the device a delightful convention. Mme d'Aulnoy, however, sounds as if she were following a silly (but possibly correct) tradition.

Any cat can ask for sardines in the language of Descartes, providing one is willing to accept for the moment that animals can talk, or that humans can be turned into cats. Transformation has its own kind of logic. It is allied to transmutation, once a scientifically accepted doctrine involving a world view that stressed the impermanence of both form and substance. Objects could be changed into other objects through their shared characteristics: the pumpkin is yellow and vaguely coach- shaped; some babies would make handsome pigs; some people are as prickly as rosebushes. However, the Salon tales often fail to respect this logic. When we find a blue bird lamenting his present form, we wonder why the young king should have become this particular bird, rather than an ermine, for example. An author who does not understand the principles of transformation may accidentally alter just those elements which justify the metamorphosis.

By the late seventeenth century, belief in transformation had become less and less tenable. The transformations and transmutations in the Salon tales often suggest that their authors no longer understood the mechanism, whether or not they still accepted old ideas about the impermanence of form. They generally avoid any hint of occultism, the most notable exception being, again, Mme d'Aulnoy, where a mannequin of reeds is given the appearance of a king. The old beliefs have disappeared, and only the outward appearance is left in the treatment of transformation, as in that of magic potions and talismans.

IV. Conclusions

When critics of fairy tales move beyond the most superficial messages, they tend to concern themselves with the spread of folk motifs through Europe and Asia, or with the psychiatric implications of fairy tales. The most popular expression of the latter approach is Bruno Bettelheim's *The Uses of Enchantment*. Bettelheim argues that, through fairy tales, children can be helped to surmount emotional and developmental problems, but he asserts that only the told tale (e.**g.**,"Cinderella") is truly nourishing, not the composed, literary fairy tale (e.g., Wilde, Andersen).[31] I doubt that this distinction would hold up for most of the classic tales of French

---

30 Delarue, p. xx.
31 *The Uses of Enchantment* (New York: Knopf, 1976), especially pp. 149–156.

provenance. What is more disturbing, Bettelheim treats fairy tales as if they were composed outside time and space, not as products of a specific culture. As a critic and literary historian, I wish to suggest the contrary: that these tales reflect the serious concerns of particular social and intellectual circles in late seventeenth- century France, and that they reveal a mood of hostility or ambivalence toward important elements in the official culture of the age of Louis XIV. An example of these concerns is the treatment of love and marriage, where within and through the conventions of the fairy tale, serious issues are presented from the point of view of *the précieux*. Less specific, but perhaps more important, is the apparent repudiation of contemporary France which appears from the opening formula in many of the tales. Mile L' Héritier insists that she is refashioning tales from the troubadours, thus restoring a national treasure.[32] Perrault says that he is recounting the tales of "nos aieux," who put into their versions true morality where virtue is rewarded and vice punished.[33] Both reflect a vision of the past as somehow better than the present. In this, they go beyond tale-telling conventions, or at least make a choice among tale-telling conventions. It is as though "Once upon a time" were not enough as an opening formula, and one ought to use "In the olden days, when wishes really mattered."

The political tone of the Salon tales is strikingly archaic. Although many of the writers lived in Paris and some of them frequented the court at Versailles, or perhaps because they did, their kings and princes reflect an earlier, less centralized and less complicated era. Such a picture of kingship is not uncommon in fairy tales from other times and places, but it is not essential to the genre. Perhaps one reason why the fairy tale was so popular in sophisticated, upper-class French circles at this time is that it was an unobtrusive, politically safe vehicle for some of the muffled aristocratic disaffection that we know surrounded the Sun-King.

What is archaic in one age may become revolutionary in another. These tales did not disappear with the death of Louis XIV. They became the literature of children and of the unsophisticated. The stories of Perrault and Mme d'Aulnoy that were reprinted in the *Bibliothèque bleue* became especially widely known, and in these stories the despotic ruler is clearly condemned and sometimes killed.

That rulers ought to be virtuous and to rule in person was part of the ideology of Bourbon France, of course, however distant it was from the reality; but that they should be killed if they did not live up to this ideal was a thought more appropriate to the antityrannical literature of the sixteenth century than to what was officially countenanced in the eighteenth. Through the fairy tale (among other media), and particularly through these tales, the notion that bad rulers deserve to be eliminated became (or remained) an integral part of what French children were taught in the eighteenth century.

The social values of the Salon tales could not, however, lend themselves to such political transformation, for they are impeccably aristocratic. Noble status reflects inner virtue. The persons living nobly who lack virtue are in reality ogres or ogresses, and they are eventually destroyed. But the virtue which underlies and justifies nobility is displayed not in virtuous actions (which are rarely seen, except insofar as to avoid acting cruelly or meanly is to act virtuously), but in a noble appearance, noble attire, good looks, and the general capacity to lead a noble life. We are hardly ever presented with a nobleman or a king doing very much, not even winning battles. The good king consults and makes decisions, but he is never busy, and the nobleman is not even shown making decisions.

Leisure is the proper reward for the nobleman, who earns it by doing nothing. Those who end as rich nobles or royalty usually do little to earn their good fortune except allow themselves to be recognized and, perhaps, transformed. It is assumed they will continue to do nothing except, perhaps, rule a kingdom or bear children for the king. It may be unintentional but it is fitting that in "Le Petit Poucet," where the hero actually uses his own wits to dispose of the ogre and becomes rich as a result, he and his brothers barely reach the officer class at the end of the story. None of the Salon tales suggests for a moment the mood of LaFontaine's version of *The Ant and*

32 *Oeuvres meslées …* (Paris, Guignard, 1696), p. 296.
33 Contes, *p. 5.*

the Grasshopper, and none of them could contain the remark that LaFontaine makes in *Le laboureur et ses enfants* (Book 5, 9), that "work is a treasure."

To give the appurtenances of daily life—the clothes, the recreations—to an unreal world is to create some tensions but to remove others. The real world can be manipulated, as it is in any fiction, to conform to the writer's beliefs and desires, but the "childish" fairy tale allows the author to dismiss anything he wishes, and its allegedly peasant origins absolve him of any responsibility for his material (save, in more recent times, for the fidelity of his transcription).

However, it is in their treatment of religion and magic that these tales reflect most profoundly the particular moment in the history of French culture in which they were written or received their final form. Superficially, the tales accept magic as all fairy tales must; upon analysis, as I have shown, their attitude to magic must be seen as quite ambivalent. Similarly, the absence of religious feeling and the relative insignificance of religious ritual in most of the Salon tales may reflect the nature of the genre and its pre-Christian or "folk" origins, but this does not explain why writers chose to express themselves in this genre and why educated and upper-class Frenchmen took to it so avidly at the close of a century that saw a profound revival of Catholic religiosity in all sectors of French society.

There has always been tension between orthodox Christianity and the practice of magic: keeping religion insignificant in these stories reduces that tension and avoids an open clash between what are at base rival ways of viewing the world. From this point of view, religion must be absent from fairy tales told in and written for a Christian society. But this is not a fully convincing explanation, though it may account in part for the absence of religion from the Salon tales. From the birth of Christianity until the practice of magic disappeared or went underground in the West in the course of the seventeenth and eighteenth centuries, devout Christians often combined religious faith with belief in magic and even with attempts to practice it. And the attempt to show that all schools of magic and religion are part of one intellectually respectable and theologically orthodox system occupied some of the best minds in Europe in the Renaissance and after.

I would like to suggest, tentatively, that it may not be a coincidence that fairy tales suddenly appealed to educated and sophisticated Frenchmen just when Cartesian rationalism and the new science were eliminating Renaissance "pseudo-science" and its philosophy as a serious intellectual force and were beginning to undermine orthodox religious belief as well. The attitude of the Salon tales to religion and magic may reflect the threat of the new science to both traditional modes of understanding the world. For if religion demands an act of faith, so does science, at least for the layman. The threat which the new science and the new philosophy posed to traditional beliefs, what Paul Hazard called *La Crise de la conscience européenne*, was forcing the intellectual elite into unaccustomed roles, into accepting as true that which did not appear to be true either to the senses or in terms of older epistemologies. "So that the philosophers spend their lives in not believing at all what they see, and in trying to guess what they do not see at all: an unbearable situation."[34] It is one thing to refuse to believe in witches—such skepticism can be found during the height of the witch-burning craze. It is another to see astronomy and astrology as mutually incompatible, and to wonder whether orthodox theology and astronomy are ultimately compatible.

Bruno Bettelheim argues that fairy tales instruct the child on how to order his emotional world, for they allow him to encounter his own fears and desires in a structured form with a happy ending.. For Bettelheim, the child needs the fairy tale because he literally does not think like an adult, because his is a world where magic and transformation are more real than the scientific explanations which he is forced to accept by adults. But in earlier times, magic and transformation were real to adults too, and not only to the ignorant but to the most educated

---

34 *La Crise de la conscience européenne (1680–1715)*, 2 vols. (Paris: Boivin, 1935) 1: 185. Hazard finds the vogue for fairy tales odd, but he does not connect it with the "crisis," except as a frivolous relief from it. See 2: 171–173.

and sophisticated Europeans. It was precisely in the late seventeenth century that the educated European was forced to accept scientific explanations of a new kind, incompatible with magic and transformation.

Can the fairy tale be seen as performing functions for adults similar to those Bettelheim asserts it plays for children? Since fairy tales contain magic elements by definition, the Salon writers were able to talk about magic as if they and everyone else still believed in it. But they treated magic prosaically, as if to make it clear to their audience that, of course, neither they nor their audience really believed in magic any longer. Did they protest too much?

The absence of religion except on a formal level in these tales is as remarkable as their prosaic treatment of magic. It is possible that their authors believed it inappropriate to mix Christian elements with magic, but this does not explain the absence of classical pagan deities, which were so ubiquitous in seventeenth-century art and literature. The failure to present us with any guiding deities or with anything that might be termed a religious view of the world and man's fate, reflects, I would suggest, not the irreligion or "secularism" of the authors (for which there is little or no evidence), but that uneasiness about the traditional religious beliefs which Hazard saw as constituting a central element in the *Crisede la conscience*. Fénelon, who was firm in his piety, peopled his tales with pagan gods and goddesses. The others took advantage of the form of the fairy tale to create a world in which religious practice serves only secular purposes, religious feeling and religious guidance are absent, and the problem of coming to terms with the crisis in faith is avoided.

* * *

The popularity of the fairy tale as adult, sophisticated literature did not last long. As the generation of Hazard's *Crise de la conscience européenne* drew to a close, about the time of Galland's translation into French of *The Thousand and One Nights* (1704–1717), the European fairy tale faded from aristocratic adult circles in France. It was replaced, to some extent, by the oriental tale, which is often a fairy tale from another culture, and by the brief licentious tale, in which the implicit sexuality of the fairy tale has become explicit and, instead of marrying and living happily ever after, our hero and heroine seize the opportunity presented by *La Nuit et le moment*.

But the fairy tale has continued to thrive, and not only in beautifully illustrated editions for the nursery. It is today, as in the seventeenth century, more than occasionally a genre of high literature practiced by sophisticated authors. Their work may be ostensibly Aiméd at children (James Thurber), but often it is never thought of as juvenile (Elinor Wylie, Sylvia Townsend Warner). Perhaps the contemporary adult, too, feels ill at ease with the scientific explanations he has learned to accept—it was only six impossible things before breakfast in Lewis Carroll's time.

Chapter II

Charles Perrault's Fairy Tales

Little Red Riding Hood

Charles Perrault

Once upon a time there was a little village girl, the prettiest in the world. Her mother doted on her, and her grandmother even more. This good woman made her a little red hood which suited her so well that wherever she went, she was called Little Red Riding Hood.

One day, after her mother had baked some biscuits, she said to Little Red Riding Hood, "Go see how your grandmother's feeling. I've heard that she's ill. You can take her some biscuits and this small pot of butter."

Little Red Riding Hood departed at once to visit her grandmother, who lived in another village. In passing through the forest she met old neighbor wolf, who had a great desire to eat her. But he did not dare because of some woodcutters who were in the forest. Instead he asked her where she was going. The poor child, who did not know that it is dangerous to stop and listen to a wolf, said to him, "I'm going to see my grandmother, and I'm bringing her some biscuits with a small pot of butter that my mother's sending her."

"Does she live far from here?" the wolf asked.

"Oh, yes!" Little Red Riding Hood said. "You've got to go by the mill, which you can see right over there, and hers is the first house in the village."

"Well, then," said the wolf, "I'll go and see her, too. You take that path there, and I'll take this path here, and we'll see who'll get there first."

The wolf began to run as fast as he could on the shorter path, and the little girl took the longer path. What's more, she enjoyed herself fey gathering nuts, running after butterflies, and making bouquets of small flowers that she found along the way. It did not take the wolf long to arrive at the grandmother's house, and he knocked:

"Tick, tock."

"Who's there?"

"It's your granddaughter, Little Red Riding Hood," the wolf said, disguising his voice. "I've brought you some biscuits and a little pot of butter that my mother's sent for you."

The good grandmother, who was in her bed because she was not feeling well, cried out to him, "Pull the bobbin, and the latch will fall."

The wolf pulled the bobbin, and the door opened. He pounced on the good woman and devoured her quicker than a wink, for it had been more than three days since he had eaten last. After that he closed the door and lay down in the grandmother's bed to wait for Little Red Riding Hood, who after a while came knocking at the door.

"Tick, tock."

"Who's there?"

When she heard the gruff voice of the wolf, Little Red Riding Hood was scared at first, but she thought her grandmother had a cold and responded "It's your granddaughter," Little Red Riding Hood. I've brought you some biscuits and a little pot of butter that my mother's sent for you."

The wolf softened his voice and cried out to her,"Pull the bobbin, and the latch will fall."

Little Red Riding Hood pulled the bobbin, and the door opened.

Upon seeing her enter, the wolf hid himself under the bedcovers and said to her,"Put the biscuits and the pot of butter on the bin and come lie down beside me."

Little Red Riding Hood undressed and got into the bed, where she was quite astonished to see how her grandmother appeared in her nightgown.

"What big arms you have, grandmother!" she said to her.

"The better to hug you with, my child."

"What big legs you have, grandmother!"

"The better to run with, my child."

"What big ears you have, grandmother!"

"The better to hear you with, my child."

"What big eyes you have, grandmother!"

"The better to see you with, my child."

"What big teeth you have, grandmother!"

"The better eat you with!"

And upon saying these words, the wicked wolf pounced on Little Red Riding Hood and ate her up.

MORAL

One sees here that young children,
Especially pretty girls,
Who're bred as pure as pearls,
Should question words addressed by men.
Or they may serve one day as feast
For à wolf or other beast.
I say a wolf since not all are wild
Or are indeed the same in kind.
For some are winning and have sharp minds.
Some are loud, smooth, or mild.
Others appear plain kind or unriled.
They follow young ladies wherever they go,
Right into the halls of their very own homes.
Alas for those girls who've refused the truth:
The sweetest tongue has the sharpest tooth.

The Grandmother's Tale

Catherine Orenstein

[handwritten: —generations]

There was once a <u>woman</u> who had some bread, and she said to her <u>daughter</u>: "Take this hot loaf and a bottle of milk to your granny." The little girl set off. At the crossroads she met a *bzou*.[35]

"Where are you going?"

"I'm taking a hot loaf of bread and a bottle of milk to my granny's."

"Which path are you taking," said the bzou, "the path of needles or the path of pins?" *[handwritten: - peasant class - told by women who sewed - girls pin, womens sew permanently]*

"The path of needles," said the little girl.

"Well then, I'll take the path of pins."

The little girl amused herself picking up needles. Meanwhile the bzou arrived at her grandmother's, killed her, put some of her flesh in the pantry and a bottle of her blood on the shelf. The girl arrived and knocked at the door.

"Push the door," said the bzou. "It's closed with a wet straw."

"Hello, Granny; I'm bringing you a hot loaf and a bottle of milk."

"Put them in the pantry. Eat the meat that's there, and drink the bottle of wine on the shelf." *[handwritten: - coming of age]*

As she ate, a little cat said: "She is slut who eats the flesh and drinks the blood of her granny!"

"Undress, my child," said the bzou, "and come to bed beside me."

"Where should I put my apron?"

"Throw it on the fire, my child; you won't be needing it anymore."

And she asked where to put the other garments, the bodice, the dress, the skirt, and the stockings, and each time the wolf replied:

"Throw them in the fire, my child. You won't be needing them anymore."

"Oh, Granny, how hairy you are!"

"It's to keep me warmer, my child."

"Oh, Granny, those long nails you have!"

"To scratch me better, my child."

"Oh, Granny, what big shoulders you have!"

"All the better to carry firewood, my child."

"Oh, Granny, what big ears you have!"

"All the better to hear with, my child."

"Oh, Granny, what a big mouth you have!"

"All the better to eat you with, my child!"

"Oh, Granny, I need to go badly! Let me go outside."

---

35   A werewolf.

"Do it in the bed, my child."

"No, Granny, I want to go outside."

"All right, but don't stay long."

The bzou tied a woolen string to her foot and let her go out, and when the little girl was outside she tied the end of the string to a big plum tree in the yard. The bzou became impatient and said: "Are you making a load out there? Are you shitting a load?"

When he realized that no one answered him, he jumped out of bed ;and saw that the little girl had escaped. He followed her, but he arrived father house just at the moment she was safely inside.

—Translated by Catherine Orenstein from P.
Delarue & M.-L. Tenèze, Le conte populaire française (Erasme, 1957)

Centuries ago in the remote hills of France, a grotesque and peculiar tale circulated by word of mouth about a girl who eats her grandmother. The tale begins, familiarly enough, with a strange encounter in the woods. At a fork in the path to her grandmother's house, the girl meets a *bzou*, a werewolf or devil. The bzou learns her destination, and upon parting he takes the way of the "pins," while she takes the path of the "needles." But the bzou arrives at the grandmother's house first. He murders the old woman, minces her flesh and decants her blood into a bottle. When the girl arrives, she eats the "meat" and "wine" that he has left in the pantry. Then she removes her clothing piece by piece, from petticoat to stocking, announcing each item before throwing it into the fire, and climbs into bed beside the bzou.

In 1951 the French folklorist Paul Delarue published a study of this, bizarre story, which he called "The Grandmother's Tale." Parts of it had appeared in a scholarly journal many years earlier, adapted from a manuscript in the possession of the folklorist Achille Millien, who in turn had been told the tale by Louis and Francois Briffault, at Montigny-aux-Amognes, Nièvre, in or around 1885. Strange as the story was, it was not unique. During the course of his research, Delarue found dozens of versions of the tale from France and from French-speaking areas, some of which had been passed on by word of mouth for generations, they varied in local color, but the great majority of them shared in abundance of details as well as the same general plot.

What's more, around the time that Delarue was collecting these French tales, scholars and collectors became aware of other, nearly identical tales from elsewhere in fiurope and beyond. Italo Calvino included "The False Grandmother," a tale from Abruzzo, in his collection *Italian Folktales*, published in 1956. Its heroine passes through a river and a gate, instead of through the forest, and she encounters an ogress, rather than a bzou, who fries up her grandmother›s ears and stews her teeth. Upon climbing into bed, the girl discovers that the ogress is large and hairy and has a tail—much like the French bzou. In Asia, the sociologist and folklorist Wolfram Eberhard documented and analyzed a group of 241 Taiwanese tales that closely resembled the one from Montigny-aux-Amognes except that instead of a bzou, a tiger is tucked under the covers in the grandmother's or grandaunt's bed. He gobbles up the girl's younger sisters and in some versions hands her one of their fingers to chew on. In the Chinese tale "Lon Po Po" a mother goes off through the woods while the wolf, disguised as Grandmother (Po Po), approaches the children in their own home. In these versions there are sometimes two or three girls, not one; yet the tale is undeniably the same.

Bawdy and gruesome, these oral tales share themes of cannibalism, sexuality, defecation, mistaken identity, and an encounter in bed with a dangerous foe. They lack the usual fairy-tale moral that scolds the heroine. And most of them share one more remarkable element: The heroine escapes. In the French story collected by Delarue, she pulls a clever, and typical, ruse. Realizing she has climbed into bed with danger, she pretends she has to relieve herself. In one memorable variation, the bzou tells her to do it in the bed, but she refuses—"Oh no, that will smell bad!" So the bzou ties a cord around her ankle and lets her out on the leash. Once outside, the girl unknots the cord and ties it around a tree. With the bzou in belated pursuit, she makes her escape.

The discovery of this global sisterhood of oral tales has potentially profound implications for understanding "Little Red Riding Hood" and more broadly the role of women in folklore. Previously, scholars had thought the literary tales of female folly and punishment penned by Charles Perrault and the brothers Grimm to be typical of folk tradition. Many of them believed the Grimms' "Little Red Cap" to be a timeless tale, chock full of details that were either very ancient or archetypal. The heroine's red cloak, in particular, attracted their attention. The myth-ritualist Emile Nourry (who published under the pseudonym P. Saintyves) thought the tale described an ancient rite celebrating the coming of spring. The heroine's red headdress, he said, was a vestigial symbol of the flowers once worn by the May Queens. Folklorist Arthur Lang saw the tale's heroine as a symbol of the sun, the dawn, or the recurring springtime. The advent of psychoanalysis brought alternative, generally sexual theories from two famous sources—Erich Fromm and Bruno Bettelheim. According to Fromm, the tale represented a riddle from: the collective unconscious, easily decipherable, in which the red cap symbolized the onset of menstruation, the heroine's bottle of wine symbolized her virginity, and the stones which she later sews in the wolf's belly symbolized sterility.

Bettelheim, whose theories had enormous popular appeal, piought "Little Red Cap" had an antecedent as far back as the Latin story *Fecunda ratis*, written in the year 1023 by Egbert of Lieges, in which a little girl in red is found with a company of wolves. For Bettelheim, the enduring red cloak stood for precocious sexuality:

> Red is the color symbolizing violent emotions, very much including sexual ones. The red velvet cap given by Grandmother to Little Red Cap thus can be viewed as a symbol of a premature transfer of sexual attractiveness, which is further accentuated by the grandmother's being old and sick, too weak even to open a door. The name "Little Red Cap" indicates the key importance of this feature of the heroine in the story. It suggests that not only is the red cap little, but also the girl. She is too little, not for wearing the cap, but for managing what this red cap symbolizes, and what her wearing it invites.

Such interpretations fascinated a generation raised on psychoanalysis and were welcomed in a scholarly climate that embraced theories of universalism. However, with the discovery of "The Grandmother's Tale" and its variants, it became evident that many of the so-called "archetypal" motifs that scholars had latched on to, including the beloved red cloak, were not universal at all but on the contrary relatively recent and unrepresentative inventions. What's more, with the advent of new folkloric methodology, it became increasingly obvious that Charles Perrault—whose 1697 text is the presumed source of the Grimms' "Little Red Cap"—had dramatically revised the original folk tradition.

Folklorists trace tales just like scientists trace the evolution of species, by collecting, dating and comparing samples and by looking for traits that suggest a common ancestry. For paleontologists, an opposable thumb or a spinal cord can indicate a species' place in the phylogenetic tree. For folklorists, motifs—the tiny, immutable elements of a plot that persist in telling after telling—are the details that suggest a tale's lineage. A motif can be an object, a person, or a particular plot development: a magic key, a wicked stepmother, or the rubbing of a lamp that recurs in tale after tale, from one place to another and from generation to generation. By dating and comparing tales and noting the earliest appearance of particular motifs, folklorists can follow a tale's development.

The so-called "science of folklore"—a seemingly unlikely combination of terms—began with the brothers Grimm, who were among the first to date tales and record their sources (however deceptively). Their results inspired scholarly followers around the world. An annotated bibliography attached to the Grimms' 1850 edition of *Children's and Household Tales* lists hundreds of folktale collections that had appeared since the Grimms' 1812 work. In their introduction to the 1850 edition, the brothers claim that most of these foreign collectors had attributed their inspiration to the Grimms, either by personal letter ,or in their prefaces. Initially, when these international scholars came across variations of well-known tales, they identified them either by their number in the Grimms' table of contents or simply by a short, descriptive phrase. Soon, however, it became evident that a better and more systematic method was needed—and the Finnish folklorist Antti Aarne emerged as the "Linnaeus of folklore."

In the early twentieth century, Aarne collected vast numbers of tales and classified them according to what he determined to be their most elemental "type." His *Types of the Folktale*, published in 1910 and augmented and updated by his disciple Stith Thompson in 1928 and again in 1961, enabled scholars to distinguish and identify related tales as they appeared around the world. The Aarne-Thompson Tale Type Index, as it is called, has since become standard study for college folklore students and one of the most important folklore Reference books. The bizarre, even comical, charm of the index is its complete lack of reverence for the intangible magic of a story. Within its jungle of cross-referenced entries and coded legends, wedged between 333–H, "The Treacherous Cat," and 334, "Household of the Witch," is "Little Red Riding Hood"—tale type 333, a strange cipher of references and cross-references called "The Glutton":

> TT 333: *The Glutton* (*Red Riding Hood*). The wolf or other monster devours human beings until all of them are rescued alive from his belly. Cf. Types 123, 2027, 2028.

> *Wolf's Feast*, (a) By masking as mother or grandmother the wolf deceives and devours (b) little girl (RRH) whom he meets on his way to her grandmother's. Rescue, (a) the wolf is cut open and his victims rescued alive; (b) his belly is sewed full of stones and he drowns; (c) he jumps to his death.

> [Motifs:] K2011. Wolf poses as grandmother and kills child. Z18.1 What makes your ears so big? F911.3 Animal swallows man (not fatally).

> F913. Victims rescued from swallower's belly. Q426. Wolf cut open and filled with stones as punishment.

Just imagine reading *that* at bedtime!

Though its European bias and heavy reliance on the brothers Grimm (whose tales, as we have already seen, were not as representative of oral folk tradition as they claimed) make the Aarne-Thompson index a rough and sometimes unreliable guide, it performs the great service of clearing away local foliage to reveal a tale's trunk and roots, allowing folklorists to see where splits in the family tree begin. Perhaps even more important, since its publication a legion of international folklorists has embarked on the endless task of recording and classifying tale traditions from around the world. These folklorists, followers of the historic- geographic or simply "Finnish" school, after Antti Aarne, have compiled a growing matrix of regional tale-type indices that fill in the gaps between the Aarne-Thompson codes. One such follower was Paul Delarue, who was in the process of creating a French tale-type index when he produced his mid-century study of "The Grandmother's Tale."

Together with fellow folklorist Marie-Louise Tenéze, Delarue classified some 10,000 tales from France and its former territories using the Aarne-Thompson scheme. The particular importance of their work is that it provides a folkloric context and suggests an oral history for what have since become some of the most popular tales in the world. Their collection, *Le Conte populaire français* (The French popular tale), includes parallel versions of "Rapunzel," in which the heroine invites her prince up into the tower to make love (tale type 310); a frightening Bluebeard, who displays his dead wives' corpses on the wall (312); a more cynical set of Cinderellas (510A and 510B}; and bawdy variations on "Sleeping Beauty" (410). It includes tales of sex, cannibalism,—rape, incest, shitting, pissing, sodomy, cheating the Devil and tricking God. And of course, it includes the thirty-five oral sisters of Little Red Riding Hood—the evidence of her buried past.

Some of Delarue's collected oral cognates of "Red Riding Hood" had been "contaminated" by exposure to Charles Perrault's "Le petit chaperon rouge"; that is, they possessed identifying details like the telltale motif of the red hood, one of Perrault's inventions. But others had not. These tales, which apparently owe nothing to the literary fairy tale, indicate a narrative ancestor that predates Perrault's story. Their discovery has enabled folklorists to say with a fair degree of certainty that "The Grandmother's Tale" is how Little Red Riding Hood's adventure was told many years ago, around the fire or in the fields, long L before she found her way to print.

The revelation about Little Red Riding Hood's oral sisters delivers two lessons: the danger of interpreting a tale without knowing its history; and the importance of examining its broader folkloric patterns. Bettelheim and Fromm made the first mistake. Princeton historian Robert Darnton, who was familiar with "The Grandmother's Tale," made a merciless summation of Fromm's psychoanalytic blunder:

> Fromm made a great deal of the (nonexistent) red riding hood as a symbol of menstruation and of the (nonexistent) bottle carried by the girl as a symbol of virginity: hence the mother's (nonexistent) admonition not to stray from the path into wild terrain where she might break it. The wolf is the ravishing male. And the two (nonexistent) stones that are placed in the wolf's belly after the (nonexistent) hunter extricates the girl and her grandmother stand for sterility, the punishment for breaking a sexual taboo.

In contrast to Fromm, who employs the psychoanalyst's universalistic approach, Darnton is an eloquent spokesman for reading the tale as an historical document with clues to the premodern past. In an essay in his book *The Great Cat Massacre,* Darnton applies this historical approach to the French oral tales of the Delarue-Ténéze collection, asking, What if these tales sprang not simply from the imagination, but also from real life? Through the lens of his historical expertise he plucks fascinating insights from previously mysterious fairy-tale motifs.

In the overcrowded, underfed households of France's Old Regime, illiterate peasants sometimes gathered around the fire on cold winter evenings for a *veillée,* to share gossip, work, and stories. Not stories of fantasy, but of observation. Hunger, infanticide, and abandonment—all the cruel "fictions" of popular fairy-tale plots—were very real in these peasant communities at a time when the land was far less fertile than the population and life was a constant Malthusian struggle against starvation. Peasants labored from dawn until dusk on pathetic strips of soil. They survived on porridge made of bread and water. They ate meat only a few times a year. Those who couldn't make it farming became highwaymen and prostitutes. Childbearing was Russian roulette—thus, the stepmother, a trope for family woe in fairy tales, was a fixture of rural France. Step-siblings were extra mouths to feed and, like Cinderella's dreaded sisters, presented direct competition for the patrimony. As for the scatological and sexual elements of oral folktales like "The Grandmother's Tale," households were small, grown children lived at home for a long time, and family members often shared beds—and the chamber pots beneath them. The intimacies arid indelicacies of bodily functions were no secret in the Old Regime's peasant households.

Yet while fruitful, Darnton's historical approach fails to explain, just as he fails to notice, the most exceptional element shared by the oral cognates of "Red Riding Hood": the happy ending, with its heroine triumphant. This ending is no mere incidental motif. Its recurrence suggests that it is fundamental.

Scholars know of many tale types, or cycles, that recur around the world. Certain tales are ubiquitous—perhaps even universal. The flood myth of the Bible is echoed in the Epic of Gilgamesh from ancient Babylon, a tale recorded on stone tablets in the seventh century B.C. and composed some 4,000 years ago. There is not one but many quests for the Holy Grail. And the same mythic hero, in many different guises, appears over and over again across the globe. There are several theories as to why this is. Some have suggested that there was once an Original tale, a narrative Adam and Eve, or even an entire "mythogenic" zone from which tales first emerged and diffused throughout the world. The *Panchatantra,* a collection of Indian folktales believed to have entered

Europe after the eighth century during the Muslim conquest, is thought by some to be the original source of all our tales. Jungians, on the other hand, believe in "polygenesis," rooting the phenomenon in the common human experience: We all possess a human body, a human psyche, and these universal aspects of humanity give rise to collective dreams and symbols, which Jung called "archetypes." But all explanations ultimately lead to the same point: If a tale is important enough, it will be found amongst many peoples and will last a long time.

A narrow focus on history, such as that found in Darnton, can obscure the big picture. The specific details of life under the French Old Regime cannot account for the appearance of "Little Red Riding Hood" cognates in China, Korea, Japan, or Italy. The recurrence of stories remarkably similar to "The Grandmother's Tale" in countries separated by land and sea suggests that only by looking at the tale's global pattern can we get a sense of its broader, older, deeper meaning as an oral folktale—or "wives' tale."

FAIRY TALES TEND TO FOLLOW a familiar pattern, which the anthropologist Arnold van Gennep calls a *rite de passage*. It is the same pattern that characterizes human rituals marking life transitions: birth, death, and especially puberty or initiation rites. This pattern follows a sequence of three stages: a separation, a "liminal" or gestational period, and finally a return to society in a new form or with new status. Indeed, most fairy tales end in marriage, a symbol of social and sexual maturity.

In the popular literary fairy tales, heroines tend to follow a passive version of the rite of passage. Sleeping Beauty, Snow White, and the Grimms' Little Red Cap all wait, asleep or in a deathlike state, for rescue (and resurrection) by a prince (or hunter-woodsman) who frees the heroine from her slumber in a castle, a glass coffin, or the belly of the wolf. But, beyond fairy tales, there is a more heroic version of this pattern that has been widely studied—as it pertains to stories about boys and men.

The myth of the hero, or Hero Cycle, has been written about since the late nineteenth century by such diverse scholars as Carl Jung, the Viennese psychoanalyst Otto Rank, the English folklorist Lord Raglan, and most famously, the American mythographer Joseph Campbell. Campbell observed that the same hero appears all over the globe: Theseus, Odysseus, Siddhartha, Buddha, Jacob, Moses, Luke Skywalker, and even (as folklorist Alan Dundes has argued) Jesus Christ. In each incarnation, the hero looks different and has a different name but acts out a remarkably consistent script.

The myth begins when the hero's royal or marvelous birth is concealed from commoners or from those who raise him. Moses is sent downstream in a basket and is found by Pharaoh's daughter. Jesus is born of God but raised by Joseph and Mary. Oedipus, the son of a king, is cast away after birth to avoid the Sphinx's prophesy that he will kill his father. Untested, the young hero may be naive, perhaps arrogant or even self-doubting, but he is nonetheless full of promise. Clues suggest a great calling—superhuman strength or skill. The youthful David bests Goliath, years before becoming king. Superman the child rescues his mother from a car wreck by single-handedly lifting the vehicle. Still, little beyond this brief foreshadowing is heard of the hero until early adulthood, when he must undertake a journey by which he proves himself. Later he will rise to power and confront his father, as Zeus battled the Titan Cronos (Time) and freed his sibling gods to reign on Mount Olympus. Ultimately he will face death, hung on the cross or in the stars—but not before he has passed his tests and completed his journey. In brief form, this journey parallels; the pattern of heroes marching through the fairy-tale woods, a passage that some have called a "wisdom journey."

This journey, the central episode of the hero's voyage, is a test of mettle. The hero's search of self is fraught with danger and promises enlightenment. He faces demons, both literal and figurative. They may be ogres or giants, death in the form of a dark figure, or the underworld itself. The passage is so important that it may become synonymous with the hero's identity: During his twenty-year journey, Odysseus voyages to Hades, where he meets the ghosts of Greek warriors and heroes. Or the hero may encounter the "dark side," the term used by movie director George Lucas, who spent time with Campbell and styled his *Star Wars* epic after the scholar's insights. This dark side is symbolic not only of physical danger but of inner demons, one's doubts and weaknesses.

The fundamental lesson of the hero's journey is self-reliance. Neither Yoda nor Obi Wan Kenobi, Luke Skywalker's warrior mentors, comes to help him when he confronts and defeats his nemesis, the villainous Darth Vader—his father. The hero must always pass this test alone. His journey leads toward wisdom and maturity, in many forms: acceptance of responsibilities to family, community, kingdom, or God.

Fairy tales, of course, are not myths. Myths are sacred and grand in scope; fairy tales are specific, secular, and local. Campbell observed that the accomplishment of the mythic hero is world-historical, representing macrocosmic human triumphs, whereas the protagonist of the fairy tale achieves a domestic, microcosmic triumph—a personal victory. More frankly, perhaps, myths tend to glorify man's accomplishments, while fairy tales—at least those that are best known today—focus on women. According to Otto Rank, mythic heroes are never female. Campbell limited his early analysis to male heroes, although many of his examples were female—and he later acknowledged childbirth as one form of heroism. Yet, "The Grandmother's Tale" follows a pattern similar to that of the mythic hero's wisdom journey. Might the lesson of her tale—a coming of age, represented by a test of self-reliance—or even heroism—be the same?

In fact this oral ancestor of "Red Riding Hood" contains the classic signs and symbols that might support this interpretation. A girl leaves home heading into the dark area of the forest, beyond the boundaries of society, where danger in all forms—physical, spiritual, and sexual—lurks. She must choose a path of pins or needles— the tools and symbols that appear in female initiation rites around the world, and in particular in France, where sending a young girl to apprentice with the seamstress for a year or so was, according to one scholar, a bit like sending her to finishing school, and carried a sense of sexual maturation. The girl meets a bzou, which some scholars interpret as a nefarious sexual encounter. The bzou might be a male figure; it might also be an ogress, the symbol of maternal oppression, when motherly protection becomes a hindrance to independence. The bzou or ogress attempts to tie the girl to the bed, but she slips the leash and goes off on her own—a classic metaphor for attaining independence.

As for the cannibalistic meal, a motif that Delarue found in a great many of the folk versions of the tale: Perhaps the act of cannibalism is a symbolic reminder that the old will be reborn in the young, in a reversal of the maternal tide. In more literal terms, our bodies carry the genes of our ancestors; we are flesh of their flesh, blood of their blood. Children are born and come of age as grandparents die.

THE HEROIC HEROINE of "The Grandmother's Tale" stands in stark contrast to the passive female protagonists of Perrault and the brothers Grimm. Why? The explanation, perhaps, is that the story and its cognates come from a different set of authors—or rather, tellers. The clues to this lie in the stories themselves. In "The Grandmother's Tale," the girl meets a bzou at the fork in the path between pins and needles. This is no isolated reference. Sewing terms appear in many variants of this oral tale—just as they are practically omnipresent in our surviving literary fairy tales. A princess can't fling a dead cat without hitting a spinning wheel or a loom. Sleeping Beauty pricks her hand on an old spindle. Rumplestiltskin spins straw into gold. None of this is coincidence.

Because today few people sew their own clothes, much less produce the fabric from which garments are made, it is difficult to grasp that for most of history, spinning was *the* consuming labor of women everywhere in the world, and France was no exception. In the seventeenth century, textiles represented France's national industry, a patriotic duty driven by the need to clothe the nation's growing armies. Spinning rooms were attached to orphanages. Jailed or hospitalized women were made to spin, and prostitutes were expected to produce a certain number of bobbins of yarn in their off hours. Prizes were awarded to women who spun the most. And in the countryside, it was the incessant and deforming labor of the peasant woman, who sought distraction and relief in conversation, gossip, and stories. Women told tales to the repetitive rhythm of work, weaving in the signs of their labor, until telling a tale and spinning a yarn became one and the same.

"The Grandmother's Tale" suggests how their tales changed Mien put on paper. Perrault, the brothers Grimm, and their early Neapolitan predecessor Giambattista Basile all credited female sources for their tales: Mother Goose, Frauen, and the ugliest old crones around, respectively. But the sense of female authorship—literally, female authority—is absent from their tales. The Stories of the fairy tale canon little resemble oral tales like those recorded by Delarue, and the heroine triumphant has all but disappeared. The best-known tales have until relatively recently been written and studied almost exclusively by men who lived In a world where women never came of age, where even well into middle age, unmarried women were "girls of the house."

In this vein, it is also particularly interesting to note that in his insightful essay drawing on "The Grandmother's Tale," Darnton hardly considers—and indeed has entirely omitted from his transcription—the happy ending recorded by Delarue in which the girl escapes by her wits. This ending's appearance in so many of the oral French variants, as well as in other cultures' versions of the tale, suggests that it is fundamental to the tale's broad meaning. But Darnton's interest lies in the tale as an historical document, and so he misses its broader elements. They are not part of his story—just as, all too frequently, they are left out of history.

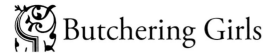# Butchering Girls

Red Riding Hood and *Bluebeard*

Graham Anderson

For heroines of the 'innocent slandered maiden' type we can expect a murder attempt, but the tale does not really centre on the murder episode as such, and the heroine for her part does not do a great deal to avert her fate, although she may show considerable initiative in variants where she is disguised as a man. Other tale-plots are, however, considerably more inclined to indulge an appetite for ghoulish horror, at times apparently for its own sake, and the 'compassionate executioner' is not likely to be oil standby either. Tales of plucky young girls who elude being devoured or murdered by an animal or human predator are well entrenched in the modern repertoire. The best known are *Little Red Riding Hood (Little Redcap)* and *Bluebeard*; both are often felt to be tales of relatively limited distribution and obscure early history. Once more there is a great deal of further exploration still to be done.

Red Riding Hood (AT Type 333)[1]

The Perrault version of *Little Red Riding Hood* is the first available example of the modern tale, and also the best known:

The girl in the red cape has to cross the wood on an errand to her grandmother. In conversation the wolf elicits details of her errand, comes to the grandmother's house by a different route, and swallows both.

Not until the Grimms does there appear to be a happy ending, in which the wolf is forced to disgorge the victims still alive and is then himself killed by having his belly weighted with stones; a second wolf in a clumsy doublet attack is then drowned in a water butt. There is also an all-animal version, in which a wolf swallows all but one of seven goat's kids, and once more is drowned *(AT* Type 123).

In the most extensive modern discussion, Jack Zipes accepts the theory that the tale itself is of little more than local distribution in western Europe in the first instance, with an evident epicentre in lycanthropy trials as late as the seventeenth century in provincial France.[2] But the picture is always changing. We should note an earlier and different looking tale at least in neighbouring north Italy. In Boccaccio's *Decameron* (9.7) there is a rather more ordinary wolf- meets-girl story:

Talano d'Immolese dreams that his wife Margarita is caught by a wolf, and warns her not to go to the wood the next day. She is at the best of times a quarrelsome wife and goes into the wood, suspecting that her husband has a lover's assignation there. She is indeed caught by the neck by a wolf, and is only rescued by chance by some shepherds; she bears the marks on her neck and is more respectful of her husband in future.

This is obviously, like Red Riding Hood itself, capable of being 'read' as a cautionary tale, but this time a more obviously adult one: the woman is married and there is the suspicion of the husband's affair. The wolf does catch the woman, and is forced to let her go; but there is no gross violation of probability as there is in the wolf's disgorging a child alive—let alone talking to her in the first place. The anticipatory dream of capture in an animal's mouth and dispute between husband and wife over the value of the dream gives the story affinities with Chaucer's *Nun's Priest's Tale;* but it does deserve at least a mention in the context of Red Riding Hoods.

Equally unmentioned in discussion of any Red Riding Hood canon are examples where the victim is not a girl but a boy—a possibility which might serve to qualify some of the more extreme feminist readings of the tale. A modern Persian example runs as follows:[3]

> A little boy is sent through a wood by his mother to take food to his father who is working in the fields at the other side. He meets the wolf and the usual conversation takes place; the wolf gets to the house where the father is staying, but he is not at home. When the boy comes home the wolf invites him to rest in bed. The boy takes his clothes off and comes to bed beside the wolf, and once more the usual conversation takes place; the boy is under the impression till the last moment that the wolf is his father—who returns in time to kill the wolf with a single stroke.

It is not clear whether this is a radical remodelling of the Perrault version: it certainly owes nothing to the oral strain of the tale that survives in France in Delarue's now well-known nineteenth-century peasant version from Nièvre,[4] with the girl forced to drink the grandmother's blood, but pleading a call of nature to escape. It seems odd that the wood is there and the dialogue so closely identical, even though oral recital tends to maintain the 'jingle' element as the most stable. ('All the better to "x" you with …'). It seems suspicious that the two paths through the wood are kept as they occur in Perrault, and oddly inconsistent to have it necessary for the father to be staying far enough away to require lodgings if a child is to be sent on an ordinary errand. It may simply be the case that this is a 'remake' for a more male-oriented society, or that it is a man's version in a society where women may have their own tales.[5] But even if that is so, it establishes that there may be reason for a male version in the Near East. There are other such versions: Tom Thumb may be swallowed first by a cow, then by a wolf, and is able to entice the wolf home and encourage it to eat too much to escape before calling on his father, who kills the wolf and rescues him.[6] Andrew Lang published a French literary version in which the girl is called Little Golden-hood ('the colour of fire') in which the magic golden cap was made by the witch-grandmother and is eaten by the wolf, burning his throat and bringing about his capture.[7]

Little attempt has been made to ask whether this much-loved fairytale is as old as the Ancient World. Perhaps the most completely satisfactory all-round analogue from antiquity is to be derived from a notice in Pausanias (6.6.7–11) about the famous boxer Euthymus of Locri in southern Italy. He was visiting nearby Temesa when he heard about a custom currently taking place there. Every year they had to offer a virgin 'bride' to a local spirit—of one of Odysseus' crew, long ago stoned to death as a rapist. The spirit—known by the neutral term of *Heros*—had a temple precinct in which the virgin had to be left (in Callimachus the spirit simply calls for a bed, and for those who brought her not to look back).[8] Euthymus entered the shrine, took pity on the girl, accepted her offer of marriage in return for saving her, fought and defeated the spirit, and drove it into the sea. Pausanias had also seen a picture of Euthymus' feat—in which the spirit was depicted as dark and terrifying *and wearing a wolfskin*. We have no actual swallowing of the girl and no red in her clothing, but the evidence relating to Callimachus' version indicates that in the rite defloration normally took place. Otherwise we have everything we need: deaths for the wolf-man involving first stoning, then (presumably) drowning; Euthymus as the huntsman; an enclosure with a bed, as in the fairytale's cottage scene; and a sexual motif. We have the wolf named in the picture as Lykas ('Mr Wolf'); but the 'girl that got away' remains unnamed.

There are a number of other, candidates. If none is so good a match, a number actually involve the element or implication of 'red' in the girl's name or general identity. We can begin by asking whether any ancient hunter associated with a girl named 'Miss Red' *also* killed a wolf-man? No single mythographic source offers us an answer, but when we combine two scraps of evidence, one from Greek tragedy and one from later mythological narrative, we find a candidate. We are told in Euripides' *Heracles* that the hero has an enemy Lycus ('Mr Wolf'), who has lolled Heracles' father-in-law Creon and the hero's own wife Megara and her children; Heracles will of course despatch him in due course. And we also know from the *Megara* attributed to Moschus that Megara, the wife of Heracles, had a sister Pyrrha ('flame-red'). We have no details, but we are entitled to infer that the reasons for Heracles' vengeance on Lycus include the desire to protect the surviving members of his wife's family.[9] We might put it briefly like this: 'hunter Heracles kills wife-killer Wolfman; sister Redgirl survives'.

Nor is this obscure Pyrrha the only 'flame-red' candidate available. A scholiast to Lycophron reports that Thetis was able to turn a real wolf to stone with her gaze when the wolf is sent to ravage her husband Peleus' flock.[10] Apollodorus credits her with the ability to change to fire, and so she too can be claimed as a 'flame-girl', though not in name; her activities in galvanising her son Achilles with fire point in the same direction. She doubtless had plenty of time to learn the craft; she and Eurynome held Hephaestus concealed for nine years, and he provided them with ornamental buckles, floral ornaments and necklaces *(Iliad* 18.398–405). We might note that lithifying the wolf by a look is a more supernatural and efficient variation on filling the sleeping wolf's belly with stones, the nearest to 'lithification' we find in the Grimms. We might also notice that the proverbially stormy relationship between Thetis and Peleus interestingly corresponds to the bad relationship between the husband and wife in the Boccaccio tale already noted.[11]

We have however no information that either Pyrrha, Heracles' sister-in-law, nor Thetis was actually *swallowed* by a wolf (a detail not always present in modern variants either).[12] But there is yet another candidate—we do have the story of Lycaon and Nyktinus, in which the father sacrifices his *son* to Zeus: Mie offering is unacceptable and he is miraculously reconstituted, while Lycaon is transformed into a wolf.[13] In Ovid's flood story Miss Flame-red (Pyrrha) is one of the survivors of the flood *(Met.* 1.348ff.), while the wolf is among the victims who drown. In all these cases, except that of Euthymus and Lykas, we have a sense of looking at the essential ingredients but never being able to assemble them in quite the right way, although the drowned wolf *does* actually occur in Grimm, as we have noted.[14] There is yet another version involving a Pyrrha in a quite different way: a mother, the nymph Thetis, sends her child for safekeeping to the home of King Lycomedes ('wolf-sly'?); the child comes as Pyrrha ('flame- red girl'); she is flame-red because she has been galvanised by her mother in a fire, and is almost entirely indestructible. But she is really a boy in disguise, and it is not long before she has made Lycomedes' daughter Deidameia pregnant.[15] This of course is part of the story of Achilles. The possibility of a cross-dresser's dialogue ('O what an "x" to "y" you with') suggests itself in such a situation, but we have no trace of any such. Yet it is really taxing coincidence very hard to see all this as random. The girl's dangerous enemy in woman's clothes is in the text, but the wrong way round. It is as if this is a counter-Red Riding Hood, like the satirical Thurber version where she slugs the wolf with the revolver she has been carrying in her basket. On the other hand, this particular Pyrrha's mother has herself turned a wolf to stone, as we have seen.[16]

We might also note an anonymous tale casually alluded to by Horace where a male child is brought alive from the belly of the Lamia: *neu pransae Lamiae uiuum puerum extrahat aluo* ('do not [in a poem] drag out the boy alive from the belly of the Lamia').[17] It might be objected that the Lamia is a cannibal ogress, not a wolf, but de Nino knew an Italian version in which the wolf's part in what is otherwise quite clearly a Red Riding Hood tale is indeed played by an ogress (and once more where the resourceful heroine escapes and kills the ogress rather than being swallowed).[18] The Red Riding Hood story may be relatively uncommon in Italy, but on this evidence it ought to be very old indeed.

Modern tellers and students of the story have not been slow to find sexual symbolisms in the close association of the young girl and the wolf, especially in the frequent instances of the wolf's requiring the girl to strip prior to entry into the wolf's bed. These elements, too, are to be found at least hinted at in antiquity. There are two pastoral pieces in Greek, one by Theocritus and one by Longus, in the same general tradition that deal with the adventures of someone with a wolf-related name. In Longus, a lustful girl called 'Little Shewolf' (Lykainion) entices the naive young Daphnis into the depths of the wood and offers to initiate him into lovemaking; there is a pretext that one of her geese has been captured by an eagle and needs to be rescued. He even offers her the produce of his flock as a 'reward'.[19] There is also an earlier episode in the same text in which the oxherd Dorcon puts on a wolfskin in order to rape the heroine Chloe, until he is foiled by dogs, then killed by pirates.[20] In the case from Ps.-Theocritus 27, Daphnis is the son of Lycidas (i.e. 'son of Wolfson'). He entices into the woods a daughter of Menalcas; after laying her down on his sheepskin he forces her to make love, having torn her dress so that she is naked.[21] There is also a standard sexual symbolism in Latin: a brothel was a *lupanar,* and prostitutes were required to wear purple-bordered togas. It does not take much adjustment of vision to see the modern tale as 'scarlet woman en route to the wolf-lair …'. The sexual symbolism was realised early enough in the modern history of the tale, as underlined by Perrault and his first English translator Robert Samber [22]

What conclusion, then, can we suggest overall? It seems clear enough that, despite the absence of a name for the heroine in Pausanias' story of Euthymus and Lykas, we do have one good clear 'take' of the traditional Red Riding Hood in antiquity; and a whole dossier of other partly converging hints surrounding a girl with a 'flame-red' name and associations;[23] the circumstantial evidence of a 'Heracles and Pyrrha' version is likewise strong. The available materials offer us two things: the skeleton of a story in which a child, male or female, is threatened, raped or eaten by a figure with wolf or ogre associations, then disgorged or otherwise reconstituted with or without the substitution of a stone, while the wolf-figure is drowned or killed, and a 'flame-girl' (in whatever sense) survives the drowning to see new life brought from stones. The tally of Red Riding Hood candidates is quite impressive: Pyrrha, sister of Megara, on the sidelines of a story in which Heracles disposes of the murderous Lycus; Pyrrha, wife of Deucalion, surviving the flood in which the wolf-king Lycaon is drowned after murdering a victim reconstituted by Zeus, and herself drawing life from stones; two Rheas—one married to a cannibal ogre from whom she saves both male and female children, including a flame-girl Hestia, by placing a stone in the ogre's belly, and another associated with a wood, worshipper of Vesta, frightened by a wolf; Thetis, a fire-goddess in several senses, who turns a wolf to stone; her son/daughter Pyrrha who seduces a wolf-king's daughter; the unnamed boy disgorged from the belly of the female ogress; and the unnamed girl rescued by Euthymus from the wolf ghost earlier stoned and later drowned. But there is also just a hint of some kind of 'allegories of adolescence' in which the form of a wolf is associated with the role of a predator, often and obviously enough with sexual overtones.[24] I do not doubt that wolf stories can emerge wherever there are wolves; but it is difficult to dislodge local tradition from the tale-type both in Italy and elsewhere in antiquity.

Bluebeard (AT Types 311/312)[25]

Hitherto it has not been possible to produce a clear connection between the celebrated Bluebeard tale and ancient mythography: the story of a serial killer whose victims know too much might so readily be rooted in recurrent reality as to make an ancient prototype unnecessary. Nonetheless, there are at least some stylised features of the story that will indeed point to one or more versions from the classical world. The modern tale can be described as follows:

A single sinister aristocratic figure, Bluebeard, engages a series of (usually) three servants or wives from the same set of sisters. Each is subjected to a test taboo: they have the free run of the house except for a forbidden door. Bluebeard absents himself and tests each wife: the first two open the door but betray their deceit by letting an egg fall into the blood of the forbidden chamber, a flower wither, a key become bloody,[26] or the like. The third takes a precaution so as to remain undetected, and is able to revive her sisters, smuggle them out, and send for the help of a brother or similar agent in the nick of time; Bluebeard himself is usually killed.

That represents the tale as familiar from Perrault. The resourceful surviving wife in the Grimm's version, 'Fitcher's Bird', makes her escape in a peculiar disguise of bird feathers stuck to her body with a coating of honey. There are also two closely related tale-types that tend to merge with *Bluebeard*: a *Robber Bridegroom* tale *(AT* Type 955) tends to have only the one girl; there is also a version where the Bluebeard figure is quite clearly detected to be the devil, and his house as hell *(AT* Type 312B). The oral tale enjoys wide circulation in northern European traditions, being particularly strong in Scandinavia; samples elsewhere tend to be sporadic, but a full modern investigation. has not been done. Particularly suggestive is the fact that some versions, notably Italian examples, have the devil as the bridegroom and hell as the forbidden chamber; or they feature a dragon as the horrid bridegroom or employer, and his efforts to make the reluctant wife or servant eat human remains; similar motifs occur in 'primitive' renderings of Red Riding Hood, and some filiation between the two is not to be ruled out entirely.

The Opies produce a respectable trickle of literary versions going back as far as a hagiographic tale of St Tryphine set as early as the fifth century AD, and thus already edging back, at least in their dramatic date, to the very threshold of antiquity.[27] But it can be pushed back a good deal further. The story has a number of connections with the lore attached to Minos of Crete. The principal theme would be the fact that he is cursed with being unable to sleep with women without fatal results to the women themselves. This in itself would produce a string of fatalities, until he is apparently cured by the ministrations of Procris, who is herself, as we shall see, already involved in *another* Bluebeard-type adventure as a daughter of Erechtheus.[28] But Minos also possesses the palace at Cnossus whose abundance of rooms and labyrinthine character is archaeologically attested; the right kind of site for the motif of the 'forbidden door'. Bluebeard put each disobedient wife into the bloody chamber with the corpses of her predecessors. We know that Minos is not above shutting a living person in with a corpse, as he does in the separate adventure of Glaucus and Polyeidos;[29] that he demanded the tribute from the Athenians including seven young women at a time; and that he was sexually attracted to at least one of the victims who travelled over with Theseus.[30] We do not know the circumstances under which he would have introduced them to the Minotaur, but there would certainly have been a suitable context for a 'room taboo' test here. Minos could have tested the women by courting each of the victims until she opened the forbidden door, after which, as a result of her disobedience, she might conceivably have been killed by being shut in with the Minotaur behind it.

More certainly, however, Minos *did* possess a peculiarity close to the Bluebeard of the fairytale: he bribed Nisus' daughter Scylla to let him have her father's purple lock on which the safety of the city of Megara depended.[31] One notes that in Ovid's retelling of this adventure Minos rides a white horse and wears a purple covering: Charles Dickens' nurse's version of the story, *Captain Murderer,* by far the ghastliest known to me, has the villain ride a white horse with a red stain on its back covered by harness.[32] Minos himself also has subterranean associations, since he becomes a reputable judge of the dead, following a Homeric tradition friendly to his reputation. But this could easily help to account for die conflation of his story with that of devils. The end of Minos in his human form, killed by Coccalus' daughters with boiling water or pitch while he vindictively pursues Daedalus, would not be inconsistent with the usual end of Bluebeard tales where he is murdered by the last of his intended victims.[33] Minos, then, has more than enough qualifications to take the Bluebeard accolade in his own right, and the purple lock is likewise hard to argue away when associated with someone sexually destructive to women; though there is no single simple narrative thread, and no single source that preserves the tale intact. Procris cures his trait of being fatal to women, but has her Bluebeard-style come-uppance with someone else, her own absent husband Cephalus, and that is treated as a romantic fatal accident in Ovid's classic version in *Metamorphoses 7*.

It might be emphasised that traditions concerning Minos are as fluid as those concerning Bluebeard himself. What has hampered identification is the stability of details like the Minotaur and the Bull of Pasiphae, which tend to obscure the more incidental and no less sinister other tales of this elusive and tantalising figure. One factor in favour of Minos is that once more his story has a legendary character to it: someone something like this existed in

Bluebeard's wife	*Procris*
Sisters are killed by murderous husband with blue beard	Sisters are sacrificed during threats from enemy king Eumolpus, son of sea-god Poseidon, a deity described as caeruleus (sea-blue)[34]
Husband has forbidden chamber	Eumolpus is a priest of Demeter and the underworld queen Persephone, and institutes mystery rites at Eleusis
Husband tests wives by going absent	Procris' husband Cephalus, son of Deion ('Murderous') or of Hermes,[35] goes off to see whether his wife will remain faithful; she fails the test, by sleeping with a stranger, or husband in disguise, for gold
Bluebeard locks women in with corpses	Minos locks a living man in with a dead one
Brides of Bluebeard do not survive to tell the tale	Procris goes to Minos, the man with the purple lock, whose lovers do not survive sleeping with him
She takes precautions against the bride-test	She takes precautions against his fatal embrace and survives
She leaves Bluebeard disguised as 'Fitcher's Bird'	She disguises herself as a man and rejoins Cephalus under the name *Pterelas* ('winged')

some sense, and so he joins the murderer of St Tryphine among the rogue's gallery of forebears for *Captain Murderer*. We may be tempted to strengthen our suspicions by looking at the story through the perspective of Procris herself:

These matches work well on the whole once we grasp that it is Procris who seems to move from one Bluebeard scenario to another. But we must stress the sense that we almost always seem to be dealing in this context with halves of stories.

There are also other candidates in antiquity for Bluebeard's victims. Curiosity in opening a forbidden object is central to the tale, and- the Opies noted in passing the story of Pandora and the forbidden jar, though only to make the point that 'the effect of female curiosity' offers a theme of great antiquity.[36] But the Pandora theme deserves to be pursued further.[37] It has to be noted that another, or an apparently other, girl by the name of Pandora is, like Procris, one of the daughters of the ancient King of Athens, Erechtlieus, and in their tale we may have something of what is missing in Hesiod. One of the daughters has to be sacrificed at the behest of Delphi to ensure Athenian survival in the war against Eumolpus of Eleusis,[38] and two other daughters give their lives in sympathy. A fourth daughter, Procris, fails a fidelity test set by an absent husband with an ominous pedigree: Cephalus, son of Deion ('murderous').[39] Any conflation of the two Pandoras, and any attempt to conflate the fortunes of the daughters of Erechtheus, will produce a further Bluebeard tale automatically—and a conveniently expurgated example at that, with simply a forbidden box of evils rather than a forbidden bloody chamber.[40]

The motif of 'the devil's bride' can also be pursued through a further mythological route: the story of Persephone has the girl taken from a flower meadow by force by Hades into the underworld;[41] there she violates a food taboo and the breaking of the taboo puts her into Hades' power for at least part of the year. Our mythographic sources do not explicitly represent the eating of the pomegranate seeds as a food taboo as such,[42] but it might be inferred nonetheless: if one touches the egg in Bluebeard's forbidden chamber, one must join the rest of the dead; if one eats the pomegranate seeds in Hades' kingdom, one must stay in the realm of the dead.[43] Underworld taboos can be shown to operate inexorably much earlier in a similar context (the confinement of the Sumerian Enkidu in the Nether World).[44] And indeed the Sumerian story of *Inanna's Descent to the Nether World* already has the goddess stripping off her seven garments to enter the Nether World, only to remain as a corpse on a hook until her extradition can be arranged.[45] Her death has occurred after her admission beyond the Seventh Door.

There is also a related girl in the underworld story reflected in a modern German version (Ranke 1966: 26), where an innocent girl goes in search of her godmother, who turns out to be the devil's wife; one of the sights seen in hell is the burning of infants in the chimney piece; another is the godmother wearing a horsehead. Both features can be compared to adventures of Demeter, mistress of Poseidon (once more a 'sea-blue' god).[46]

The Robber Bridegroom *(AT Type 955)*

The Bluebeard type-tale is closely associated with another, that of the Robber Bridegroom. A clutch of modern Spanish examples serves to convey the nature of the type:

A group of thieves prepare to rob a house, with one of their number as the 'inside man'. The youngest of three sisters in the household notices his suspicious behaviour. As he is calling his fellow thieves she pushes him out the window. He recovers and comes back for his knives: she opens the door just wide enough to allow her to mutilate his hand. Eventually the thief with the distinguishing mutilation becomes rich, and parental pressure forces the canny daughter to marry him; he prepares to kill her with the knife that caused the mutilation; but she manages to drown him in a well.[47]

In an extended version of the same tale we have the thief taking the girl to the robbers' den;[48] she kills the gangsters' moll who has been commissioned to cook her, and escapes. In a further version each of three sisters has to handle the corpses: the first two refuse and are killed; a third rescues a sick prisoner and they escape; one of the robbers is disguised in a dogskin and finds her,[49] but she gives the alarm; she marries her co-escapee.

This sequence of distinctively bloodcurdling robbers' episodes in which a humble, weak creature eludes the artful organisation of a robber band is already to be found in only slightly rearranged form in the robbers' tales in Apuleius. There are three tales—of a robber who loses a hand nailed to the door by the owner, a second thrown out of a window by an old woman, and a third trapped in a bearskin and betrayed by a slave *(Met.* 4.9–21). In the Spanish group these are all perpetrated by the same quick-thinking youngest daughter. But Apuleius does offer the girl at the robber's house in the person of Charite, and she too finally mutilates a robber, her husband's murderer (in this case,

Robber Bridegroom	Tale of Charite
Youngest sister	Young girl
is detained at robber's den, but escapes	is detained at robber's den
She detects and wounds robber by cutting off his fingers in a door;	She hears tale of robber wounded by having hand cut off in door;
by pushing him through a window;	of a second robber pushed through window;
by killing him in an animal skin	of a third robber killed in animal skin
She marries the man she has mutilated, and has great difficulty in being rescued at the last minute	She is prepared to sleep with murderous robber, but mutilates him before bringing about both their deaths

by blinding, *Met.* 8.13); he certainly has a robber's name, Thrasyllus, and indeed is said to have associations with robbers *(Met.* 8.1), though not specifically with the band already mentioned. The correspondence works like this:

Apuleius' complex web of robber stories is considerably more romanticised than the folktale versions by the complication that Charite marries a fiance who merely *poses* as one of the robbers, Haemus, ('Captain Blood') before being killed; but the basic framework is in place and must reinforce the view that Apuleius' novel has close affinities to folktale in general.

We are in a position to see, then, that the tales of extreme cruelty to resourceful women exhibited in *Red Riding Hood*, *Bluebeard* and *The Robber Bridegroom* are indeed to be found in antiquity, though seldom in an obviously coherent form. We should stress the importance of looking at the whole of the mythological tradition of any given story: a well-known version in Ovid or elsewhere is unlikely to present all the details necessary to relate any given ancient version to the modern tale-type, and it often requires the assembly of a good many hybrid outlines before we are in a position >to see that most of the features now known in a tale already exist in antiquity in- some sort of stable relationship to one another. Seldom, too, are we able to make any progress towards constructing an archetype of any given tale. The variants encountered in surviving literature are at least as varied and confused as their modern counterparts, suggesting that the tales themselves are already old.

NOTES

1. Bolte-Polivka 110. 26, 1.234–237; for a useful casebook approach, Dundes (1989' die editor himself emphasising die link with *AT* type 133. Zipes (1993a) offers detailed survey of the major shifts in emphasis since Perrault, as well as a respectable cross-section of retellings, including those of Perrault and Grimm. See also Opie and Opie (1974: 119–121); Tatar (1999: 3–10).
2. Zipes (1993a: 18–20).
3. Text in Boulvin and Chocourzadeh (1975), no. 11.
4. Delarue 1 (1957: 373f.); tr. in Zipes (1993: 21ff.).
5. But in fact there is a French male version as well, from lower Poitou, printed by Massignon (no. 16). In this instance the grandmother sets about the wolf before the father kills him, and neither boy nor grandmother is swallowed. Note the gender differentiation in what is taken to the grandmother: girls take some kind of dainties, the boy black puddings.
6. Grimm 37, *AT Type* 700.
7. Lang, *Red Fairy Book* (1890: 215–220).
8. According to the Diegesis relating to *Aetia* fr. 98f.
9. A Pindaric scholium contributes the unusual detail that Lycus was responsible for the death of Heracles' three children (Schol. *Isthmian* 4.104f., in contrast to the general tradition that Heracles murdered them himself during his madness); Gantz (1993: 380).
10. Gantz (1993: 227).
11. At this juncture we might also note the tale of the Teumessian Fox (Antoninus Liberalis 41, cf. Apollodorus 2.4.7): it is unhuntable, and requires child sacrifice once a month from the Thebans until it too is lithified by Zeus (to prevent the problem of its being hunted by Minos' inescapable hunting dog).
12. We have, however, another flame-girl who *was* swallowed and recovered alive, though not this time from a wolf: in Hesiod, Hestia is among the offspring of the cannibal Cronos, who is swallowed alive by her father and recovered by Zeus when a stone is substituted for him in his father's belly (Hesiod *Theogony* 453–495). As she became goddess of the hearth, an association embodied in her name, she too can be claimed in some sense as a 'flame-girl'.
    We should note also that there are further ramifications of Hestia and her mother Rhea in connection with a wolf and the substitution of a stone: Cronos's disgorging of his children shows at least one distinctive ingredient of the tale—the substitution of a stone for the swallowed child (in this case a single stone

rather than a lethal load of them). However, coincidence does not end there: the name of Cronos's wife is Rhea, and her Latin namesake Rhea Silvia is recorded as having been frightened by a wolf in Servius Auctus (valuable assembly of testimonia in Wiseman 1995). Rhea was frightened by the wolf while attending to her business as a vestal virgin, a devotee of the Latin Hestia, Vesta. The two Rlieas cannot immediately be identified, as one is a vestal under oath of celibacy and the other is a mother of several children. Or so it seems, except that Vesta herself was supposedly a virgin with the tide of *mater* (R. Gordon in OCD, 3rd edn, s.v.), and so the objection is rather lessened. Rhea Silvia ('Rhea of the Woods') is as a vestal associated with a sacred flame and some sort of errand as well, sanctioned by Vesta.

If the two Rheas were presented as identical, then the story when reconstructed would indeed resemble ours:

> There once was a girl who belonged to the wood. She used to tend the flame of the goddess Vesta, but while she was performing a task for the goddess, she was frightened by the sight of the wolf. She went home to her husband to find that he ate their children. She substituted a stone for one of them, and Gaia—Hestia's grandmother, be it noted—made him bring all the other five out alive. Her husband was punished for his crime by the son he had swallowed, and confined to Tartarus.

There is a further connection. The famous literary werewolf story in Petronius *Satyrica* 61f. has a man setting out to see his would-be lover Melissa now that her husband has died. The soldier he takes with him changes into a wolf and gets to Melissa's first, but is driven off wounded and resumes his human form the next day with the wounds still showing. Melissa and her household had driven him off themselves. What is interesting in the light of the foregoing discussion is that in one context at least the name Melissa was a cult tide of Rhea *(OCD3 s.v.)*.

13. For the classical sources, Gantz (1993: 728f.); Ovid *(Met.* 1.199–243) as usual offers the most detail, but omits the name of the victim, who in this case is a man; cf. also Ps.-Eratosthenes 8D (Lycaon's own grandson Arkas); a child (Hesiod) fr. 163 MW = Katast. 8R *et al*

14. *Grimm 26* (Little Redcap).

15. Hyginus 96 furnishes the critical detail of Achilles' pseudonym among the girls; for other sources, Gantz (1993: 581). A further instance of rape of a wolf's daughter occurs in the story of Sisyphus and Autolycus, where Sisyphus seduces Mr Wolfself's daughter in revenge for the stealing of his cattle. I suspect that the ancient and difficult to etymologize Sisyphus is really a simplification of Xisouthros, an oriental name for the Greek Deucalion (cf. Sumerian Ziusudra). If that is indeed the case, then *both* Deucalion and Pyrrha had a victory over the wolf-figure. Aid of course both have a key adventure with reconstituting the human race out of stones—yet another way of paraphrasing the idea that stones can be used to procure regeneration (put stones in the wolf's belly, and you can take swallowed children out alive; throw them over your shoulder, and they turn into people).

16. Zipes (1993: 229), from James Thurber (1939) cThe Girl and the Wolf', in *Fables for Our Time and Famous Poems* (New York).

17. Horace, *Ars Poetica* 340, with Brink's commentary *ad loc.*.

18. De Nino 12 (= Calvino 116).

19. Longus 3.15–18.

20. Longus 1.20f.,29f.

21. Ps.-Theocritus 27.42, 49–59.

22. In Zipes (1993: 95f.).

23. Other elements of wolf-lore may be relevant to details of Red Riding Hood. We might recall some of the oddities of the Lupercalia where young men, dressed in goatskin capes, strike women with a strip of hide to make them fertile (discussion in Wiseman 1995: 80–87). The two Luperci run by different routes, as do Red Riding Hood and wolf through the wood, but otherwise it is not easy to fit our random assortment of ancient wolf-lore to the contours of our story. For further treatment of lykanthropy, W. Burkert, *Homo Necans* (1983: 84–90); R. Buxton in J. Bremmer (1987: 60–79); also *OCDo* s.v. Lycaon. For the possibility of temporary wolf-men, cf. Marie de France's *Lai Bisclavret*.

24. There may be a symbolism of incest in the idea of a father devouring his own daughter, cf. the incest riddle in *Apollonius of Tyre* 4.

25. Bluebeard: Grimm 46 (Fitcher's Fowl); Bolte and Polivka 1.398–412; Opie and Opie (1974: 133–141) with R. Samber's first printed English version (1729: 137–141).

26. A possible euphemism for loss of virginity, as modern fairytale scholarship has not been slow to argue: for strong reservation, Tatar (1999: 141).

27. For St Tryphine and Commorre, Opie and Opie (1974: 136).

28. For this account, Apollodorus 3.15.1; Antoninus Liberalis 41; cf. Palaiphatos 2. The detailed form of the story in Antoninus is that he ejaculates snakes, scorpions and millipedes into his partners, rather than that he executes his wives.

29. For discussion, Gantz (1993: 270) (Apollodorus 3.3.1f.; Hyginus *Fab.* 136).

30. That is, (P)eriboiia, as in Bacchylides 17.

31. At any rate in Aeschylus' version, *Choephori* 612–622; and evidendy implied in the Ps.-Virgiiian *Ciris* 187; Ovid has him refusing die lock in horror, *Met.* 8.95f.

32. *Met.* 8.33f.; *The Uncommercial Traveller* (Dickens) ch.15. Note that modern Bluebeards often have the heroine helped by a dog: here Scylla's own name means 'puppy'.

33. For this episode in die tradition hostile to Minos, Diodorus 4.79.1ff.; Apollodorus, *Epitome* 1.14f.; and Gantz (1993: 275).

34. Bluebeard can be naturally related to the tide *caeruleus*, appropriate to sea deities (Poseidon, Triton, Nereus, Proteus, or die like: *caeruleos habet unda deos*, Ovid *Met.* 2.8).

35. For the sources, Gantz (1993: 238f.). Hermes, widi his underworld associations, might be no less obvious than Deion himself in this context.

36. Opie and Opie (1974: 133).

37. Epimetheus, the husband of Pandora, would as a Titan have spent a period of imprisonment underground after the revolt against Zeus, and might dierefore qualify for devil as well as mortal status. (On Epimetheus, Gantz (1993: 154): Hesiod's *Theogony* leaves any role of Prometheus and his brother in the Titanomachy unexplained). But the story as offered in Hesiod is presented as a misogynist tale: die beautiful woman brings destruction on mankind by breaking the taboo of die forbidden jar, and no punishment is offered for opening it. If the story of Pandora is a 'Bluebeard's wife' story, we do not have the whole of it here.

38. For the sources, Gantz (1993: 242f.): Euripides' *Erechtheus*, fr. 360N2; Demosthenes 60.27; Apollodorus, *Eibl.* 3.15.1; Hyginus *Fab.* 46, 238; Suda (with a variety of details).

39. Sources, Ovid *Met.* 7.672–862; Antoninus Liberalis 41; cf. Hyginus *Fab.* 160, 189; Gantz (1993: 238). (In general there are attempts to distinguish between Cephalus, son of Deion, and Cephalus, son of Hermes, but occasional conflation). It should also be noted that the name Deion/Deioneus has overtones of 'destroyer', while Hermes himself has his own underworld associations as escort of souls to the nether world. There is a prominent role for fox and dog in the Cephalus story; English Bluebeatds sometimes carry the tide 'Mr Fox'.

40. A similar range of daughters of another early Athenian king, Cecrops, are taboo breakers as well: all are given a casket of snakes by Athena and told not to open it, which diey do (sources in Gantz (1993: 235–239)). I am grateful to my colleague Jim Neville for drawing this parallel to my attention.

41. On whom see further C. Sourvinou-Inwood, *Reading Greek culture* 147–88. For the analogy between Bluebeard's consort and Persephone, Krappe (1930: 5).

42. Ovid *Met.* 5.533–50; Apollodorus *Eibl.* 1.5.3, 2.5.12; for other accounts, Gantz (1993: 64–68).

43. We might think also of the scene in *Cupid and Psyche* where die heroine has to take a 'Pandora's box' from the Underworld and opens it to find a fateful sleeping drug instead, Apuleius *Met.* 6.20f.

44. Text in Heidel (1949: 97ff.) (a great variety of taboos relating to clothing and actions, but curiously not about food).

45. Sumerian: Jacobsen (1976: 55–63); cf. *AT Type* 312C.

46. For example, burning of infants: *Homeric Hymn to Demeter*; Ovid *Fasti* 4.502–560; as mare: Pausanias 8.25.5. Note, too, the apparent conflation of Pandora and Persephone mythology in scenes depicting satyrs beating the ground, or Epimetheus depicted with a hammer, as Pandora/Persephone comes out of the ground: ‹there is clearly something here that we do not understand›, Gantz (1993: 68). The rescue of a Bluebeard victim who has just broken the taboo seems eminently plausible.

47. Spanish oral tradition in Taggart (1990: 60ff£).

48. Ibid.: 68.

49. Ibid.: 73.

# Bluebeard

Charles Perrault

Once upon a time there was a man who had fine town and country houses, gold and silver plates, embroidered furniture, and gilded coaches. Unfortunately, however, this man had a blue beard, which made him look so ugly and terrifying that there was not a woman or girl who did not run away from him.

Now, one of his neighbors was a lady of quality who had two exceedingly beautiful daughters. He proposed to marry one of them, leaving the choice up to the mother which of the two she would give him. Yet neither one would have him, and they kept sending him back and forth between then], not being able to make up their minds to marry a man who had a bfee beard. What increased their distaste for him was that he had already had several wives, and nobody knew what had become of them.

In order to cultivate their acquaintance, Blue Beard took the sisters, their mother, three or four of their most intimate friends, and some , young people who resided in the neighborhood, to one of his country estates, where they spent an entire week. Their days were filled with excursions, hunting and fishing, parties, balls, entertainments, and feasts. Nobody went to bed, for their nights were spent in merry games and gambols. In short, all went off so well that the younger daughter began to find that the beard of the master of the house was not as blue as it used to be and that he was a very worthy man.

The marriage took place immediately upon their return to town. At the end of a month Blue Beard told his wife that he was obliged to take a journey concerning a matter of great consequence, and it would occupy him at least six weeks. He asked her to amuse herself as best as she could during his absence and to take her closest friends into the country with her if she pleased, and to offer them fine meals.

"Here are the keys to my two great storerooms," he said to her. "These are the keys to the chests in which the gold and silver plates for special occasions are kept. These are the keys to the strongboxes in which I keep my money. These keys open the caskets that contain my jewels. And this is the passkey to all the apartments. As for this small key," he said,"it is for the little room at the end of the long corridor on the ground floor. Open everything and go everywhere except into that room, which I forbid you to enter. My orders are to be strictly obeyed, and if you dare open the door, my anger will exceed anything you have ever experienced."

She promised to carry out all his instructions exactly as he had ordered, and after he embraced her, he got into his coach and set out on his journey. The neighbors and friends of the young bride did not wait for her invitation, so eager were they to see all the treasures contained in the country mansion. They had not ventured to enter it while her husband was at home because they had been frightened of his blue beard. Now they began running through all the rooms, closets, and wardrobes. Each apartment outdid the other in beauty and richness. Then they ascended to the storerooms, where they could not admire enough the elegance of the many tapestries, beds, sofas, cabinets, stands, tables, and mirrors in which the> could see themselves from head to foot. Some mirrors had frames of glass and some of gold gilt, more beautiful and magnificent than they had eve seen. They could not stop extolling and envying the good fortune of the new bride.

In the meantime, she was not in the least entertained by all these treasures because she was so impatient to open the little room on the ground floor. Her curiosity increased to such a degree that, without reflecting how rude it was to leave her company, she ran down a back staircase so hastily that she nearly tripped and broke her neck on two or three occasions. Once at the door she paused for a moment, recalling her husband›s prohibition. What misfortune might befall her ^if she disobeyed? But the temptation was so strong that she could not withstand it. She took the small key, and with a›"trembling hand she opened the door of the little room.

At first she could make out nothing, since the windows were shuttered. After a short time, though, she began to perceive that the floor was covered with clotted blood of the dead bodies of several women suspended from the walls. These were all the former wives of Blue Beard, who had cut their throats one after the other. She thought she would die from fright, and the key to the room fell from her hand. After recovering her senses a little, she picked up the key, locked the door again, and went up to her chamber to compose herself. Yet she could not relax because she was too upset. Then she noticed that the key to the room was stained with blood. She wiped it two or three times, but the blood would not come off. In vain she washed it, and even scrubbed it with sand and grit. But the blood remained, for the key was enchanted, and there was no way of cleaning it completely. When the blood was washed off one side, it came back on the other.

That very evening Blue Beard returned from his journey and announced that he had received letters on the road informing him that the business on which he had set forth had been settled to his advantage. His wife did all she could to persuade him that she was delighted by his speedy return. The next morning he asked her to return his keys. She gave them to him, but her hand trembled so much that he did not have any difficulty in guessing what had occurred.

"Why is it," he asked,"that the key to the little room is not with the others?"

"I must have left it upstairs on my table," she replied.

"Bring it to me right now," said Blue Beard.

After several excuses she was compelled to produce the key. Once Blue Beard examined it, he said to her,"Why is there blood on this key?"

"I don›t know," answered the poor woman, paler than death.

"You don't know?" Blue Beard responded. "I know well enough. You wanted to enter the room! Well, madam, you will enter it and take your place among the ladies you saw there."

She flung herself at her husband's feet, weeping and begging his pardon. One glance at her showed that she truly repented of disobeying him. Her beauty and affliction might have melted a rock.

"You must die, madam," he said,"and immediately."

"If I must die," she replied, looking at him with eyes bathed in tears,"give me a little time to say my prayers."

"I shall give you a quarter of an hour," Blue Beard answered,"but not a minute more."

As soon as he had left her, she called for her sister and said,"Sister Anne"—for that was her name—go up, I beg you, to the top of the tower and see if my brothers are coming. They promised me that they would come to see me today. If you see them, give them a signal to make haste."

Sister Anne mounted to the top of the tower, and the poor distressed creature called to her every now and then,"Anne!, Sister Anne! Do you see anyone coming?"

And sister Anne answered her,"I see nothing but the sun making dust, and the grass growing green."

In the meantime Blue Beard held a cutlass in his hand and bellowed to his wife with all his might,"Come down quickly, or I'll come up there."

"Please, one minute more," Replied his wife. Immediately she repeated in a low voice,"Anne! Sister Anne! Do you see anyone coming?"

And sister Anne replied,"I see nothing but the sun making dust, and the grass growing green."

"Come down quickly," roared Blue Beard,"or I shall come up there!"

"I'm coming," answered his wife, and then she called,"Anne! Sister Anne! Do you see anyone coming?"

"I see," said sister Anne "a great cloud of dust moving this way."

"Is it my brothers?"

"Alas! No, sister, I see a flock of sheep."

"Do you refuse to come down?" shouted Blue Beard.

"One minute more," his wife replied, and then she cried,"Anne! Sister Anne! Do you see anything coming?"

"I see two horsemen coming this way," she responded,"but they're still at a great distance." A ,moment afterward she exclaimed,"Heaven be praised! They're my brothers! I'm signaling to them as best I can to hurry up."

Blue Beard began to roar so loudly that the whole house shook. So his poor wife descended to him and threw herself at his feet, all disheveled and in tears.

"It's no use," said Blue Beard. "You must die!"

He seized her by the hair with one hand arid raised his cutlass with the other. He was about to cut off her head when the poor woman looked up at him. Fixing her dying gaze upon him, she implored him to allow her one short moment to collect herself.

"No, no," he said, lifting his arm,"commend yourself as best you can to Heaven."

At that moment there was such a loud knocking at the gate that Blue Beard stopped short. The gate was opened, and two horsemen burst through. With drawn swords they ran straight at Blue Beard, who recognized them as the brothers of his wife—one a dragoon, the other a musqueteer. Immediately he fled, hoping to escape, but they pursued so quickly that they overtook him before he could reach the step of his door and passed their swords through his body, leaving him dead on the spot. The poor woman, who was nearly as dead as her husband, did not have the strength even to rise and embrace her brothers.

Since Blue Beard had no heirs, his widow inherited all his wealth. She employed part of it to arrange a marriage between her sister Anne and a young gentleman who had loved her a long time. Another part paid for commissions for her two brothers so they could become captains. The rest she used for her marriage to a worthy man who made her forget the miserable time she had spent with Blue Beard.

Moral

Curiosity, in spite of its charm,
Too often causes a great deal of harm.
A thousand new cases arise each day.
With due respect, ladies, the thrill is slight,
For as soon as you›re satisfied, it goes away,
And the price one pays is never right.

Another Moral

Provided one has common sense
And learns to study complex texts,
It's easy to trace the evidence
Of long ago in this tale's events,
No longer are husbands so terrible,

Or insist on having the impossible.
Though he may be jealous and dissatisfied,
He tries to do as he's obliged.
And whatever color his beard may be,
It's difficult to know who the master be.

Bluebeard

On The Problem of the Destructive Animus

Verena Kast

By means of wealthy prestige, and power, and despite their uneasy feelings, Bluebeard succeeds again and again in binding women to him and then he tries to kill them, like all their predecessors, when they discover his secret. The interpretation presented here detects a sadomasochistic pattern of relationship: a dominating, destructive man stands in relationship to a woman who identifies herself with his apparent power until she realizes that her femininity must inevitably be destroyed by this relationship. If this closed circle in the male-female relationship is to be opened up, the woman can no longer merely project the Bluebeard animus on actual men so as to be able to struggle with it there; it is important for her to deal with it also in herself Bluebeard in a woman is her destructive animus. If she becomes conscious of this, she can free herself from his power.

There was once a man who possessed beautiful houses in town and county, gold and silver table service, furniture and embroideries, and gilded coaches. But unfortunately this man had a blue beard. This made him so ugly and repulsive to look at that there was no woman and no girl who did not fly from him.

One of his neighbors, a lady of high degree, had two very beautiful daughters. Bluebeard asked for one of them for his wife and left it to the mother to decide which of the two she would give him. But neither wanted him. One pushed him off on the other, because neither could reconcile herself to marrying a man with a blue beard. Besides, they found it frightening that he had already married several women, and no one knew what had become of them.

In order to get to know them better, Bluebeard invited the sisters, along with their mother and three or four of their best girlfriends and a number of young people from the neighborhood, to come to one of his country houses. They spent eight entire days there, making excursions, hunting and fishing, and at dances and feasts where tides and honors were conferred. They never slept at all but passed the nights in diversions and games. At last it reached the point where the youngest sister no longer found the beard of the master of the house so blue and even found him worthy of all honors. As soon as they returned to the city, the wedding was celebrated.

When a month had passed, Bluebeard told his wife that he had a journey to make in the provinces on important business that would take at least six weeks and he hoped she would amuse herself well in his absence. She could invite her girlfriends to visit and go to the country with them if she so desired. She should serve the best from kitchen and cellar. "Here are the keys," he then said. "These are for the two big rooms where the furnishings are kept, these are for the gold and silver tableware that are not used every day, these are for the iron chests where my gold and silver is kept, these are for the coffers with my precious jewels, and this is the main key for all the rooms and apartments. And this little key here, this is the key to the small room at the end of the long corridor on the ground floor. You may open everything and *go* into every room, except for this small room. I strictly forbid you to enter it. Should you nevertheless do so, you will be the object of my most formidable wrath." She promised to obey all his orders. He embraced her, climbed into his coach, and departed on his journey.

The neighbor woman and her girlfriends did not wait to be invited to visit the young married girl, for they were burning with curiosity to see all the riches of the house. So long as the husband had been there, they had not dared to come, because they were afraid of his blue beard. Now, however, they rushed through the rooms, through the bedchambers and clothes closets, each one more splendid than the next. Then they climbed up to the rooms where the furnishings were kept, and there was no end to their amazement over the many magnificent carpets, beds, sofas, chests with secret compartments, tables, the mirrors in which one could see oneself from head to foot that had frames of glass, of silver, of gilded silver, the most beautiful and splendid they had ever seen. There was no end to their extravagant praise nor to their envy of their friend's good fortune. But the young woman took no real joy in seeing all these treasures, so impatient was she to open the little room on the ground floor.

She was so driven by curiosity that she gave no thought to the rudeness of leaving her guests to themselves. Down a small secret stairway she hurried with such great haste that she almost broke her neck two or three times. When she arrived at the door of the little room, she paused for a moment and thought about her husband's prohibition and considered that her disobedience might cause her unhappiness. But the temptation was so great that she yielded to it. She took the key and tremulously opened the door to the room.

At first she saw nothing because the window shutters were closed. After a few seconds she could make out that the floor was stained with blood. And in this blood was reflected the bodies of a number of female corpses that were fastened around the walls. The young woman thought she would die of fright, and the key, which she had taken out of the lock, fell from her hand. When she had come to her senses a bit, she picked up the key, locked the door again, and climbed up to her room in order to regain her composure. But this she did not succeed in doing; her agitation was too great. Noticing that the key was flecked with blood, she wiped it two or three times, but the blood would not come off. Try as she might to wash it, and scrub it with sand and sandstone, the key remained bloody, for it was bewitched. There was no way to clean it; if she managed to get the blood off one side, it reappeared on the other.

On that very same evening, Bluebeard returned from his journey. He said that he had received letters en route saying that the business on account of which he had undertaken the journey had already been settled in his favor. His wife did everything in her power to show him how charmed she was over his early return. The next day he asked her to return his keys. She trembled so as she gave them to him that he had no trouble guessing what had occurred.

"How does it come about that the key to the little room is not among them?" he asked.

"I must have left it upstairs on my table," she replied.

"Don't forget to give it to me later," said Bluebeard.

She delayed as long as possible, but finally she had to bring him the key. When Bluebeard had examined it, he said to his wife: "Why is there blood on this key?"

"That I don't know," responded the poor woman, paler than death.

"That you don't know?" cried Bluebeard. "But I know!

You had to go into the little room! Now, my love, you shall go in—and take your place next to the other ladies you saw there."

She threw herself sobbing at her husband's feet, begged for mercy, and showed genuine remorse at having been so disobedient. She was so beautiful and so desperate she would have softened a rock. But Bluebeard's heart was harder than a rock.

"You must die, my love, and indeed, at once!"

"If I must die," she answered, looking at him with her eyes streaming with tears,"give me a little time to pray to God."

"I'll give you half a quarter-hour," responded Bluebeard,"but not an instant longer."

Once upstairs in her room alone, she called to her sister, saying: "My dear Anne" (for that was her sister's name),"please climb up to the tower and see if our brothers are coming. They promised to visit me today. If you see them, give them a sign to hurry."

The sister climbed up to the tower and the poor desperate girl called to her from time to time: "Anne, my sister Anne, don't you see something coming?"

And the sister answered her: "I see only the sun shining and the grass growing green."

Then Bluebeard, with a big hunting knife in his hand, shouted with all his might to his wife: "Come down immediately, or I'm coming up!"

"Just another moment, please," his wife begged and called softly to her sister: "Anne, my sister Anne, don't you see something coming?" And the sister answered: "I see only the sun shining and the grass growing green."

"Come down now, immediately!" shouted Bluebeard.

"I'm coming," his wife replied and then called: "Anne, my sister Anne, don't you see something coming?"

"I see a big cloud of dust coming toward us," the sister replied.

"Is it our brothers?"

"Oh no, dear sister, it is a herd of sheep."

"Once and for all, will you come down?" Bluebeard roared.

"Just another second," replied his wife and then called: "Anne, my sister Anne, don't you see something coming?"

"I see two riders coming toward us," the sister answered,"but they are still far away!" And then right afterward: "Thanks and praise to God! It is our brothers! I'll give them a sign as best I can to get them to hurry."

Then Bluebeard shouted so loud that the whole house shook. The poor woman went down and threw herself at his feet, dissolved in tears, her hair all disheveled. "All that will do you no good," said Bluebeard. "You must die." With one hand, he took her by the hair and with the other he raised the hunting knife to cut off her head. The poor woman looked at him with deathly fear in her eyes and begged him to grant her a last moment so she could compose herself. "No, no," he said,"commend your soul to God." He raised his arm.

At that instant, there was such a loud knock at the door that Bluebeard paused briefly. The door opened and two cavaliers with swords in their hands dashed straight at Bluebeard. He recognized his wife's two brothers, the dragoon and the musketeer, and immediately took flight in order to save himself. But the two brothers were on his heels and caught him before he could reach the staircase. They ran him through with their swords and left him lying dead.

The poor woman was almost as dead as her husband. She no longer had the strength to stand up and embrace her brothers.

It turned out that Bluebeard had no heirs, and so all his wealth fell to his wife. She used a portion of it to marry off her sister Anne to a young nobleman whom she had long loved. With another part she acquired for her brothers the rank of captain, and the rest she brought as a dowry to her marriage with a very worthy man who made her forget the bad time she had spent with Bluebeard.[1]

There are many versions of "Bluebeard," but they all have in common that Bluebeard chops his wives up and always wants a new one. In some versions, as in ours, he is killed. In other versions, the heroine escapes from him, or escapes at least with her life. He is never transformed. Bluebeard is always portrayed as very rich, and always it is his possessions that cause the women to marry him in spite of the fact that they always find his blue beard frightening.

What is there about this blue beard?

According to Bolte and Polivka, in the sixteenth century a man whose black beard shone with bluish highlights was called a *"barbe bleue"*[2] Such men were regarded as womanizers. Perrault saw in this blue beard something abnormal and eerie. Some fairy tales present a figure with a red or green beard. Some other odd feature can also appear in place of the blue beard. Thus Bluebeard appears in the Italian version as a bridegroom with a silver nose, and in a Finnish version as a bridegroom with a golden nose. In both the Italian and Finnish versions, Bluebeard eats corpses. From this Bolte and Polivka conclude that the Bluebeard figure might originally have been a god of death.

Presumably this tale is related to the ballads found throughout Europe that tell of the sex murderer who is killed by a maiden he has carried off into the woods, or by her brother (Bolte and Polivka). In our version, the forbidden room is a new component. We find it also in many other tales, for example,"Mary's Child" (Grimm's no. 3).

The story says that the blue beard makes the man so "ugly and repulsive" that all women fly from him. So this blue beard also makes people afraid of him. Since no one has a blue beard, this blueness characterizes him as somehow beyond what is normal and human. It is something extraordinary in both a positive and a negative sense. If Bluebeard had not wanted to demonstrate his extraordinariness, he could easily have shaved off this blue beard.

The story makes the blueness of his beard an expression of his future wife's alienation from him. Later she suddenly no longer finds the beard so blue, that is, she no longer finds the man so repulsive. This is not because his beard has somehow become less blue, but because she has become captivated by his wealth.

The fact that he seems to have a trade in women, even one with a high turnover, is no longer referred to. His wealth and power overcome all the justified feelings of uneasiness; material values replace eros, identification with someone else's property replaces one's own potential: in short, a marriage takes place.

Bluebeard does not wait long to put his wife to the test. Is she the obedient mate? Does he want to be sure that he is still the master of the household?

He lures his wife into disobeying him with a show of generosity. He confers on her the authority connected with the keys, while at the same time mentioning the room she may not enter. In this way, he more or less seduces her into entering this forbidden room, for this is where his secret is.

But what is Bluebeard's secret? Murdered women. We knew it from the beginning: Bluebeard is a consumer of women. Bluebeard is often envisaged as a corpse-devouring god of death. If he is a god of death, he is a god of death for women only.

So the secret is that he kills women, and indeed always at the point when they discover his secret. But obviously he wants them to discover his secret. Otherwise, why would he provide each woman with the little key?

As we have pointed out, every fairy tale can be interpreted on different levels. In one way, it can be interpreted as an expression of a typical individual psychological problem; in another, as a general problem of the times. These two are directly related.

Bluebeard is, on one hand, the representative of a patriarchal society that is in a state of war with women—or with the feminine principle altogether. Here relationships with women are based on blind obedience. He tests the women he is supposed to have relationships with and then kills them. However, he seems to make up for this quite well through his relationship with materiality. Materiality, material goods, after all, represent an aspect of the feminine principle (the *mater materia*), and though Bluebeard cannot have any genuine personal relationship, he can at least have wealth. Thus we have a situation depicted in which an enthrallment with materiality has become demonically acute. A real woman cannot survive alongside a demonic attachment to matter. The tragedy is that the women, despite their justifiably uneasy feelings, play along with Bluebeard: they allow themselves to be dazzled by his wealth and the honor of being the wife of such a rich man; they even indulge their vanity by trying to dazzle their envious female friends.

It is important to see Bluebeard in his relationship to women, because by himself he is not a problematic figure. The essential problem is that, having been lured into his realm, the women are killed. But the women would not be killed if they did not go along with Bluebeard. Bluebeard never kidnaps the women; he merely seduces them. That is the difference between him and the so- called sex murderer.

In terms of the psychology of an individual, Bluebeard can be seen as an animus figure. From that point of view, the blue beard marks the animus as other-worldly—there is always a quality of unreality about him. It might be frightening or bewitching, but it is also always fascinating.

The color blue expresses something spiritual; but in this case it seems to me that "eerie" is perhaps a more accurate word. At the same time, his blue beard can be seen as an expression of his cold-bloodedness.

By means of riches, power, and role-playing, Bluebeard has once again caught himself a woman. If we take Bluebeard as an animus figure, this would mean that through fascination with these things and through drowning out one's uneasy feelings—one's own emotional reaction, which is undoubtedly present—an enthrallment with this animus is constellated that murders the feminine principle in oneself. In terms of the wife, this means that she gives up her own values in favor of Bluebeard's.

The extreme to which this is carried is shown by the fact that she is unable to tame her curiosity; she is urgently compelled to learn her husband's innermost secret. Let us imagine this for a moment in a real relationship. Wanting so urgently to penetrate into the innermost sphere of the other, not allowing the other any secrets, does not indicate a sense of close relationship; what it really indicates is possessiveness. This is confirmed by all the impatience: Bluebeard's wife runs down the secret staircase with such haste that she nearly breaks her neck two or three times.

This seems to me emblematic of the entire psychological situation. In a sense she has already broken her neck, or very nearly. In any case, there is need for a fundamental transformation. And, in this impatient seeking, we can see one form of obsession. The wife of Bluebeard as an image represents the desire to possess, however far this desire to possess might go.

However, she does not get to see what she wanted to see; instead she sees the murdered women. It is as though the room shows the cost at which the riches were accumulated: one's own missed or murdered potentialities. One cannot help thinking of the lot of so many women who have been totally assimilated into the lives of their husbands and have really become somewhat like children. They are unable to live out their own potentialities, which they have quietly and unobtrusively buried in some ground-level room. Bluebeard was too fascinating.

And now the young woman believes she is going to die of fright—and the key falls from her hand, the key that is the living witness of her disobedience. She can no longer deny what she has seen. There is no longer any possibility of denial; she has passed the point of no return. She must acknowledge her deed. She is terrified. Being terrified about something is not a terribly gentle form of consciousness expansion. Here it is a case of being gripped by panic. All the feelings that were hitherto repressed now seem to break through with concentrated force.

This fright is ongoing: the key can no longer be cleansed of blood; the relationship with Bluebeard is disrupted. Now she knows about this horrible side of Bluebeard's wealth and power. And that is not all. She also knows that he wanted to hide that side. Thus it is only logical that he will kill her too.

Once more, this can be seen on two levels: the personal and the collective. On the collective level, in a society where power and tyranny are the dominant values, if a few people "see the corpses" that have been hidden away, those people have to be eliminated for the sake of the system. This is a very common mechanism and it is not by any means reserved for women. It is easier to call somebody an idiot than to really open the last room, admit the errors of the system, and take responsibility for making changes.

This mechanism can also be seen to function in the women's liberation movement. Women who see that they are unable to realize their potential (that they themselves play a part in this is something they recognize somewhat less often) lay the blame in a way that hurts men. And men, as is usual when something hurts too much, react irascibly and strike back.

On the more personal level, what we have is a woman who suddenly realizes that although she does share in the power and authority, something in her is not participating, and that her own life is clearly hanging by a single thread.

Here the sudden fear of not having really lived and not really being able to live what is essential to her seems to be quite on the mark. Her shock is over the fact that so much of her cannot live within this constellation where she thought everything was so ideal, as well as her realization that she herself is in some way Bluebeard—in other words, somehow very brutal herself. What the woman also encounters in this forbidden room is death. This is true in our version of the tale as well as in those versions in which she sees her husband eating corpses. These phenomena have to be seen together. It is not just death but murder, violent death, that, we feel did not have to happen, therefore it seems even more brutal. She becomes conscious of death and in doing so, she "thought she would die of fright."

What is the significance of becoming conscious of death? We are talking here about becoming conscious, not coping. This nevertheless means seeing death as a possibility that has hitherto been excluded—especially in the midst of the flashy lifestyle embodied by Bluebeard—and to see it as a possibility for *oneself*. It is a peculiar feeling when one realizes—not intellectually but existentially—that at some point one is going to die. Only when this has happened does it become possible to immerse oneself fully into the eternal ebb and flow of life as a whole, not merely to experience the pain that is part of all passing away, but also to sense the meaningfulness of it, to feel there is space for the fresh and new. At the same time the value of being here and of things being as they are here and now is infinitely increased. In the face of change, life places much greater value on the here and now. Life itself acquires that unique quality that we so often think we have to manufacture.

In his essay on authority, Wilke writes that it is only possible to solve the problem of authority when one is confronted with the problem of death.[3] I would like to take that further: this not only applies to the authority problem as a specific form of the problem of power, but to the problem of power in general. The exercise of power can be seen as a desperate attempt to evade, in the broadest sense, the necessity of dying. In this way the lust for power appears as an attitude of avoidance. The exercise of power can often be seen as an attempt to gain power over death. Death can be understood as a very profound change, a change from which no one knows how he or she will emerge. The attitude of power is to stubbornly hold onto its conscious position and thus, so to speak, enforce the status quo. But then it is also important to build up power on the concrete level so as to have something to oppose to death. This is expressed in our fairy tale in which it becomes necessary to outwit death.

A further example, and there are many others, is the French fairy tale "How Death Was Made a Fool." In this story, a kindly old woman prevails upon a saint to grant her the power to cast a spell that forces people up the tree in front of her house. She casts the spell on Death as well. After a few years, with nobody dying in the world and the distress resulting from this becoming so great, she begins to feel sorry for those who have to suffer so much without being able to die, and she lets Death come down from the tree. But first she makes him promise to spare her for a few years.

In the tale "The King's Son and Death," the king's son stays in the forest with Death for three years and Death teaches him secret knowledge. Death tells him that if he sees Death at the head of a sick bed, then the patient belongs to him (Death), but if Death is sitting at the foot of the bed, then the king's son, as the doctor, will be able to cure him. After a hundred years, the king's son, who of course in the meantime has become king, grows old and weak and sees his master sitting at the head of the bed. He asks to be spared long enough to say the Lord's Prayer, a request Death gladly grants. But he recites only the first half of the prayer. He waits a hundred years to say the second half and by then he has nothing against dying.

When we realize on an existential level that we have to die, we momentarily have feelings that are illuminating, clear, and transparent. These feelings show us life in a new, broader perspective. At that point, power becomes something totally futile. Faced with another person's death, we experience a similar shift in our sense of life. The experience of death always separates the divine from the supposedly divine and thus once again opens us up to that divine quality which broadens our circumference. By contrast, power makes us narrow and destructive.

Once a woman realizes how dangerous it is to commit herself to Bluebeard, her fascination with him is lost—not least because he is relativized by death. Then comes the phase of defending oneself against him. There now takes place in the woman a complete rejection of everything Bluebeard stands for, be it authority, power, or aggression—if we needed a catchword, we might call it general possessiveness. None of these qualities are inherently bad. But when they manifest themselves *exclusively*, no longer permitting other sides to be lived, whether these are other sides of one's own personality, other people, other feelings, or other views, then they become mortally dangerous. Bluebeard is perhaps more often at work than is generally thought.

The confrontation with Bluebeard consists of the woman no longer being involved with Bluebeard but rather consciously allying herself with everything that he doesn't stand for. In her mortal fear, she pretends to want to pray. She does not, however, do this, not at least in this version of the tale. All the same, this is interesting as an intention or an idea, and meaningful as a possibility of concentrating on a more all-embracing divinity. In a French parallel version of this tale, there is a little grayhaired man called Father Jacques to whom the wife rushes for protection. Again in other versions—such as the Spanish "Girl without Arms," the middle part of which contains a very clear Bluebeard parallel in which Bluebeard is the devil—the girl calls upon the pure Virgin Mary for help.

In all the versions in which the woman turns to a power opposed to Bluebeard and more all-embracing than he is, Bluebeard is conquered and eliminated. In the other versions, in which the woman outwits Bluebeard on her own, he is sometimes burned but sometimes he simply goes back to his house where he presumably waits for his next victim.

If we see Bluebeard as an animus figure—one who embodies a typical transpersonal experience—then only a superior spiritual principle can provide a remedy against him. For the animus in whatever form is always something that fascinates us. And that which has this fascinating quality always leads us to spirituality.

In our tale, the woman calls to her sister, who is supposed to tell her if her brothers are coming. Thus she turns to a side of herself that is not under Bluebeard's spell: "I see only the sun shining and the grass growing green." This statement throws some light on the sister. Even in this situation, she still sees the sun shining and the grass growing green—she still sees life. This is a great contrast to the death chamber below on the ground floor. This sister, however, is the intermediary for the wife's two swashbuckling brothers. In the image of the sun shining and the grass growing green, we have an enormous contrast to Bluebeard sharpening his knife below and to the tense atmosphere altogether. One must contemplate these images inwardly to appreciate the consoling counterpoise they provide. (Here the meditative approach to fairy tales suggests itself.) The grass can grow even while Bluebeard threatens. It is a wonderful image of continuous growth, of letting things take their course until the brothers arrive. There is also again a strong sense of distancing oneself, of remaining uninvolved—even at the point where there is almost no way out anymore. And just as Bluebeard is about to lose patience entirely, a cloud of dust appears—but it is a herd of sheep and not the brothers.

We can of course take the point of view that the narrator devised this herd of sheep in order to heighten the suspense, but even so the image is quite well chosen. Sheep are dependent on a bellwether, which they follow uncritically. And since the bellwether itself is not necessarily very intelligent, we have the strange phenomenon of herds of sheep charging about without direction, even into abysses if abysses happen to be there. In this symbol, the authority-related dependency on Bluebeard as a mortally dangerous inhibition is represented and given a value. Nonetheless, the herd of sheep is there primarily to indicate the complete hopelessness of the situation. Distancing oneself now is no help; even this kind of defense must some time or other lose its effectiveness. Something new has to enter the picture: the brothers.

The brothers are swashbuckling companions, a dragoon and a musketeer. They run Bluebeard through before he can reach the staircase. Brothers are often animus figures who are very close to consciousness. They are not at all like Bluebeard; they are energetic comrades who represent here a very resolute kind of action—the elimination of the Bluebeard situation.

But before this solution could occur, it was important to fully experience the tension in the image of Bluebeard sharpening his knife and the helpless wife who has finally recognized his hideousness.

By the end the poor wife is nearly as dead as her husband. This shows what she has been through, but it is also an indication of a transformation: If Bluebeard is no longer her husband, then she is a new person, someone much more closely identified with herself. As a proper consequence of this, the riches fall to her. She divides these very justly among her siblings. This sounds so logical and matter of fact, but it is not if we consider how up till now all Bluebeard's riches have been hoarded. The brothers are raised in status. They become captains, in other words, leading figures.

We can interpret this second part of the fairy tale on a more collective level. In a situation dominated by power and aggression, the first step is to realize what is being murdered and to be frightened by it. This kind of a patriarchal situation can be maintained by women as well as by men—in essence this has nothing to do with men as opposed to women.

Distancing oneself is the next step. One does this in the knowledge that it is simply "inflated" to fight things that go far beyond one's powers, where there is little doubt who in the long run will be the stronger party. This means distancing oneself but at the same time realizing that one is in the danger zone. Next, one must mobilize all available forces that do not belong to Blue- beard's sphere. A solution cannot be forced, it must be eked out. For women in this situation, the idea would be to seek solidarity with their sisters. This leads to a reinforcement of self-esteem once the Bluebeard-related elements of jealousy and power struggle have disappeared. On the basis of this reinforcement, indeed in direct connection with it, active self-defense develops.

On the whole then, this fairy tale is about how to free oneself from an extreme situation of domination and destructiveness. And this situation can be found both inwardly and outwardly—each presumably affecting the other.

But in this story a particular pattern of relationship is also presented. We have a domineering, aggressive, destructive man and a woman who identifies with his strength, but then becomes aware that she herself is no longer really living. This is a pattern of relationship that is nowadays very heavily under fire. But it is a relation-ship *pattern*, and that means that it is not only the man who is to blame for it. Precisely in this kind of situation, a Bluebeard animus is often projected onto the man. In this projection the woman fights and defeats herself. It seems important for the woman's movement that women experience Bluebeard not only as a projection, but as a part of themselves as well—someone they must deal with in themselves, if he is there.

Once again, we have a sadomasochistic context, but this fairy tale seems to go at this problem much more from the point of view of feminine psychology. I think we should see the sadomasochistic problem in broad terms the way Schorsch and Becker do in their book *Angst, Lust, Zerstörung*.[4]

The essential point here is domination of the other, total power over the other. The other is dominated and submits. These roles are interchangeable or can persist onesidedly. As soon as a society is split up into inferior and superior people, the way is open for sadistic practices. We are acquainted with this from the Inquisition, war, torture, and so on.

Though it is covered up in our society, there is a whole sector that functions in accordance with the Bluebeard pattern of power and impotence. We have only to think of schools, orphanages, prisons, and to some extent, families.

It is always interesting in this context how much interest the "real sadists," for example, sex murderers, arouse in the entire population. Here projection has a field day; one's own sadistic tendencies can be lived out in fantasy.

Incidentally, Schorsch and Becker show in their book that for the sex murderer, pleasure is hardly the point. Rather, the criminal act is an expression of the collapse of his defenses. The primary part of his defense was to shift sadism onto sexuality, so that outside of this realm he could still function normally.

In this fairy tale and in the previous one,"The Cursed Princess," but quite clearly in reality as well, the circular behavior pattern of sadomasochism makes relationship to a great extent impossible. On one hand, one would like to fuse with one's partner, but at the same time one would like to remain detached.

Schorsch and Becker definitely regard sadomasochism as a partnership problem. However, it can also be seen in the relationship that we have with ourselves, that is, on the subjective level. It appears in all forms of suppressing and being suppressed.

As a partnership problem, as already indicated, it goes something like this: One partner feels and behaves like the strong one; the other feels and behaves as the weak one and identifies with the strength of the partner, much in the same way a child identifies with the strength of his father. In this way he himself becomes weaker and weaker and can simply surrender, or he can also begin to defend himself—indirectly, through the power tactics of the weak (such as sickness), or, ultimately, directly as well. This is a relationship pattern that we often encounter when someone is trying to "save" someone else. The problem with such a relationship is that the weakness of the dominant party and the strength of the subordinate one are both projected onto the other. Both are then lacking something that should be part of their own personalities. Thus the resolution of such a relational pattern can only take place through one party seeing and accepting his strength and the other seeing and accepting his weakness. Obvious examples of this pattern leap easily to mind. But in every relationship there are quite subtle sadomasochistic patterns—for example, in an analytic relationship in which one of the parties tends to play the victim. When one party plays the victim, the role of dominator or sadist is immediately delegated. The other is made into something evil, and from that the victim derives the right and obligation to defend himself.

What is the point of this roundabout approach? It is quite simple: one finagles for oneself the right to be aggressive without having to take responsibility for it—after all, one is only defending oneself! At the same time one builds up authority as an objective where it is not necessary at all. We want authority, but at the same time we do not want it. This ambivalence is a vestige of the transitional period when we still needed a mother and father but at the same time wanted to be independent. The problem with remaining stuck in the ambivalence of that phase is that one ends up cutting one's own potentialities to pieces.

NOTES

1. Perrault, *Märchen aus alter Zeit* (Melzer Verlag, 1976).
2. J. Bolte and G. Polivka, *Anmerkungen zu den Kinder- und Hausmärchen der Brüder Grimm*, vol. 1 (Hildesheim: 011115,1963), p. 409.
3. H.-J. Wilke,"Autoritàtskomplex und autoritàre Persönlichkeitsstruktur," in *Zeitschrift für Analytische Psychologie,* no. 8 (1977): 33–40
4. E. Schorsch and N. Becker, *ngst, Lust, Zerstörung* (Hamburg, 1977).

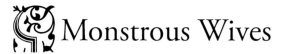# Monstrous Wives

Bluebeard as Criminal and Cultural Hero

Maria Tatar

> Look how he suffers. … He is no longer so monstrous.
> —Paul Dukas, *Ariane et Barbe-bleue*

That little Frenchman beats them all," declares an avid follower of crime fiction in Alfred Hitchcock's *Shadow of a Doubt* (1943). Today most viewers are unlikely to divine the identity of "that little Frenchman," but Hitchcock could count on audiences to recognize in that reference an allusion to Henri Landru, the short, bald, bearded con artist who came to be known to readers of the *New York Times* as the French Bluebeard, or as *Landru, dit Barbe-Bleue*, for readers of *Le Figaro*. Executed in 1922 at Versailles for murdering ten women and one boy and disposing of their bodies by incinerating them in a stove, Landru gained notoriety both in France and abroad during his trial and after his sentence to death by the guillotine. The appellation of Bluebeard did much to enhance his reputation, erasing the sordid facts of his crimes and charging the man himself, despite his unattractive appearance and lack of charm, with the charisma of a mythic figure. "An entire legend stands between the awful little hovel at Gambais and Bluebeard's castle," as *Le Figaro* put it.

Henri Landru's powerful cultural effect can be divined from his trial, which was attended by literary notables such as Colette, along with press from all over the world. Ranked +2.27 on a scale of—25 to +25 for creative merit in a literary review put out by the French wing of the Dada movement, the Bluebeard of Gambais (as he came to be known in the popular press) received a rating higher than Nobel Prize-winning author Anatole France and the poet Henri de Regnier, two men who had made the mistake of rewriting Bluebeard's story instead of re-enacting his crimes.[1] Chaplin's *Monsieur Verdoux* (1947), whose title figure, like the historical Landru, cultivates roses and cremates corpses, and Hitchcock's Uncle Charlie in *Shadow of a Doubt* were inspired in part by Landru's notoriety. What became evident at his trial was how his rather unexceptional physical presence was transformed by his criminal charisma. Here was a completely unremarkable man who managed to fashion himself into a figure of real public attention, whose crimes attracted unprecedented attention from the public and from the media and who himself gave rise to endless amounts of chatter,

Landru's association with the folkloric Bluebeard has a certain logic to it, for Bluebeard had figured prominently not only in fairy tales but also in ballads and. broadsheets, where his crimes were seen as sensational abominations, deeds that inspired awe as well as horror. Like many illustrious lawbreakers whose criminal offenses were broadcast by balladeers and showmen of an earlier age and whose stories circulated in pamphlets and almanacs, Bluebeard had become an important part of a culture of distraction that featured figures designed to entertain and provide diversions on long winter evenings. Arousing the kind of curiosity and suspense to which Bluebeard's wife succumbs, the sadistic deeds of Landru and his folkloric predecessor produced untold pleasures for listeners and readers. It is no accident that Landru, like Bluebeard, has not faded from cultural memory, with Claude Chabrol's 1963 film *Landru* keeping the name of the French Bluebeard alive as a code word for a dangerous womanizer.

By the beginning of the eighteenth century, a "new literature of crime" had emerged from ballads and broadsheets, one that positioned criminals as legendary figures, both infamous and admirable. Michel Foucault tells us that "there were those for whom glory and abomination were not dissociated, but coexisted in a reversible figure." What distinguished the criminal was not only the "beauty and greatness" of his crime but also his "cunning" and "tricks;" If ballads and broadsheets had once focused on the sensational side of crime, on the acts' clever execution and cultural effects, the literature on crime emerging in the eighteenth century turned to the more intellectual side of the matter, investigating perpetrators and focusing on the struggle between the lawbreaker and law.[2]

Bluebeard, once an iniquitous brute who had excited the popular imagination with his bloody deeds, developed an intellectual side that aligned him with reason and cunning rather than with passion and wrath. He was to emerge as the champion of antibourgeois ideologies that are fully justified by the pathologies of modern marriage. What drove Bluebeard to a life of crime in the twentieth century is clearly established in the nineteenth century as the unbearable state of matrimony. As we shall see, the logic of Bluebeard as the victim of marriage produces a Bluebeard who becomes something of a cultural hero in his effort to combat social evils (as in Chaplin's *Monsieur Verdoux*), to thwart the boredom of everyday life (as in Hitchcock's *Shadow of a Doubt),* and to struggle against existential isolation (as in Béla Bartók's *Bluebeard's Castle).*

"Mythical heroes, even infamous villains," one commentator on the Bluebeard story writes,"are part of our heritage; we can learn from them our basic aspirations and motivations." That critic mourned the fact that Anatole France, in his "Seven Wives of Bluebeard," turned the title figure into a "sheepish hero, robbed of all his prestige."[3] These observations are a compelling reminder that old myths die hard and that we treasure our villains, perhaps in part because they mirror, if not our aspirations, then at least our motivations. More important, Bluebeard, in all his mythical glory, helps us get to the bottom of the pathologies that lead him, from one century to the next, to a life of crime.

In a surge of sympathy with Bluebeard, Sam Weiler of Charles Dickens's *Pickwick Papers* explains just why the fairy-tale villain deserves pity rather than censure: "I think he's the victim of connubiality."[4] Wedlock does Bluebeard in, and Weiler is moved to tears. Bluebeard has had many other defenders, both fictional and real, as becomes evident from the titles of countless nineteenth-century theatrical scripts that reworked the fairy tale. *Bluebeard; or, Dangerous curiosity & justifiable homicide*, published in London in 1841, is symptomatic of a trend that perceived the domestic tyrant as a domestic casualty, a man whose murderous deeds are fully sanctioned by the outrageous behavior of his wives. Francis Egerton El-lesmère's two-act burlesque reveals that "womankind are all alike, rebellious and unruly, / And can't be trusted any more … I/Than in a henroost can a fox, or a cat in a china closet."[5]

When Ludwig Tieck, the German playwright and novelist who was also a contemporary of the Brothers Grimm, dramatized Bluebeard, he also framed one of the most severe indictments of the heroine's character. In his rendition, even Bluebeard's wife is appalled by her inability to resist temptation: "O curiosity," she declaims,"damned, scandalous curiosity! There's no greater sin than curiosity!" Her self-accusations are uttered in full view of. a scene of carnage for which her brutish husband bears responsibility. Bluebeard confirms his wife's appraisal of her criminal behavior and links her transgressions not only with sexual betrayal but more deeply with original sin: " 'Cursed curiosity! Because of it sin entered the innocent world, and even now it leads to crime. Ever since Eve was curious, every single one of her worthless daughters has been curious. … The woman who is curious cannot be faithful to her husband. The husband who has a curious wife is never for one moment of his life secure. … Curiosity has provoked the most horrifying murderous deeds.' "[6] Anatole France, as noted earlier, thought along similar lines when he presented the "cold, naked Truth" about Bluebeard to the public. His "Seven Wives of Bluebeard" (1909) was to be a "true history," a corrective to the "glittering enchantments of Falsehood" produced in an earlier age by

Charles Perrault. Bluebeard, France maintains, was not at all the "perfect model of cruelty" that Perrault made him out to be, but "generous and magnificent," the "victim" of a venal, corrupt, and ruthless family of conspirators. France's counternarrative, like today's upside-down stories which retell a traditional tale from the villain's point of view, systematically contests every point made in Perrault's "Bluebeard."

Although France's historical truths are told tongue in cheek, they are also consonant with the interpretive history of the Bluebeard story, which positions Bluebeard as victim of his wives' infidelities. Corrupt, licentious, and avaricious, the wives in France's story are guilty of more than intellectual curiosity. One betrays him "with every man of quality in the neighborhood"; another arranges for a tryst with her lover in the forbidden chamber. It is the seventh wife who concocts what the narrator perceives to be a moronic story about mutilated corpses, when in reality the so-called Cabinet of the Unfortunate Princesses contains nothing but wall paintings depicting scenes from tragic mythological stories. Those paintings show Dirce bound to the horns of a bull, Niobe pierced by arrows, and Procris inviting to her breast the javelin of Cephalus: "These figures had a look of life about them, and the porphyry tiles with which the floor was covered seemed dyed in the blood of these unhappy women."[7]

The story of Bluebeard as told by Perrault fits squarely into this sequence of tales about women threatened by some form of bodily mutilation yet France insists that the artworks on display in the cabinet (along with the stories underlying the paintings) gave rise to myths that have distorted the historical truth. In other words, if the history of art—visual and verbal—tells one story about women imperiled by male assailants, history itself (in the form of "authentic documents" and "reliable evidence") tells quite another story. That the so-called evidence on which "The Seven Wives of Bluebeard" is based consists of Bluebeard's own version of the events, along with an anonymous complaint against his murderers, does not seem to unsettle the narrator's conviction that his character is the victim of malicious scandalmongers.

Bluebeard's murder is described by France as the "most atrocious, treacherous, and cowardly domestic crime of which the record has come down to us."[8] Despite the narrator's assurances that he will record the facts "with all possible restraint," "The Seven Wives of Bluebeard" is more emphatically an exercise in excess than virtually any other retelling of Perrault's tale. Its aggregation of superlative forms alone—"most atrocious, treacherous, and cowardly"—is telling. With a hero who is as shy, gentle, and benevolent as his wives are unscrupulous, deceptive, and malicious, France's Bluebeard story reveals just how powerfully a rewriting of the tale can reconfigure its sexual politics.

Donald Barthelme's "Bluebeard" (1987) intensifies the message of France's account by giving us a wife who, in the course of giving her side of the story, reveals the full extent of her deceitful behavior. In an almost offhand manner, Bluebeard's wife refers to the nun's habit that she wears during the midnight masses at which she meets her lover. Claiming to be "not at all curious by nature" and "obedient to the valid proscriptions my husband might choose to impose," this is a woman who is goaded into opening her husband's forbidden chamber once she realizes that there might be something there besides the corpses of her predecessors. Yielding to her "intense curiosity," she rushes to the prohibited chamber, turns the key, and finds "on hooks, gleaming in decay and wearing Coco Chanel gowns, seven zebras."[9] Monstrous hybrid figures, the zebras combine repulsive putrefaction with designer glamour to produce a surreal effect. "Jolly, don't you think?" is the lapidary comment of this Bluebeard who has finally succeeded in duping a conniving wife.[10]

France's "Seven Wives of Bluebeard" and Barthelme's "Bluebeard" may both be cast in the satirical mode, but the "truth" they reveal about the protagonists and their wives only reinforces myths about female duplicity that are embedded even in the stories that present Bluebeard's wives as victims. Though France's narrator claims to write against the grain of Perrault's story and Barthelme's wife of Bluebeard claims to know the story and hence is able to subvert its terms, both narrators deliver tales that are consonant with the ideological position articulated in the story found between the covers of *Tales of Mother Goose*. An appetite for knowledge rhymes with the desire for sexual adventures.

Given the wobbly ethics and loose morals of Bluebeard's wife, is it any wonder that Bluebeard himself begins to look like a cultural hero, a man who, even when he murders, has a mission to rid the world of women characterized by duplicitous behavior and predatory sexuality? As Aline Kilmer puts it, in her essay "The Case of Bluebeard" (1923), Bluebeard's wife is a "monster of ingratitude" who plays the "miserable, low, contemptible trick" of going through the pockets of a man who, at the least, deserves our "sympathy."[11] In both Chaplin's *Monsieur Verdoux* and Hitchcock's *Shadow of a Doubt*, women are the real monsters and both Monsieur Verdoux and Uncle Charlie are driven to a life of crime by their hatred of feminine excesses.

In a film subtitled "A Comedy of Murders," Charlie Chaplin gives us a Bluebeard who, though guilty of murder as well as of the infidelities with which Bluebeard's wives are usually charged, remains a victim. The long-suffering Monsieur Verdoux must not only subject himself to women with disagreeable dispositions, but also falls prey to an unstable economy, losing first his job, then his small fortune. *Monsieur Verdoux* begins with the voice-over confession of its title character, who explicitly identifies himself with Bluebeard: "For thirty years I was an honest bank clerk until the Depression of 1930, in which year I found myself unemployed. It was then I became occupied in liquidating members of the opposite sex. This I did as a strictly business enterprise to support a home and family. But let me assure you that the career of a Bluebeard is by no means profitable. Only a person with undaunted optimism could embark on such a venture. Unfortunately, I did. What follows is history."

Verdoux is not the only one to refer to himself as Bluebeard. A police detective also uses the term to describe the man whom he is pursuing: "He's a Bluebeard. A mass killer working in cities all over the country." And Chaplin himself used "Bluebeard" as the working title for the script, which was inspired by Orson Welles's idea of writing a screenplay about the crimes of Henri Landru.[12]

But Monsieur Verdoux does not at all look or sound the part of a Bluebeard. Our first glimpse of him is in a garden, cutting roses in a manner that is both effete and effeminate. This is a man who, like Max Frisch's Bluebeard (in the novel of that name), would not hurt a fly, and indeed he stoops to the ground to rescue a wayward caterpillar from the walkway. Cutting the figure of a narcissist rather than of a murderer, he stops to admire himself in the mirror and is endlessly sniffing the roses. But this is a man with a secret, and we get a hint of it from the puffs of smoke in the rear of the garden (Verdoux has disposed of his latest wife in his backyard incinerator). When the doorbell rings, Verdoux is cautious, putting his eye to the keyhole to ensure that no one is planning to violate the privacy of his domestic space.

Verdoux leads a double life: he is both cold-blooded serial murderer and tender-hearted husband, a man who thinks nothing of slipping poison into a woman's drink, then catching a train in time for drinks and dinner with his disabled wife. But the film makes it clear that Verdoux's split personality has a certain logic, for it is symptomatic of what it takes to survive in a capitalist economy. As important, Verdoux's crimes are given a certain justification in that they target only the "grossly materialistic" half of the population. When Verdoux is told that he appears to dislike women, he protests: "On the contrary, I love women, but I don't admire them." The source of Verdoux's contempt has something to do with women's lack of spirituality, their innate incapacity to transcend material things. "Women are of the earth, realistic, dominated by physical facts," he declares, and, from its opening scene in a dining room, the film repeatedly shows us women engaged in practical chores: raking, clearing dishes, dusting, and doing laundry.

Mona, Verdoux's wife, is another matter: we see her for the first time in an ethereal setting—a domestic angel seated in a wheelchair, reading a book. And indeed, when she senses that her husband's health is suffering, Mona appeals to him to trade their newly won prosperity for poverty. "If it means losing your health, I'd sooner go back to living in one room again," she pleads with him. Mona seems not of this world, and before the film ends, she has been translated into a higher sphere. In a sense, *Monsieur Verdoux* suggests that there are two regimes of women: one frail, self-sacrificing, and doomed to die young, the other robust, insatiable, and deserving to die, if not young, then at least middle-aged.

No one could form a more perfect contrast to Verdoux's wife than one of his intended victims, played by Martha Raye, a comedian whom the French film critic Andre Bazin aptly described as "Hollywood's number one pain in the neck."[13] Vulgar and shrewish, with an abrasive voice and abusive manner, her character Annabella recoils in fright from what she sees in the waters of a lake—"It's a monster," she shrieks, only to realize that it is her own reflection that has frightened her. In a grotesque reprise of the lake scene in Dreiser's *An American Tragedy* (doubled also in Humbert Humbert's failed murder attempt in Nabokov's *Lolita),* Verdoux unsuccessfully seeks to rid himself of this harridan.

It is Annabella, rather than the ethereal Mona, who in the end redeems Verdoux. She vindicates Verdoux's murderous career, turning him into an object of our compassion rather than our antipathy. Verdoux, as Bazin points out, manages to have his revenge on women without having to sacrifice his splendid role as victim. This is a Bluebeard who mobilizes our sympathy, not simply because he has lost his job as bank teller but because he is the little man perpetually tyrannized by the big woman.

A failure at the box office, *Monsieur Verdoux* has come under fire for sending mixed messages. One critic suggests that the film makes the fatal mistake of breaking the implied aesthetic contract between Chaplin and his audiences, offering social criticism rather than the pleasures of slapstick.[14] The film's critique of capitalism did hot sit particularly well with United States citizens, who had little patience for what they saw as a leftist denunciation of capitalism from a guest in their country. Verdoux's exoneration of himself as nothing more than a petty businessman whose crimes pale by comparison with state-sanctioned murders stretched the limits of their tolerance. "As for being a mass killer," Verdoux proclaims, "doesn't the world encourage it? Is it not building weapons of destruction for the sole purpose of mass killing? Has it not blown unsuspecting women and little children to pieces and done it very scientifically? As a mass killer, I am an amateur by comparison." And in a final declaration citing the Reverend Beilby Porteus's famous aphorism about state-sanctioned crime, Verdoux grandstands for himself by proclaiming: "One murder makes a villain, millions a hero. Numbers sanctify."

But what must have been more troubling—and what remains disturbing to audiences today—is the paradox of Verdoux's character. He is a devoted father and husband, an underdog who deserves our sympathy, the victim of a cold capitalist machine, yet he is also a hardened criminal. Chaplin referred to Verdoux as a "paradox of virtue and vice," and it is disconcerting to most audiences to find themselves rooting for a character who is so ruthlessly calculating (it is no coincidence that Verdoux starts out as a bank teller) as to try out a new poison on a bedraggled young woman who has lost her home.[15] Verdoux's vices—his pitiless attitude toward female victims, young and old—make it something of a challenge to embrace fully his virtues as a representative of the little man.

Yet in the end Verdoux, whose voice speaks to us from beyond the grave at the beginning of the film, triumphs, for his victims prove relentlessly unsympathetic, while the beneficiaries of his murders, his wife, Mona, and his son, Peter, are emphatically idealized. In pathologizing the victims of Verdoux's crimes, Chaplin's film sanctifies the homicidal impulses of its protagonist, turning him into a cultural hero who rids society of those guilty of enjoying in excess the things to which we ourselves feel entitled.

Dean MacCannell has precisely identified the flaws in the moral logic of Chaplin's character. Verdoux, MacCannell argues, is throughout "the perfect model of the modern man in general," a man who believes that he is at liberty to do whatever he wants so long as it is for the family. "Perfectly correct in every way," he is also "absolutely pitiless toward his victims" and "as a kind of by-product of the sense of propriety that causes him to kill—he enjoys wealth, freedom, exotic entertainments, and limitless sexual conquests, all of these being necessary to the performance of his duty toward his wife and child."[16] Verdoux's parting shot, "I will see you all very soon," implies that he is no guiltier than the rest of us, that we all participate in the perversions of a capitalist economy that dictates a ruthless appropriation of surplus value.

If the death of Perrault's Bluebeard brought a sigh of relief from readers, the execution of Monsieur Verdoux produces tragic effects from a man who was the master of comedy. Verdoux's crimes, committed in the name of financial survival, turn him into a saintly figure who claims to sacrifice himself, not his victims, on the altar of the family.

Uncle Charlie, the villain of Hitchcock's *Shadow of a Doubt*, is as shrewd and cynical as Monsieur Verdoux, but with the idealistic veneer removed. His pathology runs deeper than that of Verdoux and has the virtue of revealing more clearly what is at stake for this Bluebeard figure, who also murders for cash. In a speech delivered at the dinner table of his sister's family, the "Merry Widow murderer" reveals his powerful contempt for women. For Uncle Charlie, murder is not just a business, it is a passion:

> Women keep busy in towns like this. In the cities, it's different. The cities are full of women. Middle-aged widows, husbands dead, husbands who've spent their lives making fortunes, working and working. Then they die and leave their money to their wives. Their silly wives. And what do the wives do? These useless women. You see them in the hotels, the best hotels, every day by the thousands, drinking their money, eating their money, losing their money at bridge. Playing all day and all night, smelling of money. Proud of their jewelry, but nothing else. Horrible. Faded, fat, greedy women.

Charlie Newton, Uncle Charlie's niece and namesake, is an odd candidate for Bluebeard's wife. For starters, she is, of course, a blood relation rather than a spouse. But the relationship between Uncle Charlie and Charlie is a complicated one. "We're not just uncle and niece," Charlie asserts. "It's something else. I know you." Charlie and her uncle are the first characters we meet in the film, both introduced through Peeping Tom shots in which the camera tracks from shots of their respective towns into their bedrooms to observe both, recumbent on their beds, meditating on the dead ends in which they find themselves. "This coupling of the two characters lying in beds separated by a continent is the most striking indication of the relationship that exists between them," one critic writes. "There is a sly hint that what Charlie and her uncle are thinking about while lying in bed is of the other in bed."[17] In these paired scenes, there seems to be as much a touch of the morbid as of the erotic, for both characters are posed in such a way as to suggest a deathbed scene. With what appears to be telepathic precision, Charlie and her uncle simultaneously frame plans to telegraph the other with proposals for a family reunion.

If there is any doubt that the kinship between the two Charlies transcends blood ties, it is eliminated when the uncle takes his niece's hand and slips a ring on it. "Give me your hand, Charlie," he asks, and the profile of the two suggests a romantic engagement scene more than anything else. This symbolic marriage caps a scene that decisively takes us into the territory of the Bluebeard story. Charlie confides a powerful sense of kinship to her uncle at the same time that she asserts her knowledge of a secret in his past, an enigma that endows him with an aura of mystery. As her uncle's double, she not only feels confident that she can identify it, but also feels entitled to know it:

> Charlie: I know you. I know that you don't tell people a lot of things. I don't either. I have a feeling that inside you somewhere there's something nobody knows about.
> Uncle Charlie: Something nobody knows …
> Charlie: Something secret and wonderful, and I'll find it out.
> Uncle Charlie: Not good to find out too much.
> Charlie: But we're sort of like twins, don't you see. We have to know.

Charlie, like a true wife of Bluebeard or daughter of Eve, feels compelled to penetrate the mystery of her uncle's past. Slipping into the role of detective, she embarks on an investigation that transforms her from dutiful daughter in a family repeatedly described, albeit it tongue in cheek, as "average" to transgressive agent who becomes a disruptive presence both in her uncle's plans and in her "ordinary little town."

Determined to know her uncle (and here Charlie walks a treacherous tightrope between intellectual knowledge and carnal knowledge), she enters the forbidden space of the room in which he sleeps. That room, in a wonderful

Hitchcockian twist, is her own bedroom converted into a guestroom for the visiting uncle. From it, she retrieves a clue that leads her to continue her investigation at the public library. On her way to the library, Charlie has two significant brushes with law and order. First she is halted by a policeman who takes her to task for jaywalking; then she is reprimanded by the librarian ("I'm surprised at you, Charlie!") for demanding entrance after the closing hour has struck. On the trail of her uncle's secret, she becomes contaminated by his criminal past, turning into something of a renegade herself who is perpetually disturbing the peace and enacting in unexpected new ways the powerful bond that links niece to uncle.

If Charlie becomes a true wife of Bluebeard, Joseph Cotten as Uncle Charlie slips right into the role of enraged husband, who feels, compelled to murder the "clever" young woman who has gotten to the bottom of his past. His three foiled attempts to murder Charlie follow hard on his discovery of her detective work:

> "You think you know something, don't you? You think you're the clever little girl who knows something. There's so much you don't know. So much. What do you know really? You're just an ordinary little girl living in an ordinary little town. You wake up every morning of your life and you know perfectly well there's nothing in the world to trouble your life. You go through your ordinary little day, and at night you sleep your untroubled ordinary sleep, filled with peaceful, stupid dreams. And I brought you nightmares. Or did I? Or was it a silly, inexpert lie? You live in a dream. You're a sleepwalker, blind."

Uncle Charlie, for all his craft and shrewdness, has grossly miscalculated his niece. Charlie's life is troubled, but only because it feels so ordinary and average. What agitates her is the fact that she seems destined for a life of bovine stupidity: "You sort of go along and nothing happens. We're in a terrible rut…. Eat and sleep, and that's about all," Charlie complains to her father from her bed. "A family should be the most wonderful thing, and this family has just gone to pieces." Uncle Charlie brings melodrama and passion into the household, creating romance, mysteries, enigmas, and terrors that break the tedium of life in the average family. The excitement may turn out to be the excitement of a nightmare, but Charlie still manages to get out of the rut, to awaken from the stupor in which she finds herself, to witness the rejuvenation of her mother, and to experience real disturbances in what, until Uncle Charlie's arrival, has been an untroubled existence. In an ironic twist, it is precisely the brush with death that saves Charlie from the morbid boredom of small-town life, from the simulacrum of death that she stages for the viewer as she lies stretched out on her bed at the beginning of the film. And it is Uncle Charlie's undoing that his niece is unwilling to lie down and die in order to let him lie low and survive in the average little town of Santa Rosa.

Both Verdoux and Uncle Charlie are "ideal" men,"handsome, well- dressed, well-built, intelligent, entertaining, middle-class, and democratic." Functioning as what one critic calls "capitalist 'angels of death,' " they execute "fat cows feeding off of excess," those who have more than their fair share of material pleasures, but they also bring dash, charisma, and drama into the world.[18] Verdoux becomes a kind of tragic hero whose murders seem justified by the vulgarity of his victims and by the evils of capitalism; Uncle Charlie becomes a dark rescuer, a man who, though a scoundrel, saves Charlie from the humdrum routines of small-town life and also enables her to embrace the family life for which she once felt such deep scorn.

Charlie is one of the boldest of Hitchcock's many female investigators, yet for all her investigative savvy and her near clairvoyance when it comes to her uncle's secrets, she returns, after the excitement has died down, to a blissfully benighted state. The last scene, described by one critic as "maliciously ambiguous," shows Charlie and her new boyfriend, a detective named Graham, outside the church at which Uncle Charlie's funeral is taking place.[19] The conversation between Charlie and Graham forms an ironic counterpoint to the words spoken by the priest:

> Priest: Santa Rosa has gained and lost a son. A generous, kind …
> Charlie: He hated the whole world. He said people like us had no idea of what the world is like.

> Graham: It's not as bad as all that.
> Priest: … their sterling characters..
> Graham: Sometimes, the world needs a lot of watching. It goes a bit crazy now and then, like your Uncle Charlie.
> Priest: … the beauty of their souls, the sweetness of their characters live on with us forever.

Charlie has rid herself of her uncle and of his contaminating influence over her, but she has done so at the price of acquiescing to the lethal boredom of family life. "Those desires of independence and freedom almost do kill her," James McLaughlin points out,"yet she rids herself of them only to land in the tomb of marriage and family life."[20] Charlie's career as investigator and outlaw comes to an end after a brutal murder (she manages to push her uncle into the path of an oncoming train when he tries to kill her), and she reclaims her innocence by taking refuge in the family, declaring her allegiance to the hypocrisies of bourgeois family life uttered by the priest. In a flagrant betrayal of the heroic spirit that guided her to uncover her uncle's past, Charlie closes the door to self- knowledge and integrity, disavowing the quest on which she had embarked. Once a daughter of Eve, she willingly adapts to cultural expectations, bonding with a man of the law as the voice of a priest intones sacred lies in the background.

Marriage to Graham, as William Rothman observes, is not Charlie's "dream come true."[21] In the end, we are not even absolutely certain that Charlie will marry Graham. What we do know, however, is that Charlie's body language in the presence of Graham does not reveal anything of the passion, agitation, and excitement that appeared on screen when Uncle Charlie entered Santa Rosa. Can Charlie, her uncle's double and twin, ever settle for a life that lacks the romantic chemistry, the profound mysteries, and the investigative excitement that marked her affair with Uncle Charlie? Will she, like her father and his quirky friend Herb, resign herself to reading and analyzing detective stories? Beyond a shadow of a doubt, Charlie will have trouble finding a match to the charismatic criminality of her Uncle Charlie.

The cultural critic George Steiner has read one of the many cultural variants of "Bluebeard" as a map for un-derstanding the human quest for knowledge. For Steiner, we are all—men and women alike—-wives of Bluebeard, unable to reverse the move from innocence and ignorance to knowledge. Like Judith, in Béla Bartók's opera *Bluebeard's Castle*,"we cannot turn back." "We cannot choose," Steiner adds,"the dreams of unknowing. We shall, I expect, open the last door in the castle even if it leads, perhaps *because* it leads, onto realities which are beyond the reach of human comprehension and control. We shall do so with that desolate clairvoyance, so marvelously rendered in Bartók's music, because opening doors is the tragic merit of our identity." Steiner further celebrates the irresistible appetite for knowledge that is symbolized by the curiosity of Bluebeard's wife: "We open the successive doors in Bluebeard's castle because 'they are there,' because each leads to the next by a logic of intensification which is that of the mind's own awareness of being. To leave one door closed would be not only cowardice but a betrayal—radical, self-mutilating—of the inquisitive, probing, forward-tensed stance of our species. We are hunters after reality, wherever it may lead. The risk, the disasters incurred are flagrant. But so is, or has been until very recently, the axiomatic assumption and a priori of our civilization, which holds that man and the truth are companions, that their roads lie forward and are dialectically cognate."[22]

Charlie's likely decision to choose the "tomb of marriage and family" over intellectual excitement and melodra-matic peril can be read as an abdication of the quest for self-knowledge, but on a deeper level it signifies a wholesale betrayal of Western cultural values that endorse the search for wisdom, truth, and personal integrity. In marrying Graham, Charlie would be tacitly accepting the false pieties of the priest ("the beauty of their souls, the sweetness of their characters live on with us forever") and acquiescing to the patriarchal values embodied in Graham's words about the need for supervision ("Sometimes, the world needs a lot of watching"). Turning back and choosing the "dreams of unknowing," Charlie would be losing Bluebeard and the intellectual energy he released, and, along the way, losing what is in some ways her better self.

If Steiner, in a curious twist to the customary affiliation of knowledge with patriarchy, identifies Enlightenment ideals with Bluebeard's wife, it is because his familiarity with the tale seems limited to the operatic tradition, in which the husband is associated with violence, darkness, and pessimism while the wife carries the banner for warmth, illumination, and knowledge. In Bartók's *Bluebeard's Castle*, Bluebeard remains a figure tragic in his existential isolation, while his wife, unable to turn back as Steiner observes, presses on with her quest for knowledge, even when it means facing self-defeating realities. Yet Bartók's Bluebeard, like the Bluebeards of the nineteenth-century operatic tradition who rarely murder any wives at all, is less ladykiller than a figure heroic in his tragic isolation.[23]

Paris and Budapest: in these two capitals, Bluebeard made, if not his operatic debut, his most celebrated operatic appearances.[24] In Paul Dukas's *Ariane and Blue Beard (Ariane et Barbe-bleue,* 1907), as in Bartók's opera, Bluebeard becomes a figure trapped in permanent existential loneliness. For the Belgian symbolist poet Maurice Maeterlinck, who wrote the libretto for *Ariane and Blue Beard,* the wealthy nobleman plays a subordinate role to the spirited Ariane. In Dukas's opera, as in Bartók's Hungarian work, Bluebeard's wife is given a name, in this case a name that aligns her with the heroic Greek woman who enabled Theseus to escape from the labyrinth and who was subsequently abandoned by him. Courageous and resourceful, the Greek Ariadne nevertheless fell victim to a treacherous spouse.

Maeterlinck's Ariane resists the role of tragic martyr. Recognizing the absurdity of dogged loyalty to an untrustworthy husband, she sets out to resurrect Bluebeard's previous wives. The subtitle to the libretto, "The Useless Rescue," is telling in its anticipation of Ariane's failed mission to liberate the wives, who seem to find perverse enjoyment in languishing in the cellar of Bluebeard's estate. Ariane herself triumphs in the end, refusing to relinquish hope despite the defeatist attitudes of the previous wives.

Maeterlinck's Ariane represents a radical break with the folkloric tradition, for this wife of Bluebeard is fearless in her resolve to undo the evils of a despot. The work in which she appears has been described as "a feminist answer to the male tyranny which has dominated … the Bluebeard tradition," and she herself has been heralded as "the prototype of the liberated woman."[25] Ariane is the first wife of Bluebeard to exult in defiance and to proclaim that she has an obligation to disobey orders that seem questionable. "He loves me," she declares, "I am pretty, and I'll know his secret. I must disobey him, that's the first duty when an order is threatening or incomprehensible." Dissatisfied with the treasures she finds behind the six doors to which she has been allowed access, Ariane presses on, despite the warnings from her nurse to avoid the seventh door, with its golden lock. "What we are allowed to see won't teach us anything," Ariane asserts in words that resonate with Steiner's views on forbidden doors as gateways to knowledge.[26]

Carrying a lamp to illuminate the dungeon in which Bluebeard's wives are imprisoned, Ariane brings light and life to the five women. Yet in the end these wives choose to stay with the wounded Bluebeard, and Ariane alone departs as the dawn is breaking to reveal a "world of hope" that stands in sharp contrast to the doom and gloom of Bluebeard's castle.[27] Ariane, alone of all her sex, becomes the champion of truth, the probing, inquisitive spirit who offers redemption even when it is spurned. Associated with "light and nature" and "opposed to the unnatural literal and metaphorical darkness of Bluebeard, his home and his past," Maeterlinck's heroine is positioned as a seeker of truths, who reverses an operatic tradition that—since Mozart's *Magic Flute*—associates bass and tenor voices with Enlightenment ideals.[28] And yet because her rescue is "useless" and she ends by saving no one but herself (and perhaps Bluebeard), her story can also be read as an antifeminist parody of woman's missionary zeal. Indeed, the biographical facts of Maeterlinck's life suggest that he may have been lampooning the passionate efforts of Georgette Leblanc, the actress and singer who was his companion for twenty years, to liberate beauty from oppression. "Will you help me," she wrote in *The Choice of Life* published in 1904,"… deliver beauty which doesn't know how to show itself and conviction which doesn't dare to act." "To deliver," she added with dazzling artlessness,"what a magical word!"[29]

Béla Balázs, an ardent admirer of Maeterlinck, wrote an essay on the author of *Pélleas et Mélisande* for a Hungarian journal. There he expressed his profound respect for the murky mysteries of Maeterlinck's dramas:

That silence, that motionlessness locked up in those sullen castles, does it not undulate around me here as well? That invisible, all-ruling great mystery. For *that* is the hero of Maeterlinck's plays. ... And as for the vast Unknowable, within whose breast we live as if in a dark forest: its most visible, most dramatic manifestation is death. Death is the hero of these dramas. But death here is not the terrible sad end, not burial pit and skeleton, but the dark secret, the lurker. *It is only a symbol of the great mystery.*[30]

The obsession with the unknown became evident in Balàzs's publication of a collection of plays with the title *Mysteries: Three One-Acters*, a volume that appeared in 1912. Among the three plays, whose composition dates back to 1908, was *Bluebeard's Castle,* which was to serve as the libretto for Béla Bartok.[31] Although the opera was finished in 1911 in time for a competition organized in Budapest, the work was rejected as "unperformable," and its premiere did not take place until 1918.[32]

What is clear from reading Balàzs's remarks on Maeterlinck's *Ariane and Blue Beard* is the librettist's lack of passion for the figure of Ariane. Balàzs is less impressed with Ariane's heroic move to rescue Bluebeard's victims than with the bleak loneliness of the site at which Bluebeard has stored his victims. The librettist seems indifferent to what is usually the motor of the plot for Bluebeard tales—the secret that drives a wedge between husband and wife—and instead remains fixated on the mystery of life and how death is one manifestation of that impenetrable mystery.

Bartók's opera has only two voices, but there is a third presence that manifests itself in the form of the castle, a forbidding structure that asserts its dominance already in the work's title. Bluebeard's domicile, as many critics hasten to point out, stands for the soul of its inhabitant and becomes the stage on which the conflict between husband and wife is played out. In a gesture emphasizing the centrality of the structure and its symbolic significance, Balázs had included the castle in the list of dramatis personae in the first published version of the play (Bartók later removed the castle from the list). Some years after he had written the libretto, Balázs emphasized the identity between Bluebeard and his spectral habitation: "The castle is his soul. It is lonely, dark, and secretive: the castle of locked doors. ... Into this castle, into his own soul, Bluebeard admits his beloved. And the castle (the stage) shudders, sighs, and bleeds. When the woman walks in it, she walks in a living being."[33]

The prologue to the opera situates Balázs's libretto squarely in a folkloric tradition by enunciating the traditional opening for Hungarian folktales: "Where did it happen? Where did it not happen?" That question is answered with another question—"Where is the stage: outside or inside?"—which in turn places the play within the tradition of symbolist literature (where appearances mirror essences) and also challenges members of the audience to ponder the relevance of the script to their own lives. This may be a familiar story, but it will take new twists and turns to create a more robust message with a new meaning for contemporary audiences.

The curtain to *Bluebeard's Castle* rises on an "empty, dark, cold cave of stone," with a staircase to one side, seven large doors to the other. Bluebeard returns home, accompanied by his wife, Judith, who opens each of these doors as she makes her way into Bluebeard's soul. "I will open up the darkness. / Light will shine here, breezes blow here, love will live here, / In this house as light unending," she confidently declares.[34] Each of the doors opened by Judith emits a specific color of light, the first producing a blood-red glow to symbolize what Bluebeard describes as his "torture chamber." The second door is awash in yellow-red light and contains "instruments of terrible war." A golden beam of light emanates from the third door, behind which is Bluebeard's treasure chamber, filled with golden coins, diamonds, emeralds, and rubies. Behind a fourth door is the secret garden of Bluebeard's castle, lit up by blue-green hues. The fifth door is the gateway to Bluebeard's kingdom, and it is the last of the doors to produce light. The two remaining doors, once opened, bring darkness back onto the stage. The sixth door, with its "motionless mysterious waters," represents "weeping," though whether the tears are Bluebeard's or those of his former wives is not clear. The final door, which Judith insists on opening in order to discover the "terrible truth" about Bluebeard's past, reveals Bluebeard's three previous brides, bedecked with jewels and representing dawn, noon, and eventide. For her transgression, Bluebeard's wife will incarnate night and bring darkness back to the castle as she joins the three other living brides entombed behind the seventh door, while Bluebeard remains alone.

In the folkloric tradition, Bluebeard's wife usually remains unnamed. When she is given a name, it is, as noted earlier, usually the generic Fatima, an orientalizing nod in the direction of the *Arabian Nights*. Judith is a name so powerfully allusive and yet also so remote from the world of Bluebeard that it cries out for an explanation. Why would Balázs name Bluebeard's wife after a biblical heroine who saves the Israelite town of Bethulia by taking up the scimitar and beheading the Assyrian general Holofernes? The apocryphal story of Judith, after all, reverses the positions found in the Bluebeard tale, with the woman wielding a sword in the just defense of her people and the man falling victim to her blade.

The Judith of *Bluebeard's Castle* seems to have many kindred spirits, both literary and operatic. Like Ariane in Dukas's opera, Judith brings light, illuminating the castle through her vigorous curiosity. But Judith's project backfires. The tenacity of her desire to explore the darkest recesses of every chamber in the castle leads to separation and loss. In this sense, Judith's operatic trajectory closely resembles that of Elsa in Richard Wagner's *Lohengrin*. Both Lohengrin and Bluebeard plead with their wives to curb their curiosity, and both wives are unable to resist the desire to know what lies in the past of their husbands. Judith has also been linked to Wagner's *Flying Dutchman*, for she can be seen as a latter-day Senta, whose faith and grace hold the promise of redeeming a dark, brooding man in a state of spiritual crisis.

With the name Judith, however, Balázs firmly affiliated the heroine of his libretto with the long and venerable line of Judiths in the visual and literary arts. From Caravaggio and Artemisia Gentileschi to Friedrich Hebbel and Jean Giraudoux, Judith has figured prominently in the imagination of European artists. While the biblical account of Judith celebrates the courage of a woman who dares to challenge the power of an evil Oriental tyrant, the modern period transformed Judith from a heroic protector of her people to a woman who seduces through her beauty and deceives with her words. The story of her triumph was transformed into a cautionary tale warning men of the hazards of lust, or *luxuria*. In these rescriptings of the biblical narrative, Holofernes became the tragic protagonist whose hubris brought about his downfall. Symptomatic of the way he came to take center stage are the titles given to sixteenth- and seventeenth-century dramas based on the Book of Judith.[35] Just as Bluebeard's wife is effaced from the title of her story, Judith also yields the limelight to her antagonist in titles like *Holofernes* and *The Tragedy of Holofernes*.[36] And like Bluebeard, Holofernes becomes tragic victim rather than menacing threat.

Militant, seductive, and deceitful, the nineteenth-century Judith became, like Salome, with whom she was often confused, a kind of femme fatale.[37] Friedrich Hebbel's 1840 play *Judith*, which Balázs knew well from his dissertation on Hebbel's dramatic theories, so powerfully sexualized its title figure that a biblical icon of feminine courage was suddenly transformed into an idol of perversity.[38] Balàzs was surely aware of Judith's checkered past when he chose her name to attach to his construction of Bluebeard's wife. The curiosity of his Judith may have some positive overtones, but it also poses a threat so lethal to her husband that she must be entombed before she does any further harm.

The Judith of *Bluebeard's Castle* leaves her sword behind when she enters her husband's abode, just as Bluebeard wields no scimitar and proves to be more tenderhearted than tyrannical. If the biblical Judith is renowned as a man-slayer and the folkloric Bluebeard builds his reputation on murdering wives, the Judith and Bluebeard of Bartók's opera are devoid of homicidal impulses and seem bent on establishing marital intimacy and accord. To Bluebeard, Judith reveals her deep love: "I came here because I love you: / Let each door be open for me."[39] Judith may be unable to resist the temptation to open those last two doors, but she seems to be a model of domestic devotion, resolved to ignore the rumors circulating about her husband, willing to part ways with her family, and determined to bring heat and light to a castle that resembles a dungeon. And Bluebeard seems genuinely grateful for the warmth that Judith's "fair hand" has brought to the castle.

Although folkloric versions of "Bluebeard" veered away from exploring the psychological complexities of the relationship between husband and wife, *Bluebeard's Castle* seems to focus almost single-mindedly on the mysteries of intimacy and love. As one commentator on the opera observes,"The story of Bluebeard and his wives came to be seen as one of mutual unhappiness between the lonely man who yearned for the enriching presence of a woman in his life but could not tolerate the spiritual closeness love demands, and the woman, or newest wife, who felt a mysterious attraction to this darkly violent man but could not—or would not—break down the emotional walls he had erected around his soul."[40] Bluebeard was no longer connected with murder and mayhem and instead became a target of compassion.

Despite the allegorical turn taken when Bluebeard anoints his fourth wife as night, *Bluebeard's Castle* resembles nothing so much as a story of domestic friction. Judith's undoing comes when she insists on learning about her husband's sexual history: "Tell me truly beloved, / Who possessed your love before me?" She wants full disclosure and demands details: "Tell me of the way you loved them, / Fairer than me? Dearer than me? / More than you love me, beloved?"[41] That she loses much of her sympathy through her insistence becomes evident when one critic refers to her "badgering," which becomes progressively more aggressive.[42] Another critic roundly condemns Judith for her lack of discretion and emphasizes the emotional "truth" of Bluebeard's need to protect his secrets: "In man's interior world, perhaps, there are secrets locked away; each one of us contains the best and the worst, by our material condition. Only the shining intoxication of fresh love can sometimes dissipate this dark threat: but let the new woman in a man's life be discreet; the hidden places of the masculine self are forbidden to her and, above all, those where … past love lives."[43]

Bluebeard's warnings, for all their obvious gravity, fall on deaf ears, and Judith opens the final door to face the "terrible truth" of her husband's past. The previous wives, Bluebeard reveals, are part of his past and present: "They will always live beside me."[44] *Bluebeard's Castle* displays the perils of wanting to know too much, of pushing so hard for the truth about a husband's past that that past comes to life to destroy a marriage. Caught in the paradox of opening the door that is intended for her even as she loses her husband, Judith falls victim to her insistent curiosity and to her failure to take things on trust. Bluebeard, as tragic protagonist, is left alone on stage, engulfed by the darkness that symbolizes his lot when he puts an end to the quest for knowledge.

Recent commentators on the Bluebeard operatic tradition, most notably Stephen Benson, have contested readings that position Bluebeard as tragic victim of existential loneliness. Seeking to understand the significance of the darkness that engulfs Bluebeard, these observers have reflected on why the operatic tradition gives u§ "narratives of failure." The dystopian endings leave one heroine "defiant and vulnerable," the other incorporated into the very series of repetitions that she attempted to escape. For Benson, Bluebeard represents a "masculine darkness" that is symptomatic of "historically obsessed decline, a state of being borne down by the past." Ariane and Judith incarnate a "questing and questioning femininity" that avoids being "seduced into submission by the commodities Bluebeard has shored against his ruin," commodities that represent a retreat into preserving and sanctifying a questionable past, one that has been memorialized as torture chambers, tools of warfare, treasure chambers smeared with blood, secret gardens with blood seeping through them, endless domains beneath clouds of red, and mournful waters created from tears. These wives of Bluebeard are on a mission that transcends personal happiness and engages them with the troubled political as well as personal histories of their husbands.[45] They tell us that the tale of Bluebeard's domestic life has a larger significance and that the castle that is his home represents more than a marital space.

More recently, Claude Chabrol's *Landru* reminds us, once again, of the powerful link between private vices and public virtues and of how the carnage in the Bluebeard story is repeatedly implicated in military violence. Landru, for whom women are "monsters" with "cruel hearts," commits his crimes in secret on the home front, while his fellow countrymen enter war zones to murder other men. The Frenchman's crimes, enacted on screen in Technicolor, are cross-cut with historical footage from black-and-white newsreels documenting what goes on in combat. Whether Landru's crimes are a cynical comment on military violence or whether the military violence ennobles Landru's crimes and turns him into a heroic figure, it becomes clear that the battle of the sexes cannot be divorced from the broader social violence practiced on a grand scale by nations at war. The story of Bluebeard, for all its intense focus on the home front, mirrors problems writ large in the public sphere.

NOTES

1. Robin Walz, *Pulp Surrealism: Insolent Popular Culture in Early Twentieth-Century Paris* (Berkeley: University of California Press, 2000), pp. 76–77.

2. Michel Foucault, *Discipline and Punish: The Birth of the Prison*, trans. Alan Sheridan (New York: Random House, Vintage Books, 1979), pp. 68–69.

3. Diane Wolfe Levy,"History as Art: Ironic Parody in Anatole France's *Les Sept Femmes de la Barbe-Bleue*" *Nineteenth-Century French Studies* 4 (1976): 361.

4. Charles Dickens, *The Pickwick Papers* (Harmondsworth: Penguin, 1972), p. 355.

5. Francis Egerton Ellesmère, *Bluebeard; or Dangerous curiosity & justifiable homicide* (London: T. Brettell, 1841), p. 27.

6. Ludwig Tieck, *Ritter Blaubart: Ein Ammenmàrchen in vier Akten*, in *Tieck, Werke*, ed. Richard Plett (Hamburg: Hoffmann und Campe, 1967), pp. 226,238.

7. Anatole France,"The Seven Wives of Bluebeard," in *Spells of Enchantment: The Wondrous Fairy Tales of Western Culture*, ed. Jack Zipes (New York: Viking, 1991), p. 568.

8. Ibid., p. 580.

9. Donald Barthelme,"Bluebeard," in Barthelme, *Forty Stories* (New York: Putnam, 1987), p. 97.

10. Casie Hermansson describes the zebras as "a bizarre simulacrum emptied of all possible pre-texts." See *Reading Feminist Intertextuality through Bluebeard Stories* (Lewiston,.N.Y.: Edwin Mellen Press, 2001), p. 258.

11. Aline Kilmer,"The Case of Bluebeard," in *Kilmer, Hunting a Hair Shirt and Other Spiritual Adventures* (New York: George H. Doran, 1923), pp. 94, 97.

12. On "Bluebeard" as working title for *Monsieur Verdoux*, see David Robinson, Chaplin: His Life and Art (New York: Da Capo, 1985), p. 520.

13. André Bazin,"The Myth of Monsieur Verdoux," in Bazin, *What Is Cinema?* trans. Hugh Gray (Berkeley: University of California Press, 1967), p. 116.

14. Charles J. Maland, *Chaplin and American Culture: The Evolution of a Star Image* (Princeton: Princeton University Press, 1989), p. 233.

15. Charles Spencer *Chaplin, My Autobiography* (New York: Simoijt and Schuster, 1964), p. 435.

16. Dean MacCannell,"Democracy's Turn: On Homeless *Noir*," in *Shades of Noir: A Reader* ed. Joan Copjec (London: Verso, 1993), pp. 292–93.

17. James McLaughlin,"All in the Family: Alfred Hitchcock's *Shadow of a Doubt*" in *A Hitchcock Reader*, ed. Marshall Deutelbaum and Leland Poague (Ames: Iowa State University Press, 1986), p. 142.

18. MacCannell,"Democracy's Turn," p. 293.

19. McLaughlin,"*All in the Family*," p. 148.

20. Ibid., p. 149.

21. William Rothman, *Hitchcock: The Murderous Gaze* (Cambridge,.Mass.: Harvard University Press, 1982), p. 244. "Graham," he adds,"knows only that realm of the ordinary within which, but also apart from which, Charlie is fated to stand."

22. George Steiner, In B*luebeard's Castle: Some Notes towards the Redefinition of Culture* (New Haven: Yale University Press, 1971),'pp. 140, 136. Note Susan McClary's identification of Bluebeard's wife with Judith in her discussion of feminism and musicology in "Introduction: A Material Girl in Bluebeard's Castle," in McClary, *Feminine Endings: Music, Gender; and Sexuality* (Minnesota: University of Minnesota Press, 1991), pp. 3–5.

23. Pierre Cadars,"Sept compositeurs pour une Barbe-Bleu," *L'avant-scéne opéra* 149–50 (November/December 1992): 82–85.

24. On other musical works, including ballets, that invoke the Bluebeard story, see Carl Leafstedt, *Inside Bluebeard's Castle: Music and Drama in Béla Bartók's Opera* (New York: Oxford University Press, 1999), p. 174.

25. Mike Ashman,"Around the Bluebeard Myth," in *The Stage Works of Béla Bartók* (London: John Calder, 1991), p. 38. Ivan Sanders describes Ariane as the "liberated" woman. See his "Symbolist and Decadent Elements in Early-Twentieth-Century Hungarian Drama," *Canadian-American Review of Hungarian Studies* 4 (1977): 30.

26. Maurice Maeterlinck, *Ariane and Blue Beard: A Lyric Story in Three Acts* (New York: Rullman, 1910), p. 6.

27. Ibid., p. 35.

28. Stephen Benson,"The Afterlife of 'Bluebeard,'" *Marvels and Tales* 14 (2000): 244–67.

29. Austin B. Caswell,"Maeterlinck's and Dukas' Ariane et Barbe-Bleue: A Feminist Opera?" *Studies in Romanticism* 27 (1988): 219.

30. Cited by Leafstedt, *Inside* Bluebeard's Castle, p. 39.

31. Emil Haraszti sees Balázs's play as an attempt "to compress Maeterlinck's three-act tragedy into a one-act drama." See his *Béla Bartók: His Life and Works* (Paris: Lyrebird Press, 1938), p. 72.

32. Paul Banks,"Images of the Self: 'Duke Bluebeard's Castle,'" in *The Stage Works of Béla Bartók* (London: John Calder, 1991), p. 12.

33. Quoted in Leafstedt, *Inside* Bluebeard's Castle, p. 126.

34. Béla Bartók, *Duke Bluebeard's Castle*, trans. John Lloyd Davies, in *The Stage Works of Béla Bartók* (London: John Calder, 1991), p. 49.

35. As Mary Garrard puts it, Judith's image changed "from that of a paragon of chastity, strength, and courage to a dangerous and deceitful femme fatale." See her *Judith: Sexual Warrior. Women and Power in Western Culture* (New Haven: Yale University Press, 1998), p. 301.

36. Garrard lists these titles in ibid., p. 291.

37. Nadine Sine,"Cases of Mistaken Identity: Salome and Judith at the Turn of the Century," *German Studies Review* 11 (1988): 9–29.

38. The term is borrowed from Bram Djikstra, who points out how Judith was a "paragon of self-sacrificial martyrdom for a noble cause" in the Bible and was then unmasked by nineteenth-century painters as "a lustful predator, an anorexic tigress." See *Idols of Perversity: Fantasies of Feminine Evil in Fin-de-Siecle Culture* (New York: Oxford University Press, 1986), p. 377. Marina Warner points out that although Judith is "the foremost biblical exemplar of Fortitude and Justice, the pattern of heroic virtue," in visual depictions of her, we see "a killer all the same." See Warner's *Monuments and Maidens: The Allegory of the Female Form* (New York: Atheneum, 1985), p. 175.

39. Bartók, *Duke Bluebeard's Castle*, p. 52.

40. Leafstedt, *Inside Bluebeard's Castle*, p. 176.

41. Bartók, *Duke Bluebeard's Castle*, p. 57.

42. Julian Grant,"A Foot in Bluebeard's Door," in *The Stage Works of Béla Bartók* (London: John Calder, 1991), p. 30.

43. Serge Moreux, *Béla Bartók* (London: Harvill Press, 1953).

44. Bartók, *Duke Bluebeard's Castle*, p. 58.

45. Benson,"The Afterlife of 'Bluebeard,' " pp. 259–60. See also McClary,"Introduction: A Material Girl in Bluebeard's Castle," pp. 3–34, and Anja Suschitzky,"Ariane et Barbe-Bleue: Dukas, the Light, and the Well," *Cambridge Opera journal* 9 (1997): 133–61.

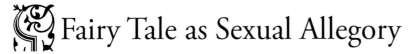

Fairy Tale as Sexual Allegory

Intertextuality in Angela Carter's *The Bloody Chamber*

Mary Kaiser

ANGELA CARTER, IN HER 1990 introduction to *The Old Wives' Fairy Tale Book,* makes a distinction between folklore, emerging from oral "unofficial" culture, and the fairy tale, product of a literary "official" culture. Folklore, she explains* is anonymous and fluid, resulting in "stories without known originators that can be remade again and again by every person who tells them, the perennially refreshed entertainment of the poor" (ix). Literary fairy tales, on the other hand, according to Garter, transformed an oral tradition into texts that become middle-class commodities. This analysis accords with Jack Zipes's economic reading of fairy tales in *Breaking the Magic Spell: Radical Theories of Folk and Fairy Tales,* wherein he argues that folk tales represent a "pre-capitalist folk form" that was transposed by the Grimm Brothers and others into a "bourgeois art form" (20). Carter's narrative of the transition from oral tradition to written tales also suggests Julia Kristeva's notion of intertextuality as the transposing of as entire system of codes or signs.

Distinguishing it from allusion, Kristeva writes in *Revolution in Poetic Language* that in its "passage from one signifying system to another," intertextuality "demands a new articulation of the thetic—of enunciative and denotative positionality" (60). In other words, the stance of the speaker—the "thetic"—is significantly altered when intertextual transposition takes place, while allusion merely gestures toward another text without taking on its entire context. As Carter suggests in her introduction to *The Old Wives' Fairy Tale Book,* intertextuality was embedded into the history of the fairy tale when Charles Perrault, the Grimm Brothers, and other compilers of the eighteenth and nineteenth centuries transposed oral folk tales into fairy tales. This transfer Involved what Kristeva refers to as "a new articulation of the thetic," as the politics, economies, fashions, and prejudices of a sophisticated culture replaced the values of rural culture that form the context of oral folklore. Part of this transfer, Carter argues, was the transposing of an essentially feminine form, the "old wives' tale," onto a masculine one, the published text. Referring to the tradition of «Mother Goose," Carter asserts that oral folktales record the "strategies, plots, and hard work" with which women have coped with the conditions of their lives but that in their oral form these narratives are considered "Old wives" tales—that is, worthless stories, untruths, trivial gossip, a derisive label that allots the art of storytelling to women at the exact same time as it takes all value from if" (xi). In her 1979 collection of retold fairy tales, *The Bloody Chamber,* Carter shows an acute awareness of the changes that result from an oral to written transposition and calls attention to them by heightening the intertexuality of her narratives, making them into allegories that explore how sexual behavior and gender roles are not universal, but are, like other forms of social interaction, culturally determined. This theme is closely related to that of Carter's 1978 study of the writings of the Marquis de Sade, *The Sadeian Woman,* where she attacks what she calls the false universalizing of sexuality, which, tending to enforce the archetype of male aggression and female passivity, merely confuses "the main issue, that relationships between the sexes are determined by history and by the historical fact of the economic dependence of women upon men"(6–7).

Mary Kaiser, "Fairy Tale as Sexual Allegory: Intertextuality in Angela Carter's The Bloody Chamber," *Review of Contemporary Fiction*, vol. 14, issue 3, pp. 30–36. Copyright © 1994 by Dalkey Archive Press. Reprinted with permission.

I wish to argue that Carter's use of intertextuality in *The Bloody Chamber* moves the tales from the mythic timelessness of the fairy tale to specific cultural moments, each of which presents a different problem in gender relations and sexuality. Although she recounts the plots of the same fairy tales—"Beauty and the Beast" twice,"Little Red Riding Hood" three times—Carter changes the cultural context from tale to tale, and, as a result, each retelling generates a different narrative. The outcomes for her protagonists can be tragic or triumphant, the tone can be serious or farcical, depending on the historic and cultural circumstances. To demonstrate the range of the collection, I will consider two tales with the same scenario, a young, powerless woman under the domination of an older, powerful male figure who is not only a threat to her virginity but a threat to her life. '"The Bloody Chamber." a retelling of "Bluebeard," is set in the world of decadent turn-of-the-century French culture, among the operas of Wagner and the fashions of Paul Poiret. "The Snow Child" is set in medieval Europe, deep in a forest, and is based much more closely on its original, a version of "Snow White." "The Bloody Chamber" is a tale of feminine courage triumphant, while "The Snow Child." as its chilling title suggests, is a stark, uncompromising tale of sexuality as a function, of overwhelming male power.

The lengthiest and perhaps the paradigmatic story of the collection,"The Bloody Chamber" explores the sexual symbolism of the secret room, making explicit the Freudian interpretation given by Bruno Bettelheim in *The Uses of Enchantment* that the "bloody chamber" is the womb. In addition to making the tale's latent sexual symbolism manifest, Carter also addresses in this story what she calls in *The Sadeian Woman* the "mystification" associated with the womb. The "bankrupt enchantments of the womb" led, she writes, to the segregation and punishment of women (109); in "The Bloody Chamber," Bluebeard, the connoisseur of women, makes his womblike secret chamber into a museum of tortured and murdered women.

Following the tradition recorded by Iona and Peter Opie, that the original of Bluebeard was a notorious Breton nobleman (103–5), Carter places her version of the tale in a castle on the coast of Brittany but makes its owner a wealthy aesthete who is as much at home at a performance of *Tristan* at the Paris Opera as he is within his ancestral hall. If the secret room containing the corpses of his dead wives is likened to a womb, Bluebeard's castle is a metaphor for his sexuality. A phallic tower, it floats upon the "amniotic salinity of the ocean," reminding Bluebeard's bride of an "anchored, castellated ocean liner" (12, 14), and becomes the stage for a symbolist version of the battle of the sexes, The fin de siécle time period Is critical to Carter's interpretation of "Bluebeard," because she sees the bride's fate as possible only at the moment in history when images of female victimization and of female aggression con verged.

Combining, like J. K, Huysmans, a taste for Catholic ritual and for sensual experimentation, Carter's Bluebeard displays an edition of Huysmans's *Là-bas* "bound like a missal" among an extensive collection of eighteenth- and nineteenth-century pornography (16). Like Huysmans also, Bluebeard has discovered a group of symbolist painters whose imagery accords with his temperament.[1] Among these images of young, attenuated, passive women, Carter includes some imaginary symbolist paintings, such as Moreau's "famous *Sacrificial Victim* with the imprint of the lacelike chains on her pellucid skin" and "Two or three late Oauguins, his special favourite the one of the tranced brown girl in the deserted house" (20). A willowy young music student, living in poverty with her widowed mother, the bride becomes a vehicle for Bluebeard's attempt to realize the decadent image of the dependent, virginal child-woman, ripe for tragedy.

Avis Lewallen has commented that she finds "The Bloody Chamber" the most disturbing of the tales in the collection, because of its lush, seductive descriptions of sexual exploitation and victimization,[2] Carter,—however, uses the language of the story not to—lull the reader into ignoring the dangers posed by Bluebeard but instead to heighten the reader's awareness of the threat posed by the sadomasochistic underpinnings of much of decadent culture, which created a dangerously passive and readily victimized feminine ideal. In *The Sadeian Woman*, describing the ideal presented by Sade's victimized Justine, she writes,"She is obscene to the extent to which she is beautiful. Her beauty, her submissiveness and false expectations that these qualities will do her some good are what make her obscene" (57). The decadent sign system that surrounds this version of Bluebeard brings the sadomasochistic subtext of the original to the foreground by giving its murderous episodes the lush refinement of Beardsley's illustrations of *Salome*,

Bluebeard, like his historical precursor the Marquis de Sade, is a producer of theatrical effects. His rooms are deliberately planned as stages for symbolic action, the bloody chamber a kind of wax museum of his previous wives, preserved in their last moments of agony, the mirrored bedroom with its "grand, hereditary, matrimonial bed" a set for "a formal, disrobing of the bride" (14, 15). Clothing, in this theatrical context, becomes costume, in which, as in theater and religious ritual, the individual, is subsumed by a role. The bride's dress (designed by Poiret, the inventor of the "hobble" skirt) and her wedding gift,"A choker of rubies, two inches wide, like an extraordinarily precious slit throat" (11), not only situate her in fin de siécle Prance but also reflect the image of innocence, vulnerability, and victimization that Bluebeard desires. Nakedness becomes a kind of costume as well, in the overdetermined imagery of Bluebeard's bedroom. Watching herself being disrobed by him, the bride perceives herself as a pornographic object: "He in his London tailoring; she, bare as a lamb chop. Most pornographic of all confrontations" (15). In this scene the bride has been reduced to an unaccommodated body, while Bluebeard retains all the accoutrements of power, wealth, and taste,

However, Bluebeard has conveniently excised from his collection of fin de siècle imagery the era's complement to the woman-as-victim, the avatar of the New Woman,"She-who-must-he-obeyed," Sandra Gilbert and Susan Gubar point, out that these complementary images appeared almost simultaneously in the late 1880s, when the harrowing mutilations and murders of women by Jack the Ripper took, place at the same time as Rider Haggard's enormously popular novel *She* introduced a heroine who, by combining virtue with authority, represented "an entirely New Woman" (6). Gilbert and Gubar suggest that the emergence of female aggression in the suffrage movement generated a backlash of images of suffering, victimized women. Carter, in *The Sadeian Woman,* shares this interpretation when she argues that the real threat posed by the emancipation of women was the removal of "the fraudulent magic from the idea of women" (109). If Bluebeard's murders mirror those of Jack the Ripper, who was also obsessed with the womb, then Bluebeard's murders are avenged by a figure who also seems to have stepped out of the *Zeitgeist* of the 1880s. The bride's mother rides onto the scene just as Bluebeard is preparing to dispatch his latest wife and kills him with a single shot, from her dead husband's service revolver. Like Haggard's fearsome heroine, she is woman-as-avenger on a grand scale. At the tale's opening the bride calls her mother "eagle-featured, indomitable," recalling that she "had outfaced a junkful of Chinese pirates, nursed a village through a visitation of the plague, shot a man-eating tiger with her own hand and all before she was as old as I (7). Appropriately, she reappears at the conclusion as a complement to her daughter's masochistic passivity, just at the point when the bride herself has begun to act in her own behalf and emancipate herself from Bluebeard's pornographic scenario.

Patricia Duncker reads the ending of "The Bloody Chamber" as carrying "an uncompromisingly feminist message" (12), while all of the other tales in the collection, she feels, merely recapitulate patriarchal patterns of behavior. What Duncker perceives as an inconsistent application of feminist principles is, I believe, merely a reflection of Carter's project in this collection, to portray sexuality as a culturally relative phenomenon. The feminism, às well as the masochism of «The Bloody Chamber,» is a feature of its turn-of-fhe-century setting. The same scenario, when it is transposed to a medieval Northern European setting in «The Snow Child,» will have a much darker resolution since its cultural context lacks an image of power for women.

"The Snow Child" is a stark, two-page version of «Snow White,» reducing the fairy tale to its skeletal outlines as a fable of incest. Carter uses, rather than the Grimm Brothers' version, in which a queen wishes for a child,"another version, quoted by Bruno Bettelheim in *The Uses of Enchantment,* in which a count wishes for a daughter (200), The girl appears, just as he imagined her, but he is forced to abandon her through the jealous stratagems of his wife. Bettelheim argues that all versions of Snow White are myths of Oedipal conflicts between mothers and daughters, but certainly the harsh simplicity of this version heightens the Oedipal tension.

Its opening paragraphs in exact parallel with the traditional tale, Carter's version veers away as the Countess's stratagem for leaving the girl behind is intercepted by the Count: 'The Countess dropped her glove in the snow and told the girl to get down to look for it; she meant to gallop off and leave her there but the Count said: 'I'll buy you new gloves''' (92), From this point, the tale becomes a fable of the struggle between masculine power and women's sexuality. In the traditional tale the Count must choose between the Countess and the Child. In Carter's version the Count, who has all the real power, does not have to choose; he can have both Countess and Child. The Countess, in fact, is as powerless as the Child, since both are held in the tyranny of the Count's desire. He has granted a subsidiary power to his wife, signaled by her title and indicated by her horse, furs, boots, and gloves, but as a sign of their mutual dependence on his favor, the furs, boots, and jewels fly off the Countess, onto the girl, and back onto the Countess again depending on the whims of the Count.

In its harsh reduction of sexual desire to a function of power, the story's scenario echoes the sexual politics of Sade. The Child, like Bluebeard's bride in "The Bloody Chamber," is a version of Sade's masochistic Justine, whose situation is summed up by Carter in *The Sadeian Woman:* "To exist in the passive case is to die in the passive case—that is, to be killed. (1] This is the moral of the fairy tale about the perfect woman" (77). Like Sade's Justine, the Snow Child will die, a victim of the Count's tyrannous desire and of the Countess's realization that they' are rivals in a life-and-death struggle. Duncker has noted the resemblance between the Countess and Sade's sadistic Juliette: "with one small touch Carter reveals the Mother [the Countess] as a sister to Sade's Juliette, the sexual terrorist" in the image of her high-heeled, spurred boots (7), Instead of a fiery suffragette, then, the Snow Child finds a mother-figure who colludes in her subjugation. In the feudal culture of "The Snow Child" power is masculine, and in this tale Carter portrays the sexual consequences of a feudal system of absolute power.

When she picks up the Countess's rose, the Snow Child is pricked in the finger and dies. After her death, her body is raped by the Count, and then it melts into the snow, leaving only a feather and a bloodstain. This closing image underlines the portrayal of the Snow Child as a creature of the forest, who, naked and mute, confronts the culture of the dressed and mounted Count and Countess. The Countess, though associated with the Count, is also compared to a wild animal, "wrapped in the glittering pelts of black foxes" (91), and she, too, is naked when her clothing flies onto the body of the girl. In their wildness and in their nakedness both women are contrasted with the Count, who not only represents culture but also bestows a cultural status on women. Like the bride in "The Bloody Chamber," the women in "The Snow Child" are placed in a pornographic contrast with the Count who is always clothed, always embedded in culture. Thus Carter introduces the notorious analogy that in Western culture male is to female as culture is to nature. Although some feminist theorists claim to find a kind of liberation in the position of woman as Other in phallogeocentric culture, Carter finds the situation more complex and more troubling. Always suspicious about universal» and never romantic about oppression, Carter sees the real suffering involved in the politics of gender. It is hardly liberating to be likened to an animal, if that implies entrapment, control, exploitation, and even violent death. Sally Robinson, in her discussion of Carter's fiction, adds that "for Carter, denigration and celebration of Woman as Other are both masculinist strategies within patriarchal cultures, whereby Man secures his hegemony over the places of enunciation" (98). In 'The Snow Child" Carter demonstrates the deadly consequences of the nature/culture analogy's denial of cultural status to women.

In *The Sadeian Woman* Carter writes, "the notion of a universality of female experience is a clever confidence trick" (12), a statement that neatly sums up her deuniversalizing of fairy tale plots in *The Bloody. Chamber,* Situating her tales within carefully defined cultural moments, Carter employs a wide-ranging intertextuality to link each tale to the Zeitgeist of its moment and to call attention to the literary fairy tale as a product, not of a collective unconscious but of specific cultural, political, and economic positions. In addition, focusing on the "strategies, plots, and hard work" of women allows Carter to reappropriate the "old wives' tale" as feminine narrative. In *The Bloody Chamber,* then, Carter deconstructs the underlying assumptions of the "official" fairy tale: that fairy tales are universal, timeless myths, that fairy tales are meant exclusively for an audience of children, and that fairy tales present an idealized, fantastic world unrelated to the contingencies of real life. Instead, Carter pushes Bruno Bettelheim's reading of fairy tales as Freudian fables even further and presents them as studies in the history of imagining sexuality and gender.

NOTES

1. In his *Symbolist Art* Edward Lucie-Smith writes,"the fact, however, is that the literary Symbolists, when they at last achieved an identity of their own by bringing together ideas which had existed in a state of potentiality for some years previously,, also looked about for artists who seemed to echo and to justify their own announced programme in another field of creative activity. The best-known example of this is I. K. Huysmans's discovery of the work of Gustave Moreau and Odilon Redon, and the use which he made of it in Ms novels *rebours (Against Nature.),* published in 1S84, Gauguin was also to be taken up in this way, at a slightly later date, after the Caf6 Volpini exhibition of 1889" (51).

2. Lewallen writes.,"Of all the tales in the volume I found 'The Bloody Chamber' most troubling in terms of female sexuality, largely because of the very seductive quality of the writing itself; As readers we are asked to place ourselves imaginatively as masochistic victims in a pornographic scenario and to sympathise in some way with the ambivalent feelings this produces" (151).

WORKS CITED

Bettelheim, Bruno. *The Uses of Enchantment: The Meaning and Importance, of Fairy Tales.* New York: Random House, 1977.

Carter, Angela. *The Bloody Chamber.* 1979. New York: Penguin, *1992.*

—Introduction. *The Old Wives' Fairy Tale Book.* Ed, Angela Carter, New York: Pantheon, 1990.

—*The Sadeian Woman and the Ideology of Pornography.* New York: Pantheon, 1979.

Duncker, Patricia. "Re-Imagining the Fairy Tales.* Angela Carter's Bloody Chambers." *Literature and History.*10 (1984): 3–14.

Gilbert, Sandra M,, and Susan Gubar, *Sexchanges,* Vol. 2 of *No Man's Land.: The Place of the Woman Writer in the Twentieth Century,* New Haven: Yale University Press, 1989.

Kristeva, Julia, *Revolution in Poetic Language.* Trans. Margaret Waller, New York: Columbia University Press, 1984.

Lewallen, Avis. "Wayward Girls but Wicked Women?: Female Sexuality in Angela Carter's *The Bloody Chamber.*" In *Perspectives on Pornography: Sexuality in Film and Literature.* Ed. Gary Day and Clive Bloom. New York: St. Martin's Press, 1988. 144–58.

Lucie-Smith, Edward. *Symbolist Art.* New York: Oxford University Press, 1972.

Opie, Iona, and Peter Opie. *The Classic Fairy Tales.* 1974. Oxford: Oxford University Press, 1992.

Robinson, Sally, *Gender and Self-Representation in Contemporary Women's Fiction.* Albany: State University of New York Press, 1991.

Zipes, Jack. *Breaking the Magic Spell: Radical Theories of Folk and Fairy Tales.* New York: Methuen, 1979.

The Sleeping Beauty in the Woods

Charles Perrault

Once upon a time there was a king and a queen who were quite disturbed at not having any children. Indeed, they were so disturbed that no words can express their feelings. They visited all the baths in the world. They took vows, pilgrimages—everything was tried, and nothing succeeded. At last, however, the queen became pregnant and gave birth to a daughter. At the christening all the fairies who could be found in the realm (seven altogether) were asked to be godmothers so that each would give the child a gift. According to the custom of the fairies in those days, the gifts would endow the princess with all the perfections that could be imagined.

After the baptismal ceremonies the entire company returned to the king's palace, where a great banquet was held for the fairies. Places were laid for each, consisting of a magnificent plate with a massive gold case containing a spoon, fork, and knife of fine gold, studded with diamonds and rubies. But as they were all about to sit down at the table, an old fairy entered the palace. She had not been invited because she had not left the tower in which she resided for more than fifty years, and it was supposed that she had either died or had become enchanted.

The king ordered a place to be set for her, but he could not give her a massive gold case as as he had with the others because the seven had been made expressly for the seven fairies.. The old fairy thought that she was being slighted and muttered some threats between her teeth. One of the young fairies who chanced to be nearby overheard her, and thinking that she might wish the little princess bad luck, hid herself behind the tapestry as soon as they rose from the table. "That way I'll have the last word and repair any evil the old woman might do."

Meanwhile, the fairies began to bestow their gifts upon the princess. The youngest fairy decreed,—"She will be the most beautiful person in the world." The next fairy declared,"She will have the temperament of an angel." The third,"She will evince the most admirable grace in all she does." The fourth: "She will dance to perfection." The sixth:,"She will play every instrument in the most exquisite manner possible."

Finally the turn of the old fairy arrived. Her head shook more with malice than with age as she declared,"The princess will pierce her hand with a spindle and die of the wound."

This terrible gift made the entire company tremble, and no one present could refrain from tears. At this moment the young fairy stepped from behind the tapestry and uttered in a loud voice,"Comfort yourselves, King and Queen, your daughter will not die. It's true that I don't have sufficient power to undo entirely what my elder has done. The princess will pierce her hand with a spindle. But instead of dying, she'll only fall into a deep sleep that will last one hundred years. At the end of that time, a king's son will come to wake her."

In the hope of avoiding the misfortune predicted by the old fairy, the king immediately issued a public edict forbidding all his subjects to spin with a spindle or to have spindles in their house under pain of death.

After fifteen or sixteen years had passed, the royal couple and their court traveled to one of their country residences, and one day the princess happened to be exploring it. She went from one chamber to another, and

Charles Perrault; Jack Zipes, trans., "The Sleeping Beauty in the Woods," *Beauties, Beasts, and Enchantment: Classic French Fairy Tales*, pp. 44–51. Copyright © 2009 by Crescent Moon Publishing. Reprinted with permission.

after arriving at the top of a tower, she entered a little garret, where an honest old woman was sitting by herself with her distaff and spindle. This good woman had never heard of the king's prohibition of spinning with a spindle.

"What are you doing there, my fair lady?" asked the princess.

"I'm spinning, my lovely child," answered the old woman, who did not know her.

"Oh, how pretty it is!" the princess responded. "How do you do it? Let me try and see if I can do it as well."

No sooner had she grasped the spindle than she pricked her hand with the point and fainted, for she had been hasty, a little thoughtless, arid moreover, the sentence of the fairies had ordained it to, be that way. Greatly embarrassed, the good old woman called for help. People came from all quarters. They threw water on the princess's face. They unlaced her stays. They slapped her hands. They rubbed her temples with Queen of Hungary's water. Nothing could revive her. Then the king, who had run upstairs at the noise, remembered the prediction of the fairies and wisely concluded that this must have happened as the fairies said it would. Therefore, he had the princess carried to the finest apartment in the palace and placed on a bed of gold and silver embroidery. One would have said she was an angel, so lovely did she appear, for her swoon had not deprived her of her rich complexion: her cheeks preserved their crimson color, and her lips were like coral. Her eyes were closed, but her gentle breathing could be heard, and that indicated she was not dead. The king commanded that she be left to sleep in peace until the hour arrived for her waking.

The good fairy who had saved her life by decreeing that she should sleep for one hundred years was in the Kingdom of Mataquin, twelve thousand leagues away. When the princess met with her accident, she was informed of it instantly by a little dwarf who had a pair of seven-league boots (that is, boots that enable the wearer to cover seven leagues at a single stride). The fairy set out immediately, and an hour afterward she was seen arriving in a chariot of fire drawn by dragons. The king advanced and offered his hand to help her out of the chariot. She approved of all that he had done. Yet since she had great foresight, she thought to herself that when the princess awoke, she would feel considerably embarrassed at finding herself all alone in that old castle. So this is what the fairy did:

With the exception of the king and queen, she touched everyone in the castle with her wand—governesses, maids of honor, ladies-in-waiting, gentlemen, officers, stewards, cooks, scullions, boys, guards, porters, pages, footmen. She also touched all the horses in the stables, their grooms, the great mastiffs in the courtyard, and little Pootsie, the princess's tiny dog lying on the bed beside her. As soon as she touched them, they all fell asleep, and they were not to wake again until the time arrived for their mistress to do so. Thus they would all be ready to wait upon her if she should want them. Even the spits that had been put down to the fire, laden with partridges and pheasants, went to sleep,* and the fire as well.

All this was done in a moment, for the fairies never lose much time when they work. Then the king and queen kissed their dear daughter without waking her and left the castle. They issued a proclamation forbidding anyone to approach it. These orders were unnecessary, for within a quarter of an hour the park was surrounded by such a great quantity of trees, large and small, interlaced by brambles and thorns, that neither man nor beast could penetrate them. Nothing more could be seen than the tops of the castle turrets, and these only at a considerable distance. Nobody doubted but that was also some of the fairy's handiwork so that the princess might have nothing to fear from the curiosity of strangers during her slumber.

At the end of the hundred years, a different family from that of the sleeping princess had succeeded to the throne. One day the son of the king went hunting in that neighborhood and inquired about the towers that he saw above the trees of a large and dense wood. Every person responded to the prince according to the story he had heard. Some said that it was an old castle haunted by ghosts. Others, that all the witches of the region held their Sabbath there. The most prevalent opinion was that it was the abode of an ogre who carried away all the children he could catch and ate them there at his leisure, since he alone had the power of making a passage through the wood. While the prince tried to make up his mind what to believe, an old peasant spoke in his turn and said to him,"Prince, it is more than fifty years since I heard my father say that the most beautiful princess ever seen is in that castle. He told me that she was to sleep for a hundred years and was destined to be awakened by a chosen king's son."

Upon hearing these words, the young prince felt all on fire. There was no doubt in his mind that he was destined to accomplish this wonderful adventure, and impelled by love and glory, he decided on the spot to see what would come of it. No sooner had he approached the wood than all those great trees and all those brambles and thorns opened on their own accord and allowed him to pass through. Then he began walking toward the castle, which he saw at the end of the long avenue that he had entered. To his surprise, the trees closed up as soon as he passed, and none of his attendants could follow him. Nevertheless, he continued to advance, for a young and amorous prince is always courageous. When he entered a large forecourt, everything he saw froze his blood with terror. A frightful silence reigned. Death seemed to be everywhere. Nothing could be seen but the bodies of men and animals stretched out and apparently lifeless. He soon discovered, however, by the shining noses and red faces of the porters that they were only asleep; their goblets, which still contained a few drops of wine, sufficently proved that they had dosed off while drinking. Passing through a large courtyard paved with marble, he ascended a staircase. As he entered the guardroom, he saw the guards drawn up in a line, their carbines shouldered, and snoring their loudest. He traversed several apartments filled with ladies and gentlemen all asleep; some standing, others seated. Finally he entered a chamber completely covered with gold and saw the most lovely sight he had ever looked upon—on a bed with curtains open on each side was a princess who seemed to be about fifteen or sixteen. Her radiant charms gave her such a luminous, supernatural appearance that he approached, trembling and admiring, and knelt down beside her. At that moment the enchantment ended. The princess awoke and bestowed on him a look more tender than a first glance might seem to warrant.

"Is it you, my prince?" she said. "You have been long awaited."

Charmed by these words, and still more by the tone in which they were uttered, the prince hardly knew how to express his joy and gratitude to her. He assured her he loved her better than he loved himself. His words were not very coherent, but they pleased her all the more because of that. The less eloquence, the more love, so they say. He was much more embarrassed than she was, and one ought not to be astonished at that, for the princess had had time enough to consider what she should say to him. There is reason to believe (though history makes no mention of it) that the good fairy had procured her the pleasure of very charming dreams during her long slumber. In short, they talked for four hours without expressing half of what they had to* say to each other.,

In the meantime the entire palace had been roused at the same time as the princess. They all remembered what their tasks were, and since they were not all in love, they were dying with hunger. The lady-in-waiting, as hungry as any of them, became impatient and announced loudly to the princess that dinner was ready. The prince assisted the princess to rise. She was fully dressed, and her gown was magnificent, but he took care not to tell her that she was attired like his grandmother, who also wore stand-up collars. Still, she looked no less lovely in it.

They passed into a salon of mirrors, in which stewards of the princess served them supper. The violins and oboes played antiquated but excellent pieces of music. And after supper, to lose no time, the chaplain married them in the castle chapel, and the maid of honor pulled the curtains of their bed closed.

They did not sleep a great deal, however. The princess did not have much need of sleep, , and the prince left her at sunrise to return to the city, where his father had been greatly worried about him. The prince told him that he had lost his way in the forest while hunting, and that he had slept in the hut of a charcoal-burner, who had given him some black bread and cheese for his supper. His father, who was a trusting soul, believed him, but his mother was not so easily persuaded. Observing that he went hunting nearly every day and always had some story ready as an excuse when he had slept two or three nights away from home, she was convinced that he had some mistress. Indeed, he lived with the princess for more than two years and had two children by her. The first was a girl named Aurora, and the second, a son, called Day because he seemed even more beautiful than his sister.

In order to draw a confession from him, the queen often said to her son that he ought to settle down. However, he never dared to trust her with his secret. Although he loved her, he also feared her, for she was of the race of ogres, and the king had married her only because of her great wealth. "It was even whispered about the court that she had the inclinations of an ogress: whenever she saw little children passing, she had the greatest difficulty restraining herself from pouncing on them. Hence, the prince refused to say anything about his adventure.

Two years later, however, the king died, and the prince became his successor. Thereupon, he made a public declaration of his marriage and went in great state to fetch his queen to the palace. With her two children on either side of her, she made a magnificent entry into the capital.

Some time afterward the king went to war with his neighbor, the Emperor Cantalabutte. He left the regency of the kingdom to his mother, the queen, and placed his wife and children in her care. Since he was likely to spend the entire summer in battle, the queen mother sent her daughter-in-law and the children to a country house in the forest, as soon as he was gone, so that she might gratify her horrible longing more easily. A few days later, she followed them there, and one evening she said to her steward, "I want to eat little Aurora for dinner tomorrow!"

"Ah, madam!" exclaimed the steward.

"That is my will," said the queen (and she said it in the tone of an ogress longing to eat fresh meat), "and I want her served up with *sauce Robert.*"

The poor man plainly saw that it was useless to trifle with an ogress. So he took his knife and went up to little Aurora's room.. She was then about four years old, and when she skipped over to him, threw her arms around his neck with a laugh, and asked him for some sweets, he burst into tears. The knife fell from his hands. Soon he went down into the kitchen court, killed a little lamb, and served it with such a delicious sauce that his mistress assured him she had never eaten anything so good. In the meantime he carried off little Aurora and gave her to his wife to conceal in the lodging she occupied at the far end of the kitchen court.

A week later, the wicked queen said to her steward, "I want to eat little Day for supper."

Determined to deceive her as before, he did not reply. He went in search of little Day and found him with a tiny foil in his hand, fencing with a large monkey, though he was only three years old. He carried him to his wife, who hid him where she had concealed his sister. Then he cooked a tender little goat in place of little Day, and the ogress thought it most delicious.

Thus far all was going well, but one evening this wicked queen said to the steward, "I want to eat the queen with the same sauce that I had with the children."

This time the poor steward despaired of being able to deceive her again. The young queen was now twenty years old, not counting the hundred years she had slept. Her skin was a little tough, though it was white and beautiful. Thus, where in the menagerie was he to find an animal that was just as tough as she was?

To save his own life he resolved he would cut the queen's throat and went up to her apartment. intending to carry out this plan. He worked himself up into a fit and entered the young queen's chamber, dagger in hand. However, he did not want to take her by surprise and thus repeated respectfully the order he had received from the queen mother.

"Do your duty!" said she, stretching out her neck to him. "Carry out the order given to you. Then I shall behold my children, my poor children, that I loved so much."

She had thought they were dead ever since they had been carried off without explanation.

"No, no, madam!" replied the poor steward, touched to the quick. "You shall not die, and you shall see your children again, but it will be in my house, where I have hidden them. And I shall again deceive the queen mother by serving her a young hind in your stead."

He led her straight to his own quarters, and after leaving her to embrace her children and weep with them, he cooked a hind that the queen ate at supper with as much appetite as if it had been the young queen. She felt content with her cruelty and intended to tell the king on his return that some ferocious wolves had devoured his wife and two children.

One evening when she was prowling as usual around the courts and poultry yards of the castle to inhale the smell of fresh meat, she overheard little Day crying in a lower room because his mother wanted to slap him for having been naughty. She also heard little Aurora begging forgiveness for her brother. The ogress recognized the voices of the queen and her children and, furious at having been duped, she gave orders in a tone that made everyone tremble,"Bring a large copper vat into the middle of the court early tomorrow morning."

[margin note: S.B. takes action]

When it was done the next day, she had the vat filled with toads, vipers, adders, and serpents, intending to fling the queen, her children, the steward, his wife, and his maidservant into it.

"Bring them forth with their hands tied behind them," she commanded.

When they stood before her, the executioners began preparing to fling them into the copper vat when the king, who was not expected back so soon, entered the courtyard on horseback. He had ridden posthaste, and greatly astonished, he demanded to know the meaning of the horrible spectacle, but nobody dared to tell, him. Then the ogress, enraged at the sight of the king's return, flung herself headfirst into the vat and was devoured by the horrible reptiles that she had commanded to be placed there. The king could not help but feel sorry, for she was his mother, but he speedily consoled himself in the company of his beautiful wife and children.

[margin note: those who want to devour will be devoured themselves]

Moral

To wait so long,
To want a man refined and strong,
Is not at all uncommon.
But: rare it is a hundred years to wait.
Indeed there is no woman
Today so patient for a mate.

Our tale was meant to show
That when marriage is deferred,
It is no less blissful than those of which you've heard.
Nothing's lost after a century or so.
And yet, for lovers whose ardor
Cannot be controlled and marry out of passion,
I don't have the heart their act to deplore
Or to preach a moral lesson.

[margin note: · Marriage not that blissful — prince is always leaving her]

[margin note: 2nd part (ogress) not included in morals]

Sleeping Beauty Must Die

The Plots of Perrault's "La belle au bois dormant"

Carolyn Fay

The cannibalism, storyline in Charles Perrault's "La belle au bois dormant" ("The Sleeping Beauty in the Woods") is both disturbing and fascinating, eliciting a wide range of critical response, even as the entire plot has been dropped from most children's editions and many subsequent adaptations.[1] Readers of Perraults 1697 tale know that after her long sleep the princess is threatened by her ogress mother-in-law, who wants to eat her and her two children. Thanks to the intervention of the ogress's steward, Sleeping Beauty and her children manage to avoid being eaten; however, when the ogress discovers them all alive, she prepares to throw the. whole lot—grandchildren, daughter-in-law, steward, and his family—into a vat of snakes, vipers, and toads. At that moment, Sleeping Beauty's husband, now king, returns from war. Rather than face her angry son, the ogress throws herself into the vat and is devoured by her own creatures. Thus a story about sleep ends as a tale of forbidden appetite, prompting Marc Soriano to assert that "La belle au bois dormant" is not one tale but two (125).

Indeed, the cannibalism plot raises many questions about the narrative coherence and structure of the tale. The prince hides his family from his mother for two years, because he fears her appetite for young flesh. Why, then, does he place the whole family under her protection when he becomes king? Furthermore, as the son of an ogress, would the prince not also be subject to ogrelike tendencies?[2] Why did Perrault include the cannibalism plot when his own moral alludes only to the sleep plot? Many critics account for the ogress story line through source study noting the similarities between the character and the spurned wife in Giambattista Basile's "Sole, Luna, e Talia" ("Sun, Moon, and Talia")[3] Jeanne Morgan maintains that the narrative incongruities in the tale result from Perrault's twin desire to remain true to his source and to adhere to the literary rules of *bienséances* (85–86). Psychoanalytic treatments of "La belle au bois dormant" often read the ogress as a necessary foil for Sleeping Beauty.[4] Two recent sociocultural analyses of the tale treat the ogress plot as integral to the text's overarching themes: Jean-Pierre van Elslande suggests that the ambivalent behavior of the prince/king toward his mother betrays a kind of powerlessness, which reflects Perrault's own ambivalence toward "les Grands" (453–54). In his study of food, visual spectacle, and the processes of acculturation in "La belle au bois dormant; Philip Lewis reads the cannibalism plot as central to Perrault's exploration of the tensions between the civilizing process and nature (133), Moreover, Lewis argues that the tale achieves symmetry through repetition: in each story line the princess is threatened by death and saved by her Prince Charming (150).

Although the narrative structure of the tale does seem, guided by repetition—or what Tzvetan Todorov calls the ideological organization, where different adventures are linked through the application of a higher, abstract rule (42)—the two plots diverge in their treatment of Sleeping Beauty's would-be assassins, Although the ogress, who serves as the agent of evil in the cannibalism plop meets a horrible death, the old fairy who curses

Carolyn Fay, "Sleeping Beauty Must Die: The Plots of Perrault's "La belle au bois dormant"," *Marvels & Tales: Journal of Fairy-Tale Studies*, vol. 22, no. 2, pp. 259–276. Copyright © 2008 by Wayne State University Press. Reprinted with permission.

the baby princess with death in the sleep plot goes unpunished and fades from the story For Bruno Bettelheim, this missing punishment is reason enough for the story line of the ogress, whose gruesome death ensures that "fairy-story justice" is accomplished (230).[5] The purpose of the cannibalism plot, then, would be to punish the ogress in the place of the old fairy substituting one woman, one death, for another. This suggests that the relationship between the two plots "is more complicated, and that, they are bound together by more than repetition. Reading Bettelheim's comment back through Lewis's observation about the repetitive structure of the tale opens up a slightly different question about this dual plot tale. Instead of "Why did Perrault include the cannibalism plot?" we may ask,"How does a tale of a sleeping princess become that of a hungry ogress?" In other words, what are the narrative processes that transform one plot into another, and what do these processes reveal about "La belle au bois dormant" as a whole?

This essay will trace the narrative progression of "La belle au bois dormant," showing that substitution is the organizing principle of the tale. Substitution underlies many of the repetitions in the story but more significantly it operates as the motor of the narrative, drawing the story out, through both metaphor and metonymy the "master tropes" of story in Peter Brooks's words (338), By following the metaphoric and metonymic substitutions that drive the tale, I will elucidate not only the transformation of the sleep plot into the cannibalism plot, but also the transformation of the central character: from sleeping princess to devouring mother-in-law. Each serves as a substitute for the other. The narratological reading of "La belle au bois dormant" allows us to understand the crucial role of the ogress and the function of her death in the tale's imagination. It also exposes the tale's underlying preoccupation: women who would, withdraw from, the societal *and* the narrative order must die.

A Detour from Death

It is Sleeping Beauty, of course, who is supposed to die. The king and queen, who had long prayed for her birth, throw a lavish christening party, followed by a banquet for her seven fairy godmothers. Each of the godmothers is given a magnificent golden case filled with jewel-encrusted cutlery. However, an eighth fairy shows up unexpectedly. She had not been invited, because no one had seen her for the last fifty years. Miffed that the royal family had neither invited her nor given her one of the golden cases of cutlery, the old fairy curses the baby princess: she will prick her hand on a distaff and die. Luckily, a younger fairy, who had not yet bestowed, a gift on the princess, is able to mitigate the curse, changing death to a hundred years' sleep.

The first half of "La belle au bois dormant" hinges upon the substitution of sleep for death. Before examining the effect of this substitution, let us consider how it works. Sleep and death have a long association with each other in Western culture, a relationship crystallized in their personification in Greek mythology as the identical twin brothers Hypnos and Thanatos. The brothering of sleep and death suggests that there is something other than mère resemblance that connects them. Montaigne, for example, writes that sleep serves to instruct and prepare us for death. While death is unknowable by the living, sleep is the next closest state: "Si nous ne la pouvons joindre [la mort], nous la pouvons approcher, nous la pouvons reconnoistre. ... Ce n'est pas sans raison qu'on nous fait regarder à nostre sommeil mesme, pour la ressemblance qu'il a de la mort" ("If we cannot contact death, we can approach it, we can recognize i t . ... It is not without reason that we see a resemblance to death in our own sleep" [351]).[6] For Montaigne, sleep and death are related on both metaphorical and metonymical registers. Sleep's immobility and passivity make it an apt metaphor for death, which in turn reinforces the metonymical relationship between them. Metonymy is a figure of substitution based not on analogy but on contiguity. In Montaigne's model sleep and death are related practically, separated only by degrees.

Moreover, Montaigne makes it clear that the metaphorical and the metonymical support each other. Whereas the tropes were once considered dichotomous by rhetoricians and linguists, an idea cemented by Roman

Jakobson's 1956 article on aphasia, recent scholarship has emphasized their interconnectedness, especially in regard to narrative prose.[7] Jakobson aligns metaphor with poetry and argues that metonymy is the dominant figure of prose, and realist fiction in particular, which uses contiguous digressions to advance the story (111). Subsequent theorists, however, have asserted that metaphor and metonymy must function together to ensure narrative progression. Gérard Genette convincingly argues that the interplay of metaphor and metonymy is crucial to the madeleine scene that gives rise to the entire narrative of Marcel Proust's *A la recherche du temps perdu.* While the taste of the cookie dipped in tea evokes involuntary memory in a way that seems purely metaphorical, Genette demonstrates that the event sets off a chain reaction that progresses through contiguity, calling forth successive pieces attached to Combray and to each other: room, house, village, and people (55). "C'est la métaphore qui retrouve le Temps perdu, mais c'est la métonymie qui le ranime, et le remet en marche" ("It is metaphor that finds Lost Time, but it is metonymy that reanimates it and sets it going again" [63]).

Genette's analysis of Proust suggests that metonymy and metaphor each play a vital and particular role in narrative progression. While metonymy moves us from point to point in the narrative, metaphor provides an organizing image that is "totalizing," in Brooks's words (91). Moreover, Brooks argues that this totalizing image is where the narrative wants to end. "We read the incidents of narration as 'promises and annunciations' of final coherence, that metaphor may be reached through the chain of metonymies" (93–94). The chain of metonymies must not only lead toward the metaphor at the end, but must also lead to the right end. One common tension in narrative, writes Brooks, is the possibility of a premature ending, or the wrong ending. The baby princess cursed with an early death is a good example of the threat of everything—her life and the story—ending too quickly. The necessary narrative response, according to Brooks, is delay or detour, until the correct end can be reached. "The complication of the detour is related to the danger of short- circuit: the danger of reaching the end too quickly, of achieving the improper death" (103–04). Thus, the "master tropes" of substitution, metaphor and metonymy, are the tools of proper narrative progression. Drawing the story out, meandering toward the final meaning, metaphor and metonymy create that middle space between beginning and conclusion, the "squiggle toward the end" (Brooks 104)—or 'l'espace dilatoire' ("the dilatory space"), as Barthes calls it—the space of deviation, false leads, twists, and turns (82).

Reading these observations back into "La belle au bois dormant," we see how the tale is one long detour from death, whose pronouncement at the banquet "fit frémir toute la compagnie" ("makes the whole gathering tremble" [188]). This is the fear of the wrong death at the wrong time. The story, after ail, has just begun. If we take a close look at the moment of the death curse, we see that in breaking off the expanding list of the princess's gifts, the curse forecloses the future narrative that the fairies are spinning. Each gift or talent relates to the previous one, a chain driven by metaphoric and metonymic associations between, key words. The first gift,"elle serait la plus belle personne du monde" ("she will be the most beautiful person, in the world") is followed by "l'esprit comme un Ange" ("a mind like an Angel's" [186]). On one level, beauty shifts laterally to intellect, while on another level, the princess's superlative, worldly beauty leads to the angel association. Another figurative shift takes us to the third gift,"une grâce admirable" ("an admirable grace"), which angels surely possess. Grace applies to the idea of movement, thus talent in dance, which then leads to singing: "elle chanterait comme un Rossignol" ("she would sing like a Nightingale" [186]). Although the nightingale is a common metaphor for singing, it also is the name of a particular organ stop that mimics the warbling of birds.[8] Thus "Rossignol" prepares the sixth gift: "qu'elle jouerait de toutes sortes d'instmments dans la dernière perfection" ("that she would play all sorts of instruments to the highest, perfection" [186–88]). The use of "dernière" is interesting because while in this context it conveys a sense of superiority the adjective also subtly evokes an ending, as its primary denotation is "last." Thus the next gift will be the last: death, which follows associatively from "la dernière perfection," and which halts the stream of gifts. Moreover, the death curse throws into doubt all of the previous talents bestowed on the princess, who may not live long enough to accomplish them fully Just as the curse short-circuits the chain of gift giving, it threatens to short- circuit the entire narrative. The pronouncement of the early death is also a pronouncement of an early end to the story

Death must be avoided for the story to continue. The attenuation of the death, curse to one hundred years' sleep constitutes the first substitution, the first step in the necessary delay. The enchanted, sleep does not. circumvent death entirely since presumably the princess is still mortal. She will die one- day but far in the future. This is underscored by the futility of the kings actions. He would rather foil death than delay it, so he behaves as though the death curse were still in effect, banning all spinning instruments "pour tâcher d'éviter le Malheur annoncé par la vieille" ("to try to avoid the Curse announced by the old fairy" [188]). The king is out of step with the story for the young fairy's sleep modification has already replaced the death curse. And of course, despite his edict, the princess does prick herself on a spindle: "comme elle était fort vive, un peu étourdie, et que d'ailleurs l'Arrêt des Fées l'ordonnait ainsi" ("as she was quite lively a little careless, and besides the Law of Fairies commanded it thus" [188]). The narrative follows the law of the enchantment, which has replaced premature death with sleep but has not ruled out eventual death. Always lurking beneath the enchanted sleep is the specter of death. When the prince comes to the enchanted chateau, he is startled by the sight of inert bodies lying everywhere: "c'était un silence affreux, l'image de la mort" ("there was a horrible silence, the image of death" [192]). Though the prince quickly realizes that everyone is slumbering, sleeps uncanny resemblance to death, reminds the reader of the original curse, and also foreshadows the future deaths threatened by the ogress.

But in the meantime, the substitution of sleep for premature death balloons the life span of the princess and the life span of the story, opening up new possibilities,"the dilatory space." Indeed, this movement is evident when the princess does succumb to her sleep. Arriving shortly afterward, the young fairy decides to extend the sleep enchantment spatially: she puts to sleep nearly everyone and everything in the castle—courtiers, ladies-in-waiting, maids, cooks, guards, horses, the princess's dog, and even the fires in the hearth. The princess's sleep is thus spread metonymically, touching the people and things around her. With great foresight, the young fairy imagines that the princess will need these supports when she awakens (189). In expanding the sleep curse outward, the young fairy has effectively expanded or dilated the future narrative forward: the princess will be able to resume her old life in one hundred years. The metonymic magic, wand of the young fairy has delayed death and guaranteed the progression of the narrative.

Metonymic and Metaphoric Magic

Although the young fairy fades from the story at this point, the chain of substitution that she has initiated with the sleep enchantment continues. Each substitution, whether it operates patently through metaphor or metonymy or both, functions to drive the story forward while creating the necessary delay of death.. After the sleep plot comes to its anticipated resolution—a hundred years later the prince penetrates the sleeping chateau and the princess awakens—the narrative effects the next shift. This is a much more subtle transition than the previous replacement of sleep for premature death. Indeed, as I noted earlier, many subsequent versions of the Sleeping Beauty tale end the story with the marriage of the prince and princess. There is a marriage in Perrault's account; however, it is preceded by a short episode that serves as a hinge between the sleep plot and the ensuing cannibalism plot. When sleep ends, it is replaced by hunger:

> Cependant tout le Palais s'était réveillé avec la Princesse; chacun songeait à faire sa charge, et comme ils n'étaient pas tous amoureux, ils mouraient. de faim; la Dame d'honneur, pressée comme les autres, s'impatienta, et dit tout haut à la Princesse que la viande était servie. (194–95)

[However, the entire palace had awakened with the princess; each thought of his tasks, and as they were not all in love, they were dying of hunger; the lady in waiting, as hurried as the others, grew impatient and announced to the princess that the meal was served.]

While the princess is distracted with her new love, her servants have awakened from their long sleep to hunger, and they prepare a banquet. They fulfill their duties precisely as the young fairy intended when she expanded the sleep enchantment to include them, ensuring the welfare of the princess and the household. In addition, they provide the next link in the chain of substitutions. Hunger quite naturally follows sleep, especially after one hundred years, and thus constitutes another metonymic substitution in the narrative. The servants' hunger works metaphorically too, as a substitute for the romantic appetites of the royal couple: "comme ils n'étaient pas tous amoureux" ("as they were not all in love" [99]). But it is the subsequent description of their hunger that anticipates and prepares the cannibalism plot: "ils mouraient de faim" ("they were dying of hunger" [194]). The servants are starving to death—figuratively of course—but the metaphor revives the idea of death. Just as when the prince beholds "the image of death," "they were dying of hunger" recalls both the initial death curse and the restored mortality and temporality of the chateau's inhabitants. No longer protected from the ravages of time in the bubble of sleep, the princess and her people awaken to the inevitability of appetites and of death. Moreover, the notion of "dying of hunger" foreshadows the story plot to come, where the princess and her children almost die from the ogress's hunger. Thus, while the shift from sleep to hunger prolongs the story and delays the end—the death—of the narrative, this shift also anticipates death *as* the end. At the tale's conclusion, of course, the ogress will die as a result of her own monstrous hunger.

What transports us from the servants' dying of hunger and the death of the ogress is a series of small substitutions that draw the story out. After the wedding and his first night with the princess, the prince returns to his own land, but lies to his parents about his whereabouts the night before. His fabricated story—of spending the night in the hut of a charcoal burner who gave him black bread and cheese to eat—is a veiled account of his wedding night and the banquet. The charcoal burner's occupation, after all, recalls the prince's fiery passion to find the princess—"il se sentait tout de feu" ("he felt himself on fire")—and likely refers also to the consummation of that passion (192). As the narrator slyly says, "ils dormirent peu" ("they slept little" [19.5]). The replacement story and the prince's subsequent lies allow him to lead a secret life for two years, the purpose of which is not unlike the hundred years of enchanted sleep. In terms of the plot, hiding the princess keeps her safe from the uncivilized appetite of the prince's ogress mother. In terms of the narrative progression, hiding the princess once again prolongs the story, long enough indeed for her to bear two children. Even the naming of the children follows the mechanism of substitution that fuels the narrative: the first is named "Aurore" ("Dawn") and the second "Jour, parce qu'il paraissait encore plus beau que sa soeur" ("Day, because he seemed even more beautiful than his sister" [195–97]). The names are chosen for both their metaphoric and metonymic power. Since Day necessarily follows Dawn, the brother is in some sense a substitute for the sister, aesthetically but also politically, as the male offspring will one day inherit the crown.

Accordingly, inheritance functions as the next substitution that spurs the story forward. When the king dies, the prince assumes the royal crown and brings his marriage out into the open. Having replaced his father, he perhaps believes that his authority alone will be enough to guarantee the safety of his family. The substitution of father for son affects the status of all the principles in the story: hereafter, the prince will be referred to as "le Roi" ("the King"), the princess as "la Reine" ("the Queen") or "la jeune Reine" ("the young Queen"), and the ogress as "la Reine-mère" ("the Queen-Mother"). When the new king leaves to make war on his neighbor, another shift in power must take place: "Il laissa la Régence du Royaume à la Reine sa mère, et lui recommanda fort sa femme et ses enfants" ("He left the Regency of the kingdom to the Queen, his mother, and left his wife and children under her protection" [197]). The substitution of ogress mother-in-law for loving father and husband allows the story to develop the cannibalism plot: the queen mother will now attempt to eat her daughter-in-law and grandchildren.

Once again death seems certain, as the ogress holds all of the power. She orders her chief steward to kill her granddaughter Aurore and cook her in a *sauce Robert* But just as death is circumvented by the substitution of the sleep enchantment, the steward saves Aurore by serving a baby lamb instead. Thus begins a game of substitution of animals for people, a ruse aided by the *sauce Robert,* which, Louis Marin argues, functions as a complex culinary sign that makes it impossible for the ogress to discern the difference between human flesh and animal meat (153). But the steward's choices of animal meat are far from accidental. Metaphor plays a significant role. The lamb is a suitable replacement for Aurore, who throws her arms around the steward's neck "en *sautant* et en riant" ("while *jumping* and laughing" [198; emphasis added]). When it is Jour's turn to be eaten, the steward kills a small kid, whose horns perhaps recall the fencing foil Jour plays with (198). Finally, the ogress demands to eat her daughter-in-law. The steward despairs, as he does not believe he can pull off the ruse one more time, precisely because it will be difficult to find an adequate animal substitute for the queen, whose skin is "un peu dure, quoique belle et blanche; et le moyen de trouver dans la Ménagerie une bête aussi dure que cela?" ("a little tough, although beautiful and white; and where in the menagerie could he find an animal as tough as that?" [198]). When the chain of substitution fails, death seems imminent. The steward resolves to kill her, but relents when she willingly extends her neck to his dagger. Instead, he reveals that, her children are alive, and. he prepares in her place "une jeune biche" ("a young doe"), perhaps inspired by the queen's compliant behavior.

Death is averted once more, until the ogress discovers the queen and her children. Enraged at the deception, she prepares to have them thrown into a vat ,of toads, snakes, and vipers—"lowly beasts," as Lewis calls them (133). Why does she prepare this end for the family when she could just order them slaughtered for her own consumption? Something has changed; her appetite for revenge is now greater than her appetite for flesh. As Lewis suggests, the ogress's culinary practice degenerates: from her demands to eat human flesh prepared in a *sauce Robert,* to her plan to tell her son that his family was devoured by wolves, to her preparation of the vat of toads and snakes. Because the humans were replaced by farm and game animals, we can trace a downward, descent, of animal hierarchy in the narrative's imagination: from, domesticated or herbivorous animals (lamb, goat, and deer), to violent carnivores (wolves), to reptilian and amphibian creatures often associated with evil or sorcery. Marin reminds us that this last group would not likely eat human flesh (155); however, the snakes are an apt choice for the ogress since some species are cannibalistic. The lowly beasts thus function as a metaphoric substitute for the ogress. And just when it seems that death can be deferred no longer, the "rex ex machina" allows the final substitution that both saves the family and provides the proper death for the end of the narrative. Rather than face her son, the ogress throws herself into the vat of beasts and is instantly devoured. The mother-in-law takes the place of the family; and for the king, the family takes the place of his mother: "Le Roi ne laissa pas d'en être fâché: elle était sa mère; mais il s'en consola bientôt avec sa belle femme et ses enfants" ("The King could not help but be upset: she was his mother; but he soon consoled himself with his beautiful wife and children" [200]). The chain of substitution functions to delay death long enough to reach the "right" end, which encompasses both death and happiness, however ambiguous.[9] The narrative has now come full circle—from death announced, to death averted, to death achieved—via the mechanism of substitution.

The Sleeping Woman and the Devouring Woman

Substitution allows Sleeping Beauty to avoid death three times. However, the particular supplanting that closes "La belle au bois dormant" is a bit more complex than the previous substitutions. When the ogress dies in the place of Sleeping Beauty, the latter assumes the full place of the former in the kingdom and in the king's heart. This is an exchange that occurs on a couple of levels. Sleeping Beauty replaces the ogress socially and politically a shift marked by the transfer of the "queen" title. Submitting herself to the death meant for Sleeping Beauty; the ogress functions as a narratological replacement for her daughter-in-law. Both substitutions are metonymic: the ogress is the final victim in the chain of consumption; Sleeping Beauty is the next queen after the ogress. Indeed, the in-law relationship appears to operate patently through contiguity: the new spouse becomes related to the parent-in-law through marriage with his or her child.[10] However, there may also be a relationship of similarity if the child chooses a spouse who resembles one of his or her parents in some way. While the princess seems to be the polar opposite of her monstrous mother-in-law, the two women share key characteristics that make them apt, if also surprising, substitutes for each other. In other words, there is a strong metaphorical connection between Sleeping Beauty and the ogress.

How do these two figures resemble each other? Let us first consider the nature of the sleeping woman and her function in the sleep plot. The Sleeping Beauty tale, in its many versions, is often read as a tale of renewal, rebirth, and resurrection, similar to the myth of Demeter and Persephone. The princess's long sleep and subsequent reawakening would represent the cycle of nature.[11] Reading more specifically, Bettelheim interprets the episode as symbolic of sexual maturation, where the prick of the spindle signals the onset of menstruation (232–33). Numerous critics have discredited Bettelheim's approach to fairy tales, and Jean Bellemin-Noël in particular points out that in both the Perrault and Grimm versions there is no mention of blood when the princess pricks her finger (114–15).[12] Nevertheless, Bettelheim does offer an additional interpretation of the princess's sleep, one that can be supported by Perrault's text. While the hundred years' sleep represents a necessary period of withdrawal and focus on the self, there is also an antisocial aspect to it. Bettelheim calls this "the isolation of narcissism," noting that the princess's sleep encompasses nearly everyone else in the castle (234). When she falls asleep, the rest of the world ceases to exist for her. This observation is largely consistent with the common experience of normal sleep: closed off to the stimulus of the outside world, the sleeper is turned inward. Moreover, normal sleep is not an experience that can be shared. The sleeper is necessarily a solitary individual, inhabiting a private world.

Furthermore, the sleeper can also be closed off to narrative, as is the case with the sleeping princess. Once the chateau has been prepared for the long sleep, and the kind fairy and the king and queen have departed, what more can the narrative say about one hundred years' sleep? When the trees, brambles, and thorns grow up around the chateau,"entrelacées les unes dans les autres" ("intertwined"), it is as though the narrative sews itself up (191). Nothing can be told about the sleeping princess until it is time for the prince to part the forest and wake her up, as though reopening a book. Indeed, the narrator surmises that the good fairy must have supplied the princess with pleasant dreams, although there is no way to confirm it: "l'Histoire n'en dit pourtant rien" ("History says nothing about it" [194]). The story cannot see into sleep, and thus the hundred years' sleep constitutes a kind of narrative suspension, in addition to a suspension of the princess's life.

Of course, this suspension, or withdrawal from the external world and from the narrative, is necessary to guarantee the princess's life. But what kind of life is this? A hundred years' sleep may as well be death for an adolescent in the full bloom of youth and sexuality The story understands this: "La bonne Fée qui lui avait *sauvé* la vie, en la *condamnant* à dormir cent ans" ("The good Fairy who had *saved* her life by *condemning* her to sleep for a hundred years" [189; emphasis added]). Sleep's salvation still constitutes a horrible curse, one that resembles death too closely The servants throw water on the sleeping princess's face, they slap and. decorset her, but. "rien ne la faisait revenir" ("nothing would make her come back") [189]). She is gone. Only the sound of her breath signifies that she is not dead, a marker similar to the reddened faces of the servants whom the prince finds strewn about the chateau (192). Sleep functions as a border space: neither life nor death, it nevertheless displays characteristics of both. The sleeping princess thus embodies a kind of paradox: she sleeps to preserve her life, but her life such as it is resembles death.

The ogress shares many of the characteristics of Sleeping Beauty, mirroring the sleeping woman by virtue of her own narcissism and the paradox of her hunger. Perrault alludes to this broadly in the segment where the prince first spies the castle in the sleeping woods. Rumor has it that it may be a haunted castle, a meeting place for witches, or the abode of a child-eating ogre who alone has the power to penetrate the forest (192).[13] Noting the irony of these tall tales, Anne Duggan remarks that,"it is as if the rumors about Sleeping Beauty's castle refer instead to the [ogress] queen" (154). Indeed, the ogre-in- the-woods rumor not only foreshadows the cannibalism plot, but also slyly hints at the deeper metaphorical relationship between the two figures. Like the sleeper, the ogress is a figure turned inward upon herself. Although she adopts some of the cultural rituals surrounding the consumption of food—such as her request that the human flesh be cooked and served in a *sauce Robert*—there is a strong antisocial aspect to her eating. Once the king is away, the ogress relocates the family from the royal palace to "une maison de campagne dans les bois, pour pouvoir plus aisément assouvir son horrible envie" ("a country house in the woods, so that she could more easily satisfy her horrible desire" [197]). Once again, the forest functions as the locus of isolation, providing cover for the devourer as it did for the sleeper.[14] Furthermore, the ogress dines alone, in contrast to the two previous banquet scenes, which emphasize communal eating. Of course, the antisocial dimension of the ogress's eating is abundantly clear in her choice of food: she would eat her own kin and living companions, those closest to her in blood and in geographical proximity. The ogress's feeding is remarkably similar to the way sleep overtakes everyone surrounding the enchanted princess. At the height of her frenzy, the ogress even prepares to destroy her steward, his wife, and their servant. Both the sleeping woman and the devouring woman function as a kind of vortex, pulling in the people surrounding them.

The ogress is most destructive and most narcissistic in her desire to eat her own grandchildren. If she abandons the social and cultural functions of eating, as Lewis argues (152–53), the ogress also rejects the bio-evolutionary function of eating, through her desire to eat of her own blood. One eats to live. Sustenance provides the organism with energy to create and procreate. But though satisfying her appetite may keep the ogress alive, it would destroy future generations. In seeking to eat her own progeny, the ogress would cut off her own bloodline, a kind of self-cannibalism that she enacts at the end by jumping into her own vat of devouring creatures. Like the enchanted sleeping princess existing between life and death, the cannibalistic ogress is a paradox: by feeding her hunger, she destroys herself. This is not just consumption out of control, but a regressive hunger. The grandchildren, after all, are named "Dawn" and "Day." The ogress would turn back the clock by eating them, imaginarily returning us to the beginning of the tale, where a childless couple yearns for offspring. In this way the ogress not only threatens to cut off the royal bloodline of her own house and that of Sleeping Beauty's parents, but she also endangers the narrative's advancement, looping the story back on itself. Where the princess's sleep introduces a gap that cannot, be narrativized, the ogress's hunger represents the possibility that the story will consume itself, like the serpent devouring its own tail. Although radically different on the surface, the sleeping woman and the devouring woman are excellent substitutes for each other, because they fulfill the same narrative function in the tale. Each constitutes a central, paradoxical figure who threatens the narrative progression, and who ultimately must die.

The Death of Sleeping Beauty

But the princess does not die. That is, after all, the point of the story. However, awakening at the end of the hundred years' sleep does constitute a death of sorts: the end of the princess's role as Sleeping Beauty. No longer the immobile, silent, and closed woman who is effectively unavailable to the narrative, the awakened princess is quickly recuperated and transformed into a wife, a mother, a queen—a woman defined by societal and familial roles. In that sense, the solitary narcissistic Sleeping Beauty does die. Furthermore, she dies too by virtue of her relationship with the ogress. When the ogress literally takes the princess's place in the vat of deadly creatures, she reinforces their link as substitutes for each other Behind the satisfyingly "right" death of the evil ogress lies the symbolic death of the princess.

What does this death mean? What dies in the imaginary death of Sleeping Beauty are all of the qualities she shares with the ogress: her antisocial behavior her paradoxical nature, her ability to trouble the narrative progression. In fact, reading the ogress and Sleeping Beauty as substitutes for each other highlights the extent to which "La belle au bois dormant" is a tale about problematic women. In turning away from the outside world—the one in her sleep, the other in her appetite—they potentially disrupt the narrative. In this light, even the old fairy who curses the princess is part of the pattern, The king and queen did not invite the fairy to the baby's baptism, because "il y avait plus de cinquante ans qu'elle n'était sortie d'une Tour et qu'on la croyait morte, ou enchantée" ("it had been more than fifty years since she had left her Tower, and she was believed to be dead or enchanted" [186]). Indeed, Sleeping Beauty is targeted with the very fate of which the old fairy is suspected: death first, and then enchantment in a tower. Now we can understand the seeming disappearance of the old fairy from the tale: she functions as an anterior double to both Sleeping Beauty and the ogress. The original antisocial woman is replaced by the sleeping princess, who is then subsequently replaced by the ogress. And like her successors, the old fairy threatens the narrative progression, in her case by introducing death too soon.

In fact, the whole tale springs from the reclusive fairy's failed attempt to rejoin society "La belle au bois dormant" thus suggests that a woman's assimilation is best achieved through marriage. This is the prominent theme of the moral, appended to the story While the relationship between Perrault's verse morals and his prose narratives is an entire question in itself, we can approach the moral of "La belle au bois dormant" as just another instance of metaphorical and metonymical substitution.[15] As the hindmost piece of text attached to the tale, the moral would seem to offer the final word on the meaning of the narrative, the last link in the chain of substitutions on a macro level. The moral to "La belle au bois dormant" even mirrors the plot structure of the narrative: the author offers one meaning and then adds another, prolonging the lesson: "La Fable semble encor vouloir nous faire entendre" ("The Fable also seems to want us to understand" [200]). However, after this stirring tale of enchantment, attempted cannibalism, and gruesome death, the two morals are rather flippant. Both appear to praise the virtues of waiting for marriage. First, Perrault jokes about the idea of a woman waiting one hundred years for an appropriate spouse; then he speaks more generally about delaying marriage, declaring the tale's message to be: "Et qu'on ne perd rien pour attendre" ("And one loses nothing by waiting" [200]). As I noted earlier, there is no reference to the ogress and her attempts to eat her family. The two morals read like a deflection, as though. Perrault were applying his own *sauce Robert* to leave us with a particular taste in our mouths as we come away from the story. But in fact it is the irony of the morals that betrays their meaning and links them back to the prose narrative. Although both make jabs at women who single-mindedly pursue marriage, each moral ends on a negative that undermines the purported message of the tale:

On ne trouve plus de femelle,
Qui dormît si tranquillement.
…
Mais le sexe avec tant d'ardeur,
Aspire à la foi conjugale,
Que je n'ai. pas la force ni le coeur,
De lui prêcher cette morale. (200)

[No longer will one find a woman

Who would sleep so tranquilly.

…

But the fair sex with such ardor,

Aspires to the conjugal trust,

That I have neither the strength nor the heart

To preach to her this moral]

On the one hand, no woman exists who would wait as long as Sleeping Beauty for her prince; on the other hand, the author admits that he has neither the strength nor the *heart* to advocate waiting for marriage. Perrault thus slyly reverses his proposed lessons. The moral of "La belle au bois dormant" would be: women, marry *without* delay, a message that is consistent with the narrative's theme. Isolating oneself from the world, whether through sleep or appetite, is destructive. If such a woman cannot be reintegrated into society—and the widowed ogress is really beyond redemption—she must die.

The death of the ogress is of paramount importance. It carries a global meaning that resonates throughout the tale. It is not simply the punishment of evil, but the obliteration of the woman who withdraws from the social order, and who would trouble the narrative order as well. This death not only supplies the desired narrative end but also represents the elimination of the forces that would forestall, short-circuit, or otherwise endanger the narrative progression. The literal death of the ogress and the imaginary death of Sleeping Beauty ensure the full dilation and closure of the story. This is the right death at the right time. Thanks to the play of substitution, the original death curse comes full circle, from one problematic woman to another. And thanks to the play of substitution, one problematic woman *is* another. The self-cannibalistic, gesture that closes the narrative is thus emblematic of the whole tale: like the closed circle she is, the antisocial woman destroys herself. Ultimately, then, the original death curse holds the answer to my initial question about Perrault's two plots. The tales of enchanted sleep and forbidden appetite are the systematic means of managing and directing death to the most potent and symbolic target. And the narratological reading reveals that target to be a quite specific creature. At the heart of "La belle au bois dormant" is a warning about self- isolating women. It is not enough to banish, the hungry ogresses and mean fairies of the world. Sleeping Beauty must, die too.

Notes

A preliminary version of this article was presented at the 2004 Group for Early Modern Cultural Studies Conference, held in Orlando, Florida, from November 18 to 21, 2004. I would like to thank my fellow panel speakers and the participants for their- useful questions and suggestions.

1. The Grimm brothers' 1857 "Dornröschen" ("Briar Rose") ends with Sleeping Beauty's marriage to the prince. Most modern interpretations, such as Disney's 1959 film *Sleeping Beauty*, also drop the ogress story line among other alterations. See Heidi Anne Heiner's *SurLaLune Fairy Tale Pages* for an annotated list of contemporary versions of the Sleeping Beauty tale in literature, film, poetry, and theater.

2. Francois Rigolot pursues the prince's ogre heritage, revealing several moments in the text that suggest, or at least leave open the possibility, that he too is subject to his mother's power and inclinations (94–95).

3. "Sole, Luna, e Talia," from the *Pentamerone* (1634), is commonly held to be Perrault's chief source for "La belle au bois dormant," along with the tale of Zellandine in the fourteenth-century *Roman de Perce forest*. In Basile's tale the sleeping beauty, Talia, is impregnated in her sleep by a king who already has a wife. The jealous queen plots to have Talia's two children cooked and served to the king, but as in

Perrault's version Talia and her children are saved and the queen is killed. For more on Perrault's possible sources, see Soriano (125–34) and Robert (87–90).

4. In her Jungian analysis of the tale, Barbara Bucknall suggests that the ogress represents the shadow side of the sleeping princess (101).

5. Bettelheim's treatment of fairy tales in his 1976 *The Uses of Enchantment,* has been widely criticized for its misreading of Freudian theory and its universalizing approach to children and the tales. See, in particular, Donald Flaase (359–60) and Jack Zipes (*Breaking the Magic Spell* 185–88). Although I agree with both Zipes's and Haase's overall assessment, I find that Bettelheim makes some useful remarks about the Sleeping Beauty tale, which I will explore in this essay

6. All translations are my own.

7. Jakobson conceives of metaphor and metonymy as fundamentally opposed tropes in competition with each other (113).

8. See the 1926 *Dictionnaire pratique et historique de la musique* by Michel Brenet (395).

9. As Rigolot suggests, the son of an ogress may "console" himself by drowning his sorrows in food (95). Sleeping Beauty and her children may still be in danger. The ambiguity of the closing line of the tale indicates an additional substitution that would continue the story: the son will take the role of the mother.

10. See Marina Warner's chapter on the role of the stepmother/mother-in-law in fairy tales. With regard to Sleeping Beauty Warner suggests that the princess's sleep represents "the dark time that can follow the first encounter between the older woman and her new daughter-in-law" (220).

11. Many critics discuss the theme of renewal with regard to Sleeping Beauty, including Marie-Louise von Franz (24), Deborah Greenhill, and P L. Travers (60–61).

12. Nor is there blood in Basile's version. While she spins, a piece of stalk gets lodged underneath Talia's fingernail, and she falls down, seemingly dead. Talia awakens only when one of her babies sucks the splinter out (Basile 685–86).

13. This may provide the first clue of the prince's ogre lineage, as the forest brambles part for him quite easily leading Rigolot to assert that the prince may be more sinister than the tale would have us believe (94–95).

14. Rigolot notes this parallel, calling the woods "un lieu stratégique identique" ("an identical, strategic location") for both the sleep and the ogress episodes. He connects the princess and the ogress through the figure of Diana, goddess of the hunt, who embodies characteristics of both the mother- and daughter-in-law (96).

15. In his preface to the *Contes en vers,* Perrault defends the literariness of the fairy tale by invoking the critical standard of "plaire et instruire," whereby art should be both pleasing and instructive (77). The moral, then, would serve as proof that the fairy tale indeed has a lesson to impart. Critics, however, assert that the relationship between the morals and the prose narratives is much more intricate. See Lewis C. Seifert (51–58) and Morgan (35–54) for two different interpretations of the role of the morals in Perrault's fairy tales.

Works Cited

Barthes, Roland. S/Z. Paris: Editions du Seuil, 1970.

Basile, Giambattista. "Sun, Moon, and Talia." Zipes, *The Great Fairy Tale Tradition* 685–88.

Bellemin-Noel, Jean. *Les contes etleurs fantasmes.* Paris: PU de France, 1983.

Bettelheim, Bruno. *The Uses of Enchantment: The Meaning and Importance of Fairy Tales.* New York: Vintage, 1976.

Brenet, Michel. *Dictionnaire pratique et historique de la musique.* Ed. Amedee Gastoué. Paris: A. Colin, 1926.

Bucknall, Barbara J. "'La Belle au bois dormant' par Perrault." *Humanities Association Review* 26 (1975): 96–105.

Brooks, Peter. *Reading for the Plot: Design and Intention in Narrative.* Cambridge: Harvard UP, 1984.

Duggan, Anne E. Salonnières, *Furies, and Fairies: The Politics of Gender and Cultural Change in Absolutist France.* Newark: U of Delaware P, 200.5.

Genette, Gérard. "Metonymie chez Proust." *Figures III.* Paris: Seuil, 1972. 41–63.

Greenhill, Deborah. "Thorn Hedges & Rose Bushes: Meaning in "The Sleeping Beauty." *Folklore and Mythology Studies* 2 (1978): 20–26.

Grimm, Jacob, and Wilhelm Grimm. "Dornröschen." Zipes, *Great Fairy Tale Tradition* 696–98.

Haase, Donald. "Yours, Mine, or Ours? Perrault, the Brothers Grimm, and the Ownership of Fairy Tales." *The Classic Fairy Tales: Texts, Criticism.* Eel. Maria Tatar. New York: Norton, 1999. 353–64.

Heiner, Heidi Anne. "Modern Interpretations of Sleeping Beauty." *SurLaLune Fairy Tale Pages.* Feb. 14, 2005; Sept. 15, 2005. http://www.surlalunefaiiytales.com/sleepingbeauty/index.html

Jakobson, Roman. "Two Aspects of Language and Two Aspects of Aphasic Disturbances." *Fundamentals of Language.* By Roman Jaksobson and Morris Halle. The Hague: Mouton, 1956. 69–96. Rpt. in *Language in Literature.* Ed. Krystyna Pomorska and Stephen Rudy. Cambridge: Belknap/FIarvard UP, 1987. 95–114.

Lewis, Philip. *Seeing through the Mother Goose Tales: Visual Turns in the Writings of Charles Perrault.* Stanford: Stanford UP, 1996.

Marin, Louis. *La parole mangée et autres essais théologico-politiques.* Paris: Méridiens Klincksieck, 1986.

Montaigne, Michel de. *Essais: Oeuvres complètes.* Ed. Albert Thibaudet. and Maurice Rat. Paris: Gallimard, 1962.

Morgan, Jeanne. *Perrault's Morals for Moderns.* New York: Peter Lang, 1985.

Perceforest. Ed. Gilles Roussineau. Vol. 3. Geneva: Droz, 1993. 3 vols. 1979–93.

Perrault, Charles. "La belle au bois dormant." *Contes.* Ed. Catherine Magnien. Paris: Livre de poche, 2006. 185–200.

—Preface. *Contes en vers: Contes.* By Perrault. Ed. Catherine Magnien. Paris: Livre de poche, 2006. 77–82.

Rigolot, Frangois. "Les songes du savoir de la 'Belle endormie' à la 'Belle au bois dormant.'" *Littérature* (May 1985): 91–106.

Robert, Raymonde. *Le conte de fées littéraire en France de la fin du XVIIe à la fin du. XVIIIe siècle.* Nancy: PU de Nancy, 1981.

Seifert, Lewis C. *Fairy Tales, Sexuality, and Gender in France, 1690–1715: Nostalgic Utopias.* Cambridge: Cambridge UP, 1.996.

Sleeping Beauty. Dir. Clyde Geronimi. Walt Disney, 1959.

Soriano, Marc. *Les contes de Perrault: Culture savante et traditions populaires.* Paris: Gallimard, 1968.

Travers, P L. *About the Sleeping Beauty.* New York: McGraw Hill, 1975.

Todorov, Tzvetan. "The 2 Principles of Narrative." Trans. Philip E. Lewis. *Diacritics* 1.1 (1971): 37–44.

Van Elslande, Jean-Pierre. "Parole d'enfant: Perrault et le cleclin du Grand Siécle." *Papers on French Seventeenth-Century Literature* 26 (1999): 439–54.

Von Franz, Marie-Louise. *La femme dans les contes de fées.* Trans. Francine Saint René Taillandier. Paris: Albin Michel, 1993.

Warner, Marina. *From the Beast to the Blonde: On Fairy Tales and Their Tellers.* 1994. New York: Farrar, Straus & Giroux, 1995.

Zipes, Jack. *Breaking the Magic Spell: Radical Theories of Folk and Fairy Tales.* Rev. ed. Lexington: UP of Kentucky, 2002.

—, trans. and ed. *The Great Fairy Tale Tradition: From Straparola and Basile to the Brothers Grimm.* New York: Norton, 2001.

Wicked Stepmothers

The Sleeping Beauty

Marina Warner

This is the world we wanted.
All who would have seen us dead
are dead. I hear the witch's cry
Break in the moonlight through a sheet
of sugar: God rewards.
Her tongue shrivels into gas …

Louise Glück

The word in French for stepmother is the same as the word for mother-in-law—belle-mère. Latin, Greek, Italian, German, have distinct words for the two relations, and both feature in their romances and fairy tales. In English usage, 'mother-in-law' meant stepmother until the mid-nineteenth century, while the term 'daughter-in-law' was used for stepdaughters as well. Although the term 'stepmother' was not used, it seems, for a husband's mother, there was clearly some confusion. The Oxford English Dictionary gives examples occurring from Saint Bridget's visions (translated in 1516) to Thackeray, who, as late as 1848 in Vanity Fair, is still using the word in the sense of stepmother.

'Mother-in-law' is of course the *mot juste* for a stepmother: the new wife becomes the mother of the former wife's children by law, not by nature. It is still the custom for orphaned stepchildren to call the new wife of their father by whatever name they called their mothers, and in England today it is quite common for daughters-in-law to call their husband's mother Mum, or whatever diminutive is used in his family.

The mother who persecutes heroines like Cinderella or Snow White may conceal beneath her cruel features another familiar kind of adoptive mother, not the stepmother but the mother-in-law, and the time of ordeal through which the fairytale heroine passes may not represent the liminal interval between childhood and maturity, but another, more socially constituted proving ground or threshold: the beginning of marriage.

The absent mother may not have died in fact, though many did; she may have died symbolically according to the laws of matrimony that substitute the biological mother in a young woman's life with another. Taking the story from one vantage point, and imagining that the storyteller is remembering her own life, and is speaking as a daughter-in-law, we can hear her venting all her antagonism against the older woman who as it were bewitched her and her potential allies, including the man she married: stories of the Beauty and the Beast group conjure a spouse to whom the young woman has been sacrificed at her father's wish, and then relate how an old and wicked fairy, usually with some kind of family hold on him—in Villeneuve's version, she is his foster mother and his mother's best friend—has cast the spell on him that makes him hideous and stupid, and unable to express his love to his bride until that spell is broken.

The weddings of fairy tale bring the traditional narratives to a satisfying open ending which allows the possibility of hope; but the story structure masks the fact that many stories picture the conditions of marriage during the course of their telling. It is clearly a late, conventional moral reflex on the part of Mother Goose to make *marriage* the issue between Beauty and the Beast: Beauty is living alone with the Beast from the moment she agrees to save her father by leaving home. The issue is not sex, but love, and the pledging of lifelong mutual attachment. Similarly, the Sleeping Beauty's enchanted sleep or Rapunzel's magic imprisonment may not represent the slow incubation of selfhood, of consciousness of the Other and eventual sexual fulfilment. Rather, it may stand for the dark time that can follow the first encounter between the older woman and her new daughter-in-law, the period when the young woman can do nothing, take charge of nothing, but suffer the sorcery and the authority—and perhaps the hostility—of the woman whose house she has entered, whose daughter she has become.

Perrault's 'La Belle au bois dormant' (Sleeping Beauty) resembles, as many of his fairy tales do, a story in Giambattista Basile's collection of sixty years before, and both of them ring changes on a tale which appears **in** a vast Arthurian prose romance of the fourteenth century, *Perceforest*. *Perceforest* was first printed in 1528 and appeared in Italian as soon as three years later; it may have been known to Basile in this version. With regard to the familial conflicts represented in fairy tales, Basile and Perrault diverge, and are in turn reinterpreted by later retellings of 'Sleeping Beauty'; the changes are almost funny, they are so revealing of social prejudices and expectations.

In Basile, the saviour hero is already married to someone else at the start of the story; out hunting, he comes upon the sleeping beauty Talia, who has pricked her finger on a sliver of flax. When she will not wake up, however much he shouts, he 'plucked from her the fruits of love' (as Basile puts it), fathering two children on her in the act, twins called Sole and Luna. One of the babies, trying to nurse on the body of his comatose mother, sucks her finger instead of her breast, and so draws out the splinter of flax that has caused her to fall into her enchanted sleep. She wakes. The king, who had meanwhile forgotten about his little adventure, finds himself a year later riding in the same woods and it comes back to mind; he discovers his second family awake and flourishing. His wife suspects him, and she takes the steps that prefigure the manoeuvres of other ogresses, like Snow White's (step)mother: by a ruse, she summons the twins to court, then orders the cook 'to butcher them and turn them into various delicacies and sauces to give them to their vile father'. The cook, like the huntsman in 'Snow White', is too softhearted to kill the twins, and picks two goat's kids instead, which he serves 'in a hundred different dishes'; the king tucks in, exclaiming all the while with relish at the deliciousness of it all, while the queen grimly comments, 'Eat up, you're eating what's your very own.' To which he responds, in anger, 'I know very well I'm eating what's my own, because you have brought nothing to this house.' This taunt on the childlessness of their union does not excite Basile's pity for her; and is not intended to stir ours.

The queen is a Medea, a Lady Macbeth, a murderous and unnatural, unsexed anomaly, who then tricks Talia into coming to court to visit her, and berates her furiously, and will not listen when Talia protests she was fast asleep throughout the escapade and therefore blameless. A huge pyre is prepared for Talia's burning but the queen, at her rival's entreaties, allows her to take off her clothes beforehand—partly, says Basile sourly, because she coveted her fine embroideries and jewels. Like Bluebeard's wife, Talia screams as she plays for time, taking off each garment one by one, until at the very last moment, as she is being dragged across to the cauldron now boiling on the fire, the king at last answers her yells for help He asks for his children; his wife tells him that, like Titus Andronicus, he has eaten them. He instantly orders that she be thrown into the flames instead, along with her accomplices. But the cook pleads for his life, when it comes to his turn to die, by revealing the children he saved. The children, found again, are reunited with their father, who promotes the cook to gentleman of the bedchamber and marries Talia.

Basile's cheerful cynicism and often scabrous immoralism continues the tradition of Boccaccio; though so much closer to Perrault in time, Basile is far distant from him in spirit. In Perrault's version of 'The Sleeping Beauty', the vengeful wife, who is herself destroyed by the fire she prepared for her rival, changes into the adventurous prince's mother, who, says Perrault baldly, *'était de race Ogresse'* (was of the Ogre race) and, according to the tendency of ogres, liked eating the fresh meat of little children. The story follows the lines of Basile's version except that the queen mother specifies to the cook that she wants little Aurora dished up with a particular gourmet sauce *'la sauce Robert'*. A few days later, it is the little boy's turn. But in both cases, the tender-hearted cook has switched them, for a lamb and a kid respectively. The queen then expresses a desire to eat their mother, her daughter-in-law, as well. The once sleeping Beauty agrees meekly to her own death, as she imagines her children have preceded her. Again, the cook spares her, and serves a hind in her place; but a few days later the queen overhears one of the children crying in her hiding place, and, furious that they have escaped her, she orders a cauldron filled with toads and vipers and eels and snakes for her daughter-in-law, the babies, the steward and his wife and their servant into the bargain. The king arrives, in the nick of time, and his mother, enraged at being baulked, throws herself headfirst into the pot and 'was immediately devoured by the horrible creatures she had had put into it'. (As if the boiling water were not sufficient to kill her.) Perrault concludes, with his customary dryness: 'The king did not fail to be cross about it: she was his mother; but he soon consoled himself :with his beautiful wife and children'.

Basile told of adultery; in his harsh tale, the first wife, in her infertility, commits a crime against the family. Perrault adapted the tale to speak of a more palatable crime: cannibalism seemed then much less scandalous than rape, adultery and bigamy, and more suited to the childish fantasy of the invoked audience. But Perrault's modified, still gruesome coda to the fairy tale no longer appears, after the eighteenth century, in children's editions. The story follows instead the Grimms' more romantic and innocuous account, *'Dornröschen'*, (Little Briar Rose), and ends with the prince's famous saving kiss that wakes the sleeping beauty and leads to their wedding. Sometimes, for propriety's sake, the kiss is left, out, too. The macabre excesses of Basile and Perrault were dismaying to the same Victorian editors who, aiming at children, also dropped Perrault's *'Peau d'Ane'* The story's leading character, the terrible queen, migrated instead into the pages of the Grimms' 'Snow White'—as a wicked stepmother. It took Disney's film to make her face a familiar terror—her double face, for she appears twice over as an unsexed woman, endangering and destabilizing due order. First as the raven- haired queen ('Mirror, mirror on the wall … ') and then disguised as the old beggarwoman who gives Snow White the apple which chokes her. Basile's villain was a jealous wife, Perrault's a jealous mother-in-law; in our times, bad women come in the form of (step)mothers.

The doubling of negative female power has become very interesting to modern interpreters of fairy tales: in the recent English National Opera production of *Hansel and Gretel*, the opera by Engelbert Humperdinck, the witch doubled the , part of the mother, following a Bettelheimian reading which envisaged the children's point of view and identified the mother who could abandon them with; their persecutor in the woods.

Critics of both approaches—the Victorians' bowdlerizations, the twentieth century's appetite for maternal violence—are placed in a quandary by the matter of fairy tale when children, are the presumed audience. The space and time of, marriage and its problems—however farfetched—which were of crucial concern to the earlier, adult or mixed circle of listeners, have been pushed out of the narrative and replaced by courtship—the time before the wedding—as the generic theme of fairy tale.

Persinette, the heroine of a fairy tale of 1697 by Charlotte-Rose de La Force, is held captive in the tower by an old witch to whom she has been handed over, as in the Grimms' later version, the more famous 'Rapunzel'. (Persinette is called after the parsley from the witch's garden which her mother craves; Rapunzel after the rampion, another savoury herb, which her mother also desires so much that she promises the witch her baby in exchange.) Is Little Parsley-flower or Little Rampion the victim of a rapacious and cruel foster mother, who wants to keep her for herself, or has the old woman been allowed to take the daughter away from her real mother, install her in her own house to do her bidding, and then rob her of her freedom and denied her lover access to her? This is what the story relates, and such a reading tallies with common experience in medieval and early modern society, when a daughter-in-law worked under the direction of her husband's mother, to whom she had been handed over often by family arrangement in tender youth, even childhood. The historian Janet Nelson gives a good Merovingian example, from the *Vita* of Rusticula: as a child, Rusticula was taken by her promised husband to his natal household, and brought up by his mother. This 'private arrangement' was effectively wardship, and underlined Rusticula's legal incapacity In Shakespeare's *King John,* the conflict between France and England is patched up by bestowing Blanch on the Dauphin, but on the wedding day itself, the peace is shattered and the bride left centre stage, between her new husband, her father, her uncle the king and their competing claims on her allegiance. She cries out:

> The sun's o'ercast with blood; fair day, adieu!
> Which is the side that I must go withal?
> I am with both …
> They whirl asunder and dismember me …
> Whoever wins, on that side shall I lose …

Shakespeare's audience would have understood her feelings, and not only against a medieval backdrop. At the level of less exalted households, the conflicts in Basile's early collection of Italian fairy tales arise from the same divided loyalties; his stories seethe with married women's domestic turbulence. The wicked stepmother who has become the stock figure of fairy tale makes her first literary appearance as a mother-in-law, in 'Cupid and Psyche' by Apuleius', where Cupid's mother, the goddess Venus, orders her son to destroy Psyche, her rival in beauty. But instead Cupid falls in love with her. Though Apuleius does not say so in so many words, Cupid's mother's antagonism inspires his furtive behaviour: her envy of Psyche, his foreknowledge of her furious disapproval of his relations with her, require the clandestine, unseen lovemaking his mother turns him into a mystery presence, which Psyche, goaded by her sisters, then suspects of monstrous, beastlike form. When Venus does discover the truth about their 'marriage' she blazes with fury against Psyche and against her son for his choice. The rhetoric is comic, the accents all too familiar:

> She found Cupid lying ill in bed … As she entered she bawled out at the top of her voice: 'Now is this decent behaviour? … A fine credit you are to your divine family … "You trample your mother's orders underfoot … you have the impudence to sleep with the girl … at your age, you lecherous little beast! I suppose you thought I'd be delighted to have her for a daughter-in-law, eh?

Venus pursues Psyche with her vengeance and, when the girl is eventually brought before her, she shrieks at her with hysterical rage, and orders the cruellest punishments: 'she flew at poor Psyche, tore her clothes to shreds, pulled out handfuls of her hair, then grabbed her by the shoulders and shook her until she nearly shook her head off …' (p. 218). She then sets her various impossible tasks -   to sort lentils and millet wheat, barley, beans, poppy and vetch seeds, just as the wicked stepmother in medieval retellings and, later in Grimm, orders Aschenputtel as a condition of going to the ball (p. 204). And just as doves come to Aschenputtel's rescue, and peck the grain and seed into separate piles, much to the stepmother's astonishment, so Venus is horrified when she finds that Psyche has also managed the tasks.

Apuleius is jocular, trifling, wears his dislike of the vanity, snobbery and ruthlessness of Venus with a flourish, though at the concluding wedding feast, he relents enough to show the goddess relenting too: 'The music was so sweet that Venus came forward and performed a lively step-dance in time to it.'

In the fifteenth century, before the first extant variations on the tale were written down as fairy stories, 'Cupid and Psyche' was chosen by *cassone* painters as a fitting tale for the trousseau chests brides took to their new home; alongside other stories of wronged daughters and difficult unions, like the sufferings of Patient Griselda, the false witness of Potiphar's wife, or Paris' abduction of Helen of Troy, Psyche's troubles and eventual happiness could suitably furnish the room of a bride and help her keep in mind the pitfalls and the vindication of her predecessors in wedlock. Francesco di Giorgio (on a *cassone* panel in the Berenson Collection at I Tatti) chose the scene where Venus' vicious sidekick is dragging Psyche by her hair into the goddess's presence. 'Cinderella', 'Beauty and the Beast', 'Snow White' have directly inherited features from the plot of Apuleius' romance, as we have seen—Psyche's wicked sisters, the enchanted bounty in her mysterious husband's palace, and the prohibitions that hedge about her knowledge of his true nature. At a deeper level, they have also inherited the stories' function, to tell the bride the worst, and shore her up in her marriage.

The more one knows fairy tales the less fantastical they appear; they can be vehicles of the grimmest realism, expressing hope against all the odds with gritted teeth. Like 'pardon tales', written to the king to win a reprieve from sentence of death, fairy tales sue for mercy.

The wicked stepmother makes a savage appearance as a mother-in-law in the *Vita* of Saint Godelive, patron saint of Bruges, a historical figure who, according to a certain Drogo, the priestly author of her *Vita,* was born around 1050 and married to the nobleman Berthulphe de Ghistelles. Hagiography and fairy tale are often intertwined, and Godelive's story develops along familiar lines. It relates how she gave away food and goods to the poor against her mean husband's wishes and behind his back, and how angels saved her from detection, replacing the supplies she had taken. Berthulphe's mother was furious at the match, and ; Berthulphe himself neglected his wife by his frequent absences and maltreated her when they were together, until finally mother and son conspired to murder—her: she was held head down in a pond and throttled bv their servants. She was then put hack to bed to make out she had died in her sleep. Berthulphe remarried, but he later repented, made the pilgrimage to Jerusalem, and returned to become a monk. Godelive was canonized in 1084, very soon after her death, for miraculous cures had taken place: the blindness of one of her successor's children was suddenly lifted, and this was attributed to Godelive's intercession—a kind stepmother in this case working wonders beyond the grave and making amends for the wickedness of the rival mother in the story.

In one of Straparola's tales, yet another malignant mother-in-law substitutes three snapping curs in the childbed of her daughter-in-law for the beautiful triplets, with gold stars on their foreheads, to whom she has given birth. She orders their death, by drowning, and publicizes the disgrace of her hated daughter-in-law and her monstrous litter. Her plan is foiled, of course, though only after much suffering, and she herself is burned to death on a huge pyre built for her by her son. This is only one of dozens of fairy tales and other fictions which belong in the rich cycle of accused queens.

When a blind woman storyteller gave her account of the story set down by the Grimms as '*Das Mädchen ohne Hände*' (The Maiden without Hands), at the turn of the century in Scandinavia, she included a poisoned letter written by the hapless heroine's mother-in-law denouncing her, in the usual fairytale terms, for giving birth to a dog; interestingly enough, a male storyteller at the same time attributed this wickedness to the Devil himself The recent musical by Stephen Sondheim and James Lapine, *Into the Woods* (1988), assumes the possessiveness of a perverted mother-love between witch and captive in the Rapunzel story; a more historically based view would see that the old woman's desire for the baby girl corresponds to material needs for helping hands at home, and reflects the arranged transfer of girls to other families as prospective wives, or surrogate domestic servants. Her furious intervention between the girl and her suitor would then relate the conflicting, simultaneous fears of redundancy growing in a widowed woman whose son's marriage has made her insecure in what used to be her home, under her control. The vilification of older women in such interpretations belongs in a long tradition, as discussed in Chapters Two and Three; they bring to mind the medieval *fabliau,* in which a son-in-law performs a mock 'nutting' and pulls out from the body of his mother-in-law the bull's testicles which have made her so unfeminine.

Fairy stories relate the tensions between competitors, for a young man's allegiance; they reflect the difficulty of women making common cause within existing: matrimonial arrangements.

II

Hatred of the older woman, and intergenerational strife, may arise not only from rivalry, but from guilt, too, about the weak and the dependent. The portrait of the tyrant mother-in-law or stepmother may conceal her own vulnerability, may offer an excuse for her maltreatment.

Reversing the angle of approach, and coming at the matter of fairy stories from another vantage point, imagining that the teller speaks instead as an older woman, as herself a grandmother or a mother-in-law, we can then discover in the tales the fear she feels, the animus she harbours against her daughter-in-law or daughters-in-law: when the mother disappears, she may have been conjured away by the narrator herself, who despatches her child listeners' natural parent, replaces her with a monster, and then produces herself within the pages of the story, as if by enchantment, often in many different guises as a wonder-worker on their behalf, the good old fairy, the fairy godmother. Thus the older generation speaks to the younger in the fairy tale, prunes out the middle branch on the family tree as rotten or irrelevant, and thereby lays claim to the devotion, loyalty and obedience of the young over their mothers' heads. This structure underlies the classic Cinderella story; this ancient tussle has contributed to the misogyny in such tales.

A mother-in-law had good reason to fear her son's wife, when she often had to : strive to maintain her position and assert her continuing rights to a livelihood in the patrilineal household. If she was widowed, her vulnerability became more acute. Christiane Klapisch-Zuber, the historian, uses the chilly phrase 'passing guests' when she describes the condition of wives in the households, both symbolic and geographic, which they had married into in fifteenth-century Florence.

The divergent claims on women of their paternal, natal home on the one hand and their later, marital households on the other would begin when they first left their parents and continue throughout their lives. These conflicting demands could greatly exacerbate women's insecurity, kindling much misery and hatred in, consequence. Although the patterns of inheritance and household obviously vary;—and in highly complex ways—at different times and in different places, the burden of evidence points to the relation between mothers-in-law and daughters-in- law as the acute lesion in the social body ('la Tormenta' is the name for mother-in-law in Spanish comedy). English wills of the seventeenth century, show that widowed parents were customarily cared for in the household of their eldest child: the continuing right to shelter, to a place by the family hearth, to bed and board, was granted and observed. However, as *King Lear* reveals, even in the case of a powerful king the exercise of such a right could meet ferocious resistance and reprisals. Just as Cordelia is a fairytale heroine, a wronged youngest child, a forerunner of Cinderella, so Goneril and Regan are the wicked witches, ugly sisters; the unnatural women whom fairy tales indict.

But women lived longer than men, then as now, and there were more old: female dependants needing bed and board, if not the hundred knights King Lear; demands. In Florence, some widows who wished to return to the family of their birth, as they had a right to do, were forced to bring suits against their children in' the marital household in order to wrest back the dowry which was also theirs by' right and necessary to their survival outside. The Court of Chancery, established in England in the mid-fifteenth century, was set up to deal with abuses of widows' inheritance by heirs. Stepsons featured prominently among those who flouted their legal obligations. Chancery's attempts made matters worse, and widows' rights of inheritance were only effectively smoothed out by the Dower Act of 1833. The legal complexities are very great indeed, but in this respect England conformed more to Catholic, continental Europe than to another Protestant:, country, Holland, which offered unmarried and widowed women much greater independence.

Demographic change has affected the condition of old people. In a census taken in the small community of Eguilles, near Aix, in Provence, in 1741–70, and carefully analysed by David Troyansky in his book *Old Age in the Old Régime*, the figures show that many more widows survived and lived with their children—married and unmarried—than widowers, that half the marriage contracts notarized stipulated co-residence with the parents on one side or the other, and that the widowed mother of the husband—the mother-in-law in relation to the incoming wife—lived with her son and his wife in 25 per cent of cases. By contrast, the wife's parents lived with a married daughter only in 5 per cent of unions the wife's mother on her own lived with the couple only in 16.7 percent of the marriages. Thus a widowed woman had to get along with her daughter-in-law, and vice versa, rather more commonly than with her own daughter. Troyansky sums up: 'In the day-to-day fact of co-residence, the husband's family took precedence … Of 111 cases of co-residence [in the sample], 100, or 90 percent, lived with the husband's parents and only 11 families (10 percent) lived with the wife's [parents].' Almost a decade passed before the younger couple could expect to live on their own: the average length of time between their marriage and the death of (his) parents living with them was 9.8 years.

This interval could represent exactly that time of trial, of forged alliances, of varied struggles, which many fairy tales told by women across the generations record in code.

In France, after the Revolution, a widow did not retain her keys to the house- hold or to the family's business. Thus dispossessed by her husband's death, she was often only grudgingly provided for by his legatees; co-residence declined as the population moved to the cities to work, and destitute and homeless old women became a feature of nineteenth-century society. At the same time, the rights of grandparents began to be considered: in 1867, for instance, an important law was passed in France allowing the mother's parents to visit children who had remained in their father's custody after a divorce. This sign that the grandparents' role in a child's upbringing was being recognized and valued coincides exactly with the publication of dozens of editions of *contes* in which an old woman is felling children tales by a fireside, both in France and England. Through the medium of children's literature, the old were shown to be entitled to continuing respect in society and a place in the family, and the fairy tales in which they play a part did not attempt to conceal the bitter conflicts within the romance of marriage that fairy tale spins.

Like gossip, fairy tales defame their objects in their attempt to establish—and extend—the speaker's influence.

III

The kind of woman who threatens society by her singleness and her dependency was not always a clinging mother, or a desperate or abusive widow. She could be a spinster, an unmarried mother, an old nurse or servant in a household—any woman who was unattached and ageing was vulnerable. In the centuries when the image of Mother Goose was being disseminated through numerous editions of fairytale collections, 'there was,' writes the historian Michelle Perrot, 'in a radical sense, no place for female solitude in the conceptual framework of the time'. She quotes Michelet: 'The woman who has neither home nor protection dies.' Yet there were many such, and they had to survive, however precariously. The census of 1851 in France showed that 12 percent of women over fifty had never married, and 34 percent were single; this ratio remained the same nearly fifty years later. The parish churches of England reveal, in the pious record of donations made to the 'oldest poor widows or single women living in the [said] ward', the chronic indigence of this social group in the same era: in 1824, in St Nicholas's church, King's Lynn, a bequest of £60 was made by Francis Boyce for the distribution of *4d.* loaves on certain feast days to these needy women.

The old wives who spin their tales are almost always represented as unattached:* spinsters, or widows. Mother Goose appears an anomalous crone, an unhusbanded female cut loose from the moorings of the patriarchal hearth; kin to the witch and the bawd. It is not difficult to see that such a storyteller may be speaking from a position of acute vulnerability, the kind that makes enemies in the heart of the family. In one of the most power- ful scenes in *The Three Sisters* Chekhov dramatized the old nurse Anfisa's plight when a new woman is brought: into the family. Natasha, who marries the three sisters' brother, is the classic daughter-in-law head of household of fairytale nightmares, in that she does not feel she owes the family nurse anything—neither board nor lodging. Natasha comes in and adjusts her hair in the mirror, then notices that Anfisa is sitting by the fire. She turns on her 'coldly', say the stage directions, and bursts out, 'How dare you sit in my presence? Get up! Get out of here!' The old woman obeys, and Natasha then says to Olga, one of her sisters-in-law, 'I can't understand why you keep that old woman in the house.' Olga defends the old woman: 'Forgive me for, saying it, but I can't understand how you …' But Natasha interrupts her. 'She's , quite useless here. She's just a peasant woman, her right place is in the country. I don't like having useless people about.' In the end, Olga has to leave home, too^t and she moves her old nurse in with her so that she will be looked after.

In fairy tales, such a useless old woman reappears in the form of the beggar whom the heroine meets by chance, and who turns out to be a powerful fairy in disguise. She has the secret power to reward virtuous sweet-talking girls (the Olgas of this world), who perform acts of kindness like giving her food and drink, and to punish the wicked mother and her unkind daughter (the Natashas) who scorn old women as useless. Again, paying attention to the internal structure of this story, one can assemble a picture of strain across three generations, in which the old struggle to survive and plead for the mercy of the young.

'La Mère Cigogne' (Mother Stork), for instance, a woodcut strip fairy tale from the *Imagerie Pellerin* at Epinal of around 1900 (pp. 232–3), reveals the full pathos of wishful thinking on the part of the old, as well as familiar moral instruction to the young to be good: 'Mother Stork had had from three dead husbands, over time, some thirty or more children, girls and boys.' But they have driven her out to beg for her wherewithal on the street. There a good fairy finds her who announces: 'May your sons who have wicked hearts change instantly into windmills!' No sooner said than done: the windmill-sons have to work on their mother's behalf, grinding flour for her bakery—as they should have in the first place. The worst offender of all becomes an ass, and provides her with the transport she was previously denied. She becomes rich, and distributes her cakes only to good little children. Eventually her own see the error of their ways, and all is forgiven. The story reproduces transparently an old woman's protest that she can be of use, directed : past the next generation to the more sympathetic young who come after.

Such a *bande dessinée* literally tells an 'old wives' tale', full of threats, fear, and pathos. It provides a hinge between the instrumental use of literature to form the young, a process that has long been recognized, and the earlier annexation of narrative by speakers who were trying to help themselves.

The protagonist here, bearing one of the traditional names for a storyteller, talks about her indigence. Walter Crane, in 'My Mother' (1873), using the same Toy Book format as his illustrated 'Beauty and the Beast', turned to remind his readers of their future duties in characteristic Victorian fashion. Mother is pictured through the stages of life, first young and vigorous and playful ('Who dress'd my dolls in clothes so gay? My Mother'), then ageing and weakening, until she lies in bed dying: 'And when I see thee hang thy head, / 'Twill be my turn—to watch thy bed.' If this book was read by a mother to her child, its injunction carried a special force.

The hostility shown towards the mother figure in modern fairytale interpretations narrows its sights too sharply; other women besides stepmothers, mothers-in-law and guardians were placed *in loco matris* and excited the powerful emotions pupillage always arouses. In 'Peau d'ours' (Bearskin), one of the tales attributed to Henriette-Julie de Murat, Princess Hawthorn's godmother makes intermittent, dazzling appearances arrayed in jewels and flowers, but she trifles capriciously with her godchild, putting her to the test to discover the strength of her love, punishing the lovers for failing, or sometimes just for the pleasure of it, at whim, like her classical precursor the goddess of love. She refuses to help Hawthorn after her unwanted marriage to the predatory ogre Rhinoceros, for instance, because she was not consulted by her father earlier. In this she resembles the fairies in Murat's tales in general, as well as her contemporaries': arbitrary, tyrannical, self-interested and untender, they have djinn-like powers of life and death over their charges' movements, prospects, wealth. These powers are defined as social and economic: when the father hands over the heroine to be brought up by a fairy, Murat writes, 'The power of the fairies does not extend to the qualities of the heart.' The fairies, not knowing gentleness or, in this particular story, constancy, cannot bestow it on their protégés. In some tales, fairies *in loco matris* have explicit designs on humans: in Villeneuve's '*La Belle et la bête*', the Beast has come to this pass because he turned down his guardian's propositions. Marie-Catherine d'Aulnoy's stories deal obsessively with these powerful, indeed fateful figures of female authority who are abusive of their position: Hidessa is plagued by Magotine's perverted desires, the Blue Bird is metamorphosed by another wicked fairy. In Murat's stories equally malign termagants bear self-explanatory names: Formidable, Danamo, Mordicante. Louise, Comtesse d'Auneuil, another aristocrat who put her hand to the writing of fairy stories, encapsulated the general antagonism against these designing females in the title of her one extant tale,' *La Tyrannie des fées détruite*' (The Fairies' Tyranny Destroyed), which appeared in 1702. There, the lovers are kept apart, in hideous animal shapes, by the jealous fairy, Serpente.

All these older malevolent women stand in some degree of parental or guardian relation to the young on whom they prey and whose romances they attempt to spoil. Perrault's sprightly *moralité*, appended to his 'Cinderella', means more than might appear when he says that talent will never be enough for a young person's advancement in the world: a powerful godparent is required. Godmothers acted as co-maters: they stood *in loco parentis*. According to the laws of affinity in the early medieval Church, even god-siblings committed incest if they married, as their spiritual generation of the child into the Christian family made them true kin, even if there was no blood relation.

Fairy power in the stories borrows the clothes of the romance and mythological pantheon and assumes the kinship patterns of an earlier social organization in order to mirror female power within the extended kinship and patronage systems of the contemporary elite: the Vicomtesse of Kernosy, who wants to marry off her niece to cancel a debt, may love listening to fairy tales of an evening, but only because, in her overweening self-regard, she fails to see her own face in their looking glass.

Murat identified fairies with informal, aristocratic female power in the *ancien régime* very clearly. D'Aulnov made the connection even more explicit when she dedicated one volume of her fairy tales, *Nouveaux Contes des fées,* to Madame, the sister-in-law of Louis XIV She wrote: 'Here are Queens and Fairies, who having made the happiness of all who were most charming and most commendable in their own times, have come to seek at the court of your Royal Highness the most illustrious and delightful aspects of ours Flattery, perhaps, a courtier's cunning, a smokescreen veiling the pullulating evil fairies of Mme d'Aulnoy's tales who hamper true lovers. Her good fairies often fail to command enough magic to withstand the enemy's,evil machinations: at the end, the mermaid godmother in 'The Yellow Dwarf' cannot resuscitate the dead lovers, but only manages to turn them into intertwined palm trees. In the preamble to this same volume, D'Aulnoy describes walking with friends in the Pare de Saint Cloud, and sitting down by herself for a while. When her friends rejoin her, she describes how '*une jeune Nymphe*' with 'gracious and polite manners', who was able to remember the bygone days when Rhea ruled, had approached her there. Her friends press D'Aulnoy to tell them a story. The implication is that the nymph was a messenger, and D'Aulnoy will pass on what she said. But our storyteller confounds this expectation; she produces a notebook, and coquettes with the circle around her, saying that it contains tales which are treasures. Then she adds: 'All my friends the Fairies have been niggardly with their favours towards me hitherto, so I assure you that I am resolved to neglect them, as they have neglected me.'Distinguishing herself from classical nymphs on the one hand, and fairies on the other, she begins to read a tale from the book she has written herself. A tiny detail of nomenclature becomes significant, in this respect: Mme d'Aulnoy's first editions are entitled *Contes des fées* in the sense of 'about' not 'by'(Latin *de* not *a*). Tales *about* fairies, from a point of view that may take issue with the patronage of the fairies themselves. It is only in later editions and translations that the phrase 'tales of the fairies' takes root, and implies broad agreement between story and subject in an atmosphere of benign and happy 'fairytale' enchantments. Many early literary fairy tales tell stories of the fairies' undoing.

Echoing the prevalent abuses of wardship, Villeneuve also rings complicated changes on the theme of deviant motherhood within the social, rather than the natural or biological, family; in '*La Belle et la bête,* Beauty, the heroine, was brought up in a foster home, discarded by her biological mother, like many other protagonists, when the fairies cast her out (the fairies figure as thinly disguised Versailles *mignons* and schemers) and compelled her to give up her child. For his part, the Beast has been raised by his mother's closest friend, and it is she who attempts to seduce him. In counterpoise to these wrongs, Villeneuve then multiplies different figures of female benevolence who make up for the false mothers' failings: sisters, godmothers, female friends abound in her elaborately constructed extended family, and at the end it is the maternal, sacrificial act of a fairy on behalf of her sister's child that brings about the completion of the story and the union of Beauty and the Beast. Improvised and entangled families of this sort were not uncommon in the *ancien régime*. Mme de Villeneuve herself lived under the protection of Crébillon *pére,* and was writing at the same time as his son, the playwright Crébillon *fits,* was himself composing oriental fairy tales in a satirical, semi-licentious tone that became *à la mode* in the 1720s.

The proliferation of mother figures does not only reflect wishful thinking on the part of children, though fantasies of gratification and power over parents play their part; the aleatory mothers of Mme de Villeneuve's 'Beauty and the Beast' reflect the conditions of aristocratic and less than aristocratic life in early modern France. In Marie-Jeanne L' Héritier's apparently farfetched tales *'Ricdin-Ricdon'* and *'La Robe de sincérité,* the relations of wetnurses, foster parents, guardians, court patrons and godparents can be glimpsed as family networks interpenetrating and combining with the natural, biological family.

In English, French, and Italian, the very title 'mother' formerly designated many women who were not natural mothers, nor women acting directly in lieu of , her, like a foster parent, but women who were occupied in some way with the care of other, often younger colleagues—sometimes including men: nuns on the one hand, like the celebrated Mère Arnault at the convent of Port Royal, brothel- keepers on the other, like the notorious real-life madam Ma Needham in Hogarth's *Progress of a Harlot,* who welcomes young Kate Hackabout to London. As with Mother Goose and Mother Stork, midwives and layers-out were granted maternal status. Until the mid-nineteenth century wetnurses were the regular ; object of sentimental idealization, in spite of the abuses which flourished (and the 1 high death rate of the children). In the mid-eighteenth century, when the fairy tale was being domesticated for the nursery, Greuze was also painting uplifting scenes like *Le Retour au village,* showing a young man arriving rapturously to visit a nurse; surrounded by a multiplicity of offspring, like an allegory of Charity, she appears a paragon of natural bounty and health. Jonathan Swift, as a year-old baby, was farmed out to England for three years, and was taught to read from the Bible by his nurse and to 'spell', just as in *Gulliver's Travels* (1726) Gulliver is taught languages by his giant nurse, Glumdalclitch, and another servant, the sorrel nag. In the nineteenth century, George Sand passed her childhood, and laid the foundations of her fiction, in the company of her *vieille confidente,* her nurse. Freud was devastated by the disappearance of his nurse when he was two and a half. She was dismissed for stealing, and went to prison. In 1897, in the course of his self-analysis, Freud recalled her 'an ugly, elderly but clever woman, who told me a great deal about God Almighty and hell and instilled in me a high opinion of my own capacities. Freud as Cinders, his nurse as the fairy godmother. Elsewhere Freud added, 'she was my teacher in sexual matters and complained because I was so clumsy and unable to do anything': the secret enterprise of Mother Goose's narratives. If any of these maternal substitutes had told their nurslings stories, the mother might well have been absent; again the differences in rank between the wetnurse in the village and the mother in the town are reflected in so many fair} tales' frank assault on women with power over others and affection for others with less authority.

In French, bawds were also called mothers: *la mère maquerelle* in colloquial speech. 'Mother' was used in English as 'a term of address for an elderly woman of the lower class'. In usage, it also implies something subtly marginal, with a whiff of the comic, to do with taboo mysteries of the body and the associated matters of life and death. Mother Trot, for instance, as in 'Tell-troth's New Year Gift' of 1593, would be related to Old Dame Trot, of nursery-rhyme witchery, and both are popular descendants of Trotula, the author of the midwifery manual of the middle ages, who may or may not be a historical figure, but certainly gave her name to venereal and obstetric lore of all kinds. In North London until recently two pub names recalled two such characters, Mother Red Cap and Mother Shipton, the last a byword in witchcraft and prophecy who was first mentioned in a pamphlet of 1641 and went on to an illustrious afterlife as a pantomime dame; Both pubs have changed their names: the one to The End of the World, the other to *The Fiddler's Elbow*. The old names no longer held any meaning for their customers—a symptom of the historical forgettings that drain our culture, as well as a reflection of a deep shift in consciousness: the meanings of the word 'mother'. are becoming more and more restricted to the biological mother in the nuclear;; family Mothers cannot appoint themselves, or be assigned the role at will; they even need to be biologically proven by matching DNA. And with the coming of, bottle-feeding, the practice of wetnursing has died out.

Oddly, this intense focus on the legitimacy of the maternal bloodline and the flesh bond of mother and child has implications in the reading of fairy tales. Our understanding of the stock villain, the wicked stepmother, has been dangerously attenuated and even misunderstood as a result. In the stories, she may not even be a stepmother, and the evil she does is not intrinsic to her nature, or to the strict maternal relation, or to her particular family position. It cannot and should not be extended to all women, for it arises from the insecurity of her interests in a social and legal context that can be changed, and remedied.

If the narrator's ambition to influence her audience, as a licit or illicit surrogate "mother, if the storyteller's competition with a powerful woman in control of the Household, emerge from the story, the targets of narrative hatred begin to fit in to the economy of family life. For although it does not appear clearly in the teller's , interest to insist on the wickedness of women, as she might be tainted by association, the instrumental character of storytelling means that scaring children can be useful, too. Nannies use bogeymen to frighten children into obedience, and a woman storyteller might well displace the harsher aspects of her command on to another woman, a rival who can take the blame. But this is a social stratagem, not an ineluctable or Oedipal condition, and mothers or stepmothers today need not be inculpated *en masse*. As remarriage becomes more and more common, stepmothers find they are tackling a hard crust of bigotry set in the minds of their new children, and refreshed by endless returns of the wicked stepmother in the literate of childhood.

Fairy tale's historical realism has been obscured. One of the reasons may be the change in audience that took place through the nineteenth century, from the mixed age group who attended the *veillée* or the nursery reading of the tales, as in the seventeenth- and eighteenth- and early nineteenth-century evidence, towards an exclusively young audience who had the great enterprises like marriage still ; ahead of them. Furthermore, certain tales which star children have gained world-wide popularity ('Cinderella' and 'Jack and the Beanstalk'), while the range of the familiar problems dramatized in the stories reflects the youth of the dominant target audience of recent times. The increasing identification of fantasy with the child's mentality has also contributed to the youth of the protagonists.

Stories collected in Alaska in the 1960s often deal frankly with matters sunk deep beneath the surface of European fairy tales destined for children to hear. In one example, a mother-in-law, in the absence of her son, provides her daughter- in-law with food—seals she has hunted—and in return asks for the attentions of a wife—grooming, delousing, and sex, making love to her with the help of a penis of sealbone. When her husband returns from fishing and spies on them, he fetches his mother such a blow he kills her; his wife is disconsolate: '"You've ' killed my dear husband," she cried. And would not stop crying.' "

This could be a concocted folk tale, and this brand of incest certainly remains ^ Undocumented further south. But its very anomalousness reveals how an alliance between a man's mother and his wife does not spring easily from the soil of Western, exogamous, patrilocal marriage, especially when the mother is widowed, and both women are competing for their material welfare and the man's attention. It is significant that when the Russian folklorist Vladimir Propp analysed the wonder tale, he broke the form down into seven spheres of action, to which correspond different functions of the dramatis personae: the villain, the hero, the donor, the helper, the princess and her father, the dispatcher and false hero.

When it came to the princess, Propp could not sever her function from her father's but treated them as belonging to a single sphere of action: 'The princess and her father cannot be exactly delineated from each other,' he wrote, thus disclosing, unwittingly, the strictly patriarchal character of the traditional marriage plots, the steps by which the narrative moves, the dynamic of the contract made according to her father's wish. Propp did not analyse the wonder tale's function from the point of view of a mother, did not probe the structure for the inverse rubbing of the father-daughter design: the mother-son. Mothers are distributed according to their part in the plot, as donors or villains, rather than their place in the system of family authority, like the father. Their disappearance from the foreground of his taxonomy replicates their silencing and absence from some of the stories themselves. "Vet the tales' deeper, invisible structure can be differently anatomized, as a bid for authority on the part of women. Propp inadvertently reproduces the weight of male power in the wonder tale, and the consequent alliances which set women against women; the tension erupts within the stories as female dissension and strife.

The experiences these stories recount are remembered, lived experiences of women, not fairytale concoctions from the depths of the psyche; they are rooted in the social, legal and economic history of marriage and the family, and they have all the stark actuality of the real and the power real life has to bite into the psyche and etch its design: if you accept Mother Goose tales as the testimony of women, as old wives' tales, you can hear vibrating in them the tensions, the insecurity, jealousy and rage of both mothers-in-law against their daughters-in-law and vice versa, as well as the vulnerability of children from different marriages. Certainly, women strove against women because they wished to promote their own children's interests over those of another union's offspring; the economic dependence of wives and mothers on the male breadwinner exacerbated—and still does—the divisions that may first spring from preferences for a child of one's flesh. But another set of conditions set women against women, and the misogyny of fairy tales reflects them from a woman's point of view: rivalry for the prince's love. The effect of these stories is to flatter the male hero; the position of the man as saviour and provider in these testimonies of female conflict is assumed, repeated and reinforced—which may be the reason why such 'old wives' tales', once they moved from the spinning rooms and the nurseries on to the desks of collectors and folklorists, into the public forum of the printed page and the video screen, have found such success with mixed audiences of men and women, boys and girls, and have continued to flourish in the most popular and accessible and conventional media, like Disney cartoons.

When history falls away from a subject, we are left with Otherness, and all its power to compact enmity, recharge it and recirculate it. An archetype is a hollow thing, but a dangerous one, a figure or image which through usage has been uncoupled from the circumstances which brought it into being, and goes on spreading false consciousness. An analogy—a harmless one—occurs in metaphors of sunrise and sunset, familiar metaphors which fail to represent the movement of the sun or the relation of the planet to it.

In Greece, the women of the Thesmophoria rituals and the Eleusinian mysteries kept their disclosures to themselves, and forbade men access; they understood the risks involved in speaking of female matters. The open circulation of women's experiences in fairy tales has certainly given hostages to fortune, handed ammunition to the very figures—the princes—who often cause the fatal rivalry in the first place. Women were trapped on the fine reverse-barbed hooks of allegiances and interests, on which like trout they became more and more ensnared the more they attempted to pull away. It is revealing that one or two of the peasant or artisan sources to whom the Grimms were alerted were highly reluctant to share their stories with the keen scholars; these women may have felt abashed at the difference in education, social status, but they may also have felt uncomfortable with the idea of broadcasting their contents beyond predominantly female and worker- class circles. In one case, Wilhelm resorted to using the children of the manager of the Elizabeth Hospital (the poorhouse) in Marburg in which one storyteller was living to learn two of the tales she had previously refused to pass on to either his sister Lotte or himself. One of these was 'Aschenputtel', the Grimms' version of 'Cinderella', which includes of course some of the bloodthirstiest moments of interfemale vengeance of all the famous tales.

A storyteller invites the audience to sympathize with the heroine; with Cinderella, with Beauty, with Snow White: she deals death—physical and moral—to the mother of the heroine; she effectively tells the audience that mothers abandon children to witches in return for the fruits she craves from their warden, as in D'Aulnoy's 'The White Cat' or La Force's 'Persinette', that mothers order daughters to cut off their toes to please the prince, that they die and leave them to the mercies of the wicked. She is killing off the mother, replacing her, and can be aligned with the mother-in-law who talks to her grandchildren, and claims them for her own, overlooking, disparaging, undoing the work of her son's wife, their mother, and hoping she will not end in the poorhouse.

Yet, even as the voice of the fairy tale murders the mother who is her rival for the children, she remembers how she herself was maltreated: how she entered the house of another as an outsider and was reviled. One of the reasons for the fairytale prince's impeccable reputation is that, in a marriage where a bride enters the husband's family, he becomes her chief ally, and his love her mainstay against the interests of others. Many of the most famous and best-loved tales, like 'Bluebeard', and 'Beauty and the Beast', tell of the struggles the heroine undergoes in the quest to secure this love.

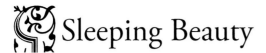

Sleeping Beauty

Passivity, Introspection, and Silence

Bettina Knapp

Unlike the strong and down-to-earth Donkey-Skin, the female protagonist in *Sleeping Beauty is* passive and introspective. Nonetheless, in some strange way she is sufficiently wise to know that by maintaining her reserve, and most importantly her silence, her fondest hopes will be realized.

The sources for *Sleeping Beauty* are many and varied. The oldest dates back to Epimenides (c.sixth and fifth cent. B.C.E.), the Cretan philosopher and legislator, who supposedly slept for fifty-seven years in a cave, after which he awakened and prophesied. In the tale of *The Seven Sleepers*, referred to in the Muslim world as the "Two-Horned One," the protagonists remain dormant for two hundred years *(Koran,* Sura 18). Other sources include, the *six*teenth-century prose romance, *Perceforest;* the *Volsung Saga*, in which the Walkyrie Brunhilde is awakened from her slumber by Sigurd (Siegfried); and Sun Moon *and Talia* in Basile's *Pentameron* (Barchilon and Flinders, *Charles Perrault* 93).

Perrault's tale begins on a religious note, with the enumeration of many pilgrimages, prayers, and pieties undertaken by a royal couple in an unsuccessful attempt to conceive a child. In due course, their wishes are granted and the queen is delivered of a baby girl. Seven fairy godmothers are invited to the baptism. Following the ceremony, they repair to the palace for a feast during the course of which they bestow, as is customary, perfections on the newborn. Magnificent place settings, including a solid gold case containing a spoon, fork, and knife decorated with diamonds and rubies, have been—placed before each fairy. As the banquet commences, an old fairy angrily enters the great hall, protesting her exclusion from the ceremony and feast Greatly embarrassed, the king explains that, since she had not stepped out of her tower lodgings for fifty years, he thought her dead or bewitched. To rectify a wrong, however, the host has a place setting put before her on the table. Since only seven solid gold cases had been ordered for the occasion, and these had already been distributed among the young fairies, an eighth could not be produced at a moments notice. The old fairy considered such an omission an unpardonable slight.

Muttering veiled threats under her breath, she is overheard by one of the young fairies who decides to hide behind a tapestry to wait for the old fairy to utter her imprecation, after which she will step forward to mitigate the evil. Predictably, the old fairy places a curse on the newborn: the princess's hand will be pricked by a spindle and she will die. Above the din of the weeping guests, the disarmingly gentle voice of the young fairy is heard speaking her reassuring words: the spindle will prick the princess's hand, but rather than die, she will fall into a deep sleep that will last a hundred years, after which a king's son will come and awaken her.

Spinner-Fairies: Fates. Just as the Fates in ancient Greek, Roman, and Germanic lore played a role in carving out an infant's future, the fairy godmothers bestowed physical and spiritual qualities on the newborn, while the old fairy called down a curse, Etymologically, the words "fairy," and "fate" are connected: "fairy," from M.E. *fais;* M.F. *fei, fée;* Lat. *Fata;* and the English *Fate* (Harf-Lancner, *Les Fées au Moyen Age 9),* The mythological Fates included the Greek Moerae, the Roman Parcae, and the German Norns. The Greek Clotho, for example, spun the thread of life; Lachesis determined its length; and Atropos cut it. In that the gifts the seven fairy godmothers were to bestow on the newborn were designed to protect the infant from harm, these suprapersonal women may be compared to Clotho and Lachesis. Endowed with both negative and positive maternal qualities, the Fates, as karmic powers, had the capacity to cherish, sustain, devour, or terrify all living beings. Thus, everyone may be said to be connected in some way with these spinning women—or with predestination. Hesiod, understandably, referred to them as "Daughters of the Night," and sisters of the Goddesses of death *(Theogony* 211–217).

The identification of wisdom and understanding with old age was not applicable in the case of the uninvited fairy in our tale. As a negative aspect of the Great Mother, she bore the royal family a grudge, revealing her feelings of spite and mean-spiritedness, which are characteristic of those who have never known or dispensed love. Unfulfilled, introverted, unable to relate to others, she had chosen to live a reclusive existence, erroneously assuming that isolation would protect her from further hurt. Deep in her collective unconscious were factors that she either ignored or repressed. Instead of attempting to dislodge them, she suffered the fate of those who try to relieve their pain without attempting to resolve the reasons for its existence. In her resentment, her unredeemed, dark, unlived shadow forces took on dimension, flooded her ego, and transformed it into an ever-festering instrument of destruction. Like the archetypal witch, the old fairy released her life-threatening haplessness on the helpless (Franz, *Shadow and Evil in Fairy Tales* 104, 5). As a prisoner of her own deadly powers, she may be identified with the third Greek Fate—Atropos—whose spectral form stands behind every individual as she cuts the thread of life.

Like the old fairy of Perrault's tale, so the quarreling and fighting Eris, a Greek Goddess, later assimilated to the Roman allegorical figure Discord, had not been invited to the marriage of Peleus,(king of the Myrmidons)4 to Thetis, the Nereid. Eris avenged herself for the affront by offering a golden apple to Paris who was to award it to the most beautiful of three deities—Hera, Athena, or Aphrodite. That he chose Aphrodite set off the Trojan War, As in life, so agents of violence and hurt are perpetually evident in religions, history, fairy tales, and fables.

Numerology and Alchemical Symbolism, In numerology and alchemical symbolism, widespread during Europe's Middle Ages and in Perrault's time as well, the number 7 (cf. the seven fairy godmothers in our tale) was considered to have mystical significance. According to Jung, numbers are archetypal. As such, they were not invented by the conscious mind, but emerged from the unconscious spontaneously, when the need arose, in the form of archetypal images. Like archetypes, numbers are psychic energy *(libido),* thus fomentors of dynamic processes or virtualities in the psyches. They may lie latent in the unconscious as events or shapes until consciousness experiences them in the form of "images, thoughts, and typical emotional modes of behavior" (Franz, *Number and Time* 18; Jung, 92'31).

The number 7 brings to mind the paradoxical worlds of abstractions and of concretions: the days of the week, the seven petals of the rose, the seven heavens, the seven spheres of angels, the seven alchemical operations, the seven planets, and so forth. The ability of the fairy godmothers to circulate from one world to another enabled these supernatural beings to transcend the workaday domain, As inhabitants of both physical (earthly) and spiritual (heavenly) spheres, they would bestow qualities on the infant girl that would incorporate tangible and intangible values. Not only would she be beautiful, but she would also possess artistic accomplishments, such as dancing, singing, and musicianship. The child would bear the grace and spirit of an angel, thereby likening her to themselves. *Earth,* as previously mentioned, was associated by numerologists and alchemists with 4, and heaven with 3, the two adding up to 7, suggesting a harmony of opposites that would ultimately prevail in the child's psyche (Jung, 9, #425).

THE KING'S ATTEMPT TO ALTER FATE. So destabilized was the king upon hearing of his daughter's fate that his psychic functioning became impaired to the point that he sought to dominate what has and would always elude mortals, the chance factor. Unlike Abraham who, in total humility, was willing to sacrifice his son Isaac (psychologically speaking, his ego or center of consciousness) to God (the Self, i.e., the whole psyche), and thus was spared the loss of his son (Gen. 22: 7–18), the king in our fairy tale refused to submit, and thus failed in altering his child's fate. Unwilling to surrender his ego-power to the Self—perceived psychologically as a "matrix out of which the conscious individual develops"—the king attempted to play God, the "creator and preserver," and would suffer the consequences for his hubris (Cox, *Modern Psychology 162*).

Believing himself authorized to circumvent the infinite—God's world of imponderables—he tried to sidestep the old fairy's prognostication by concentrating his energies on ways of protecting his daughter. To this end, he issued an edict banning, under pain of death, all spinning and spindles from the palace.

TO LIVE UNDER A SPELL. A spell—in our case, the one cast by the old fairy- may be likened, psychologically speaking, to a *poisoning* (an autonomous content introduced into an individual's subliminal world). The implantation of a terrible fear in someone's mind may take on the aspects of a malediction, and if the malediction comes from several sources it acquires a cumulative power that may suck up the life force of the person involved. Thus, the imprecations of sorcerers, witches, astrologers, soothsayers, handwriting experts, enemies, and even friends, may vitiate the life of the vulnerable as well as the strong person,   *

In the case of the royal couple—emotionally fragile parents who had suffered a difficult conception and were concerned about the newborn's good health—the old fairy's spell exacerbated an already built-in sense of panic. However, the careful planning and vigilant supervision on the part of the royal parents succeeded in protecting their beautiful daughter from harm's way until she became of marriageable age. As fate would have it, an accident occurred on the day chosen by the royal couple to oversee repairs to one of their country homes. The unsupervised princess, imbued with a sense of excitement, and perhaps taking advantage of her parents' absence, yielded to her yearning to discover something on her own. Although she was wobbly emotionally, infantile in her expectations, and unsteady in her direction, curiosity had become her psychopomp. Having been imprisoned by understandably excessive restrictions imposed upon her by her parents, she took advantage of her day of freedom to investigate the, until-now, unseen upper floors of the palace. Gleefully, she climbed the stairs and peered into what must have been a thrilling but forbidden realm, where she happened upon a dungeon. There, she came upon a nice old lady spinning.

THE DUNGEON: ASCENSIONAL IMAGERY. Not a dark underground prison cell usually associated with medieval castles, the dungeon in Perrault's tale is a *donjon,* a massive inner; tower located on the castle's top floor. The inner stairs, leading to what the adolescent considered a wondrously mysterious area, served to enhance the thrill of her ascension.

Ascensional symbols, such as stairs, ladders, and pyramids, are designed to encourage earthbound creatures to shed their mundane cares and opt for divine preoccupations. Although the tower-dungeon in Perrault's tale suggests a remote, repressed, virtually forgotten, and certainly neglected area of the palace, it may also be looked upon as a paradigm for the head or the human rational sphere (as cellars or underground areas are frequently identified with the body, instinct, and/or unconscious). The princess's climb up the stairs corresponded to a directional alteration, filling her with an increasing sense of freedom and release from a highly structured and imprisoning life style, But it served as well to cast all judgmental faculties to the wind.

Might her rapid and unheeding ascent have been motivated by an unconscious rejection of her fearful parents' apprehension? The headiness she felt in the tower's rarefied atmosphere, while serving to dispel ,the pall of fear that had weighted her down since infancy, triggered in her an oppositional mode of behavior as well: *enantiodromia.* This condition, now dominating her actions, is defined as "a one-sided conscious attitude [which] constellates its opposite in the unconscious" (Edinger,"An Outline of Analytical Psychology" 2). So exaggerated were the feelings of release and self-confidence in her adolescent ego that her imaginary world became her reality Never before having seen anyone practicing the art of spinning or weaving, it is no wonder that the princess stood in awe before the "nice" old lady.

The "Nice" Old Lady and Her Spindle. Who was this seemingly endearing old lady living in a dungeon? Like the Fates, she spun, wove, and sewed, thus performing activities identified with creating, shaping, and structuring, but also with cutting the fabric of a person's earthly existence. As an aspect of the Great Mother or matrix, she stood for the transitory nature of the life process. As a personification of a disguised appeal for acceptance, love and recognition, she would entrap the princess, but on a positive note, she would offer her new possibilities of developing her consciousness within, of course, the preestablished or fated design of her future (Jung, 91, #187). Although seemingly destructive in Perrault's tale, the "nice" old lady may be considered a positive force in fulfilling the adolescent's life: for it is she who will bring her to the next stage of her emotional development. Like Lachesis, in charge of measuring time, the old lady, as spinner and weaver of the young girl's web of earthly activities, redraws and retwists the fibers into thread, thus altering the previous focus of her existence. No sooner, therefore, does the old lady allow the princess to take hold of the spindle than the young girl pierces her finger and falls into a dead faint. Predictably, all attempts to revive her are in vain.

Although needles, spindles, pins, darts, and other pointed instruments inserted into someone's skin or body may be considered phallic symbols, in the princess's case, they are to be looked upon as protective devices as well. She is psychologically unprepared for marriage (symbolized by her syncopal reaction to the phallic image—the piercing of her finger), and the hundred- year sleep would serve to impede any matrimonial union, cut her off from mundane pursuits, and, most importantly, shield her from the effects of puberty. The time allotted to her during her long slumber—not a death—will permit her to indwell, that is, to evolve subliminally, thereby preparing her for her future love and parenting experience.

The Great Sleep. Upon being alerted that the princess had fainted, the king had her carried into the most beautiful room in the palace and placed on a bed whose spread was embroidered in silver and gold. Although her eyes remained closed, the princess's cheeks retained their rosy hue and her lips their coralflush. Her audible breathing indicated that she was alive,

The good fairy, who had altered the curse placed on the princess, although a thousand leagues away, was instantaneously apprised of the catastrophe by a dwarf. Dwarfs or elves, often appear in fairy tales focusing on children for, like them, they may be devilish, roguish, and impulsive. Known for their skills and their diligent work habits, they frequently figure as helpers to the young. Their small size was not considered a deformity, but rather identified them with "tiny" or remote possibilities of finding alternative means of handling dangerous situations (Jung, 91, #268).

No sooner was she informed of the princess's condition than the good fairy hopped into her flaming chariot drawn by dragons (Gr. *drakon, derkomai;* see, sharp-sighted), which took her by air to the castle. Positive attributes are here ascribed to the fairy's dragons, in sharp contrast to the symbolism of the principle of evil in Christian lore. St. George, St. Michael, St. Patrick, and a host of other men proved their heroism as slayers of dragons and thus destroyers of evil By contrast, dragons in ancient times were often considered guardians of treasures, as in the Greek legend of the Golden Fleece. In China, to these same fabulous monsters were ascribed dynamic intelligence, strength, and wisdom, so that they became identified with imperial power. Because many Christians thought that subhuman psychological characteristics were lodged in dragons, the animals became associated, psychologically, with a seemingly equally fearsome beast—the feminine. Throughout the Middle Ages and thereafter, the dragon as a female force was featured as spewing flames—thus as a monstrous destroyer of everything in her wake. What was not taken into consideration in the rigid patriarchy of the times was the meaning of fire in general, and of its issuance from the dragon's gullet in particular. Fire as energy, if properly directed, could produce positive results: it could cook and thereby transform what formerly was raw. As ably demonstrated by Claude Lévi-Strauss in his *The Raw and the Cooked*, fire transforms and acculturates what was formerly crude and unrefined. The fairy's choice of dragons to guide her chariot to the tower indicated not only a need to take her to her destination as rapidly as possible, but demonstrates as well that fire/energy, if directed toward positive purposes, may turn what originally was a curse into a carefully nurtured, fruitful life experience.

Upon arrival at the palace, the deeply sensitive fairy, foreseeing how lonely the princess would be when she awoke one hundred years later to find herself surrounded by strangers took it upon herself once again to protect her from sorrow. By touching with her magic wand everyone (except the king and queen) and everything (even the fires used for cooking) in the castle, she put them all to sleep. Psychologically fascinating is the fairy's intent to allow the parents to die at their allotted hour, thereby permitting the princess upon awakening to make her own decisions and take responsibility for her own wellfare. Indeed, she was endowing her with the prerogative of grown-ups, Moments after sleep had engulfed the palace, a protective wall of trees, shrubs, and thorny bushes was set in place to safeguard the area from intruders. Only the castle's towers remained visible from a distance.

THE MEANING OF SLEEP. Sleep, throughout ancient times, was recognized as crucial to the healing process, whether physical or psychological. Had not the Greeks in one of their most famous healing centers—Epidaurus, devoted to the physician God, Aesculapius—effected cures of the physically ill by analyzing their incubation dreams? Using procedures very different from today's psychiatric hours, the priests at healing centers in Greece first gave their patient a drink from the the spring of forgetfulness (Lethe) and then from that of re-membrance (Mnemosyne), permitting the forgetting of the past and the recall of dreams. Interestingly, instances of Aesculapius's miraculous cures were identified during the early centuries of the Common Era with those of Jesus. Fearing the power this Greek physician exercised over the people, the early Church regarded Aesculapius as one of its greatest foes. Because some of Jesus' miracles had been confused with those of Aesculapius, it was claimed that the former's name derived from Jaso (Aesculapius's daughter), and from *lashtai* (to heal) (Pongracz and Santner, *Les rêves à travers les ages* 55).

When the princess fell asleep, her adolescent ego was still weak and unprepared for marriage and motherhood. That the fairy had the genial idea of putting everyone in the castle to sleep, while also endowing the princess "with the pleasure of pleasant dreams," indicated her understanding of sleep as a working period, instrumental in the adolescent's maturation process. Although the princess's ego was submerged in repose, that is, in timelessness, dream activity continued, encouraging her, paradoxically, to grow in understanding. In a process like that of as-sociation in filmic sequences, the princess's unconscious took charge of linking together the separate images that were being formed in her subliminal sphere. The capacity to transform the disparate feelings, sensations, and/ or ideations cohabiting within her unconscious into what might be called a scenario, encouraged her to "spin her yarn," so to speak, or fantasize freely in her sleep. Upon the princess's awakening, she might perhaps be able to articulate her inner drama coherently, by bringing subliminal sequences or happenings onto conscious levels.

Like the spinning, weaving, and cutting processes that are interwoven throughout *Sleeping Beauty*, dream images are also to be understood as threads connecting an ambiguous or visionless past with a still-undeciphered future. Wasn't it thanks to the thread Ariadne gave Theseus before he entered the labyrinth that he was able to find his way out of the dark and confusing maze—into enlightenment in the outside world?

So the princess's magical sleep, unlike death when the body decomposes, is to be regarded as a transitional and beneficial period in her life. This kind of *regressus ad uterum*, as in Orphic ritualistic descents, invited the princess's psyche to penetrate preexistent spheres of being: those matriarchal folds linking feelings of love, wholeness, and the sexual experience into one. The princess's passive acceptance of the dream sphere enabled her to descend into the chthonic domain of the nourishing Great Mother. That her body experienced a condition of physical stasis in no way, as previously mentioned, deterred her activity in subliminal spheres. The period of indwelling, which sleep had forced upon the princess, encouraged her to develop a broader approach to life that would, upon her awakening, endow her with a greater understanding of human nature. As written in the Mandukya Upanishad: "The life of man is divided between waking, dreaming, and dreamless sleep. But transcending these three states is superconscious vision—called The Fourth" (*The Upanishads* 49).

THE PRINCE'S ARRIVAL AND SEXUAL INTERCOURSE. After a hundred years had elapsed, the son of a neighboring king who had been hunting in the vicinity caught site of towers in the distance. Upon questioning several people, he was told that they were inhabited by spirits and sorcerers, as well as ogres who fed on little children. An old peasant, having heard a different story, reported that the towers housed a beautiful sleeping princess. Inflamed by the very thought of this exquisite creature, the prince, like any hero of old, braved the fearsome stillness and deathly immobility of the premises. Making his way through the thickly forested area, he noticed that the trees, thorns, and brambles parted before him, as though helping him walk with ease directly toward the castle. Guided, seemingly, by some unknown inner power, he proceeded through the great marble courtyard, ascended a stairway, continued through some rooms, and then beheld the most "divinely luminous" young maiden he had ever seen. Consumed with excitement, he knelt atremble before this resplendent creature.

As an *anima* image, defined as an "autonomous psychic content in the male personality," the princess took on the most exalted of qualities for the prince: not merely the incarnation of beauty and love, but of connectedness as well (Edinger, *Melville's Moby Dick* 5). Sensing, then recognizing her beloved from the many dreams she had had during her hundred-year sleep, the princess looked at him most tenderly, then asked: "Is it you, my prince? I have long awaited your arrival" (*Sleeping Beauty* 252). Charmed and moved by her words, the prince, traumatized by the sight of such exquisiteness, was unable to convey his joy and gratitude coherently. Finally mustering sufficient self-control, he told her he loved her more than himself. Warmed and comforted by each other's presence, the two spoke for four hours, at the end of which they realized they had still not told each other half the things they wanted to say. A note of levity is injected into the narrative when the prince, loath to hurt her feelings, refrains from mentioning her outmoded clothes.

What would be the role the princess would play in the prince's life? Would she be his *femme inspiratrice*, the idealized mate for whom he had evidently been waiting? Or would her love serve as a catalyst to arouse him sexually? Certainly, their meeting redirected the lives of both—giving them a new awareness of their great love for one another, and a mutual sense of commitment. The princess's awakening brought joy and a mood of ebullience to the palace. The entire court had begun to stir with activity. The hall of mirrors served as the lovers' dining hall, a metaphor perhaps for certain ancient sacred spaces. The continuous motility and interplay of glimmering reflections may be considered an externalization of their impassioned mutual love. Their marriage was celebrated that very evening in the palace's chapel, and was consummated in the princess's bedroom, A note of frivolity was interjected by the author after the princess's lady-in-waiting drew the curtain around the bed, and commented "they slept very little for the princess was not in need of it" (*Sleeping Beauty* 253).

Upon returning to his own castle the following morning, the prince did not inform his parents of his marriage. Seeking to allay his father's anxiety, he accounted for his absence by telling both parents that he had lost his way in the forest. His trusting father believed him. His mother, inured to the ways of the world, concluded that he had fallen in love.

Although time sequences are muddled in fairy tales, and those in *Sleeping Beauty* are no exception, readers learn that for the next two years the prince settled into a routine; by night he lived with his wife, by day, with his parents. Two beautiful children—a girl, Aurora, and a boy, Day—were born to the couple.

THE VAGINA DENTATA—OGRESS/MOTHER. Knowing that his mother was descended from a race of ogres, the prince took every precaution to protect his wife and children from her aggressive, vicious, and devouring proclivities. Although the queen was a veritable *vagina dentata* type, the prince nonetheless loved his piranha-like mother. In keeping with similar mother/son relationships, his was fraught with ambiguity.

The Terrible Mother archetype in myths is not in short supply; Kali, Hecate, Empusa, Gorgon, Lamia, Lilith, female demons, witches, and countless destructive spirits whirl about individuals who realize their helplessness against, and dependency upon, these devastating and overpowering mothers/maws (Neumann, The Origins and History of Consciousness 40), The benumbing dynamism of the ogress in Sleeping Beauty emphasizes the lengths to which the Terrible Mother would go to assuage her appetite.

Inhabitants of dark, hidden, and forbidding areas within the psyche, ogress mothers usually draw on vulnerable, malleable, and still-unformed beings for food. Although the prince in our narrative would have liked to be loved and cared for by his mother, her flesh-eating instinct had not gone unnoticed by him. While she inspired dread in those about her, the prince must have learned during his formative years how best to protect himself from this castrating predator. Rather than adopting a confrontational attitude toward her, which would have undoubtedly led to a dismemberment of his ego, he sidestepped, obfuscated, or clearly lied in order to ward off her maniacal outbursts. Such tactics caused neither a diminution of his ego's directive powers, nor a weakening of the masculine side of consciousness.

Imprisoned in her blind anthropophagous need to consume whatever might deter her from realizing her inborn phobic hunger to dominate, rule, stunt, and arrest the development of individuals who seek to evolve and mature, she, like the Terrible Father Kronos/Saturn, also sought to subvert time—or the life/death factor—by devouring his progeny. It comes as no surprise, then, that Kronos/Saturn was later called the God of time. Having rejected her role as genetrix, the ogress in Sleeping Beauty sought to destroy her genitors. Amoral rather than immoral in her flesh-driven appetite, she was oblivious of the suffering she brought to her entourage.

The prince had noticed on repeated occasions that in the presence of children, his mother was barely able to control her ravenous need to devour them. Indeed, her unappeasable appetite was nearly always focused on children—a metaphor for futurity—indicating an inborn terror of having her power usurped by younger, and eventually stronger, elements. Anxiety for those he loved dictated his unwillingness to confide in her the secret of his marriage and the birth of his children. Although he had succeeded to a great extent in becoming emotionally separated from his mother, the threat of matriarchal castration must have nonetheless loomed large on his horizon, urging him forever to take precautions. Nor did he trust his father. Not because of any malice on the part of his parent, but for his naivete and his weakly structured ego which, under pressure, the prince feared, might easily be urged to reveal his closely guarded secret Important as well was the fact that his father, having married his mother for her wealth, had never known the meaning of love. How could he possibly understand his son's feelings for his wife and children? Or his fears for their well-being? Although the ties of a mitigated love for the prince's mother and father remained, the young man was no Attis. The princes psychological hiatus between him and his parents had already been effected; therefore, he suffered no guilt with regard to them. On the contrary, his ability to reason and his understanding of their positive and negative attributes, had set him well on the way toward independence (Neumann, *Origins* 117).

THE CHILDREN, The prince's daughter having been named Dawn, and his son, Day, suggests that their birth may have symbolized their mother's rebirth, her awakening to the light of consciousness, and her fulfillment in marriage and motherhood.

Dawn (Aurora), meaning to begin, to appear, to develop, suggests the birth of a series of days and the possibilities of realizing one's dreams and hopes. Such a time frame allows for a maturation process ands a birth of light, or God's victory over darkness:

Hast thou commanded the morning since thy days; and caused the day spring to know his place;
That it might take hold of the ends, of the earth, that the wicked might be shaken out of it;
It is turned as clay to the seal; and they stand as a garment.
And from the wicked their light is witholden, and the high arm shall be broken. (Job 38:12–15)

While day represents both sunrise and sunset, as well as a succession of definite time periods, it contains not only each day's residue, but that of a lifetime as well. Whenever short or long expanses of time are activated, and past memories recalled, lessons may be drawn from the variety of each individual's experience. The birth of Dawn and Day, therefore, suggests a turning point in the lives of their parents. Just as every individual must live out her or his own rite of passage, so the protagonists in *Sleeping Beauty*, must confront theirs.

Only after the prince's father had died, and the kingship had passed to him, did he publicly announce his marriage and the birth of his children. With pomp and circumstance, he then went to his wife's castle and bought his family to live with him. Aware of his mother's anthropophagous inclinations, the reader may wonder why the prince, upon being called to war shortly after assuming the kingship, left his mother in charge not only of his domain but of his greatest treasures—his wife and children.

A NONINTERFERENCE COURSE» Instances arise when noninterference may be the most appropriate means of resolving life-threatening situations/With her son gone, free from his judgmental eye, the ogress mother—experiencing perhaps the same kind of freedom the princess had felt with the departure of her parents on that fateful day—allowed her instincts free rein. Repairing to the family's country home with her daughter-in-law and her grandchildren, she ordered her steward to *cook* the four-year-old Dawn and serve her in a sauce of spices and vinegar, symbolically masking her flesh-eating needs. The steward, sickened at the thought of committing such a heinous act and catching sight of the delightful little girl running happily toward him, dropped his knife and began to cry. Reversing his steps, he went to the barnyard, severed the neck of a little lamb, cooked it, and served it to the queen mother, who complimented him on the succulence of the dish. Unseen by the queen mother, he took Dawn for safekeeping to his wife's lodgings in the far corner of the barnyard. A week later, the ogress asked that Day, her three-year-old grandson, be served to her with the same sauce. This time, the steward substituted a baby doe for the boy, who was also sent into hiding with his sister. And again the queen mother consumed the morsels of flesh with intense gusto. Shortly afterward, she requested that the steward kill and cook her daughter-in-law. Again the steward refused to comply. Failing, however, to find an appropriate animal to serve to the ogress, he went to the young queen and apprised her of his dilemma. Since the demise of her children, she confided in him, life held no more meaning for her. It was, therefore, his duty to kill her. Moved to the extreme by the gentle woman's loving manner, the steward took her to her children, after which he slaughtered a young hind, which he served to the satisfied ogress.

One evening, however, while the ogress was prowling around the farmyard in search of fresh meat, she heard voices, which she recognized as those of Dawn, Day, and their mother. So outraged was she at the deception that she ordered a fire to be lit under a huge vat filled with toads, vipers, snakes, and a variety of serpents. After the queen, her children, the steward, his wife, and her servant had been bound, and just as the executioner was about to cast them all into the vat, the king entered the courtyard on horseback and demanded to know the meaning of this "horrible spectacle" (*Sleeping Beauty* 257). Foiled, the ogress threw herself headlong into the vat and was instantaneously devoured.

The very human king who had always loved his mother despite her anthropophagous instincts, was saddened by her death. Soon, however, he found consolation, joy, and enrichment in his wife, children, and kingship.

Fate, the supernatural, wish fulfillment, verisimilitude, and fabulous events such as a hundred-year sleep, were instrumental in paving the way for the maturation process of both the princess and her prince in *Sleeping Beauty,*

Generally passive, neutral, and apathetic, the adolescent princess acted overtly only once—on the day her parents had gone away. Aggressively and spunkily, she demonstrated a need to enter into the life experience. Her mother and father had so feared for their child's well-being that they had prevented her from stepping out into the world to carve out a life for herself. Like an infant taking her first steps, she, not surprisingly stumbled at the outset. In time, however, she ceased falling and developed a relatively strong self-image. With glee, abandon, and a tinge of rebellion, she found a sense of excitement and fortitude in her newly achieved independence.

The healing sleep from which the princess awakened brought her understanding and the capacity to love without fear or guilt. Prepared for the responsibilities of marriage and motherhood, she not only accepted the prince's difficult familial situation, but understood the importance of biding her time. The prince's ability to protect his wife and children against the continuous threat of his ogress mother indicated his strength of character and augured well for the rulership of his kingdom and for his role as husband and father. That he neither feared nor despised, nor took overt action against his mother, revealed his ability to cope with a panoply of vastly different personality types—necessary for any ruler. The ogress,"unable to satisfy her own inner rage," took her life, thereby ending the possibility of malevolence—at least temporarily—in the royal couple's world.

Donkey Skin

Charles Perrault

Once upon a time lived the most powerful king in the world. Gentle in peace, terrifying in war, he was incomparable in all ways. His neighbors feared him while his subjects were content. Throughout his realm the fine arts and civility flourished under his protection. His better half, his constant companion, was charming and beautiful. Such was her sweet and good nature that he was less happy as king and more happy as her husband. Out of their tender, pure wedlock a daughter was born, and she had so many virtues that she consoled them for their inability to have more children.

Everything was magnificent in their huge palace. They had an ample group of courtiers and servants all around them. In his stables the king had large and small horses of every kind, which were adorned with beautiful trappings, gold braids, and embroidery. But what surprised everyone on entering the stables was a master donkey in the place of honor. This discrepancy may be surprising, but if you knew the superb virtues of this donkey, you would probably agree that there was no honor too great for him. Nature had formed him in such a way that he never emitted an odor. Instead he generated heaps of beautiful gold coins that were gathered from the stable litter every morning at sunrise.

Now, heaven, which always mixes the good with the bad, just like rain may come in good weather, permitted a nasty illness to suddenly attack the queen. Help was sought everywhere, but neither the learned physicians nor the charlatans who appeared , were able to arrest the fever, which increased day by day. When her last hour arrived, the queen said to her husband,"Before I die, you must promise me one thing, and that is, if you should desire to remarry when I am gone—"

"Ah!" said the king,"your concern is superfluous. I'd never think of doing such a thing. You can rest assured about that."

"I believe you," replied the queen,"if your ardent love is any proof. But to make me more certain, I want you to swear that you'll give your pledge to another woman only if she is,more beautiful, more accomplished, and wiser than I." ~ like a challenge   most important quality

Her confidence in her qualities and her cleverness were such that she knew he would regard his promise as an oath never to remarry. With his eyes bathed in tears, he swore to do everything the queen desired. Then she died in his arms.

Never did a king make such a commotion. Day and night he could be heard sobbing, and many believed that he could not keep mourning so bitterly for long. Indeed, some said-he wept about his deceased wife like a man who wanted to end the matter in haste.

In truth, this was the case. At the end of several months he wanted to move on with his life and choose a new queen. But this was not easy to do. He had to keep his word, and his new wife had to have more charms and grace than his dead one, who had become immortalized. Neither the court, with its great quantity of beautiful women, nor the city, the country, or foreign kingdoms, where the rounds were made, could provide the king with such a woman.

The only one more beautiful was his daughter. In truth, she even possessed certain attractive qualities that her deceased mother had not had. The king himself noticed this, and he fell so ardently in love with her that he became mad. He convinced himself that this love was reason enough for him to marry her. He even found a casuist who argued logically that a case could be made for such a marriage. But the young princess was greatly troubled to hear him talk of such love and grieved night and day.

Thus the princess sought out her godmother, who lived at some distance from the castle in a grotto of coral and pearls. She was a remarkable fairy, far superior to any of her kind. There is no need to tell you what a fairy was like in those most happy of times, for I am certain that your mother has told you about them when you were very young. '

Upon seeing the princess, the fairy said,"I know why you've come. I know your heart is filled with sadness. But there's no need to worry, for I am with you. If you follow my advice,! there's nothing that can harm you. It's true that your father wants to marry you, and if you were to listen to his insane request, it would be a grave mistake. However, there's a way to refuse him without contradicting him. Tell him that before you'd be willing to abandon your heart to him, he must grant your wishes and give you a dress the color of the sky. In spite of all his power and wealth and the favorable signs of the stars, he'll never be able to fulfill your request."

So the princess departed right away, and trembling, went to her amorous father. He immediately summoned his tailors and ordered them to make a dress the color of the sky without delay. "Or else, be assured I will hang you all."

The sun was just dawning the next day when they brought the desired dress, the most beautiful blue of the firmament. There was not a color more like the sky, and it was encircled by large clouds of gold. Though the princess desired it, she was caught between joy and pain. She did not know how to respond or get out of her promise. Then her godmother said to her in a low voice,"Princess, ask for a more radiant dress. Ask for one the color of the moon. He'll never be able to give that to you."

No sooner did the princess make the request than the king said to his embroiderer,"I want a dress that will glisten greater than the star of night, and I want it without fail in four days."

The splendid dress was ready by the deadline set by the king. Up in the night sky the luster of the moon's illumination makes the stars appear pale, mere scullions in her court. Despite this, the glistening moon was less radiant than this dress of silver.

Admiring this marvelous dress, the princess was almost ready to give her consent to her father, but urged on by her godmother, she said to the amorous king,"I can't be content until I have an even more radiant dress. I want one the color of the sun."

Since the king loved her with an ardor that could not be matched anywhere, he immediately summoned a rich jeweler and ordered him to make a superb garment of gold and diamonds. "And if you fail to satisfy us, you will be tortured to death."

Yet it was not necessary for the king to punish the jeweler, for the industrious man brought him the precious dress by the end of the week. It was so beautiful and radiant that the blond lover of Clytemnestra, when he drove his chariot of gold on the arch of heaven, would have been dazzled by its brilliant rays.

The princess was so confused by these gifts that she did not know what to say. At that moment her godmother took her by the hand and whispered in her ear,"There's no need to pursue this path anymore. There's a greater marvel than all the gifts you have received. I mean that donkey who constantly fills your father's purse with gold coins. Ask him for the donkey skin. Since this rare donkey is the major source of his money, he won't give it to you, unless I'm badly mistaken."

Now this fairy was very clever, and yet she did not realize that passionate love counts more than money or gold, provided that the prospects for its fulfillment are good. So the forfeit-was gallantly granted the moment the princess requested it.

When the skin was brought to her, she was terribly frightened. As she began to complain bitterly about her fate, her godmother arrived. She explained,"If you do your best, there's no need to fear." The princess had to let the king think that she was ready to place herself at his disposal and marry him while preparing at the same time to disguise herself and flee alone to some distant country in order to avoid the impending, evil marriage.

"Here's a large chest," the fairy continued. "You can put your clothes, mirror, toilet articles, diamonds, and rubies in it. I'm going to give you my magic wand. Whenever you hold it in your hand, the chest will always follow your path beneath the ground. And whenever you want to open it, you merely have to touch the ground with my wand, and the chest will appear before you. We'll use the donkey's skin to make you unrecognizable. It's such a perfect disguise and so horrible that once you conceal yourself inside, nobody will ever believe that it adorns anyone so beautiful as you."

Thus disguised, the princess departed from the abode of the wise fairy the next morning as the dew began to drop. When the king started preparations for the marriage celebration, he learned to his horror that his bride-to-be had taken flight. All the houses, roads, and avenues were promptly searched, but in vain. No one could conceive of what had happened to her. Sadness and sorrow spread throughout the realm. There would be no marriage, no feast, no tarts, no sugar-almonds. The ladies at the court were quite disappointed not to he able to dine, but the priest was most saddened, for he had been expecting a heavy donation at the end of the ceremony as well as a hearty meal. *[handwritten margin note: approval ← *of marriage in court]*

Meanwhile the princess continued her flight,, dirtying her face with mud. When she extended her hands to people she met, begging for a place to work, they noticed how much she smelled and how disagreeable she looked, and did not want to have anything to do with such a dirty creature, even though they themselves were hardly less vulgar and mean. Farther and farther she traveled and farther still until she finally arrived at a farm where they needed a scullion to wash the dishclothes and clean out the pig troughs. She was put in a corner of the kitchen, where the servants, insolent and nasty creatures all, ridiculed, contradicted, and mocked her. They kept playing mean tricks on her and harassed her at every chance they had. Indeed, she was the butt of all their jokes.

On Sundays she had a little time to rest. After finishing her morning chores, she went into her room, closed the door, and washed herself. Then she opened the chest and carefully arranged her toilet articles in their little jars in front of her large mirror. Satisfied and happy, she tried on her moon dress, then the one that shone like the sun, and finally the beautiful blue dress that even the sky could not match in brilliance. Her only regret was that she did not have enough room to spread out the trains of the dresses on the floor. Still, she loved to see herself young, fresh as a rose, and a thousand times more elegant than she had ever been. Such sweet pleasure kept her going from one Sunday to the next.

I forgot to mention that there was a large aviary on this farm that belonged to a powerful and magnificent king. All sorts of strange fowls were kept there: chickens from Barbary, rails, guinea fowls, cormorants, musical birds, quacking ducks, and a thousand other kinds, which were the match of ten other courts put together. The kings son often stopped at this charming spot on his return from the hunt to rest and enjoy a cool drink. He was more handsome than Cephalus and had a regal and martial appearance that made the proudest batallions tremble. From a distance Donkey-Skin admired him with a tender look. Thanks to her courage, she realized that she still had the heart of a princess beneath her dirt and rags.

"What a grand manner he has!" she said, even though he paid no attention to her. "How gracious he is, and how happy must be the woman who has captured his heart! If he were to honor me with the plainest dress imaginable, I'd feel more decorated than in any of those I have."

One Sunday the young prince was wandering adventurously from courtyard to courtyard, and he passed through an obscure hallway, where Donkey-Skin had her humble room. He chanced to peek through the keyhole, and since it was a holiday, she had dressed herself up as richly as possible in her dress of gold and diamonds that shone like the sun. Succumbing to fascination, the prince kept peeking at her, scarcely breathing because he was filled with such pleasure. Her magnificent dress, her beautiful face, her lovely manner, her fine traits, and her young freshness moved him a thousand times over. But most of all, he was captivated by the air of grandeur mingled with modest reserve that bore witness to the beauty of her soul.

Three times he was on the verge of entering her room because of the ardor that overwhelmed him, but three times he refrained out of respect for the seemingly divine creature he was beholding.

Returning to the palace, he became pensive. Day and night he sighed, refusing to attend any of the balls even though it was Carnival. He began to hate hunting and attending the theater. He lost his appetite, and everything saddened his heart. At the root of his malady was a deadly melancholy.

He inquired about the remarkable nymph who lived in one of the lower courtyards at the end of the dingy alley where it remained dark even in broad daylight.

"You mean Donkey-Skin," he was told. "But there's nothing nymphlike or beautiful about her. She's called Donkey-Skin because of the skin that she wears on her back. She's the ideal remedy for anyone in love. That beast is almost uglier than a wolf."

All this was said in vain, for he did not believe it. Love had left its mark and could not be effaced. However, his mother, whose only child he was, pleaded with him to tell her what was wrong, yet she pressured him in vain. He moaned, wept, and sighed. He said nothing, except that he wanted Donkey-Skin to make him a cake with her own hands. And so, his mother could only repeat what her son desired.

"Oh, heavens, madam!" the servants said to her. "This Donkey-Skin is a black drab, uglier and dirtier than the most wretched scullion."

"It doesn't matter," the queen said. "Fulfilling his request is the only thing that concerns us." His mother loved him so much that she would have served him anything on a golden platter.

Meanwhile, Donkey-Skin took some ground flour, salt, butter, and fresh eggs in order to make the dough especially fine. Then she locked herself alone in her room to make the cake. She washed her hands, arms, and face and put on a silver smock in honor of the task that she was about to undertake. It is said that in working a bit too hastily, a precious ring happened to fall from Donkey-Skin's finger into the batter. But some claim that she dropped the ring on purpose. As for me, quite frankly, I can believe it because when the prince had stopped at the door and looked through the keyhole, she must have seen him. Women are so alert that nothing escapes their notice. Indeed, I pledge my word on it that she was convinced her young lover would gratefully receive her ring.

There was never a cake kneaded so daintily as this one, and the prince found it so good that he immediately began ravishing it and almost swallowed the ring. However, when he saw the remarkable emerald and the narrow band of gold, his heart was ignited by an inexpressible joy. At once he put the ring under his pillow. Yet that did not cure his malady. Upon seeing him grow worse day by day, the doctors, wise with experience, used their great science to come to the conclusion that he was sick with love.

Whatever else one may say about marriage, it is a perfect remedy for love sickness. So it was decided that the prince should marry. After he deliberated for some time, he finally said," I'll be glad to get married provided that I marry only the person whose finger fits this ring."

This strange demand surprised the king and queen very much, but he was so sick that they did not dare to say anything that might upset him. Now a search began for the person whose finger might fit the ring, no matter what class or lineage. The only requirement was that the woman be ready to come and show her finger to claim her due.

A rumor was spread throughout the realm that to claim the prince, one had to have a very slender finger. Consequently, every charlatan, eager to make a name for himself, pretended that he possessed the secret of making a finger slender. Following such capricious advice, one woman scraped her finger like a turnip. Another cut a little piece off. Still another used some liquid to remove the skin from her finger and reduce its size. All sorts of plans imaginable were concocted by women to make their fingers fit the ring.

The selection was begun with the young princesses, marquesses, and duchesses, but no matter how delicate their fingers were, they were too large for the ring. Then the countesses, baronesses, and all the rest of the nobility took their turns and presented their hands in vain. Next came well-proportioned working girls who had pretty and slender fingers. Finally, it was necessary to turn to the servants, kitchen help, minor servants, and poultry keepers, in short, to all the trash who with their reddened or blackened hands hoped for a happy fate just as much as those with delicate hands. Many girls presented themselves with large and thick fingers, but trying the prince's ring on their fingers was like trying to thread the eye of a needle with a rope.

Everyone thought that they had reached the end because the only one remaining was Donkey-Skin in the corner of the kitchen. And who could ever believe that the heavens had ordained that she might become queen?

"Why not?" said the prince. "Let her try."

Everyone began laughing and exclaimed aloud,"Do you mean to say that you want that dirty wretch to enter here?"

But when she drew a little hand as white as ivory and of royal blood from under the dirty skin, the destined ring fit perfectly around her finger. The members of the court were astonished. So delirious were they that they wanted to march her to the king right away, but she requested that she be given some time to change her clothes before she appeared before her lord and master. In truth, the people could hardly keep from laughing because of the clothes she was wearing.

Finally, she arrived at the palace and passed through all the halls in her blue dress whose radiance could not be matched. Her blonde hair glistened with diamonds. Her blue eyes, so large and sweet, whose gaze always pleased and never hurt, were filled with a proud majesty. Her waist was so slender that two hands could have encircled it. All the charms and ornaments of the ladies of the court dwindled in comparison. Despite the rejoicing and commotion of the gathering, the good king did not fail to notice the many charms of his future daughter-in-law, and the queen was also terribly delighted. The prince, her dear lover, could hardly bear the excitement of his rapture.

Preparations for the wedding were begun at once. The monarch invited all the kings of the surrounding, countries, who left their lands to attend the grand event, all radiant in their different attire; Those from the East were mounted on huge elephants. The Moors arriving from distant shores were so black and ugly that they frightened the little children. People embarked from all the comers of the world and descended on the court in great numbers. But neither prince nor king seemed as splendid as the bride's father, who had purified the criminal and odious fires that had ignited his spirit in the past. The flame that was left in his soul had been transformed into devoted paternal love. When he saw her, he said,"May heaven be blessed for allowing me to see you again, my dear child."

Weeping with joy, he embraced her tenderly. Everyone wanted to share in his happiness, and the future husband was delighted to learn that he was to become the son-in-law of such a powerful king. At that moment the godmother arrived and told the entire story of how everything had happened and culminated in Donkey-Skin's glory.

Evidently, the moral of this tale implies it is better for a child to expose oneself to hardships than to neglect one's duty.

Indeed, virtue may sometimes seem ill-fated, hut it is always crowned with success. Of course, strongest reason is a weak dike against mad love and ardent ecstacy, especially "if a lover is not afraid to squander rich treasures.

Finally, we must take into account that clear water and brown bread are sufficient" nourishment for all young women provided that they have good habits, and that there is not a damsel under the skies who does not imagine herself beautiful and somehow carrying off the honors in the famous beauty contest between Hera, Aphrodite, and Athena.

The tale of Donkey-Skin is hard to believe,
But as long as there are children on this earth,
With mothers and grandmothers who continue to give birth,
This tale will always be told and surely well received.

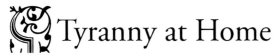# Tyranny at Home

"Catskin" and "Cinderella"

Maria Tatar

> *Anna will never marry until she finds a man exactly like her father.*
>
> Martha Freud

I N "THE MAIDEN WITHOUT HANDS," the Grimms made a spirited effort to mask a father's desire for his daughter. Where most European versions of the tale type (including many of the Grimms' own sources) show a father so enraged by his daughter's refusal to marry him that he chops off her hands (and occasionally her breasts or tongue as well), the Grimms' story places the father in the dreadful—but by no means scandalous—situation of having to choose between forfeiting his own life or maiming his daughter. That he chooses the latter may make him cowardly, graceless, and mean-spirited, but it emphatically removes him from the class of ruthless fiends that his folkloric cousins join when they first court their daughters, then lift the sword against them.

The miller in the Grimms' "Maiden without Hands" makes a pact with the devil. In exchange for untold wealth, he promises to give the devil whatever is standing behind his mill—his daughter, as it turns out, and not the apple tree on which the miller had counted. The doomed maiden succeeds in protecting herself from satanic advances by cleansing herself, first in bathwater, then in tears. In a rage, the devil orders the miller to chop off his daughter's hands or to face perdition. When the terrified miller elects to sacrifice the girl's hands and begs her to forgive him for the injury he is about to inflict on her, his dutiful daughter replies: "Dear Father, do what you want with me. I'm your child."[1] The girl's tears miraculously sanctify her wounds, thereby thwarting the devil's designs on her soul, but she is left with dismembered hands that she binds to her back before setting out on a journey that culminates in her accession to a throne.

Slotting the devil rather than the father into the role of villain in "The Maiden without Hands" was a brilliant move on the part of the Grimms. A tale of family conflict in which a father's sexual desire is turned on his daughter, and thereby instantly demonized, turned into a plot about devilish, rather than human, agency. What was once a frightening, sensational story about a father's illicit passion became a religious exemplum about the devil's drive to capture a girl's soul. In the Grimms' version of the tale, the father is absolved of serious blame and turned into a well-meaning though cowardly figure—one not unlike the fathers in "Hansel and Gretel," "Snow White," and "Beauty and the Beast."[2]

We can see this same tendency to blot out all signs of a father's obstructed incestuous desires as the motive for mutilating his daughter in the Italian tale "Olive." In that story, a Jewish widower leaves his daughter with devout Christians, who promise to raise the girl while he is off on business in distant lands. Not until Olive is eighteen does her father return to claim her, and by then she has become so thoroughly assimilated that she evidently cannot resist reading a copy of the Office of the Blessed Virgin on the sly. In punishment, Olive's father cuts her hands "clean off," then has her taken into the woods and abandoned.[3] Here the sexual conflict is transformed into a contest between the daughter's faith and the father's will, with the Jew, in an interesting example of projection, guilty of religious intolerance. In making the father a Jew who abandons his daughter to Christians, the tale probably suggested to its audience that this father's cruelty and willfulness were uniquely deviant, not at all homologous with the behavior of most fairy-tale fathers and their real-life counterparts.

In most unadulterated versions of "The Maiden without Hands"—including several collected by the Grimms—the heroine is the victim of a father who first demands her hand in marriage, then chops both hands off in retaliation for her refusal of his proposal. Even the literary rewritings of the folktale cannot fully conceal what is behind the father's violent mutilation of the daughter's body. The maiming episode is generally reported in the dispassionate, factual style of the folktale, with no searing descriptions of pain and no particular explanation provided for the mutilation of the arms. It is tempting to argue with Alan Dundes that "since the father is after his daughter's hand, he takes it literally'" especially in view of the highly charged meaning of a woman's hand as reflected in the church marriage ceremony of Western tradition dating from the thirteenth century[4]—a service in which the father relinquishes power over his daughter by transferring physical possession of her hand to her husband (he must stand and observe the priest placing :he bride's hand into that of the groom).[5] But it is not particularly satisfying to rely on an explanation for mutilation that rests on a linguistic foundation alone. Besides, what are we to make of variant episodes that show a father cutting off his daughter's breasts or cutting out her tongue? In point of fact, the latter two acts square more closely with the psychological twists and turns taken by the tale. Removing the breasts [think of the martyrdom of Saint Agnes and Saint Barbara) would symbolically de-sexualize the daughter and hence diminish the number of rivals in competition with the father.[6] Cutting off the tongue (think of Tereus's rape and mutilation of his sister-in-law Philomela in Ovid's *Metamorphoses*) would silence the daughter and prevent her from broadcasting her father's base deeds.[7]

In "The Girl with Maimed Hands," Basile goes to such great lengths to motivate the removal of his heroine's hands that we get a vivid sense the motif's problematic opaqueness. Basile's Penta is beside herself when her brother (an occasional substitute for the father in this tale type) reveals his plans to marry her. Once she has collected herself, she demands to know just what it is that stirs her brother's desire for her. He replies with a speech so extraordinary in its baroque detail that it deserves to be cited in full:

> "My Penta, you are lovely and perfect from the crown of your head to the soles of your shoes, but above all things it is your hands that enchant me; that hand, like a fork, draws the entrails from the cauldron of my heart; that hand, like a hood, lifts up the bucket of my soul from the well of this life; that hand, like pincers, grips my spirit while Love works on it like a file. O hand, O lovely hand, ladle which pours out sweetness, pliers which rend my desires, shovel which piles on coals to make my heart boil over!"[8]

Penta cuts his speech short, summons a servant, and orders him to sever her hands from her body. After placing the hands in a porcelain bowl covered with a silk cloth, she sends a message to her brother, entreating him "to enjoy what delighted him most" and "wishing him good health and fine sons."[9]

"The Maiden without Hands" gives us the extreme form of a heroine disempowered by a coercive male—usually a father. We shall see that the many stories about beauties and beasts ("The Search for the Lost Husband" [AT 425]) illustrate the perils of forced marriages, unions in which women must submit unquestioningly to matches made by then- fathers and must follow a standard cultural script that privileges filial obedience over the free choice of a sexual partner.[10] "The Maiden without Hands," by contrast, violates every cultural script, if we are to believe, as Freud and Lévi-Strauss assert, that the incest taboo marks the beginning of social organization and signals the passage from nature to culture.[11] With hands severed from their arms, the heroine's body stands as an emblem of disempowerment, helplessness, and victimization. Deprived of the very appendages that have served the creation of culture, she has been moved, through a double violation—the mutilation of her hands as well as the attempted assault on her body—into the realm of nature, the sphere traditionally associated with women by virtue of their privileged biological role and assigned social role in the reproductive process. As Simone de Beauvoir concluded some years ago, the female is "more enslaved to the species than the male, her animality is more manifest."[12] When we learn how the maimed heroine pathetically shakes an apple tree with her body to reap its harvest, or nibbles at pears hanging from low branches, we realize the extent to which her bodily state has forced her to become a foraging creature and reduced her to pathetic dependency on nature's bounty.

The heroine's status as victim is doubly enacted in the tale. In the second phase of the plot, the heroine marries die king in whose garden she had sought nourishment, but becomes the target of a jealous mother-in-law's evil designs while the king is at war with a neighboring land. (The Grimms' version, once again, veers away from family conflict by resurrecting the devil as the source of mischief in the second part of the tale as well as the first.) When the queen gives birth, the mother-in- law writes her son that a dog or some kind of monster has been delivered, whereupon the king orders that his wife and child be abandoned or murdered (the queen is then sent into the forest with her nursing infant bound to her back). If it is not the devil who engineers the murder of queen and child, it is almost invariably a female figure, usually the king's mother but in some cases his sister.

The girl without hands thus becomes the fairy-tale victim par excellence, the prey of paternal power rim wild and of maternal jealousy that knows no limits. Bent by the burden of the child bound to her back, and with two stumps for hands, she represents a supremely abject portrait of helplessness. Yet this pathetic figure, who has no sooner escaped incestuous violation than she is driven out of her marital home by a fiendish mother-in-law, has been read by folklorists as the real villain of the story. What Alan Dundes has to say succinctly summarizes their argument:

> The maiden without hands is *a girl who wants to marry her father,* but this taboo cannot be expressed directly. So through projective inversion, it is the father who wants to marry his daughter. This is not to say that there may not be fathers who are sexually attracted to their own daughters, but only that in fairy tales, it is the daughter's point of view which is articulated. … Since … *it is the girl who is guilty of the original incestuous thought,* it is appropriate that it is the girl who is punished for this thought, [p. 61; my emphasis][13]

For Dundes, a story that describes the tyrannical demands of a father on his daughter is, in reality, nothing more than the pretext for a plot detailing a daughter's desire for her father. Dundes bases his argument on the assumption that fairy tales "represent the child's point of view" and are thus constantly turning parent-victims into parent-oppressors, a line of thinking similar to the one followed by Freud in his qualified rejection of patients' stories about incestuous seduction.[14] (Our earlier look at children's literature has shown us just how "successful" adults have been in capturing the child's point of view when they create stories about children for children.) The "guilty" child simply projects its own sins and transgressions onto the "innocent" parent. Were this so consistently the case as Dundes would have us believe, then "Hansel and Gretel" would be a story that is ostensibly about children abandoned by their parents in the woods, but in reality about parents who are left to starve by their children. Or, more to the point for our context,"Beauty and the Beast" would not really be about a girl who is forced into marriage with a beast by her father, but about a father who is forced into an undesirable marriage by his daughter. That the propositions are so preposterous for these two tales suggests something amiss in Dundes' model of projective inversion.

Dundes' interpretation of "The Maiden without Hands" is a perfect illustration of the hazards of giving too much weight to "hidden meanings" while neglecting the significance of a tale's manifest content. A fairy tale's surface events often work in tandem with latent undercurrents to generate the productive ambiguities that engage our attention as listeners and readers. In "The Maiden without Hands," the father's sexual desire for his daughter may elicit her repudiation of his advances in the chain of the tale's events, but that desire has deep psychological resonances that implicate the daughter in all her vulnerability. To see a daughter as wholly detached from the drama of her father's desire is just as absurd as labeling her "guilty of the original incestuous thought" when it is the father who makes the advances. Dundes makes the error of ignoring textual realities that unequivocally show us a father (who as male parent stands in the most asymmetrical possible power relationship to a female child) taking coercive action against his daughter.[15] Dundes sees "The Maiden without Hands" as a text that blames the victim, when in fact he himself engages in the very practice he identifies at work in the psychological dynamics of the tale.

Stories of father/daughter incest invariably show the father as aggressor, with the daughter as successful resister or unwilling victim. But note how a daughter becomes tainted by her father's evil no matter what the circumstances. Here is how Gower tells the story of the King of Antioch in Shakespeare's *Pericles:*

> This king unto him took a peer,
> Who died and left a female heir,
> So buxom, blithe, and full of face,
> As heaven had lent her all his grace;
> With whom the father liking took,
> And her to incest did provoke:
> Bad child; worse father! to entice his own
> To evil should be done by none.
>
> *(Pericles,* prologue: 21–28)

The father may be the instigator of the incest and may be condemned in the harshest possible terms, but his daughter, by responding to the "provocation," becomes by implication a "bad child."[16]

The Aarne/Thompson tale type index fails to note the obvious links between "The Maiden without Hands" (AT 706) and "The Dress of Gold, of Silver, and of Stars" (AT 510B), a tale type that—following the practice of Marian Roalfe Cox—I will henceforth refer to as "Catskin."[17] Both tale types dictate the presence of a father intent on marrying his unwilling daughter and chart the successful evasive action she takes. They also illustrate the perils of excessive paternal devotion and stand in sharp contrast to "Cinderella," the story paired with "Catskin" in the tale type index as AT 510A. In place of the overly affectionate father in "The Maiden without Hands" and "Catskin," "Cinderella" (and for that matter "Snow White" [AT 709]) gives us an insufficiently affectionate mother who withholds love from her (step) daughter.

In all these tale types, a persecuted heroine must flee home in order to escape a parental oppressor, either one who overwhelms her with too much (paternal) love *or* who punishes her with too little (maternal) love, but rarely both. The two stories give us different aspects of one plot—each demonizing only one of the two parental actors in that drama of family conflict.[18] That the two plots really constitute only one story becomes clear from the ease with which "The Maiden without Hands" can cross over from tale type AT 706 to become a "Cinderella" or "Snow White" tale.

A late nineteenth-century German variant of "The Maiden without Hands" from the region of Mecklenburg, for example, describes the fate of a girl whose father remarries after his wife has died. After the death of the father, the heroine's stepmother runs an inn and becomes enraged by the attention paid to her stepdaughter by guests. She takes the girl down to the cellar and gives her a choice between two grisly options: "to be burned with sulfur or to have her arms and feet cut off (the arms right up to the elbows, the feet right up to the knees)."[19] The remainder of the tale charts the heroine's sufferings and redemption, capped by the obligatory punishment of the stepmother who is "torn into pieces by four oxen." The ease with which the stepmother moves into the slot of villain in "The Girl without Hands," without for one moment altering the motivation for her hatred of the heroine, illustrates the essential unity of what has turned into one plot about fathers driven by incestuous desires and another about stepmothers whose murderous schemes are fueled by sexual jealousy.

Interestingly, however, our own age has suppressed tales of paternal incestuous desire even as it has turned stories about maternal evil into cultural icons.[20] Given the radical shift in audience for fairy tales as they moved from the workroom into the nurseiy, it is easy enough to understand why the forbidding theme of incest—along with any sexually-charged matters—would be erased as quickly as possible. As early as 1816, when Albeit Ludwig Grimm (no relation to the brothers) published *Lina's Book of Fairy Tales*, the father in "Catskin" was declared innocent: The court councillors in Grimm's "Fairy Tale of Brunnenhold and Brunnenstark" are the ones to blame, for they are intent on arranging a marriage between father and daughter. The morally unimpeachable king tries to defy their orders and delivers stern lectures on the duties of a monarch: "He explained … that such a thing would be a sin in the eyes of man and God, for it had never before happened that a father wanted to take his daughter for a wife, and even as a king he could not allow himself what no man had ever done."[21]

In an age that accepted the biblical wisdom of husbands as gods ("Wives submit yourselves unto your own husbands, as unto the Lord" [*Ephesians* 5.22]) and told young women that "to you your father should be as a god," it was near sacrilege to depict a father whose conduct was so shocking as to sanction disobedience.[22] But it is less obvious why "Catskin" came to be used as an opportunity to dilate on maternal malice. The tale type offers an interesting case study of the way in which rewriters of a tale ingeniously exonerated fathers and shifted the burden of guilt for a father's crimes to the mother.

Let us begin with what is perhaps the best known of all versions of "Catskin": Perrault's "Donkey-Skin" ("Peau d'Ane"). The tale begins with a dying queen's last words to her husband: "'Promise me that if, when I am gone, you find a woman wiser and more beautiful than I, you will marry her and so provide an heir for your throne.'"[23] The king, who is "inconsolable in his grief," is not eager to remarry, but his courtiers urge him to find a new wife. As it turns out, only the king's daughter has "a charm and beauty that even the queen had not possessed," and so the king is maneuvered by his dead wife's pronouncements into proposing an incestuous union to his daughter. The story clearly implies that it is the queen who has engineered the alliance and thus removes much of the blame from the father/king. To ensure that no one could ascribe malice to the tale's "innocent" monarch, the narrator observes that the king's grief has also so "confused" his mind that he imagines himself to be a young man and believes his daughter to be "the maiden he had once wooed to be his wife."

Like Perrault, most of the men who produced written versions of this tale implicate the wife in the father's bid for his daughter's hand. Fidelity to the wishes of a dying spouse thus comes to supplant incestuous desire as the motive for the father's attempted seduction of his daughter, and the heroine's mother rather than her father becomes the villain of the piece. In "La Peau d'Anon" (a tale recorded at the close of the nineteenth century in France), the prince/father explains his peculiar dilemma to his daughter with pointed Gallic logic: "I want to remarry, but your mother made me promise that I would marry only a woman who looked liked her. Therefore I can only marry you."[24] Under the circumstances, it becomes difficult to blame the man for turning to his daughter. The text goes beyond suggesting that the king's loyalty to his wife and distress about her death have led to his mad proposal of marriage; here, the king becomes the *victim* of his wife's unreasonable demands. Some versions of the tale make it clear that the wife has targeted one and only one candidate for the king's remarriage. The dying queen gives her husband a shoe or a ring—the woman who can wear the one or the other ("not too slack and not too tight") is destined to be his wife. That woman is always the daughter.[25]

In Perrault's tale, Donkey-skin turns to her fairy godmother for advice. This godmother, in keeping with the spirit of the tale and its conspiracy to muffle the shock of incest, suppresses the possibility of expressing outrage, shame, or fear at the father's demands. "In your heart there is great sadness," she tells Donkey-skin, in an observation that can only be seen as a wild understatement of how a girl would react to her father's proposal of marriage. "You must not disobey your father," she adds, in a sentence that flies in the face of all cultural logic. Nonetheless, the godmother gives advice on how to dodge her father's desire—first by asking him to have three impossibly beautiful dresses made for her, then by asking him for a donkey's skin. When it finally becomes clear that the king will go to any lengths to secure his daughter as bride, the godmother counsels flight from the kingdom.

Straparola also makes the king of his "Catskin" tale something of a victim of his wife's dying wishes. Throughout the tale we hear about the "evil designs of [the] wicked father," of his "execrable lust," his "accursed design," and his "wicked and treacherous passion." Yet it is his wife who decrees that the object of his lust and passion will be his daughter Doralice. On her deathbed, the queen beseeches her husband Tebaldo never to take anyone as wife whose finger does not perfectly fit the wedding ring she is wearing. Faithful husband that he is, Tebaldo "made it a condition that any damsel who might be offered to him in marriage should first try on her finger his wife's ring, to see whether it fitted, and not having found one who fulfilled this condition—the ring being always found too big for this and too small for that—*he was forced to dismiss them all without further parley.*"[26] As Tebaldo puts it, he must marry his daughter, for it is the only way "I shall satisfy my own desire without violating the promise I made to your mother." Thus husband and wife conspire in crafting this assault on the daughter.

Both Perrault and Straparola seem to use similar tactics, if for different reasons, when it comes to rewriting "Catskin." In order to retain the potentially offensive episode in which a father proposes to his daughter, they resort to the strategy of lifting blame for the desired marriage from the father and shifting it to the mother. The incestuous proposal on which the plot turns continues to exist, but without the underlying scandal of the father's incestuous wishes. It is interesting to observe how both critics and rewriters of "Catskin" come at the tale in similar ways. While critics of all persuasions bend over backwards to demonstrate that a story about a father who wants to marry his daughter is really about a seductive daughter, rewriters of the tale insist that the father's proposal of marriage is nothing more than the fulfillment of a mother's desire. Thus the seductive daughter and the collusive mother, the two major culprits for apologists of incestuous fathers, make then- appearances in folktales, and in commentaries on them, long before they emerge in the psychoanalytic literature and in legal arguments.[27]

"Catskin," as recorded by the British folklorist Joseph Jacobs, goes one step further in the direction of eliminating the father as villain by replacing him with "a nasty rough old man" to whom the daughter is promised. "Let her marry the first that comes for her," the girl's father proclaims in a fashion reminiscent of the father/king in the Grimms' "King Thrushbeard." The urgency of removing all signs of incestuous desire is underscored by the narrator's move to separate father from daughter as much as possible: "Her father never set eyes on her till she was fifteen years old and was ready to be married."[28] (Interestingly, age fifteen would be precisely when a father might, for the first time, consciously take note of his daughter as an object of sexual desire, and the story here unwittingly betrays its thematic origins.) Jacobs' need to choose a variant of the tale that swerves as far away as possible from the theme of incest is also made clear in his notes to "Catskin." "A Mr. Mutt [the folklorist Alfred Nutt]," he observes,"is inclined to think, from the evidence of the hero-tales which have the unsavoury motif of the Unnatural Father, that the original home of the story was England. ... I would merely remark on this that there are only very slight traces of the story in these islands nowadays, while it abounds in Italy."[29] Jacobs numbered among those who ensured that there remained "only very slight traces" of the story in collections of British folktales. The conclusion to his "Catskin" is, ironically, one of the few endings that reunite the heroine with her father. Catskin marries a lord, but cannot find happiness until her husband locates Catskin's father, a widower "all alone in the world ... moping and miserable." Husband and father return to the castle, where with Catskin they form a curious trio that "lives happily ever afterwards."

In "Cinderella" tales, (step)mothers are regularly boiled in oil, rolled down hills in barrels spiked with nails, and torn to pieces by wild animals. The fate of the witch in the Russian 'White Duck' shows us just how important it is to eliminate every trace of a malignant female:

As for the witch, she was tied to the tail of a horse and dragged over a field; where a leg was torn off her, a fire iron stood; where an arm was torn off, a rake stood; where her head was torn off, a bush grew. Birds came swooping down and pecked up her flesh, a wind arose and scattered her bones, and not a trace or a memory was left of her.[30]

In view of this radical elimination of evil women in tales the world over, it seems more than odd that the fathers in variants of "The Girl without Hands" and "Catskin" almost to a man escape penalty and in many cases live happily ever after with their daughters. The Grimms' notes on "Allerleirauh" (their version of "Catskin") observe that two unrecorded oral stories did in fact end with the father's punishment: "He has to pronounce his own sentence and say that he no longer deserves to be king."[31] The gulf between this mild form of self-imposed punishment and the bodily tortures to which (step)mothers and their like are subjected could hardly be greater, but the distance is entirely predictable in view of the tendency in literary versions of these tales to exonerate fathers with incestuous intent and to make mothers responsible for the evil that befalls their daughters. The Grimms' elimination of any punishment for the father in "Allerleirauh" was part of a trend followed by virtually all who had a hand in producing the great nineteenth-century collections of folktales—the very collections that form the basis of tales read by and to children today.

Nowhere is this need to effect a reconciliation between father and daughter more evident than in "Love Like Salt" (AT 923), a tale type that has been recognized to be a diluted version of "Catskin."[32] The folktale plot, which will be familiar in its tragic form to readers of *King Lear*, begins with a test of love: a king demands declarations of filial devotion from his three daughters. When the youngest states that she loves her father like salt, he flies into a rage and banishes her from the kingdom. The daughter marries a prince, invites her father to the wedding celebration, and in a finale that marks reconciliation with the father, teaches him the value of her declaration by serving him an unsalted meal.

Variants of "Catskin" pose the very real threat of sexual violation in its most shocking form to their heroines. In Basile's "She-Bear," the father responds in the following fashion to his daughter's protest against their marriage: "'Stop your voice and keep your tongue quiet; make up your mind to tie the marriage knot this very night, for otherwise your ear will be the biggest bit left of you!'"[33] Fathers in versions of "Love Like Salt," by contrast, never demand more than verbal pledges of filial love, and their daughters remain devoted to them even though their words are seen as indicators of a dearth of affection. Hence the road to reconciliation remains open, for it is only the father's misreading of his daughter's pledge that has driven a wedge between the two. In the end, the daughter can reestablish warm familial relations with her father, even in the context of marriage to another man—she can live happily ever after as dutiful daughter *and* as loving wife. This is the same happy ending Bettelheim praises in "Beauty and the Beast," where Beauty is seen to transfer the oedipal love for her father to her husband, but is still able to give her father "the kind of affection most beneficial to him"—an affection that "restores his failing health and provides him with a happy life in proximity to his beloved daughter."[34]

While the mother-daughter dyad in fairy tales rarely tolerates a third element, and slips into the pairing of daughter with husband (eliminating the mother) if there is to be a happy ending at all, the triangular, father-daughter-husband relationship can weather the most severe strains and conflicts, as in "Love like Salt" and even in many versions of "Catskin." One clear sign of a cultural bias working in favor of keeping the triangle intact appears in the staging of *King Lear*, which for many years was performed with a happy ending that reunited Cordelia with Lear and married her to Edgar.[35] We shall see an analogous operation at work in "The Juniper Tree," a tale that culminates in an idyllic final scene that removes the mother from the family circle to leave a trio consisting of father, daughter, and son.

We have seen the extent to which literary versions of "The Maiden without Hands," "Catskin," and "Love Like Salt" either erase, rationalize, or mute the transgressions of the father. One father becomes guilty of greed rather than of incestuous desire; another is the victim of temporary insanity; a third wants nothing more than a declaration of filial love. All of them, however, are responsible for the flight of their daughters from home into nature. That flight into the woods, with its concomitant degradation of the heroine into a creature of nature, remains the lasting mark of the father's attempted incestuous violation. The flight may not be psychologically motivated in rewritten texts (as was the case in the Grimms' version of "The Maiden without Hands"), but it remains an ineradicable trace of the tale's genealogy.

The Grimms' "Allerleirauh" (their variant of "Catskin") gives us an interesting take on the heroine's flight from her father. Allerleirauh dodges her father's marriage proposal by fleeing into a forest, where she finds a hollow tree that becomes her home. We are reminded of Mary's Child, who makes an "old hollow tree" in the forest her "dwelling place." These fairy-tale outcasts live like animals, sleeping in woodland sanctuaries and foraging for food. When the king's huntsmen discover Allerleirauh's dwelling, they report to their ruler: "There's a strange animal lying in the hollow tree. We've never seen anything like it. Its skin is made up of a thousand different kinds of fur.'"[36] Mary's Child, who lives like a "poor little animal," must rely on her hair to cover her body when her clothing disintegrates in the course of her exile. As all remnants of culture disappear from the bodies of these heroines, they become affiliated with nature alone and take on its protective coloring.

A flight into nature offers numerous imperiled women an unlikely, but surprisingly common, refuge from sexual pursuit. Perieus, we recall from Ovid's *Metamorphoses*, turns his daughter Daphne into a laurel tree to avert Apollo's assault on her chastity.[37] Here the father intervenes to *protect* the daughter by moving her back to nature—though who can rule out the possibility that sexual jealousy motivates the "protection" to one degree or another? Yeats, in a very different context, but one that still concerns a father's desire to shelter his daughter, celebrates the transformation of girl into rooted tree in "Prayer for My Daughter":

> May she become a flourishing hidden tree
> That all her thoughts may like the linnet be,
> And have no business but dispensing round
> Their magnanimities of sound,
> Nor but in merriment begin a chase,
> Nor but in merriment a quarrel
> O may she live like some green laurel
> Rooted in one dear perpetual place.

It took Sylvia Plath to recognize the coercive violence of these transformations from flesh into bark, of the cultural edict that places the daughter's fate into the hands of the father, but more importantly wedges her between violation and entrapment. In "Virgin in a Tree," Plath exposes the implications of the cultural story that celebrates the transformation of woman into tree:

> … chased girls who get them to a tree
> And put on bark's nun-black
> Habit which deflects
> All amorous arrows.[38]

Thrown back into a state of nature through the threat of paternal violation, Allerleirauh becomes a treed animal, a living being with no father, no possessions, and hence no palpable exchange value. Lévi-Strauss's observations on the incest prohibition indirectly reveal the exact implications of the violation of the incest taboo—the woman in question is not only coerced into an inappropriate "marriage," she also loses her value as a gift. "The prohibition of incest," we learn in *The Elementary Structures of Kinship*," is less a rule prohibiting marriage with the mother, sister, or daughter, than a rule obliging the mother, sister, or daughter to be given to others. It is the supreme rule of the gift, and it is clearly this aspect, too often unrecognized, which allows its nature to be understood."[39] Once the incest taboo is violated, a woman is withdrawn from circulation, no longer available to be "given away," as we say even today, by a father to another man. In the case of "Allerleirauh," the incest taboo may never actually be violated, but the heroine loses her exchange value—hence also her social status—once the father makes known his desire for her. The isolation born of incest (threatened or real) is aptly captured in the formulation of one anthropological observer: "An incestuous couple as well as a stingy family automatically detaches itself from the give-and-take pattern of tribal existence; it is a foreign body—or at least an inactive one—in the body social."[40]

Allerleirauh returns to civilization when the dogs of a king's huntsmen follow her scent to the hollow tree in which she is sleeping. "You'll be perfect for the kitchen, Allerleirauh,'" the huntsmen tell the heroine, who can occupy only the lowest rung on the social ladder now that she has been divested of all exchange value. In the kitchen where the king's meals are prepared, Allerleirauh toils away: "She carried wood and water, kept the fires going, plucked the fowls, sorted the vegetables, swept up the ashes, and did all the dirty work." Enslaved as a domestic, Allerleirauh suffers the same trials and tribulations that beset such fairy-tale heroines as the bride of King Thrushbeard and, most notably, Cinderella.

The story of Allerleirauh, as the Grimms tell it, is curiously disjointed. The two kings mentioned in the tale (father and master/groom) seem curiously undifferentiated (both are designated as "the king")—a fact that has led a number of critics to question whether this is really a story that charts a course from incest averted to the legitimate fulfillment of desire.[41] The first version of the Grimms' "Allerleirauh" makes it clear that the golden ring placed in the king's soup to alert him to the presence of the beloved was originally the gift of the man to whom the heroine was once betrothed and whom she marries at the end of the tale. All of this might lead us to believe that the heroine's father and master/groom are one and the same, were it not for the evidence produced by Heinz Rölleke that the many enigmas and inconsistencies in the story stem from the Grimms' reliance on a literary source unacknowledged in their notes to the tale.[42] Interestingly, the literary source begins with the flight of the heroine from a cruel stepmother, not from a menacing father. Allerlei-Rauch, in Carl Nehrlich's novel *Schilly* (1798), becomes the target of her stepmother's wrath because of the attentions of a suitor, to whom she becomes betrothed. She is abandoned in the woods, rescued by hunters, and obliged to polish boots and clean the kitchen in the castle where she takes up residence. By putting the ring given to her by her betrothed into the soup served up to him, she ensures her recognition and weds the duke.

The genesis of the Grimms' tale, its amalgamation of plot lines from both "Catskin" and "Cinderella," demonstrates the close degree of kinship between the two stories. A folktale heroine can become an outcast because of either a father's desire for her or a (step)mother's envy of that desirability. Basile's "Cat Cinderella" shows us just how closely knit the two passions are, though—like most tellers of tales—Basile does not spell out the connection between them:

> There was once … a Prince who was a widower, and he had a daughter so dear to him that he saw with no other eyes but hers. … The father, however, shortly remarried, and his wife was an evil, malicious, bad-tempered woman who began at once to hate her stepdaughter and threw sour looks, wry faces and scowling glances on her enough to make her jump with fright.[43]

This introduction allows the tale to move in the direction of "Cinderella," but it could easily be truncated to frame the opening situation of "Catskin."

Whether the heroine is oppressed by a father or a (step)mother, she finds herself in dire straits. Becoming a slave to her father's love represents an intolerable situation, and the prospect leads her to become a fugitive. Becoming a domestic slave for her mother brings abuse and humiliation, though it does not force the heroine to take immediate flight. The heroine pursued by her father may hightail it into the forest, but she eventually ends up in the kitchen, where she suffers the lot of Cinderella. In a British variant of "Catskin," the voice of the chief cook in the king's kitchen is uncannily close to that of the wicked stepmother in "Cinderella." When Catskin hints to "Mrs. Cook" that she would like to attend the ball honoring the young lord of the castle, the cook responds in familiar tones and Catskin, like Cinderella, suffers in silence as insults are hurled at her:

> "What! you dirty impudent slut," said the cook,"you go among all the fine lords and ladies with your filthy catskin? A fine figure you'd cut!" and with that she took a basin of water and dashed it into Catskins face. But she only briskly shook her ears, and said nothing.[44]

It is at this juncture in the tale that the kinship between "Catskin" and "Cinderella" becomes most clearly evident. Cooks, as we know from looking at different variants of other tales (the Grimms' "Fledgling," for instance) often occupy the same functional slot as mothers. "The Juniper Tree," in which a stepmother chops up the hero and cooks him up in a stew, gives us clear evidence of just how readily the activity of preparing food slides into the monstrous. Cinderella's persecution by her stepmother is entirely homologous with Catskin's victimization at the hands of a cook. But where the one tale turns the mother into the chief villain and virtually eliminates the father as actor, the other—in its literary renditions—habitually tones down the father's villainy and continually allows the mother to resurface in the role of fiend.

That the drama of maternal evil (which involves sexual jealousy and domestic enslavement) came to be favored over that of paternal evil (which involves the expression of forbidden sexual desires) comes as no surprise. What is astonishing, however, is that the dual tyrannies exercised by mother and father display such stability in the manner of their representation among different eras and cultures. No matter how far and wide we look, there are just not many fathers who browbeat their daughters with requests for fresh laundry or clean floors, while the number of mothers who turn their daughters into domestic slaves is legion. By the same token, mothers never seem tempted to propose to their sons, though widowers find their daughters virtually irresistible. The domains of the father and mother are clearly marked in "Cinderella" and "Catskin." Control of marriage, and hence the regulation of desire and sexuality, are in the hands of the father; the organization of the domestic sphere, which also determines the availability and desirability of daughters, is orchestrated by the mother. It is at just the point when father and mother wield their power to wall the heroine in, to keep her "at home" through an endogamous marriage or through a form of labor that prevents exogamy (by making her as unattractive as possible), that the heroine becomes either a fugitive or a victim awaiting rescue.

"Catskin" offers the fullest depiction of parental tyranny in its description of a father who withholds the gift of his daughter and of a cook/mother who keeps the heroine at home in a perpetual state of degradation. The only hope for the heroine depends on finding the right clothes and getting a chance to sneak off to the ball. From the father, guardian of her desirability, the heroine receives the clothing that she needs to attract the prince, but only because she has succeeded in hoodwinking him. In many versions of "Catskin," it is the cook, too, who allows the heroine to slip off for half an hour to observe the festivities at the ball—an opportunity that the quick and clever heroine uses to attend the ball. Somehow, despite the control and oppression exercised by those at home, the heroine finds a way to escape and to establish a new home. That she can do so only by proving her domestic skills and presenting herself as dazzling in her physical attractiveness sends a distinct message to the tale's audience, one that has rarely been refashioned by the many cultures in which the tale has flourished.

Ironically, it is our own day and age that, in the tales of "Cinderella" and "Snow White," has intensified maternal malice while placing a premium on physical beauty as the source of salvation for a woman. Walt Disney's "Cinderella," based on Perrault's version of the tale, shows us a stepmother whose harsh, angular features and shrill, arrogant voice conspire to present a portrait of evil incarnate. While her daughters are no lambs, they are never presented as the primary movers in this version of the tale, which privileges mother/daughter rivalry over sibling rivalry. Incessantly barking orders at Cinderella, the stepmother does everything in her power to obstruct the girl's rise from ashes to throne. Cinderella's father, as it turns out, never even enters the animated portion of the movie. In stills that form a preface to the film, we learn that Cinderella's father died in untimely fashion—but he was "kind and devoted," giving his "beloved" child "every luxury and comfort." The only mistake that he made was to marry a "cold," "cruel" woman who was "bitterly jealous of Cinderella's charm and beauty" and "grimly determined to follow the interests of her own two awkward daughters."

In "Snow White," Disney went a step further than in "Cinderella" by revealing in visual terms the monstrous nature of the wicked queen. While the Grimms' stepmother dresses up as an old peddler women (Disney based his film on the Grimms' version), Disney's stepmother transforms herself into a hag of such startling ugliness that she bears no resemblance whatsoever to the wicked queen. The images of this cinematic witch's physiognomy dominate the film and give us its most arresting, and controversial, moments. So frightening was the figure of the old hag that many parents kept their children away from the film. "All over the country," Richard Schickel writes," there were earnest debates about the appropriateness of *Snow White* for children, and everyone seemed to have a story about someone's child who had had hysterics in the theater or bad dreams for weeks after seeing the film."[45] Fifty years later the debate repeated itself when the film was rereleased to mark its anniversary.

Just as Disney gives us maternal evil in its most extreme manifestation, so too he strengthens the emphasis on female attire and physical beauty. This might seem logical in a cinematic version of these tales, but the amount of footage devoted in "Cinderella" to that perennial "female" problem of what to wear is extraordinary. Disney's subplot concerned with the relationship between Cinderella and the mice in the castle is also based almost entirely on costumes of one sort or another. Snow White may not go through any costume changes, but it is no exaggeration to say that the focus on her physical appearance, highlighted most dramatically when she lies in repose under glass, is remarkable.

The Disney version does not, however, represent a revolutionary turn in the development of these two tales, but rather the logical culmination of a trend that diminished the part of the father even as it magnified the role of the mother. We have seen just how important it was to eliminate fathers and to write large the villainy of mothers as folktales were turned into storybooks. Since then, the invisible father and the monstrous mother have come to serve as twin anchors of many fairytale plots and will remain stationed there until the tellers of tales receive new messages to inscribe on their narratives.

Notes

1. "The Maiden without Hands," in *The Complete Fairy Tales of the Brothers Grimm*, pp. 118–23.

2. For an analysis of the motivation underlying the substitution, see John M. Ellis, *One Fairy Story Too Many: The Brothers Grimm and Their Tales* (Chicago: Univ. of Chicago Press, 1983), pp. 77–78.

3. "Olive," in *Italian Folktales*, comp. Calvino, pp. 255–61.

4. Dundes, "The Psychoanalytic Study of the Grimms' Tales," pp. 50–65.

5. On the church ritual, see Lynda E. Boose, "The Father's House and the Daughter in It: The Structures of Western Culture's Daughter-Father Relationships," in *Daughters and Fathers*, ed. Lynda E. Boose and Betty S. Flowers (Baltimore: Johns Hopkins Univ. Press, 1989), pp. 19–74.

6. Margaret R. Miles discusses a painting that depicts one of Saint Barbara's executioners slicing off her left breast and observes that Saint Agnes was subjected to a similar fate—both her breasts were cut off. See her *Carnal Knowing*, p. 156.

7. For a fascinating analysis of the episode in Ovid and the way in which weaving and spinning become the literal and metaphorical equivalents of storytelling for women who are literally or metaphorically silenced, see Karen E. Rowe, "The Female Voice in Folklore and Fairy Tale," in *Fairy Tales and Society: Illusion, Allusion, and Paradigm*, ed. Ruth B. Bottigheimer (Philadelphia: Univ. of Pennsylvania Press, 1986), pp. 53–74.

8. "The Girl with Maimed Hands," in Basile, *The Pentamerone*, 1: 232–41.

9. Thelma S. Fenster has argued that the self-mutilation of another heroine "ensures that Joie is no longer a perfect copy of her mother, and is therefore no longer participating in the doubling" (49). See "Beaumanoir's *La Manekine*: Kin D(r)ead: Incest, Doubling, and Death," *American Imago* 39 (1982): 41–58.

10. For elaboration on this point, see Lynda E. Boose, "The Father's House and the Daughter in It," p. 32.

11. "If social organization had a beginning," Lévi-Strauss writes, "this could only have consisted in the incest prohibition, since … the incest prohibition is, in fact, a kind of remodeling of the biological conditions of mating and procreation (which know no rule, as can be seen from observing animal life) compelling them to become perpetuated only in an artificial framework of taboos and obligations. It is there, and only there, that we find a passage from nature to culture, from animal to human life." See his essay "The Family," in *Man, Culture, and Society*, ed. Harry Shapiro (New York: Oxford Univ. Press, 1956), p. 278. Freud's most complete statement on the cultural implications of the incest prohibition appears in *Totem and Taboo: Some Points of Agreement between the Mental Lives of Savages and Neurotics*, vol. 13 of the *Standard Edition*. Robin Fox disputes the notion of incest taboos as "the great gateway and bridge to culture" (14). See *The Red Lamp of Incest* (New York: E. P. Dutton, 1980).

12. For an extensive discussion of the nature/culture opposition and of de Beauvoir's observations, see Sherry B. Ortner, "Is Female to Male as Nature Is to Culture?" in *Woman, Culture, and Society*, ed. Michelle Zimbalist Rosaldo and Louise Lamphere (Stanford: Stanford Univ. Press, 1974), pp. 67–87.

13. Dundes, "The Psychoanalytic Study of the Grimms' Tales," p. 61. Dundes even goes so far as to assert that *King Lear*, since it is based on a folkloric source, must entail "a *projection of incestuous desires on the part of the daughter*. In this sense, the plot revolves around Cordelia, not Lear" (p. 236; Dundes' emphasis). For Dundes, Lear is truly "a man more sinn'd against than sinning." See also Jack Zipes's critique of Dundes' reasoning in "Recent Psychoanalytical Approaches with Some Questions about the Abuse of Children," in *The Brothers Grimm: From Enchanted Forests to the Modern World*, pp. 110–34.

14. Nancy Chodorow astutely observes that the "absence of actual paternal seduction is not the same thing as absence of seductive fantasies toward a daughter or behavior which expresses such fantasy." Similarly, fairy tales about paternal seduction may have as much to do with seductive behavior as with actual paternal seduction. See *The Reproduction of Mothering: Psychoanalysis and the Sociology of Gender* (Berkeley and Los Angeles: Univ. of California Press, 1978), p. 160.

15. As Judith Lewis Herman observes,"the relationship between father and daughter, adult male and female child, is one of the most unequal relationships imaginable. It is no accident that incest occurs most often precisely in the relationship where the female is most powerless." See her study conducted with Lisa Hirschman: *Father-Daughter Incest* (Cambridge: Harvard Univ. Press, 1981), p. 4.

16. On incest in Shakespeare, see Diane Elizabeth Dreher, *Domination and Defiance: Fathers and Daughters in Shakespeare* (Lexington: Univ. Press of Kentucky, 1986). I am grateful to Elizabeth Archibald, who sent me the typescript of a talk given at Harvard University on women and incest in medieval literature. In it, she refers to the passage in *Pericles* and also draws attention to the late medieval morality play *Dux Moraud* in which is found an exception to the rule of evil father and innocent heroine in father-daughter incest plots. The maiden without hands, as Archibald makes clear, is a prominent figure in medieval romance as well as in folklore.

17. Cox was the first to undertake a systematic study of Cinderella variants. In *Cinderella: Three Hundred and Forty-five Variants of Cinderella, Catskin, and Cap o' Rushes*, ed. Andrew Lang (London: David Nutt, 1893), Cox uses the three names in her subtitle as categories for collecting tales about an "ill-treated heroine" ("Cinderella"), an "unnatural father" who forces the heroine to flee ("Catskin"), and a "King Lear judgment" that turns the heroine into an outcast ("Cap o' Rushes"). Cox's three groups were modified by Anna Birgitta Rooth *(The Cinderella Cycle* [Lund: Gleerup, 1951]).

18. For a full discussion of the Oedipal dimensions of the plot, see Bettelheim, *The Uses of Enchantment*, pp. 236–77.

19. "The Girl without Hands," in *Folktales of Germany*, ed. Kurt Ranke, trans. Lotte Baumann (Chicago: Univ. of Chicago Press, 1966), pp. 84–89.

20. On this point, see my *Hard Facts of the Grimms' Fairy Tales*, pp. 137–55.

21. A. L. Grimm, *Lina's Màrchenbuch: Eine Weynachtsgabe* (Frankfurt: Wilmans, 1816), pp. 191–216.

22. The phrase comes from A Midsummer Night's Dream, when Duke Theseus counsels Hermia to marry the man chosen by her father (I.i.47).

23. "Donkey-Skin," in Perraults Complete Fairy Tales, pp. 92–99. On the tale, see Réné Démoris,"Du littéraire au littéral dans Peau d'Ane de Perrault," Revue *des sciences humaines* 43 (1977): 261–79.

24. "La Peau d'Anon," in *Le Conte populairefrangais*, ed. Delarue and Tenèze, pp. 256–60.

25. Critics have been quick to use these cues from the tellers of tales to blame mothers for the heroine's misfortune. W.R.S. Ralston, for example, notes that "Rashie-Coat's degradation is consequent upon her dying mother's unfortunate imprudence," and in the Sicilian tale of "Betta Pilusa," the marriage from which the heroine flees "would never have been suggested to her had not her mother obtained a promise from her husband on her death-bed that he would marry again whenever any maiden was found whom her ring would fit." See Ralston's essay "Cinderella," in *Cinderella: A Casebook*, ed. Alan Dundes (New York: Garland, 1982; Madison: Univ. of Wisconsin Press, 1988), pp. 30–56. The phrase about the fit comes from a Brazilian "Catskin." See "Dona Labismina,' in *The Cinderella Story: The Origins and Variations of the Story Known As "Cinderella,"* ed. Neil Philip (London: Penguin, 1989), pp. 70–73.

26. Straparola, *The Facetious Nights*, pp. 79–103.

27. On the seductive daughter and the collusive mother, see Herman, *Father- Daughter Incest,* pp. 36–49.

28. "Catskin," in *English Fairy Tales*, comp. Jacobs, pp. 268–71.

29. *English Fairy Tales*, comp. Jacobs, p. 341.

30. "The White Duck," in Afanasev, *Russian Fairy Tales,* pp. 342–45.

31. *Brüder Grimm. Kinder- und Hausmärchen*, ed. Heinz Rölleke (Stuttgart: Re- clam, 1980), vol. 3, pp. 117.

32. As Alan Dundes points out,"the love like salt' plot appears to be a weakened form of the folktale plot in which a 'mad' father tries to marry his own daughter." See his essay "To Love My Father All,'" in *Cinderella: A Casebook*, pp. 229–44.

33. "The She-Bear," in Basile, *The Pentamerone*, 1:170–78.

34. Bettelheim, *The Uses of Enchantment*, p. 308.

35. Dreher, *Domination and Defiance*, p. 108.

36. "All Fur," in *The Complete Fairy Tales of the Brothers Grimm*, pp. 259–63. Since the title of this tale has been translated in so many different ways, I have chosen to retain the Grimms' original title to identify the tale.

37. Elizabeth Butler Cullingford discusses the literary topos of the virgin in the tree in "W B. Yeats and Sylvia Plath," in *Daughters and Fathers*, ed. Boose and Flowers, pp. 233–55.

38. Sylvia Plath, *Collected Poems*, ed. Ted Hughes (New York: Harper & Sr Row, 1981), pp. 81–82.

39. Claude Lévi-Strauss, *The Elementary Structures of Kinship*, rev. ed., trans. James Harle Bell, John Richard von Sturmer, and Rodney Needham, and also ed. Rodney Needham (Boston: Beacon Press, 1969), p. 481. The effectiveness of the loss of exchange value as a barrier to father-daughter incest is recognized by Jane Gallop, who writes that "the father must not desire the daughter, for to do so would threaten to remove him from the homosexual commerce in which women are exchanged between men, for the purpose of power relations and community for the men" (47). See "The Father's Seduction," in *The (M)other Tongue: Essays in Feminist Psychoanalytic Interpretation*, ed. Shirley Nelson Garner, Claire Kahane, and Madelon Sprengnether (Ithaca: Cornell Univ. Press, 1985), pp. 33–50.

40. G. Devereux,"The Social and Cultural Implications of Incest among the Mohave Indians," *Psychoanalytical Quarterly* 8 (1939): 510–33.

41. Peter Brooks describes the story as representing the move from "one desire that w e … know to be prohibited, to a legitimate desire whose consummation marks the end of the tale." See his *Reading for the Plot: Design and Intention in the Narrative* (New York: Random House, Vintage Books, 1984), p. 8. Marianne Hirsch challenges Brooks' reading by calling attention to the tale's "fundamental power structure" and revealing "possible responses to it." See "Ideology, Form, and 'Allerleirauh': Reflections on *Reading for the* Plot," *Children's Literature* 14 (New Haven: Yale Univ. Press, 1986), pp. 163–68. Finally, Sandra M. Gilbert finds that the "two kings are one, paternal figures from both of whom the 'fair princess' tries to escape, though not, perhaps, with equal vigor" (275). See "Life's Empty Pack: Notes toward a Literary Daughteronomy," in *Daughters and Fathers,* ed. Boose and Flowers, pp. 256–77.

42. Heinz Rölleke,"Allerleirauh: Eine bisher unbekannte Fassung vor Grimm," *Fabula* 13 (1972): 153–59.

43. "The Cat Cinderella," in Basile, *The Pentamerone*, pp. 56–63.

44. "Catskin," in *English Fairy Tales*, comp. Jacobs, pp. 268–71.

45. Richard Schickel, *The Disney Version: The Life, Times, Art and Commerce of Walt Disney* (New York: Simon and Schuster, 1968), p, 220.

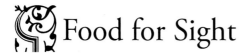

Food for Sight

Perrault's "Peau d'âne"

Philip Lewis

> En ajoutant d'autres dimensions au modèle, on intègrera les aspects diachroniques, tels ceux qui concernent l'ordre, la prsentation et les gestes du repas. … Ainsi peut-on espérer découvrir, pour chaque cas particulier, comment la cuisine d'une société est un langage dans lequel elle traduit inconsciemment sa structure, à moins que, sans le savoir davantage, elle ne se résigne à y dévoiler ses contradictions.
>
> —Claude Lévi-Strauss, *L'Origine des manières de table* [p. 4 1 1]

In academic inquiry into the typology of foods, dietary systems, and eating practices, it has become almost obligatory to reckon with the analytical framework and general claims that Lévi-Strauss elaborates in his *Mythologiques*. The insight most commonly appropriated from this work has to do with understanding the relation between nature and culture through the opposition of raw food, a product of nature, to cooked food, a product of culture. In the penultimate chapter of *L'Origine des manières de table*, a kind of theorizing summation aptly entitled "Petit traité d'ethnologie culinaire," that duality is actually converted into a triangular schematic distinguishing three states of food, *raw, cooked, and rotten [le pourri]*, as well as three modes of food preparation, *roasting, smoking, and boiling*. The analysis of a given dish and its place within the nature/culture relation has to take into account not only the condition of the food after it has been prepared for eating, but also the process of cooking itself. Between the three major terms, moreover, there are gradations that depend on a number of differential factors: the type of cooking utensil or apparatus used, the distance of the food from the source of heat, the time of cooking and the level of heat required, the succulence or dryness of the food, the time food will last before spoiling, and so forth.

The play of these variable factors makes for the apparent ambiguity or insecurity that emerges within the nature/culture opposition. For example, roasted meat may be well done or cooked on the outside, and thus on the side of culture, yet rare or raw on the inside, and thus still on the side of nature as well. Or, from the standpoint of the cooking method, a categorizer would place roasted meat on the side of nature, with smoked and boiled on the side of culture; whereas from the standpoint of the resulting foodstuffs, the smoked, since thoroughly transformed, would lie on the side of culture, while the roasted and boiled, when they retain their texture and succulence, end up on that of nature. These multiple ambiguities prompt Lévi-Strauss to draw the following conclusion: "le système atteste que l'art de la cuisine ne se situe pas tout entier du côté de la culture. Répondant aux exigences du corps, et déterminée dans chacun de ses modes par la manière particulière dont, ici et là, l'homme s'insère dans l'univers, placée donc entre la nature et la culture, la cuisine assure plutôt leur nécessaire articulation. Elle relève des deux domaines, et reflète cette dualité dans chacune de ses manifestations"

Philip Lewis, "Food for Sight: Perrault's 'Peau d'âne'," *MLN*, vol. 106, no. 4, pp. 793–817. Copyright © 1991 by The Johns Hopkins University Press. Reprinted with permission.

[405]. Insofar as this claim is valid for any society, ancient or modern, primitive or advanced, exotic or familiar, it can doubtless be qualified as "structuralist" and construed as an invitation to conduct synchronic analyses that regard a given culinary system as a variant on a general model of the vital, if ambiguous nature/culture relation.

Moreover, as a practical matter (given humankind's relatively decisive distaste for starvation) it is hardly surprising that the culinary system is vitally enmeshed in the processes of socialization and acculturation. For insofar as this system extends to prescriptions and prohibitions concerning the production, preparation, and consumption of food, it exercises a double function. On the one hand, Lévi-Strauss writes, dietary regimens, good manners, hygienic or table utensils are muting or mediating objects that play the role of "insulators or transformers" [isolants ou médiateurs, 420] suppressing or reducing the potentially dangerous tension between the social being and that person's (natural) body, or between the clothed and groomed body (of culture) and its physical drives. On the other hand, they also function as evaluative or prescriptive standards, as regulators that assign to physiological processes and social gestures an appropriate rhythm or duration, securing for individual and communal life a needed sense of periodicity. In short, to the extent that the culinary system serves simultaneously to hold individuals at a safe distance from one another or to mute the tensions within a single individual, yet still to keep them together, individually and collectively integrated through the bonding of society, its operation overlaps integrally with the moderating and mediating functions of culture itself. With this analytic superstructure in place, we can formulate a first hypothesis concerning the representation of food: to the extent—perhaps quite limited—that it embraces and discloses the operations of the culinary system, it is no less revelatory of a culture's vital ordering principles than representations of the other normative social systems—language, money, or kinship—with which it is presumably homologous.

No doubt the overarching framework of Lévi-Strauss' theoretical or philosophical reflections can indeed be reduced, in the end, to a set of oppositions—simple/complex, inside/outside, cause/effect, nature/culture, the raw/the cooked, and so forth. Once the systemic articulations or mediations between these terms, which prove to be subtle and multi-faceted, have been grasped analytically, the ethnologist can construct his celebrated characterization of the dignity and complexity of primitive or mythic thought and venture to compare "traditional" models of social behavior with the ideologies of modern western civilization. But in commenting on the order of the elaborated European culture that necessarily dominates the ethnologist's enterprise, Lévi-Strauss is not content with describing the practices of our civilization as if it were a monument or a continuum. Notwithstanding the commonplace critical characterization of the structuralist theses that Lévi-Strauss articulated in his *Mythologiques* as ahistorical, the ethnologist repeatedly punctuates this monumental work with an explicitly historical point of view. In particular, he takes pains to evoke a constant evolution of the culinary system, comparable to the evolution of linguistic usage. In the final chapters of *L'origine des manières de table*, in the process of building up a double-edged contrast between "peoples we call primitive" and "our civilization" [414], he has occasion to refer to texts about table manners from the middle ages, the sixteenth century, the great *Encyclopedia* of the French Enlightenment, and the nineteenth century.

The first of the two major contrasts Lévi-Strauss evokes is a social one. For primitive peoples "table manners formed a sort of free code, the terms of which could be combined so as to convey distinct messages." For us, on the other hand, table manners have become so uniform that they are just good or bad,"no longer constitute a *free code*" [414]. The evidence provided by texts of the last few centuries suggests that this shift has been subtle, gradual, and consummated only recently. The second and more celebrated contrast is a moral one. For the so-called primitive peoples, the commitment to good manners or to prescribed dietary and hygienic practices is grounded in the need to protect others, or society, or the human environment from danger or corruption, whereas for us, says Lévi-Strauss, it is a matter of self-protection, of preserving the internal integrity of the subject against others or the outside world. Like the change in the signifying status of the code of table manners, this second shift is also, he suggests, a relatively modern one. It appears to start taking hold only in the Renaissance or early modern period of European history.

From the attention to these overlapping historical processes, we can derive a second hypothesis about the representation of food: as this quiet socio-moral transformation slowly develops, the representation of food and of cooking and eating practices can hardly fail to manifest its effects. No doubt this broadly stroked historical hypothesis about our own culture that we can tease out of the speculative passages in *L'Origine des manières de table* is at one with his claims that the frames of cultural understanding have to be temporal as well as spatial. But unlike the first hypothesis, which the ethnographer tests massively in his analyses of South American cultures, it can hardly be qualified as more than a sketchy footnote to Lévi-Strauss' work. Thus it is necessary to look elsewhere for pursuit and refinement of the historical inquiry that this second hypothesis subtends. One highly instructive instance in which important scholarly investigations into cultural representation, its structure and processes have focussed upon food is provided by the works of two formidably original scholars, Norbert Elias and Louis Marin. Their probing into the significance of alimentary production and consumption might be regarded as constituting a kind of fountainhead or watershed on which studies of specific cases in the culture of modern Europe can hardly fail to draw. Elias' socio-historical account of the culinary system is a key element of two fascinating volumes, *The History of Manners* and *Power and Civility*, that comprise a study entitled *The Civilizing Process*. After recalling very briefly and partially the thrust of this work's general thesis, I shall dwell at some length on Marin's remarkable study, *La parole mangée*, distilling from it a third hypothesis about the culinary system that focusses much more squarely on the problematics of representation itself.

Elias tracks the civilizing process in Western societies over the past eight centuries in two distinct orbits: (1) the social and psychological existence of individuals and groups in their everyday life, their habits, customs, fears and anxieties, and (2) the political and economic existence of feudal estates and modern nation-states understood as monopolizers of power. The historical process he evokes is a long-term, slow-moving evolution, largely imperceptible to those caught up in it. It has three main stages: a medieval period of *courtoisie*, characterized by dispersion of political power and by diversity in the forms of social control; an intermediate, early modern period of *civilité* running from the fifteenth through the eighteenth centuries, in which the rise of the absolutist state—epitomized by the France of Louis XIV—is accompanied by the development of codes of social behavior; and our own modern period of pervasive normalization and conformity, marked by the consolidation of state power and a very high degree of individual self-regulation in society. Predictably enough, Elias' general claim is that the developments in the two dimensions, civilized behavior and state power, go hand in hand, enabling and conditioning one another. This functional interdependence comes into view as one studies the spread of civility and the attitudes, emotions, and practices associated with it from the aristocratic court, where it originated, through the nobility at large, and then outward and downward through the bourgeoisie and eventually through all social classes: conformity to the centrally constituted model of behavior and personality structure at one and the same time enables the king's subjects to partake of the power, military and monetary, concentrated in the hands of the monarch and enables the latter to extend his power ever more decisively over his subjects.

In describing what he sometimes terms the civilization curve, Elias devotes considerable attention to two phenomena that may concern us here, the development of a ritual of eating habits and a change in the attitude toward the eating of meat. After a medieval phase marked by eating with the hands and by a relaxed standard of manners that imposes relatively minimal restraint on the play of emotions, the sixteenth century ushers in a phase of rapid development. During this phase, which is complete by the end of the eighteenth century, a new standard of table manners and the psychological condition corresponding to this behavior model will extend across the whole of French society. The transformation that, for example, eliminates common dishes in favor of plates for each individual, introduces the fork and spoon, and builds up a bevy of taboos around the knife, has little to do with hygiene; rather, developments such as the "fork ritual" *[History of Manners, 126]* have to do with a trend toward the formation of good taste and a sense of decency that depends fundamentally on the mechanisms by which individuals come to experience feelings of shame and revulsion. "The fork," Elias writes, "is nothing other than the embodiment of a specific standard of emotions and a specific level of revulsion. Behind the change in eating techniques between the Middle Ages and modern times appears the same process that emerged in the analysis of other incarnations of this kind : a change in the structure of drives and emotions" [127].

Unsurprisingly, the key among these other phenomena that incarnate the advance in the threshold of embarrassment happens to be speech. In language, the all-encompassing medium of human contact, we encounter a spreading and tightening control of usage that closely parallels the regulating of eating; and just as the rules for serving and eating food are not driven by a practical concern with hygiene, the code governing language-use can hardly be understood as the effect of a rational concern with accurate expression. Rather, the control of usage serves the same sense of delicacy and politeness that the refinement of eating habits promotes, and it also demonstrates in the same way the power of the court and aristocratic circles to determine the standards and sensitivities to be adopted by the bourgeoisie and imposed on society at large by the bourgeoisie. No doubt we should point out here that economic exchange is also a crucial parallel factor in this process. The development of money and taxation at the base of the economic system first provides for the king's power to monopolize the definition of standards; then it subsequently makes for the monarchy's cooptative exercise of power in society with an ascendant bourgeoisie that gradually takes over socio-economic dominance from a waning aristocracy and helps recast the social order as an extension of the arm of state. The argument of *Power and Civility* makes it clear that one can discern still other parallels in the value-forming process disclosed by the regulation of eating and speaking by tracing the development of the monetary system or the regulation of property. In any case, the economic hegemony of the bourgeois class is what gradually enables it to coerce all facets of society into the civilizing process. Bourgeoisified civilization ultimately entails making the acquisition and internalization of the class' values, feelings, and standards of conduct a matter of course, an unconscious and seemingly natural experience for children growing up in a society.

In elaborating on his claim that this socio-historical process transforms personality structures and the psychological dynamics of human relationships, Elias suggests that the example of meat-eating is particularly instructive. In the seventeenth century, the serving of whole animals or large parts of large animals and their carving at table disappears; the century's rapidly articulated standard of taste suppresses reminders that meat-eating is connected with the killing of an animal and the eating of the dead animal by live human animals. Elias writes that "people, in the course of the civilizing process, seek to suppress in themselves every characteristic that they feel to be 'animal.' They likewise suppress such characteristics in their food" [120]. "The curve running from the carving of a large part of the animal or even the whole animal at table, through the advance in the threshold of repugnance at the sight of dead animals, to the removal of carving to specialized enclaves behind the scenes is a typical civilization curve" [121]. We can readily see, in this case, how the requirements of the culinary system affect the presentation of meat to its consumer, i.e., the people who buy it from a butcher as well as those who gather at the table and participate in the ritual of eating it as food: the food we see and eat, that we represent in our culinary discourse, is a product of this acculturation or civilization, and contributes not simply to meeting our natural need for nourishment, but just as vitally, on the side of culture, to our practice of self-conception, of human identification.

Elias' studies give substance to the second (general, historical) thesis we drew above from the writings of Lévi-Strauss. In the work of Louis Marin on the thought and culture of seventeenth-century France, there are numerous intersections with the investigatory horizons we have encountered in Lévi-Strauss and Elias. On the one hand, Marin appropriates the structuralist's view that the culinary system is a language, isomorphic with other cultural formations. On the other hand, he takes up, in *La parole mangée*, a historical correlation that Elias sketches in broad strokes, the consolidation of political power under the absolute monarch in conjunction with the elaboration of neo-classical values and thought. In relation to this over-arching background, Marin's insights on food in western culture inevitably have a special flavor simply because his analytical focus is relatively precise and propels him into a detailed reckoning with seminally important texts and artefacts of mid-to-late seventeenth-century France. But if he manages from the start to put a particularly original and challenging spin on his work in this domain, it is surely because the very ground of his reflections is the problematics of representation. Vis-à-vis the ethnologist's assimilation of cuisine to language, the import of this term and the framing it effects is considerable. For in its range and grasp, representation, subsuming not only language but the dimension of images and graphic forms as well, extends across the full spectrum of cultural formations, all of which become subject to conscious elaboration by virtue of being re-presentable. It is, one might say, the system of systems, the embracing fulcrum on which the recognition of cultural spheres and patterns, as well as the very possibility of articulating particular systems with one another, depends. To study representation is, we might say, to study the general order of culture, the complex of materials, relations, and processes of which culture is made.

It is not, moreover, a merely structural or historical account of representation that comes into play in *La parole mangée* it is, supplementally, an analysis of language, of images, of what Marin terms, rather than the culinary system, the culinary sign, that pushes beyond the apprehension of functional relations and systemic developments toward the disclosure of what is absent, insecure, or dissembled within the processes of representation. From Marin's perspective on the cultural representation of food, it is necessary to add to the two hypotheses—one structural and one historical—that we have posited a third one, according to which the role of food within the representational order is that of a *transignifier,* i.e., of an operator or articulator uniquely well suited to playing in a double or multiple and transitive register so as, on the one hand, to dissimulate and to compensate for a potentially discomfitting inadequacy or missing link, an excess or lack in the general order of culture, which is that of representation, and on the other hand, to provide for links or transfers or modulations, or indeed for jumps or slides, between orders or levels or terms that appear to be disconnected. To restate this hypothesis somewhat more simply, and in Marin's own terms, it suffices to refer to a passage in which he describes the culinary sign as the mechanism of the marvelous in the fairytales of Perrault: in this fictional world the culinary sign is a place or process, Marin writes, in and through which "the dialectic of *logos, eros,* and *sitos* is formed," [131] i.e., where the figurative processes of *transsignifiance*—metonymy, synecdoche, and metaphor—convey and indeed carry out the articulation of society's major systems of exchange: words in a discursive system, wives in a matrimonial system, worldly goods in an economic system. The third hypothesis thus posits the representation of food as a privileged sign, uniquely positioned for revealing the tensions and transactions between the various orders or spheres of culture.

Now, before looking more closely at Louis Marin's intriguing line on the tales of Charles Perrault, we should outline the larger historical scheme in which his reading of the tales takes root. Marin's understanding of the culinary sign stems from the study of representation and representationality that he elaborates in *La critique du discours,* a study that takes the *Logique* of Port-Royal to be the pivotal text in French intellectual history of the seventeenth century. The *Logique* endeavors to construct for Cartesian rationalism a theory of representation and of signification that Descartes left in a conspicuously underdeveloped state in his work. To put it crudely, that theory perceives the sign to be an adequate representation of or stand-in for an idea, which is an adequate representation or mental image of an object. Objectivity depends on a correspondence between object and idea and between idea and sign so perfect that representation as such—the activity of image- or thought- formation and the representing material (words, pictures)—passes unnoticed: the sign is transparent, the image translucent, access to the represented is immediate. But for many reasons the authors of the *Logique* cannot make do with such a simple construct.

In the first place, like their colleague Pascal, Arnauld and Nicole realize of course that signs and images are produced by a subject whose awareness of the activity and medium of represent*ing* cannot be suppressed and whose use of signs inflects them with the effects and motives of desire. Hence the moral imperative to understand representation in order to restrict it to the service of truth. In the second place, and perhaps more significantly, the logicians of Port-Royal, working in the Augustinian tradition of semiotics, are obliged to reckon with the mystery and the implications of the eucharistic sign. The singular utterance within the eucharistic ritual, *Hoc est corpus meum*—"this is my body"—is, Marin writes,"at once the productive source of the representational model of the sign and what throws the model into question" *[La parole mangée* 126]. Whereas Arnauld and Nicole were constrained to conceal this origin, to treat the sacramental speech act, not as the enabling condition of their general model for explaining the transformative capacity of the word, but merely as an illustration of the model, Marin asks if the magical phrase should not be accorded a seminal theoretical and critical position. He proposes to set forth explicitly the problem of language brought to a head by the eucharistic mystery, and to study its ramifications throughout the order of representation.

The thesis advanced here is a bold one. For Marin, the eucharistic sign provides the original model of *transsignifiance,* of a metamorphosis he also designates with the theological term *transsubstantiation* (defining the process of conversion whereby the bread becomes the spoken word and the word becomes the body eaten, whereby, under the proper conditions, the authoritative speech act produces the divine body as the food of the sacramental meal). As such, as the agent of an ontological transformation effected by the force of signs, by effects of *transsignifiance,* the eucharistic formula is not only the model of the culinary sign, but is also, Marin suggests, the general model of the communal process by which the force of signs is transformed into power. Thus the utterance "this is my body" prefigures various representations—historical narratives, panegyrics, paintings, medals, portraits—that will serve to consecrate the power of the state, the solemn discourse of the king being precisely an instance of speech capable of transforming words into consumable goods. The parallel between the theological or ecclesiastical operation carried out by the words of Christ and the political operation carried out by the words of the king underlies Marin's reading of Perrault's tales. "Perhaps one might say," he writes,"… that every culinary sign is in some sense and to some extent eucharistic; likewise, that all cooking is a theological, ideological, political, and economic operation by means of which a non- signified edible foodstuff is transformed into a sign-body that is eaten. It is this story, this dialectic of the edible and the consumed, of the thing and the body, of what is shown and its sign, of need and desire, that the tales never stop telling in their manner" [128].

So for Louis Marin, to read the culinary signs in Perrault's tales turns out to entail a further exploration of the eucharistic sign and thereby to be a(n un)cannily double-edged operation. On the theoretical side, ferreting out the effects of *transsignifiance* will expose the order of representation as an exercise of power; it will reveal the complicities of the rationalist theory of representation and signification with theological, ideological, and psychological operations that, in structuring human relations by as well as in representation, repeat essentially the same power play. Describing these operations analytically serves to shore up the general thesis on power and civility set forth by Norbert Elias. On the critical side, disclosing the forces—the forcing—at work in the processes of *transsignifiance* will expose the strains and fissures that plague the order of representation; it will reveal the transactions and slippages that make representational practice an opportunity for strategic manipulation, for cooking up an enticing dish that hungry consumers will take from the *chef*—the chief—on faith. Describing the process that makes the enigmatic utterance efficacious opens onto the spectacle of fiction and illusion, onto the forces of dissension within representation.

Insofar as Louis Marin's thesis and his critical gambit in *La parole mangée* consist in ressurrecting the move- ment of the eucharistic sign in every culinary sign, it ties the operations structuring French culture and society under Louis XIV to a quite particular ground—one which is not simply theological in general and thus readily assimilable to a certain theocentric version of Cartesian rationalism, but which is a specifically religious event, the biblical meal understood to be constitutive of the body of the Christian church. In the introduction to *Food for Thought*, the admirable English translation of *La parole mangée,* Marin refers explicitly to the withdrawal of the divine body from the institution of the church in the very sacramental meal that founds it. He suggests that in Perrault's *Contes* we can read traces of this scenario, situating the real presence of the mystical body of Christ as the object of the church's communal desire: "The displacements and transformation of the culinary sign in Perrault's *Tales* may be viewed as the figurative traces of this desire for the divine body" [xix]. What is at stake here is perhaps less the value of a Christological interpretation of Perrault's writings, the plausibility of which can be reinforced by various details from the author's life and works,[36] than a very pointed account of the way in which Cartesian rationalism is appropriated by seventeenth-century French culture. On Marin's account, to put the point indelicately, the Cartesian scheme is Christianized in the theory and practice of representation, and the ramifications of that historical movement, while given to be read in many places, receive their "most precise and suggestive narrative expression" [xviii] in Perrault's *Tales.*

Since Louis Marin has demonstrated the applicability of his reading hypothesis in a host of essays on Perrault, as well as in diverse analyses of texts and icons that disclose the figural status of the king and explain its effects, his perspective on the cultural representation of food is hardly subject to refutation or correction. The question is rather whether his description of the dynamics by which the rationalism of Descartes is complicated and recuperated by subsequent cultural formations is the only workable account, or the most satisfactory one. Concomitantly, in the case of Perrault's tales the question is not whether the narratives' persistent invocation of the culinary sign yields reinscriptions of the eucharistic sign and deploys its capacity to bridge across the other systems of exchange that are caught up in the mechanisms of the marvelous tale; rather, the question is whether those moments of *transsignifiance* are indeed the most telling or dominant effects of the play of representation, and secondarily whether other, essentially esthetic signs—such as terms that evoke vision and intellection—are not just as capacious and pivotal as the culinary sign in exercising the trans- signifying function. In a moment, I shall venture a necessarily preliminary and tentative response to this latter question by looking at a tale,"Peau d'âne," that, in *La parole mangée,* Marin treats as crucial, owing to its inaugural and in many respects exemplary status. In tandem with it, I shall comment as well on a second, quite celebrated tale,"Cendrillon," that he evokes only in passing, precisely because the fairy godmother's transformation of the pumpkin into a carriage offers a fine illustration of the marvelous and of *transsignifiance.* Let me first comment briefly, however, on the former question, concerning the framework in which Perrault's narratives relate to Cartesian rationalism and to Port-Royal's theory of representation.

In work on Perrault's esthetics that I intend to incorporate into a study of the seventeenth-century sublime, I appeal to a somewhat different framework for understanding Perrault's recuperation of Descartes and his handling of the difficulties Cartesian rationalism encounters in its reckoning with the problems of representation. I take the crucial turn in Descartes' foundational texts to be the tightly controlled conversion of knowledge inherent in the speech of the subject into knowledge in the form of an image. What I term the Cartesian turn is the initial and, as it were, immediate envisualization of the proposition "I think," the folding or displacement of thought onto sight in a manner that marks their continuity and near-coincidence. Thus the representational movement or signifying event that a Cartesian theory of language or signification has to deal with is indeed a metamorphosis effected by a pivotal proposition, but one far more confined and discreet than the process of transsubstantiation in the eucharist or *transsignifiance* in the realm of the marvelous; it is the subtle, metaphorical shift or shuttle or *tropos* whereby the sayable is shunted—or "raised"—into the visible, speech into image, assertion into figuration, knowledge into representation, the mind into the sphere of natural light; in short, a movement generative of the most elemental representation, a primary imaging that underlies the fundamental value of the visual—the clear and distinct idea—in Descartes' epistemology.

It is above all through this accreditation of the compelling visual image, faithfully reproducing its object for a thinking subject, that Descartes' influence makes itself felt in Perrault's *Parallèle des andern et des modernes.* In this important treatise on the culture and esthetics of the age of Louis XIV, the position of Perrault's spokesman, the abbot, is generally one of solidarity with the rationalist construction of a conventional mimeticism; this stance, a kind of mainstream, domesticated Cartesianism, supports the privileging of the visual in the work's esthetics. However, when the work of Descartes is encountered directly, a counterposition appears that stresses not the

---

36   See, in particular, Perrault's *Pensées chrétiennes,* ed. Jacques Barchilon. Paris: Biblio 17, vol. 34, 1987.

continuity in the Cartesian turn, but the difference between the enabling ground of representation, visibility, and that of knowledge, mind. The latter engages reason and intelligence and communicative powers that Cartesian rationalism reserves for man, whereas animals, while lower than man, can perfectly well be endowed with the faculty of representation. Through this reversal that disconnects the image from cognition and leads Perrault's spokesman to posit a certain necessary inconceivability or irrepresentability within or beneath the knowledge he extols, the prestige of visual representation is momentarily thrown into doubt and Perrault's Cartesianism takes on an intriguingly critical edge or twist. The result is a compromise formation in which a simple, mainstream rationalism accrediting a stable, technological, continuist account of representation is dominant, but in which a space for a critical position, antagonistic to the dominant scheme, is preserved. One may ask if the fairytales do not display a similar compromise formation and if such compromises do not constitute, from tale to tale, a dominant horizon on which the work of the marvelous (including such transsignifiers as the culinary sign)—insofar as it is not fully assimilable to the tenets of rationalism—appears and, as it were, comes into perspective. Were one to develop this suggestion as a systematic argument, it would quickly become necessary to show how the model of representation constructed in Louis Marin's work fits into it. The working hypothesis would presumably be that the signifying operations vehiculated by the culinary sign belong to the apparatus of compromise formation. Thus, while they may serve to expose and on occasion to disturb or contest the mechanisms of power, their essential place would be one of complicity in a movement that, whether textual or historical, enables the dominant order to sustain itself, to incorporate and use productively the very play of representation that threatens it. As a corollary to this hypothesis, we might suppose that the *moralités* or lessons attached to Perrault's tales would typically rearticulate a distilled version of such a compromise.

In *La parole mangée,* Louis Marin offers a reading of "Peau d'âne" that stresses Perrault's artful writing down of a story so emblematic of the oral tradition of folktales that one could refer to such tales as *contes de Peau d'âne.* By writing down a paradigmatic or master-tale that is also a story of a king and a father, Perrault the author positions himself as a surrogate father and surrogate king, inasmuch as the king is a kind of originary author of all written cultural production. From this position, he—Perrault—dramatizes "what was at stake at a given time and place in a writing of orality and in the orality of writing" [46] and enables the reader—Marin—to grasp all the ambivalences that are captured and figured by the mouth, that flexible organ of speaking and eating that is also an erogenous zone, the locus of an anaclitic relation mingling libidinal impulses with the instinct for self-preservation. This relation, says Marin, amounts to the inscription of a bodily desire, a bodily writing that takes place in the mouth. Hence the proposal to read the tale as a kind of dismantling of the opposition between the oral and the written.

Now, taking this account of "Peau d'âne"'s context-setting status to be valid, it is instructive to pursue a somewhat different tack, reading the story as a densified elaboration on the narrative structure of a sister-tale, "Cendrillon," which initially resembles "Peau d'âne" because it is entitled with the nickname of its heroine and because each of these degrading names points to the sordid, bedraggled state into which a virtuous maiden has fallen. "Cendrillon" is the story of a lovely young girl whose mother dies and whose father remarries with a thoroughly disagreeable woman who has two self-centered daughters. Once Cinderella and her father have moved in with these three women, we hear no more of the father: the haughty stepmother and her daughters persecute Cinderella, relegating her to the role of household servant. Both her nicer nickname, Cendrillon, and her less nice nickname, Cucendron ("Cinderseat," "Cinderfanny"), are derived from her habitual, lowly sitting place in cinders by the chimney; both suggest a kind of seating of her identity in the material her body contacts, just as Peau d'âne's name suggests a kind of displacement of her identity onto that of the animal whose skin she wears. When the son of the King gave a ball for notables in the kingdom, of course the two daughters of Cinderella's stepmother were able to attend, decked out in splendid costumes, whereas poor Cinderella, clothed in her tattered rags, was expected to stay at home. But fortunately the good fairy godmother struck, using her magic wand to make a coach and coachmen from pumpkins and mice, then outfitting Cinderella in a beautiful jewel-studded gold and silver dress and dainty glass slippers. Thus she could attend the ball, provided she made it home before midnight. All went well: the prince was so taken with her that during the banquet he ate nothing,"tant il était occupé à la considérer" [174]—and he invited her back the next night. This time all went so delightfully that Cinderella forgot to leave on time. Thus her costume and coach disintegrated as she ran from the ball at midnight, losing one of her glass slippers during her exit. We learn that the prince picked up the glass slipper and until the ball was over did nothing but gaze at it. A few days later, the prince announced that he would marry the woman whose foot would fit the delicate little glass slipper.[37] In the ensuing shoefitting contest, after watching her stepsisters fail to squeeze the slipper on, Cinderella of course succeeds. After she pulls out the other glass slipper, the fairy godmother turns up to dress her splendidly one last time. The tale ends with her marriage to the prince and her reconciliation with the two stepsisters.

In what sense does "Peau d'âne," the master-tale, enact essentially the same plot we encounter here? In the opening sequence of "Peau d'âne," the heroine becomes, like Cinderella, a kind of disinherited victim of her parents. The sequence that reduces her to a plight comparable to Cinderella's is, to be sure, much longer and weightier in connotations. Peau d'âne is a princess who loses her beautiful and virtuous mother, just as Cinderella had lost her mother, whom the narrator simply qualified as "la meilleure personne du monde" [171]. But the dying queen had a vengeful streak: she made her husband, the greatest king on earth [98], swear not to remarry unless he found a woman superior to her in beauty and goodness. Entrapped, the king eventually discovers that only his lovely daughter can fill the bill and hatches a violent incestuous passion for her. On advice from her fairy godmother, she tries to fend him off by erecting impossible obstacles: before marrying him she requires a dress the color of time; when the king's tailors produce the most beautiful blue dress imaginable, she adds a second demand, a dress the color of the moon, and a comparable silver dress is produced; she then calls for a third dress, the color of the sun, which yields another marvel made of cloth laced with gold and diamonds. At her wit's end, she follows her fairy godmother's suggestion to request of her father the skin of his prize donkey, an animal formed by Nature, we are told [98–99], so that, instead of feces, it excreted only silver and gold. "Comme il est toute sa ressource," i.e., as the ass is the source of the great king's wealth and power, says the fairy, reason dictates that he will not grant this exorbitant request. But of course passion defeats reason and the poor young girl, clothing herself in the donkey-skin and covering her extremities with dirt, takes flight. Peau d'âne is aided by the fairy, who enables her to take along the three beautiful dresses and other personal effects in a magic trunk that follows her underground.

All this elaboration of an Oedipal calamity compounded by an economic fiasco reduces Peau d'âne, as a family outcast, to the position that Cinderella occupied when she was at the bottom of the domestic ladder, unable to go to the ball. Our heroine ends up in another kingdom, working as a lowly kitchen servant on a royal farm and living in a miserable hovel. There she is sustained by the pleasurable experience she enacts on Sundays and holidays, when she puts on one of the three magnificent dresses and contemplates herself in a mirror. One holiday the king's son happens into the barnyard, walks about, and eventually looks through the hole in Peau d'âne's doorlock, contemplates her, and is ravished with passion. After learning what people call her and that they consider her an ugly beast, the prince falls into a drastic lovesickness. Refusing to eat, he wastes away, saying his only desire is to have a cake made by Peau d'âne. While making him a fine cake, she drops a ring of gold and emerald into the cake batter. Famished, he eats this dessert so ravenously that he nearly swallows the ring,

---

37 Gilbert Rouger, in his edition of the *Contes* (Paris: Classiques Garnier, 1967; pp. 154–56), provides a persuasive justification of the reading "pantoufles de vair," as opposed to the claim of some readers (Balzac, Littré, Gide) that the homonymic "pantoufles de vair" makes better sense. The line of insight developed here would reinforce Rouger and his predecessor, Paul Delarue, with two points: (1) a slipper made of fur would be flexible, less well suited than the rigid glass for the shoefitting contest that Cendrillon wins; (2) a glass slipper, perceived as a refined, perhaps light-conducting artefact, makes a rather more appropriate object for the prince's gaze than would a fur slipper.

but saves it under his pillow. Thereafter, his illness worsens. The doctors diagnose lovesickness and recommend treating it with marriage. The prince agrees and proposes a contest: he will marry the woman whose finger will fit into the ring extracted from Peau d'âne's cake. Like Cinderella fitting her foot into her glass slipper, the victorious Peau d'âne is the last contestant allowed to try the ring. With the ring on her finger, she then puts on one of her dresses and is accepted by the royal family, to whom the fairy recounts her story. Her marriage, like Cinderella's, is marked by a familial reconciliation, as her father, wisened and chastened, turns up for the wedding.

To recapitulate the parallels between the stories of Cinderella and Peau d'âne, it is helpful to distinguish schematically [cf. the tree diagram] a principal narrative structure, the locus of a drama within the heroine's family, and an embedded structure, which consists of the recovery from her downtrodden state through an amorous adventure outside the family. On the global level, the initial situation results from the death of the mother; the transgression that fuels the drama is the parental aggression against the heroine; the heroic response is the joint resistance undertaken by the heroine allied with the fairy godmother; and the dénouement is the family reconciliation. On the embedded level, which in each case is simply an extension or specification of the heroine's quest in the global sequence, the parallelism is still more striking. In each tale the prince is quickly enraptured by the unknown beauty he discovers, the transgression stems from her mysterious identity and lowly status, the problem is solved in a vestmental ceremony that enables the heroine to don a key part of her costume that she alone can wear, and the denouement is her marriage with the prince. The comparative framework provided by this schematic framework enables us to launch a series of observations that will, I hope, lead to a comment on the representation of food and its role in the structuring work on the family, society, economy, and political order that "Peau d'âne," by filling in the blanks or gaps left in the sparer story of Cinderella, evokes with a comprehensiveness that does indeed make it exemplary in the Perraldian corpus.

Following the classical procedure of structural narratology, let us begin by noting some further parallelisms in the two tales, then veer toward the differences that emerge, on the assumption that it is ultimately the latter that are suggestive.

In both *Cendrillon* and *Peau d'âne,* the trajectory of the heroine may be taken as an illustration of what Norbert Elias terms the civilizing process. Each heroine, in servitude, is characterized by insistent associations with dirt and with animality. In *Cendrillon,* the first case of a magical transformation of the type that Cinderella undergoes both instantly, before the ball, and gradually, as her story unfolds, is the fairy's nifty reincarnation of the pumpkin, mice, and rats as her coach and coachmen. That conversion illustrates a crossing over from nature to culture that *Peau d'âne* redoubles: the donkey first appears in the tale having already crossed the nature/culture divide and occupied a position of splendid luxury, as the idol at the center of the immaculate, manureless royal stable. When Peau d'âne takes on the donkey's skin and its name, she is treated as a "pauvre bête," so that her itinerary—like that of another Perraldian hero marked by a natural ugliness, Riquet à la houppe—involves shedding her visible animal features for human ones. For both Cinderella and Peau d'âne, the mark of their civilization that is stressed most decisively, however, is a passage from a milieu of filth and dirt—Cinderella's cinders, and the *crasse* or grime that Peau d'âne puts on as make-up—into their brilliant costumes, dresses that become progressively more scintillating and more compelling in impact as each story develops. The principal emblems of court society, the magnificent dresses and the heroine's glittering appearance, are indeed the exclusive locus of supernatural effects, as the fairies' artful deeds—as distinct from their words—bear upon nothing else: the supernatural here lies in the costuming and appointments of high society—in the embellishment of visible bodies and objects and in the control of appearances, which are the hallmarks of neoclassical culture.

While the visual effects of dress seem paramount in the society of these tales, manifestations of the consonant culinary system are assuredly in evidence. At the ball, in a gesture connoting her charm and cleverness as well as the flavor of the event, Cinderella gives to her stepsisters the oranges and lemons (expensive fruits that were signs of luxury) the prince had given to her to express his favor. After Peau d'âne's disappearance from her father's castle, the pall that has been cast is evoked in these verses:

Partout se répandit un triste et noir chagrin;
Plus de Noces, plus de Festin,
Plus de Tartes, plus de Dragées;
Les Dames de la cour, toutes découragées,
N'en dînerent point la plupart …

But what seems to bear out our initial hypothesis about the representation of food particularly well is the eating behavior of the two princes. In "Cendrillon," as we have noted, the prince's infatuation with the unknown young woman's beauty is signaled by his less than impeccable table manners: instead of eating he stared at her. The prince in "Peau d'âne" likewise gets away with not eating when he should eat during his seemingly self-styled lovesickness, and when he does punctuate his abstinence with food, rather than proper nourishment he gorges down Peau d'âne's delectable dessert. In each case, the suppression of appetite correlates with visual behavior that seems excessive, as the prince gives himself over to contemplation of a beautifully clothed stranger. The predominance of the visual over the oral as a channel of desire seems no less decisive than the capacity of apparel to signify beauty, wealth, and above all social station.

Now in "Peau d'âne," there is one scene that seems to record the dominance and significance of visual experience with an insistence that has no parallel in "Cendrillon." While the prince gazes at Peau d'âne through the keyhole, looking long enough moreover to pass through three rounds of temptation to break through the door before he could tear himself away, Peau d'âne is inside the room, decked out magnificently, going through her ritual of gazing at herself in a full-length mirror. Upon evoking these conjoined spectacles of voyeuristic and narcissistic pleasure, which is not exactly a commonplace concatenation in neo-classical French literature, the Perraldian narrator glosses lightly over the effects of eroticism, quickly shifting the focus from the scopic dynamics to the objects seen and what they reveal, to the conventional critical opposition of the French *moralistes,* appearances to being. The prince's moral interpretation of the scene he observes is reassuring, as he discerns the perceptible marks of the young woman's beautiful soul and noble birth. The spectacle of seeing a scene of self-admiration thus coordinates the sphere of pleasure and desire, animated by Peau d'âne's natural beauty, with the sphere of economic resources, evoked by the magnificence of her dress, jewelry, and full-length mirror, and those of social and psychological relations, which are accessible to the prince's penetrating gaze. This process of coordination and communication, through the play of the visual dynamics, is further marked, moreover, by a narratorial intervention suggesting that Peau d'âne had noticed she was being observed by the prince, owing to a kind of magnetic interaction of the two gazes at work in this scene, and thus that her dispatch of the ring in the cake was not accidental, but contrived.

The extended development of a visual dynamics and metaphorics in "Peau d'âne" differentiates the tale in degree, but not in kind, from "Cendrillon." There are two features, however, that distinguish the two tales decisively. The first is the extended elaboration, in "Peau d'âne," of the mediation function in the global narrative, where the young woman and the fairy godmother pursue their unsuccessful attempts to fend off the father. The second is the scene of cake-baking and eating, which brings into play an intriguing operation of the culinary sign. It is, we shall now see, the linkage of these segments—and specifically of their key signifiers, the gold-defecating donkey and the ring-bearing cake—that the narrative constructs and invites us to ponder.

In the strategy of the fairy godmother and her fearful daughter in setting marital conditions they imagine to be impossible, there is a curious echo of the dying mother's prohibition on remarriage by her husband: they attempt, as she had done, to set impossible conditions, and their failures tend to reinforce the aspersions that the narrative casts on the mother-figure. A comparably disparaging view of the domineering mother figure is developed in "Cendrillon," moreover; it is as if the mothers were somehow to blame for the irresponsibility of the fathers toward their daughters; yet in the denouements of each tale, it turns out that the scenes of familial recognition incorporate the satisfaction of the mothers' wishes. In any case, Peau d'âne's imitation of the problem- causing maternal gesture appears to occasion her downfall, although for her, too, the strategy will eventually appear to have been a successful one. But the telling difference between "Peau d'âne" and "Cendrillon" lies in the transformation itinerary through which Peau d'âne passes: a deeper, steeper fall from a royal station to which she already belongs, into an apparent abjection that is nonetheless shrouded in an ambivalence missing from Cinderella's experience—followed by a drama of return toward her elevated social origin, crowned by a classic scene of recognition, whereas Cinderella's itinerary is more straightforwardly one of social ascension toward a new identity in a higher class.

The ambivalence of Peau d'âne's position stems, of course, from her costume: superficially, it is the ass's skin around her neck that causes the attendants of the queen, mother of the Prince, to describe her as "la bête en un mot la plus laide/Qu'on puisse voir après le Loup" [108] and again as "une noire Taupe/Plus vilaine encore et plus gaupe/Que le plus sale Marmiton" [109]. But for the reader of the tale, who understands that her clothing comes from the marvelous, idolized animal that had been worshipped as the creator of her royal father's wealth, the significance of her identity is rather more complex. Given the power of clothing in the tale to invest the wearer with identifying marks, to the extent that the skin masking her identity confers on her some of the identity of the donkey, the prized centerpiece of domestic life—of the economy—in her father's kingdom, Peau d'âne—thanks to her father's sacrifice of the ass, a gift made to her *without reserve*—bears the value, a certain quality, derived from that supernatural beast—*non-* or *super-natural* precisely because it excreted no waste, but only gold. In other words, the animalization of Peau d'âne effected by the donkey-skin, the fourth and ultimate garment she receives (after the three dresses) in the series of failed mediations, places her, not squarely on the side of nature, but in the donkey's position, straddling the nature/culture dichotomy. The donkeyskin's capacity to work as a garment, as one of the heroine's possible costumes or guises, is immediately signaled by the fairy, who refers to it as a "masque admirable" [104], an admirable mask or disguise; and the employment she acquires as a dishwasher in a distant corner of the royal kitchen is granted to her because of the steadfastness with which she maintains her practice of what the narrative pointedly describes, when she puts on the skin, as *travesty:* "la princesse ainsi travestie …" [105]. The verb *travestir*—literally cross-dressing, costume switching—suggests that Peau d'âne is caught up in the practice of changing identities by changing clothes, a seesaw movement between public and private faces that she maintains by shifting back and forth between the donkey-skin and her three gorgeous dresses. Her problem in the visual order—in the sphere of being and appearances—will be solved precisely when she is able to eliminate the screen that shields the private side of her existence from view. The interest of the reader thus tends to focus on the mechanism that will enable her full visibility to be restored.

It is here that we meet the culinary sign, functioning unmistakably in the manner Louis Marin describes. Miraculously, Peau d'âne brings to her confection the quality of a master-baker who, significantly, retires to her room, grooms herself, and puts on a silver vest in order to concoct her dessert in a worthy ("pour faire dignement son ouvrage" [109])—i.e., adjusting the situation so that the scene's setting and costumes are in harmony with the reality of her production itself, so that being and appearance are at one with one another. The crucial feature of her performance, however, has to do with the product, a cake so fine that, according to the narrator, "On ne pétrit jamais un si friand morceau" [110]. But the feature that makes this culinary work of art so remarkable is what connects it with the production of the donkey : the unnatural, inedible object that emerges from the baking process and falls thereby into the hand of the prince ("il désire/que Peau d'âne lui fasse un gâteau de sa main" [109]) from the hand of the heroine ("De son doigt par hasard il tomba dans la pâte/Un de ses anneaux de grand prix" [110]), just as the gold coins from the donkey—*écus* and *Louis*—turned up on the litter where one would expect to find, not valuable, manufactured objects of culture, but a passably natural waste product. Moreover, it is as if, by dint of the metonymic effects conveyed by the ring as an identifying part of the princess' hand and as an ingredient of the cake destined to be seen and held, but not eaten, the cake has linked product and producer

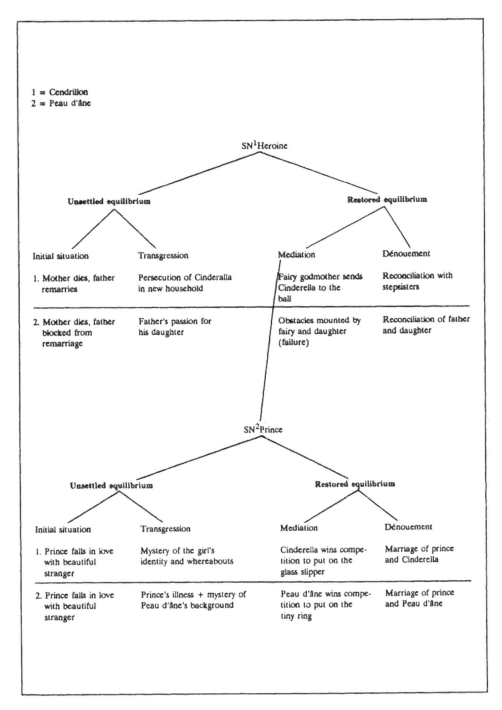

1 = Cendrillon
2 = Peau d'âne

SN¹Heroine

Unsettled equilibrium   Restored equilibrium

Initial situation	Transgression	Mediation	Dénouement
1. Mother dies, father remarries	Persecution of Cinderalla in new household	Fairy godmother sends Cinderella to the ball	Reconciliation with stepsisters
2. Mother dies, father blocked from remarriage	Father's passion for his daughter	Obstacles mounted by fairy and daughter (failure)	Reconciliation of father and daughter

SN²Prince

Unsettled equilibrium   Restored equilibrium

Initial situation	Transgression	Mediation	Dénouement
1. Prince falls in love with beautiful stranger	Mystery of the girl's identity and whereabouts	Cinderella wins competition to put on the glass slipper	Marriage of prince and Cinderella
2. Prince falls in love with beautiful stranger	Prince's illness + mystery of Peau d'âne's background	Peau d'âne wins competition to put on the tiny ring	Marriage of prince and Peau d'âne

and become a dessert not only made with her hands but *of her hand,* so that the cake provides, for the prince, a symbolic meal through which he is almost literally taking her hand. The narrative pointedly notes that the cake, quickly consumed, supplies more than one form of nourishment to the Prince, satisfying and whetting another appetite that eating does not assuage:

> Quand il en vit l'émeraude admirable,
> Et du jonc d'or le cercle étroit,
> Qui marquait la forme du doigt,
> Son coeur en fut touché d'une joie incroyable. [110]

What Peau d'âne cooked up for the Prince supplied not only edible food to be consumed in the natural processes of ingestion and digestion, but a food supplement, we might say., in the form of an inedible object to be seen with the eyes—"il en vit l'emeraude admirable"—and prized for its form. The value of the ring here is doubtless very close to that of the glass slipper, a readily fetishizable object that Cendrillon's prince contemplated from the moment he picked it up until the end of the ball. For "Peau d'âne" 's prince, the pleasure derived from imagining that erotic moment when the impeccably shaped bodily part slips delicately into the receiving hole is made rather more explicit. The key point, in any case, is that what Peau d'âne brings with her, in her ambivalence, via the metamorphosis that invests her first with the traits of the donkey and then, in the kitchen, with the donkey's alchemical skills of production, turns crucially on her success in drawing the food she cooks into her practice of travesty and in making that food the carrier of an enduring, visible object, the ring, that functions as a conventional symbol of a matrimonial exchange in the works, but also, more generally, as an artefact embodying the overriding articulatory power of the visual image in the civilizing process represented in Perrault's tales. Indeed, the prince's consumption of the cake, because it offers up the beautiful bodily adornment for enduring contemplation, is perhaps the exemplary figuration in Perrault's work not only of the signifying power of the visual mark, but also of the dynamics through which it comes, in the tales, to embrace and be privileged over all others, including the culinary sign. So if the narrator of "Peau d'âne," as Louis Marin suggests, invites us to grasp a certain writing in or with the mouth or the voice, the tale itself invites us to apprehend a scopic culture, given over to eating with the eyes.

WORKS CITED

Elias, Norbert. *The Civilizing Process, I: The History of Manners,* Tr. Edmund Jephcott. New York: Pantheon, 1978.
— *The Civilizing Process, II Power and Civility*, Tr. Edmund Jephcott. New York: Pantheon, 1982.
Lévi-Strauss, Claude. *L'origine des manières de table.* Paris: Plon, 1968.
Marin, Louis. *La parole mangée.* Paris: Méridiens Klincksieck, 1986. Translated as *Food for Thought* by Mette Jhort (Baltimore: Johns Hopkins University Press, 1989).
La critique du discours. Paris: Minuit, 1975.
Perrault, Charles. *Contes,* ed. Jean-Pierre Collinet. Paris: Gallimard [Folio], 1981.
—*Parallèle des anciens et des modernes.* Réimpression de la seconde édition, Paris, 1692–97. Geneva: Slatkine Reprints, 1979.

The Master Cat or Puss in Boots

Charles Perrault

A MILLER bequeathed to his three sons all his worldly goods, which consisted just of his mill, his ass, and his cat. The division was made quickly, and neither notary nor attorney were called, for they would have soon consumed all of the meager patrimony. The eldest received the mill; the second son, the ass; the youngest got nothing but the cat.

Of course, the youngest was upset at inheriting such a poor portion. "My brothers may now earn an honest living as partners," he said, "but as for me, I'm bound to die of hunger once I have eaten my cat and made a muff of his skin."

The cat, who had heard this speech but pretended not to have been listening, said to him with a sober and serious air, "Don't trouble yourself, master. Just give me a pouch and a pair of boots to go into the bushes, and you'll see that you were not left with as bad a share as you think."

Although the cat's master did not place much stock in this assertion, he had seen the cat play such cunning tricks in catching rats and mice- hanging himself upside down by the heels or lying in the flour as if he were dead—that he did not abandon all hope.

As soon as the cat had what he had asked for, he boldly pulled on his boots. Then he hung the pouch around his neck, took the strings in his forepaws, and went to a warren where a great number of rabbits lived. He put some bran and lettuce into his pouch and, stretching himself out as if he were dead, he waited for a young rabbit little versed in the wiles of the world to look for something to eat in the pouch. He had hardly laid down when he saw his plan work. A young scatterbrain of a rabbit entered the pouch, and master cat instantly pulled the strings, bagged it, and killed it without mercy. Proud of his catch, he went to the king's palace and demanded an audience. He was ushered up to the royal apartment, and upon entering, he made a low bow to the king. "Sire," he said, "here's a rabbit from the warren of my lord, the Marquis de Carabas (such was the name he fancied to call his master). He has instructed me to present it to you on his behalf."

'Tell your master/' replied the king, "that I thank him and that he's given me great pleasure."

After some time had passed, the cat hid in a wheatfield, keeping the mouth of the pouch open as he always did. When two partridges entered it, he pulled the strings and caught them both. Then he went straight to the king and presented them to him just as he had done with the rabbit. The king was equally pleased by the two partridges and gave the cat a small token for his efforts.

During the next two or three months the cat continued every now and then to carry presents of game from his master to the king.

One day, when he knew the king was going to take a drive on the banks of a river with his daughter, the most beautiful princess in the world, he said to his master, "If you follow my advice, your fortune will be made. Just go and bathe in the river where I tell you, and leave the rest to me.

[margin note: in quotes, still virtual]

The "Marquis de Carabas" did as his cat advised, little expecting that any good would come of it. While he was bathing, the king passed by, and the cat began to shout with all his might, "Help! Help! My lord, the Marquis de Carabas is drowning!"

At this cry the king stuck his head out of the coach window. Recognizing the cat who had often brought game to him, he ordered his guards to rush to the aid of the Marquis de Carabas. While they were pulling the poor marquis out of the river, the cat approached the royal coach and told the king that some robbers had come and carried off his master's clothes while he was bathing/even though he had shouted "Thieves!" as loud as he could. But in truth the rascal had hidden his master's clothes himself under a large rock. The king immediately ordered the officers of his wardrobe to fetch one of his finest suits for the Marquis de Carabas. The king embraced the marquis a thousand times, and since the fine clothes brought out his good looks (for he was handsome and well built), the king's daughter found him much to her liking. No sooner did the Marquis de Carabas cast two or three respectful and rather tender glances at her than she fell in love with him. The king invited him to get into the coach and to accompany them on their drive.

Delighted to see that his scheme was succeeding, the cat ran on ahead and soon came upon some peasants mowing a field.

[margin note: peasants to lie to king — why? accept master so ogre is another real threat power so could form be cat]

"Listen, my good people," he said, "you who are mowing, if you don't tell the king that this field belongs to my lord, the Marquis de Carabas, you'll all be cut into tiny pieces like minced meat!"

Indeed, the king did not fail to ask the mowers whose field they were mowing.

"It belongs to our lord, the Marquis de Carabas," they said all together, for the cat's threat had frightened them.

"You can see, sire," rejoined the marquis, "it's a field that yields an abundant crop every year."

Master cat, who kept ahead of the party, came upon some reapers and said to them, "Listen, my good people, you who are reaping, if you don't say that all this wheat belongs to my lord, the Marquis de Carabas, you'll all be cut into tiny pieces like minced meat!"

A moment later the king passed by and wished to know who owned all the wheatfields that he saw there.

"Our lord, the Marquis de Carabas," responded the reapers, and the king again expressed his joy to the marquis.

Running ahead of the coach, the cat uttered the same threat to all whom he encountered, and the king was astonished at the great wealth of the Marquis de Carabas. At last master cat arrived at a beautiful castle owned by an ogre, the richest ever known, for all the lands through which the king had driven belonged to the lord of this castle. The cat took care to inquire who the ogre was and what his powers were. Then he requested to speak with him, saying that he could not pass so near his castle without paying his respects. The ogre received him as civilly as an ogre can and asked him to sit down.

"I've been told," said the cat, "that you possess the power of changing yourself into all sorts of animals. For instance, it has been said that you can transform yourself into a lion or an elephant."

"It's true," said the ogre brusquely. "And to prove it, watch me become a lion."

The cat was so frightened at seeing a lion standing before him that he immediately scampered up into the roof gutters, and not without difficulty, for his boots were not made to walk on tiles. Upon noticing that the ogre resumed his previous form a short time afterward, the cat descended and admitted that he had been terribly frightened.

"I've also been told," said the cat, "but I can't believe it, that you've got the power to assume the form of the smallest of animals. For instance, they say that you can change yourself into a rat or mouse. I confess that it seems utterly impossible to me."

"Impossible?" replied the ogre. "Just watch!"

Immediately he changed himself into a mouse, which began to run about the floor. No Sooner did the cat *moral-* catch sight of it than he pounced on it and devoured it. *strongest always win*

In the meantime the king saw the ogre's beautiful castle from the road and desired to enter it. The cat heard the noise of the coach rolling over the drawbridge and ran to meet it.

"Your Majesty," he said to the king,"welcome to the castle of my lord, the Marquis de Carabas."

"What!" exclaimed the king. "Does this castle also belong to you, Marquis? Nothing could be finer than this courtyard and all these buildings surrounding it. If you please, let us look inside."

The marquis gave his hand to the young princess, and they followed the king, who led the way upstairs. When they entered a grand hall, they found a magnificent repast that the ogre had ordered to, be prepared for some friends who were to have visited him that day. (But they did not presume to enter when they found the king was there.) The king was just as much delighted by the accomplishments of the Marquis de Carabas as his daughter, who doted on him, and now, realizing how wealthy he was, he said to him, after having drunk five or six cups of wine,"The choice is entirely yours, Marquis, whether or not you,want to become my son-in-law." , After making several low bows, the marquis accepted the honor the king had offered him; and on that very same day, he married the princess. In turn, the cat became a great lord and never again ran after mice, except for his amusement.

Moral

> Although the advantage may be great
> When one inherits a grand estate
> From father handed down to son,
> Young men will find that industry
> Combined with ingenuity,
> Will lead more to prosperity.

Another Moral

> If the miller's son had quick success
> In winning such a fair princess,
> By turning on the charm,
> Then regard his manners, looks, and dress
> That inspired her deepest tenderness,
> For they can't do one any harm

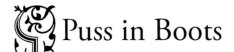

Puss in Boots

Power of Signs—Signs of Power

Louis Marin

The essay which follows can be considered in several ways: as a contribution to the long and respectable intellectual tradition of the history of ideas and ideologies in their expression by literary texts; as a possible element of comparison in the field of mythological studies between myths and tales belonging to different cultures; as an approach, through an example, to a theory of the text, reading and their effects—an approach roughly characterized by the use of some procedures of structural analysis; as an attempt to define a kind of logic which is not the logic of truth as representation, as *adequatio rei et intellectus* but the logic of will and desire, or to be more precise, a logic of the weak, of the marginal, of minorities that is a logic of deceit, trick, simulation, lie, a cunning logic that serves as a weapon against the powerful and a way of capturing their power while subverting it. Moreover, this essay is a kind of byproduct of my book *La critique du discours, études sur la Logique de Port-Royal et les Pensées de Pascal,* an application of some hypotheses 1 articulated therein to an unexpected set of texts: the seventeenth- century tales.

I propose to read a tale which is not actually a folk-tale since it was written by an author whom I consider one of the greatest writers of the seventeenth-century. To be sure, my reading will not be a very serious one: it just deals with a tale, a children's tale from which I shall extract only what seems *to me* the most pleasurable, the most delightful features of the story. But at the same time, I have imagined my essay as bearing *some very pedantic subtitles: "Power of signs or Signs of power,"* or "how to do things with words," or "language as representation and power," the latter being a kind of Schopenhauerian parody. Subtitles I might rephrase to be more explicit and more pedantic if possible in the manner of the historian of ideas and in the wake of my previous work on the *Port-Royal Logic* and Pascal: "Deception words—powerful speech: a mythical Eucharist in a French seventeenth-century tale." The tale is the *Master-Cat* or *Puss-in-Boots* by Charles Perrault. It was published in Perrault's *Mother Goose's Tales, Histories or Tales of Past Time with Morals,* in 1697. I shall read "Le Chat-Botté" in an English translation made in 1729 by Robert Samber. As it may now be evident, my first task is to explain the various subtitles of the essay, to justify my pedantry and in so doing, to reveal my secrets, my tricks, I mean the reading hypotheses I have and that I shall attempt to prove.

When I read the tale, I am struck by the important role played by a certain use of language. The main character of the tale, the Cat, appears to be the Master of words in this particular sense that he is always speaking and always lying and nonetheless that at the end his deceptive words are true. Everything he said when he deceived his interlocutors finally turns out to be just as he had claimed. The most direct way of understanding this process is to consider it as magical. His "parole" or speech, I mean his *use* of language, has the power of changing his representations, his words into real things. This power of language over reality is my leading thread in the reading of the story. In this respect, the tale recalls the basic conception of language, and more generally speaking the seventeenth- century model framing the relationships of mind and reality, of thought and word: the model we find explicitly developed in the *Port-Royal Logic,* a treatise, first published in 1662, which met with extraordinary success. My purpose, then, is to explore this particular aspect of the ideological and philosophical context of Perrault's text, or in other words, to show that in "Puss-in-boots," Perrault restates the traditional content of the folktale on a literary level in such a way as to provide us with a good tool for displaying and criticizing the implicit presuppositions of such a model of language and thought, a model that patterns basic problems with which we still are concerned today; similarly, Perrault's version of the tale is a good tool for pointing out some interesting historical and social changes that occurred at that time. I shall leave the tale for a while and quickly specify the paradigm of my reading: the representational theory of language and its use in the *Port-Royal Logic.*

As you know, in the first edition, language is not considered as a specific problem deserving a specific analysis: it is because words are constantly present in all the operations of mind that they do not have to be studied as such. This very fact leads me to rephrase it as a basic principle of the whole theoretical attempt of the Port- Royal logicians: the principle of representation that relates language and thought to each other. Mind is the mirror of things: ideas are things themselves within the mind, ideas represent things in the mind and for it. Language is the mirror of mind: signs and especially verbal signs, words, are things that represent ideas. Signs represent the representations of things. To give an idea a sign is to give mind an idea whose object represents what constitutes the idea.

The principle of representation has a correlated principle which concerns the very structure of a sign or of a signifying system. A sign divides the relation of representation characterizing an idea into two subrelations: a relation between ideas and signs and between signs and things. But a sign allows a process of substitution to take place between its object and the idea of the signified object, a substitution that works, in the case of language, from the thing to the sign: the idea of the signified object is substituted for the sign. Because of their arbitrariness, words are transparent to the primary relation or representation: they are necessary only to permit communication between minds and within the mind itself.

Now we can consider the additions of the fifth edition of the *Logic* (1683): their occasion is explicitly found in polemics with Reformers about the Eucharist. However these, theological discussions are directly related to fundamental parts of the logical and grammatical theories. Two main problems concerning language come into the foreground in the revised *Logic.* First the structure of the sign as a representation becomes a problem once the distinction between signified and referent is questioned. The very notion of representation had concealed this distinction beneath the unity of a presence that makes equivalent thing, sign, idea. Second, the relation between words and sentences: how can judgment, an assertive operation relating two representations to each other, have an ontological effect in the world? How can it articulate things in the world, making the world significant?

But at the same time, all these additions are provided by a privileged example, that of the Catholic interpretation of the Eucharist ritual formula "This is my body," a statement that conveys Jesus' Real Presence in the Host. This utterance raises the theological problem of a *power speech* in the sense that it transforms a thing into another thing. However it also gives to the philosophy of language-as-representation a new dimension: that of an analysis of a speech act that links to a deictic (this) by an ontological statement (is) a predicate (my body) that is nothing else than the very being of the subject who utters the sentence. Is this sentence only metaphorical?

That is the Reformers' interpretation. Or does it mean that the thing pointed out by the deictic becomes the speech act itself represented in the sentence by the speaker's body? If there is a metaphor, it is an ontological one, the transference being operated within the thing itself by the speech act, by its force. It explains, but within the religious mystery, what remains concealed in the representational process of signs themselves: the fact that through them things become ideas ready to be exchanged or consumed by the speakers community.

I do not want to discuss in a detailed way the functioning, in the Port-Royal representational system, of the two key-terms of the Eucharist formula, the deictic "this" and the verb "is" (third person of the present indicative). I shall present only the two axes of my comments: first, the deictic operates characteristically on the limits of the representational system; second, the verb, because of its theoretical reduction to the verb "to be," to the indicative present and to the third person, operates right in the center of the model. These two key-terms signify two fundamental operations of the model construction that cannot be included as such in the model, the first by which the representational system is closed, the second by which it is given a center that only allows and justifies its functioning.

With the deictic, we encounter a word that escapes a defined representational function, but at the same time it produces the representational function itself, since, on the limits of language, it operates simultaneously as having no distinct meaning and as the origin of all the possible signifieds. The metalinguistic discourse can only name, in its analysis of the deictic, Being in general, the outside of the representational system. However, in its speech use, the deictic points out a pure individual. It marks out the place where a name will be uttered. I should add that, in the *Port-Royal Logic,* the analysis of the deictic is related to the problem of proper names and to that of nominal definitions.

Now the verb. I quote again its famous definition given by the Port-Royal logicians: "The verb is a word whose principal use is to express affirmation, that is to say to denote that the discourse wherein the word is employed is the discourse of a man who not only conceives things but who judges and affirms them." I shall give here just the conclusion of my commentary: when verbs are reduced to the third person, there is no longer, in the utterance, a marker of this subject of enunciation, and for this reason, the representations connected to each other in the sentence by the verb "is" can ontologically appear as the things themselves they represent, as things ordered as they really are in a rational and universal discourse. And at the same time, through reduction of the verbs to the indicative mood and the present tense, the sentence is related to a mind, or better to a power or a desire that makes judgments concerning these things and makes an assertion.

Now why, according to my hypothesis, does the Eucharist formula appear as the core or the matrix of the representational models of the sign, the sentence, the discourse? Because it shows us, in the domain of non-rational religious practice, the theoretical *process* of the representation itself, a process concealed by the models themselves. The religious practice, with all its social, political, ideological implications, shows us the basic truth of the philosophy of representation: how it grounds the claim that the representational systems are equivalent to things themselves? It is possible to assume such an equivalence if we understand these systems as the results of an operation by which a subject inscribes himself as their center and transforms himself into them by transforming things through them—as an operation by which a subject has the right to possess things legitimately because he has substituted for things *his* signs that represent them adequately. This process is a practical one in religion. By his enunciative operation, Jesus transformed an external thing which is not signified but pointed to by "this," into a signified element of the signifying system of representation: the word "body" related to him by the possessive "my." Thus he becomes a product, a "word-thing," so to speak, to be exchanged in a communicative process, through a practical ritual of consumption in a religious community that thinks of itself as a universal one.

Now the tale. I shall use a very simple technique of reading: I shall follow the syntagmatic narrative order of the episodes while analyzing the feed-back of the successive segments of the tale upon each other. In fact, what can be looked at as a rather innocent, unsophisticated procedure is required by what seems to me the specific problem raised by this tale: how to acquire a maximum from a minimum. This is a problem of strategy and tactics unsolvable in the terms in which it is posed. This is the reason why the syntagmatic organization is important insofar as it would display by the sequence of episodes and actions some principles of this strategy. By strategy I mean determined ways of structuring will or desire toward a goal.

So the Miller left as an inheritance three objects to his three sons, the Mill to the eldest, the ass to the second, and the cat to the youngest: three objects that are ranked according to an order of decreasing value related to the age order. By excluding the scrivener and the attorney from the legal partition of the estate, the family as such is meant to have its own rules and as the youngest son observes, the eldest and second sons, by joining their stocks together, can reconstitute a stable self- reproductive social community, from which the youngest son is excluded.

With his cat, he cannot participate in the social process of production. At the very beginning of the tale, he is defined as an individual located out of the social community, on its limits, in a cultural marginality. For him, the question is not to produce commodities but to survive. However his exclusion from culture makes him an adventurer socially unbound and gives him a kind of absolute freedom vis-à-vis social regulations. His first project, in this state of affairs, has to do with food—to eat his cat"—and it is a socially transgressive project since a domestic cat is culturally not edible. (To be sure, it is not a very strong prohibition: a common story among hunters tells how an unlucky hunter substitutes a cat for a rabbit when he offers a hunting party dinner to his friends. But the cat is *his* cat and in a certain sense we may say that the situation of lack in relation to culture *is* inversely a situation of excess outside culture.) In fact, the youngest son's freedom will be actually invested in language. Language, or better a certain use of language, will be the natural instrument of the individual. The questions—what to eat? how to survive?—are changed into this one: how to transform the linguistic use value into economic and social use value? Paradoxically, this investment in language is represented by the cat: when we read the tale, we shall observe that, contrary to our implicit expectation and contrary to one of its morals, it is not the Miller's son, but the cat who is the actual hero, and above all, the cat is a "speaker," all his activity throughout the tale consists in talking, in communicating with others. Here occurs a kind of scission or duplication of the hero into a passive principle, the beneficiary of gifts, things, and an active principle that obtains them. By active principle, I mean a certain use of language.

Or to push a little further in that direction, I might say more abstractly that the cat is an operator of change: he articulates a spatial continuum (he differentiates space) by a temporal program or better a strategy. The cat as the trickster figure in North American Indian myths is always wandering in the different parts of the world. But his trips in our tale cannot be separated from his tricks, I mean his use of language. This use is manifested in the tale by the fact that the cat always anticipates his master's itinerary toward the cultural (social and economic) maximum. Everything occurs as if his master's coming in a place actualizes what his cat says just before. Textually speaking, the cat is the representative of the narrative modalizations (mainly the modality of desire) and his master, the vehicle of narrative assertions (or wish fulfilments).

Then the cat, the real hero of the tale, is endowed with two qualities belonging to two different levels of the semantic content. On the level of qualifications he is depicted as a liar or as a trickplayer. But what is important is that the very first trait of his deceiving nature is related to language: the cat hears his master's bitter remarks which concern him directly since he is in danger of being eaten, but he makes as if he does not. He behaves *as if:* he responds to the real situation as if he had not understood it. Related to language, the cat is also related to pretense, simulation, appearance as opposed to truth, reality. On the level of narration, the cat is transformed from being a gift given by the Miller to his youngest son into a receiver of gifts and through this transformation, into a potential donor. And if so, it is because he asks his master for a bag and a pair of boots as *if* he has not heard his master's expressed intention to eat him and he receives these gifts because *he pretends to be* in the future a possible giver. A contract is suggested by the cat to his master and if his master accepts it, it is because he knows his cat as a trickplayer.

Now when we read just after that the cat catches a young rabbit not yet acquainted with the deceits of the world, we might conclude that the contract between the cat and his master is going to be fulfilled: the cat could now bring back to his master the rabbit he caught and in so doing, he would have succeeded in substituting the rabbit for himself as an object to be eaten and transforming himself from a non-productive object of consumption into a productive instrument to the benefit of his master. Thanks to their deceptive illocutory force, the cat's words would have entailed a transformation from death (starvation to death and his own death) into life (a minimal survival) at the lowest level of the exchange cycle.

Instead of choosing this closed exchange cycle, the cat gives his prey to the king. He institutes someone else—different from his master—as the receiver of his gifts and he chooses as the receiver the opposite upper limit of the social scale. His communicational strategy consists in substituting the maximal extreme pole for the minimal extreme one. But he can play his hand only by deception: First, he behaves deceptively vis-à-vis his master since he does not observe the terms of the contract. Second, he says deceptive words vis-a-vis the king since it is not the Marquis of Carabas who gives a rabbit of his warren to the king. However with the king, he behaves truly: it is true that a cat gives the king a warren rabbit. The episode is repeated three times with a quantitative amplification at each step (one rabbit, two partridges, game). And each time, the king answers the gifts by countergifts that are signs: words of thanks and money. Some interesting transformations here occur in the narrative. First, the Master of the cat is excluded from the exchange cycle. Second, this exchange consists in exchanging things (that can be eaten) and words. Natural things (game) are exchanged with arbitrary signs. Third, the fact that the natural gifts (hunted preys) are signified by deceptive words allows the transformation of natural things into arbitrary signs to occur: the rabbit is no longer a thing good to be eaten but the social sign of the feudal homage of the marquis to his king. Fourth, this transformation now reintroduces the Master of the cat within the exchange cycle not as a person but as a *name*, the Marquis of Carabas, a proper name that is a social title too. In this sense, the Miller's son receives a gift from his cat, a name: "Marquis of Carabas that was the name the cat was pleased to give his Master." Certainly, it is a false name that actually denotes nobody. However we do not know the true name of the young son. In the terms of the *Port-Royal Logic*, it is a nominal definition: I am free, I am pleased to *name this* man I point out in the world the Marquis of Carabas or to announce that "this is the Marquis of Carabas."

It is worth recalling here some passages from the *Port-Royal Logic* about definitions of names. Definitions of names have three basic characteristics: first,"they are arbitrary. For every sound being indifferent in itself, I may be allowed, for my own use and provided I forewarn others of it, to select a sound to signify precisely a certain thing." This is the first trick of the cat: he names explicitly his master, the Marquis of Carabas ("from now on, I shall call my master, the Marquis of Carabas") and he conforms in the story to the basic logical requirement of the definition of name: not to change the definition in the discourse that uses it. Second,"because they are arbitrary, the definitions of names cannot be contested, for we cannot deny that a man (here a cat) has given to a sound (here Marquis of Carabas) the signification which he says he has given to it, neither that he has that signification only in the use which he makes of it after we have been forewarned of it." Third,"every definition of a name, since it cannot be contested, may be taken as a principle," This is the case in our tale. The logicians add: "But we ought not to infer from this idea that, because we have given it a name, it signifies anything real. For example, I may define a chimera by saying I call a chimera that which does imply contradiction, and yet it will not follow from this that a chimera is anything." This is true for common nouns but what about a proper name? If the logical structure of a proper name is to point out an actual individual person, in this case, says and thinks the cat, the proper name "Marquis of Carabas" designates someone real,"my master." But naming his master the Marquis of Carabas, the cat does more than just name *this* "individual" who is his master. He gives him a title of nobility—and, we shall see in a moment, much more. So he uses deceptively a right definition of a name as if it were a definition of a thing. However the episodes which follow will transform this deceptive use of a right definition of a name into a right use of a right definition of a thing.

We may consider now the three episodes of the bath in the river, the meeting with the countrymen and the encounter with the ogre as three phases of such a transformation, i.e., three ways of giving a semantic content to the name "Marquis of Carabas" or of expanding it narratively.

The first phase—the bath in the river—is a repetition of the first contract between the cat and his master, but with an important change: in the first contract, the master has to give a bag and a pair of boots to the cat in order to receive something to eat from him. But the cat has deceived his master. In the second contract, the master actually has to give himself to the cat (to take a bath, to be undressed) without knowing anything about the purpose of the advice, in order to obtain an undefined maximal gift. The cat has nothing to give back and he has no obligation vis-à-vis his master and the master has nothing to expect from his cat. The master is becoming the servant of his cat; and the cat, his master's master. The Miller's youngest son reached *really* the extreme minimal limit of the social scale, but at the same time, in language, as a *name,* he is at the top. Now the cat speaks to the king: "Help! Help! My lord the Marquis of Carabas is going to be drowned." Again he utters deceptive words, but symbolically they are true since his master is at his last extremity. This time, the cat does not give something to the king, he asks the king for something: to help his master. The king who has answered by words to the things given by the cat, now has to respond by deeds and things to the cat's words: first by helping his master; second, by giving him his royal clothes. This is the beginning of the fulfillment or realization of the name: to bear a noble name means to wear noble clothes. We have a textual sign of such a transformation in the tale itself. From this point on the narrator will name the Miller's son the Marquis of Carabas. The name which was arbitrary as a word and as a sign without a real referent becomes a definition of the man who is named by it. And suddenly as his name gets some content with the help of the king's clothes, the master of the cat becomes a beautiful young man and the king's daughter falls in love with him. He becomes a possible receiver of a woman, a princess. Having nothing to give, he is now in a position to receive the maximal gift.

After the clothes, an estate: this is the second step of the transformation of the name. The acquisition of the estate is operated through three repetitive episodes ranked in order of increasing value: hay, corn, everything. What is here the strategy of the cat? He no longer says deceptive words. He asks others to lie. And if they do not, he affirms that they will be eaten: "You shall be chopped up as meat for meat-pies." In other terms, if you do not say my own words, you will be eaten. Then the deceptive words the cat asks the countrymen to say define the estate of the marquis, that is, his name. They refer truly to the agricultural products, edible things, but falsely to the name of their owner.

Edible things have to be stated falsely, as parts of a name: this means that they have to be named in such a false way as to give a semantic content and a truth value to a proper name. If the countrymen refuse to speak, the speakers themselves become edible things (meat for the meat-pie). The speaker has to say that food is a part of name. If not, he becomes food. The speaker has to change things, food, (bread for example) into a name (Carabas or "my body"). If not (or so that) the speaker or his name will be changed into food.

Now a very important question: why is the cat's speech so powerful? Where does the basis of his linguistic power lie? The first answer is—I should say—textually empirical: the cat's threats had made the countrymen terribly afraid because they belong to the ogre and by definition, an ogre is an absolute eater, a super cannibal. The second one is linguistic: the power of the cat's speech rests upon the formulaic power of his expression, a curse which destroys by the power of its own words the people toward whom it is directed.

Now the episode of the ogre's castle. In a sense, it is the third step of the semantic filling-up of the name, Carabas. But it is also the ultimate moment when either the name will acquire its final truth-value or it will be reduced to an empty sound. The castle is the place of truth. If it appears that the estate belongs to the ogre, the king will take back his clothes and the Marquis of Carabas will be changed into the poorest and youngest son of a dead Miller.

Now in the tale the ogre is not characterized by his usual feature as the maximal eater, a man-eater (but his name ogre is sufficient to suggest this trait in all readers' minds). So the ogre—through his name—is the opposite of the Miller's son (without a name) who was characterized as the minimal eater: he did not eat his cat and the first contract has not yet been fulfilled. Against this implicit background an essential trait stands out: the ogre is the richest that ever was known. He is absolute wealth, as in a sense the Marquis of Carabas is: but the latter's riches lie in his "name," in a false one, a name without referent, while the former's wealth is real.

Again the cat speaks—and the most socially conventional language: "He would not pass so near his castle, without having the honour of paying his respects to him." Again the cat is a speaker, a donor of words, a master of language. He acts upon things and beings through words. He articulates reality by words and in so doing, he succeeds in a sense, in making real things correspond to words. He substitutes names for things; his words stand for things. The time now comes for the reverse substitution: to substitute things for words, to speak a true language instead of a deceptive one.

The ogre is the reverse of the cat: he has not the natural power of linguistic deception (the false natural use of words) like the cat, but the magical power of true metamorphosis (the real supernatural use of his body). The ogre joins together supernature and infraculture (cannibalism). The ogre is a god who behaves like a beast. The cat joins together nature (he is an animal, a domestic one) and culture: he speaks very cleverly. The cat is an animal who behaves like a man. Or we may put the things in this way: the ogre can perform a supernatural transsubstantiation of himself by negating language; the cat, a representational transsubstantiation of things by stating language.

Then the two challenges of the cat: the ogre is invited by the cat to use his power without need, just to be admired. The ogre uses his power falsely because of the linguistic power of the cat's flattery. The cat successively calls upon the ogre to change himself into the two extremes of the animal order: the lion, the king of animals and the mouse, a parasite. But what is important is this: the lion can eat the cat in a real situation, but here, since the ogre just wants to show the cat his power, the lion does not eat him. The situation is not real but simulated. But the cat eats the mouse: he does not play according to the rules of the game. He considers the simulated situation as a real one. This is his ultimate trick that is the reverse of a trick and in the narrative, the reverse of the situation at the beginning of the tale: in danger of being eaten by his master, he escapes death by speaking like a man and by taking the real situation as a simulated one. Now he eats the cannibal eater, the god-beast, by behaving like a cat and by taking simulation as reality. The cat eats the cannibal eater. The master of words eats the monstrous master of food. The true transsubstantiation is to transform things into words in order to change words into things. The power of the cat is to substitute words for things and his power is effective because finally he substitutes things for words and his deceptive words become a language objectively valid because language is power.

The representational transsubstantiation or metaphor I evoked at the beginning with commentary on the *Port-Royal Logic* is here represented by a mythical Eucharist. By eating the ogre as a mouse the cat gives an objective value to his deceptive words. By eating or assimilating the master of food to himself, the master of language, he represents the true metamorphosis of things into words. Now words and things are exactly corresponding.

But at the same time, the cat answers also a question we asked at the beginning, a question which is not different from the other one concerning language: how can a man—a cultural being who is excluded from culture—reintegrate the cultural world? Moreover how can a man reduced to a cultural (social and economic) zero reach a cultural, social, economic maximum, a supercultural position, that of the king? Before his ultimate trick, the cat as the vehicle of the nature/culture relation has to transform wild and cultivated nature into culture: first, as we have seen by changing wild animals into cultural signs, second by converting the agricultural products into parts of an estate and ultimately of a name and a noble title, (and the cat achieved that by threatening the producers with being changed into infracultural food, food for the supercannibal, the ogre). Language is representation *and* power. Discourse is structural strategy of desire and will, a social will, an epistemological desire as well. Is the Cartesian process of hyperbolic skepticism toward the statement of *cogito ergo sum ergo Deus est* so different from the trips and tricks of the master-cat? Is the encounter of the philosophical mind with the Evil Genius in Descartes's *Méditations* not akin to Puss-in-boots' encounter with the ogre?

We can read now the final episode: the king arrives in the castle with the princess and the Marquis of Carabas. For the last time, the cat speaks, offering conventional words of welcome—but now they are true words: "Your Majesty is welcome to *this* castle of my lord the Marquis of Carabas." The king answers by words of congratulation that are also words of recognition of Carabas as a Marquis. For the first time in the tale, he addresses the Miller's son as My Lord Marquis. There is no better proof of our preceding analysis than the fact that immediately after he asks precisely: "Does this castle also belong to you?" The deictic in the cat's address to the king signals the end of the transformation that began with the nominal definition of the Miller's son as Marquis of Carabas now transformed into an ostensive definition of being.

Then the king enters the castle and coming into a great hall, he finds a magnificent collation. In a sense, this meal has no narrative necessity except the strongest, i.e., to recover and to neutralize the negative function with which the story began: starvation to death of the Miller's son. The sudden apparition of the collation proves the truth value of all the cat's words: the meal is the concrete Eucharist that realizes explicitly what has already occurred in the previous episodes. All the characters of the tale eat together, they eat the ogre, the cannibal, at least symbolically. And this communal meal is the ultimate proof that the performative linguistic activity of the cat has worked successfully: words are changed into consumable food.

On the other hand, the collation has the interesting function of excluding from the community of true eaters/ speakers those who did not participate in the exchange cycle and in its transformational process. The magnificent collation was prepared by the ogre "for his friends who were that very day to come to see him but dared not enter knowing the king was there." The ogre's friends obviously belong to the "class" of ogres. They are only eaters, they come just to eat with their friend; but they are excluded from the banquet by the king's presence—as heretics and pagans are excluded from the Holy Table, that is from a place where a thing is changed into a word, but a word which is God's body, *symbolically his* body as a priest and *really* Christ's body, Christ of whom the priest is the representative. The representational signifying system is at one and the same time closed in itself and completely equivalent to the Being it represents.

Like other tales, *Puss-in-Boots* ends by a marriage. Nevertheless it is remarkable that the king decides to give the Marquis of Carabas his daughter only "after having drunk five or six glasses." The ultimate gift, the princess is given only after the consumption of the meal: it is its last course. In other terms, in a kind of generalized potlatch—but only through the representation of this total consumption—it is the king who gives himself to be consumed through his daughter who genealogically represents him and in this way, he responds to the total consumption of Carabas through the meal he offers him, the king; for we know that the meal ultimately signifies his castle, his estate, his clothes, his title, his name, all that he is.

A last word about the reward of the cat: he became a great lord and never again ran after mice but for his diversion. To become a noble means that one no longer needs to eat. Life becomes play, not a vital necessity; it is no longer a matter of survival, but an entertainment. At the beginning of the tale, the cat came within a hairbreadth of being eaten by his master like a mouse. At the end he does not need to eat mice for a vital purpose, he just plays at eating them. An infinite abundance succeeds to a total scarcity. And now he can assume his basic nature. The cat is by nature a player, a trickmaker. But at the beginning his trickmaking aimed at eating mice in order to survive. Now it is trickmaking for the pleasure of hunting. A biological purpose is changed into an aesthetic-aristocratic activity, into a finality without end.

Nevertheless in order to reach this ultimate goal, his trickmaking ability has been diverted into a serious game: of how to change things into words in order to change words into things; of how to use language, how to play with words in order to use things or to possess things in order to consume them.

According to Hegel in the *Phenomenology of Mind*, that was the great discovery made by the noble consciousness during the seventeenth-century. He calls this dialectical phase, the way from the heroism of the feudal service to the heroism of the courtier, flattery. By giving words of flattery to the king, the courtier receives money, but through this process, the king's self becomes the state and the noble self a pure futility. Perhaps it is another exemplification of the functioning of the representational system of language with its central core, the Eucharist matrix; or of the charming tale of Charles Perrault I have just read; or of my own essay announced as a diversion, a diversion itself diverted into very pedantic questions and ending as the intellectual game—half funny, half serious—whose name is structural analysis. But "serio ludere," serious playing may be the only way to conduct a radical criticism.

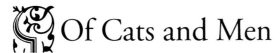# Of Cats and Men

Framing the Civilizing Discourse of the Fairy Tale

Jack Zipes

I t is said that a man's best friend is his dog, but those of us who read fairy tales know better. Time and again, cats have come to the aid of poor, suffering young men, much more often than dogs. In two of the more famous examples, Charles Perrault's "Puss in Boots" (1697) and Mme. D'Aulnoy's "The White Cat" (1697), cats enabled disadvantaged and often maltreated youngest sons to attain wealth and power. In the case of "Puss in Boots," a miller's son becomes a rich marquis and marries the king's daughter, thanks to a cat. In "The White Cat," a young nobleman is helped by a strange, gracious cat, in reality a princess, who marries him and makes him a wealthy man. Indeed, there are hundreds if not thousands of oral folk tales and literary fairy tales throughout the world in which a cat either takes pity on an unfortunate young man or helps him advance in society. Why, then, do we still proclaim that man's best friend is his dog? Is it because cats have frequently been associated with females and goddesses, and men must worship them or pay the consequences? Is it because men and women are supposedly opposites and often fight like cats and dogs? Is it because cats are allegedly duplicitous and devious and cannot be trusted? Or is it because cats have learned that men are dumb and ungrateful and not worth maintaining as friends?

It is difficult to answer these questions because the folklore about the relations between cats and men is so rich and varied. One need only glance at *Nine Lives : The Folklore of Cats* (1980), by the renowned British folklorist Katharine Briggs, or *The Folktale Cat* (1992), edited by the noted American scholar Frank de Caro, to ascertain this fact, to name but two of the more fascinating books on the subject. Yet no matter how mysterious and variegated the folklore is, one aspect is clear: In both the oral and the literary tradition in Europe and America, cats play a very special role in *civilizing men* and in explaining how the civilizing process operates in Western society. In fact, I want to suggest that by studying the *literary* tradition of "Puss in Boots" from Giovan Francesco Straparola's 1550 version through Walt Disney's silent animated film of. 1923, we can learn, thanks to an assortment of gifted cats, an immense amount about the sociohistorical origins of the literary fairy tale in the West and why honorable cats perhaps have decided not to be man's best friend.

To speak about the honor of cats in literary fairy tales necessitates redeeming the honor of two neglected writers of fairy tales, namely, Giovan Francesco Straparola and Giambattista Basile, and to set the record straight about the historical origins of fairy tales in the West. It also means grasping how the narrative discourse of the fairy tale as a genre was essentially framed by men who unconsciously and consciously set a gender-specific agenda for the manner in which we expect the miraculous turn of events to occur. If we study the formative "Puss in Boots" versions of Giovan Francesco Straparola, Giambattista Basile, and Charles Perrault, we shall see that the narrative strategies of these authors, the transformations of motifs and characters, the different styles, and the implied historical symbolical meanings and overtones constitute a generic mode of discourse that establishes the frame for the manner in which we discuss, debate, and propose standards of behavior and norms in Western civilization. As Marina Warner has demonstrated in her remarkable and comprehensive study, *From the Beast to the Blonde: On Fairytales and Their Tellers*, it is a male frame that needs to be expanded and questioned if not subverted.

But let us begin by trying to understand how this frame may have originated, which means beginning with Giovan Francesco Straparola. Frankly, we do not know much about this man, but our lack of knowledge does not mean he deserves the neglect that he has suffered. In fact, he could even be called the "father" of the modern literary fairy tale in the West, for Straparola was the first truly gifted author to write numerous fairy tales in the vernacular and to cultivate a form and function for this kind of narrative that made it an acceptable genre among the educated classes in Italy and soon after in France, Germany, and England.

Straparola was born about 1480 in Caravaggio, a town in the region of Lombardy. His name may even be a pseudonym, for it means someone who is loquacious. Perhaps his family or friends used it as a nickname, or perhaps Straparola used the name in a satirical sense. Whatever the case may be, we do know that he moved to Venice and published a collection of sonnets under the title *Opera nova da Zoan Francesco Streparola da Caravazo novamente stampata Sonetti* in 1508. Forty-two years later, in 1550, the first part of his major work *Le Piacevoli Notti (Pleasant Nights)* appeared, followed by the second part in 1553. The work seemed to have met with a favorable reception because a second edition was printed in 1556, and by 1560 it had also been translated into French. Comments in the Italian editions indicate that Straparola probably died in 1558.

Straparola was not an original writer, but he was the first to make a substantial contribution to the shaping of the literary fairy tale and to give it a prominent place in his unusual collection of tales. The frame for the *Le Piacevoli Notti,* first translated into English as *The Facetious Nights* by W. G. Waters in 1894, was modeled after Boccaccio's *Decameron* and had strong political implications. The prologue reveals how Ottoviano Maria Sforza, the bishop-elect of Lodi (most likely the real Sforza, who died in 1540) is compelled to leave Milan because of political plots against him. He takes his widowed daughter, Signora Lucretia, with him; and since her husband has died in 1523, we can assume that the setting for the *Nights* is sometime between 1523 and 1540. The bishop and his daughter flee first to Lodi, then to Venice, and finally settle on the island of Murano. They gather a small group of congenial people around them: ten gracious ladies, two matronly women, and four educated and distinguished gentlemen. Since it is Carnival time, Lucretia proposes that members of the company take turns telling stories during the two weeks before Lent, and consequently there are thirteen nights on which stories are told, amounting to seventy-four tales in all.

As was generally the case in upper-class circles, a formal social ritual is followed. Each night there is a dance by the young ladies. Then Lucretia draws five ladies' names from a vase, and those five are to tell the tales that evening. But before the storytelling, one of the men must sing a song, after which a lady tells a tale, fallowed by a riddle in verse. Most of the riddles are examples of the double entendre and have strong sexual connotations, especially those told by the men. The object is to discuss erotic subjects in a highly refined manner. During the course of the thirteen nights, a man is invited every now and then to replace a woman and tell a tale. In addition, Lucretia herself tells two tales.

There are very few "tragic" tales among the seventy-four, and the optimism, humor, and graceful style of the narratives may be due to the fact that Straparola was writing in Venice at a time when there was relative harmony in that society. To a certain extent, the fictional company on the island of Murano can be regarded as an ideal representation of how people can relate to one another and comment in pleasing and instructive ways about all types of experience. The stories created by Straparola are literary fairy tales, revised oral tales, anecdotes, erotic tales, buffo tales of popular Italian life, didactic tales, fables, and tales based on the work of writers who preceded him, such as Boccaccio, Franco Sacchetti, Ser Giovanni Forentino, Giovanni Sercambi, and others.

During the eleventh night, the lady Fordiana begins the storytelling by relating the first known literary version of "Puss in Boots" in Europe. Yet, as we shall see, there are no boots, and the cat is really not a cat. The story goes as follows:

There was once a poor woman in Bohemia named Soriana, who had three sons named Dusolino, Tesifone, and Constantino. Right before she dies, she leaves her two oldest sons a kneading trough and a pastry board and her youngest, Constantino, a cat. The older sons are able to earn a good living with their inheritance, but they treat Constantino cruelly and do not share anything with him. The cat, who is a fairy in disguise, takes pity on him and helps him by providing the king with rabbits and winning his good graces with many other gifts. Because the cat frequently returns to Constantino with wonderful food and drink, the two older brothers are jealous, but there is nothing they can do. The cat cleans Constantino's blotched face with her tongue and eventually takes him to meet the king. When they near the castle, the cat tells Constantino to take off his clothes and jump into the river. Then the cat yells for help, and the king sends his men to rescue Constantino and dress him in noble garments. Of course, the king wants to know why the now good-looking young man almost drowned, and Constantino, who is baffled, must depend on the cat, who tells the king that Constantino was bringing a great treasure of jewels to the king when he was robbed and thrown into the river to drown. Impressed by Constantino's alleged wealth, the king arranges for him to marry his daughter. After the ceremonies and festivities, Constantino is given ten mules with gold and rich garments, and he is expected to take the princess and a group of other people to his castle, which he does not have. Again, the cat comes to his rescue by riding in advance and warning cavaliers, shepherds, and herdsmen to beware of a great troop of armed men. Unless they say they serve Master Constantino, they will be in trouble. Then the cat arrives at a castle, which is weakly defended. In fact, Signor Valentino, the lord of the castle, has recently died during a journey to seek his wife. So the cat easily convinces the guards and company of people at this castle to say they serve Constantino too. When Constantino finally arrives with his bride, he easily establishes himself as the lord of the castle. Soon after, the king of Bohemia dies, and Constantino inherits the throne. He and his wife have many children and live a long life. When they die, their children inherit the kingdom.

Although this tale, alone cannot represent how the literary fairy tale came to be established and institutionalized in Europe, and although it cannot be considered representative of all the tales in Straparola's *Pleasant Nights*, I should nevertheless like to use it to illustrate a possible means for opening perspectives and questions about the origins of the literary fairy tale and the ramifications of such origination and institutionalization.

It is possible to approach this tale as a literary adaptation of an oral tale that may have been common in Italy, generally involving an animal that comes to the rescue of a forlorn human being, usually a man, who manages to pull himself up by his bootstraps in the end. Folklorists generally categorize this type as AT 545b "Puss in Boots." But the fact is, we do not know exactly what oral tale Straparola used as the basis for his literary narrative. We can only assume that he had heard some version of "Constantino" and decided to write his own. In other words, Straparola appropriated popular lore to represent it in his own manner and comment on the mores and values of his time. If we regard his tale as a mode of representation that was intended to indicate how a young man was to behave in a certain social situation, we see that it has a great deal to say about Venetian society of Straparola's time.

What are the important features of the tale?

1. A young peasant, who is ugly and has no manners, is placed at a disadvantage in life because he is poor and his mother leaves him nothing but a cat when she dies.
2. The cat, however, turns out to be a fairy, or his good fortune.
3. The cat endows him with good looks, clothes, and manners and puts him on display.

4. Only through her intercession, her good fortune and knowledge of the civilizing process, does Constantino have a chance of moving up in society, from a poor peasant to king of Bohemia.

5. The cat uses threats and the show of force to help Constantino succeed.

6. Constantino's climb is based on duplicity, spectacle (display of gifts, clothes, richness), a marriage of convenience, and patriarchal absolute rule. The king's word is the final word, and Constantino's word will also become absolute after he becomes king of Bohemia.

Using these features, we can draw some interesting parallels between the world of the tale and Venetian and Italian sixteenth- century society that have ramifications for the later development of the literary tradition. In many city and state republics in Italy, it was difficult but possible to rise from the lower classes and become a rich lord. Such advancement depended on making the right connections, luck, a good marriage, shrewdness, and the ability to wield power effectively. This kind of social mobility was more accessible to men than to women, and the social institutions created in the cities benefited men just as the family structure was centered around the male as the seat of all power. Women's role was to grace the home and serve men, providing them with the means to establish themselves and their families.

Though "Constantino" features a poor, dismal peasant boy in Bohemia, there is little doubt that literate Italians of that time, who were very few and were from the upper classes, read the tale metaphorically as the "lucky" rise of a man who learns how to use the civilizing process to his advantage. In Straparola's version of the "Puss in Boots"-type tale, the highest virtue that a man can achieve is the status of lord or king, no matter what it takes. There is no real rational or moral basis for Constantino's rise and success, and the only thing that he must learn is how to fool other people, wear the right clothes, pretend to be what he is not, and take power through force. Clearly, the strategy of the narrative, the purposeful unfolding of the author's desire, is to rationalize and legitimate patriarchy; women play a key role, but they are dispensable in the end, just as they become dispensable at the end of *Pleasant Nights*, when Lent arrives and it is time to repent for one's sins.

Now, if Straparola set the scene for a particular literary manner in which the tales of cats and men were to be told, how did other authors consciously respond to this initial tale? Do we have proof that other writers knew of Straparola's tale and changed it to comment on their own times? Were they interested in representing power relations within the civilizing process?

The next literary version of the "Puss in Boots"-type tale was written by Giambattista Basile. We know a great deal about him, unlike Straparola, including the fact that he had probably read Straparola's "Constantino" and may have been familiar with other oral versions. But let us first turn to a quick synopsis of his version,"Cagliuso."

This tale concerns an old beggar in Naples who bequeaths his eldest son, Oraziello, a sieve so he can earn a living and his younger son, Cagliuso, a cat because he is the baby of the family. While Oraziello goes out into the world and begins to have success, Cagliuso bemoans his fate and worries that he now has two mouths to feed. However, the cat tells him,"You are complaining too soon, and you've more luck than wits! You don't know your good fortune, for I am able to make you rich if I put myself to it."

Cagliuso apologizes to her catship, who goes fishing and hunting and carries her catch to the king as humble presents from Lord Cagliuso. At one point the cat tells the king that Lord Cagliuso would like to place himself at the king's service and would like to visit him the next day. When the next day arrives, however, the cat tells the king that Cagliuso's servants have robbed him and left him without even a shirt to his back. In response, the king sends clothes to Cagliuso from his own wardrobe, and soon the beggar's son appears at the king's court dressed as a lord. A banquet is prepared, but the dumb Cagliuso can think only of regaining his proper beggarly rags, and the cat must constantly tell him to keep his mouth shut. Eventually, the cat manages to have a private conversation with the king in which she praises Cagliuso's intelligence and wealth and wants to arrange a marriage of convenience with the king's daughter. Since she knows that the king will want some proof of Cagliuso's immense wealth, the cat suggests that the king send trusty servants with her to Cagliuso's estates around Rome and

Lombardy to procure information about the young man's situation. The cat runs ahead of the king's servants and threatens shepherds, gamekeepers, and farmers that robbers are on their way; if they do not say that everything belongs to Lord Cagliuso, they will be killed. Consequently, the king's servants hear the same message wherever they go and are convinced that Cagliuso owns a tremendous amount of property.

Now the king becomes, anxious to bring about a marriage between his daughter and Cagliuso and promises the cat a rich reward if she can arrange everything, which she does. After an entire month of feasting, the cat advises Cagliuso to take his wife's dowry and buy some land in Lombardy, The beggar's son follows this advice and soon becomes a wealthy baron. He continually thanks the cat and promises her that whenever she should die, he will have her embalmed and placed inside a golden cage. To test Cagliuso, the cat pretends to die and learns how ungrateful her master is when Cagliuso wants to take her by the paws and simply throw her out the window. All at once the cat jumps up and exclaims,"Get out of my sight, and may a curse be on everything I've done for you because you're not even worth spitting on! What a fine golden cage you prepared for me! What a beautiful grave you've assigned me! I go and serve you, work and sweat, only to receive this reward. Oh, woe is he who boils his pot for the hope of others! That philosopher put it well when he said, 'Whoever goes to bed an ass wakes up an ass.'"

Though Cagliuso tries to make amends, the cat runs through the door and keeps on running while muttering the following moral to end the tale:

> *Oh God keep you from those rich men turned poor*
> *And from beggars grown rich who now have more,*

As we can see, Basile's version of "Puss in Boots" is immensely different from Straparola's, and obviously the changes have a lot to do with the different life that Basile led and wanted to represent. Born in Naples in 1576, Basile came from a middle-class family and spent his youth in his native city. In 1600 he took a trip to Venice, where he became a soldier to earn a living and began writing poetry. By 1609 he had begun publishing his poetry, and thanks to his sister, a famous singer, he was appointed to à position at the court of Mantua in 1613. After that, throughout his life, Basile held various positions as administrator or magistrate. In 1620 he returned to Naples and was appointed a captain in Lagonegro. He continued to be successful as a poet and became a member of various literary academies. Yet it was not his poetry that would make him famous but his book of fairy tales in Neapolitan prose dialect. He began writing this book, titled *Lo Cunto de li Cunti (The Tale of Tales)* in the early 1630s, but unfortunately he never saw the published version, for he died of a disease contracted during an epidemic in 1632. His sister arranged for the publication of *Lo Cunto de li Cunti*, which appeared in four separate books between 1634 and 1636. When the fourth edition was published in 1674, the title of the collection of tales was changed to *Il Pentamerone.*

Like Straparola, Basile set a frame for his tales, but unlike Straparola, he used a fairy tale as his "tale of tales" to set the stage for fifty marvelous stories. In this frame tale, Zoza, the daughter of the king of Vallepelosa, cannot laugh, and her father is so concerned about her happiness that he invites people from all over the world to try to make her laugh. Yet nobody can succeed until an old woman who attempts to sop up oil in front of the palace has her jug broken by a mischievous court page. The ensuing argument between the old woman and the page, each hurling coarse and vulgar epithets at one another, is so delightful that Zoza bursts into laughter. However, this laughter angers the old woman, and she curses Zoza, saying,"Be off with you, and may you never see the bud of a husband unless it is the Prince of Camporotondo!"[7] To her dismay, Zoza learns that this prince, named Tadeo, is under the spell of a wicked fairy and is in a tomb. He can only be wakened and liberated by a woman who fills with her tears a pitcher that is hanging on a nearby wall.

In need of help, Zoza visits three different fairies and receives a walnut, a chestnut, and a hazelnut as gifts. Then she goes to Tadeo's tomb and weeps into the pitcher for two days. When the pitcher is almost full, she falls asleep because she is tired from all the crying. While she is sleeping, however, a slave girl steals the pitcher, fills it, wakens Tadeo, and takes the credit for bringing him back to life. Tadeo marries her, and she becomes pregnant.

But Zoza, whose happiness depends on Tadeo, is not about to concede the prince to a slave girl. She rents a house across from Tadeo's palace and manages to attract Tadeo's attention. However, the slave girl threatens to beat the baby if Tadeo spends any time with Zoza, who now uses another tactic to gain entrance into Tadeo's palace. On three different occasions she opens the nuts. One contains a little dwarf who sings; the next twelve chickens made of gold; and the third a doll that spins gold. The slave girl demands these fascinating objects, and Tadeo sends for them, offering Zoza whatever she wants. To his surprise, Zoza gives the objects as gifts. Yet the final one, the doll, stirs an uncontrollable passion in the slave girl to hear stories during her pregnancy, and she threatens Tadeo again: unless women come to tell her tales, she will kill their unborn baby. So Tadeo invites ten women from the rabble known for their storytelling: lame Zeza, twisted Cecca, goitered Meneca, big-nosed Tolla, hunchback Popa, drooling Antonella, snout-faced Ciulla, rheumy Paola, mangy Ciommetella, and diarrhetic Iacoba. The women spend the day chattering and gossiping, and after the evening meal, one tale is told by each of the ten for five nights. Finally, on the last day, Zoza is invited to tell the last tale, and she recounts what happened to her. The slave girl tries to stop her, but Tadeo insists that Zoza be allowed to tell the tale to the end. When he realizes that Zoza's tale is true, Tadeo has the pregnant slave girl buried alive, and he marries Zoza to bring the tale of tales to a happy conclusion.

If we were to compare just the frame tales of Straparola's *Notti* and Basile's *Pentamerone*, it is again apparent that there are major differences between the two. Basile is much more witty, vulgar, and complex than Straparola. He wrote in a mannered Neapolitan dialect to address a new reading public that had begun to form at the beginning of the sixteenth century and was not interested in the courtly culture of representation. This reading public was open to dialect and materials from the oral culture. According to Barbara Broggini, Basile shifted the perspective of the folk tale so that both the peasant and aristocratic classes are critiqued. For instance, the value system of civility transformed in the tales to favor the standards of the rising middle classes that were in the process of establishing their interests throughout Italy. As a consequence, Basile parodied the peasantry and condemned the corruption of court society, arguing for self-determination and the ethics of fairness through hard work. One of the reasons why Basile chose dialect and popular tales is that he could incorporate many levels of meaning in these tales and escape aristocratic censorship.

If we now return to "Gagliuso," we can see that there is definitely a shift in ideological perspective and style from Straparola's "Constantino." Whereas Straparola celebrated the good fortune of a deprived young man who is the hero of his story and represents the continuity of patriarchal rule as the new king of Bohemia, Basile focuses on the cat as the "tragicomic" heroine who serves a stupid and ungrateful peasant and a greedy and gullible king. Caught in the middle, the cat can literally be taken for a middle-class protagonist who speaks for a middle-class morality (not to mention, the role of women). In some ways, the cat's situation resembles that of Basile, who was expected to act as an administrator of the popular class, while serving the whims of the aristocracy. The cat's power is not "magic," like that of the fairy cat in Straparola's tale, but resides in her shrewdness, cunning, and industry. She knows the court is interested in nothing but show (clothing) and wealth, and she also knows that it is important to have the right manners and speech if one is to succeed in society. She takes pride in her work, her ability to arrange contracts and to maintain loyalty, and she expects only justice and due compensation in return. When she realizes that Cagliuso will behave like any other rich lord, she parts company with him for good.

Basile's tale, though humorous, contains a devastating critique of the feudal system of his time and represents a moral code that was not yet fully instituted within the civilizing process in Europe. Throughout the tale the cat is completely loyal to her master, works hard, and demonstrates that wits are more important than fortune. Indeed, the cat saves her own life and sees through the facade of the servant-master relationship because she is smart and knows how to use the feudal system to her advantage. The difficulty is that she cannot achieve the security that she would like—and that Basile apparently also desired.

This lack of gratitude and security is not the case with Charles Perrault's cat, the famous Puss in Boots, the first literary cat to wear boots. Indeed, the security and destiny of this master cat may be due to the fact that the high bourgeoisie was more secure and respected at Louis XIV's court, as was Perrault himself. Though the aristocracy established most of the rules and behavioral codes in the civilizing process of the ancien régime, the norms and values of civilité, and their modalities, would have been impossible to maintain without the cooperation of the middle classes.

Perrault himself was an important administrator, a member of the Academic Francaise, a noteworthy poet, and a cultural critic who challenged Nicolas Boileau's theories in the controversial *Quarrels of the Ancients and the Moderns*. Perrault regarded himself as a modernist and wanted to break away from the neoclassicist rules dependent on Greco-Roman models; he published his famous *Histoires ou Contes du temps passé (Stories or Tales of Past Times)* in 1697 in part to prove that France had its own unique traditions that could be cultivated in innovative ways. In fact, the fairy tale had gradually become *en vogue* during the 1690s, and Perrault was only one among many writers in the literary salons to begin promoting this genre. The other prominent writers were mostly women. Mme. D'Aulnoy, Mlle. L' Héritier, Mlle. de La Force, Mme. Lubert, and Mlle. Bertrand all published important collections of tales to establish the genre as a literary institution, but we remember Perrault mainly because, I suggest, the frame for our reception of the tales was set by male writers, who have more or less marked the ways in which we are to interpret and analyze them. Certainly, male writers have inscribed their concerns and desires in such a way that they play a role in determining our readings of the tales.

Let us take Perrault's "The Master Cat or Puss in Boots." As Denise Escarpit has demonstrated in her immense study, *Histoire d'un Conte: Le Chat Botté en France et en Angleterre*, there is a strong probability that Perrault knew the literary versions of Straparola and Basile,and he most likely knew some of the oral versions that had become common in France. Whatever the case may be, Perrault was not satisfied with those stories, and by writing his own version, he entered into a dialogue with them and sought to articulate his position regarding the position of the cat, his hero, as a mediator between a miller's son and a king. Again it is important to review the essential components of the plot.

A miller dies and bequeaths his three sons, respectively, a mill, an ass, and a cat. The youngest son is so dissatisfied with inheriting the cat that he wants to eat it and make a muff of its skin. To save his life, the cat responds,"Don't trouble yourself, master. Just give me a pouch and a pair of boots to go into the bushes, and you'll see that you were not left with as bad a share as you think." The extraordinary cat goes into the woods, where he proceeds to catch rabbits, partridges, and other game, and he gives them to the king as presents from the Marquis de Carrabas. On a day when the cat knows the king will be taking a drive on the banks of a river with his daughter, the cat instructs his master to take off his clothes and bathe in the river. When the king comes by, the cat pretends that robbers have taken his master's clothes. Consequently, the king provides the miller's son with royal clothes, and the princess immediately falls in love with him. The young man gets into the royal coach, while the cat runs ahead and warns peasants, who are mowing and reaping in the fields, that if they do not say that the estate belongs to the Marquis de Carrabas, they will be cut into tiny pieces like minced meat. Of course the peasants obey, and in the meantime, the cat arrives at a beautiful castle owned by an ogre. He flatters the ogre, who can change himself into anything he wants, by asking him to transform himself into a lion. Then he dares the ogre to change himself into a rat or mouse, and after the ogre performs this feat, he is promptly eaten by the cat. When the king, his daughter, and the miller's son arrive at this beautiful castle, they are all overwhelmed by its splendor, and after the king has had five or six cups of wine, he proposes that the marquis become his son-in-law. No fool, the "marquis" accepts, and after he marries the princess, the cat becomes a great lord and never again runs after mice except for his own amusement.

Perrault's version combines elements of the Straparola and Basile tales to forge his own statement, which he presents in two ironic verse morals at the end of his tale:

Although the advantage may be great
When one inherits a grand estate
From father handed down to son,
Young men will find that industry
Combined with ingenuity,
Will lead to prosperity.

Another Moral

If the millers son had quick success
In winning such a fair princess,
By turning on the charm,
Then regard his manners, looks, and dress
That inspired her deepest tenderness,
For they can't do one any harm.

These morals reflect two of the major themes in Perrault's tale that were also significant in the tales of Straparola and Basile. In the first instance, Perrault asserts that the best means of becoming a rich nobleman is brains and industry. In the second instance, he maintains that show and the proper clothing (spectacle and display) can also enable a man from the lower classes to move up in society. But Perrault deals with more than just these two themes in his tale: He also demonstrates that speech and writing can be used to attain power within the civilizing process.

In his highly perceptive essay, *"Puss-in-Boots:* Power of Signs—Signs of Power," Louis Marin points out that

> the cat is an operator of change: he articulates a spatial continuum that differentiates space by a temporal program or better strategy. The cat as trickster figure in North American Indian myths is always wandering in the different parts of the world. But his trips in our tale cannot be separated from his tricks. I mean his use of language. This use is manifested in the tale by the fact that the cat always anticipates his master's itinerary toward the cultural (social and economic) maximum. Everything occurs as if his master's coming in a place actualizes what his cat says just before. Textually speaking, the cat is the representative of the narrative modalizations (mainly the modality of desire) and his master, the vehicle of narrative assert ions (or wish fulfillments).

It is not only the manipulation of speech within the tale that outlines how men can succeed in society; it is in Perrault's very writing of the text itself that generic prescriptions take hold, assume power, and become established models for reading and writing. If we begin by examining the text, it becomes evident that Perrault's tale consolidates crucial elements from the Straparola and Basile versions to transform the cat into the *master cat,* whose story effaces all those before it and determines the direction of all those to come. Perrault's Puss demonstrates what it takes for a mid- dle-class administrator to succeed in French society of his time:

1. Loyalty and obedience to one's master; otherwise one will be killed;
2. the proper tools to do one's job; the cat needs a pouch to capture his prey and boots of respectability to gain entrée to the king's castle;

3. gracious speech that is also duplicitous;
4. cunning to take advantage of those who are more powerful;
5. the acquisition of land and wealth by force;
6. the readiness to kill when necessary;
7. the ability to arrange business affairs such as a marriage of convenience that will lead to permanent security.

In the process, it is important to note that women are pushed to the margins in this tale, just as they are in the real world of men. They exist as display, as chattel, as bargaining items. They are speechless. The words of the cat that generate and mediate the action are crucial for attaining success. The cat knows how to plead, flatter, advise, threaten, dupe, and generate a proposition from the opposing side.

But we must remember that these are the words of Perrault, who manipulated, arranged, and played with them on the page. In one of the most thorough and insightful readings of Perrault's tales in recent years, Philip Lewis demonstrates that Perrault was strongly influenced by Descartes and developed a "rationalist aesthetics" that was the governing principle in all his tales.[13] Yet Perrault did not slavishly incorporate Cartesian ideas into his aesthetics. Lewis comments,

> By forgetting the vigilant rigor with which Descartes structures and verifies the passage from saying to seeing, by dispensing with the methodic analysis of experience in the service of truth in favor of constructing elaborate comparisons and analogies that promote an accommodation of reason with verisimilitude, Perrault manages to restructure the relation of the verbal to the visual, enabling them to function as the polar terms of a reciprocal exchange. That drastic relaxation of the foundationalist, scientific impulse is perhaps typical of what happens to philosophical reflection in the hands of a so-called man of letters; it is certainly anticipatory of the pattern that thinkers from the eighteenth century onward would appropriate in representing the passage of ideas into art as a process of sublimation.[14]

The dominant perspective in Perrault's tales is the result of a compromise formation "in which a simple, mainstream rationalism accredits a stable, technological continuist account of knowledge as well-formed representation."[15] On the one hand, this means that Perrault's compromise of Cartesian rationalism served to represent the magnificence of King Louis XIV and his court, that is, to reinforce the ideological import of courtly manners and mores and the dominance of French language and culture. On the other hand, Perrault did not force "the transcendental model that would finally assimilate all cognitive experience of the subject to conception modeled on the forming of an image,"[16] but he left room for reflection and resistance to this model, making his tales somewhat ambivalent. This ambivalence is crucial to the appeal of his tales because it creates subtle and profound contradictions. However, I argue that it is Perrault's compromising mentality, which seeks to legitimate the power of patriarchal order, that demands our attention, for this mentality generates a rational aesthetics that feeds into the domestication of the fairy tale in the nineteenth century and its commodification in the twentieth century. Of course, the aesthetics of literary fairy tales and their function within the civilizing process cannot be traced entirely to Perrault. Nevertheless, his case is highly indicative of a certain mode of thinking and writing basic to the approach that many Western authors after him took. Perrault carefully contemplated known literary and oral versions of fairy tales, changed them in his mind and on paper, represented his own society and literary debates to himself and his readers, and sought to endow his words with the power of conviction so that they might become exemplary.

And become exemplary they did. Almost all of the eight tales that he published in *Histoires ou Contes du temps passé*—"Sleeping Beauty," "Cinderella," "Little Red Riding Hood," "Little Tom Thumb," "Bluebeard,"

Riquet with the Tuft," "The Fairies," and "Puss in Boots"—have become classics in Western society. And his verse tales,"The Foolish Wishes" and "Donkey-Skin," have also achieved classical status. In the case of "Puss in Boots," the tale was disseminated through chapbooks and broadsides at the very beginning of the eighteenth century, translated into English and German by 1730, and became firmly embedded in the oral tradition. Obviously, there were many different versions that continued to be told and spread, but for the most part, the literary tradition of "Puss in Boots" was now based mainly on Perrault's version. For all intents and purposes, the versions of Straparola and Basile were erased from Western memory. Indeed, they were no longer necessary, for Perrault's literary text became the standard-bearer of a male civilizing process at a time when French culture was setting the dominant cultural standards in Europe, and at a time when the fairy tale was being firmly established as a literary institution by Perrault and numerous other French writers.

It is interesting to note that by the time the Brothers Grimm began publishing their collection of fairy tales in 1812, they reproduced a version of "Puss in Boots" that was very similar to Perrault's. In fact, they decided to drop the tale from their collection because it was either too much within the French literary tradition or too commonly known as a literary tale to be considered a "true" folk tale. Although nobody could claim true authorship or ownership of "Puss in Boots" by the nineteenth century because it had been appropriated in many different ways by both the literary and oral traditions, it is important to note that the dominant paradigm resembled Perrault's tale. In other words, that version became the classical reference point or touchstone in publishing and in oral folklore, and it did not matter whether the tale was attributed to or signed by Perrault because his signature and his social-class and gender signatures had become deeply woven into the tale itself through the relations between cat and master. Furthermore, the tale became one of many more or less fixed classical tales like "Sleeping Beauty," "Cinderella," and "Little Red Riding Hood" that have determined the manner in which we socialize children and ourselves and set up "civilized" standards of behavior in the West. It is a male frame that is not entirely rigid, but it is within this enunciated symbolic code and order, whether oral or literary, that we discuss and debate norms, values,, and gender roles.

Whether for children or adults, fairy tales in all forms have played and continue to play a crucial role in the socialization process and in aesthetic development. The genre of the fairy tale has developed through oral, literary, and cinematic means, and "Puss in Boots" again enables us to grasp how the frame for our absorption and appropriation of fairy tales is determined through a male denominator in the films and videos of the twentieth century. Here the case of Walt Disney is very important. Of all the early animators, Disney was the one who truly revolutionized the fairy tale as institution through the cinema. One could almost say that he was obsessed by the fairy-tale genre, or to put it another way, Disney felt drawn to fairy tales because they reflected his own struggles in life. After all, Disney came from a relatively poor family; suffered from the exploitative and stern treatment of an unaffectionate father; was spurned by his early sweetheart; and became a success through his tenacity, cunning, and courage and his ability to gather talented artists and managers such as his brother Roy.

One of his early films,"Puss in Boots" (1922), produced in Kansas City, is crucial for understanding his approach to the literary fairy tale and how he used it as a form of self-figuration that would mark the genre for years to come. As Russell Merritt and J. B. Kaufman remark,"In many ways, Disney's first films in Kansas City seem as accomplished as his later Hollywood silents. We have to wait several years to find a film as well-paced, as thematically rich, or with backgrounds as provocative and well-drawn as his earliest surviving Laugh-O-Gram fairy tales such as 'Little Red Riding Hood,' 'Puss in Boots,' and 'Cinderella.'"[18] In the case of "Puss in Boots" Disney did not especially care whether one knew the original Perrault text or some other popular version. It is also unclear which text he actually knew. However, what is clear is that Disney sought to replace all earlier versions with his animated version and that his cartoon is astonishingly autobiographical.

The hero is a young man, a commoner, who is in love with the king's daughter, and she fondly returns his affection. At the same time, the hero's black cat, a female, is having a romance with the royal white cat, who is the king's chauffeur. When the gigantic king discovers that the young man is wooing his daughter, he kicks him out of the palace, followed by Puss. At first, the hero does not want puss's help, nor will he buy her the boots that she sees in a shop window. Then they go to the movies together and see a film with Rudolph Vaselino, a reference to the famous Rudolph Valentino, as a bullfighter that spurs Puss's imagination. She tells the hero that she now has an idea that will help him win the king's daughter, providing he will buy her the boots. Of course, the hero will do anything to obtain the king's daughter, and after he disguises himself as a masked bullfighter, Puss explains to him that she will use a hypnotic machine behind the scenes so he can defeat the bull and win the approval of the king. When the day of the bullfight arrives, the masked hero struggles but eventually manages to defeat the bull. The king is so overwhelmed by his performance that he offers his daughter's hand in marriage, but first he wants to know who the masked champion is. When the hero reveals himself, the king is enraged, but the hero grabs the princess and leads her to the king's chauffeur. The white cat jumps in the front seat of the car with Puss, and they speed off with the king vainly chasing after them.

Although Puss as cunning cat is crucial in this film, Disney focuses most of his attention on the young man who wants to succeed at all costs. In contrast to the traditional fairy tale, the hero is not a peasant, nor is he dumb. Read as a "parable" of Disney's life at that moment, the hero can be seen as young Disney wanting to break into the industry of animated films (the king) with the help of Ub Iwerks (Puss), his friend and best collaborator at that time. The hero upsets the king and runs off with his prize possession, the virginal princess. Thus, the king is dispossessed, and the young man outraces him with the help of his friends.

But Disney's film is also an attack on the literary tradition of the fairy tale. He robs the literary tale of its voice and changes its form and meaning. Since the cinematic medium is a popular form of expression and accessible to the public at large, Disney actually returns the fairy tale to the majority of people. The images (scenes, frames, characters, gestures, jokes) are readily comprehensible to young and old alike and to different social classes. In fact, the fairy tale is practically infantilized, just as the jokes are infantile. The plot records the deepest oedipal desire of every young boy: The son humiliates and undermines the father and runs off with his most valued object of love, the daughter/wife. By semiotically simplifying the Oedipus complex in black-and-white drawings and making fun of it so that it had a common appeal, Disney also touched on other themes:

1. Democracy—the film is very *American* in its attitude toward royalty. The monarchy is debunked, and a commoner causes a kind of revolution.
2. Technology—it is through the new technological medium of the movies that Puss's mind is stimulated. Then she uses a hypnotic machine to defeat the bull and another fairly recent invention, the automobile, to escape the king.
3. Modernity—the setting is obviously the twentieth century, and the modern minds are replacing the ancient. The revolution takes place as the king is outpaced, and he will be replaced by a commoner who knows how to use the latest inventions.

But who is this commoner? Was Disney making a statement on behalf of the masses? Was Disney celebrating "everyone" or "every man"? Did Disney believe in revolution and social change in the name of socialism? The answer to all these questions is simply "no."

Disney's hero is the enterprising young man, the entrepreneur, who uses technology to his own advantage. He does nothing to help the people or the community. In fact, he deceives the masses and the king by creating the illusion that he is stronger than the bull. He has learned, with the help of Puss, that one can achieve glory through deception. It is through the artful use of images that one can sway audiences and gain their favor. Animation, is trickery—trick films—for still images are made to seem as if they move through automatization. As long as one controls the images (and machines) one can reign supreme, just as the hero is safe as long as he is disguised. The pictures conceal the controls and machinery. They prevent the audience from really viewing the production and manipulation, and in the end, audiences can no longer envision a fairy tale for themselves, as they can when they read one. The pictures deprive the audience of the ability to visualize their own characters, roles, and desires. At the same time, Disney offsets the deprivation with the pleasure of scopophilia and inundates the viewer with delightful images, humorous figures, and erotic signs. In general, the animator, Disney, projects the enjoyable fairy tale of his life through his own images, and he realizes through animated stills the basic oedipal dream that he was to play out time and again in most of his fairy-tale films. The repetition of Disney's infantile quest—the core of American mythology:—enabled him to strike a chord in American viewers from the 1920s to the present, a chord that has also resounded across the ocean in Europe, for Disney continued framing the discourse of civility within a male frame in the tradition of writers like Straparola, Basile, Perrault, the Brothers Grimm, Ludwig Bechstein, Henri Pourrat, J. R. R. Tolkien, and C. S. Lewis as well as illustrators like George Cruikshank, Gustav Doré, Richard Doyle, Walter Crane, Charles Folkard, Arthur Rackham, and Charles Robinson. All of these men bonded, so to speak, or collaborated for the same reason: to use cats for their own self-figuration and to rationalize the manner in which power relations are distributed to benefit men in Western society.

Perhaps this is why cats are not man's, best friend. In the literary and cinematic fairy-tale tradition of "Puss in Boots," they have been manipulated to extol male prowess and to represent the difficulties of middle-class writers and administrators in establishing a secure position for themselves in societies that are dominated by display and force. The only writer who spoke for cats and against servility was Basile, but who remembers his version? Who remembers his smart cat who long ago grasped the duplicity of the men who tried to frame her life? She escaped the frame, but the tradition of "Puss in Boots" reveals how the origins of this frame and its borders of enclosure are still very much with us as we approach the twenty-first century.

Chapter III

His and Her Versions of *Riquet with the Tuft: French Women as Writers of Fairy Tales*

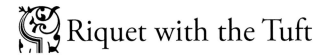
Riquet with the Tuft

Charles Perrault

Once upon a time there was a queen who gave birth to a son so ugly and misshapen that for a long time everyone doubted if he was in fact human. A fairy who was present at his birth assured everyone, however, that he could not fail to be pleasant because he would have a great deal of intelligence. She added that he would also have the ability to impart the same amount of intelligence to that person he came to love by virtue of this gift she was giving him. All this somewhat consoled the poor queen, who was very much distressed at having brought such a hideous little monkey into the world. Sure enough, as soon as the child was able to talk,^ he said a thousand pretty things. Furthermore, there was an indescribable air of thoughtfulness in all his actions that charmed everyone. I have forgotten to say that he was born with a little tuft of hair on his head, and this was the reason why he was called Riquet with the Tuft (Riquet being the family name).

At the-end of seven or eight years, the queen of a neighboring kingdom gave birth to two daughters. The first of them was more beautiful than daylight, and the queen was so delighted that people feared her great joy might cause her some harm. The same fairy who had attended the birth of little Riquet with the Tuft was also present on this occasion, and to moderate the queens joy, she declared that this little princess would be as stupid as she was beautiful. The queen was deeply mortified by this, but a few minutes later her chagrin became, even greater still, for she gave birth to a second child who turned out to be extremely ugly.

"Don't be too upset, madam," the fairy said to her. "Your daughter will be compensated in another way. She'll have so much intelligence that her lack of beauty will hardly be noticed."

"May heaven grant it," replied the queen. "But isn't there some way to give a little intelligence to my older daughter who is so beautiful?"

"I can't do anything for her, madam, in the way of wit," said the fairy, "but I can do a great deal in matters of beauty. Since there's nothing I would not do to please you, I shall endow her with the ability to render any person who pleases her with a beautiful or handsome appearance."

As these two princesses grew up, their qualities increased in the same proportion. Throughout the realm everyone talked about the beauty of the older daughter and the intelligence of the younger. It is also true that their defects greatly increased as they grew older. The young daughter became uglier, and the older more stupid every day. She either gave no answer when addressed, or she said something foolish. At the same time she was so awkward that she could not place four pieces of china on a mantel without breaking one of them, nor drink a glass of water without spilling half of it on her clothes. Despite the great advantage of beauty in a young person, the younger sister always outshone the elder whenever they were in society. At first everyone gathered around the more beautiful girl to admire her, but soon left her for the more intelligent sister to listen to the thousand pleasant things she said. In less than a quarter of an hour, not a soul would be standing near the elder sister while everyone would be surrounding the younger. Though very stupid, the elder sister noticed this and would have willingly given up all her beauty for half the intelligence of her sister.

The queen, discreet though she was, could not help reproaching the elder daughter whenever she did stupid things, and that made the poor princess ready to die of grief. One day, when she had withdrawn into the woods to bemoan her misfortune, she saw a little man coming toward *her. He was extremely ugly and unpleasant, but was dressed in magnificent attire. It was young Riquet with the Tuft. He had fallen in love with her from seeing her portraits, which had been sent all around the world, and he had left his fathers kingdom to have the pleasure of seeing and speaking to her. Delighted to meet her thus alone, he approached her with all the respect and politeness imaginable. After paying the usual compliments, he remarked that she was very melancholy.

"I cannot comprehend, madam," he said,"how a person so beautiful as you are can be so sad as you appear. Though I may boast of having seen an infinite number of lovely women, I can assure you that I've never beheld one whose beauty could begin to compare with yours."

"It's very kind of you to say so, sir," replied the princess, and there she—stopped.

"Beauty is such a great advantage," continued Riquet,"that it ought to surpass all other things. If one possesses it? I don't see anything that could cause one much distress."

"I'd rather be as ugly as you and have intelligence," said the princess,"than be as beautiful and stupid as I am."

"There's no greater proof of intelligence, madam, than the belief that we do not have any. It's the nature of the gift that the more we have; the more we believe we are deficient in it."

"I don't know whether that's the case/' the princess said,"but I know full well that I am very stupid, and that's the cause of the grief which is killing me."

"If that's all that's troubling you, madam, I can easily put an end to your distress."

"And how do you intend to manage that?" the princess asked.

"I have the power, madam, to give as much intelligence as anyone can possess to the person I love," Riquet with the Tuft replied. "And as you are that person, madam, it will depend entirely on whether or not you want to have so much intelligence, for you may have it, provided that you consent to marry me."

The princess was thunderstruck and did not say a word.

"I see that this proposal torments you, and I'm not surprised," said Riquet with the Tuft. "But I'll give you a full year to make up your mind."

The princess had so little intelligence, and at the same time had such a strong desire to possess a great deal, that she imagined the year would never come to an end. So she immediately accepted his offer. No sooner did she promise that she would marry Riquet with the Tuft twelve months from that day than she felt a complete change come over her. She found she possessed an incredible facility to say anything she wished and to say it in a polished yet easy and natural manner. She commenced right away, maintaining an elegant conversation with the prince. Indeed, she was so brilliant that he believed that he had given her more wit than he had kept for himself.

When she returned to the palace, the whole court was at a loss to account for such a sudden and extraordinary change. Whereas she had formerly said any number of foolish things, she now made sensible and exceedingly clever observations. The entire court rejoiced beyond belief. Only the younger sister was not quite pleased, for she no longer held the advantage of intelligence over her elder sister. Now she merely appeared as an ugly woman by her side, and the king let himself be guided by the elder daughter's advice. Sometimes he even held the meetings of his council in her apartment.

The news of this change spread abroad, and all the young princes of the neighboring kingdoms exerted themselves to the utmost to gain her affection. Nearly all of them asked her hand in marriage, but since she found none of them sufficiently intelligent, she listened to all of them without promising herself to anyone in particular. At last a prince arrived who was so witty and handsome that she could not help feeling attracted to him. Her father noticed this and told her that she was at perfect liberty to choose a husband for herself and that she only had to make her decision known. Now, the more intelligence one possesses, the greater the difficulty one has in making up one's mind about such a weighty matter. So she thanked her father and requested some time to think it over.

By chance she took a walk in the same woods where she had met Riquet with the Tuft to ponder with greater freedom what she should do. While she was walking, deep in thought, she heard a dull rumble beneath her feet, as though many people were running busily back and forth. Listening more attentively, she heard voices say,"Bring me that cooking pot." "Give me that kettle." "Put some wood on the fire." At that same moment the ground opened, and she saw below what appeared to be a large kitchen full of cooks, scullions, and all sorts of servants necessary for the preparation of a magnificent banquet. A group of approximately twenty to thirty cooks came forth, and they took places at a very long table set in a path of the woods. Each had a larding pin in hand and a cap on his head, and they set to work, keeping time to a melodious song. Astonished at this sight, the princess inquired who had hired them.

"Riquet with the Tuft, madam," the leader of the group replied. "His marriage is to take place tomorrow."

The princess was even more surprised than she was before, and suddenly she recalled that it was exactly a year ago that she had promised to marry Prince Riquet with the Tuft. How she was taken aback! The reason why she had not remembered her promise was that when she had made it, she had still been a fool, and after receiving her new mind, she had forgotten all her follies. Now, no sooner had she advanced another thirty steps on her walk than she encountered Riquet with the Tuft, who appeared gallant and magnificent, like a prince about to be married.

"As you can see, madam," he said,"I've kept my word to the minute, and I have no doubt but that you've come here to keep yours. By giving me your hand, you'll make me the happiest of men."

"I'll be frank with you," the princess replied. "I've yet to make up my mind on that matter, and I don't believe I'll ever be able to do so to your satisfaction."

"You astonish me, madam."

"I can believe it," the princess responded,"and assuredly, if I had to deal with a stupid person—a man without intelligence—I'd feel greatly embarrassed. A princess is abound by her word,' he'd say to me, 'and you must marry me as you promised to do so.' But since the man with whom I'm speaking is the most intelligent man in the world, I'm certain he'll listen to reason. As you know, when I was no better than a fool, I could not decide whether I should, marry you. Now that I have the intelligence that you've given me and that renders me much more difficult to please than before, how can you expect me to make a decision today that I couldn't make then? If you seriously thought of marrying me, you made a big mistake in taking away my stupidity and enabling me to see clearer."

"If a man without intelligence would be justified in reproaching you for *your* breach of promise," Riquet with the Tuft replied,"why do you expect, madam, that I should not be allowed to do the same? This matter affects the entire happiness of my life. Is it reasonable that intelligent people should be placed at a greater disadvantage than those who have none? Can you presume this, you who have so much intelligence and have so earnestly desired to possess it? But let us come to the point, if you please. With the exception of my ugliness, is there anything about me that displeases you? Are you dissatisfied with my birth, my intelligence, my temperament, or my manners?"

"Not in the least," replied the princess. "I admire you for everything you've just mentioned."

"If so," Riquet with the Tuft responded,"I'll gain my happiness, for you have the power to make me the most pleasing of men."

"How can that be done?"

"It can if you love me sufficiently to wish that it should be. And to remove your doubts, you should know that the same fairy who endowed me at birth with the power to give intelligence to the person I chose also gave you the power to render handsome any man who pleases you."

"If that's so," the princess said,"I wish with all my heart that you may become the most charming and handsome prince in the world."

No sooner had the princess pronounced these words than Riquet with the Tuft appeared to her eyes as the most handsome, strapping, and charming man she had ever seen. There are some who assert that it was not the fairy's spell but love alone that caused this transformation. They say that the princess, having reflected on her lover's perseverance, prudence, and all the good qualities of his heart and mind, no longer saw the deformity of his body nor the ugliness of his features. His hunch appeared to her as nothing more than the effect of a man shrugging his shoulders. Likewise, his horrible limp appeared to be nothing more, than a slight sway that charmed her. They also say that his eyes, which squinted, seemed to her only more brilliant for the proof they gave of the intensity of his love. Finally, his great red nose had something martial and heroic about it. However this may be, the princess promised to marry him on the spot, provided that he obtained the consent of the king, her father.

On learning of his daughter's high regard for Riquet with the Tuft, whom he also knew to be a very intelligent and wise prince, the king accepted him with pleasure as a son-in-law. The wedding took place the next morning, just as Riquet with the Tuft had planned it.

Moral

That which you see written down here
Is not so fantastic because it's quite true:
We find what we love is wondrously fair,
In what we love we find intelligence, too.

Another Moral

Nature very often places
Beauty in an object that amazes,
Such that art can ne'er achieve.
Yet even beauty can't move the heart
As much as that charm hard to chart,
A charm which only love can perceive.

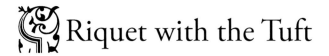

Riquet with the Tuft

Catherine Bernard

A GRAND nobleman of Grenada, whose wealth was equal to his high birth, experienced a domestic calamity that poisoned all the treasures of his fortune. His only daughter was so stupid that her naturally beautiful features only, served to make her appearance distasteful. Her movements were anything but graceful. Her figure, though slender, made an awkward impression since it lacked sprightliness.

Mama—that was the name of this girl—did not possess enough intelligence to know that she was not intelligent, but she did have, enough to realize she was looked upon with disdain, even though she could not figure out why. One day, when she was out walking by herself, as was her habit, she saw a man hideous enough to be a monster emerge from the ground. As soon as she caught sight of him, she wanted to flee, but he called her back.

"Stop," he said to her. "I have something unpleasant to tell you, but I also have something nice to promise you. Even with your beauty you have something—and I don't know, what's caused it—that makes people regard you with disfavor. It has to do with your incapacity to think, and without my making a value judgment, this fault makes you as inferior as I am, for my body is like your mind. That's the cruel thing I have to say to you. But from the stunned manner in which you're looking at me, I think I've given your mind too little credit, for I fear I've insulted you. This is what makes me despair as I broach the subject of my proposition. However, I'm going to risk making it to you. Do you want intelligence?"

"Yes." Mama responded in a manner that might have indicated no.

"Very good," he said. "Here's the way. You must love Riquet with the Tuft. That's my name, and you must marry me at the end of the year. That's the condition I'll impose on you. Think it over. If you can't, repeat the words that I'm going to say to you as often as possible. They'll eventually teach you how to think. Farewell for a year. Here are the words that will dissipate your indolence and at the same time cure your imbecility:

Love can surely inspire me
To help me shed stupidity.
And teach me to care with sincerity
If I have the right quality."

As Mama began to utter these words properly, her poise improved immensely—she became more vivacious, and her movements more free. She kept repeating the verse and soon departed for her father's house, where she told him something coherent, then a little later, something intelligent, and finally, something witty. Such a great and rapid transformation did not go unnoticed. Lovers came in droves. Mama was no longer alone at the balls or during promenades. Soon she made men unfaithful and jealous. People talked only about her and for her.

Among the men who found her charming, it was easy for her to find someone more handsome than Riquet with the Tuft. The mind that her benefactor had given her started to work against him. The words that she conscientiously repeated filled her with love, but the effect was contrary to Riquet's intentions: the love was not for him.

She favored the most handsome of those men who sighed for her, although he was not the best match with regard to his wealth. Thus her father and mother, who saw that they had wished this misfortune on their daughter by desiring she should have a mind, and who realized that they could not deprive her of it, thought at least they should give her lessons against love. But prohibiting a young and pretty person from loving is like preventing a tree from bearing leaves in May. She only loved Arada more—that was the name of her lover.

She made sure not to tell anyone about how she happened to obtain her mind. Her vanity caused her to keep this a secret. She had enough intelligence to understand the importance of hiding the mystery of how she had managed to become so.

The year that Riquet with the Tuft had given her to make a decision drew to an end. With great anguish she awaited the deadline. Her mind, now her bane, did not let one single torturous consequence escape her. To lose her lover forever, to be under the power of someone about whom the only thing she knew was his deformity, which was perhaps his least fault, and finally to marry someone and to accept his gifts that she did not want to return—these thoughts kept passing through her mind.

One day, when she was contemplating her cruel destiny and wandering off alone, she heard a loud hubbub and subterranean voices singing the words Riquet with the Tuft had taught her. She shuddered when she heard them, for it was the signal of disaster! Soon the ground opened. She descended gradually and saw Riquet with the Tuft surrounded by creatures who were just as deformed as he was. What a spectacle for a person who had been pursued by the most charming men in her country! Her torment was even greater than her surprise. Unable to speak, she let loose a flood of tears. This was the only human quality she possessed that was beyond the control of the mind that Riquet with the Tuft had given her. In turn, he regarded her sadly.

"Madam," he said, "it's not difficult to see that I'm more distasteful to you than when I first appeared before you. I myself am bewildered by what has happened in giving you a mind. But in the last analysis, you're free to make a choice: marry me or return to your former condition. I'll send you back to your father's house the way I found you, or I'll make you mistress of this kingdom. I am king of the gnomes, and you would be queen. If you can excuse my shape and overlook my repulsive deformities, you could enjoy a great many pleasures here. I am master of all the treasures locked up in the earth, and you would be mistress of them. With gold and intelligence, who could want more from life?" Seeing she was unconvinced, he continued, "I'm afraid that you've developed some kind of false squeamishness. I must seem inadequate in the midst of all my riches. But if I and my treasures don't please you, just speak up. I'll take you away from here and bring you home because I don't want anything to trouble my happiness here. You have two days to become acquainted with this place and to decide my fate and yours."

After leading her into a magnificent apartment, Riquet with the Tuft left her. She was attended by gnomes of her sex, whose ugliness did not repel her as much as that of the men. They entertained her with a meal and good company. After dinner she saw a play in which the deformities of the actors prevented her from developing any interest in the subject of the drama. That evening a ball was held in her honor, but she attended it without desiring to please anyone. Indeed, she felt an innate disgust that made it impossible for her to show Riquet her appreciation for all the pleasures he provided.

In order to save herself from this odious husband, she would have returned to her stupidity without feeling grief if she had not had a lover, but it would have meant losing a lover in a most cruel manner. It is also true that she would lose her lover by marrying the gnome—she would never be able to see Arada, speak with him, or send him news about herself, for Riquet would suspect her of infidelity. In sum, by getting rid of the man she loved, she was going to marry a husband who would always be odious even when he was pleasant. Moreover, he was a monster.

The decision was a wrenching one to make. When the two days had passed, her mind was not any more made up than before. She told the gnome that it had not been possible for her to reach a decision.

"That's a decision against me," he told her. "So now I'll return you to your former condition that you didn't dare to choose."

She trembled. The idea of losing her lover through the disdain he would show her provided such a powerful spur that she felt compelled to renounce him.

"Well, then!" the gnome said to her. "You've decided. It must be up to you.

Riquet with the Tuft did not make it difficult. He married her, and Mama's intelligence increased even more through this marriage. Her unhappiness, though, increased in proportion to the growth of her mind. She was horrified to have given herself to a monster, and she couldn't comprehend how she spent one moment with him.

The gnome realized very well how much his wife hated him, and he was hurt by it, even though he prided himself on the force of his intelligence. This aversion was a constant reproach to his deformity and made him detest women, marriage, and curiosity so much so that he became distraught. He often left Mama alone, and since she was reduced to 'just thinking, she became convinced that she had to make Arada see with his own eyes that she was not unfaithful. She knew he could get to this place because she had so easily managed to get there herself. At the least she had to send him news about herself and explain her absence because of the gnome who had abducted her. Once Arada saw him, he would know she was faithful.

There is nothing that an intelligent woman in love cannot do. She won over a gnome attendant, who carried news about her to Arada. Fortunately, this was still during the time that lovers were faithful to each other. He had become despondent over Mama's absence without becoming bitter about it. He was not even plagued by suspicion. He maintained that if he died, he would not have the least negative thought about his mistress and did not want to seek a cure for his love. It is not difficult to believe that with such feelings, he was willing to risk his life to find Mama as soon as he knew where she was. Nor did she forbid him from coming there.

Mama's cheerfulness returned gradually, and her beauty made her even more perfect, but the amorous gnome caused her to worry. He had too much intelligence and knew Mama's repugnance for him too well to believe that she had become accustomed to being there and had become sweeter so suddenly. Mama was imprudent enough to get dressed up, and he was smart enough to realize that he was not worthy of this. Long did he search until he discovered a handsome man hiding in his palace. As a result, he thought up an extremely fine way both to revenge himself and take care of the lover. First, Riquet ordered Mama to appear before him.

"It doesn't amuse me to make complaints and reproaches," he said. "I let human beings have their share of them. When I gave you a mind, I presumed I would enjoy it. However, you've used it against me. Still, I won't deprive you of it completely. You've submitted to the law that was imposed on you. But even if you did not break our agreement, you didn't observe it to the letter. Let us compromise. You shall have a mind during the night. I don't want a stupid wife, but you shall be stupid during the day for whomever you please."

All at once Mama felt a dullness of mind that she did not understand anymore. During the night her ideas were aroused again, and she wept over her misfortune. She was not able to console herself or find the ways through her wisdom to help herself.

The following night she noticed that her husband was sleeping soundly. She placed an herb on his nose that increased his oblivion and made it last as long as she wished. She got up and crept away from the object of her wrath. Led by her dreams, she went to the place where Arada was dwelling. She thought that he might be looking for her and found him in a lane where they had often met. He asked her all kinds of questions. Mama told him about her misfortunes, which abated because of the pleasure she derived in relating them to him.

The next night they met at the same place without being followed, and their meetings continued for such a long time that their misfortune now enabled them to taste a new kind of happiness. Mama's mind and love provided her with a thousand ways to be charming and to make Arada forget that she lacked intelligence half the time.

Whenever the lovers felt the dawn of day approaching, Mama went to wake the gnome. She took care to remove the herb that made him drowsy as soon as she was beside him. Although she now became an imbecile again, she used the time to sleep.

Such bittersweet happiness could not last forever. The leaf that made Riquet sleep also made him snore, and, thinking his master was grumbling, a half-asleep servant ran to him, saw the herb that had been placed on his nose, and removed it because he thought that was disturbing him—a cure that made three people unhappy all at the same time. Riquet saw that he was alone and searched for his wife in a rage. Either chance or his bad luck led him to the place where the two lovers had abandoned themselves to each other. As he approached, he heard them swear eternal love to each other. He did not say a word. He touched the lover with a wand that transformed his shape into one exactly like his own. And after looking back and forth and back and forth, Mama could no longer distinguish who her husband, was. Thus she lived with two husbands instead of one, never knowing whom she should address her lamentations for fear of mistaking the object of her hatred for the object of her love.

But perhaps she hardly lost anything there. In the long run lovers become husbands anyway.

Twice Upon a Time

Women Writers and the History of the Fairy Tale

Elizabeth Wanning Harries

> In appropriating folklore genres, the literay tradition is able to create an Idealization of itself through a separation of speech and writing. Such a separation … always posits speech as a form of nature.
>
> —Susan Stewart, *Crimes of Writing*

> [W]e must give up the fiction that collects all these sounds under the sign of a "Voice," of a "Culture" of its own—or of the great Other's. Rather, orality insinuates itself … into the network—an endless tapestry—of a scriptural economy.
>
> —Michel de Certeau, *The Practice of Everyday Life*

Fairy tales and orality seem intimately connected. We think of written tales as transcribing-stories handed down orally for hundreds of years, as simply "putting into print" the traces of that long-standing tradition. Most writers of fairy tales have done their best to reinforce that impression. Charles Perrault's alternative title, Tales of Mother Goose, suggests a traditional, spoken, origin. The Brothers Grimni work hard to create a simple and naive narrative voice. Hans Christian Andersen's stories often begin with formulas like "Now then, here's where we begin" that imitate oral storytelling. I am not denying that many fairy tales have been (and continue to be) part of an ongoing oral, popular culture, but I do want to show that our sense of access to that culture through reading written fairy tales is an illusion—an illusion carefully and deliberately created by many fairy-tale collectors, editors, and writers.

We can become conscious of that illusion by looking further at another strand in the tangled history of written fairy tales—the tales written by women in the 1690s in France. Unlike Perrault, their contemporary, these women only occasionally appealed to the oral, popular tradition and never attempted to imitate an illiterate or uneducated voice. Bather, they simulated a different kind of orality—the conversation that framed the tales they knew by Straparola and Basile, and that animated the salons of the later seventeenth century in France. Most of the long, elaborate tales they wrote are set within a conversational frame, a frame that often reproduces the milieu and the carefully formulated repartee that was part of salon culture.

The frontispiece of thee 1697 edition of Perrault's Contes that I discussed in the first chapter defines the traditional version of the oral storytelling situation. If we look at it again, from a slightly different angle, we can see die kind of orality Perrault means to suggest. The central female figure, dressed in the simple costume and sabots of a domestic servant or nurse, is simultaneously spinning and telling a story, spinning wool or flax and "spinning a yam."1 The thumb and forefinger of her left hand, carefully delineated, are guiding the filament; the next two are raised in the traditional gesture that asks for a listening audience's attention. The frontispiece sets her in the tradition of the spinning woman with distaff, a tradition that also links her to the oral transmission of stories. The simple peasant woman in Perrault's frontispiece may be simply that, but the distaff and her raised fingers suggest her unsettling verbal power, a power that Perrault both mimes and controls. Her distaff and her dress mark, the storyteller's gender, social position, and place in the literary economy: she is an emblem of the mythical oral tradition that Perrault claimed to draw on and at the same time carefully distanced himself from..

The distaff is always a mark of gender; it often anchors the woman in the domestic sphere but sometimes is used to stress her unruly distance from it. Witches and harridans often carry one. In two engravings of about 1500, Albrecht Dürer's savage depiction of a witch riding backward on a goat and Israhel van Meckenem's The Angry Wife, the spindle is thrust through the distaff, suggesting that the domestic implement is no longer used for spinning but rather has become a subversive banner or a weapon. The distaff often stirs up undercurrents of misogyny and fear of women's voices and gossip. One particularly telling woodcut from a French seventeenth-century pamphlet, an example of the old "silent woman" topos; shows a headless woman holding a distaff with the motto "Si Tu La Cherche La Voicy" (If you are looking for her [the silent woman], here she is).[2]

The presence of the distaff suggests that the woman has effectively been silenced and relegated to her domestic functions; she is no longer a speaker or a teller of tales, but rather a mute sexualized object. As Marina Warner says,"Women dominated the domestic webs of information and power"; this domination always made male observers uneasy.[3] In Perrault's choice of frontispiece, however, all these negative connotations are subdued. The central figure continues to spin while she is telling her stories; she is both nurse and tale-teller, trustworthy domestic and *raconteuse*.

Women are often supposed to be tellers of tales: those anonymous, lower- class nurses and grandmothers who taught and entertained children by telling them stories. The murky legend of "Mother Goose" is an instance of this belief; Sévigné s well-known letter of October 30,1656, refers to it casually as if this were part of the common lore about fairy tales:

> Et si, Mademoiselle,…, ce n'est pas un conte de ma mere Foie,
> Mais de la cane de Montfort
> Oui, ma foi, lui resemble fort.
> (And if, Mademoiselle, …, this is not a tale of Mother Goose, but of the drake of Montfort, there are strong resemblances between them.)

For Sévigné, the Mother Goose tale is the generic title for a whole group of popular stories. The *Dictionnaire de l'Academie* (1694) gives many folk synonyms for *conte*:

> *Le vulgaire appelle* conte au vieux loup, conte de vieille, conte de ma Mère l'Oye, conte de la cicogne, conte à la cicicogne, conte de peau d'asne, conte à dormir debout, conte jaune, bleu, violet, conte borgne, *Des fables ridicules telles que sont celles dont les vielles gens entretiennent et amusent les enfants.*[4]
> (*The common people call* old wolfs tale, old wives' tale, Mother Goose tale, tale of the stork, tale told by a stork, donkey skin tale, tale to fall asleep by standing up, yellow, blue, violet tale, one-eyed tale, *all those ridiculous tales told by old women to entertain and amuse children.*)

Many, if not all, of these definitions are linked to the traditions of gossip and tale-telling by women—not only the old wives' and Mother Goose tales, but also the tales of and by the stork, as Warner has pointed out. Angela Carter has described the situation in her usual trenchant prose: "Old wives' tales—that is, worthless stories, untruths, trivial gossip, a derisive label that allots the art of storytelling to women at the exact same time as it takes all value from it."[5] Perrault's frontispiece perpetuates the prevailing myth about the appropriate role for women in the transmission of fairy tales: as aging, patient, nurturing conduits of oral culture or spinners of tales.

This belief has not completely faded. Vladimir Propp in his essay "The Nature of Folklore" imagines the prehistory of literature using exclusively feminine metaphors: "Folklore is the womb of literature; literature is born of folklore. Folklore is the prehistory of literature … Literature, which is born of folklore, soon abandons the mother that reared it. Literature is the product of another form of consciousness."[6] He locates folklore at the beginning of time, in a feminine realm. Or, as Trinh Minh-ha says, in her *Woman, Native, Other* (1989),"The world's earliest archives or libraries were the memories of women. Patiently transmitted from mouth to ear, body to body, hand to hand   Every woman partakes in the chain of guardianship and of transmission."[7] Trinh still imagines oral culture as literally handed down by women, in a particularly physical, intimate way ("from mouth to ear, body to body, hand to hand"). Women are still said to be the guardians of tradition, passing on to their children and grandchildren the stories of their culture. But, as folklorists like Linda Degh have shown, women are and were not the only, or even the primary, storytellers in most oral cultures.[8] The myth of the anonymous female teller of tales, particularly strong in the legends of Mother Goose and Mother Bunch, is just that: a myth—but a myth that has several important functions and corollaries. If women are the tellers of tales, storytelling remains a motherly or grandmotherly function, tied (to use the language of French feminist criticism) to the body and nature, as we see in the quotation from Trinh. Stories are supposed to flow from women like milk and blood. And if women are thought of as *tellers* of tales, it follows that they are not imagined as the collectors or writers of tales. As fairy tales were transmuted from oral tales into "book tales" *(Buchmàrchen,* or tales that have been written down) into written, invented tales (*Kunstmàrchen*), women were subtly relegated to the most "primitive" stage. Perrault's frontispiece may have been an attempt to etch his female writing competitors out of existence.

As Catherine Velay-Vallantin has shown us, the frontispiece also suggests the fictive reading situation that Perrault and his printer wanted to prescribe, a simulation of oral tale-telling, or what she calls "factitious orality."[9] In his prose tales, Perrault mimes the voice of the peasant storyteller, always elegantly walking the line between the practices of writing and supposed "oral" transmission "within a culturally more aristocratic mode of reading."[10] He presents the voice as "authentic," as a transcription of traditional storytelling. As we have seen, contemporary commentators like the abbe de Villiers particularly admired his ability to feign this voice, to be clever enough to sound naive. But we must remember that this voice is a deliberate simulation, existing in an uneasy tension with the more sophisticated language of the worldly verse morals at the end of each tale and with the sophisticated verse tales he wrote earlier. Perrault abandons the intricate, courtly style he used for those verse tales in his *Contes,* choosing instead a simpler narrative voice.

The frontispieces of volumes of tales women wrote in the 1690s often seem to be designed to contest the ideological force, of. Perrault's. In the frontispiece of early editions (1698 and 1711) of d'Aulnoy's *Contes nouveaux,* a woman dressed in the flowing robes and turban usually associated with a sibyl is writing the title of one of d'Aulnoy's tales,"Graeceuse et Percinet," in a large folio or book. Again she has children as her audience, but these children are dressed in rather the same way and probably are of the same class as the storyteller. The storyteller is represented *not* with the domestic and gendered spindle, but rather with a large book that demonstrates her literacy. There is a fireplace, but the fire is out. Instead of the simple candlestick, there are sconces surrounded with elaborate scrollwork. Instead of the locked door, there is a window opening out on a summer country scene. Instead of the domestic cat, there is an exotic monkey—again perhaps a reference to another of d'Aulnoy's tales,"Babiole," published earlier that same year. This mirror effect-—the reflection of some of the tales in the introductory picture—heightens the conscious artificiality of the scene and of the tales that follow.[11]

The frontispieces of a 1725 Amsterdam edition of d'Aulnoy's *Contes nouveaux ou les Fées à la mode* also work against the image of the woman as lower-class storyteller. The frontispiece of volume 1 shows a fashionably dressed woman seated on an elevated dais, gesticulating as she speaks to an audience, similarly dressed, that seems to be primarily adult. Far from an enclosed, domestic, fireside scene, this is a large room with classical columns and an open window that looks out on a faintly classical landscape with obelisks and a tower. The decorative rocaille around the title at the top of the page underscores the aristocratic milieu of this storyteller.

The frontispiece of volume 2 again represents a woman writing, a woman with a helmet on her head—probably Pallas Athena, since she is accompanied by an owl—writing on a large tablet with a quill and apparently speaking at the same time. Behind her a spear replaces the distaff. In the foreground there is an audience of fashionably dressed adults, sitting at leisure on the ground. The scene in the background might represent, in miniature, the plot of one of d'Aulnoy's tales, with its fleeing figures and pursuing horseman.

The frontispieces used for the *conteuses'* tales, then, usually represent them as sibyls, or as aristocratic storytellers, or as Greek goddesses, not as spinning peasant women.[12] In another paradoxical illustration of the interweaving of the oral and the written, they often are represented as "writing to an audience," inscribing words on a tablet or folio in front of a listening group. Because women have been perennially associated with the *telling* of tales—in nurseries, in spinning and weaving circles, in quilting bees, by the fireside—it has been difficult for them to think of themselves, and to be thought of, as fairy-tale *writers*. As Joan DeJean points out in *Tender Geographies,* France was the only country where "the written transcription of fairy tales was not totally controlled by men,"[13] at least until the nineteenth century. It was not primarily the traditional passivity of most female protagonists of fairy tales that made it difficult for women to take the active step of writing them down and inventing them, but rather the pervasive notion that women were the designated oral transmitters of those tales.

But the women who wrote tales in the 1690s chose frontispieces and created narrative structures that contested this limiting prescription. The tales the women wrote—again in contrast to Perrault's—are full of references to a feminine, aristocratic, listening audience: "Perhaps you are going to think, Madame." Isn't it true, Countess, that …"; "I'm sure you have heard, Madame… ." The typographical forms in which their tales were printed rarely reflect any interest in suggesting popular origins for the tales; rather, they tend to be identical with those forms in which the many novels and "nouvelles" of the late 1600s in France were printed. Perrault's tales in his 1697 volume always have a crude, illustrative engraving on the first page; the tales in the women's collections often have only the same decorative, stylized headpieces that they use for their other writing. The tales embedded in the women's novels are sometimes not set off from the rest of the text at all, as in d'Aulnoy's "L'île de la Félicité" (in her 1690 novel *Histoire d'Hipo-yte, comte du Duglas);* sometimes they are separated by a chaste and simple border of florets. The *conteuses'* words do not often appear "in costume" to delight children or to simulate popular orality;[14] their fairy tales are in part reflections of an ongoing (though perhaps fading) salon practice.

Sometimes, in fact, they present their tales in deliberate opposition to Perrault's model. Murat, in the introduction to her *Histoires sublimes et allegoriques* (1699), explicitly dedicates her tales to "Les Fées Modernes" (modern fairies), the writers who are anything but the old-fashioned, naive, female storytellers of times past:

> Les anciennes Fées vos devancieres ne passent plus que pour des badines auprés de vous. Leurs occupations étoient basses & pueriles, ne s'amusant qu'aux Servantes & aux Nourrices. Tout leur soin consistoit à bien ballayer la maison, mettre le pot au feu, faire la lessive, remuer & endormir les enfans, traire les vaches, battre le beurre, & mille autres pauvretez de cette nature;… Leur divertissement étoit de dancer au clair de la Lune, de se transformer en Vieilles, en Chats, en Singes, & en Moynes-bourus, pour faire peur aux enfans, & aux esprits foibles. C'est pourquoy tout ce qui nous reste aujourd'hui de leurs Faits & Gestes ne sont que des Contes de ma Mere l'Oye. Elles étoient presque toûjours vielles, laides, mal-vétuës, & mal logées.[15]

(The old fairies, your predecessors, were just gossips compared to you. Their occupations were low and child-ish, amusing only for servants and nurses. All they did was to sweep the house well, put the pot on the fire, do the washing, rock the children and put them to sleep, take care of the cows, churn the butter, and a thousand other little things of that kind … their diversions were to dance by the light of the moon, or to transform themselves into old women, cats, monkeys, or bogeymen, to frighten children and feeble minds. That is why all that remains today of their deeds and actions are only tales of Mother Goose. They were almost always old, ugly, badly dressed and badly housed.)

Murat here deliberately mocks the kind of tale that Perrault produced, his "Contes de ma mere l'Oye" that had been published only two years earlier.[16] She suggests that these tales are only old wives' tales," crude and outmoded, certainly not suitable for an adult and sophisticated audience. She contrasts his model storytell-ers, the nurse/gossips busy doing mundane and menial female tasks, with the elegant and educated *conteuses*:

Mais pour vous mesdames, vous avez bien pris une autre route: Vous ne vous occupez que de grandes choses, dont les moindres sont de donner de l'esprit à ceux & celles qui n'en ont point, de la beauté aux laides, de l'éloquence aux ignorans, des richesses aux pauvres, & de l'éclat aux choses les plus obscures. Vous estes toutes belles, jeunes, bien-faites, galament & richement vétuës & logées, & vous n'habitez que dans la Cour des Rois, ou dans des Palais enchantez.[17] •

(But you, my ladies, you have chosen another way: you occupy yourselves only with great things, the least of which are to give wit to the men and women who have none, beauty to the ugly, eloquence to the ignorant, riches to the poor, and luster to the most hidden things. You are all beautiful, young, well formed, nobly and richly dressed and housed, and you live only in the courts of kings, or in enchanted palaces.)

Murat insists on the distinction between the traditional lower—class female storyteller and the late-seventeenth-century *conteuses*, a group she both praises and implicitly includes herself in. Her literary con-temporaries are often aristocratic, certainly well born, well »dressed, and well housed; their writing reflects the elegance of their milieu. As modern "fees," they have a magical power of discourse that transforms their lowly materials into stories fit for a discerning audience. They form and frame their narratives echoing the voices heard in the salons.

II

To trace the tales written in the 1690s by women, then, is to trace a kind of writing based on a very different conception of the "oral" from Perrault's dominant model. The *conteuses* do write stories based on traditional material, though their sources are usually written (Straparola in particular); they also occasionally echo traditional formulas that seem to define women as the oral conduits of popular culture. For example, Perrault, in his verse tale "Peau de l'âne" (1694), and his niece Marie-Jeanne Lhéritier, in her tale "Les en-chantemens de l'éloquence" (1696), include almost identical verses:

Ils ne sont pas aisez à croire;
Mais tant que dans le monde on verra des enfants,
Des meres & des mere-grands,
On en gardera la memoire.

(These stories are not easy to believe, but as long as there are children, mothers, and grandmothers in the world, they will be remembered.)[18]

These lines, and other similar ones, occur once in a while in the women's tales, linking the written stories to an ongoing tradition of storytelling and marking that tradition as transmitted by women to children. But much more often, and sometimes simultaneously, the *conteuses* place their tales in the complex and playful ambience of salon conversation. The "oral" for them is not primarily naive and primitive, but rather a highly charged, high-cultural event.

We still tend to identify the oral with peasant, illiterate, or "folk" culture. Like the Grimms, we tend to think of the oral as coming before the written, or as part of the origins of culture. As John Guillory has pointed out,"the generic category of the popular continues to bear the stigma of nonwriting, of mere orality, within writing itself, since popular works are consumed, from the point of view of High Culture, as the textual simulacra of ephemeral speech."[19] Or, to translate, popular writing is usually treated as simply a transcription or a written echo of the speech of the "folk," a less sophisticated, less intellectual activity. (Perrault's imitation of the voice of a member of the folk could be seen as an early instance of this practice.) But, as folklorists like Alan Dundes have shown, there are many different kinds of "folks" and illiteracy is not a requirement.[20] The "oral" can appear in many different social contexts and does not necessarily precede writing. In many cultures, oral narrative and written texts continually influence and change each other.[21]

Walter J. Ong has pointed to a different kind of orality: the residues of ancient rhetorical practices that continued to be taught in schools for boys throughout the seventeenth century.[22] In his book *Orality and Literacy*, Ong makes an interesting guess about women's leading role in the invention of the novel:

> A great gap in our understanding of the influence of women on literary genre and style could be bridged or closed through attention to the orality-literacy-print shift. …[E]arly women novelists and other women writers generally worked from outside the oral tradition because of the simple fact that girls were not commonly sub-jected to the orally based rhetorical training that boys got in school. … Certainly, non-rhetorical styles congenial to women writers helped make the novel what it is: more like a conversation than a platform performance.[23]

It seems to me, however, that Ong's guess about the relationship of early women writers to orality is off the mark, at least in France. Or rather, his primary conception of secondary orality (orality that persists after, the introduction of writing) is in fact a very narrow, academic, and elite one—and not very "oral" at all. The women who wrote fairy tales, though they were "outside" the oral tradition he *is* considering, were interested in simulating another kind of oral transmission, a practice that Ong never mentions. He suggests, at the end of the passage above, that women's writing tended to be based on "conversation" rather than on platform rhetoric—but he never acknowledges that conversation, including the ritualized conversation of the salons, is after all an oral practice too. In spite of his laudable attempt to think about women in relation to orality and writing, he in fact defines the oral tradition in a way that excludes them.

We need to develop more nuanced categories of the oral—categories that will permit us to see the ways oral practices that do not derive from supposed "folk narrative" or from the ancient techniques of rhetoric taught in schools continue to leave their traces in written texts. The nostalgia for the oral that permeates most written narrative can take on very different forms. The orality that has left its marks in many fairy tales is rarely the disputational "harangue" of Ong's school-based oratorical rhetoric, and not always the pseudo-folk situation that is sketched in Perrault's frontispiece. Rather, the women of the 1690s attempted to reproduce the conversational ambience of the salons that had formed them as writers. As Joan DeJean has shown in *Tender Geographies,*"the conversational style … is originally a female concept, invented in the salons and reinscribed in prose fiction when, following Seudery's example, women found a new power base in the republic of letters."[24] While her claim seems too broad, ignoring the conversational basis of earlier texts like Plato's dialogues, or the *Decameron*, or the collections of tales by Straparola and Basile, DeJean rightly emphasizes the importance of conversation in women's writing of the later seventeenth century in France.

Like the earlier novels by Scudéry or Villedieu, the *conteuses'* tales grew in part out of the competitive, scintillating dialogues that were an integral part of the salons. First the tales were probably a diversion, one of the many collaborative "divertissements" that formed part of salon culture, like riddles, metamorphoses, portraits, and "maximes d'amour"; then they were written down. But both practices seem to have continued simultaneously throughout the 1690s; as Roger Chartier has said,"the opposition of oral and written fails to account for the situation that existed from the sixteenth to the eighteenth century when media and multiple practices still overlapped."[25] This was true in popular culture, where evening tale-telling probably coexisted with the publication of fairy tales in chapbooks and *colporteur* literature. And it was equally true in the aristocratic practices of the salons. Tale-telling and tale writing went on simultaneously, as many of the frontispieces suggest.

Like all oral cultures, the culture of the salons is difficult to recover, because it was fluid, ephemeral, constantly changing. We know much more about it than about many other oral cultures, however, since the participants were literate; they wrote about what went on at the salons in their letters, memoirs, even novels. The evidence we have of the ways stories were told and received is spotty and unreliable—found mostly in letters like Sévigné's and novels like Segrais's *Les nouvelles franqaises ou les divertissements de la princesse Aurélie* (1656), about the group around the Grande Mademoiselle during her exile at Saint—Fargeau, or La Force's *Jeux d'esprit* (1701), about the "divertissements" that the princesse de Conti promoted during her exile at Eu in the early seventeenth century. Madame de Sévigné, in another well known letter—this one dated August 6, 1677—suggests all the artificiality and the incongruities of a fairy—tale-telling scene at court, as well as its links with the opera, in order to establish the oral situation in which it took place:

> Mme de Coulanges, qui m'est venue faire ici une fort honnête visite qui durera jusqu'à demain, voulut bien nous faire part des contes avec quoi Ton amuse les dames de Versailles: cela s'appelle les *mitonner*. Elle nous *mitonna* donc, et nous parla d'une île verte, où l'on élevait une princesse plus belle que le jour; c'étaient les fées qui soufflaient sur elle à tout moment.[26]

> (Mme de Coulanges, who has come here to pay me a gracious visit that will last until tomorrow, wanted to acquaint us with the stories that are currently amusing the ladies of Versailles: that is called cajoling [literally, simmering] them. She cajoled us then, and told us about a green island, where a princess more beautiful than the day was being brought up;, it was the fairies who breathed on her at every moment.)

Sévigné, with her usual clear-eyed irony, is not much amused by the fantastic fairy tale, with its pastoral "green island," or its length: it lasts "une bonne heure" (a good hour). She makes use of the new word *mitonner* in order to mock the tone and flavor of the storytelling.[27] But in 1677, neither Mme de Coulanges, her court source, or Mme de Sévigné herself thinks of fairy tales primarily as written material; they see the tales, rather, as part of a concrete social milieu—a milieu that is far from the homely, domestic milieu sketched in Percault's frontispiece.

Recently several writers have attempted to look at the conversation of the salons in its relationship to French intellectual and artistic life in the seventeenth and eighteenth centuries.[28] While acknowledging its elusiveness, they have brought out some of its crucial features: the allusive wordplay, the emphasis on repartee and collaborative exchange, the emphasis on improvisation, the absence of weighty "sujet." Erica Harth believes that the salons became "a discursive dead end for women"[29]—and, if one is primarily interested in women's becoming recognized as philosophers, this is probably true. But I see the discourse or, to use a less weighty term, "talk" of the salons as a literary proving ground—not only for the novel, as DeJean has shown, but also for fairy tales. Just as salon talk influenced the suggestive brush strokes of Watteau's canvases, it also provided the airy framework for the castles and enchanted islands that were staples of the fairy tales women wrote.

And here I mean "framework" in a rather literal way. Though Perrault often used the dialogue form in his more "serious" works—the *Parallèle des anciens et des modernes* (1692), for example—he abandoned it when he wrote his *Contes*, preferring to create the naive, solitary voice of "Ma Mére Loye." His women contemporaries, however, saw in the give-and-take of salon dialogue a useful way to introduce and frame the stories they were writing. Though they may not have collaborated on individual stories (I have found no evidence that they did), they situated themselves and their stories in this sparkling, collaborative interchange. Both Raymonde Robert and Lewis Seifert argue that the framing device functioned primarily to give a nostalgic illusion of "social cohesion" or class solidarity.[30] I want to argue here, however, that the frames had a different, and important, narrative function.

Reading tales like Lhéritier's "The Adroit Princess" (1696) in their original form, in fact, we discover that most later editions and translations have wrenched her tales out of their conversational frame. "The Adroit Princess" is dedicated to the comtesse de Murat and begins as if Lhéritier were carrying on a dialogue with her:

Vous faites les plus jolies Nouvelles du monde en Vers; mais en Vers aussi doux que naturels: je voudrois bien, charmante Comtesse, vous en dire une à mon tour; cependant je ne sai si vous pourrez vous en divertir: je suis aujourd'huy de l'humeur du Bourgeois-Gentilhomme; je ne voudrois ni Vers, ni Prose pour vous la conter: point de grands mots, point de brillans, point de rimes; un tour naif m'accomode mieux; en un mot, un recit sans façon et comme on parle.[31]

(You create the most beautiful "nouvelles" in the world in verse, but in verse as sweet as natural: I would like, charming Countess, to tell you one in my turn; however, I'm not sure it will amuse you: today I feel like [Molière's] Bourgeois Gentilhomme; I don t want to use verse or prose to tell it to you: no grand words, no startling effects, no rhymes; a naive tone suits me better; in a word, a story ["récit," which retains the aura of the oral] told without any ceremony and as one speaks.)

There are lots of interesting things here, particularly Lhéritier's claim that she has used a language that is simple and "naive," a language that is not formal but rather is written "as one speaks." Simplicity, a key word for both Perrault and these women writers when they talk about the language of their tales, is never a pure transcription, but rather a constructed and carefully pruned version of actual speech.[32] In his similar dedication of one of his verse tales, "Les souhaits ridicules," to "mademoiselle de la C***," Perrault emphasizes her ability to tell stories "dont l'expression est toujours si naïve" (in which the language is always so naïve) and her understanding of the importance of style:

Qui savez que c'est la manière
Dont quelque chose est inventé,
Qui beaucoup plus que la matière
De tout Récit fait la beauté   (*Contes*, 81)

(who understands that it is the *manner* of invention, much more than the *matter*, that is the beauty of any story)

Like Perrault, Lhéritier is creating a special, stripped-down language for her tales. Unlike Perrault, however, she does not claim to be reproducing the voice of a peasant storyteller. Rather, she is interested in recapturing the elegant simplicity of the language current in the salons, always characterized as "naive" even at its most artificial and constructed. In his recent "Origins of the Fairy Tale," Jack Zipes describes the rhetoric of the *conteuses* this way: "[T]hey placed great emphasis on certain rules of oration such as naturalness and formlessness. The teller of the tale was to make it 'seem' as though the tale were made up on the spot and did not follow prescribed rules."[33] This assumed "naïvete" and simplicity is a crucial feature of the language promoted in the salons.[34] As Murat said of d'Aulnoy's writing, in an unpublished manuscript, "elle écrivoit comme je fais par fantaisie, au milieu et au bruit de mille gens qui venoient chez elle, et elle ne donnoit d'application à ses ouvrages qu'autant que cela la divertissoit" (she wrote the way I do, as her whims took her, in the middle of the noise of the many people who came to her house, and she concentrated on her works only as much as it amused her).[35] Murat here suppresses the labor of writing; what is important is the natural *sprezzatura* of the born aristocrat, writing without constraint and without effort.

We also do not hear this informal, apparently improvisational language as a monologue, the uninterrupted voice of a single storyteller. In the passage above, Lhéritier speaks of telling a story *in her turn*; that is, she conceives of storytelling as an exchange.[36] She imagines a situation rather like the situation in Boccaccio's *Decameron,* or in Marguerite de Navarre's *Heptaméron,* or in Basile's *Pentamerone,* in which the characters in the frame-tale tell stories. This seems to have been the way fairy tales played a role in the salons: members of the group took turns, often adding to and elaborating on the tales others had just told. Lhéritier echoes this reciprocal, sometimes competitive, sometimes collaborative storytelling (a version of what Joan De- Jean calls "salon writing") in her written tales.[37]

In the earliest novels that included fairy tales—d'Aulnoy's *Histoire d'Hipolyte, comte de Duglas* (1690), for example—the tale is always told by a character in the novel, sometimes in very contrived situations. The hero of d'Aulnoy's novel tells the tale of the "île de la Félicité" to an abbess to distract her while her portrait is being painted. He is in disguise as the painter's assistant; his beloved Julie is quasi-imprisoned in the abbey. The tale—a long story that mingles classical references and motifs that the hero remembers from the "contes des fées" he has heard on his travels—seems in part to be a retarding moment, designed to build up the suspense that leads to the lovers' reunion. But it also establishes the convention followed by many of the later writers of fairy tales (though significantly *not* Perrault): the creation of a conversational frame for the tales.

At the height of fairy-tale production, five years later, the tales become a more motivated and "natural" part of the action. In Catherine Bernard's novel *Inés de Cordoüe* (1696), two rival ladies at the Spanish court of the late sixteenth century tell contrasting tales, each trying to outdo the other,, Since the queen of Spain, Elizabeth, is French—a point that the novel underlines—she has preserved the custom of holding "conversations" for four or five *hours* a day; she *is always* thinking up new amusements for the group that gathers in her "cabinet."[38] Bernard carefully establishes Elizabeth's salon as the place where the court could escape the legendary severity of Philip II, a retreat to French "galanterie" and arts.39

In this milieu, the heroine Inés tells the story of "Le Prince Rosier," a story that features appearances of fairies in miniature chariots of ivory, and princes transformed into rosebushes, but that is essentially about the impossibility of unchanging true love. Her rival Leonor responds by telling the story of "Riquet à la houppe," a story that Perrault also retold. As we saw in the first chapter, this is also, unlike Perrault's, a tale in which no one lives "happily ever after." Like "Le Prince Rosier," her version of the tale runs counter to the form we expect fairy tales to take. Both women tell stories that are marked by the marvelous: in "Le Prince Rosier" a guardian fairy and miraculous transformations; in "Riquet à la houppe" fairies and a subterranean realm occupied by gnomes. But though the decor is fantastic, the emotional climate is in fact quite grimly realistic: in both 'le mariage, selon la coustume, finit tous les agrémens de leur vie" ("Riquet," 43) (marriage, as is the custom, ended all the pleasures of their lives).

These stories suggest some of the distinctiveness of the tales the women wrote, their tendency to work against the "happily ever after" we now expect as an ending. But, in the context Bernard provides for them, they also show us the way the tales grew out of salon culture, its diversions and rivalries. Inés's tale, for example, is praised by the queen and many other members of the court; her rival Leonor, however, ~

> fit à Inés plusieurs questions sur ce conte avec autant de malice que d'aigreur. Inés y repondit avec une douceur qui acheva de la faire paroistre une personne parfaite.
>
> Le lendemain Leonor se prepara à conter une Fable, & n'oublia rien pour l'emporter s'il se pouvoit sur Inés. (45)

> (asked Inés several questions about the story with as much malice as animosity. Inés answered with a sweetness that had the effect of making her seem to be a perfect person. The next day Leonor got ready to tell a Fable, and did everything she could to make it superior to Inés's.)

To tell a fairy tale well is a way to shine in the salon; Leonor is unable to attract the attention of the marquis de Lerme, who clearly prefers Inés's story, "Prince Rosier." The entire plot of the novel—incredible though it often seems—is driven by Leonor's jealousy of Inés and her desire for revenge; the tale-telling sessions in the queen's salon mark the beginning of the conflict between the perfect Inés and her most imperfect competitor.

When they begin writing fairy tales down, then, d'Aulnoy and Bernard and Lhéritier set them in an oral situation, but an oral situation that is far from the supposed ur-situation that Perrault evokes in his frontispiece. D'Aulnoy continues to frame her tales; in her *Nouveaux contes des fées* (1697, the third and fourth volume of her first collection of stories), for example, she sets them in a double frame: first within the conversational milieu at Saint-Cloud, then within a Spanish "nouvelle": *Dom Gabriel Ponce de Leon* in the third volume, *Dom Ferdinand de Tolède* in the fourth. As the Madame D*** of the preface (a transparent stand-in for d'Aulnoy herself) says,

> Voici un cahier tout prêt à vous lire; &, pour le rendre plus agréable, j'y ai joint une nouvelle Espagnolle, qui est très-vraie & que je sais d'original, *(iContes,* 1:296).

> (Here is a notebook ready to read to you; and to make it more charming, I have connected it with a Spanish novella, which is very true and also I think original.)

The fictionalized "author" of the tales, after being visited by a nymph in the park at Saint-Cloud, offers to *read* her tales aloud to her listeners; again reading and the oral are explicitly invoked together. This motif persists throughout the volumes, as various characters in the Spanish novellas read fairy tales to each other and comment on them. D'Aulnoy, as Patricia Hannon has suggested,[40] blurs the boundaries between novel and *conte de fée,* insisting on the similarities between them. She exploits the conventions of the novel, its digressions and interpolated tales, in the *contes* themselves; the tales crystallize many strategies of the seventeenth-century romance in miniature. At the same time, however, the novellas frame the tales as verbal artifacts, as simulations of an aristocratic dialogue.

D'Aulnoy published another four-volume collection of tales a year later, *Contes nouveaux ou les fées à la mode* (1698). Again she includes a frame- tale in the last two volumes. This one, however, gives us not a series of miniromances within a romance but rather a series of tales that are constantly in friction with, and sometimes interrupted by, a frame-tale that mocks them and questions their validity: "Le gentilhomme bourgeois." The principal figure of this frame-tale—one can hardly call him a hero—begins life as the son of a draper on the rue St. Denis but decides to pass himself off in Normandy as the nobleman M. de La Dandinardiére. He's clearly a descendant of Moliére's Georges Dandin, but also of Don Quixote; his experience is always at odds with the fairy tales he begins to dream of, listen to, and even write. At the beginning, the daughters of a neighbor offer to send him a "conte" (tale) to read; he says he does not want any more "comptes" (accounts) (*Contes*, 2:161), attempting to erase his mercantile origins. (The pun on "conte" and "compte" suggests d'Aulnoy's persistent play with the tropes of the literary and the fashion marketplaces.) He must be persuaded by one of the daughters that tales are fashionable: "[C]es sortes de Contes sont à la mode, tout le monde en fait, & comme je me pique d'imiter les personnes d'esprit, encore que je sois dans le fond d'une Province, je ne laisse pas de vouloir envoyer mon petit ouvrage a Paris" {*Contes,* 2:161—62) (This kind of tale is à la mode, everyone writes them, and since I pride myself on imitating talented people, even though I'm in the depths of a province, I still plan to send my little work to Paris).

Throughout the frame-tale, d'Aulnoy identifies the writers and the readers of fairy tales as badly educated, provincial or bourgeois, and credulous to an extreme. The tales they are said to write and read out loud, however, do not seem markedly different from the tales in her earlier collection—and, in fact, are among her best known: "La chatte blanche," "Belle-belle ou le chevalier Fortuné," "Le pigeon et la colombe" among them. How are we to understand her strategy? Raymonde Robert claims that the comic and disruptive frame does not and should not affect our reading of the tales, that d'Aulnoy's aim here is not parody. But d'Aulnoy consistently stresses the discrepancies between the frame-tale and the tales themselves, at one point even interrupting "La princesse Belle-Étoile et le prince Cheri" in the middle for a long discussion (*Contes,* 2:373–74). (This interruption is omitted without comment in most versions of the tale I have seen.) The reader must move from the remote elegance of the world of the tale to a farcical conversation in which all the characters of the frame-tale pretend to learning they do not have. (For example, M de la Dandinardiére uses a Latin tag he does not really understand and is accused by the provincial baroness of having used dirty language. There is a feminist speech, as Patricia Hannon points out, but the ridiculous self-importance of the speaker effectively nullifies any impact it might have.) D'Aulnoy constantly points up the ignorance and the pretensions of the characters, mocking them and their love for her own *contes*.

Perhaps the most telling moment—the moment when this reader, at least, knows without doubt that d'Aulnoy is fooling—is when the narrator describes the manuscript of a tale that is about to be read as "fort grifonné, car c'étoit une Dame qui l'avoit écrit" (*Contes,* 2:342) (badly scribbled, since it was a woman who wrote it). Here d'Aulnoy insists on the reader's knowledge that this book is written by a woman—and slyly asserts her own literary authority while pretending to undermine it. Like Cervantes, d'Aulnoy plays with the distance between a misguided narrator and her authorial self, as well as with conflicting narrative styles. The crude narrative frame, full of comic dialogue and farcical pratfalls, highlights the ethereal dream-settings of her later fairy-tale romances—and at the same time calls their otherworldliness into question.

Her tactics here also undermine claims that her tales are nostalgic utopia, born of a desire to re-create lost aristocratic SPACES or to create new ones. In these *Contes nouveaux,* her last collection of fairy tales, she insists on the comic disparities between the worlds the characters of the tales and of the frame inhabit. The romance drama of the unrecognized princess in a story like "La chatte blanche" is juxtaposed with the comic class drama of the merchant's son trying to rise in a sharply stratified world. Dandinardière's reaction to "La chatte blanche," read to him by the local prior, is typical in its naïveté:

> [J]'étois si charmé de Chatte blanche, qu'il me sembloit estre à la noce, ou ramassant à l'entrée qu'elle fit, les fers d'Emeraudes & les clouds de Diamans de ses chevaux. Vous aimez donc ces sortes de fictions? reprit le Prieur: Ce ne sont pas des fictions, ajouta le Dandinardière, tout cela est arrivé autrefois, et arriveroit bien encore sans que ce n'est plus la mode. (208)

(I was so charmed by "The White Cat" that I seemed to be at the wedding, or at her entrance, collecting the emerald horseshoes and the diamond nails of her horses. So you like this kind of fiction, replied the Prior. These are not fictions, added Dandinardière, all this happened long ago, and would still happen now except that it's no longer fashionable.)

Dandinardière seems completely unable to recognize a fiction when he sees it—and dreams of living in a time when he could make his fortune by collecting the jewels that are always a feature in the *conteuses'* tales. D'Aulnoy mocks his ridiculous belief that he actually could be present at the marvelous events the tales depend on, his clumsy faith in their literal truth. He and most of the other readers in the frame-tale see neither the joyfully fictive embroidery of the tales nor their subversive social commentary. The White Cat's jewels intrigue him; her political wisdom and power as ruler of her realm and as writer do not.

Why have readers ignored the frames of these tales? Why have most editors (including those who produce versions of the early collections called "complete") omitted them? Why have critics in general failed to discuss the strange comic frame of d'Aulnoy's last printed tales? Partly this is the result of publishing practices, the habit of presenting fairy tales as isolated and unmediated fantasies that exist in a "world apart." (Many of these tales were published alone in chapbooks throughout the eighteenth century. Though the *Nouveau cabinet des fées*, a collection of most of the tales written after 1690, published from 1785 to 1789, included the frame-tales, most publishers continued the practice of printing them as isolated texts.) The *conteuses* often frame individual tales in typical fairy-tale style, beginning with "Once upon a time" and ending with a marriage, but they do not intend these generic gestures to become impermeable barriers between the tales and their world. Setting the tales in a wider frame, the milieu of the Parisian salons—or even in the clumsy and comic imitation salons of the provincial nobility that we see in the "Le gentilhomme bourgeois"—the *conteuses* situate them in a recreation of a vibrant oral economy. They are not simply symbolic structures, though of course they must be read as symbolic; they are also tokens of an ongoing exchange, an exchange that is part of their meaning and their value.

The conception of the oral that pervades the tales written by women, then, is not the "factitious orality" that Perrault created, the simulation of the supposed stripped-down language of the "folk." And their tales were even less designed for children than Perrault's. Rather, their written fairy tales grew in part out of an aristocratic oral culture, a culture that, though often in opposition to the official culture of the court, always distinguished itself from die culture of the "menu peuple" as well. In the dedication of his prose *Contes* to Louis XIV's niece, Perrault argues that he has included tales that show what goes on "dans les moindres familles" (in the least important families) to give her and other potential rulers some idea of what the life of their subjects is like. Lhéritier, on the other hand, explicitly distinguishes her tales from popular ones; she says that tales told and retold by the folk must have picked up impurities, much as pure water picks up garbage as it flows through a dirty canal: "if the people are simple, they are also crude (*grossière*)"

Lhéritier also claims that stories she tells come from the Provençal troubadours, and that she has attempted to imitate the purity of their morals and style—unlike the writers of the many bad novels being published in her day. Other *conteuses* appeal to other written traditions. For example, Murat in her "Avertissement" to the reader of her *Histoires sublimes et allegoriques* (1699) acknowledges that her source for three of the four tales in her volume is Straparola:

[J]'ai pris les idées de quelques-uns de ces Contes dans un Auteur ancien intitulé, *les Facecieuses nuits du* Seigneur Straparole, imprimé pour la seiziéme fois en 1615. Les Contes apparemment étoient bien en vogue dans le siecle passé, puis que l'on a fait tant d'impressions de ce livre. Les Dames qui ont écrit jusques icy en ce genre, ont puisé dans la même source au moins pour la plus grande partie.

(I've taken the ideas for these stories from an old author, *The Entertaining Nights* of M. Straparola, printed for the sixth time in 1615. Fairy tales must have been popular in the past century, because there were so many reprintings of this book. The women who have written in the genre so far have also drawn on the same source, at least for the most part.)

This passage is fascinating for several reasons. Murat makes no bones about taking the outlines of most of her tales from another, written source. ("Le sauvage," "Le roy porc," and "Le turbot" all come directly from the first volume of Straparola's tales, though her versions are much longer and more complex.) She also suggests her interest in the history of written tales, and in the publishing history of Straparola's collection. (Six editions of the French translation of Straparola between 1573 and 1612 does seem like a lot.) She places herself—and her fellow *conteuses*—squarely in the tradition of *written* tales, just as Lhéritier does by appealing to the *troubadours* and medieval romance. But they framed their tales the way they did in part to make it clear that they had little to do with the simple, uneducated teller of tales Perrault gives us. They saw their tales not as a continuation of an illiterate female tradition but as a new and powerful intervention in the world of letters.

III

Though the *conteuses* often refer to and simulate oral practices, then, they do not attempt to re-create a mythical or ur-storytelling situation. Theirs is not primarily a nostalgic art. Rather, they attempt to resist or undo the cultural notions that were coming into being as they wrote: the equation of the oral with the unformed and primitive, the equation of the written with the sophisticated. As Michel de Certeau once said, modern Western culture defines the oral as "that which does not contribute to progress; reciprocally, the 'scriptural' is that which separates itself from the magical world of voices and tradition." In their simulation of interwoven voices, in the elaborate conversational frames of their tales, the *conteuses* show that the oral can be progressive, and that the written can and often must bear the traces of tradition and myth. They implicitly challenge the contemporary assumption that the language of history, of science, of learning in general must necessarily be an abstract written language, divorced from the language of the everyday—and that women's language is necessarily trivial and childish.

The *conteuses* also do not pretend that the language of their tales had anything to do with the language of the "folk." Unlike Perrault, they do not suggest that the voices they simulate are primitive, unlettered, grounded in a long peasant oral tradition. Rather, they evoke the voices they heard every day, in the palaces, in the salons. As Marc Fumaroli has pointed out, they were interested in "l'art de la conversation et de l'entretien entre honnêtes gens, où l'art de narrer joue un si grand rôle" (the art of conversation and of dialogue between gentlefolk, where the art of narrating plays such a great role). Their tales are based primarily on written models—Straparola, Basile,. medieval romances, accounts of Greek mythology, probably the chapbooks that circulated in all levels of society during the seventeenth century. But their "scriptural economy," as de Gerteau calls it, is a celebration and interweaving of narrative voices.

Written simulations of the oral are nothing new, of course. The old tradition of frame-tales is only one example of this persistent strategy of writing. (Think of Boccaccio's nobles outside Florence, or Chaucer's pilgrims, or Basile's wicked old women.) But our persistent romantic identification of the oral with the unlettered has made it difficult for us to appreciate the many possibilities of voice in writing that the *conteuses* exploit. D'Aulnoy, for example, gives us many different voices, from the aristocratic sibyl of Saint-Cloud to the bumbling nouveau-riche Dandinardiére. The voice she never mimics, however, is the voice of the old peasant woman telling her tales.

This leads to a final series of paradoxes: Perrault in his prose *Contes* manipulates conventions of the book, both typography and illustration, in order to create the illusion of "folk orality"—in the frontispiece, on the title page, and in the crude illustrative headpieces of the tales. Lhéritier, Bernard, Murat, d'Aulnoy, and the other women writers of the 1690s, on the other hand, usually rely on the apparent transparency or neutrality of current print practices to carry on what seems to have been a living oral tradition. Instead of surrounding their tales with all the typographical signals of folk origins, they frame them in a conversational setting, a setting that marks their tales as part of an aristocratic and highly literate milieu.

Perrault, like the king in the *Thousand and One Nights*, pays apparent homage to the skills and cultural power of the female storyteller. He pretends to reproduce her voice, in a peculiar kind of narrative cross-dressing. But he appropriates that voice and that female figure for his own purposes—and, at the same time, represents her as unable to write. The storyteller is female, but the story-writer is male. Perrault creates the illusion that he is reproducing storytelling as it had always existed in oral popular culture; his simulation of its practices became the dominant style and ideology of the fairy tale, as we see in the Grimms' prefaces and most writing on the fairy tale up to our time. But the women who also participated in the invention of the written fairy tale in France created a very different illusion—the illusion that the *story is* told within the conversational space of the salons.

All these writers try to give the impression that the stories are being told aloud. They all simulate oralities, but the oralities they simulate are radically different and their methods of producing the illusion of orality even more so. Perrault simulates the oral by imitating (or inventing) the language and world of the folk and the image and voice of the lower-class woman taleteller. D'Aulnoy, Lhéritier, Murat, and Bernard, however, reject the models—of orality and of femininity that Perrault both accepts and promotes. By framing their tales with traces of salon conversation, they represent their tales as part of an aristocratic oral culture. By writing their tales down, they contest the notion that women can only tell the tales that men transcribe and transmit in print. By explicitly setting their work within the traditions of fairytale *writing*, they establish themselves as not only literate but learned. And, in a final paradox, by including traces of the oral culture of the salons, they create a new model of femininity: the woman who not only talks—by the fireside to children or in the salon—but also writes.

NOTES

1. Karen E. Howe explores the history of this connection, beginning with the story of Philomela, in her essay "To Spin a Yarn."
2. Thanks to my colleague Ann Rosalind Jones for bringing these images to my attention. (Restaurants called "Silent Woman," with a headless female torso as their logo, still existed in Maine and California in the 1970s; one advertised regularly in the *New Yorker*.)
3. Warner, *From the Beast to the Blonde*, 34. Warner concentrates on the fear of woman's speech and mentions the "headless woman" motif in her third chapter, "Word of Mouth: Gossips II," 27–50.
4. Quoted by Warner, *From the Beast to the Blonde*, 52. Warner details the connections among storks, geese, donkeys, and women at some length.
5. Carter, introduction to *The Old Wives' Fairy Tale Book*, xi.
6. Propp, "The Nature of Folklore," in *Theory and History of Folklore*, 14. Katie Trumpener's analysis of this passage in *Bardic Nationalism* brings out its crucial characteristics: "Folklore, in Propp's description, becomes the mother and prehistoric nurse, and literature the son who suckles himself in infancy

on the folkloric but who eventually must leave his mother's arms to follow his destiny" (341 n. 9). Her whole fifth chapter, "The Old Wives' Tale," is a telling deconstruction of German and Anglo-American romantic myths about the nurse figure.

7. Trinh, *Woman, Native, Other*, 121. Trinh's last chapter, "Grandma's Stories," is a remarkable treasure trove of myth about female storytelling; see, for example, these lines: "Salivate, secrete the words. No water, no birth, no death, no life. No speech, no song, no story, no force, no power. The entire being is engaged in the act of speaking-listening-weaving-procreating" (127). Warner repeats a version of it, linking mother's milk and vernacular language, in *From the Beast to the Blonde,* 169–70.

8. See Dégh's *Folktales and Society*, particularly chapter 6, and Schenda's doubts about the association between fairy tales and middle- or lower-class mothers in *Von Mund zu Ohr*, chapter 5.' •

9. Catherine Velay-Vallantin, "Tales as a Mirror," 130, and see 95–97 and 128–32. Louis Marin's analysis of the frontispiece, in "Les enjeux," also suggests the ways it plays into Perrault's literary strategies in designing his collection.

10. Velay-Vallantin, "Tales as a Mirror," 132.

11. Gabrielle Verdier, in her excellent article "Figures de la conteuse," has studied this frontispiece and others in later editions of d'Aulnoy in order to show that she rejects the model of the storytelling woman with the spindle in favor of a Sibyl-like figure. But her contention that these frontispieces show women writing seems too simple. (They often seem to be writing and speaking at the same time.) And she does not discuss the traces of salon conversation and practices that are present in the tales written by women.

12. Occasionally, as in the volume of tales by La Force in the same edition, the publishers use Perrault's frontispiece for tales by the *conteuses*. It seems impossible to determine who chose the frontispieces—publisher or author—and why. Perrault's frontispiece may have become a kind of default position: when printers were unable to find another frontispiece, they slapped Perrault's on any collection of tales. The other, more unusual frontispieces I have discussed above were consciously selected to show a different kind of tale transmission.

13. DeJean, *Tender Geographies*, 233n.

14. On words "in costume" and the effects of the materiality of print in literature for children, see Jeffrey Mehlman, *Walter Benjamin for Children*, 6.

15. Murat, *Histoires sublimes et allegoriques,* iii.

16. See Seifert's discussion of this passage in "*Les Fées Modernes* ," 142–43, and in *Fairy Tales, Sexuality, and Gender,* 90–91. In his article, he emphasizes Murat's celebration of "a distinctively gendered literary enterprise" and the rarity of dedications to other writers. Hannon in her *Fabulous Identities,* 185–86, talks about the way Murat ridicules not only the ancient fairies but the kind of story, told by Perrault

17. Murat, *Histoires sublimes et allegoriqües,* iii-iv.

18. Perrault, *Contes,* 75, and Lhéritier, *Oeuvres meslées,* 163–64 (also reprinted in Perrault volume, 239).

19. Guillory, *Cultural Capital*, 24.

20. See Dundes's essay "Who Are the Folk?" in *Interpreting Folklore,* and Roger Chartier's analogous redefinitions of "popular culture."

21. See Jan M. Ziolkowski's penetrating discussion of these issues in folklore research in his article "A Fairy Tale from before Fairy Tales."

22. In his essay "Latin Language Study as a Renaissance Puberty Rite," Ong makes it clear that "oral memory skills" and Latin were taught almost exclusively to boys. But, as far as I can tell, he does not see how narrow—and by the seventeenth century, how un-oral—his definition of "orality" is.

23. Ong, *Orality and Literacy*, 159–60.

24. DeJean, *Tender Geographies*, 47.

25. Chartier, "Texts, Printing, Readings," 170. Marc Fumaroli, in "Les enchantements de l'eloquence," argues that both Perrault and the *conteuses* use a language that is based on worldly conversation, rather than the language of the schools (184–85). See also Ruth Finnegan in *Oral Poetry*: "In practice, interaction between oral and written forms is extremely common, and the idea that the use of writing *automatically* deals a death blow to oral literary forms has nothing to support it" (160). She gives examples from British and American balladry, Irish songs, and American cowboy laments, as well as from modern Yugoslavia.

26. Sévigné, *Correspondance*, 516.

27. The neologism "mitonner" derived from cookery, where it means to simmer slowly. (It is related to the word "mie," the soft part of a loaf of bread, the noncrusty part—a word that was also used in seventeenth-century France for a governess, though that is usually thought to be short for "amie.") The word tends to have connotations of flattery, buttering someone up so that that person will do something for you. (Examples Furetière gives in his *Dictionnaire* of 1693 include "This nephew *mitonne* his uncle, so that he will make him his heir," and "This cavalier *mitonne* the old woman, so that she will give him her daughter in marriage.") But the word here seems to have slightly different connotations: the storytellers at court seem to be treating their audience, the ladies of Versailles, as governesses treat spoiled children, catering to their wishes (perhaps in order to get into their good graces).

28. These include Erica Harth's *Cartesian Women* and Mary Vidal's *Watteau's Painted Conversations*. Benedetta Craven summarizes their efforts and others' in "The Lost Art."

29. Harth, *Cartesian Women*, 17.

30. See Robert, *Le conte de fées littéraire*, 330–35, and chapter 1 of Seifert's *Fairy Tales, Sexuality, and Gender*. Armine Kotin Mortimer, "La clôture féminine," also emphasizes the frame primarily as a representation of a closed and exclusive society. For a recent discussion of d'Aulnoy's use of the frame, one that is closer to my emphasis on literary form and play (though I first read it after this chapter was completed), see Anne Defrance, *Les contes de fées et les nouvelles de Madame d'Aulnoy*, 31–91.

31. Lhéritier, *Oeuvres meslées*, 229–30.

32. For a stimulating account of the sources and principles of "simplicité naïve" in Perrault's work, see Fumaroli's "Les enchantements de l'eloquence," particularly 156–60.

33. Zipes, "Origins of the Fairy Tale," in, Fairy *Tale as Myth / Myth as Fairy Tale*, 21.

34. See Seifert's *Fairy tales, Sexuality, and Gender*, 76–78, for a very interesting discussion of salon interaction and the stylistic principle of *négligence*.

35. Quoted by Hannon, *Fabulous Identities*, 184. The manuscript, written after Murat was exiled from court, is in the Bibliothèque de l'Arsenal, 3741.

36. See Stewart, *On Longing*: "The exchange value of language, a value we see at work in oral genres even in modern society (e.g., the reciprocity of puns, the joke- swapping session) is replaced by a form of what we might, in analogy, call surplus value. Literary discourse is performed not within the ongoingness of conversation but in the largely private production and apprehension of the text …" (5). The conversational frames of the *conteuses*' tales could be seen as an attempt to preserve or replicate the "exchange value" of tale-telling in the salons.

37. See DeJean, *Tender Geographies*, 22–24, 71–77. For a brief account of the way these practices affected the transmission of fairy tales, see Zipes's introduction to *Beauties, Beasts and Enchantment*, particularly 2–4, and his "Origins of the Fairy Tale," in *Fairy Tale as Myth / Myth as Fairy Tale*, 20–23. Renate Baader (*Dames de Lettres*) also is helpful in elucidating the role fairy tales played in the salons.

38. Bernard, *Inés de Cordoüe,* 6–7. Further page numbers from this edition will be given in the text.

39. This may be a camouflaged reference to the function of the salons in the late years of Louis XIV's reign, when he was increasingly influenced by the puritanical practices of Mme de Main tenon. See Dorothy R. Thelander,"Mother *Goose* and Her Goslings," for a discussion of the "muffled aristocratic disaffection" (493) that these tales reveal.

The Green Serpent

Madame d'Aulnoy

ONCE upon a time there was a great queen who, having given birth to twin daughters, invited twelve fairies who lived nearby to come and bestow gifts upon them, as was the custom in those days. Indeed, it was a very useful custom, for the power of the fairies generally compensated for the deficiencies of nature. Sometimes, however, they also spoiled what nature had done its best to make perfect, as we shall soon see.

When the fairies had all gathered in the banquet hall, they were about to, sit at the table and enjoy a magnificent meal. Suddenly the fairy Magotine entered. She was the sister of Carabossa and no less malicious. Shuddering when she saw her, the queen feared some disaster since she had not invited her to the celebration. However, she carefully concealed her anxiety, personally went looking for an armchair for the fairy, and found one covered with green velvet and embroidered with sapphires. Since Magotine was the eldest of the fairies, all the rest made way for her to pass and whispered to one another,"Let us quickly endow the infant princesses, sister, so that we may get the start on Magotine."

When the armchair was set up for her, she rudely declined it, saying that she was big enough to eat standing. She was mistaken in this, though, because the table was rather high and she was not tall enough to see over it. This annoyance increased her foul mood even more.

"Madam," the queen said,"I beg you to take your seat at the table." : "If you had wished me to do so," the fairy replied,"you would have sent an invitation to me as you did to the others, but you only want beauties with fine figures and fine dresses like my sisters here. As for me, I'm too ugly and old. Yet despite it all, I have just as much power as they. In fact, without boasting about it, I may even have more."

All the fairies urged her strongly to sit at the table, and at length she Consented. A golden basket was placed before them, containing twelve bouquets composed of jewels. The fairies who had arrived first each took a bouquet, leaving none for Magotine. As she began to mutter between her teeth, the queen ran to her room and brought her a casket of perfumed Spanish morocco covered with rubies and filled with diamonds, and asked her to accept it. But Magotine shook her head and said,"Keep your jewels, madam. I have more than enough to spare. I came only to see if you had thought of me, and it's clear you've neglected me shamefully."

Thereupon she struck the table with her wand, and all the delicacies heaped on it were turned into fricasseed serpents. This sight horrified the fairies so much that they flung down their napkins and fled the table, While they talked with one another about the nasty trick Magotine had played on them, that cruel fairy approached the cradle in which the princesses, the loveliest children in the world, were lying wrapped in golden swaddling. "I endow you with perfect ugliness/' she quickly said to one of them, and she was about to utter a malediction on the other when the fairies, greatly disturbed, ran and stopped her. Then the mischievous Magotine broke one of the window panes, dashed through it like a flash of lightning, and vanished from sight.

All the good gifts that the benevolent fairies proceeded to bestow on the princess did not alleviate the misery of the queen, who found herself the mother of the ugliest being in the universe. Taking the infant in her arms, she had the misfortune of watching it grow more hideous by the moment. She struggled in vain to suppress her tears in the presence of their fairy ladyships, whose compassion is impossible to imagine. "What shall we do, sisters?" they said to one another. "How can we ever console the queen?" They held a grand council about the matter, and at the end they told the queen not to give into her grief since a time would come when her daughter would be very happy.

"But," the queen interrupted, "will she become beautiful again?"

"We can't give you any further information," the fairies replied, "Be satisfied, madam, with the assurance that your daughter will be happy."

She thanked them very much and did not forget to give them many presents. Although the fairies were very rich, they always liked people to give them something. Throughout the world this custom has been passed down from that day to our own, and time has not altered it in the least.

The queen named her elder daughter Laidronette and the younger Bellotte. These names suited them perfectly, for Laidronette, despite her boundless intelligence, became too frightful to behold, whereas her sisters beauty increased hourly until she looked thoroughly charming.

After Laidronette had turned twelve, she went to the king and queen, and threw herself at their feet. "Please, I implore you, allow me to shut myself up in a lonely castle so that I will no longer torment you with my ugliness." Despite her hideous appearance, they could not help being fond of her, and not without some pain did they consent to let her depart. However, since Bellotte remained with them, they had ample consolation.

Laidronette begged the queen not to send anyone except her nurse and a few officers to wait on her. "You needn't worry, madam, about my being abducted. I can assure you that, looking as I do, I shall avoid even the light of day."

After the king and queen had granted her wishes, she was conducted to the castle she had chosen. It had been built many centuries before, and the sea crashed beneath its windows and served it as a moat. In the vicinity was a large forest in which one could stroll, and in several fields leading to the forest, the princess played various instruments and sang divinely.

Two years she spent in this pleasant solitude,' even writing several volumes recording her thoughts, but the desire to see her father and mother again induced her to take a coach and revisit the court. She arrived just as they were to celebrate the marriage of Bellotte. Everyone had been rejoicing, but the moment they saw Laidronette, their joy turned to distress. She was neither embraced nor hugged by any of her relatives. Indeed, the only thing they said to her was that she had grown a good deal uglier, and they advised her not to appear at the ball. "However, if you wish to see it, we shall find some hole for you to peep through."

She replied that she had come there neither to dance nor to hear the music, that she had been in the desolate castle so long that she had felt a longing to pay her respects to the king and the queen. Painfully aware that they could not endure the sight of her, she told them that she would therefore return to her wilderness, where the trees, flowers, and springs she wandered among did not reproach her for her ugliness. When the king and queen saw how hurt she was, they told her reluctantly that she could stay with them two or three days. Good-natured as always, though, she replied, "It would be harder for me to leave you if I were to spend so much time in your good company." Since they were all too eager for her to depart, they did not press her to stay, but coldly remarked that she was quite right.

For coming to her wedding the Princess Bellotte gave her a gift of an old ribbon that she had worn all winter in a bow on her muff, and Bellotte's fiancé gave her some zinzolin taffeta to make a petticoat. If she had expressed what she thought, she would have surely thrown the ribbon and rag of zinzolin in her generous donors' faces, but she had such good sense, prudence, and judgment that she revealed none of her bitterness. With her faithful nurse she left the court to return to her castle, her heart so filled with grief that she did not say a word during the entire journey.

One day as she was walking on one of the gloomiest paths in the forest, she saw a large green serpent at the foot of a tree. As it reared its head, it said to her,"Laidronette, you aren't the only unhappy creature. Look at my horrible form. And yet at birth I was even handsomer than you."

Terrified, the princess heard not one half of this. She fled from the spot, and for many days thereafter did not dare to leave the castle, so afraid was she of another such encounter.

Eventually she tired of sitting alone in her room, however, and one evening she went for a walk along the beach. She was strolling slowly, pondering her sad fate, when she noticed a small gilt barque painted with a thousand different emblems gliding toward her. With a sail made of gold brocade, a mast of cedar, and oars of eagle wood, it appeared to be drifting at random. When it landed on the shore, the curious princess stepped on board to inspect all of its beautiful decorations. She found its deck laid with crimson velvet and gold trimmings, and all the nails were diamonds.

Suddenly the barque drifted out to sea again, and the princess, alarmed at her impending danger, grabbed the oars and endeavored in vain to row back to the beach. The wind rose and the waves became high. She lost sight of land and, seeing nothing around her but sea and sky, resigned herself to her fate, fully convinced not only that it was unlikely to be a happy one, but also that this was another one of the fairy Magotine's mean tricks. "If I must die, why do I have such a secret dread of death?" she asked. "Alas, have I ever enjoyed any of life's pleasures so much that I should now feel regret at dying? My ugliness disgusts even my family. My sister is a great queen, and I'm consigned to exile in the depths of a wilderness where the only companion I've found is a talking serpent Wouldn't it be better for me to perish than to drag out such a miserable existence?" Having thus reflected, she dried her tears and courageously peered out to discover whence death would come, inviting its speedy approach. Just then she saw a serpent riding the billows toward the vessel, and as it approached her, it said: "If you're willing to be helped by a poor green serpent like me, I have the power to save your life."

"Death is less frightful to me than you are," the princess exclaimed,"and if you want to do me a kind favor, never let me set eyes on you again."

The green serpent gave a long hiss (the manner in which serpents sigh); and without saying a word it immediately dove under the waves.

"What a horrible monster!" the princess said to herself. "He has green wings, a body of a thousand colors, ivory claws, fiery eyes, and a bristling mane of long hair on his head. Oh, I'd much rather die than owe my life to him! But what motive does he have in following me? How did he obtain the power of speech that enables him to talk like a rational creature?"

As she was entertaining these thoughts, a voice answered her: "You had better learn, Laidronette, that the green serpent is not to be despised. I don't mean to be harsh, but I assure you that he's less hideous in the eyes of his species than you are in the eyes of yours. However, I do not desire to' anger you but to lighten your sorrows, provided you consent."

The princess was dumbfounded by this voice, and the words it uttered: seemed so unjust to her that she could not suppress her tears. Suddenly, though, a thought occurred to her. "What am I doing? I don't want to cry about my death just because I'm reproached for my ugliness!" she exclaimed. "Alas, shouldn't I perish as though I were the grandest beauty in the world? My demise would be more of a consolation to me."

Completely at the mercy of the winds, the vessel drifted on until it struck a rock and immediately shattered into pieces. The poor princess realized that mere philosophizing would not save her in such a catastrophe, and grabbed onto some pieces of the wreck, so she thought, for she felt herself buoyed in the water and fortunately reached the shore, coming to rest at the foot of a towering boulder. Alas, she was horrified to discover that her arms were wrapped tightly around the neck of the green serpent! When he realized how appalled she was, he retreated from her and said,"You'd fear me less if you knew me better, but it is my hard fate to terrify all those who see me."

With that he plunged into the surf, and Laidronette was left alone by the enormous rock. No matter where she glanced, she could see nothing that might alleviate her despair. Night was approaching. She was without food and knew not where to go. "I thought I was destined to perish in the ocean," she said sadly,"but now I'm sure that I'm to end my days here. Some sea monster will come and devour me, or I'll die of hunger." Rising, she climbed to the top of the crag and sat down. As long as it was light, she gazed at the ocean, and when it became dark, she took off her taffeta petticoat, covered her head with it, and waited anxiously for whatever was to happen next. Eventually she was overcome by sleep, and she seemed to hear the music of some instruments. She was convinced that she was dreaming, but a moment later she heard someone sing the following verse, which seemed to have been composed expressly for her:

Let Cupid make you now his own.
Here he rules with gentle tone.
Love with pleasure will be sown.
On this isle no grief is known."

The attention she paid to these words caused her to wake up. "What good or bad luck shall I have now?" she exclaimed. "Might happiness still be in store for someone so wretched?" She opened her eyes timidly, fearing that she would be surrounded by monsters, but she was astonished to find that in place of the rugged, looming rock was a room with walls and ceiling made entirely of gold. She was lying in a magnificent bed that matched perfectly the rest of this palace, which was the most splendid in the universe. She began asking herself a hundred questions about all of this, unable to believe she was wide awake. Finally she got up and ran to open a glass door that led onto a spacious balcony, from which she could see all the beautiful things that nature, with some help from art, had managed to create on earth: gardens filled with flowers, fountains, statues, and the rarest trees; distant woods, palaces with walls ornamented with jewels, and roofs composed of pearls so wonderfully constructed that each was an architectural masterpiece. A calm, smiling sea strewn with thousands of vessels, whose sails, pendants, and streamers fluttered in the breeze, completed the charming view.

"Gods! You just gods!" the princess exclaimed. "What am I seeing? Where am I? What an astounding change! What has become of the terrible rock that seemed to threaten the skies with its lofty pinnacles? Am I the same person who was shipwrecked last night and saved by a serpent?" Bewildered, she continued talking to herself, first pacing, then stopping. Finally she heard a noise in her room. Reentering it, she saw a hundred pagods advancing toward her. They were dressed and made up in a hundred different ways. The tallest were a foot high, and the shortest no more than four inches—some were beautiful, graceful, pleasant, others hideous, dreadfully ugly. Their bodies were made of diamonds, emeralds, rubies, pearls, crystal, amber, coral, porcelain, gold, silver, brass, bronze, iron, wood, and clay. Some were without arms, others without feet, others had mouths extending to their ears, eyes askew, noses broken. In short, nowhere in the world could a greater variety of people be found than among these pagods.

Those pagods who presented themselves to the princess were the deputies of the kingdom. After a speech containing some very judicious ideas, they informed her that they had traveled about the world for some time past, but in order to obtain their sovereign's permission to do so, they had to take an oath not to speak during their absence. Indeed, some were so scrupulous that they would not even shake their heads or move their hands or feet, but the majority of them could not help it. This was how they had traveled about the universe, and when they returned, they amused the king by telling him everything that had occurred, even the most secret transactions and adventures in all the courts they had visited. "This is a pleasure, madam," one of the deputies added,"which we shall have the honor of occasionally affording you, for we have been commanded to do all we can to entertain you. Instead of bringing you presents, we now come to amuse you with our songs and dances."

They began immediately to sing the following verses while simultaneously dancing to the music of tambourines and castanets:

"Sweet are pleasures after pains,
Lovers, do not break your chains;
Trials though you may endure,
Happiness they will insure.
Sweet are pleasures after pains,
Joy from sorrow luster gains."

When they stopped dancing and singing, their spokesman said to the princess,"Here, madam, are a hundred pagodines, who have the honor of i being selected to wait on you. Any wish you may have in the world will be fulfilled, provided you consent to remain among us."

The pagodines appeared in their turn. They carried baskets cut to their own size and filled with a hundred different articles so pretty, so useful, so well made, and so costly that Laidronette never tired of admiring and praising them, uttering exclamations of wonder and delight at all the marvels they showed her. The most prominent pagodine, a tiny figure made of diamonds, advised her to enter the grotto of the baths, since the heat of the day was increasing. The princess proceeded in the direction indicated between two ranks of bodyguards, whose appearance was enough to make one die with laughter.

She found two baths of crystal in the grotto ornamented with gold and filled with scented water so delicious and uncommon that she marveled at it. Shading the baths was a pavilion of green and gold brocade. When the princess inquired why there were two, they answered that one was for her, and the other for the king of the pagods.

"But where is he, then?" the princess asked.

"Madam," they replied,"he is presently with the army waging war against his enemies. You'll see him as soon as he returns."

The princess then inquired if he were married. They answered no. "Why, he is so charming that no one has yet been found who would be worthy of him." She indulged her curiosity no further, but disrobed and entered the bath. All the pagods and pagodines began to sing and play on various instruments. Some had *theorbos* made out of nut shells; others, bass viols made out of almond shells, for it was, of course, necessary that the instruments fit the size of the performers. But all the parts were arranged in such perfect accord that nothing could surpass the delight their concert gave her.

When the princess emerged from her bath, they gave her a magnificent dressing gown. A pair of pagods playing a flute and oboe marched before her, and a train of pagodines singing songs in her praise trailed behind. In this state she entered a room where her toilet was laid out. Immediately the pagodines in waiting, and those of the bedchamber, bustled about, dressed her hair, put on her robes, and praised her. There was no longer talk of her ugliness, of zinzolin petticoats, or greasy ribbons.

The princess was truly taken aback. "To whom am I indebted for such extraordinary happiness?" she asked herself. "I was on the brink of destruction. I was waiting for death to come and had lost hope, and yet I suddenly find myself in the most magnificent place in the world; where I've been welcomed with the greatest joy!"

Since the princess was endowed with a great deal of good sense and breeding, she conducted herself so well that all the wee creatures who approached her were enchanted by her behavior. Every morning when she arose, she was given new dresses, new lace, new jewels. Though it was a great pity she was so ugly, she who could not abide her looks began to think they were more appealing because of the great pains they took in dressing her. She rarely spent an hour without some pagods coming to visit and recounting to her the most curious and private events of the world: peace treaties, offensive and defensive alliances, lovers' quarrels and betrayals, unfaithful mistresses, distractions, reconciliations, disappointed heirs, matches broken off, old widows remarrying foolishly, treasures discovered, bankruptcies declared, fortunes made in a minute, favorites disgraced, office seekers, jealous husbands, coquettish wives, naughty children, ruined cities. In short, they told the princess everything under the sun to entertain her. She occasionally saw some pagods who were so corpulent and had such puffed-out cheeks that they were wonderful to behold. When she asked them why they were so fat, they answered, "Since we're not permitted to laugh or speak during our travels and are constantly witnessing all sorts of absurdities and the most intolerable follies, our inclination to laugh is so great that we swell up when we suppress it and cause what may properly be called risible dropsy. Then we cure ourselves as soon as we get home." The princess admired the good sense of the pagodine people, for we too might burst with laughter if we laughed at all the silly things we see every day.

Scarcely an evening passed without a performance of one of the best plays by Corneille or Molière. Balls were held frequently, and the smallest pagods danced on a tightrope in order to be better seen. What's more, the banquets in honor of the princess might have served for feasts on the most solemn occasions. They also brought her books of every description—serious, amusing, historical. In short, the days passed like minutes, although, to tell the truth, all these sprightly pagods seemed insufferably little to the princess. For instance, whenever she went out walking, she had to put some thirty or so into her pockets in order for them to keep up. It was the most amusing thing in the world to hear the chattering of their little voices, shriller than those of puppets in a show at the fair.

One night when the princess was unable to fall asleep, she said to herself, "What's to become of me? Am I to remain here forever? My days are more pleasant than I could have dared to hope, yet my heart tells me something's missing. I don't know what it is, but I'm beginning to feel that this unvarying routine of amusements is rather insipid."

"Ah, Princess," a voice said, as if answering her thoughts, "isn't it your own fault? If you'd consent to love, you'd soon discover that you can abide with a lover for an eternity without wishing to leave. I speak not only of a palace, but even the most desolate spot."

"What pagodine addresses me?" the princess inquired. "What pernicious advice are you giving me? Why are you trying to disturb my peace of mind?"

"It is not a pagodine who forewarns you of what will sooner or later come to pass/' the voice replied. "It's the unhappy ruler of this realm, who adores you, madam, and who can't tell you this without trembling."

"A king who adores me?" the princess replied. "Does this king have eyes or is he blind? Doesn't he know that I'm the ugliest person in the world?"

"I've seen you, madam," the invisible being answered, "and have found you're not what you represent yourself to be. Whether it's for your person, merit, or misfortunes, I repeat: I adore you. But my feeling of respect and timidity oblige me to conceal myself."

"I'm indebted to you for that/' the princess responded. "Alas, what would befall me if I were to love anyone?"

"You'd make a man who can't live without you into the happiest of beings," the voice said. "But he won't venture to appear before you without your permission."

"No, no," the princess said. "I wish to avoid seeing anything that might arouse my interest too strongly."

The voice fell silent, and the princess continued to ponder this incident for the rest of the night. No matter how strongly she vowed not to say the least word to anyone about it, she could not resist asking the pagods if their king had returned. They answered in the negative. Since this reply did not correspond in the least with what she had heard, she was quite disturbed. She continued making inquiries: was their king young and handsome?

They told her he was young, handsome, and very charming. She asked if they frequently received news about him.

They replied,"Every day."

"But," she added,"does he know that I reside in his palace?"

"Yes, madam," her attendants answered,"he knows everything that occurs here concerning you. He takes great interest in it, and every hour a ; courier is sent off to him with an account about you."

Lapsing into silence, she became far more thoughtful than she had ever, been before.

Whenever she was alone, the voice spoke to her. Sometimes she was alarmed by it, but at others she was pleased, for nothing could be more polite than its manner of address. "Although I've decided never to love," the princess said,"and have every reason to protect my heart against an attachment that could only be fatal to it, I nevertheless confess to you that I yearn to see a king who has such strange tastes. If it's true that you love me, you're perhaps the only being in the world guilty of such weakness for a person so ugly."

"Think whatever you please, adorable princess," the voice replied,"I find that you have sufficient qualities to merit my affection. Nor do I conceal myself because I have strange tastes. Indeed, I have such sad reasons that if you knew them, you wouldn't be able to refrain from pitying me."

The princess urged him to explain himself, but the voice stopped speaking, and she heard only long, heavy sighs.

All these conversations made her very uneasy. Although her lover was unknown and invisible to her, he paid her a thousand attentions. Moreover, the beautiful place she inhabited led her to desire companions more suitable than the pagods. That had been the reason why she had begun feeling bored, and only the voice of her invisible admirer had the power to please her.

One very dark night she awoke to find somebody seated beside her. She thought it was the pagodine of pearls, who had more wit than the others and sometimes came to keep her company. The princess extended her arm to her, but the person seized her hand and pressed it to a pair of lips. Shedding a few tears on it, the unseen person was evidently too moved to speak. She was convinced it was the invisible monarch.

"What do you want of me?" she sighed. "How can I love you without knowing or seeing you?"

"Ah, madam," he replied,"why do you make conditions that thwart my desire to please you? I simply cannot reveal, myself. The same wicked Magotine who's treated you so badly has condemned me to suffer for seven years. Five have already elapsed. There are two remaining, and you could relieve the bitterness of my punishment by allowing me to become your husband. You may think that I'm a rash fool, that I'm asking an absolute impossibility. But if you knew, madam, the depth of my feelings and the extent of my misfortunes, you wouldn't refuse this favor I ask of you."

As I have already mentioned, Laidronette had begun feeling bored, and she found that the invisible king certainly had all the intelligence she could wish for. So she was swayed by love, which she disguised to herself as pity, and replied that she needed a few days to consider his proposal.

The celebrations and concerts recommenced with increased splendor, and not a song was heard but those about marriage. Presents were continually brought to her that surpassed all that had ever been seen. The enamored voice assiduously wooed her as soon as it turned dark, and the princess retired at an earlier hour in order to have more time to listen to it. Finally she consented to marry the invisible king and promised him that she would not attempt to look upon him until the full term of his penance had expired. "It's extremely important," the king said,"both for you and me. Should you be imprudent and succumb to your curiosity, I'll have to begin serving my sentence all over again, and you'll have to share in my suffering. But if you can resist the evil advice that you will soon receive, you'll have the satisfaction of finding in me all that your heart desires. At the same time you'll regain the marvelous beauty that the malicious Magotine took from you."

Delighted by this new prospect, the princess vowed a thousand times that she would never indulge her curiosity without his permission. So the wedding took place without any pomp and fanfare, but the modesty of the ; ceremony affected their hearts not a whit.

Since all the pagods were eager to entertain their new queen, one of them brought her the history of Psyche, written in a charming style by one of the most popular authors of the day. She found many passages in it that paralleled her own adventures, and they aroused in her a strong desire to see her father, mother, sister, and brother-in-law. Nothing the king could say to her sufficed to quell this whim.

"The book you're reading reveals the terrible ordeals Psyche experienced. For mercy's sake, try to learn from her experiences and avoid them."

After she promised to be more than cautious, a ship manned by pagods and loaded with presents was sent with letters from Queen Laidronette to her mother, imploring her to come and pay a visit to her daughter in her own realm. (The pagods assigned this mission were permitted, on this one; occasion, to speak in a foreign land.)

And in fact, the princess's disappearance had affected her relatives. They believed she had perished, and consequently her letters filled them with gladness. The queen, who was dying to see Laidronette again, did not lose a moment in departing with her other daughter and son-in-law. The pagods, the only ones who knew the way to their kingdom, safely conducted the entire royal family, and when Laidronette saw them, she thought she would die from joy. Over and over she read the story of Psyche to be completely on her guard regarding any questions that they might put to her and to make sure she would have the right answers. But the pains she took were all in vain—she made a hundred mistakes. Sometimes the king was with the army; sometimes he was ill and in no mood to see anyone; sometimes he was on a pilgrimage and at others hunting or fishing. In the end it seemed that the barbarous Magotine had unsettled her wife: and doomed her to say nothing but nonsense.

Discussing the matter together, her mother and sister concluded that she was deceiving them and perhaps herself as well. With misguided zeal they told her what they thought and in the process skillfully plagued her mind with a thousand doubts and fears. After refusing for a long time to acknowledge the justice of their suspicions, she confessed at last that she had never| seen her husband, but his conversation was so charming that just listening to him was enough to make her happy. "What's more," she told them, has only two more years to spend in this state of penance, and at the end of; that time, I shall not only be able to see him, but I myself shall become beautiful as the orb of day."

"Oh, unfortunate creature!" the queen exclaimed. "What a devious trap they've set for you! How could you have been so naive to listen to such tales? Your husband is a monster, and that's all there is to it, for all the pagods he rules are downright monkeys."

"I believe differently," Laidronette replied. "I think he's the god of love himself."

"What a delusion!" Queen Bellotte cried. "They told Psyche that she had married a monster, and she discovered that it was Cupid. You're positive that Cupid is your husband, and yet it's certain he's a monster. At the very least, put your mind to rest. Clear up the matter. It's easy enough to do."

This was what the queen had to say, and her husband was even more emphatic. The poor princess was so confused and disturbed that, after having sent her family home loaded with presents that sufficiently repaid the zinzolin taffeta and muff ribbon, she decided to catch a glimpse of her husband, come what may. Oh, fatal curiosity, which never improves in us despite a thousand dreadful examples, how dearly you are about to make this unfortunate princess pay! Thinking it a great pity not to imitate her predecessor, Psyche, she shone a lamp on their bed and gazed upon the invisible king so dear to her heart. When she saw, however, the horrid green serpent with his long, bristling mane instead of a tender Cupid young, white, and fair, she let out the most frightful shrieks. He awoke in a fit of rage and despair.

"Cruel woman," he cried,"is this the reward for all the love I've given you?"

The princess did not hear a word. She had fainted from fright. Within seconds the serpent was faraway. Upon hearing the uproar caused by this tragic scene, some pagods ran to their post, carried the princess to her couch, and did all they could to revive her. No one can possibly fathom Laidronette's depths of despair upon regaining consciousness. How she reproached herself for the misfortune she had brought upon her husband! She loved him tenderly, but she abhorred his form and would have given half her life if she could have taken back what she had done.

These sad reflections were interrupted by several pagods who entered her room with fear written on their faces. They came to warn her that several ships of puppets with Magotine at their head had entered the harbor without encountering any resistance. Puppets and pagods had been enemies for ages and had competed with each other in a thousand ways, for the puppets had always enjoyed the privilege of talking wherever they went—a privilege denied the pagods. Magotine was the queen of the puppets, and her hatred for the poor green serpent and the unfortunate Laidronette had prompted her to assemble her forces in order to torment them just when their suffering was most acute.

This goal she easily accomplished because the queen was in such despair that although the pagods urged her to give the necessary orders, she refused, insisting that she knew nothing of the art of war. Nevertheless, she ordered them to convene all those pagods who had been in besieged cities or on the councils of the greatest commanders and told them to take the proper steps. Then she shut herself up in her room and regarded everything happening around her with utter indifference.

Magotine's general was that celebrated puppet Punch, and he knew his business well He had a large body of wasps, mayflies, and butterflies in reserve, and they performed wonders against some lightly-armed frogs and lizards. The latter had been in the pay of the pagods for many years and were, if truth be told, much more frightening in name than in action.

Magotine amused herself for some time by watching the combat. The pagods and pagodines outdid themselves in their efforts, but the fairy dissolved all their superb edifices with a stroke of her wand. The charming gardens, woods, meadows, fountains, were soon in ruins, and Queen Laidronette could not escape the sad fate of becoming the slave of the most malignant fairy that ever was or will be. Four or five hundred puppets forced her to go before Magotine.

"Madam," Punch said to the fairy, "here is the queen of the pagods, whom I have taken the liberty of bringing to you."

"I've known her a long time," Magotine said. "She was the cause of my being insulted on the day she was born, and 111 never forget it."

"Alas, madam," the queen said, "I believed you were sufficiently avenged. The gift of ugliness that you bestowed on me to such a supreme degree would have satisfied anyone less vindictive than you."

"Look how she argues," the fairy said. "Here is a learned doctor of a new sort. Your first job will be teaching philosophy to my ants. I want you to get ready to give them a lesson every day."

"How can I do it, madam?" the distressed queen replied. "I know nothing about philosophy, and even if I were well versed in it, your ants are probably not capable of understanding it."

"Well now, listen to this logician," exclaimed Magotine. "Very well, Queen. You won't teach them philosophy, but despite yourself you'll set an example of patience for the entire world that will be difficult to imitate. Immediately thereafter, Laidronette was given a pair of iron shoes so small that she could fit only half her foot into each one. Compelled, nevertheless to put them on, the poor queen could only weep in agony.

"Here's a spindle of spider webs," Magotine said. "I expect you to spin it as fine as your hair, and you have but two hours to do it."

"I've never spun, madam," the queen said. "But I'll try to obey you even though what you desire strikes me to be impossible."

She was immediately led deep into a dark grotto, and after they gave her some brown bread and a pitcher of water, they closed the entrance with a large rock. In trying to spin the filthy spider webs, she dropped her spindle a hundred times because it was much too heavy. Even though she patiently picked it up each time and began her work over again, it was always in vain. "Now I know exactly how bad my predicament is. I'm wholly at the mercy of the implacable Magotine, who's not just satisfied with having deprived me of all my beauty, but wants some pretext for killing me." She began to weep as she recalled the happiness she had enjoyed in the kingdom of Pagodia. Then she threw down her spindle and exclaimed,"Let Magotine come when she will! I can't do the impossible."

"Ah, Queen," a voice answered her. "Your indiscreet curiosity has caused you these tears, but it's difficult to watch those we love suffer. I have a friend whom I've never mentioned to you before. She's called the Fairy Protectrice, and I trust she'll be of great service to you."

All at once she heard three taps, and without seeing anyone, she found her web spun and wound into a skein. At the end of the two hours Magotine, who wanted to taunt her, had the rock rolled from the grotto mouth and entered it, followed by a large escort of puppets.

"Come, come, let us see the work of this idle hussy who doesn't know how to sew or spin."

"Madam," the queen said,"it's quite true I didn't know how, but I was obliged to learn."

When Magotine saw the extraordinary result, she took the skein of spider web and said: "Truly, you're too skillful. It would be a great pity not to keep you employed. Here, Queen, make me some nets with this thread strong enough to catch salmon."

"For mercy's sake!" the queen replied. "You see that it's barely strong enough to hold flies."

"You're a great casuist, my pretty friend," Magotine said,"but it won't help you a bit." She left the grotto, had the stone replaced at the entrance, and assured Laidronette that if the nets were not finished in two hours, she was a lost creature.

"Oh, Fairy Protectrice!" the queen exclaimed,"if it's true that my sorrows can move you to pity, please don't deny me your assistance."

No sooner had she spoken than, to Laidronette's astonishment, the nets were made. With all her heart she thanked the friendly fairy who had granted her this favor, and it gave her pleasure to think that it must have been her husband who had provided her with such a friend. "Alas, green serpent," she said,"you're much too generous to continue loving me after the harm I've done you."

No reply was forthcoming, for at that moment, Magotine entered. She was nonplussed to find the nets finished. Indeed, they were so well made that the work could not have been done by common hands. "What?" she cried. "Do you have the audacity to maintain that it was you who wove these nets?"

"I have no friend in your court, madam," the queen said. "And even if I did, I'm so carefully guarded that it would be difficult for anyone to speak to me without your permission."

"Since you're so clever and skillful, you'll be of great use to me in my kingdom."

She immediately ordered her fleet to make ready the sails and all > the puppets to prepare themselves to board. The queen she had heavily; chained down, fearing that in some fit of despair she might fling herself; overboard.

One night when the unhappy princess was deploring her sad fate, she perceived by the light of the stars that the green serpent was silently approaching the ship.

"I'm always afraid of alarming you," he said,"and despite the reasons { have for not sparing you, you're extremely dear to me."

"Can you pardon my indiscreet curiosity?" she replied. "Would you be offended if I said:

"Is it you? Is it you? Are you again near?
My own royal serpent, so faithful and dear!
May I hope to see my fond husband again?
Oh, how I've suffered since we were parted then!"

The serpent replied as follows:

"To hearts that love truly, to part causes pain,
With hope even to whisper of meeting again.
In Pluto's dark regions what torture above
Our absence forever from those whom we love?"

Magotine was not one of those fairies who fall asleep, for the desire to do mischief kept her continually awake. Thus, she did not fail to overhear the conversation between the serpent king and his wife. Flying like a Fury to interrupt it, she said,"Aha, you amuse yourselves with rhymes, do you? And you complain about your fate in bombastic tones? Truly, I'm delighted to hear it. Proserpine, who is my best friend, has promised to pay me if I lend her a poet. Not that there is a dearth of poets below, but she simply wants more. Green serpent, I command you to go finish your penance in the dark manor of the underworld. Give my regards to the gentle Proserpine!"

Uttering long hisses, the unfortunate serpent departed, leaving the queen in the depths of sorrow. "What crime have we committed against you, Magotine?" she exclaimed heatedly. "No sooner was I born than your infernal curse robbed me of my beauty and made me horrible. How can you accuse me of any crime when I wasn't even capable of using my mind at that time? I'm convinced that the unhappy king whom you've just sent to the infernal regions is as innocent as I was. But finish your work. Let me die this instant. It's the only favor I ask of you."

"You'd be too happy if I granted your request." Magotine said. "You must first draw water for me from the bottomless spring."

As soon as the ships had reached the kingdom of puppets, the cruel Magotine took a millstone and tied it around the queen's neck, ordering her to climb to the top of a mountain that soared high above the clouds. Upon arriving there, she was to gather enough four-leaf clovers to fill a basket, descend into the depths of the next valley to draw the water of discretion in a pitcher with a hole in the bottom, and bring her enough to fill her large glass. The queen responded that it was impossible to obey her: the millstone was more than ten times her weight and the pitcher with a hole in it could never hold the water she wished to drink. "Nay, I cannot be induced to attempt anything so impossible."

"If you don't," Magotine said,"rest assured that your green serpent will suffer for it."

This threat so frightened the queen that she tried to walk despite her handicap. But, alas, the effort would have been for naught if the Fairy Protectrice, whom she invoked, had not come to her aid.

"Now you can see the just punishment for your fatal curiosity," the fairy said. "Blame no one but yourself for the condition to which Magotine has reduced you."

After saying this, she transported the queen to the top of the mountain. Terrible monsters that guarded the spot made supernatural efforts to defend it, but one tap of the Fairy Protectrice's wand made them gentler than lambs. Then she proceeded to fill the basket for her with four-leaf clovers.

Protectrice did not wait for the grateful queen to thank her, for to complete the mission, everything depended on her. She gave the queen a chariot drawn by two white canaries who spoke and whistled in a marvelous way. She told her to descend the mountain and fling her iron shoes at two giants armed with clubs who guarded the fountain. Once they were knocked unconscious, she had only to give her pitcher to the canaries, who would easily find the means to fill it with the water of discretion. "As soon as you have the water, wash your face with it, and you will become the most beautiful person in the world." She also advised her not to remain at the fountain, or to climb back up the hill, but to stop at a pleasant small grove she would find on her way. She could remain there for three years, since Magotine would merely suppose that she was either still trying to fill her pitcher with water or had fallen victim to one of the dangers during her journey.

Embracing the knees of the Fairy Protectrice, the queen thanked her a hundred times for the special favors she had granted her. "But, madam," the queen added,"neither the success I may achieve nor the beauty you promise me will give me the least pleasure until my serpent is transformed."

"That won't occur until you've spent three years in the mountain grove," the fairy said,"and until you've returned to Magotine with the four-leaf clovers and the water in the leaky pitcher."

The queen promised the Fairy Protectrice that she would scrupulously follow her instructions. "But, madam," she added,"must I spend three years without hearing any news of the serpent king?" • "You deserve never to hear any more about him for as long as you live," the fairy responded. "Indeed, can anything be more terrible than having made him begin his penance all over again?"

The queen made no reply, but her silence and the tears flowing down her cheeks amply showed how much she was suffering. She got into her little chariot, and the canaries did as commanded. They conducted her to the bottom of the valley, where the giants guarded the fountain of discretion. She quickly took off her iron shoes and threw them at their heads, The moment the shoes hit them, they fell down lifelessly like colossal statues. The canaries took the leaky pitcher and mended it with such marvelous skill that there was no sign of its having ever been broken.

The name given to the water made her eager to drink some. "It will make me more prudent than I've been," she said. "Alas, if I had possessed those qualities, I'd still be in the kingdom of Pagodia." After she had drunk a long draught of the water, she washed her face with some of it and became so very beautiful that she might have been mistaken for a goddess rather than a mortal.

The Fairy Protectrice immediately appeared and said,"You've just done something that pleases me very much. You knew that this water could embellish your mind as well as your person. I wanted to see to which of the two you would prefer the most, and it was your mind. I praise you for it, and this act will shorten the term of your punishment by four years."

"Please don't reduce my sufferings," the queen replied. "I deserve them all. But comfort the green serpent, who doesn't deserve to suffer at all."

"I'll do everything in my power," the fairy said, embracing her. "But since you're now so beautiful, I want you to drop the name of Laidronette, which no longer suits you. You must be called Queen Discrete."

As she vanished, the queen found she had left a pair of dainty shoes that were so pretty and finely embroidered that she thought it almost a pity to wear them. Soon thereafter she got back into her little chariot with her pitcherful of water, and the canaries flew directly to the grove of the mountain.

Never was a spot as pleasant as this. Myrtle and orange trees intertwined their branches to form long arbors and bowers that the sun could not penetrate. A thousand brooks running from gently flowing springs brought a refreshing coolness to this beautiful abode. But most curious of all were the animals there, which gave the canaries the warmest welcome in the world.

"We thought you had deserted us," they said.

"The term of our penance is not over yet," the canaries replied. "But here is a queen whom the Fairy Protectrice has ordered us to bring you. Try to do all you can to amuse her."

She was immediately surrounded by all sorts of animals, who paid her their best compliments. "You shall be our queen," they said to her. "You shall have all our attention and respect."

"Where am I?" she exclaimed. "What supernatural power has enabled you to speak to me?"

One of the canaries whispered in her ear,"You should know, madam) that several fairies were distressed to see various persons fall into bad habits on their travels. At first they imagined that they needed merely to advise them to correct themselves, but their warnings were paid no heed. Eventually the fairies became quite upset and imposed punishments on them. Those who talked too much were changed into parrots, magpies, and hens. Lovers and their mistresses were transformed into pigeons, canaries, and lapdogs. Those who ridiculed their friends became monkeys. Gourmands were made into pigs and hotheads into lions. In short, the number of persons they punished was so great that this grove has become filled with them. Thus, you'll find people with all sorts of qualities and dispositions here."

"From what you've just told me, my dear canary," the queen said,"I've reason to believe that you're here only because you loved too well"

"It's quite true, madam," the canary replied. "I'm the son of a Spanish grandee. Love in our country has such absolute power over our hearts that one cannot resist it without being charged with the crime of rebellion. An English ambassador arrived at the court. He had a daughter who was extremely beautiful, but insufferably haughty and sardonic. In spite of all this, I was attracted to her. My love, though, was greeted with so much disdain that I lost all patience. One day when she had exasperated me, a venerable old woman approached and reproached me for my weakness. Yet everything she said only made me more obstinate. When she perceived this, she became angry. 1 condemn you,' she said, 'to be a canary for three years, and your mistress to be a wasp.' Instantly I felt an indescribable change come over me. Despite my affliction I could not restrain myself from flying into the ambassador's garden to determine the fate of his daughter. No sooner had I arrived than I saw her approach in the form of a large wasp buzzing four times louder than all the others. I hovered around her with the devotion of a lover that nothing can destroy, but she tried several times to sting me. If you want to kill me, beautiful wasp,' I said, 'it's unnecessary to use your sting. You only have to command me to die, and I'll obey you.' The wasp did not reply, but landed on some flowers that had to endure her bad temper.

"Overwhelmed by her contempt and the condition to which I was reduced, I flew away without caring where my wings would take me. I eventually arrived at one of the most beautiful cities in the universe, which: they call Paris. Wearily, I flung myself on a tuft of large trees enclosed within some garden walls, and beforeI knew who had caught me, I found myself behind the door of a cage painted green and ornamented with gold. The apartment and its furniture were so magnificent that I was astounded. Soon a young lady arrived. She caressed me and spoke to me so sweetly that I was charmed by her. I did not live there long before learning whom her sweetheart was. I witnessed this braggart's visits to her, and he was always in a rage because nothing could satisfy him. He was always accusing her unjustly, and one time he beat her until he left her for dead in the arms of her women. I was quite upset at seeing her suffer this unworthy treatment, and what distressed me even more was that the blows he dealt the lovely lady served only to increase her affection.

"Night and day I wished that the fairies who had transformed me into a canary would come and set to rights such ill-suited lovers. My wish was eventually fulfilled. The fairies suddenly appeared in the apartment just as the furious gentleman was beginning to make his usual commotion. They reprimanded him severely and condemned him to become a wolf. The patient lady who had allowed him to beat her, they turned into a sheep and sent her to the grove of the mountain. As for myself, I easily found a way to escape. Since I wanted to see the various courts of Europe, I flew to Italy and fell into the hands of a man who had frequent business in the city. Since he was very jealous of his wife and did not want her to see anyone during his absence, he took care to lock her up from morning until night, and I was given the honor of amusing this lovely captive. However, she had other things to do than to attend to me. A certain neighbor who had loved her for a long time came to the top of the chimney in the evening and slid down it into the room, looking blacker than a devil. The keys that the jealous husband kept with him served only to keep his mind at ease. I constantly feared that some terrible catastrophe would happen when one day the fairies entered through the keyhole and surprised the two lovers. 'Go and do penance! the fairies said, touching them with their wands. 'Let the chimney sweeper become a squirrel and the lady an ape, for she is a cunning one. And your husband, who is so fond of keeping the keys of his house, shall become a mastiff for ten years.'

"It would take me too long to tell you all the various adventures I had," the canary said. "Occasionally I was obliged to visit the grove of the mountain, and I rarely returned there without finding new animals, for the fairies were always traveling and were continually upset by the countless faults of the people they encountered. But during your residence here you'll have plenty of time to entertain yourself by listening to the accounts of all the inhabitants' adventures."

Several of them immediately offered to relate their stories whenever she desired. She thanked them politely, but since she felt more inclined to meditate than to talk, she looked for a spot where she could be alone. As soon as she found one, a little palace arose on it, and the most sumptuous banquet in the world was prepared for her. It consisted only of fruits, but they were of the rarest kind. They were brought to her by birds, and during her stay in the grove there was nothing she lacked.

Occasionally she was pleased by the most unique entertainments: lions danced with lambs; bears whispered tender things to doves; serpents relaxed with linnets; a butterfly courted a panther. In short, no amour was categorized according to species, for it did not matter that one was a tiger or another a sheep, but simply that they were people whom the fairies had chosen to punish for their faults.

They all loved Queen Discréte to the point of adoration, and everyone asked her to arbitrate their disputes. Her power was absolute in this tiny republic, and if she had not continually reproached herself for causing the green serpent's misfortunes, she might have accepted her own misfortune with some degree of patience. However, when she thought of the condition to which, he was reduced, she could not forgive herself for her indiscreet curiosity.

Finally the time came for her to leave the grove of the mountain, and she notified her escorts, the faithful canaries, who wished her a happy return. She left secretly during the night to avoid the farewells and lamentations, which would have cost her some tears, for she was touched by the friendship and respect that all these rational animals had shown her.

She did not forget the pitcher of discretion, the basket of four-leaf clovers, or the iron shoes. Just when Magotine believed her to be dead, she suddenly appeared before her, the millstone around her neck, the iron shoes on her feet, and the pitcher in her hand. Upon seeing her, the fairy uttered a loud cry. "Where have you come from?"

"Madam," the queen said,"I've spent three years drawing water into the broken pitcher, and I finally found the way to make it hold water."

Magotine burst into laughter, thinking of the exhaustion the poor queen must have experienced. But when she examined her more closely, she exclaimed,"What's this I see? Laidronette has become quite lovely! How did you get so beautiful?"

The queen informed her that she had washed herself with the water of discretion and that this miracle had been the result. At this news Magotine dashed the pitcher to the ground. "Oh, you powers that defy me," she exclaimed,"I'll be revenged. Get your iron shoes ready," she said to the queen. "You must go to the underworld for me and demand the essence of long life from Proserpine. I'm always afraid of falling ill and perhaps dying. Once I have that antidote in my possession, I won't have any more cause for alarm. Take care, therefore, that you don't uncork the bottle or taste the liquor she gives you, or you'll reduce my portion."

The poor queen had never been so taken aback as she was by this order. "Which way is it to the underworld?" she asked. "Can those who go there return? Alas, madam, won't you ever tire of persecuting me? Under what unfortunate star was I born? My sister is so much happier than I. Ah, the stars above are certainly unfair."

As she began to weep, Magotine exulted at her tears. She laughed loudly and cried,"Go! Go! Don't put off your departure a moment, for your journey promises to benefit me a great deal." Magotine gave her some old nuts and black bread in a bag, and with this handsome provision the poor queen started on her journey. She was determined, however, to dash her brains out against the first rock she saw to put an end to her sorrows.

She wandered at random for some time, turning this way and that, thinking it most extraordinary to be sent like this to the underworld. When she became tired, she lay down at the foot of a tree and began to think of the poor serpent, forgetting all about her journey. Just then appeared the Fairy Protectrice, who said to her,"Don't you know, beautiful queen, that if you want to rescue your husband from the dark domain where he is being kept under Magotine's orders, you must seek the home of Proserpine?"

"I'd go much farther, if it were possible, madam," she replied,"but I don't know how to descend into that dark abode."

"Wait," said the Fairy Protectrice. "Here's a green branch. Strike the earth with it and repeat these lines clearly." The queen embraced the knees of her generous friend and then said after her:

"You who can wrest from mighty Jove the thunder!
Love, listen to my prayer!
Come, save me from despair,
And calm the pangs that rend my heart asunder!
As I enter the realm of Tartarus, be my guide.
Even in those dreary regions you hold sway.
It was for Proserpine, your subject, that Pluto sighed;
So open the path to their throne and point the way.
A faithful husband from my arms they tear!
My fate is harder than my heart can bear;
More than mortal is its pain;
Yet for death it sighs in vain!"

No sooner had she finished this prayer than a young child more beautiful than anything we shall ever see appeared in the midst of a gold and azure cloud. He flew down to her feet with a crown of flowers encircling his brow. The queen knew by his bow and arrows that it was Love. He addressed her in the following way:

"I have heard your tender sighs,
And for you have left the skies.
Love will chase your tears away,
And try his best in every way.
Shortly shall your eyes be blest
With his sight you love the best.
Then the penance will be done,
And your foe will be overcome."

The queen was dazzled by the splendor that surrounded Love and delighted by his promises. Therefore, she exclaimed:

"Earth, my voice obey!
Cupid's power is like my own.
Open for him and point the way
To Pluto's dark and gloomy throne!"

The earth obeyed and opened her bosom. The queen went through a dark passage, in which she needed a guide as radiant as her protector, and finally reached the underworld. She dreaded meeting her husband there in the form of a serpent, but Love, who sometimes employs himself by doing good deeds for the unfortunate, had foreseen all that was to be foreseen: he had already arranged that the green serpent become what he was before his punishment. Powerful as Magotine was, there was nothing she could do against Love.

The first object the queen's eyes encountered was her charming husband. She had never seen him in such a handsome form, and he had never seen her as beautiful as she had become. Nevertheless, a presentiment, and perhaps Love, who made up the third in the party, caused each of them to guess who the other was. With extreme tenderness the queen said to him:

> "I come to share your prison and your pain.
> Though doomed no more the light of heaven to see,
> Here let but love unite our hearts again,
> No terrors these sad shades will have for me!"

Carried away by his passion, the king replied to his wife in a way that demonstrated his ardor and pleasure. But Love, who is not fond of losing time, urged them to approach Proserpine. The queen offered Magotine's regards and asked her for the essence of long life. Proserpine immediately gave the queen a phial very badly corked in order to induce her to open it. Love, who is no novice, warned the queen against indulging a curiosity that would again be fatal to her. Quickly the king and queen left those dreary regions $nd returned to the light of day with Love accompanying them. He led them back to Magotine and hid himself in their hearts so that she would not see him. His presence, however, inspired the fairy with such humane sentiments that she received these illustrious unfortunates graciously, although she knew not why. With a supernatural effort of generosity she restored the kingdom of Pagodia to them, and they returned there immediately and spent the rest of their days in as much happiness as they had previously endured trouble and sorrow.

> Too oft is curiosity
> The cause of fatal woe.
> A secret that may harmful be,
> Why should we seek to know?
>
> It is a weakness of womankind,
> For witness the first created,
> From whom Pandora was designed,
> And Psyche imitated.
>
> Each one, despite a warning, on the same
> Forbidden quest intent,
> Did bring about her misery and become
> Its fatal instrument.
>
> Psyche's example failed to save
> Poor Laidronette from erring.
> Like warning she was led to brave.
> Like punishment incurring.
>
> Alas, for human common sense,
> No tale, no caution, schools!
> The proverb says, Experience

Can make men wise, and change dumb fools.

But when we're told, yet fail to listen
To the lessons of the past,
I fear the proverb lies quite often,
Despite the shadows forward cast.

Feminine Genealogy, Matriarchy, and Utopia in the Fairy Tale of Marie-Catherine D'Aulnoy

Anne Duggan

With the development of a proto-capitalist economy and court society, nobles, and particularly noble women who had just one generation earlier prospered in the salons, were losing their "place" in seventeenth-century France. Through an analysis of Madame d'Aulnoy's *L'île de la Félicité*, *Belle-Belle, ou le Chevalier Fortuné,* and *L'oranger et l'abeille,* I look at how d'Aulnoy creates utopic spaces based on notions of civility in order to provide a "place," or no-place (*ou-topos*) for those disenfranchised nobles.

In brief, I show that within d'Aulnoy's tales are inscribed so many salon-like spaces which are structured in a matriarchal and utopic manner. The fairy tale as a genre furthermore creates "feminine genealogies" between Amazons and fairies of times past with the salon women of the first half of the seventeenth-century. At the same time that d'Aulnoy concerns herself with gender issues, she also proposes through her tales a rehabilitated model of the feudal state in which noble men and women are equal, implicitly criticizing a patriarchal monarchy. The very genre of the fairy tale, which historically legitimated the lineage of a noble family by posting a fairy at its origin, coincides with d'Aulnoy's gender and class interests.

The rise of Louis XIV's absolutist regime marks the fall of both the nobility of the sword and the *précieuses* of the salons. Over the course of the seventeenth century, all hopes of retaining a feudal or feudal-like order were lost; consequently, the nobility lost the legitimate foundation of its political, social and economic identity. What was left of this "feudal" identity was in part recuperated by the salons. Feudalism became a sort of fashion, where nick-names functioned like titles conveying social worth earned by one's polite conversation and civility, and the salons themselves might be seen as so many chivalric orders. But what differed from previous such orders is that women were at their centers, directing conversations, prescribing a code of behavior, and affirming the equality of the sexes. Salons were influential institutions in French society, in which there developed a new nobility or elite, oftentimes including members of the Haute-Bourgeoisie.

When Louis XIV began his direct rule in 1661, the court surpassed the salons in influencing French cultural affairs. Since at least the Fronde (1648–1652),[1] salons had become rather suspect in the eyes of the monarchy as salon women such as Mademoiselle de Montpensier and Madame de Longueville, who frequented the salon of Madame de Rambouillet, became active opponents of Louis XIII's monarchy Already by the beginning of the century, nobles were losing governmental positions to the bourgeoisie and the nobility of the robe, for they represented a potential threat to the constitution of the monarchy. Writers such as Charles Perrault identified salon women, or "independent" women, as a threat both to the rule of men and to the monarchy itself. That the rule of men or parents over women was reinforced in the latter part of the century can be demonstrated in part by the laws passed requiring widows and working women to get the consent of their parents and their employers in order to marry.[2]

The modern literary fairy tale is a phenomenon of the end of the century: it is post-Fronde and post-preciosity. It might be said that the fairy tale provides a place, or rather, a no-place (*ou-topos*), in which the traditional nobility and salon women can resolve the contradiction of their very existence in a pre-capitalist, patriarchal monarchy. These fairy tale resolutions take the form of idealized feudal and matriarchal worlds, based on reciprocal relations between all nobles, regardless of their gender.

Marie Catherine d'Aulnoy, the great initiator of the literary fairy tale, created through her tales utopic spaces in which feudal lords reign independently or in harmonious co-existence with a monarch, and noble women and men live in perfect equality. Her Utopias may be characterized as matriarchal in two respects. First, women are usually the rulers, governing according to conventionally feminine values. Second, d'Aulnoy creates a female heritage or genealogy in her tales, drawing from and continuing a female mythology, indicating and inscribing in her tales a transfer of power from generation to generation of women.

This is evident in the very genre of fairy tales, for the evocation of fairies is the evocation of female powers themselves. D'Aulnoy makes this explicit in her choice of stories and characters. She draws from at least two French traditions of fairy tales, those about the fairy Morgane, who lures a mortal man into her fairy world, and Mélusine, who went to live among mortals and became the founder of a noble line. Fairies often marked the beginning of a noble family's lineage, but in d'Aulnoy's tales, they protect them. We might consider d'Aulnoy's Amazons to be fairy-like in their supernatural powers. Even princesses have fairy-powers, like their ancestors Morgane and Mélusine, both of whom where "fairy-princesses." Salon women, in their grace and virtue, are the fairies and Amazons of the recent past, leading good conversations as well as soldiers against those of an absolute monarch. By drawing from such feminine "mythologies," d'Aulnoy creates salon-like Utopias, a world in which women play an essential role in the well-being of all those worthy of entry.

That noble women are essential to a perfect society is best demonstrated in d'Aulnoy's tale, *L'île de la Félicité*, the first of her fairy tales to be published. In this tale, a mortal man, the prince Adolphe, is lured away from his cold and sterile Russia to the island of Félicité. "Félicité" refers both, and quite consequently, to the perfect happiness and satisfaction that can be acquired on the island (*eu-topos*, or place of happiness),[3] and to the princess who is the source of all things here, whose name is Félicité. Such an identification of the women Félicité with the place of the island is reminiscent of the salon, where the space of the salon is identified with and organized in conformity to the personal style of the *maîtresse de maison*. According to Joan DeJean, it was she "who dictated the style of the salon," embodying its very essence.[4] Given the structural parallel between the salon *maîtresse de maison* on the one hand, and the island-Félicité on the other, *L'île de la Félicité* could be read as the story of the rise and fall of a feminine utopic space, allegorizing the decline of the salon after its golden age as best represented by Madame de Rambouillet and Madeleine de Scudéry.

Prince Adolphe can only reach the island with the help of the wind Zéphir, for "le sort des humains est tel qu'on ne saurait la trouver."[5] Mere mortals are refused admittance onto the island, which protects itself from an undesirable "outside" by being in-suitable (in that it is no-place, *ou-topos*) and by having monsters guard its boundaries. Like admittance to an exclusive salon, only those who conform to a particular code of behavior, which consequently confers ontological superiority to them (they are not mere mortals, but wind gods, fairy princesses, characterized by their "civility"), are admitted into Félicité.

This code is indicated to us in the opposition between Zéphir and his brother winds. On his way to Félicité, Adolphe stops at the cavern of the winds. The narrator informs us of their uncivil behavior:

leurs manières n'étaient pas civiles, ni polies et lorsqu'ils voulurent parier au prince ils faillirent
à le gêler de leur haleine. L'un raconta qu'il venait de disperser une armée navale; l'autre qu'il
avait fait périr plusieurs vaisseaux ... enfin chacun se vanta de ses exploits.[6]

What makes Zéphir's brothers uncivil is their conversation: they speak only of destruction and death. In
effect, they sound like soldiers discussing battles and politics, subjects to be avoided in polite salon conversation.
So their breath (*haleine*) freezes the atmosphere. The fact that they boast (*se vantent*) their exploits shows their
bad manners and is manifested in their very nature: they are winds, or *vents*, which sounds like *se vanter.*

That Zéphir's uncivil brothers are also wind gods suggests first, that he and his brothers are all of the *noblesse
d'épée.* D'Aulnoy, as Scudéry did before her, deifies the elite for whom she writes; neither bourgeois nor peasant
have supernatural powers in her tales. Second, Zéphir's brothers seem to illustrate the violence of the traditional
nobility in their function as soldiers, defined by their physical force. They serve as negative examples of the
nobility, the image of which d'Aulnoy hopes to rehabilitate and to civilize through her tales.

But not all of the winds are so uncivil. Contrary to his cold, violent brothers, Zéphir has an agreeable "air"
about him, and is the only wind allowed onto the island of Félicité. As can be expected, his conversation is
qualitatively different from that of his brothers. Whereas his brothers speak of death and destruction, implying
relations of domination, Zéphir's language offers delectable descriptions of the island and its beautiful inhabitants, recounting not actions, but conversations:

> Zéphir disait-elle [Félicité], que je te trouve agréable! que tu me fais de plaisir! tant que tu seras ici,
> je ne quitterai point la promenade ... Je [Zéphir] vous avoue que des douceurs prononcées par une
> si charmante personne, m'enchantaient et j'étais si peu maître de moi même que je n'aurais pu me
> résoudre à la quitter, si je n'eusse appréhende de vous déplaire.[7]

Zéphir's language can be characterized by a desire to please and to satisfy his interlocutor, which, according
to Elizabeth Goldsmith, is typical of polite conversation of this period: "The classical ideal of civility, it would
seem, depends on a kind of perpetual verbal potlatch within a circumscribed social circle. Social contact is a kind
of constant circulation of verbal gifts"[8] This "verbal potlatch" assures that relations are based on reciprocity rather
than domination, for ideally everyone should strive to please everyone else within the salon, or in our case, within
the confines of the island of Félicité.

Zéphir incarnates those codes which are constitutive of the space of the island, or in other words, constitutive
of the way in which relations between people are organized: the desire to please, civility, and polite conversation. Relations in Félicité, and more generally in fairy-land, are based on reciprocity, on the mutual pleasure
or satisfaction of all those admitted. In this way, d'Aulnoy's fairy Utopias reproduce the structure of salons
such as those of Madame de Rambouillet and Madeleine de Scudéry. Although salonniers were in reality quite
politically active,"outside" politics, wars, and relations based on domination of any sort were formally excluded
from the space of the salon, from its discourse about itself, and from the conversations between its members.
When Adolphe finally arrives on the island, he discovers a world in which one need not look far to satisfy one's
needs and desires: "on trouvait dans toute L'île des tables couvertes et servies délicatement aussitôt qu'on le
souhaitait."[9] In a sense, one is like a baby in the womb, who is immediately satisfied through the umbilical cord.
This interpretation is suggested by the numerous metaphors of the womb and the female sex in d'Aulnoy's tales,
from delicious gardens to "des grottes faites exprès pour les plaisirs."[10] In one of these caves Adolphe finds a white
statue of Cupid from whose torch spurts unceasingly a jet of water, a sign perhaps of the eternal satisfaction
offered to man in this world governed by a woman.

After enjoying some of the island's pleasures, the prince finally finds the princess Félicité: "Elle était sur un trône fait d'une seule escarboucle plus brillante que le soleil; mais les yeux de la princesse Félicité étaient encore plus brillants que l'escarboucle."[11] Carbuncle has quite a marvelous history, as it was associated with both Morgane and Mélusine. By associating the carbuncle with Félicité, d'Aulnoy not only indicates Félicité's fairy-like nature, but also inscribes her in a tradition of fairy-princesses of which she is the continuation. This continuation constitutes, as it were, a "feminine genealogy," the antithesis to a patriarchal and absolutist monarchy legitimated by salic law. It is to mark an opposition to such a monarchy that d'Aulnoy alludes to Félicité as a sort of Sun Queen (Félicité's eyes, brighter than carbuncle, are like two *suns),* center and source of all light and life of the island, of this "other" heliocentric world from which linear time, changing fashions and death are excluded.

Yet, in her tale *Belle Belle ou le Chevalier Fortuné,* d'Aulnoy does find a way to overcome the apparently insurmountable opposition between the monarchy and her own aspirations as a woman of the *noblesse d'épée.* For it is not the monarchy itself that she attacks, but the way in which it is being constituted to the detriment of noble women and the feudal nobility, and to the profit of the rising bourgeoisie and those nobles who have adapted themselves to the new bourgeois order. Through this tale, d'Aulnoy proposes another solution, the re-establishment of the former alliance between the feudal nobility and the monarchy, along with the participation of noble women in political affairs.

In the beginning of the tale, the kingdom of the gentle king is being pillaged by Emperor Matapa's army In the meantime, Belle's father, a dispossessed marquis who has no sons, has been ordered to provide a son or money to support the king's war effort. D'Aulnoy parallels the situation of the dispossessed nobility to that of the pillaged king or monarch, both of whom must unite in order to ward off a dangerous and destabilizing "outside." The marquis' daughter Belle will be responsible for the economic stability of both the kingdom and of her own family, a stability accomplished only by the alliance between the nobility and the monarch. The story closes with the marriage of Belle to the monarch, a marriage which reintegrates the nobility, to the exclusion of the bourgeoisie, into a kinder, gentler monarchy.

Belle, the heroine of the tale, accomplishes such an alliance and brings stability to the kingdom by dressing up as a knight and thus passing herself off as a man. She recalls such salon women as Mademoiselle de Montpensier and Madame de Longueville, both of whom led troops against the monarchy during the Fronde. Through Belle, d'Aulnoy tries to rehabilitate the image of such women by having Belle lead troops to protect, rather than to destroy, the monarchy, at the same time that the tale pays homage to these Amazons of the Old Regime. In many of her tales d'Aulnoy contests the image of the threatening woman, demonstrating time and time again that noble women can play an active role in the constitution of a more perfect society—for both women and men. But this more perfect world is mere chimera without the complicity of noble men.

One day Adolphe asks how much time has passed since his arrival, and is more than surprised by Félicité's answer:

> Trois cent ans! ... en quel état est donc le monde? qui le gouverne à present? qu'y fait on? quand j'y retournerai, qui me reconnaîtra et qui pourrai-je reconnaître? Mes états sont sans doute tombés en d'autres mains que celle de mes proches ... je vais être un prince dépouillee, l'on me regardera comme un fantôme, je ne saurai plus les moeurs ni les coûtumes de ceux avec qui j'aurai à vivre.[12]

His first concerns are for the state of the world and of the government; that is to say, for political power which has traditionally been defined as a masculine power. His next and analogous concern is for his own lands and masculine genealogy. In this masculine world of kings and fathers, everything (*moeurs, coûtumes*) changes, is inconstant, whereas the feminine world of Félicité is constant and never-changing. By invoking linear time and patriarchal values, Adolphe threatens the matriarchal order of the island. He must therefore leave the island to meet his fate in the world of men.

It is no surprise that time, personified as an old man, takes the life of Adolphe as soon as he leaves the island. This old man symbolizes sterility and death, as opposed to Félicité, figured as the young mother.[13] By taking the life of Adolphe, Father Time also takes the life of the island, for princess Félicité, source of all life here, has now become a widow, source of tears and mourning. The departure of Adolphe leads not only to his own death, but by causing Félicité to be filled with sorrow, brings about as well the end of Utopia: the utopic world of the sun Queen has been abandoned for that of the Sun King, a world of death.

This tale is significant in that it is an introduction to all of d'Aulnoy's tales, which, although they may end with a "happily ever after," having resolved through fiction the contradictions presented by her society and can thus be qualified as "utopic," are at the same time many tales of the Félicité that was already lost. Félicité represents those salon women, centers of French cultural production in the first half of the century, who saw their decline with the rise of Louis XIV. D'Aulnoy inscribes in this tale the loss of place, of function, felt by both salon women and mothers, in a society that was becoming a court society and that was reaffirming the authority of the father in the family. Hence the need to create an-other place, a no-place or place of happiness where those disenfranchised noble women, endowed with fairy powers, find themselves again at the center of life.

While *L'île de la Félicité* tells the story of the rise and fall of the salon, *L'oranger et l'abeille* draws from the myth of Mélusine, and takes the reader back to an Amazonian past, to the "natural" matriarchal world of the "savage" ogres (or cannibals?). The tale is about princess Aimée, and her cousin, prince Aimé, who on separate occasions get stranded on the island of the ogres Tourmentine and Ravagio, far from the future destination which they will reach together, the *île heureuse*. We might envision this detour from Utopia, from the *île heureuse*, as a visit to "nature," to a lawless and thus dangerous place in which the true or natural powers of women, as well as the natural relation between the sexes, will be discovered.

Shipwrecked and then stranded on the ogres' island, princess Aimée is raised by the ogress Tourmentine, who becomes her adoptive mother. Although Tourmentine may be seen as the negative opposite of Aimée, they share, like mother and daughter, a certain "heritage" or transfer of powers. Aimée will "earn" Tourmentine's magic wand through a series of tricks to outsmart Tourmentine and Ravagio, which might be considered as Aimée's initiation into womanhood. Furthermore, they both wear animal skins, signs of women's sacredness at the time of the matriarchy.[14] Tourmentine's snake skin evokes more specifically the fairies Morgane and Mélusine,[15] both of whom took the form of snakes. In d'Aulnoy's tale, the animal skin is a sign of feminine power.

In writing his tale *Peau d'Ane*, Charles Perrault, conversely, desacrilizes the animal skin by making it a sign not of power, but of ridicule and ugliness, the result of which is becoming a social outcast:

> L'Infante … poursuivait son chemin, / Le visage couvert d'une vilaine crasse; / A tous Passant eile tendait la main, / Et tâcher pour servir de trouver une place. / Mais les moins délicats et les plus malheureux / La voyant si maussade et si pleine d'ordure, / Ne voulaient écouter ni retirer chez eux / Une si sale créature.[16]

By recuperating this ancient symbol belonging to a matriarchal past and reintegrating it into his tale in such a way as to negate its symbolism, Perrault represses an-other history or mythology in order to naturalize the domination of men over women. *L'oranger et l'abeille* and *Peu d'Ane* can be read as engagements, albeit conflicting ones, in a political debate over the definition of gender relations.

Contrary to Perrault, however, d'Aulnoy did not simply advocate the domination of women over men. Both Linda, the castrating Amazon, and Tourmentine, the cannibalistic ogre, are implicitly excluded from the *île heureuse*, or in other words, from Utopia, at the end of the tale. Like her precursor Madeleine de Scudéry, d'Aulnoy puts forth a Utopia based on reciprocity, and furthermore, on civility. Though she is stranded on a "savage" island, Aimée nevertheless builds for herself a "civil," utopic space, much as Robinson Crusoe will do one generation later. In a cave, where she takes and protects her cousin Aimé, she re-creates the comforts befitting of a princess:

> comme eile avoit beaucoup de propreté et d'adresse, elle l'avoit meublé d'un tissu d'ailes de papillons de plusieurs couleurs ... elle mettoit dans de grandes et profondes coquilles des branches de fleurs, cela faisoit comme des vases, qu'elle remplissait d'eau pour conserver ses bouquets ... ces petits ouvrages, malgré. leur simplicité, avoient quelque chose de si éelicat, qu'il étoit aise de juger par eux du bon goût et de l'adresse de la princesse.[17]

Her cave recalls those from *L'île de la Félicité*, and more generally the island itself, in that is constituted as a feminine space which provides both comfort and protection to worthy (noble) men. At the same time, the use of words such as "adresse" and "bon goût" suggests that, although she roams the island wearing a tiger skin, Aimée is nonetheless like the women of the salons.

That d'Aulnoy promotes reciprocal relations between (noble) men and women is evident in the names of the main protagonists, which mark this equality: Aimée and Aimé. In order to demonstrate this "natural" equality, d'Aulnoy temporarily inverts conventional gender roles, evident as well in the examples of Belle and Félicité. For instance, Aimée rescues the shipwrecked Aimé while hunting, then protects him from the ogres in her salon-like cave. Finally, it is by means of Aimée's wit and fairy wand that allows them to escape from Tourmentine and Ravagio. This inversion is symbolized most explicitly in the scene where Aimée turns herself into a bee, eliciting images of the natural, matriarchal society of the bees, and Aimé into a flower, conventionally a metaphor for women. The very form of the bee and the flower, in addition to their multiple attributes, further confuses (or fuses) the sexual identity of Aimé and Aimée. By situating the two in "nature," d'Aulnoy concocts a myth of a primordial matriarchal society at the same time that she affirms a "natural" equality or sameness of the sexes.

Yet, an essential feature of the constitution of Utopia is difference, or otherness. Such difference is created by the way in which the Utopian world rejects the negative or "other" outside and includes the positive or "same" within its boundaries.[18] In d'Aulnoy's Utopias, difference is not constructed on the basis of gender, but rather, on such criteria as nationality, race, class, or more generally, a failure to conform to the code of behavior constitutive of Utopia. In *L'île de la Félicité*, the uncivil winds are excluded; in *Belle-Belle ou le Chevalier Fortuné*, the alliance or sameness of the monarchy and nobility is based on their common opposition to the apparently non-European, non-French Emperor Matapa; in *L'Oranger et l'abeille,* ogres fulfill the role of the other in their cannibalism, perhaps modeled on the Indians of Brazil, so popular in sixteenth and seventeenth century *relations de voyage*; and the castrating Amazonian Linda is excluded for her extremism. In tales such as *Gracieuse et Percinet*, d'Aulnoy constructs gender sameness in opposition to the apparently bourgeoise Grognon. Only noble men and women who uphold the principles of civility and reciprocity enjoy the fruits of her Utopias.

D'Aulnoy's project is twofold. First, she is concerned with the role and representation of women, particularly noble women, in French society. By linking the salon women of the recent past to fairies and Amazons of a much earlier period, she establishes, on the one hand, a sort of female genealogy, a literary and cultural heritage or transfer of powers, and on the other, she legitimates a more active female role based on historical precedent. Second, d'Aulnoy quite nostalgically attempts to resuscitate and at the same time rehabilitate a feudal culture that has all but disappeared. Both of these objectives are opposed to the formation of a patriarchal and absolutist state that allied itself with the bourgeoisie, and whose proponents, such as Charles Perrault, call for the submission of women to men.

These objectives come together in the figure of the salon, repeated and refigured *ad infinitum* throughout all of d'Aulnoy's tales, in the nobility, civility, or more precisely, in the ontological superiority of those accepted into her salon-like Utopias, as well as in the reciprocity governing relations between the sexes. Originating in the noble milieu of the late Middle Ages and often used to legitimate a noble line by positing a fairy princess such as Mélusine at its origin, the genre of the fairy tale has historically united the notion of feminine genealogy and power to the legitimation of the nobility.[19]

It is thus no surprise that the genre attracted writers such as Charlotte-Rose Caumont de La Force and Henriette Julie de Murat, who, like d'Aulnoy, were from old noble families and provoked scandal due to their sometimes not so "feminine," and even "scandalous" behavior, questioning in their tales and their lives restrictions put to them due to their gender and an absolutist state.[20] Yet these writers often uphold the notion of nobility to the detriment of those peoples and classes who support Utopia symbolically in their otherness, and even physically, as does the virtually invisible servant class, represented in *La Chatte Blanche* "by disembodied 'little white hands.'"[21] While her status as *noblesse d'epée* and as a women impelled d'Aulnoy to question her society, she nevertheless placed restrictions on who could enjoy the freedoms and pleasures offered by her Utopias.

Notes

1. In brief, the Fronde was a general protest against the cardinal Mazarin, the principal minister under the regency of Anne d'Autriche, during the minority of Louis XIV (1648–1652). The protest was provoked by his unpopular financial policies and more generally by both popular and noble discontent with the monarchy.
2. Maïté Albistur and Daniel Armogathe, *Histoire du féminisme français,* 2 vols. (Paris: des Femmes, 1977) 1: 198–199.
3. Louis Marin argues that Utopia has two senses: "Utopie, c'est *ou-topos,* le non-lieu, mais c'est aussi *eu-topos,* le lieu de bonheur." See Louis Marin, *Utopiques: Jeux d'espaces* (Paris: Minuit, 1973) 123.
4. *Joan DeJean,* Tender Geographies: Women and the Origins of the Novel in France *(New York: Columbia UP, 1991) 77.*
5. Aulnoy, Marie-Catherine de. "L'île de la Félicité," *Le cabinet des fées,* ed. Elisabeth Lemirre, 3 vols. (Aries: Editions Philippe Picquier, 1988) 1:13.
6. Aulnoy, "L'île" 12–13.
7. Aulnoy, "L'île" 13.
8. Elizabeth C. Goldsmith,"*Exclusive Conversations*": The Art of Interaction in Seventeenth-Century France (Philadelphia: U of Pennsylvania P, 1988) 11.
9. Aulnoy, "L'île" 15.
10. Aulnoy, "L'île" 16.
11. Aulnoy, "L'île" 19.
12. Aulnoy, "L'île" 21.
13. In the tale, Félicité is surrounded by cupids, children of Venus. The tale makes of Félicité a new Morgan, who also symbolized motherhood, by virtue of the morganian plot. On the basic structure and symbolism of Morganian and Melusinian tales, see Laurence Harf-Lancer, *Les fées au Moyen Age: Morgane et Mélusine: La naissance des fées* (Genéve: Editions Slatkine, 1984).
14. Pierre Gordon,"Mélusine," *Cahiers du Sud* 324 (1954): 228.
15. Mélusine is specifically referred to when Aimé is turned into a portrait of "Merlusine," or in other words, Mélusine.
16. Charles Perrault. *Contes,* ed. Marc Soriano (Paris: Flammarion, 1989) 224.

17. Marie-Catherine d'Aulnoy, "L'oranger et l'abeille," *Le cabinet des fées ou collection choisie des contes de fées, et autres contes merveilleux, ornés de figures,* ed. Charles Joseph Mayer, 41 vols. (Amsterdam: 1785–1789) 2: 314–315.

18. Marin 141.

19. Claude Lecouteux, *Mélusine et le Chevalier au Cygne* (Paris: Payot, 1982) 36–46.

20. Jack Zipes, trans., *Beauties, Beasts and Enchantment: Classic French Fairy Tales* (New York: New American Library, 1989) 101–102, 129–130, 295–297.

21. Michele L. Farrell, "Celebration and Repression of Feminine Desire in Mme d'Aulnoy's Fairy Tale: *La Chatte Blanche,*" *Esprit Créateur* 29:3 (1989): 54.

The Heroine's Violent Compromise

Two Fairy Tales by Madame d'Aulnoy

Marcy Farrell

Violence is a fairly standard ingredient of fairy tales. In many traditional tales, protagonists suffer at the hands of their cruel adversaries, who are in turn punished, sometimes mercilessly. This essay examines two literary fairy tales that include more surprising instances of violence, wherein gentle heroines become suddenly capable of brutal acts. By examining these tales in terms of their use of and variation on popular tale types and motifs, it shows how Aulnoy's versions of these tales bring into play questions of women's power and female solidarity. Read in the light of Aulnoy's gender politics, these tales raise the issue of the betrayal of female solidarity and suggest a tragic compromise that the author's heroines must make in order to remain engaged in society.

The immensely popular literary fairy tales published in France toward the end of the seventeenth century are replete with acts of violence, committed by both antagonists and protagonists. While the rules of *bienséance* banished blood and death from the stage, scores of literary fairy tales suggesting and explicitly depicting violence, murder, and all manner of cruelty found great favor with the reading public. Most of the authors of these tales were aristocratic women, although Charles Perrault was a notable exception. Marie-Catherine d'Aulnoy, the best-known and most prolific of the *conteuses*, weaves various kinds of violence into her tales, with great imagination and evident pleasure. Based on popular folk tales and classic myths, her stories incorporate the violence that is characteristic of the oral tradition. But Aulnoy's tales are always explicitly political, and her politics play into her use of violence. While it is most often the antagonists who inflict harm and later receive cruel punishments, some of Aulnoy's noble, benevolent protagonists also prove capable of surprisingly violent acts. Here, I examine two tales by Aulnoy,"Finette Cendron" and "Chatte Blanche," wherein an otherwise exceedingly gentle, gracious protagonist erupts into momentary violence. As we shall see, this violence is tied to one of Aulnoy's most consistent themes: the critique of women who betray female solidarity in the pursuit of their own power.

For the most part, Aulnoy did not invent the violent elements of her stories. The fairy tale is a genre inclined to violence. Indeed, its basic thematic structure requires some degree of violence: fairy tales typically revolve around a protagonist who suffers unjustly at the hands of others. As a number of scholars have pointed out, even fairy tales that purport to be simple children's stories frequently involve remarkable acts of viciousness and cruelty. Such acts commonly occur as punishment for the evil deeds of the antagonist, as when Sleeping Beauty's stepmother must dance in red-hot iron shoes, or Cinderella's stepsisters' eyes are plucked out by birds. Evildoers, however, are not the only perpetrators of violence; protagonists also commit violence, often in the name of self-preservation. Thus, Hansel and Gretel burn the evil witch in her own oven, and Tom Thumb decapitates seven little ogre children, without losing their status as fundamentally good characters. Aulnoy's ^stories are full of both the sadistic violence that characterizes fairy tale villains and the punitive violence that is their just fate.

Marcy Farrell; James Day, ed., "The Heroine's Violent Compromise: Two Fairy Tales by Madame d'Aulnoy," *Violence in French and Francophone Literature and Film*, pp. 27–38. Copyright © 2008 by Rodopi B.V. Reprinted with permission.

Overtly political, her texts consistently criticize bad rulers for their abuses of power and rail against masculine power over women's lives. Violence in her tales is often a key element in her portrait of offensive monarchs or their counselors; it is also a characteristic of odious husbands. An aristocrat writing for an upper-class public, Aulnoy promotes shaking up the status quo in certain ways, particularly concerning women's place and power in society, while maintaining the aristocracy's power and privilege. Her heroines are all noble figures, conforming to the *précieuse* model of femininity[1], yet they are allowed moments of revolt. But not all the violence of her female protagonists can be understood as simple acts of rebellion. In the tales I examine here, violence is a necessary evil, a compromise that must be made in women's quest to gain power.

Although her material is largely drawn from mythology and the oral folk tradition, Madame d'Aulnoy's texts are extremely "literary" renderings, much longer and more complex than a typical oral tale. As Jean Mainil points out, Madame d'Aulnoy tends to stitch together two or three tales, though occasionally she will break a single tale into two or three separate stories. She tends to remove "popular" details and characters and replace them with aristocratic ones. She clearly had a message for her aristocratic counterparts; the "people" were not her target audience. This leads to a possibility of reading Aulnoy simply as a hypocritical elitist who stole the tales of the people for her own self-interested purposes. However, such an argument assumes that tales really belong only to a certain portion of the population, and that there is such a thing as a pure version of a tale. Like tellers before and after her, Madame d'Aulnoy adapted traditional tales according to her circumstances and her whims. Such adaptations are the right, indeed part of the art, of every teller, even ones from the privileged elite.

Indeed, no peasants rise to wealth and power in these literary tales. Aulnoy's heroes and heroines are always of high birth (although some pass through stages of rough living). Nevertheless, though Aulnoy's tales ceaselessly defend and reinforce the privileges of the aristocracy, they are simultaneously concerned with questions of oppression and resistance. Her writing is marked by an overt political and social engagement, especially given that she worked within quite severe social and political constraints. The heavy-handed censorship of the Ancien Régime is well known, and expectations for women writers presented particular difficulties.[2] Yet Aulnoy's tales offer unambiguous social critiques and call for radical social change, especially in terms of women's status and rights, but also in terms of the broader society. Aulnoy returns frequently to questions of war and injustice, and repeatedly brings up the question of monarchs acting for the benefit of their subjects. Several tales involve popular revolts against cruel, flawed, or inadequate monarchs; at least one tale includes the phrase "coup d'état"[3] The theme of social change in Madame d'Aulnoy's writing should not be overstated—it is abundantly clear that she approves of and desires to maintain the social hierarchy that favors those like her. Yet a subversive and radical current is always present. Aulnoy's tales invite us to see their seditious side—sedition not for its own sake, but as a vision of a new social order.

Above all, these tales all take on the issue of women's power in the social and political spheres. Aulnoy envisions worlds where women—aristocratic women, to be sure—wield power, both in their own lives and in the public and political world. These women are for the most part protagonists who use their power appropriately and benevolently. Yet there are more than a few evil fairies and queens in Aulnoy's work. Aulnoy's tales clearly call for change regarding women's place and possibilities in society, but they also depict the damage done by powerful women who maneuver to maintain the status quo.

---

1   See Jacques Barchilon's discussion in the preface to *Le Nouveau Cabinet des fées*.

2   Mainil notes that Aulnoy wrote during an "[é]poque où il n'était pas bon d'être 'femme écrivain' et encore moins 'femme savante,' parce que tout cela implique 'ridicule'" (26).

3   In "La Bonne petite souris" the fairy suggests: "Ne nous amusons point, il faut faire un coup d'état: allons dans la grande salle du chateau, haranguer le peuple."

Aulnoy's texts feature the two faces of the woman-mother-witch found throughout the folk tale tradition: the sage woman capable of protecting the protagonist against the wicked enemy bent on the protagonist's destruction and the evil witch-queen who persecutes the protagonist.[4] Her texts differ from more traditional, popular renderings of tales, which frequently develop either one figure or the other. Aulnoy seems to insist on the presence of both, perhaps suggesting that women must choose to act as one or the other. But this choice doesn't smack of the kind of virgin-whore or saint-witch dichotomy present in tales and texts across many cultures and eras. Rather, Aulnoy seems interested in the forms and directions that power can take and particularly in the impact of powerful women in the realms of both the personal and the political.

Taking figures and motifs from the popular, oral tradition, Aulnoy brings a critical eye to her world and writes into being new possibilities for her society. Fairy tales are typically about transformation, and often about the transformation of the powerless. They are a way for the powerless to express resistance and to envision a different, better world. Aulnoy's imagined world is defined by the presence, even the dominance, of feminine power. Yet even within this marvelous, imagined universe, this power is still limited, existing within unbreakable constraints. This is part of the realism of Aulnoy's fairy tales: the world she envisions closely resembles the aristocratic world of seventeenth-century France. It is a reality that "could be," with the help of just a little magic to make room for powerful, independent, self-determined women. Yet, as we shall see, Aulnoy's heroines are not ultimately wholly satisfied with their enchanted worlds. The real world has its attractions as well, and Aulnoy's princesses want to be part of it.

Thus, while magical, Utopian realms are a hallmark of Aulnoy's texts, a countervailing characteristic is the desire to engage fully in society. A recurring motif—that of the heroine shut away in a tower—suggests to what extent Aulnoy abhors the idea of social isolation. Again and again, her heroines are imprisoned in towers where they suffer, above all else, from the seclusion and loneliness of their plight. The marvelous universes where Aulnoy's fairies and queens reign are not depicted as lonely or isolated. But the presence of the tower, rep- resented as a harshly cruel and heartbreaking fate in so many of her texts, indicates her deep aversion to the prospect of being cut off from the rest of society. Aulnoy's heroines frequently return to society after a prolonged adventure in the marvelous. This is a pattern typical of traditional tales, where the hero or heroine usually returns to the everyday world, having gained knowledge, power, or maturity. The tales under consideration here follow this pattern, but their return to society involves a compromise not usually present in traditional tales.

"Finette Cendron" combines two well-known traditional fairy tales, or what folklorists refer to as "tale types."[5] The first part resembles the tale type "The Small Boy Defeats the Ogre" (best known in France as "Le Petit Poucet" and known in English as "Tom Thumb," or "Hop o' My Thumb"), while the second is a Cinderella story. Aulnoy's text tells of the tribulations and ultimate triumph of the youngest of three princesses. The first part of the tale, resembling the "Petit Poucet" tale, begins with the story of impoverished monarchs who wish to get rid of their too burdensome children. The family's dire straits are a result of the King and Queen having managed their affairs badly ("un roi et une reine qui avaient mal fait leurs affaires" 482), which in turn leads to their being forced into exile. The Queen is the clear authority figure of the family. Seeing the three daughters as only more mouths to feed, she accuses them of laziness (an accurate description in the case of the two elder princesses) and proposes to lead them away and abandon them in a distant forest or desert.

Finette, the youngest princess, is a clever, sensitive, virtuous heroine. Although the elder princesses are relentlessly, almost sadistically cruel to Finette, she sweetly and steadfastly forgives and protects them. Finette is twice able to outwit the Queen, but ultimately the three princesses become hopelessly lost in the wilderness. They

---

4   Merluche in "Finette Cendron" and Chatte Blanche, La Grenouille Bienfaisante, and La Bonne Petite Souris in the tales that bear their names belong to the former category; Truitonne in "L'Oiseau bleu," La Fée Carabosse in "La Princesse Printanière," and the evil fairies in "Chatte Blanche" belong to the latter.

5   The Aarne-Thompson Tale Type Index is the most widely recognized catalog of tale types.

wander together through deserted country, facing various challenges to their survival. Finally, they come to a fabulous castle, where they expect to encounter eligible young princes, only to find an ogre couple eager to devour them. Confronted with this disastrous reality, Finette not only uses her wits to overcome the situation, but she becomes remarkably aggressive, even ruthless, burning the ogre in his own oven and lopping off the ogress's head with an axe. This sudden capacity for violence is startling, given the profound virtue and gentleness that characterize Finette.

Finette's abrupt turn to ferocity is wholly justified, yet still quite surprising. At this point in the tale, she has already endured cruelty and a multitude of misadventures with grace and patience, usually finding a clever way out of her difficult situations. When the sisters come to the castle, they expect to find princes with whom to live happily ever after, but instead they find ogres. This in itself is an ironic commentary on women's experience of marriage, which Aulnoy often represents as a violent and dangerous affair. Finette's violence, however, is on one level clearly a simple act of self-defense. It is also an integral part of the tale type, which generally includes a frightful ogre who wishes to eat the protagonist, and also the ogre's wife, who provides protection, usually by hiding the hero.

In traditional tales, the hero often escapes by tricking the ogre, then fleeing. Aulnoy's text varies on this pattern in several interesting ways. While the ogress does seek to hide the girls, it is not to protect them, but so that she may eat them herself, rather than sharing them with her husband. Finette deals with the ogre by tricking him into falling into his enormous oven, a typical solution for this tale type. Her encounter with the ogress, however, is not part of the traditional pattern. She approaches the ogress with much greater caution than when dealing with the ogre, and here she does not act alone. The sisters come together to console the ogress, and Finette proposes they give her a makeover to help her attract a new husband. The sisters distract the ogress, doing her hair and chatting amicably, causing her to drop her guard. Finette deftly steps in at this moment and abruptly beheads her momentarily vulnerable enemy.

The phrase immediately following this act is striking: "Il ne fut jamais une telle allégresse" (492). Finette's violence is clearly liberating in a number of ways. The sisters are of course no longer prisoners—they are out of danger, and can now revel in the treasures of the castle. Yet Finette's act also liberates their laughter and happiness. While such joy is not unusual in this tale type, this moment of glee stands out considerably in Aulnoy's text. Ogres are, of course, an easy target for violence. Finette can hardly be reproached for defending herself, and the ogres are monsters who clearly merit their fate. Yet the scene of feminine bonding used to trick the ogress is provocative. While the ogre is simply stupid and easily fooled, the ogress must be manipulated. A parallel to the Queen who first schemes to lose the princesses in the woods and who so easily manipulates her husband, the ogress is the monstrous face of the Queen wholly revealed. This situation may of course be read as an allusion to court politics and the controversial power of women such as Mme de Maintenon.[6] Finette's violence, however, suggests more complex levels of meaning. It is not only an instinct to self-preservation, or a veiled criticism of a particular woman; it is a gesture of revolt against the figure of the powerful woman who sacrifices other women in order to maintain and enjoy her own power.

Despite the momentary joy of the three sisters, Finette is later saddened by her act. We learn that Finette "avait le coeur serré de douleur," and she tells herself,"sans moi, l'ogre et sa femme se porteraient encore bien" (493). Such regret is not common to the tale type. Moreover, Finette's sadness is explicitly tied to the behavior of her sisters, who return to their habitually cruel and nasty ways. Finette's heart aches because her turn towards violence seems to have been in vain; she is still rejected and mistreated by the sisters she unswervingly cares for. Their moment of solidarity is as fleeting as the moment of feigned bonding with the ogress. Finette's grief stems not from a sense of guilt but from a sense of loss, for she has confronted the most tragic and threatening source of

---

6   See Zipes, chap. 2, for a discussion of how literary fairy tales transformed traditional, popular tales in ways that expose the influence of the Ancien Régime.

violence in her world: women who betray feminine solidarity for their own ends. Ironically, this is what Finette herself has just done, in staging an act of feminine bonding in order to attack the ogress. If she is forced to kill the ogress in self-defense, she is also forced to take on the kind of violence she herself suffers throughout the story.

The second tale I wish to examine, Aulnoy's "Chatte Blanche," includes a tale within a tale. Like "Finette Cendron," it is a composite tale that uses structures and motifs found commonly in the popular oral tradition. It is at first the story of a prince but becomes that of a princess—one who takes over the narrative in order to tell her own story. The prince is the youngest of three brothers sent away on a series of quests by their father the king, who secretly fears that one of them may attempt to seize power. The youngest prince becomes lost in the forest, a common fairy tale motif wherein the hero passes from the real world into the domain of the marvelous. He encounters an enchanted castle, the center of an ideal, magical universe where political and personal power are reimagined and, in particular, are given a decidedly feminine stamp. Reigning over this universe is an extraordinary white cat capable of speech. She provides the prince with the objects needed for each quest, orchestrating each of his triumphant returns to his kingdom. Upon the third quest, the young prince proclaims that he no longer wishes to return to his kingdom, but Chatte Blanche refuses, insisting he must complete his final task. She then declares that the moment has come for him to break an evil spell that hangs over the castle; to do so, he must kill her. Though he protests, she insists so forcefully that he obeys, cutting of her head, whereupon she is transformed into a dazzling princess. Eventually, Chatte Blanche and the prince leave the realm of the marvelous, returning to the human world where they reign benevolently as beloved monarchs. While it is the prince who perpetrates the violence, it is clearly with Chatte Blanche that it originates. Throughout the story, she directs the prince's actions as if he were her puppet, and he is characterized by his profound obedience to her. We are surprised not so much by the prince's willingness to do as she commands, but by the command itself.

The figure of the white cat gifted with speech, whose disenchantment must occur through decapitation, is found in many tales.[7] Aulnoy's version is distinguished by the explicitly feminine nature of the castle and her development of Chatte Blanche's identity story, which comprises almost half of the entire text. Her own story in fact begins with that of her mother, whose transgressions are the ultimate source of Chatte Blanche's enchantment.

The prince's violent act and Chatte Blanche's insistence on this violence are the necessary conditions of the unveiling of her identity and, indeed, of her liberation. This is not an uncommon motif in folk and fairy tales. Elizabeth Harries, in an article entitled "The Violence of the Lambs," notes the link in "Chatte Blanche" between the necessary passage through violence and the newfound capacity of the heroine to tell her own story. Harries reads the decapitation as "sacrificial violence" which permits Chatte Blanche's rebirth into human form, but it is also a "necessary stimulus to story" (62). To further add to this discussion, I would suggest that Chatte Blanche sacrifices herself to violence not only to be reborn, but also in recognition of the violence she must be willing to accept in order to return to a more significant kind of power. Aulnoy's tale implies that such violence is a compromise that women must eventually make in order to achieve and retain power in the world.

Chatte Blanche, thus liberated by the act of violence, is able to return to herself and literally give voice to her true identity. However, the transformation permitted by the violence ultimately leads her away from the idyllic world of her enchanted castle. Restored to human form, Chatte Blanche leaves the realm of the marvelous—which in Aulnoy's text is a markedly feminine domain—and returns to the world to reclaim a political power that both she and her mother had previously abandoned. Her return to the world is a triumph, yet it is based on a disturbing condition: her symbolic death. This death corresponds to Chatte Blanche's renunciation of the ideal world she had reigned over while enchanted. Her castle is a Utopian model of good government and artistic pursuits, but it is also a realm of explicitly feminine power. For example, when the prince first arrives, he is greeted by hands that push him inside. The hands are insistent, even dominating, causing the prince enough

---

7   See the Aarne-Thompson Index, as well as Azzolina.

worry to reach for his sword, but they also appear quite feminine, described as "fort belles, blanches, petites, grassettes et proportionnées" (167). The hands promptly undress the prince and then provide him fine new clothes. Although receiving new clothes is a frequent motif to mark the beginning of the transformation of the hero of a traditional tale, the undressing of the hero is not a standard ingredient. The hands also ready the prince by combing his hair with "une légèrete et une adresse dont il fut fort content" (167). In Aulnoy's tale, these details and the feminine qualities of the hands establish the castle not only as the realm of the marvelous, but also as a space dominated by feminine sexuality. Other portions of the text represent the castle as a society where female collaboration and community are privileged. Chatte Blanche's return to the world signals an acknowledgement that such feminine power can only exist in an isolated, indeed imaginary realm. Real power, the power that truly matters, must be exercised in the imperfect, masculine world of human society. Aulnoy suggests that to enjoy such power, women must make painful concessions to the constraints of society, concessions that amount to calling for violence upon themselves. This violence is ultimately bearable because it permits women to become or remain significant players in society's all-important games of power. It is the violence of the bargain that the powerful woman must make with the world.

Of course, Chatte Blanche's symbolic death and return to the world do not imply a complete concession to all of the constraints of society. She does return as a triumphant and powerful monarch. And while her enchanted castle is a Utopian realm, the marvelous universe is not a wholly benevolent place. Although Chatte Blanche's castle is a female community based on egalitarian principles, the tale offers a counter-example in the collective figure of the cruel fairies who raise Chatte Blanche. Overtly described as merciless and violent, these fairies are at once more powerful and more despicable than any of the male despots found in Aulnoy's work.

The fairies are the adoptive mothers of the princess; it is they who transform her into a white cat, as a punishment for her insubordination. They raise her in luxury, but imprisoned within a tower, specifically isolating her from men. The princess falls in love with a suitor who comes secretly to her window; the fairies, however, plan to marry her off to a fairy king. Significantly, the fairy most directly involved in discovering and repressing the princess's rebellion is named La Fée Violente. She threatens to burn the princess if she does not open her heart to her; ultimately, she goes to the other fairies to develop a strategy to rein in their adopted daughter. They come to her room at night, accompanied by their dragon, planning to bind her hands and feet and turn her over to the fairy king. They surprise the princess with her lover, whom they command the dragon to devour. When the princess tries to follow her lover into death by offering herself to the dragon, the fairies prevent her from doing so, saying,"il faut […] la réserver à de plus longues peines, une prompte mort est trop douce pour cette indigne créature" (513). It is at this point that the fairies, whom the text describes as "encore plus cruelles que le dragon" (513), transform the princess into a white cat and banish her to a faraway realm. Of course, this "punishment" turns out to be a great gift in many ways, since Chatte Blanche then reigns over a marvelous, ideal universe. But the origin of the enchantment is narrated as part of the fairies' vicious cruelty, and their desire to hurt and isolate the princess. A representation of harsh, corrupted feminine power, these fairies suggest the ways in which women can be powerful in the real world, not only by adopting, but also by exaggerating, the abusive strategies that men and monarchs use in order to conserve power.

Chatte Blanche can escape the fairies' enchantment only by submitting to violence, and indeed, by inviting violence upon herself. However, Aulnoy's tale does not abandon its earlier optimism and idealism, despite the violence at its core. Chatte Blanche's return to power in the world does not require her to become cruel, vicious, and manipulative. In this way, she is spared the kind of heartbreak Finette Cendron suffers after her turn to violence.

Both Finette and Chatte Blanche appear to be liberated by violence, but it is violence that is ultimately part of a tragic compromise. While these heroines are clearly rebels, the violence in these tales is not that of rebellion. In fact, one of the characteristics that distinguish these heroines is their general disinclination to violence, particularly the manipulative violence perpetrated by women against other women. This is the most tragic kind of violence in Aulnoy's work, the kind for which she cannot imagine a real solution. It is, finally, the most realistic violence represented in these magical tales—a violence that even enchantment cannot overcome.

Works Cited

Aarne, Antti. *The Types of the Folktale: a Classification and Bibliography.* Antti Aarne's *Verzeichnis der Märchentypen.* Trans, and enlarged by Stith Thompson. Helsinki: Academia Scientarum Fennica, 1961.

Aulnoy, Marie-Catherine. "Chatte Blanche," "Finette Cendron." *Le Nouveau Cabinet des fées.* Ed. Jacques Barchilon. Geneva: Slatkine, 1978.

Azzolina, David. *Tale Type and Motif Indexes: An Annotated Bibliography.* New York: Garland, 1987.

Barchilon, Jacques. *Le Nouveau Cabinet des fees.* Geneva: Slatkine, 1978.

Harries, Elizabeth. "The Violence of the Lambs." *Marvels and Tales* 19.1 (2005)54–66.

Mainil, Jean. *Madame d'Aulnoy et le rire des fées: essai sur la subversion féerique et le merveilleux comique sous l'Ancien Régime.* Paris: Kime, 2001.

Zipes, Jack. *Fairy Tales and the Art of Subversion.* New York: Routledge, 1991.

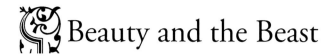

Beauty and the Beast

Madame Leprince de Beaumont

There was once a very rich merchant, who had six children, three boys and three girls. As he was himself a man of great sense, he spared no expense for their education. The three daughters were all handsome, particularly the youngest; indeed, she was so very beautiful that in her childhood everyone called her the Little Beauty; and being just as lovely when she was grown up, nobody called her by any other name, which made her sisters very jealous of her. This youngest daughter was not only more handsome than her sisters, she was also better tempered. The two eldest were vain of their wealth and position. They gave themselves a thousand airs, and refused to visit other merchants' daughters; nor would they condescend to be seen except with persons of quality. They went every day to balls, plays, and on public walks, and always made game of their youngest sister for spending her tithe in reading or other useful employments. As it was well known that these young ladies would have large fortunes, many great merchants wished to get them for wives; but the two eldest always answered that for their parts they had no thoughts of marrying anyone below a duke or an earl at the very least. Beauty had quite as many offers as her sisters, but she always answered with the greatest civility that though she was much obliged to her lovers, she would rather live some years longer with her father, as she thought herself too young to marry.

It happened that by some unlucky accident the merchant suddenly lost all his fortune, and had nothing left but a small cottage in the country. Upon this he said to his daughters, while the tears ran down his cheeks,"My children, we must now go and dwell in the cottage, and try to get a living by labour, for we have no other means of support." The two eldest replied that they did not know how to work, and would not leave town; for they had lovers enough who would be glad to marry them, though they had no longer any fortune. But in this they were mistaken, for when the lovers heard what had happened, they said,"The girls were so proud and ill-tempered, that all we wanted was their fortune: we are not sorry at all to see their pride brought down: let them show off their airs to their cows and sheep." But everybody pitied poor Beauty, because she was so sweet-tempered and kind to all, and several gentlemen offered to marry her though she had not a penny; but Beauty still refused, and said she could not think of leaving her poor father in his trouble. At first Beauty could not help sometimes crying in secret for the hardships she was now obliged to suffer; but in a very short time she said to herself,"All the crying in the world will do me no good, so I will try to be happy without a fortune." When they had removed to their cottage, the merchant and his three sons employed themselves in ploughing and sowing the fields, and working in the garden. Beauty also did her part, for she rose by four o'clock every morning, lighted the fires, cleaned the house, and got ready the breakfast for the whole family. At first she found all this very hard; but she soon grew quite used to it, and thought it no hardship; indeed, the work greatly benefited her health. When she had done she used to amuse; herself with reading, playing her music, or singing while she spun. But her two sisters were at a loss what to do to pass the time away: they had their breakfast in bed, and did not rise till ten o'clock. Then they commonly walked out, but always found themselves very soon tired; when they would often sit down under a shady tree and grieve for the loss of their carriage and fine clothes, and say to each other,"What a mean-spirited poor stupid creature our young sister is, to be so content with this low way of life!" But their father thought differently: and loved and admired his youngest child more than ever,

After they had lived in this manner about a year, the merchant received a letter, which informed him that one of his richest ships which he thought was lost had just come into port. This news made the two eldest almost mad with joy; for they thought they should now leave the cottage and have all their finery again. When they found that their father must take a journey to the ship, the two eldest begged he would not fail to bring them back some new gowns, caps, rings, and all sorts of trinkets. But Beauty asked for nothing; for she thought to herself that all the ship was worth would hardly buy everything her sisters wished for. "Beauty," said the merchant,"how comes it that you ask for nothing: what can I bring you, my child?"

"Since you are so kind as to think of me, dear father," she answered,"I should be glad if you would bring me a rose, for we have none in our garden." Now Beauty did not indeed wish for a rose, nor anything else, but she only said this that she might not affront her sisters; otherwise they would have said she wanted her father to praise her for desiring nothing. The merchant took his leave of them, and set out on his journey; but when he got to the ship, some persons went to law with him about the cargo, and after a deal of trouble he came back to his cottage as poor as he had left it. When he was within thirty miles of his home, and thinking of the joy of again meeting his children, he lost his way in the midst of a dense forest. It rained and snowed very hard, and besides, the wind was so high as to throw him twice from his horse. Night came on, and he feared he should die of cold and hunger, or be torn to pieces by the wolves that he heard howling round him. All at once he cast his eyes towards a long avenue, and saw at the end a light, but it seemed a great way off. He made the best of his way towards it, and found that it came from a splendid palace, the windows of which were all blazing with light. It had great bronze gates, standing wide open, and fine courtyards, through which, the merchant passed; but not a living soul was to be seen. There were stables too, which his poor, starved horse, less scrupulous than himself, entered at once, and took a good meal of oats and hay:'-His master then tied him up, and walked towards the entrance hall, but still without seeing a single creature. He went into a large dining parlour, where he found a good fire, and a table covered with some very nice dishes, but only one plate with a knife and fork. As the snow and rain had wetted him to the skin, he went up to the fire to dry himself. "I hope," said he,"the master of the house or his servants will excuse me, for it surely will not be long now before I see them." He waited some time, but nobody came: at last the clock struck eleven, and the merchant, being quite faint for want of food, helped himself to a chicken and to a few glasses of wine, yet all the time trembling with fear. "He sat till the clock struck twelve, and then, taking courage; began to think he might as well look about him: so he opened a door at the end of the hall and went through it into a very grand room, in which there was a fine bed; and as he was feeling very weary, he shut the door, took off his clothes, and got into it.

It was ten o'clock in the morning before he awoke, when he was amazed to see a handsome new suit of clothes laid ready for him, instead of his own, which were all torn and spoiled. "To be sure," said he to himself,"this place belongs to some good fairy, who has taken pity on my ill luck." He looked out of the window, and instead of the snow-covered wood where he had lost himself the previous night, he saw the most charming arbours covered with all kinds, of flowers. Returning to the hall where he had supped, he found a breakfast table, ready prepared. "Indeed, my good fairy," said the merchant aloud,"I am vastly obliged to you for your kind care of me." He then made a hearty breakfast, took his hat, and was going to the: stable to see his horse; but as he passed under one of the arbours, which was loaded with roses, he thought of what Beauty had asked him to bring back to her, so he took a bunch of roses to carry home. At the same moment he heard a loud noise, and saw coming towards him a beast, so frightful to look at that he was ready to, faint with fear. "Ungrateful man!" said the beast in a terrible voice,"I have saved your life by admitting you into my palace,, and in return you steal my roses which I value more than anything I possess. But you shall atone for your fault: you shall die in a quarter of an hour."

The merchant fell on his knees, and clasping his hands, said,"Sir, I humbly beg your pardon: I did not think it would offend you in gathering a rose for one of my daughters, who had entreated me to bring her one home. Do not kill me, my lord!"

"I am not a lord, but a beast," replied the monster; "I hate false compliments: so do not fancy, that you can coax me by any such ways. You tell me that you have daughters; now I will suffer you to escape, if one of them will come and die in your stead. If not, promise that you will yourself return in three months, to be dealt with as I may choose."

The tender-hearted merchant had no thoughts of letting any one of his daughters die for his sake; but he knew that if he seemed to accept the beast's terms, he should at least have the pleasure of seeing them once again. So he gave his promise, and was told he might then set off as soon as he liked. "But," said the beast,"I do not wish you to go back empty-handed. Go to the room you slept in, and you will find a chest there; fill it with whatsoever you like best, and I will have it taken to your own house for you."

When the beast had said this, he went away. The good merchant, left to himself, began to consider that as he must die—for he had no thought of breaking a promise, made even to a beast- he might as we'll have the comfort of leaving his children provided for. He returned to- the room he had slept in, and found there heaps of gold pieces lying about. He filled the chest with them to the very brim, locked it and, mounting his horse, left the palace as sorrowful as he had been glad when he first beheld it. The horse took a path across the forest of his own accord, and in à few hours they reached the merchant's house. His children came running round him, but instead of kissing them with joy, he could not help weeping as he looked at them. He held in his hand the bunch of roses, which he gave to Beauty saying,"Take these roses, Beauty; but little do you think how dear they have cost your poor father"; and then he gave them an account of all that he had seen or heard in the palace of the beast.

The two eldest sisters now began to shed tears, and to lay the blame upon Beauty who, they said, would be the cause of her father's death. "See," said they,"what happens from the pride of the little wretch; why did she not ask for such things as we did? But to be sure, miss must not be like other people; and though she will be the cause of her father's death, yet she does not shed a tear."

"It would be useless," replied Beauty,"for my father shall not die. As the beast will accept one of his daughters, I will give myself up, and be only too happy to prove my love for the best of fathers."

"No, sister," said the three brothers with one voice,"that cannot be; we will go in search of this monster, and either he or we will perish."

"Do not hope to kill him," said the merchant,"his power is far too great. But Beauty's young life shall not be sacrificed: I am old and cannot expect to live much longer; so I shall but give up a few years of my life, and shall only grieve for the sake of my children."

"Never, father" cried Beauty. "If you go back to the palace you cannot hinder my going after you; though young I am not over-fond of life; and I would much rather be eaten up by the monster than die of grief for your loss."

The merchant in vain tried to reason with Beauty,, who still obstinately kept to her purpose; which, in truth, made her two sisters glad, for they were jealous of her, because everybody loved her.

The merchant was so grieved at the thoughts of losing his child that he never once thought of the chest filled with gold, but at night, to his great surprise, he found it standing by his bedside. He said nothing about his riches to his eldest daughters, for he knew very well it would at once make them want to return to town; but he told Beauty his secret, and she then said that while he was away two gentlemen had been on a visit at their cottage, who had fallen in love with her two sisters. She entreated her father to marry them without delay, for she was so sweet-natured she only wished them to be happy.

Three months went by, only too fast, and then the merchant and Beauty got ready to set out for the palace of the beast. Upon this the two sisters rubbed their eyes with an onion, to make believe they were crying; both the merchant and his sons cried in earnest. Only Beauty shed no tears. They reached the palace in a very few hours, and the horse, without bidding, went into the same stable as before. The merchant and Beauty walked towards the large hall, where they found a table covered with every dainty, and two plates laid ready. The merchant had very little appetite; but Beauty, that she might the better hide her grief, placed herself at the table and helped her father; she then began to eat herself, and thought all the time that, to be sure, the beast had a mind to fatten her before he ate her up, since he had provided such good cheer for her. When they had done their supper they heard: a great noise, and the good old man began to bid his poor child farewell, for he knew it was the beast coming to them. When Beauty first saw that frightful form she was very much terrified, but tried to hide her fear. The creature walked up to her, and eyed her all over—then asked her in a dreadful voice if she had come quite of her own accord.

"Yes," said Beauty.

"Then you are a good girl, and I am very much obliged to you."

This was such an astonishingly civil answer that Beauty's courage rose: but it sank again when the beast, addressing the merchant, desired him to leave the palace next morning, and never returned to it again. "And so good night, merchant. And good night, Beauty."

"Good night, beast," she answered, as the monster shuffled out of the room.

"Ah! my dear child," said the merchant; kissing his daughter,"I am half dead already, at the thought of leaving you with this dreadful beast; you shall go back and let me stay in your place."

"No," said Beauty, boldly,"I will never agree to that; you must go home tomorrow morning."

They then wished-each other good night and went to bed, both of them thinking they should not be able to close their eyes; but as soon as ever they had lain down, they fell into a deep sleep, and did not awake till morning. Beauty dreamed that a lady came up to her, who said','"I am very much pleased, Beauty, with the goodness you have shown, in being willing to give your life to save that of your father. Do not be afraid of anything: you shall not go without a reward."

As soon as Beauty awoke she told her father this,dream; but though it gave him some comfort he was a long time before he could be persuaded to leave the palace. At last Beauty succeeded in getting him safely away.

When her father was out of sight poor Beauty began to weep sorely; still, having naturally a courageous spirit, she soon resolved not to make her sad case still worse by sorrow, which she knew was vain, but to wait and be patient. She walked about to take a view of all the palace, and the elegance of every part of it much charmed her.

But what was her surprise when she came to a door on which was written, BEAUTY'S ROOM! She opened it in haste, and her eyes were dazzled by the splendour and taste of the apartment. What made her wonder more than all the rest was a large library filled with books, a harpsichord and many pieces of music. "The beast surely does not mean to eat me up immediately," said she,"since he takes care I shall not be at a loss how to amuse myself." She opened the library and saw these verses written in letters of gold on the back of one of the books:

"Beauteous lady, dry your tears.
Here's no cause for sighs or fears.
Command as freely as you may,
For you command and I obey."

"Alas!" said she, sighing; "I wish I could only command a sight of my poor father, and to know what he is doing at this moment." Just then, by chance, she cast her eyes at a looking- glass that stood near her, and in it she saw a picture of her old home, and her father riding mournfully up to the door. Her sisters came out to meet him, and although they tried to look sorry, it was easy to see that in their hearts they were very glad. In a short time all this picture disappeared, but it caused Beauty to think that the beast, besides being very powerful, was also very kind. About the middle of the day she found a table laid ready for her, and a sweet concert of music played all the time she was dining, without her seeing anybody. But at supper, when she was going to seat herself at table, she heard the noise of the beast, and could not help trembling with fear.

"Beauty," said he,"will you give me leave to see you sup?"

"That is as you- please," answered she, very much afraid.

"Not in the least," said the beast; "you alone command in this place. If you should not like my company, you need only to say so, and I will leave you that moment. But tell me, Beauty, do you not think me very ugly?"

"Why, yes," said she,"for I cannot tell a falsehood; but then I think you are very good."

"Am I?" sadly replied the beast; "yet, besides being ugly, I am also very stupid: I know well enough that I am but a beast."

"Very stupid people," said Beauty,"are never aware of it themselves."

At which kindly speech the beast looked pleased, and replied; not without an awkward sort of politeness,"Pray do not let me detain you from supper, and be sure that you are well served. All you see is your own, and I should be deeply grieved if you wanted for anything."

"You are very kind—so kind that I almost forgot you are so ugly," said Beauty, earnestly.

"Ah! yes," answered the beast, with a great sigh; "I hope I am good-tempered, but still I am only a monster."

"There is many a monster who wears the form of a man; it is better of the two to have the heart of a man and the form of a monster."

"I would thank you, Beauty, for this speech, but I am too senseless to say anything that would please you," returned the beast in a melancholy voice; and altogether he seemed so gentle and so unhappy that Beauty, who had the tenderest heart in the world, felt her fear of him gradually vanish.

She ate her supper with a good appetite, and conversed in her own sensible and charming way till at last, when the beast rose to depart, he terrified her more than ever by saying abruptly, in his gruff voice,"Beauty, will you marry me?"

Now Beauty, frightened as she was, would speak only the exact truth; besides, her father had told, her that the beast liked only to have the truth spoken to him. So she answered, in a Very firm tone,"No, beast."

He did not go into a passion or do anything but sigh deeply, and depart.

When Beauty found herself alone she began to feel pity for the poor beast. "Oh!" said she,"what a sad thing it is that he should be so very frightful, since he is so good-tempered!"

Beauty lived three months in this place very well pleased. The beast came to see her every night, and talked with her while she supped; and though what he said was not very clever, yet, as she saw in him every day some new goodness, instead of dreading the time of his coming, she soon began continually looking at her watch, to see if it were nine o'clock; for that was the hour when he never failed to visit her. One thing only vexed her, which was that every night before he-;went away he always made it a rule to ask her if she would be his wife, and seemed very much grieved at her steadfastly replying "No." At last, one night, she said to him,"You wound me greatly, beast, by forcing me to refuse you so often; I wish I could take such a liking to you as to agree to marry you: but I must tell you plainly that I do not think it will ever happen. I shall always be your friend; so try to let that content you."

"I must," sighed the beast,"for I know well enough how frightful I am; but I love you better than myself. Yet I think I am very lucky in your being pleased to stay with me: now promise me, Beauty, that you will never leave me."

Beauty would almost have agreed to this, so sorry was she for him, but she had that day seen in her magic glass, which she looked at constantly, that her father was dying of grief for her sake.

"Alas!" she said,"I long so much to see my father, that if you do not give me leave to visit him I shall break my heart."

"I would rather break mine, Beauty," answered the beast. "I will send you to your father's cottage: you shall stay there, and your poor beast shall die of sorrow."

"No," said Beauty, crying,"I love you too well to be the cause of your death; I promise to return in a week. You have shown me that my sisters are married and my brothers are gone for soldiers, so that my father is left all alone. Let me stay a week with him."

"You shall find yourself with, him tomorrow morning," replied the beast; "but mind, do not forget your promise. When you wish to return, you have nothing to do but to put your ring on a table when you go to bed. Good-by, Beauty!" The beast sighed as he said these words, and Beauty went to bed very sorry to see him so much grieved. When she awoke in the morning, she found herself in her father's cottage. She rang a bell that was at her bedside, and a servant entered; but as soon as she saw Beauty, the woman gave a loud shriek; upon which the merchant ran upstairs, and when he beheld his daughter he ran to her, and kissed her a hundred times. At last Beauty began to remember that she had brought no clothes with her to put on; but the servant told her she had just found in the next room a large chest full of dresses, trimmed all over with gold, and adorned with pearls, and diamonds.

Beauty, in her own mind, thanked the beast for his kindness and put on the plainest gown she could find among them all. She then desired the servant to lay the rest aside, for she intended to give them to her sisters; but as soon as she had spoken these words the chest was gone out of sight in a moment. Her father then suggested that perhaps the beast chose for her to keep them all for herself: and as soon as he had said this they saw the chest standing again in the same place. While Beauty was dressing herself, a servant brought word to her that her sisters were come with their husbands to pay her a visit. They both lived unhappily with the gentlemen they had married. The husband of the eldest was very handsome, but was so proud of this that he thought of nothing else from morning till night, and did not care a pin for the beauty of his wife. The second had married a man of great learning; but he made no use of it except to torment and affront all his friends, and his wife more than any of them. The two sisters were ready to burst with spite when they saw Beauty dressed like a princess, and looking so very charming. All the kindness that she showed them was of no use, for they were vexed more than ever when she told them how happy she lived at the palace of the beast. The spiteful creatures went by themselves into the garden, where they cried to think of her good fortune.

"Why should the little wretch be better off than we?" said they. "We are much handsomer than she is."

"Sister!" said the eldest,"a thought has just come into my head: let us try to keep her here longer than the week for which the beast gave her leave; and then he will be so angry that perhaps when she goes back to him he will eat her up in a moment."

"That is well thought of," answered the other,"but to do this, we must pretend to be very kind."

They then went to join her in the cottage, where they showed her so much false love that Beauty could not help crying for joy.

When the week was ended, the two sisters began to pretend such grief at the thought of her leaving them, that she agreed to stay a week more: but all that time Beauty could not help fretting for the sorrow that she knew her absence would give her poor beast; for she tenderly loved him and much wished for his company again. Among all the grand and clever people she saw she found nobody who was half so sensible, so affectionate, so thoughtful, or so kind. The tenth night of her stay at the cottage she dreamed she was in the garden of the palace, that the beast lay dying on a grass-plot, and with his last breath put her in mind of her promise, and laid his death to her forsaking him. Beauty awoke in a great fright and burst into tears. "Am not I wicked," said she,"to behave so ill to a beast who has shown me so much kindness? Why will not I marry him? I am sure I should be more happy with him than my sisters are with their husbands. He shall not be wretched any longer on my account; for I should do nothing to blame myself all the rest of my life."

She then rose, put her ring on the table, got into bed again, and soon fell asleep. In the morning to her joy she found herself in the palace of the beast. She dressed very carefully, that she might please him the better, and thought she had never known a day pass away so slowly. At last the clock struck nine, but the beast did not come. Beauty, dreading lest she might truly have caused his death, ran from room to room, calling out,"Beast, dear beast"; but there was no answer. At last she remembered her dream, rushed to the grass-plot, and there saw him lying apparently, dead beside the fountain. Forgetting all his ugliness she threw herself upon his body, and finding his heart still beat, she fetched some water and sprinkled it over him, weeping and sobbing the while.

The beast opened his eyes: "You forgot your promise, Beauty; so I determined to die; for I could not live without you. I have starved myself to death, but I shall die content since I have seen your face once more."

"No, dear beast," cried Beauty, passionately,"you shall not; die; you shall live to be my husband. I thought it was only friendship I felt for you, but now I know it was love."

The moment Beauty had spoken these words the palace was suddenly lighted up, and all kinds of rejoicings were heard around them, none of which she noticed, but hung over her dear beast with the utmost tenderness. At last, unable to restrain herself, she dropped her head upon her hands, covered her eyes, and cried for joy; and when she looked up again, the beast was gone. In his stead she saw at her feet a handsome, graceful prince, who thanked her with the tenderest expressions for having freed him from enchantment.

"But where is my poor beast? I only want him and nobody else," sobbed Beauty.

"I am he," replied the Prince. "A wicked-fairy condemned me to this form and forbade me to show that I had any wit or sense, till: a beautiful lady should consent to marry me. You alone, dear Beauty, judged me neither by my looks nor by my talents, but by my heart alone. Take it then, and all that I have besides, for all is yours."

Beauty, full of surprise but very happy, suffered the Prince to lead her to his palace, where she found her father and sisters who had been brought there by the fairy-lady whom she had seen in a dream the first night she came.

"Beauty," said the fairy,"you have chosen well; and you have your reward, for a true heart is better than either good looks or clever brains. As for you, ladies"—and she turned to the two' elder sisters—"I know all your ill deeds, but I have no worse punishment for you than to see your sister happy. You shall stand as statues at the door of her palace, and when you repent of and have amended your faults, you shall become women again. But, to tell you the truth, I very much fear you will remain statues forever."

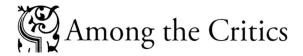

Among the Critics

Jerry Griswold

Only after Beauty decides to leave her fathers house to be reunited with the Beast—that is, after she has resolved her oedipal ties with her father—does sex, which before was repugnant, become beautiful.
　　　—Bruno Bettelheim, *The Uses of Enchantment* (1976)

The theme of this aristocratic tale involves "putting the bourgeoisie in their place."
　　　—Jack Zipes, *Breaking the Magic Spell (1979)*

Beauty stands in need of the Beast, rather than vice versa. … He holds up a mirror to the force of nature within her, which she is invited to accept and allow to grow, [namely] … her female erotic pleasures in matching and mastering a man who is dark and hairy, rough and wild.
　　　—Marina Warner, *From the Beast to the Blonde (1994)*

Beauty and the Beast" provides a convenient way to examine how meaning is discovered in, or imposed on, fairy tales. Professionals, scholars, and various kinds of specialists have explained the tale in dozens of ways.

Among these, we can detect three main trends. Psychological critics have focused attention on Beauty and suggested she has a "problem" (with sex). Socio-historical critics have seen the tale as a reactionary condemnation of social-climbing by the bourgeoisie or merchant class. Finally, feminist critics—while at first faulting the tale for advocating womanly sacrifice and submissiveness—have come to endorse "Beauty and the Beast" for presenting a desirable exploration of feminine erotics.

Psychological Readings

Among the earliest interpreters of "Beauty and the Beast" were Jungian critics Maria Von Franz and Joseph Henderson.[8] Typically, the followers of Carl Jung see the various characters in a tale as representations of different facets of a single individuals personality. Problems arise, they suggest, when individuals reject a part or parts of their personality. The aim of Jungian therapy is for an individual to acknowledge and integrate all the parts of their personality into a harmonious whole, and this resolution is often symbolized in a tale by a marriage.

8　Joseph Henderson,"Beauty and the Beast," and Marie-Louise Von Franz,"The Process of Individuation," *Man and his Symbols,* ed. Carl G. Jung (Garden City, NJ: Doubleday, 1964) 137–40 and 193–95, respectively.

A concept important to Jungians is the *"anima"* and the *"animus."* Jungians noticed that in men s dreams what is forbidden, dangerous, and erotic often comes in the form of a woman (an *anima); in the case of women's dreams, the forbidden, dangerous, and erotic often comes in the form of a male (an *animus*). In their interpretation of "Beauty and the Beast," then, Jungian critics see the Beast as Beauty's *animus*—as a part of her personality that she has denied and excluded, a part that is animal-like and sexual. Jungians argue that Beauty's task in the tale is to face reality rather than turn away from it, to acknowledge and integrate that part of her personality she regards as beastly and has rejected[9]

Two things make this task difficult, they suggest. First, Beauty is something of a Goody Two Shoes. Events early in the story suggest that she has embraced an unreal and exaggerated life of virtue, and Beaumont certainly goes to great lengths to tell us of Beauty's supernal goodness and her self-sacrificing ways. If she is to be saved, Beauty must venture forth from her antiseptic existence and make contact with the Beast. Moreover, this too good girl must fall: the all-too-virtuous Beauty must sin and betray the Beast and recognize that she has done so. Only in this way can she escape her Shirley-Temple-like life of saccharine goodness and dutiful self- denial.

A more significant impediment to Beauty's coming to acknowledge and accept her *animus* is the incest taboo. Growing up with her father, Beauty has driven all thought of sexuality out of her mind. By means of the Beast, however, she comes into contact with the erotic and awakens to the possibility of love. In her prolonged contact with the Beast, her childhood sexual repression (originally maintained because of the incest taboo) must give way and be replaced by trust and love.

If these remarks fairly represent the Jungians' view of the story, the Freudians are best represented by the ideas of Bruno Bettelheim in his *The Uses of Enchantment* (1977).[10] With regard to "Beauty and the Beast," Bettelheim generally follows the lead of the Jungians but differs slightly in identifying Beauty's problem as an oedipal one.

v A Freudian concept, the oedipal complex refers to a period in most children's lives when they feel a rivalry with the same-sex parent and a special bond of affection with the opposite-sex parent. Interestingly enough, many of Bettelheim's analyses of other fairy tales focus on the rivalry between the child and same-sex parent; numerous stories, he points out, feature antagonistic relationships between young women and mother figures like the witch or stepmother. But "Beauty and the Beast" focuses on the other side of the oedipal relationship, on the special bond of affection that exists between Beauty and her father. Indeed, we can only wonder how this tale might have been different had Beauty's mother (or her surrogate) been present.

Freudians, we should add, see nothing necessarily sick or. aberrant about the oedipal complex; most children go through a period when they are a "momma's boy" or a "daddy's girl." The oedipal complex only becomes a problem when someone gets frozen at this developmental stage and does not outgrow it. In fact, as Bettelheim suggests, when the oedipal period is successfully negotiated, love for a parent can be a prelude to the transfer of affection to someone outside the family:

> No other well-known fairy tale makes it as obvious as "Beauty and the Beast" that a child's oedipal attachment to a parent is natural, desirable, and has the most positive consequences of all, if during the process of maturation it is transferred and transformed as it becomes detached from the parent and concentrated on the lover. Our oedipal attachments, far from being a source of our greatest emotional difficulties (which they can be when they do not undergo proper development during our growing up), are the soil out of which permanent happiness grows if we experience the right evolution and resolution of these feelings.[11]

---

9 Von Franz 194.

10 Jacques Barchilon was probably the first to employ Freudian thinking in understanding the tale, and Bettelheim appears to have borrowed from him. Barchilon,"Beauty and the Beast: From Myth To Fairy Tale," *Psychoanalysis and the Psychoanalytic Review 46,4.* (Winter 1959): 19–29.

11 Bruno Bettelheim, *The Uses of Enchantment* (New York: Vintage Books, 1977) 307.

To support his diagnosis of Beauty's oedipal difficulties, Bettelheim points to the young woman's special connections with her father. First, while her sisters go out to parties and are concerned with courtship, Beauty shuns this kind of romantic life and prefers to remain at home with her father. And second, while her sisters are eager to marry, Beauty twice turns down suitors, saying she wishes to stay longer with her father.

But in marshaling evidence to suggest that Beauty has a special bond of affection with her father, Bettelheim overlooks additional proofs that might be used to support his view. For instance, when Beauty resides at the Beast's castle, we learn that every second thought of hers concerns her father and his well-being, so much so that she regularly looks in the Beast's magic mirror to get news of him; and when given permission by the Beast to leave his castle, she flies to her father's side. Indeed, following Bettelheim's ideas, we might view Beaumont's story as a series of Beauty's trial separations from her father until, finally, she can leave the nest and remain with her admirer.

Understanding Bettelheim's view of the story as essentially recounting Beauty's transference of her love from her father to the prince, we can begin to understand Bettelheim's notion of how beastliness enters the story. According to this psychologist, as long as Beauty has a special bond of affection with her father, she sees sex as animal-like and loathsome because of the incest taboo. Or, to say this differently, as long as Beauty has a special bond of affection with her father, she sees other men as beastly. Once she works through her relationship with her father and separates from him, Beauty can then see the handsome prince as he is.

Though this is not exactly said by Bettelheim, the logical implication of his view is that the Prince has *always* looked like the Prince. Beauty—because of the incest taboo and her oedipal attachment to her father—has not seen the prince correctly and has imagined him a beast. Once she works through her relationship with her father and separates from him, she can see the Prince as he is—*and as he has always been.*

And it is here where we might begin a critique of psychological interpretations of the tale, by noticing how both the Jungians and Freudians have narrowed the story to a discussion of Beauty and *her* problems. Such a view is not wrong, but it is incomplete. After all, the title of "Beauty and the Beast" suggests dual billing; and while Beauty may certainly have a problem with her relationships, the Prince (trapped in the form of a beast) has manifest problems of his own that should not be overlooked.

Moreover, in directing attention away from the Beast's physical transformation and towards Beauty's emotional transformation, both Jungians and Freudians have come to see the tale as an account of *feminine* maturation. Beauty passes through various developmental stages. She learns and matures. But if this is, equally, the Beast's story, then we may need to consider his development. What is it that *he* learns? In what ways, does *he* need to mature?

We might even hazard some answers here. Perhaps the prince was changed into a beast, as is the case in some folk tales, because of unwelcome sexual misconduct and animal-like aggressiveness with women. If that is so, then "Beauty and the Beast" might talk about *a male's* needing to learn not to force himself on women and his demonstration that he can be a gentleman. In other words, the tale presents a test of his ability (in amorous engagements) to wait patiently until the woman says "Yes."

Again, in overlooking the Beast's story and in remaking Beaumont's tale into the story of "Beauty and Her Problems," psychological critics have not erred but they have limited our understanding of the story. Other kinds of myopia can be noticed*, when we pay attention to the ideology behind these psychological approaches. Consider the Jungians, for example. In their formulations of the *anima* (the female dream figure of men) and the *animus* (the male dream figure of women), Jungians, we should note, display a distinct predisposition to heterosexuality. This same predisposition plays itself out in the way Jungians focus on male/female relationships in "Beauty and the Beast." While these relations are important and are foregrounded in this romantic story, attention to them should not come at the expense of ignoring female/female and male/male relations in the story—all of which, we might note, are conflicted.

A similar kind of shortsightedness limits Freudian understandings of the story. Bettelheim emphasizes that it is *Beauty's* oedipal affection which makes difficult her detaching from her father and her aligning herself with the Beast. But we might ask: Is she the only one who has problems with separating? Is attachment only *her* problem? Beauty's father, we might note, collapses in illness and very nearly dies when he is separated from his daughter, and he bounces back to health upon her return. Oedipal attachment, we might observe, is not a one-way street.[12]

And Beauty's father is not the only one to suffer from deathlike swoons—or, perhaps, the self-indulgent tantrums we associate with spoiled children—when Beauty absents herself. The Beast, too, collapses and is near death when Beauty leaves his side. If Bettelheim's argument is that such dependency is a kind of immaturity, then we might argue that poor Beauty is surrounded by masculine whiners desperate for her nurturance, and this unfairly compels Beaumont's Florence Nightingale to shuttle between needy males, at her father's home and the Beast's castle. Indeed, Beauty is only permitted happiness at the end, when her family comes to the Beast's castle and she is no longer asked to choose between father and husband.

Again, in offering these reservations to the Jungian and Freudian interpretations of the tale, I am not suggesting that these psychological readings of "Beauty and the Beast" are wrong. Instead, my aim is to add more complexity and depth to them. In raising questions about the consistency and thoroughness of their arguments, however, I am still playing within their ballpark and working within the mind-set of psychological criticism. Other critics might raise more comprehensive questions and ask whether this is the right ballpark, at all, in which to take up the meanings of Beaumont's story.

Socio-Historical Readings

Jack Zipes is a well-known and prolific commentator on fairy tales whose methodology is socio-historical or Marxist. Zipes vehemently objects to Bettelheim's psychological approach to the fairy tales, arguing that Bettelheim sees these stories as ahistorical documents that address timeless human problems. Instead, Zipes insists, these tales must be seen precisely within their historical and cultural contexts. And when this is done, we notice how they have been reshaped in different times and locales not to address universal human issues, but to push specific social agendas.[13]

In "Beauty and the Beast," Zipes suggests, we see class struggle: the story presents the quarrel between the nobility and the rising merchant class or bourgeoisie. The aim of Beaumont's aristocratic tale, Zipes explains, is to "[put] the bourgeoisie in their place."[14]

With regard to the role of class in the story, Zipes is entirely convincing. Unlike the classic folk tale, at the outset of Beaumont's tale, we are not introduced to, say, a king and queen. Instead, front and center is an entirely new set of characters—a merchant and his family. They are *nouveau riche*. Moreover, Beauty's sisters are vulgar social climbers who insist they will only marry a duke or an earl. And, of course, these *arrivistes* get their comeuppance when their father loses his fortune.

---

12   This notion that other characters have problems in the tale—and that psychological critics are shortsighted in viewing the story only as an account of Beauty and *her* problems—is also suggested in another way. Bettelheim's ideas lead to the interesting suggestion that the prince has always looked like the prince but Beauty (because of her oedipal attachment to her father) mistakenly views him as a beast. But here is the catch: Beauty's father *also* sees the Beast. If we wish to be consistent then, we need to say that the father s equally mistaken vision of the Prince reveals the father's own oedipal attachment to his daughter: his unwillingness to give up his daughter and his notion that her suitors are unsuitable beasts.

13   Cf. Jack David Zipes, *Breaking the Magic Spell: Radical Theories of Folk and Fairy Tales* (Austin, TX: University of Texas Press, 1979; London: Methuen, 1984) 160–82.

14   *Zipes*, Breaking the Magic Spell *9.*

Opposite the merchant and his family stands the Beast. Zipes suggests he is a figure for the aristocracy, "old money," a nobleman living in a castle. According to Zipes, the message of the story, then, is that the merchant class (in the face of their aristocratic betters) ought to be humble like Beauty and not put on airs like her sisters.

Zipes's approach to Beaumont's tale suggests how meaning can be found by positioning "Beauty and the Beast" within its historical context, particularly in terms of the rise of the bourgeoisie. In that regard, we might follow his example but go a bit further in order to gather an even more comprehensive understanding of the story.

One of the principal architects of the rise of the bourgeoisie was Jean Baptiste Colbert (1619–83), the minister of Louis XIV. Faced with massive government debts and looking for advice, the king turned not to the members of his court or to the nobility, but to this professional civil servant, the son of a prosperous merchant family. Colbert thought the way to put France on a sound financial footing was to run the government as a business and put the merchant at center stage. Moreover, he was impressed by how the English and the Dutch had increased their wealth by becoming commercial nations with ships that sailed the world and engaged in trading enterprises. Colbert saw to it that France followed their examples. He encouraged the building of ships, the formation of private trading companies among groups of investors, and the extension of commerce to the East and West Indies as well as northern Europe and the eastern Mediterranean.

At home, Colbert hated idlers and slackers—landlords, bureaucrats, nobles, clergymen, and others who wiled away their days with luxurious pastimes, who lived in the cities and depended upon the labors of others who worked on their distant estates. Convinced that every citizen should work and produce, Colbert developed a number of economic measures meant to frustrate the privileged and undermine their lives of ease. Under his mercantile system, productive merchants and manufacturers were rewarded, and wealth began to gradually shift to this merchant class and away from the privileged whose families for years had derived their income from others.

In the decades following Colbert and his policies, the gradual erosion of the *ancien régime* left the nobility in a sorry state. While they might claim the grandeur of their titles and possibly the ownership of vast estates, aristocrats were often at the brink of financial ruin and unable to pay taxes—especially because they were now required to do so in a new way, by using money and paying in the new currency. Moreover, they could not easily find a solution to their financial woes by engaging in activities like trade or manufacturing since such commercial pursuits were often viewed as common and beneath members of the nobility.

So, on the one hand, those who laid claim to titles like "Duke" or "Earl" seemed to be headed towards extinction. On the other hand, the bourgeoisie, the merchant class, was on the rise. To be sure, wealth fluctuated. Great fortunes were both made and lost as a result of investments in tobacco, mining, foundries, cotton mills, banks, maritime trade, and other activities. But boom or bust, the merchant class (as a whole) was gaining the upper hand.

Of course, the nobility (on their way down) and the merchant class (on their way up) did occasionally find a meeting ground. Cash-poor, the nobility at least had the grandeur of their titles. Class-less, the bourgeoisie had money—even though it might have been acquired in the sordid and common world of commerce, and even though aristocrats might look down their noses at them as *nouveau riche*. Typically enough, a happy compromise was reached when, say, the wealthy owner of cotton mills arranged for his daughter to be married to a destitute nobleman. In this way, the aristocrat could pay his taxes and keep the family estate, while the merchant and his family gained a title and an entrance into high society.

It may be immediately obvious how the historical circumstances described here reappear in the situation found in Beaumont's "Beauty and the Beast." Beaumont sets her story in a world of merchants and nobility, of trading ships and fluctuating fortunes, of merchants' daughters with aspirations to upward mobility, and so forth. But what is perhaps more interesting is how Beaumont's tale differs from, or reacts to, its times. Most obvious is the fact that the union between Beauty and the Beast is not presented as a marriage of convenience between a wealthy merchant's daughter and an impoverished nobleman. Instead, we have the opposite.

In Beaumont's tale, the nobleman is not hurting for cash; it is the merchant's family that is down on its luck.)Moreover, the merchant the meanings of beauty and the beast and his family are considerably helped by the magnanimous Beast and his chests of gold, his largesse and sense of *noblesse oblige*. In fact, as a figure for the aristocrat, the Beast presents an appealing picture—landed and kind, generous and refined, and in every way noble. In other words, in the midst of changing times, Beaumont seems to offer a kind of backwards-looking endorsement of the nobility, a flattering and conservative portrait of the *ancien régime*.

But, besides honoring the aristocrat, we should also notice how Beaumont responds to changing times by offering a reactionary criticism of the new and rising merchant class. Beauty's sisters and their vulgar class aspirations are particularly singled out for disapproval. Moreover, in her vision of the merchant's slide from urban prosperity to rural poverty, Beaumont seems to go out of her way to emphasize that status is a precarious thing among the bourgeoisie because (unlike the landed gentry) social station is tied to money and wealth, and fortunes could and did fluctuate. Ultimately, Beaumont seems to suggest that the merchant class would be better if they were more like Beauty—that is to say, if they went back to the farm and became once again hardworking and uncomplaining peasants; in the evenings, she suggests, they can turn to improving books and music.

When Beaumont's tale is seen in its historical context, then, we can detect the author's aristocratic airs, patronizing attitudes, and conservative views, Seen in this way, her tale is not so much a reflection of her era as it is a reaction to it: a kind of aristocratic backlash to changing times.

Feminist Readings

The fortunes of the fairy tales among feminist critics may be divided into two phases. A first generation of feminist critics condemned the tales as reflections of a patriarchal culture and found abundant evidence in them of the victimization of women.[15]

However, a second generation of feminists:—a loose collection of writers, Jungian essayists, and critics—came to endorse them as female stories and saw in these "old wives' tales" visions of feminine empowerment.[16] What has been the history of fairy tales in general has also been the history of "Beauty and the Beast" in particular.

Those feminists who object to "Beauty and the Beast" see it as an admiring portrait of a self-sacrificial maiden and argue that Beaumont's story conveys the objectionable lesson that women should be submissive. Beauty puts others' interests before her own, especially her father's interests, when she rejects suitors, resettles in the country in order to comfort the old man, and finally takes his place at the Beast's castle. When the family moves

15   Cf. Marcia K. Lieberman's "Some Day My Prince Will Come: Female Acculturation Through the Fairy Tale" and Karen E. Rowe's "Feminism and Fairy Tales" in *Don't Bet on the Prince: Contemporary Feminist Fairy Tales in North America and England*, ed. Jack Zipes (New York: Methuen, 1986) 185–200 and 209–26, respectively. See also Ruth B. Bottigheimer, *Grimm's Bad Girls and Bold Boys: The Moral and Social Vision of the Tales* (New Haven, CT: Yale University Press, 1987).
16   Cf. Warner; Pinkola Estes; Angela Carter, ,*The Bloody Chamber* (New York: Penguin Books, 1993); Maria Kolbenschlag, *Kiss Sleeping Beauty Good-Bye* (New York: Bantam Books, 1981).

to the country, Beauty (like some uncomplaining Cinderella) represses her own feelings and remains upbeat, rising at four in the morning and doing the chores. In Beauty's going to the Beast's castle and in her agreeing to marry him, these feminists also see the situation of women pledged to arranged marriages by their fathers; in that case, the message to young aristocratic girls in Beaumont's story seems to be that they should acquiesce to arrangements that have been made for them. Moreover, the tale suggests that if her selected spouse should strike her as a beast, a young woman should know that a clever and well-meaning woman can change a brute into a companionable husband.[17] In summary, as one critic suggests, when we consider the admirable heroine who gives her name to this tale, we are obliged to conclude that "the mark of beauty for a female is to be found in her submission, obedience, humility, industry, and patience."[18]

When the story is seen in this way, first-generation feminists seem entirely correct and Beaumont emerges from their assessments as a matronly co-conspirator coaching young women to bow to traditional and patriarchal values. Other evidence, however, suggests that this is too simple an understanding. Indeed, it might be possible to construct a counter-argument and argue that Beaumont was an early feminist.

"Beauty and the Beast" appeared in Beaumont's book for young women, *The Young Misses Magazine*, and in the introduction to that work Beaumont presented strikingly radical and forward-looking views for her times. Against the commonly held opinion that only boys should be schooled, Beaumont declared her conviction that young women should be educated and encouraged to be intelligent, not just viewed as fodder for marriage:

> Some will think, that the instructions to be given here are too serious for ladies from fifteen to eighteen years of age. But to satisfy this objection, [I need only say] that I have merely [written] down the conversations that have passed between me and my [students]; and experience has taught me that those instructions are not above their reach. ... We don't have a true [understanding] of the capacity of [young women]; nothing is out of their reach Now-a-days ladies read all sorts of books, history, politicks, philosophy and even such as concern religion. They should therefore be in a condition to judge solidly of what they read and able to discern truth from falsehood.[19]

If we admit the possibility that Beaumont might be considered a proto-feminist, then we may question the opinions of first-generation feminists who condemned her and her tale. For example, note that Beaumont's Beauty is not always submissive. When she first sees the Beast, she recoils in horror and does not repress her feelings; and when he asks her if she finds him ugly, her answer is direct and candid and in the affirmative. When Beauty returns to visit her father, she is not catering to the Beast's wishes but indulging her own desires. In fact, self-indulgence, more than self-sacrifice, seems to characterize her time at the Beast's castle, where she has a room of her own and every kind of luxury. At these moments, it might be argued, the tale does not speak of compliance but of feminine independence and autonomy.

Moreover, it can be argued further, first-generation feminists do not offer a complete view of Beauty when they regard her as a self-sacrificial and powerless victim. In several ways, Beaumont offers a tale in which Beauty is in charge. Although the Beast is a huge and formidable creature, it is Beauty who calls the shots: she is the mistress of the house, the Beast insists, and everything and everyone (including the Beast himself) is at her command. Moreover, the tale dramatically emphasizes Beauty's power of choice: she must come to the Beast's castle of her own free will; she is not to be coerced but must freely choose to marry; she alone holds the power to transform the Beast; and, indeed, through much of the tale he waits upon her decision. In fact, Beauty seems to inhabit a world where males (her father, the Beast) are weak and where women have power.

---

17 Cf. Warner 293.

18 Jack Zipes, *Fairy Tales and the Art of Subversion: The Classical Genre for Children and the Process of Civilization* (New York: Wildman Press, 1983) 38,40–41.

19 Quoted in *Visions and Revisions* 17.

These facts suggest something important: that "Beauty and the Beast" is not a story of feminine submissiveness but of feminine empowerment. Here may be found the reason for something noted earlier in this book—namely, the story's unusual popularity among women.

This is the point at which second-generation feminists, such as Marina Warner, have taken up the story and endorsed it. Inspired by the "pagan" and "earthy" feminism of writer Angela Carter, Warner sees "Beauty and the Beast" as not only dealing with power transactions but with "the complicated character of the female erotic impulse."[20]

In a fashion, Warner sees Beaumont's "Beauty and the Beast" as the familiar kind of story seen in popular women's romance novels: the charged encounter between the nice girl and the dark or dangerous male. In Warner's eyes, Beauty is going for "a walk on the wild side." And in this way, "Beauty and the Beast" addresses the attraction women feel towards males who are appealing not so much because of their looks but because of their dark and sexy nature, their animal magnetism.

In advancing her views, Warner subsumes and answers other interpretations of the tale. Jungian and Freudian critics, for example, have suggested that the Beast represents Beauty's own sexual or animal nature which she is resisting because of her special bond of affection with her father and the incest taboo. Warner is willing to accept the view that the Beast represents Beauty's sexual nature, but she steadfastly refuses to find a "problem" in that. Instead, she suggests, for example, that Bettelheim's views reveal his prudery and discomfort with feminine sexuality since he feels obliged to stigmatize Beauty's encounter with sexuality as showing oedipal difficulties and arrested development.^ On her part, Warner finds the encounter powerful and positive: Bettelheim's interpretation of the tale, Warner complains, "takes the exuberance and the energy from female erotic voices."[21]

At the same time, Warner also goes beyond the notion implicit in the interpretations of Marxists and first-generation feminists: namely, that Beauty is a victim. Beauty is not subjugated, Warner notes; once she gets to the Beast's castle, she is the mistress of all she surveys, and the huge and formidable Beast waits on her approval. If anything, the equation of power is tipped in her favor. She might, in fact, be seen as a dominatrix in several senses of the word, not excluding the sexual one. For Warner, "Beauty and the Beast" is a story of "female erotic pleasures in matching and mastering a man who is dark and hairy, rough and wild."[22]

Oedipal difficulties and sexual anxiety, the noblesse oblige and uppity bourgeoisie, womanly deference and feminine erotics—the spectrum of meanings this fairy tale produces is one measure of the story's potency and prism-like perfection.

---

20 Warner 313.
21 Warner 313.
22 Warner 318.

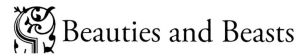

Beauties and Beasts

Descending into the Body

Joan Gould

"Cupid and Psyche," The African Queen, *the Legend of the Minotaur,*
Jane Eyre, Casablanca

In every Beauty-and-Beast story, the heroine encounters sexual passion for the first time, inside herself as well as outside in the form of a Beast. Her consciousness changes. Mind meets body, if we want to look at it that way; the soul (called the *psyche*) experiences itself through flesh, especially her own. While tracking the stages of love in a woman's life, this story raises the possibility of learning to love what we fear, which is always more erotic than learning how to get what we want. The first approach is "Beauty and the Beast," the second "Cinderella."

In our society, the transformation to adulthood takes place over a period of years. Girls reach sexual maturity early here and expect freedom in their choices, so we let our children dawdle at each stage of ripening, perhaps because we are afraid to make their mistakes for them.

When a daughter finishes high school, her parents hire a U-Haul and drive her to college, where she moves into a freshman dorm with roommates assigned at random, sharing her sleeping space and bathroom for the first time with unfamiliar bodies. The following years, she picks her own roommates, before taking an apartment with friends of the same sex. She loses her virginity, if she hasn't done so already. She moves in with a lover. Step by sanctioned and expected step, she closes doors behind her and opens new ones, heading for the goal, which is a home of her own.

Before 1950, our society was closer to the fairy-tale world than it is today. A virgin knew little about Beasts before she chose one for a husband (or was given to him in marriage), any more than she knew about paying electricity bills or figuring out her food budget. At last she came into contact with a male Beast. She touched him. Nothing more than that at first, but her senses were alerted to new messages. She married and moved, not only out of her family home and into her own but down into her body, lapped in the pleasure of the present moment, until one day she woke up, suspecting that time was passing at another rate outside the realm of enchantment. There seemed to be something else she wanted, something more demanding that was essential for her future, though she wasn't sure how to get it.

In ancient times (in a classical myth that is another version of the Beauty-and-Beast story), a princess named Psyche had the misfortune to be more beautiful than any human had a right to be—so beautiful, in fact, that her fathers subjects deserted the temples of Venus, the great goddess of love and fertility, known as "the Universal Mother," and worshiped the fresh young girl instead.

The two female spirits could not have been more different. Venus, sprung from the sea foam, represented mindless, boundless sex energy that wants fertility and nothing else, paying no attention to individual personalities, which only get in the way. ("Get married, get married," our grandmothers still tell us, not specifying to whom.) Psyche was the opposite: a human virgin, which made her a mortal affront to the sex goddess—a creature of the earth rather than of the sea. Unmarried and humble in her suffering, she never dreamed that she might embody a new ideal of love.

Wild with jealousy, the goddess Venus called her winged son, Cupid, to her side (he was always bent on mischief, anyway), kissed him long and tenderly in a way that mothers aren't supposed to kiss their sons, and begged him to avenge her by using his arrows to make the blasphemously beautiful girl fall in love with "some perfect outcast" of a man, the most degraded creature he could find, the vilest of the vile. "That wicked boy" is the way Venus thought of her son, who flies over the rooftops at night, stirring up trouble in respectable homes. But in truth he was no boy, and certainly not the cherub with dimpled knees that we see on valentines. He was the youthful god of love at the peak of masculine beauty, susceptible himself to the passion he spread so casually with his random arrows.

As a result, when Psyche's father, the King, went to the oracle of Apollo to ask why his youngest daughter was so exceptional that no man, not even a prince or king, dared to court her, he was told in fancy Latin verse that she was about to get a husband: She must be sacrificed from the top of a mountain, dressed as a bride. Her wedding ceremony would also serve as her funeral, since her bridegroom would not be a mortal but a flying demon,"fierce and wild and of the dragon breed," who would swoop through the air with fire and sword to collect her.

And so the wedding party set out with smoky torches and mournful music, interrupted by howls of grief from the heartbroken parents and their sympathizers as they followed poor Psyche to the crest of a hill. There they left her alone to weep. Suddenly a friendly west wind swirled around her ankles and billowed out her cloak, which it used as a sail to carry her down to a valley and lay her on a flowery bank, so softly cushioned that she fell asleep. When she woke up, feeling calmer, she followed a stream that led her to a palace so marvelous that she knew no human being could have built it. Passing through the gates, she saw ceilings supported by golden columns and walls faced with massive gold blocks that streamed with light of their own, even when no sun was shining. The floor was a series of mosaic pictures made from jewels. How could anyone fail to be happy who walked on a pavement like that?

A demon was what the oracle had predicted her husband would be, a winged pestilence that even Jupiter was afraid of, but this palace had to be the creation of a god, she told herself. What's more, the god must be in residence at this minute.

Wealth is the first sign of the Beast that the heroine encounters, wealth and luxury in contrast to the bleakness of her former life. This she understands in spiritual as well as material terms. The Beast who owns this castle is no starveling wolf lying in wait for Little Red Riding Hood to satisfy both of his appetites, one for gobbling up little girls and the other for getting them into bed. The proprietor here has to be a great lord—"my master" is the way Jane Eyre refers to Mr. Rochester, an erotic phrase for a woman to use if ever there was one—lord of the beasts, king of the forest, a demigod or even a god, as Psyche claims.

Because of his wealth, he needn't do what would be impossible for him to do: call any man master. This is an essential piece of information for a woman during courtship, since nothing dampens romantic ardor so quickly as to hear a lover mention "my boss." A woman may choose to be dominated in bed, often chooses just that, but it means nothing to be dominated by a man, or to dominate him, unless he's the strongest in her world. Otherwise, when she hears the words "my boss," her mind strays from the familiar arms and legs wound around her, and in their place she visualizes—who else?—her mate's boss. A Beast capable of holding her down.

Of course, the Beast's wealth does not come to him in the ordinary way, by working for it, or in the hero's way of fighting for it. He's magically rich (in his palace, tears turn into diamonds as they fall) for the same reason a mermaid is rich: because below the surface level on which we lead our everyday lives, all of us can lay claim to unimaginable treasures, of which the greatest, as Beauty's Beast claimed, is a rose. As a result, the Beast is as rich as the hero is poor.

By nature, a hero's whole life is centered on what he wants and doesn't have, even if it is as unattainable as the Holy Grail, and so he is the poorest of the poor, constantly thinking of what he must do next to get what he lacks, even while he's in bed with the heroine. The Beast, on the other hand, wants nothing except to stay locked up in his lair and wait for Beauty to arrive, and so his home looks like a castle in his eyes and hers. To her surprise, once she is cut off from home and family (a prisoner liberated by her imprisonment) she finds that she has come up in the world, not down, in terms of pleasure and power.

In real life, this is the development that scandalizes parents, when a young woman moves in with a lover, or into a college apartment shared only with age-mates: bunk beds; clothes strewn over the floor for lack of closet space; no place to hang wet towels; no reading lamp; clutter and mess in territory that is her own, where the walls radiate light even in bad weather because here, one day, she expects to be kissed.

"Do these treasures astonish your Royal Highness? They are all yours," the spirit voices inform Psyche. As long as the heroine stays home she is propertyless, no matter how rich her family may be, because nothing belongs to her, but the first time that she picks out a comforter for her bed—-even if she then leaves the bed unmade for two weeks—her body expands in space and power. Every object in the stores is potentially hers. Floating above her previous life, she says, like a magic incantation,"No one in the world knows where I am at this moment. Not even my boyfriend. No one knows what I'm going to have for supper."

Mess in the modern world equals splendor for a fairy-tale heroine: wealth that her parents cant provide, or control.

The habitat changes from palace to rain forest, the heroine's background changes, the medium in which the story is told shifts from a myth to a movie, but the theme of a woman forced out of her home who ripens sexually in a lusher setting remains the same.

This time the heroine (Katharine Hepburn) is an overaged spinster who plays the organ with quivering intensity for her missionary brother in an African village on the bank of a river, until German troops invade their compound during World War I. On the day when Roses brother dies, the skipper of the *African Queen* (Humphrey Bogart) steams up to the dock in his cranky teakettle of a boat. This Beast who rises from the river is unshaven, unwashed, with a rag tied around his neck, a cigar clamped in his teeth, and bursts of intestinal •gas erupting from his insides. Up to now, his only mate has been his gin bottle, but he is lord of the Congo all the same, the only person who can navigate the river and save her from the Germans.

Wearing a collar buttoned up to her chin and a wide-brimmed hat, Rose steps aboard the boat, and learns almost at once that ahead of them lie "a hundred miles of water like it's coming out of a fire hose." The *African Queen* enters the first stretch of rapids. Water boils around the rocks. The skipper wrestles with the tiller as the boat dives over waterfalls and fishtails from side to side. Despite his wish to stay uninvolved in the war, the virgin is about to transform him from a Beast into a hero.

"Well, miss? … How d'ya like it?" he asks when they have passed safely through the rapids. He chuckles benignly and takes a cigarette from behind his ear, while she wipes the spray off her cheeks with the back of her hand. "Like it?"

"White water. Rapids."

"I never dreamed …"

"I don't blame you for being scared, Miss. Not one little bit. Ain't no person in their right mind ain't scared of white water."

She has stars in her eyes. "I never *dreamed* that any mere physical experience could be so stimulating … I've only known such excitement a few times before. A few times in my dear brothers sermons when the spirit was really upon him!"

"You mean—you want to go on?"

"Naturally."

Isolated in the world except for the Beast, in danger of being killed at any minute, the heroine transcends downward into her body. This is a rare experience, she discovers, every bit as illuminating as transcending upward beyond her physical state, and equally difficult to sustain without interruption from the mind.

Since puberty, she has been aware of her body, but only of how it looks to others when seen from the outside and what effect her appearance will have on her future. Now, in a combination of exhilaration and terror, she sits rooted to her seat in the wildly careening riverboat, the small space allotted her on earth, existing inside a body that feels excruciatingly mortal but vividly alive in a particle of time.

Fear stimulates us to full consciousness as effectively as sensual pleasure does. Only through the body, which is our gateway to knowledge, can we understand abstractions like time, space, and willpower that we mistakenly think come from our minds. (Contrary to what we expect, time slows down for us, rather than speeding up, when we are in danger.) Through fear and sex and a brush with death, we experience mortality intertwined with its opposite—a love of life so overwhelming that we weep at the thought that some day we must leave it.

In our civilization, it's not easy to put the mind to sleep and live solely in the present like an animal, with an animal's singleness of purpose—which is what we mean by transcending downward—yet every woman must do just that at times if she is to become fully female. From here on, the heroine will experience the delights offered by the Beast as another path of descent into her body, coming at a period when she's still available. Right now, unmarried, she doesn't sense her life through the bodies of her mate, children, home. Her body is all she has, but it's her own.

"Why not go to your bedroom now, and rest your tired limbs," a bodiless voice suggests to Psyche after she wanders through rooms loaded with treasures. "When you feel inclined to bathe, we will be there to help you—this is one of your maids speaking—and after- wards you will find your wedding banquet ready for you."

Following the airborne suggestions, Psyche sits down to eat, alone like Beauty, and instantly the finest dishes float in front of her of their own accord, while an invisible singer entertains her, accompanied by an invisible player on an equally invisible lyre. (Modern women approximate these stimuli through CDs, scented candles, rings of perfumed oil to hang around lightbulbs, loofahs, aromatic bath gels, Jacuzzis. Alcohol. Drugs. Anything that arouses the senses and swathes her in pleasure, leaving the body open, without discrimination. Especially open to him.)

Even if Psyche wants to, she cant escape these luxuries by running away. She can only submit—that's the exquisitely erotic element—while her senses are massaged by the bath, followed by dinner and off to bed on silken sheets.

And then something better. Around midnight, she hears gentle whispers beside her. "Now he was climbing into bed with her. Now he was making her his wife." She learns his body (which doesn't feel the way she sup- poses a demons body feels) by touching and being touched, the way a baby learns a mother, which means she knows him more intimately than anyone else. While she has been desirable for years, at last she is desired. In fact, demanded. She is the cause of the passion that carries her along in its wake.

Before daybreak, her bedmate departs.

In this fantasy of erotic pleasure without commitment, Psyche's husband makes his presence known only in the dark, just as the brave lass who rode off with the White Bear is joined in bed every night by a man she never sees by daylight, and Jane Eyre is summoned to the library by Mr. Rochester only in the evenings. All day the heroine is free to go her own way as if she's still a single woman, while she waits eagerly, but modestly, for evening to come.

On the dot of nine every evening, Beauty's Beast comes into the dining room to talk to Beauty—with good common sense, though no cleverness—while she eats her supper. He could force himself on her, but he doesn't. Time passes agreeably until she stands up to go to bed, when the Beast turns to her and asks her to be his wife. "I shall always esteem you as a friend," she answers in the time- honored female evasion. "You must try to be satisfied with that."

The Beast moans. "Promise you will never leave me" is all he can say.

For three months the honeymoon is resumed every evening, flirtatious but not sexual in Beauty's case. Nothing is so compelling to a woman as power held on a leash by consideration for her.

PSYCHE'S HUSBAND WILL BE a creature "fierce and wild and of the dragon breed," the oracle predicted, but what else could be of the dragon breed except a serpent? Even though the body wound around Psyche feels like a mans, in older versions of the myth he was undoubtedly just what the oracle said, the Snake God as the consort of the Mother Goddess, twining himself around the tree of life. Like the White Bear, he is master of immortality: lord of death with his poisonous tongue, but, at the same time, lord of rebirth, who periodically coils himself into a spiral and casts off his old scarred skin, to emerge, a few days later as bright as a painted belt!

Bear, serpent, bull, the beast-god takes on whatever shape he pleases, and always for the same reason: to gain access to the body of a woman whom he claims as his mate—not any woman, but the Beauty he has his eye on. He is divine, and he is a Beast, but a layer in between is missing that can be filled only by a woman. As a conduit linking three levels of being—animal, human, and divine—she alone can produce children who will be as fleshly as animals but will also inherit the spiritual power of their father.

For him, she represents earth as opposed to heaven, body as opposed to spirit—daily life, which is what gives substance to transcendent ideas. In fact, she is matter. *Mater.* Mother.

FOR CENTURIES, the animal is a god, or the god slips in and out of an animal body at will. Until one day he cant do it any longer; he's stuck halfway. The last of the bull gods, known as the Minotaur (the *taurus,* or bull, of his father, Minos) bears the head and hooves of a bull on the body of a human. Earlier in his existence he was the holy bull, the sex energy that fertilized his island of Crete, but as soon as this energy no longer seemed divine he was regarded as a monster to be penned in a maze called the Labyrinth. To the Athenians, he was never a god in the first place but a devil who devoured seven Athenian youths and seven maidens in the tribute Athens paid to Crete once every nine years.

Baffled and terrifying, the Minotaur waits for the sun hero Theseus to come down from Athens with his patriarchal ideals of discipline and combat, to put an end to this monstrous energy with the help of the kings daughter, Ariadne. Both of them know that if the Minotaur is killed the civilization of Crete will crumble.

This struggle marks a breaking point in the consciousness of Western civilization: The hero, who is wholly human, conquers the male who is half beast. Mind dominates body. Law takes precedence over energy. Chastity, rather than fertility, becomes the startling new ideal for women. But first the Beast has to die, in order to guarantee that the hero will be the one to mate with Beauty and reproduce his kind.

(The struggle between Theseus and the Minotaur is still being fought out in the bullrings of Spain and Mexico, where the matador, the sun hero in his glittering *traje de luces,* or "suit of lights," confronts the power of the moon bull.)

After Theseus kills the Minotaur, he does what heroes always do: He disappears. He sails back to Athens for his next adventure, abandoning Ariadne on an island, even though he promised to make her his bride if she would help him kill her half brother, the Minotaur. The last that the heroine sees of the hero is always his back as he sails or rides into the sunset.

From this point on, for thousands of years in Europe, the wild beast is seen as the enemy, the marauder in the forests, like the wolf or boar, or at best the object of royal hunts, like the stag. Or perhaps he's a slavering fool, like a bear who dances at the end of a chain. For a man to wear the head of an animal is no longer a sign of divine power uniting two orders of being but a curse, a sign of inferiority. The hero is the ideal.

THE PENDULUM SWINGS the other way. Ever since the start of the Industrial Revolution, nature has slipped away from us: "The world is too much with us," sighed Wordsworth. Wilderness is what we long for, with its sense of authenticity, its emphasis on uninhibited growth, its reliance on body assurance.

Instead of inspiring terror, the Beast has turned into a romantic character who makes our ordinary lives look pallid. Tousled, irritable, difficult to deal with; often scarred; isolated in self-hatred, and contemptuous of worldly success, he lives in his own world. (In real life these days, we find our Beast-men on boats, in fishing and hunting camps, in workshops or garages, always in touch with bodies of one sort or another, literally in touch, since their fingertips are another kind of brain.)

Heroes are supposed to be handsome, but Beasts are ugly, or at least think they are ugly. "You examine me, Miss Eyre," says Mr. Rochester a short time after he meets the new governess he has hired. "Do you think me handsome?" Jane says that if she had stopped to think she would have given a conventionally polite reply,"but the answer somehow slipped from my tongue before I was aware: 'No, sir.' " And yet she admits to herself that if the stranger she met on the highway had been good-looking and gallant, if he had acted grateful for her help in getting up after a fall from his horse (another fall from a high horse, like that of Beauty's father in the fairy tale, when he was about to encounter sexuality), she would have known instinctively that there could be no sympathy between them.

A handsome man has had his gold plating rubbed thin by contact with the world. His life has been too easy; he knows nothing about suffering. Well aware that he can get any woman he wants whenever he wants one, he never commits to a single woman with the channeled intensity of a Beast.

A hint of ugliness, in fact, is spice for an erotic banquet. Too much ruins everything, but none at all is bland.

The hero is equal and opposite to the Beast, which is not surprising in view of the fact that they are alter egos. In stories, the hero is agreeable, polished, well mannered, dedicated to some noble undertaking larger than himself. The heroine cannot help but lean toward him, irresistibly drawn to a man so influential in world affairs that he doesn't need her.

In our terms, he's Victor Laszlo, the heroic leader of the French Resistance forces in the movie *Casablanca* (Paul Henreid). Without him, the Resistance will collapse. It s possible that no one will sing "The Marseillaise" in Morocco ever again. Meanwhile, the Beast named Rick (Bogart again) stays out of the fray, a drink in front of him and a cigarette dangling from his lips, licking his erotic wounds in his lair known as Ricks Cafe.

The heroine of *Casablanca* (Ingrid Bergman) makes no choice between them—the choice is made for her by the two men involved, which is fortunate, since she admires the sterling virtues of the hero, who happens to be her husband, but realizes the sad truth that heroes don t have much time to devote to women, not even their wives. Heroes don't wholeheartedly care for women, or for happiness either, not the way they care about their quests.

Lord Byron, Heathcliff, Edward Rochester, Rhett Butler. The intimidating Beast who isn't housebroken yet has ousted Prince Charming as the sex object of choice, even with his hands still smoking from crime (incest, wife-battering, bigamy, smuggling, in that order), though the heroine may not know her own heart at first.

Cathy Earnshaw of *Wuthering Heights* marries upper-class Edgar Linton, the master of Thrushcross Grange, but in life and death she remains the counterpart of Heathcliff, with the smells of the stables and moors about him.

Scarlett O'Hara, that Scarlett woman in *Gone with the Wind*, is madly in love with Ashley Wilkes, the hero with a classic profile who will soon ride off to fight for the Confederate cause, even though he knows it is doomed. But we understand at once that her soul mate is the mustachioed stranger with a quizzical half smile who shows up at a barbecue that is the last fling of Southern gentility before the Civil War begins.

"Who is that man? The one looking at us with a smile, the nasty dark one?" Scarlett asks another belle.

"My dear, don't you know?" her friend whispers. "Why, that's Rhett Butler. He has the most *terrible* reputation."

Scarlett peers at him over her shoulder. "He looks as if—as if he knows what I look like without my shimmy."

"My dear, he isn't received," her confidante continues. "He has to spend most of his time up North because his relatives in Charleston won't speak to him. … And then there's that business about the girl he wouldn't marry."

"Tell, tell!"

"*Well,* he took a girl out buggy-riding after dark without a chaperone, and then ..." (the girls put their heads together and whisper) "... and then he refused to marry her."

For a moment, Scarlett forgets that she's in love with Ashley, not with the Beast who has loped down from the North.

IT'S IN THIS GAP between the male hero and the Beast that the heroine finds the work of transformation laid out for her, which we accept without question as her task, not his. Women are biologically engineered for transformation. Lacking a man's strength to resist the unknown, a woman tries to enfold it when she meets it, change it if she can, or adapt to it if she cant. She takes a man s penis, which is strange to her, inside her body. She gives birth to a baby, and says to herself,"This isn't me. This is someone perfect, and I could never make any- thing perfect." (The fetus and placenta are the only foreign proteins that are not attacked and rejected by the human immune system.)

For a Beauty, this is the ultimate seduction, this sense that only she has the power to transform her Beast. If she accepts a man the way he is, because his faults are part of him, the two of them stay friends. But the moment she thinks that she can change the way he dresses, clean up his manners, persuade him to put his talents to use by getting a steady job, she admits to herself that she loves him. Her friends she can put up with the way they are, but her lovers and children must be popped into her cauldron and transformed by the heat into paragons of high achievement.

So long as the Beast remains a misfit, he attracts her, but he is of no use to her as a potential mate or to society as a whole, and so she goes out and serves society's ends without meaning to. She trans- forms him into a productive member of the group, which is harder than his job of transforming a virgin into a bedmate, even if she is still half in love with her father. A double transformation takes place: While he grows milder through her increasing acceptance of him and the love he feels, she becomes receptive to sex. He grows tender as she grows stronger.

In the end, she gets herself a Prince, whom she turns into a husband, co-signer of a mortgage, the future father of her children. She'd better hope that's what she wants instead of the sexually avid, socially marginal Beast he was in the first place.

In fiction, the heroine decides once and for all whether she chooses the hero or the Beast, but in real life every man embodies both, although one aspect or the other predominates, and only one appears at a time. Because of her ambivalence, a woman's split expectations may be too much for her mate. She wants to be loved by a Beast, vehemently, violently:

Oh, violate me in violet time
In the vilest way you know

as an old music-hall song implores. She wants Stanley Kowalski, in his sweaty wife-beater shirt *(A Streetcar Named Desire)*, to carry her into the bedroom and throw her on the bed. But she also wants to stay a virginal Beauty. She wants every move she makes to be scrutinized by a Beast focused on her, but she also wants the liberty of being ignored at times by a hero. She wants to be a hero herself, but biology keeps nudging her toward motherhood, which means an end to the time of courtship when she and an enchanted Beast lived only for the moment and for one another.

In a sense, she outgrows her Beast. She still wants him. In bed, she will always want him—if denied, she may go out looking for him—but by daylight she wants a father for her children, along with protection for herself in her role as a parent. Biology tells her to find a hero, armored with health insurance and a portable pension plan, who will work fifty, sixty hours a week at his job, whipped on by personal ambition to climb the career ladder. The price is that he'll come home too late to have supper with the children, also too exhausted to pay attention to her in bed—there's always a choice to be made between security and sex—but the family will own a house, and the children will have karate lessons, summer camp, and college tuition. If this doesn't work out according to plan, she may have to become a hero herself.

Torn between the Beast and the hero, what's a woman to do? She might listen to the anthropologist Margaret Mead (married three times herself), who said that every woman needs three mates: the first when she's young, for sex; the second for parenthood; and the third, presumably when her children are grown—when she's released at last from the dire imperatives of sex, fertility, and money——for companionship.

CENTURIES PASS. The wilderness shrinks. The predatory animals that used to be hunted (lions, tigers, crocodiles) have to be protected from extinction in wilderness sanctuaries. Sex, or at least our view of it, changes at the same time.

Nowadays, in this country a young woman more or less has to do what in the past she was forbidden to do: sleep around, or indulge in oral sex with the mistaken notion that this will protect her from the danger of AIDS. The girl may find herself freer than she wants to be, but conflicted. Once she gives up her virginity, she has to make a fresh decision at every encounter.

For a visual history of our shifting attitudes toward sex and the wilderness, we need only look at various artists' pictures of the Beast, who is never specifically described in fairy tales. In the early nineteenth century, illustrations in children's books showed Beauty's Beast as a huge black mole, or an imbecilic giant, or a wolf with the tusks and snout of a boar—whichever would be most loathsome to a virgin, in or out of marriage. By the end of the century, however, when arranged marriages were uncommon in Western countries, and when sex was not so fearsome a prospect for a virgin, the Beast's appearance undergoes a radical change. For the first time, he is shown wearing clothes and walking on two legs, revealing himself as the exiled aristocrat he is.

Suddenly, we see him as a man who carries an insupportable burden on his shoulders that cuts him off from his kind: the head of an animal, like Beauty's Beast; or a mask like the one worn by the Phantom of the Opera, to hide something worse that lies underneath; or if not a mask, then a perpetual scowl like Heathcliff or Mr. Rochester, meant to keep the world at a distance. His head is the remnant of his wild nature, the emblem of his suffering. Poised on top of the male's wide shoulders, it lets the heroine know that this creature is whatever he thinks he is, and he thinks himself a monster.

In Jean Cocteau's movie *Beauty and the Beast>* made in 1946, the Beast (as played by Cocteau's male lover, Jean Marais), is overwhelming, magnificent, noble as well as terrifying, like sex itself, a deserted god with glowing eyes and hands that gesture helplessly in jeweled gauntlets. A lace ruff supports his lionlike head, as if displaying it on a tray.

Beauty faints at her first glimpse of him. He lifts her off the ground and carries her to her room, the panels of his robe flowing up the stairs behind him. Tenderly, he lays her on the bed. His muzzle hovers over her face, the brow furrowed with lines that might have been made with a branding iron. She wakes and gasps. "You mustn't look into my eyes!" he exclaims, cringing as he raises his hands to screen his head. "Have no fear. You will see me only at seven each evening. But you must never look into my eyes." No horror, no pity—those he cannot endure. He wants a mate, not a mother. Hunched in shame, he backs out of the room and shuts the door.

In the Disney studio's version of the story, the inspiration for the Beast came from the head of a buffalo, a massive creature with crescent-shaped horns like that of the Minotaur, the ancient moon bull that is now a reminder of our former Wild West. Why a buffalo? the Disney artist was asked. Because the eyes are so sad, he replied. There is a profound seriousness in the expression of all wild creatures, but the buffalo in particular is the animal that white settlers almost exterminated in the American West, the native of the plains that once thundered in herds but must now be reestablished and fostered, primarily for the sake of their milk, which makes superior mozzarella, and their meat, which is uncontaminated by the hormones and antibiotics we pour into domestic cattle feed.

As WE KNOW THE MODERN BEAST, he lives in the wilderness we have destroyed, suffers from the erotic passion we have diluted, survives as an outcast who used to be a god. "Don't look into my eyes." he says to the heroine. Don't see my face, my suffering. Who are you to know what lies behind a mask? Something better or much worse perhaps, but not to be revealed.

And who has the right to strip away his shield?

Chapter IV

Walt Disney and French Fairy Tales

Beauties and their Beasts and Other Motherless Tales from the Wonderful World of Walt Disney

Mark Axelrod

One can clearly find commonalities in Disney's *Snow White, Sleeping Beauty, Cinderella, The Little Mermaid*, and *Beauty and the Beast*. On one level they are all Disney appropriations of works by nineteenth- and eighteenth-century writers such as the Grimms and Andersen, Perrault and Mme. Leprince de Beaumont. But they have another very interesting phenomenon in common: There are no mothers. Some of them have stepmothers, though they are evil and far removed from the matronly sacredness of a June Cleaver or a Harriet Nelson. However, none of the films have "real" mothers, that is, biological or genetic mothers. To think of the Disney phenomenon as predicated on the legitimacy of the "nuclear family," or on the notion Dan Quayle delivered at the 1992 Republican National Convention that "family" comes first, would merely be an illusion, like the "reality" imposed on celluloid itself. In a curious state of social allegiances, Quayle's admiration of family values, and, by extension, of a mother's role within the family, would be totally at odds with the rather perverted and divisive vision offered by Disney. The vision has become, for the current Disney "family," a phenomenon that approaches the role of mother in rather disparaging ways, and ultimately begs the question: How is it that some of Disney's greatest animated achievements are, if not misogynistic, works that have devalued motherhood and the role of the mother within the nuclear family?

One might think that Disney would be at the vanguard of motion picture filmmakers who produce adulating films about mothers and motherhood, since Disney is and has been clearly associated with the family, with "good, old-fashioned" family entertainment. One need not go into depth here about how important the role of mother is in the psychological development of the child. One could argue about the role of mother in terms of economics and the family, and where she has been classified in a sex-gender system which is and has been dominated by white males. One could also argue about the roles of mothers and fathers in terms of their ability or lack of ability to be nurturing. Certainly there are some men who are more nurturing than some women, and some women who are far more nurturing than other women, but clearly the role of mother is profound in the creation and maintenance of a child's self-esteem, of a child's sense of self, and of feelings about his/her mother and women. So where, then, does Disney (the company) fit into this archetypal system of mothers and mothering and nurturance? In fact, it does not.

One concern here is the issue of "adaptation" and how those works chosen by Disney and/or the Disney corporation have been adapted. There are and have been two main approaches to adaptation: fidelity to the target text and ability to manipulate the target text. In his article "The Well Worn Muse," Dudley Andrew writes that the distinctive feature related to adaptation is "the matching of the cinematic sign system to a prior achievement in some other system" and that "every representational film adapts a prior conception." But "adaptation delimits representation by insisting on the cultural status of the model" and "in a strong sense adaptation is the appropriation of a meaning from a prior text" (qtd. in McFarlane 21). Brian McFarlane goes on to say that "the stress on fidelity to the original undervalues other aspects of the film's intertextuality. By this, I mean those non-literary, non- novelistic influences that work on any film, whether or not it is based on a novel" (21). Certainly, McFarlane alludes to the notions of cinematic content or storyline, since the great majority of adaptations are not that concerned with the stylistic integrity generated by the target text. But McFarlane makes an extremely critical comment when he states,"It is equally clear, however, that many adaptations shave chosen paths other than that of the literal- minded visualization of the original or even of 'spiritual fidelity,' making quite obvious departures from the original. Such departures may be seen in the light of offering a *commentary* on or, in more extreme cases, a *deconstruction* ... of the original" (22). Disney, or the corporation that bears his name—past, present, and presumably future—has chosen certain texts for adaptation. Additionally, how it has decided to adapt those texts is critical, because, as McFarlane has argued, the Disney filmmakers make a decision on whether or not issues of "fidelity" to the target text are important. In other words, in the adaptation process, someone must make a decision as to whether the final project will adhere to or veer from the integrity of the target text. In that case, Disney has the option of "adapting" the "mothers" from those target texts as being nurturing, abusive, or absent.

Invariably, from *Snow White* to *Beauty and the Beast*, one sees in Disney "products" a clear vision of motherhood (if not the feminine) which tends to deal with matronly and/or womanly figures in one of three significant ways: (1) the role of mother is totally neglected or eliminated *{Sleeping Beauty, Beauty and the Beast*, even *Aladdin*); (2) the role of mother is reconstituted in the figure of the "cruel" stepmother *(Snow White, Cinderella)*; or (3) the role of a leading female authority figure, where no mother or stepmother exists, is transformed into an evil character *(The Little Mermaid)*. There is, of course, Cinderella's "fairy godmother," who, like Disney's stepmothers, is not a blood relative. She is neither mundane nor motherly, but ethereal and self-serving, since she exists not only as a mediating device between the "horrors" of living with an "evil" stepmother and the "joys" of living with a handsome and economically privileged prince, but exacts a price for her "matronly" consideration by reminding Cinderella that "the magic only lasts till midnight." When the clock strikes twelve, the fairy godmother's best little girl is once again in rags. The godmother does not act as a mother might, but as a mitigating medium between the sanctions of poverty and wealth. As for the good fairies in *Sleeping Beauty*, their magic acts only as a kind of "vaccine" against the "evil witch Maleficent." Yet throughout the story, the Queen, Sleeping Beauty's mother, plays no role at all in attempting to subvert Maleficent's evil intentions. It is only through the good graces of the fairies, Flora, Fauna and Merryweather, who sequester Sleeping Beauty in the woods, that she is protected at all. Once again, a mother is impotent to action and, by virtue of another woman's evil intentions, essentially abandons her child.

Examples from Disney's films are replete. There is no mention of Snow White's mother, nor of her father for that matter. From *Cinderella*: "Once upon a time a wealthy widower lived in a fine house with his daughter, Cinderella. ... Sadly the gentleman died soon after [remarriage] and Cinderella discovered that her stepmother was a cold and cruel woman." Once again there is no mention of the biological mother and the influence of her on Cinderella. Finally, from *Beauty and the Beast*:

> In a nearby village, there lived a young woman named Belle. She was the kindest and most beautiful girl in the village. Although she spent most of her time taking care of her father, Maurice, a hardworking but unsuccessful inventor, she loved to read more than anything else.

There is no mention of Belle's mother at all. As a matter of fact, there is no clear indication that any of the mothers alluded to or ignored were, in fact, the main character's biological mother, which raises some interesting questions about the biological legitimacy of the main character. It would not be out of the question to imagine Disney's vision of motherhood as the vision of a child who was either abandoned by his parents or who questioned his own birthright, an issue that has been dealt with before (see Ayres' chapter, "The Wonderful World of Disney: The World That Made the Man and the Man That Made the World").

What is curious about the Disney phenomenon of motherless children (primarily daughters) is that the same storyline has continued for over fifty years. From *Snow White* (1937) to *Beauty and the Beast* (1991), it is as if Walt Disney's predilection for commodifying virtue by selling products that either ignore or dehumanize the role of woman and/or mother has become a kind of Disney trademark, if not company policy, which has been carefully nurtured. Even mothers of nonhuman characters in animated features such as *Bambi, Dumbo,* and the most profitable of Disney's films, *The Lion King,* are either exterminated or are somehow ineffectual. In the "classic" Disney version, Bambi's mother is shot to death by a hunter. Dumbo's mother is physically restrained and can do nothing to safeguard her baby. Simba has little relation with his mother and is dependent on Timon, Pumbaa, and Rafiki. These erasures beg yet another question: Why did Walt Disney choose to reconstitute the mother figure as either absent or evil, as a creature who either abandons or abuses her young through birth or marriage, and why has The Walt Disney Company perpetuated the role?

In the biography *Walt Disney: Hollywood's Dark Prince,* Marc Eliot pays critical attention to Disney's relationship with his own mother: "Other times, during the day, Walt would sneak into his mother's bedroom and put her clothes on and her makeup. Afterward, he would stand in front of her full-length mirror to admire his reflection. He knew this version of his mother, unlike the real one, would always be there when he needed her" (7). To say Disney was a cross-dresser would be missing the point; he apparently experienced a sense of abandonment over and over again. Apparently he was plagued by doubts of his true parentage. "This infection of doubt," according to Eliot, "would eat at Walt the rest of his days, infusing his future films with a feverish passion that would deepen their dramatic themes" (12). These themes have been played out over and again in Disney as those of the *abandoned child* and the *nonexistent mother.* The culmination, at least for Disney, reached its peak with the adaptation of Carlo Lorenzini's (aka Carlo Collodi) *Pinocchio,* which was in production at the time of the death of Disney's own mother, a death which many believe to have been a suicide (Eliot 111–12). When Disney was finally able to return to production, the first thing he did was to rework the studio's plot of *Pinocchio,* eliminating almost all of the completed footage and rewriting a new script that eliminated a puppetmaker's wife (who would, of course, have become Pinocchio's mother) implied in an earlier script in favor of emphasizing the puppet's desire to become a human. The Eisnerian parallel here is, of course, the Little Mermaid, who also yearns to become a human being and in whose film one cannot overlook the role that free will presumably plays, especially in relation to capital conquest. After all, the man she loves is a prince, not a pauper.

For some unclear reason, however, the Disney magic, fabricated to engage the imagination of the ideal and not the recognition of the real, subsumes any notion of the role of mother. In speaking of *Snow White,* for example, the brilliant Russian filmmaker Sergei Eisenstein was overwhelmed by the *medium* and overlooked the *message* when he wrote, "Disney's works themselves strike me as the same kind of drop of comfort, an instant of relief, a fleeting touch of lips in the hell of social burdens, injustices, torments, in which the circle of his American viewers is forever trapped" (qtd. in Leyda 7). Though on some preadolescent level, perhaps Eisenstein was too infatuated with the techniques of Disney's animation to recognize the flaws in the subtext on an adult level. As Ariel Dorfman and Armand Mattelart have written in their brilliant analysis, *How to Read Donald Duck,*

> There are automagic antibodies in Disney. They tend to neutralize criticism because they are the same values already instilled into people, in the tastes, reflexes and attitudes which inform everyday experience at all levels.

Disney manages to subject these values to the extremist degree of commercial exploitation. The potential assailer is thus condemned in advance by what is known as "public opinion," that is, the thinking of people who have already been conditioned by the Disney message and have based their social and family life on it. (28)

Animation genius aside, *Snow White* was just the point of departure for a collection of animated films which, regardless of their animation value or the brilliance of their scores or their sizable worth in commodified objects sold in Disney stores, clearly eliminate the role of mother as a nurturing, comforting hedge against the evils in the world. Certainly Eisenstein, whose works were so preeminently humane, should have recognized that flaw. In contrast, the image of the mother is reconstituted such that the feminine is "raised" to a level in which stepparental child abuse is often an acceptable mode of behavior (*Snow White* and *Cinderella*) or in which motherhood exists only as something that may be implicitly nostalgic, but never uttered (*The Little Mermaid* and *Beauty and the Beast*).

One could make the argument that the stories Disney chose to animate were not his stories to begin with and the apparently negative role of mother is something for which Disney need not take responsibility. Accurate reproduction of details seemingly has not been a priority for Disney (the company). In the original story of *Snow White* which Disney adapted, the Grimm brothers create a mother who dies, an evil stepmother who eventually also dies, seven dwarfs (none of whom had names), and a prince who takes pity on Snow-White and takes her coffin with him:

> The prince ordered his servants to carry the coffin on their shoulders [perhaps not to soil his own], but they stumbled over some shrubs, and the jolt caused the poisoned piece of apple that Snow-White had bitten off to be released from her throat. It was not long before she opened her eyes, lifted the lid of the coffin, sat up, and was alive again. (Grimms 204)

Such an ending was not in keeping with the romantic way Disney stories should end. Regardless of how the tale is told, the fact still remains that it was Disney who, out of dozens of Grimms' tales to be told, ultimately chose both *Snow White* and *Cinderella* to adapt to the Disney formula. In both originals, the mothers are kindly and caring, even though they die while their daughters are very young. In *Cinderella* the dying mother says, "Dear child, be good and pious. Then the dear Lord shall always assist you and I shall look down from heaven and take care of you" (Grimms 86). Disney's version not only omits a mother—more strikingly—it omits a pious mother, as if no such creature could exist.

All of this psychodrama accounts for why Disney himself may have preferred to create a motherless universe for his adolescent female characters, but what of the new Disney? What of the Disney after Walt, where the board of directors do not have to ask themselves the hand-wringing question "What would Walt have done?" to get something accomplished? Hans Christian Andersen's *The Little Mermaid* is an excellent example of how a work can be "Disneyfied" (in the best Disney tradition) beyond reasonable recognition and without the authority of Disney the man. In Andersen's story, "for many years the king of the sea had been a widower, and his old mother kept house for him. She was a wise woman and proud of her royal birth. ...she deserved much praise, especially because she was so fond of the little princesses, her grandchildren" (39). Clearly the role of mother has not been relegated to an inferior position, and the figure of the Little Mermaid's grandmother plays a prominent role in the story, as do the Little Mermaid's five sisters (none having any significant role in the film). Granted, the Sea Witch is present in Andersen's tale, but she mediates between the world of the sea and the world of the humans. Though she exacts a price from the Little Mermaid (the appropriation of the Mermaid's voice), she is not destroyed in the end to exact a happy ending. To the contrary, the Little Mermaid dies. The fact that this film is a post-Walt production only accents the notion that the Disney company, at least when it comes to animation, has been and will continue to be an advocate of a motherless universe. Apparently it is proud of that accomplishment if one is to believe in the economic viability of such projects.

After Walt Disney's death in 1966, the Disney empire appeared on the verge of being swallowed by itself. According to Mark Portland Peter Behr in their book *The Leading Edge* (1987),

> the company's decline was traced to a group of managers that seemed bent on not offending the memory of Walt Disney. Under the leadership of long-time Disney employee Cardon Walker and then Ronald W. Miller—Walt Disney's son-in-law—the company meandered through the two decades after the founder's death with its output reflecting anything but the vastly changing culture of those years. … At Walt Disney Productions, it seemed, projects were being judged not so much on creative or artistic merits, but rather by one criterion: "What would Walt have done?" (153)

Though Eisner has accomplished a major economic overhaul of Disney Productions, certain components of the Walt Disney vision are still viable. Quoting Eisner, Potts writes that "the basic fabric of the company hopefully will remain, and on that fabric we will build a different company. It's clearly a different company, but at the same time, the same company" (153). It has been Eisner who has pushed the rereleasing of a number of Disney's older animated features which are also older animated visions of "mother" (or lack of her), such as *Snow White, Bambi, Dumbo,* and *Pinocchio,* violating the Disney Commandment, "Thou Shalt Not Overexpose." It is also Eisner who has promoted the new animated features which are also the new visions of mother (or the lack of her) in *The Little Mermaid, Aladdin,* and *Beauty and the Beast.* As Richard Schickel writes in *The Disney Version,*

> Before his first month in office had passed, Michael Eisner was saying things that no one at Disney had ever dared to say before. For example, he was looking at video in a new way, speculating that carefully controlled exposure in these markets could perhaps enhance the value of some of the studio's classics, teasing the public into a new awareness of their virtues—while contributing mightily to cash flow. He was proposing, as well, that there might be valid ways for the studio to use the less costly and long-eschewed techniques of limited animation to penetrate the Saturday-morning television cartoon market, which Disney had abandoned to competitors less caring about what was said and shown. (425)

The notion that Disney was "more caring" than its competitors regarding "what was said and shown" is, apparently, no longer a consideration at least in terms of the family. One of Disney's later television dalliances, *Goof Troop,* has, presumably, rendered Goofy divorced at best, a widower at worst; and Max, his son, motherless. The entire show, if not promoting the virtues of capitalism, clearly extols the apparent virtues of dysfunctional families. It is certainly too late to blame Uncle Walt for that, though the method and manner is certainly in keeping with the Disney tradition of motherless families led by Mickey and Minnie, Donald and Daisy, and all of Donald's nephews. Actually, even Pluto is without a mom to call his own.

One could argue that Walt Disney was ahead of his time, that he was prescient and foresaw the inevitable disintegration of the nuclear family into a family of "familial foreigners" controlled by "heartless stepmothers." In a way, he predated the Reagan-Bush years, in which, as Barbara Kruger maintains, there was "the substitution of an idyllic image of family life for the real life material struggles of a dissolving American family" (qtd. in Bassin 199). Supposing that Disney's vision of children in America was the correct one and that perhaps Snow White's evil stepmother (who wanted Snow White killed and her heart returned in a box) was merely reflective of the real American attitude toward children, an attitude that W.C. Fields made a part of Americana and that no V-chip could ever eliminate—one could make that argument, but it would be a feckless one, if not a cynical one, for Disney's choice in creating a motherless and faithless universe is much different than Eisner's choice in creating a motherless and faithless universe. For Disney, it seems, the choice arose out of a psychological void contingent on a family life seemingly filled less with joy and nurturance than with confusion and abuse. Eisner's perpetuation of the devalued role of mother seems to be based upon a position of profitability; and that, ironically, is "what Walt would have wanted."

Since Eisner's "coronation," Disney has gone from economically susceptible to economically resplendent. Its films have garnered billions of dollars, not only from animated features, but through ancillary spin-offs such as videos, CDs, dolls, puppets, trinkets, key chains *ad nauseum ad astra*—the stuff which Italians call "Americanata" and which Nabokov would have called "poshlost." For example, as Leonard Maltin has written,

> In 1938 it was estimated that *Snow White* had earned $4.2 million in the United States and Canada alone. After its eighth reissue in 1993 that total had swelled to more than $80 million. In 1989, *USA Today* computed that if one adjusted for inflation and changing box-office prices, *Snow White's* theatrical earnings up to that time would exceed six billion dollars! When the film made its long-awaited video debut in 1994, it outsold *Jurassic Park* (its contemporary "rival" for release that fall) to become the biggest-selling video of all time. (32)

Huge profits indeed for the animated versions of child abuse and attempted murder.

In terms of economic viability, Eisner's decisions have put the magic kingdom back in the darkest recesses of the black. But at what cost? For some, like Eisenstein, the subtext of a motherless universe seems to be unimportant. Why create an animated feature in which parents (especially mothers) play a vital role when one can do without them so effectively? So cost effectively? Certainly, to consider doing the obverse would not cost Disney anything extra in dollars, since motherhood (like the Notre Dame hunchback, who is yet another motherless character) is public domain and, therefore, free of any cost for Disney to adapt. But in an era when notions of the family from El Ché to Dan Quayle to Rush Limbaugh can actually have something in common, is it possible that the Disney company stands alone as some kind of ultra-reactionary monolith, durable in its fidelity to eliminating motherhood? The great irony in all of this is that the entire notion of "family entertainment" is brought into question. John Taylor, in *Storming the Magic Kingdom,* has written that besides the rather false image which Disney gave to others, relative to the way "good family men" are supposed to be (he swore, smoked, and drank routinely),

> it was true that a gap existed between the social standards Disney upheld and the personal behavior of many of the men who set them. But Disney's executives fussed and fretted over the company's image precisely because Disney was in the family entertainment business. More than that, Disney did market a value system. … The experience offered by the parks and by Disney films could be intermittently frightening or sad, but it was not designed to challenge the assumptions of customers or assault middle- class values. (25–26)

Not designed to assault middle-class values? If one assumes that demeaning the role of mother is not assaulting middle-class values, then certainly Disney had, and Eisner has, his finger on the pulse of American values.

And to that end, and to the Disney company's "credit," for over five decades (if not longer) it has been able to maintain the image of a family-oriented family company (albeit transnational) while at the same time producing a product that if not demeaning to mothers, then totally ignores them in the grand scheme of child rearing and in the extended name of "family values." In a way, there is something unconscionable about all of that; about that illusory image the Disney company has conceived, exploited, and maintained; about the hypocrisy which was Disney in his own fashion and which he fashioned in that image and about the commodification of that image.

Curiously,"film critics," such as Maltin and Michael Medved, seem somehow oblivious to this commodifying image. In Medved's book *Hollywood vs. America,* a work presumably "taking on" the film and television industry because of its negative attitude toward family values (and a book endorsed by Limbaugh), the chapter titled "Maligning Marriage" says practically nothing about motherhood per se, and nowhere in the book does Medved "take on" the pervasive "Disney attitude" about the family. Perhaps Medved, like Maltin, like so many others "in the business," are oblivious-to what Disney does and has done. Perhaps, like Eisenstein, they merely "see" what they want to see and disregard the rest. Perhaps it is the fact that the films are really cartoons with cartoon characters and as such remove us from those daily tragedies in which the same stories filmed with humans would render us outraged at the abuse and the violence and the indifference. Perhaps that is the greatest of Disney's achievements: to render harmless that which is harmful. In a way, each time one pays a Disney price for a Disney product, one is contributing to the exploitation of that "family image" which somehow flies in the face of any genuine notion of family and is not only disingenuous, but deceitful. In large measure, it truly validates the Disney company's monopoly on the "fiction of family" and renders large the meagerness of motherhood.

Works Cited

Andersen, H. C. *Andersen's Fairy Tales.* Trans. Pat Shaw Iversen. New York: Penguin, 1987.

Bassin, Donna, Margaret Honey, and Meryle Mahrer Kaplan, eds. *Representations of Motherhood.* New Haven:Yale UP, 1994.

Dorfman, Ariel, and Armand Mattelart. *How to Read Donald Duck: Imperialist Ideology in the Disney Comic.* Trans, and introd. David Kunzle. New York: International General, 1975.

Eliot, Marc. *Walt Disney: Hollywood's Dark Prince.* New York: Carol Publishing Group, 1993.

Grimms. *The Complete Fairy Tales of the Brothers Grimm.* Trans. Jack Zipes. New York: Bantam, 1987

Leyda, Jay, ed. *Eisenstein on Disney.* London: Methuen, 1988.

Maltin, Leonard. *The Disney Films.* New York: Hyperion Books, 1995.

McFarlane, Brian. *Novel to Film: An Introduction to the Theory of Adaptation.* Oxford: Clarendon P, 1996.

Medved, Michael. *Hollywood vs. America.* New York: HarperCollins, 1993.

Potts, Mark, and Peter Behr. *The Leading Edge: CEOs Who Turned Their Companies Around: What They Did and How They Did It.* New York: McGraw-Hill, 1987.

Schickel, Richard. *The Disney Version: The Life, Times, Art and Commerce of Walt Disney.* New York: Simon and Schuster, 1985.

Snow White and the Seven Dwarfs. Dir. David Hand. Animated. Voices: Adriana Caselotti and Harry Stockwell. The Walt Disney Company. 1937.

Taylor, John. *Storming the Magic Kingdom: Wall Street, the Raiders and the Battle for Disney.* New York: Knopf, 1987.

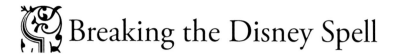

Breaking the Disney Spell

Jack Zipes

It was not once upon a time, but at a certain time in history, before anyone knew what was happening, that Walt Disney cast a spell on the fairy tale, and he has held it captive ever since. He did not use a magic wand or demonic powers. On the contrary, Disney employed the most up-to-date technological means and used his own "American" grit and ingenuity to appropriate European fairy tales. His technical skills and ideological proclivities were so consummate that his signature has obfuscated the names of Charles Perrault, the Brothers Grimm, Hans Christian Andersen, and Carlo Collodi. If children or adults think of the great classical fairy tales today, be it *Snow White, Sleeping Beauty,* or *Cinderella,* they will think Walt Disney. Their first and perhaps lasting impressions of these tales and others will have emanated from a Disney film, book, or artifact. Though other filmmakers and animators produced remarkable fairy-tale films, Disney managed to gain a cultural stranglehold on the fairy tale, and this stranglehold has even tightened with the recent productions of *Beauty and the Beast* (1991) and *Aladdin (1992).* The man's spell over the fairy tale seems to live on even after his death.

But what does the Disney spell mean? Did Disney achieve a complete monopoly on the fairy tale during his lifetime? Did he imprint a particular *American* vision on the fairy tale through his animated films that dominates our perspective today? And, if he did manage to cast his mass-mediated spell on the fairy tale so that we see and read the classical tales through his lens, is that so terrible? Was Disney a nefarious wizard of some kind whose domination of the fairy tale should be lamented? Wasn't he just more inventive, more skillful, more in touch with the American spirit of the times than his competitors, who also sought to animate the classical fairy tale for the screen?

Of course, it would be a great exaggeration to maintain that Disney's spell totally divested the classical fairy tales of their meaning and invested them with his own. But it would not be an exaggeration to assert that Disney was a radical filmmaker who changed our way of viewing fairy tales, and that his revolutionary technical means capitalized on American innocence and utopianism to reinforce the social and political status quo. His radicalism was of the right and the righteous. The great "magic" of the Disney spell is that he animated the fairy tale only to transfix audiences and divert their potential UTOPIAN dreams and hopes through the false promises of the images he CAST UPON the screen. But before we come to a full understanding of this magical spell, we must try to understand what he did to the fairy tale that was so revolutionary and why he did it.

The Oral and Literary Fairy Tales

The evolution of the fairy tale as a literary genre is marked by dialectical appropriation that set the cultural conditions for its institutionalization and its expansion as a mass-mediated form through radio, film, and television. Fairy tales were first *told* by gifted tellers and were based on rituals intended to endow with meaning the daily lives of members of a tribe. As *oral folk tales,* they were intended to explain natural occurrences such as the change of the seasons and shifts in the weather or to celebrate the rites of harvesting, hunting, marriage, and conquest. The emphasis in most folk tales was on communal harmony. A narrator or narrators told tales to bring members of a group or tribe closer together and to provide them with a sense of mission, a *telos.* The tales themselves assumed a generic quality based on the function that they were to fulfill for the community or the incidents that they were to report, describe, and explain. Consequently, there were tales of initiation, worship, warning, and indoctrination. Whatever the type may have been, the voice of the narrator was known. The tales came directly from common experiences and beliefs. Told in person, directly, face-to-face, they were altered as the beliefs and behaviors of the members of a particular group changed.

With the rise of literacy and the invention of the printing press in the fifteenth century, the oral tradition of storytelling underwent an immense revolution. The oral tales were taken over by a different social class, and the form, themes, production, and reception of the tales were transformed. This change did not happen overnight, but it did foster discrimination among writers and their audiences almost immediately so that distinct genres were recognized and approved for certain occasions and functions within polite society or cultivated circles of readers. In the case of folk tales, they were gradually categorized as legends, myths, fables, comical anecdotes, and, of course, fairy tales. What we today consider fairy tales were actually just one type of the folk-tale tradition, namely the *Zaubermärchen* or the magic tale, which has many sub-genres. The French writers of the late seventeenth century called these tales *contes de fées* (fairy tales) to distinguish them from other kinds of *contes populaires* (popular tales), and what really distinguished a *conte de fée,* based on the oral *Zaubermärchen,* was its transformation into a literary tale that addressed the concerns, tastes, and functions of court society The fairy tale had to fit into the French salons, parlors, and courts of the aristocracy and bourgeoisie if it was to establish itself as a genre. The writers, Mme D'Aulnoy, Charles Perrault, Mile L'Héritier, Mile de La Force, etc., knew and expanded upon oral and literary tales. They were not the initiators of the literary fairy-tale tradition in Europe (cf. Zipes 1989). Two Italian writers, Giovanni Francesco Straparola and Giambattista Basile, had already set an example for what the French were accomplishing.[1] But the French writers created an institution, that is, the genre of the literary fairy tale was institutionalized as an aesthetic and social means through which questions and issues of *civilité,* proper behavior and demeanor in all types of situations, were mapped out as narrative strategies for literary socialization, and in many cases, as symbolic gestures of subversion to question the ruling standards of taste and behavior.

While the literary fairy tale was being institutionalized at the end of the seventeenth and beginning of the eighteenth century in France, the oral tradition did not disappear, nor was it subsumed by the new literary genre. Rather, the oral tradition continued to feed the writers with material and was now also influenced by the literary tradition itself. The early chapbooks (cheap books), known as the *Bibliothèque Bleue,* that were carried by peddlers or *colporteurs* to the villages throughout France contained numerous abbreviated and truncated versions of the literary tales, and these were in turn told once again in these communities. In some cases, the literary tales presented new material that was transformed through the oral tradition and returned later to literature by a writer who remembered hearing a particular story.

By the beginning of the nineteenth century when the Brothers Grimm set about to celebrate German culture through their country's folk tales, the literary fairy tale had long since been institutionalized, and they, along with Hans Christian Andersen, Carlo Collodi, Ludwig Bechstein, and a host of Victorian writers from George MacDonald to Oscar Wilde, assumed different ideological and aesthetic positions within this institutionalization. These writers put the finishing touches on the fairy-tale genre at a time when nation-states were assuming their modern form and cultivating particular types of literature as commensurate expressions of national cultures.

What were the major prescriptions, expectations, and standards of the literary fairy tale by the end of the nineteenth century? Here it is important first to make some general remarks about the "violent" shift from the oral to the literary tradition and not just talk about the appropriation of the magic folk tale as a dialectical process. Appropriation does not occur without violence to the rhetorical text created in the oral tales (cf. Armstrong and Tennenhouse 1989). Such violation of oral storytelling was crucial and necessary for the establishment of the bourgeoisie because it concerned the control of desire and imagination within the symbolic order of western culture.

Unlike the oral tradition, the literary tale was written down to be read in private, although, in some cases, the fairy tales were read aloud in parlors. However, the book form enabled the reader to withdraw from his or her society and to be alone with a tale. This privatization violated the communal aspects of the folk tale, but the very printing of a fairy tale was already a violation since it was based on separation of social classes. Extremely few people could read, and the fairy tale in form and content furthered notions of elitism and separation. In fact, the French fairy tales heightened the aspect of the chosen aristocratic elite who were always placed at the center of the seventeenth- and eighteenth-century narratives. They were part and parcel of the class struggles in the discourses of that period. To a certain extent, the fairy tales were the outcome of violent "civilized" struggles, material representations, which represented struggles for hegemony. As Nancy Armstrong and Leonard Tennenhouse have suggested,

> a class of people cannot produce themselves as a ruling class without setting themselves off against certain Others. Their hegemony entails possession of the key cultural terms determining what are the right and wrong ways to be a human being. (1989, 24)

No matter where the literary tale took root and established itself—France, Germany, England—it was written in a standard "high" language that the folk could not read, and it was written as a form of entertainment and education for members of the ruling classes. Indeed, only the well-to-do could purchase the books and read them. In short, by institutionalizing the literary fairy tale, writers and publishers violated the forms and concerns of non-literate, essentially peasant communities and set new standards of taste, production, and reception through the discourse of the fairy tale.

The literary fairy tales tended to exclude the majority of people who could not read, while the folk tales were open to everyone. Indeed, the literary narratives were individualistic and unique in form and exalted the power of those chosen to rule. In contrast, the oral tales had themes and characters that were readily recognizable and reflected common wish-fulfillments. Of course, one had to know the dialect in which they were told. From a philological standpoint, the literary fairy tale elevated the oral tale through the standard practice of printing and setting grammatical rules in "high French" or "high German." The process of violation is *not* one of total negation and should not be studied as one-dimensional, for the print culture enabled the tales to be preserved and cultivated, and the texts created a new realm of pleasurable reading that allowed for greater reflection on the part of the reader than could an oral performance of a tale. At the beginning, the literary fairy tales were written and published for adults, and though they were intended to reinforce the mores and values of French *civilité*, they were so symbolic and could be read on so many different levels that they were considered somewhat dangerous: social behavior could not be totally dictated, prescribed, and controlled through the fairy tale, and there were subversive features in language and theme. This is one of the reasons that fairy tales were not particularly approved for children. In most European countries it was not until the end of the eighteenth and early part of the nineteenth century that fairy tales were published for children, and even then begrudgingly, because their "vulgar" origins in the lower classes were suspect. Of course, the fairy tales for children were sanitized and expurgated versions of the fairy tales for adults, or they were new moralistic tales that were aimed at the domestication of the imagination, as Rüdiger Steinlein has demonstrated in his significant study.[2] The form and structure of the fairy tale for children were carefully regulated in the nineteenth century so that improper thoughts and ideas would not be stimulated in the minds of the young. If one looks carefully at the major writers of fairy tales for children who became classical and popular in the nineteenth century,[3] it is clear that they themselves exercised self-censorship and restraint in conceiving and writing down tales for children.

This is not to argue that the literary fairy tale as institution became one in which the imagination was totally domesticated. On the contrary, by the end of the nineteenth century the genre served different functions. As a whole, it formed a multi-vocal network of discourses through which writers used familiar motifs, topoi, protagonists, and plots symbolically to comment on the civilizing process and socialization in their respective countries. These tales did not represent communal values but rather the values of a particular writer. Therefore, if the writer subscribed to the hegemonic value system of his or her society and respected the canonical ideology of Perrault, the Grimms, and Andersen, he/she would write a conventional tale with conservative values, whether for adults or children. On the other hand, many writers would parody, mock, question, and undermine the classical literary tradition and produce original and subversive tales that were part and parcel of the institution itself

The so-called original and subversive tales have kept the dynamic quality of the dialectical appropriation alive, for there has always been a danger that the written word, in contrast to the spoken word, will fix a structure, image, metaphor, plot, and value as sacrosanct. For instance, for some people the Grimms' fairy tales are holy, or fairy tales are considered holy and not to be touched. How did this notion emanate?

To a certain extent it was engendered by the Grimms and other folklorists who believed that the fairy tales arose from the spirit of the folk. Yet, worship of the fairy tale as holy scripture is a petrification of the fairy tale that is connected to the establishment of correct speech, values, and power more than anything else. This establishment through the violation of the oral practices was the great revolution and transformation of the fairy tale.

By the end of the nineteenth century the literary fairy tale had the following crucial functions as institution in middle-class society:

1. It introduced notions of elitism and separatism through a select canon of tales geared to children who knew how to read.
2. Though it was also told, the fact that the fairy tale was printed and in a book with pictures gave it more legitimacy and enduring value than an oral tale that disappeared soon after it was told.
3. It was often read by a parent in a nursery, school, or bedroom to soothe a child's anxieties, for the fairy tales for children were optimistic and were constructed with the closure of the happy end.
4. Although the plots varied and the themes and characters were altered, the classical fairy tale for children and adults reinforced the patriarchal symbolic order based on rigid notions of sexuality and gender.
5. In printed form the fairy tale was property and could be taken by its owner and read by its owner at his or her leisure for escape, consolation, or inspiration.
6. Along with its closure and reinforcement of patriarchy, the fairy tale also served to encourage notions of rags to riches, pulling yourself up by your bootstraps, dreaming, miracles, etc.
7. There was always tension between the literary and oral traditions. The oral tales have continued to threaten the more conventional and classical tales because they can question, dislodge, and deconstruct the written tales. Moreover, within the literary tradition itself, there were numerous writers such as Charles Dickens, George MacDonald, Lewis Carroll, Oscar Wilde, and Edith Nesbit who questioned the standardized model of what a fairy tale should be.
8. It was through script by the end of the nineteenth century that there was a full-scale debate about what oral folk tales and literary fairy tales were and what their respective functions should be. By this time the fairy tale had expanded as a high art form (operas, ballets, dramas) and low art form (folk plays, vaudevilles, and parodies) as well as a form developed classically and experimentally for children and adults. The oral tales continued to be disseminated through communal gatherings of different kinds, but they were also broadcast by radio and gathered in books by folklorists. Most important in the late

nineteenth century was the rise of folklore as an institution and of various schools of literary criticism that dealt with fairy tales and folk tales.

9. Though many fairy-tale books and collections were illustrated (some lavishly) in the nineteenth century, the images were very much in conformity with the text. The illustrators were frequently anonymous and did not seem to count. Though the illustrations often enriched and deepened a tale, they were generally subservient to the text.

However, the domination of the word in the development of the fairy tale as genre was about to change. The next great revolution in the institutionalization of the genre was the film, for the images now imposed themselves on the text and formed their own text in violation of print but also with the help of the print culture. And here is where Walt Disney and other animators enter the scene.

Disney's Magical Rise

By the turn of the twentieth century there had already been a number of talented illustrators, such as Gustav Doré, George Cruikshank, Walter Crane, Charles Folkard, and Arthur Rackham, who had demonstrated great ingenuity in their interpretations of fairy tales though their images. In addition, the broadside, broadsheet, or *image d'Epinal* had spread in Europe and America during the latter part of the nineteenth century as a forerunner of the comic book, and these sheets with printed images and texts anticipated the first animated cartoons that were produced at the beginning of the twentieth century. Actually, the French filmmaker Georges Méliès began experimenting as early as 1896 with types of fantasy and fairy-tale motifs, in his *féeries* or trick films (Jacobs 1979). He produced versions of *Cinderella, Bluebeard*, and *Little Red Riding Hood* among others. However, since the cinema industry itself was still in its early phase of development, it was difficult for Méliès to bring about a major change in the technological and cinematic institutionalization of the genre. As Lewis Jacobs has remarked,

> this effort of Méliès illustrated rather than re-created the fairy tale. Yet, primitive though it was, the order of the scenes did form a coherent, logical, and progressive continuity. A new way of making moving pictures had been invented. Scenes could now be staged and selected specially for the camera, and the movie maker could control both the material and its arrangement. (1979, 13)

During the early part of the twentieth century Walter Booth, Anson Dyer, Lotte Reiniger, Walter Lantz and others all used fairy tale plots in different ways in trick films and cartoons, but none of the early animators ever matched the intensity with which Disney occupied himself with the fairy tale. In fact, it is noteworthy that Disney's very first endeavors in animation (not considering the advertising commercials he made) were the fairy-tale adaptations that he produced with Ub Iwerks in Kansas City in 1922–23: *The Four Musicians of Bremen, Little Red Riding Hood, Fuss in Boots, Jack and the Beanstalk, Goldie Locks and the Three Bears*, and *Cinderella*.[4] To a certain degree, Disney identified so closely with the fairy tales he appropriated that it is no wonder his name virtually became synonymous with the genre of the fairy tale itself.

However, before discussing Disney's particular relationship to the fairytale tradition, it is important to consider the conditions of early animation in America and role of the animator in general, for all this has a bearing on Disney's productive relationship with the fairy tale. In his important study, *Before Mickey: The Animated Film 1898–1928*, Donald Crafton remarks that the early animated film was the location of a process found elsewhere in cinema but nowhere else in such intense concentration: self-figuration, the tendency of the filmmaker to interject himself into his film. This can take several forms, it can be direct or indirect, and more or less camouflaged. … At first it was obvious and literal; at the end it was subtle and cloaked in metaphors and symbolic imagery designed to facilitate the process and yet to keep the idea gratifying for the artist and the audience. Part of the animation game consisted of developing mythologies that gave the animator some sort of special status. Usually these were very flattering, for he was pictured as (or implied to be) a demigod, a purveyor of life itself (1982, 11)

As Crafton convincingly shows, the early animators before Disney literally drew themselves into the pictures and often appeared as characters in the films. One of the more interesting aspects of the early animated films is a psychically loaded tension between the artist and the characters he draws, one that is ripe for a Freudian or Lacanian reading, for the artist is always threatening to take away their "lives," while they, in turn, seek to deprive him of his pen (phallus) or creative inspiration so that they can control their own lives. (Almost all the early animators were men, and their pens and camera work assume a distinctive phallic function in early animation.) The hand with pen or pencil is featured in many animated films in the process of creation, and it is then transformed in many films into the tail of a cat or dog. This tail then acts as the productive force or artist's instrument throughout the film. For instance, Disney in his Alice films often employed a cat named Julius, who would take off his tail and use it as stick, weapon, rope, hook, question mark, etc. It was the phallic means to induce action and conceive a way out of a predicament.

The celebration of the pen/phallus as ruler of the symbolic order of the film was in keeping with the way that animated films were actually produced in the studios during the 1920s. That is, most of the studios, largely located in New York, had begun to be run on the Taylor system by men who joined together under the supervision of the head of the studio to produce the cartoons. After making his first fairy-tale films in close cooperation with Ub Iwerks in Kansas City, Disney moved to Hollywood, where he developed the taylorized studio to the point of perfection. Under his direction, the films were carefully scripted to project his story or vision of how a story should be related. The story-line was carried by hundreds of repetitious images created by the artists in his studios. Their contribution was in many respects like that of the dwarfs in *Snow White and the Seven Dwarfs*: they were to do the spadework, while the glorified prince was to come along and carry away the prize.

It might be considered somewhat one-dimensional to examine all of Disney's films as self-figurations, or embodiments of the chief designer's[5] wishes and beliefs. However, to understand Disney's importance as designer and director of fairy-tale films that set a particular pattern and model as the film industry developed, it does make sense to elaborate on Crafton's notion of self-figuration, for it provides an important clue for grasping the further development of the fairy tale as animated film or film in general.

We have already seen that one of the results stemming from the shift from the oral to the literary in the institutionalization of the fairy tale was a loss of live contact with the storyteller and a sense of community or commonality. This loss was a result of the social-industrial transformations at the end of the nineteenth century with the *Gemeinschaft* (community-based society) giving way to the *Gesellschaft* (contract-based society). However, it was not a total loss, for industrialization brought about greater comfort, sophistication, and literacy in addition to new kinds of communication in public institutions. Therefore, as I have demonstrated, the literary fairy tale's ascent corresponded to violent and progressive shifts in society and celebrated individualism, subjectivity, and reflection. It featured the narrative voice of the educated author and publisher over communal voices and set new guidelines for freedom of speech and expression. In addition, proprietary rights to a particular tale were established, and the literary tale became a commodity that paradoxically spoke out in the name of the unbridled imagination. In- deed, because it was born out of alienation, the literary fairy tale fostered a search for new "magical" means to overcome the instrumentalization of the imagination.

By 1900 literature began to be superseded by the mechanical means of reproduction that, Walter Benjamin declared, were revolutionary:

> the technique of reproduction detaches the reproduced object from the domain of tradition. By making many reproductions it substitutes a plurality of copies of a unique existence. And in permitting the reproduction to meet the beholder or listener in his own particular situation, it re- activates the object reproduced. These two processes lead to a tremendous shattering of tradition which is the obverse of the contemporary crisis and renewal of mankind. Both processes are intimately connected with the contemporary mass movements. Their most powerful agent is the film. Its social significance, particularly in its most positive form, is inconceivable without its destructive, cathartic aspect, that is, the liquidation of the traditional value of the cultural heritage. (1968, 223)

Benjamin analyzed how the revolutionary technological nature of the film could either bring about an aestheticization of politics leading to the violation of the masses through fascism, or a politicization of aesthetics that provides the necessary critical detachment for the masses to take charge of their own destiny.

In the case of the fairy-tale film at the beginning of the twentieth century, there are "revolutionary" aspects that we can note, and they prepared the way for progressive innovation that expanded the horizons of viewers and led to greater understanding of social conditions and culture. But there were also regressive uses of mechanical reproduction that brought about the cult of the personality and commodification of film narratives. For instance, the voice in fairy-tale films is at first effaced so that the image totally dominates the screen, and the words or narrative voice can only speak through the designs of the animator who, in the case of Walt Disney, has signed his name prominently on the screen. In fact, for a long time, Disney did not give credit to the artists and technicians who worked on his films. These images were intended both to smash the aura of heritage and to celebrate the ingenuity, inventiveness, and genius of the animator. In most of the early animated films, there were few original plots, and the story-lines did not count. Most important were the gags, or the technical inventions of the animators ranging from the introduction of live actors to interact with cartoon characters, to improving the movement of the characters so that they did not shimmer, to devising ludicrous and preposterous scenes for the sake of spectacle. It did not matter what story was projected just as long as the images astounded the audience, captured its imagination for a short period of time, and left the people laughing or staring in wonderment. The purpose of the early animated films was to make audiences awestruck and to celebrate the magical talents of the animator as demigod. As a result, the fairy tale as story was a vehicle for animators to express their artistic talents and develop their technology. The animators sought to impress audiences with their abilities to use pictures in such a way that they would forget the earlier fairy tales and remember the images that they, the new artists, were creating for them. Through these moving pictures, the animators appropriated literary and oral fairy tales to subsume the word, to have the final word, often through image and book, for Disney began publishing books during the 1930s to complement his films.

Of all the early animators, Disney was the one who truly revolutionized the fairy tale as institution through the cinema. One could almost say that he was obsessed by the fairy-tale genre, or, put another way, Disney felt drawn to fairy tales because they reflected his own struggles in life. After all, Disney came from a relatively poor family, suffered from the exploitative and stern treatment of an unaffectionate father, was spurned by his early sweetheart, and became a success due to his tenacity, cunning, courage, and his ability to gather around him talented artists and managers like his brother Roy.

One of his early films, *Puss in Boots* (1922), is crucial for grasping his approach to the literary fairy tale and understanding how he used it as self- figuration that would mark the genre for years to come. Disney did not especially care whether one knew the original Perrault text of *Puss in Boots* or some other popular version. It is also unclear which text he actually knew. However, what is clear is that Disney sought to replace all versions with his animated version and that his cartoon is astonishingly autobiographical.

If we recall, Perrault wrote his tale in 1697 to reflect upon a cunning cat whose life is threatened and who manages to survive by using his brains to trick a king and an ogre. On a symbolic level, the cat represented Perrault's conception of the role of the *haute bourgeoisie* (his own class), who comprised the administrative class of Louis the XIV's court and who were often the mediators between the peasantry and aristocracy. Of course, there are numerous ways to read Perrault's tale, but whatever approach one chooses, it is apparent that the major protagonist is the cat.

This is not the case in Disney's film. The hero is a young man, a commoner, who is in love with the king's daughter, and she fondly returns his affection. At the same time, the hero's black cat, a female, is having a romance with the royal white cat, who is the king's chauffeur. When the gigantic king discovers that the young man is wooing his daughter, he kicks him out of the palace, followed by Puss. At first, the hero does not want Puss's help, nor will he buy her the boots that she sees in a shop window. Then they go to the movies together and see a film with Rudolph Vaselino as a bullfighter, a reference to the famous Rudolph Valentino. This spurs the imagination of Puss. Consequently, she tells the hero that she now has an idea that will help him win the king's daughter, provided that he will buy her the boots. Of course, the hero will do anything to obtain the king's daughter, and he must disguise himself as a masked bullfighter. In the meantime Puss explains to him that she will use a hypnotic machine behind the scenes so he can defeat the bull and win the approval of the king. When the day of the bullfight arrives, the masked hero struggles but eventually manages to defeat the bull. The king is so overwhelmed by his performance that he offers his daughter's hand in marriage, but first he wants to know who the masked champion is. When the hero reveals himself, the king is enraged, but the hero grabs the princess and leads her' to the king's chauffeur, The white cat jumps in front with Puss, and they speed off with the king vainly chasing after them.

Although Puss as cunning cat is crucial in this film, Disney focuses most of his attention on the young man who wants to succeed at all costs. In contrast to the traditional fairy tale, the hero is not a peasant, nor is he dumb. Read as a "parable" of Disney's life at that moment, the hero can be seen as young Disney wanting to break into the industry of animated films (the king) with the help of Ub Iwerks (Puss). The hero upsets the king and runs off with his prize possession, the virginal princess. Thus, the king is dispossessed, and the young man outraces him with the help of his friends.

But Disney's film is also an attack on the literary tradition of the fairy tale. He robs the literary tale of its voice and changes its form and meaning. Since the cinematic medium is a popular form of expression and accessible to the public at large, Disney actually returns the fairy tale to the majority of people. The images (scenes, frames, characters, gestures, jokes) are readily comprehensible by young and old alike from different social classes. In fact, the fairy tale is practically infantilized, just as the jokes are infantile. The plot records the deepest oedipal desire of every young boy: the son humiliates and undermines the father and runs off with his most valued object of love, the daughter/wife. By simplifying this oedipal complex semiotically in black-and-white drawings and making fun of it so that it had a common appeal, Disney also touched on other themes:

1. Democracy—the film is very *American* in its attitude toward royalty. The monarchy is debunked, and a commoner causes a kind of revolution.
2. Technology—it is through the new technological medium of the movies that Puss's mind is stimulated. Then she uses a hypnotic machine to defeat the bull and another fairly new invention, the automobile, to escape the king.
3. Modernity—the setting is obviously the twentieth century, and the modern minds are replacing the ancient. The revolution takes place as the king is outpaced and will be replaced by a commoner who knows how to use the latest inventions.

But who is this commoner? Was Disney making a statement on behalf of the masses? Was Disney celebrating "everyone" or "every man"? Did Disney believe in revolution and socialism? The answer to all these questions is simple: no.

Casting the Commodity Spell with *Snow White*

Disney's hero is the enterprising young man, the entrepreneur, who uses technology to his advantage. He does nothing to help the people or the community. In fact, he deceives the masses and the king by creating the illusion that he is stronger than the bull. He has learned, with the help of Puss, that one can achieve glory through deception. It is through the artful use of images that one can sway audiences and gain their favor. Animation is trickery—trick films—for still images are made to seem as if they move through automatization. As long as one controls the images (and machines) one can reign supreme, just as the hero is safe as long as he is disguised. The pictures conceal the controls and machinery. They deprive the audience of viewing the production and manipulation, and in the end, audiences can no longer envision a fairy tale for themselves as they can when they read it. The pictures now deprive the audience of visualizing their own characters, roles, and desires. At the same time, Disney offsets the deprivation with the pleasure of scopophilia and inundates the viewer with delightful images, humorous figures, and erotic signs. In general, the animator, Disney, projects the enjoyable fairy tale of his life through his own images, and he realizes through animated stills his basic oedipal dream that he was to play out time and again in most of his fairy-tale films. It is the repetition of Disney's infantile quest—the core of American mythology—that enabled him to strike a chord in American viewers from the 1920s to the present.

However, it was not through *Puss in Boots* and his other early animated fairy tales that he was to captivate audiences and set the "classical" modern model for animated fairy-tale films. They were just the beginning. Rather, it was in *Snow White and the Seven Dwarfs* (1937) that Disney fully appropriated the literary fairy tale and made his signature into a trademark for the most acceptable type of fairy tale in the twentieth century. But before the making of *Snow White*, there were developments in his life and in the film industry that are important to mention in order to grasp why and how *Snow White* became the first definitive animated fairy-tale film—definitive in the sense that it was to define the way other animated films in the genre of the fairy tale were to be made.

After Disney had made several Laugh-O-Gram fairy-tale films, all ironic and modern interpretations of the classical versions, he moved to Hollywood in 1923 and was successful in producing fifty-six *Alice* films, which involved a young girl in different adventures with cartoon characters. By 1927 these films were no longer popular, so Disney and Iwerks soon developed Oswald the Lucky Rabbit cartoons that also found favor with audiences. However, in February of 1928, while Disney was in New York trying to renegotiate a contract with his distributor Charles Mintz, he learned that Mintz, who owned the copyright to Oswald, had lured some of Disney's best animators to work for another studio. Disney faced bankruptcy because he refused to capitulate to the exploitative conditions that Mintz set for the distribution and production of Disney's films (Mosley 1985, 85–140). This experience sobered Disney in his attitude to the cutthroat competition in the film industry, and when he returned to Hollywood, he vowed to maintain complete control over all his productions—a vow that he never broke.

In the meantime, Disney and Iwerks had to devise another character for their company if they were to survive, and they conceived the idea for films featuring a pert mouse named Mickey. By September of 1928, after making two Mickey Mouse shorts, Disney, similar to his masked champion in *Puss in Boots*, had devised a way to gain revenge on Mintz and other animation studios by producing the first animated cartoon with sound, *Steamboat Willie*, starring Mickey Mouse. From this point on, Disney became known for introducing new inventions and improving animation so that animated films became almost as realistic as films with live actors and natural settings. His next step after sound was color, and in 1932 he signed an exclusive contract with Technicolor and began producing his *Silly Symphony* cartoons in color. More important, Disney released *The Three Little Pigs* in 1933 and followed it with *The Big Bad Wolf* (1934) and *The Three Little Wolves* (1936), all of which involved fairy-tale characters and stories that touched on the lives of people during the Depression. As Bob Thomas has remarked," *The Three Little Pigs* was acclaimed by the Nation. The wolf was on many American doorsteps, and Who's Afraid of the Big Bad Wolf?' became a rallying cry" (1991, 49). Not only were wolves on the doorsteps of Americans but also witches, and to a certain extent, Disney, with the help of his brother Roy and Iwerks, had been keeping "evil" connivers and competitors from the entrance to the Disney Studios throughout the 1920s. Therefore, it is not by chance that Disney's next major experiment would involve a banished princess, loved by a charming prince, who would triumph over deceit and regain the rights to her castle. *Snow White and the Seven Dwarfs* was to bring together all the personal strands of Disney's own story with the destinies of desperate Americans who sought hope and solidarity in their fight for survival during the Depression of the 1930s.

Of course, by 1934 Disney was, comparatively speaking, wealthy. He hired Don Graham, a professional artist, to train studio animators at the Disney Art School, founded in November 1932. He then embarked on ventures to stun moviegoers with his ingenuity and talents as organizer, storyteller, and filmmaker. Conceived some time in 1934, *Snow White* was to take three years to complete, and Disney did not leave one stone unturned in his preparations for the first full-length animated fairy-tale film ever made. Disney knew he was making history even before history had been made.

During the course of the next three years, Disney worked closely with all the animators and technicians assigned to the production of *Snow White*. By now, Disney had divided his studio into numerous departments, such as animation, layout, sound, music, storytelling, etc., and had placed certain animators in charge of developing the individual characters of Snow White, the prince, the dwarfs, and the queen/crone. Disney spent thousands of dollars on a multiplane camera to capture the live-action depictions that he desired, the depth of the scenes, and close-ups. In addition, he had his researchers experiment with colored gels, blurred focus, and filming through frosted glass, while he employed the latest inventions in sound and music to improve the synchronization with the characters on the screen. Throughout-the entire production of this film, Disney had to be consulted and give his approval for each stage of development. After all, *Snow White* was his story that he had taken from the Grimm Brothers and changed completely to suit his tastes and beliefs. He- cast a spell over this German tale and transformed it into something peculiarly American. Just what were the changes he induced?

1. Snow White is an orphan. Neither her father nor her mother are alive, and she is at first depicted as a kind of "Cinderella," cleaning the castle as a maid in a patched dress. In the Grimms' version there is the sentimental death of her mother. Her father remains alive, and she is never forced to do the work of commoners such as wash the steps of the castle.

2. The prince appears at the very beginning of the film on a white horse and sings a song of love and devotion to Snow White. He plays a negligible role in the Grimms' version.

3. The queen is not only jealous that Snow White is more beautiful than she is, but she also sees the prince singing to Snow White and is envious because her stepdaughter has such a handsome suitor.

4. Though the forest and the animals do not speak, they are anthropomorphized. In particular the animals befriend Snow White and become her protectors.

5. The dwarfs are hardworking and rich miners. They all have names—Doc, Sleepy, Bashful, Happy, Sneezy, Grumpy, Dopey—representative of certain human characteristics and are fleshed out so that they become the star attractions of the film. Their actions are what counts in defeating evil. In the Grimms' tale, the dwarfs are anonymous and play a humble role.

6. The queen only comes one time instead of three as in the Grimms' version, and she is killed while trying to destroy the dwarfs by rolling a huge stone down a mountain to crush them. The punishment in the Grimms' tale is more horrifying because she must dance in red-hot iron shoes at Snow White's wedding.

7. Snow White does not return to life when a dwarf stumbles while carrying the glass coffin as in the Grimms' tale. She returns to life when the prince, who has searched far and wide for her, arrives and bestows a kiss on her lips. His kiss of love is the only antidote to the queen's poison.

At first glance, it would seem that the changes that Disney made were not momentous. If we recall Sandra Gilbert and Susan Gubar's stimulating analysis in their book, *The Madwoman in the Attic* (1979), the film follows the classic "sexist" narrative about the framing of women's lives through a male discourse. Such male framing drives women to frustration and some women to the point of madness. It also pits women against women in competition for male approval (the mirror) of their beauty that is short-lived. No matter what they may do, women cannot chart their own lives without male manipulation and intervention, and in the Disney film, the prince plays even more of a framing role since he is introduced at the beginning while Snow White is singing,"I'm Wishing for the One I Love To Find Me Today." He will also appear at the end as the fulfillment of her dreams.

There is no doubt that Disney retained key ideological features of the Grimms' fairy tale that reinforce nineteenth-century patriarchal notions that Disney shared with the Grimms. In some way, they can even be considered his ancestor, for he preserves and carries on many of their benevolent attitudes toward women. For instance, in the Grimms' tale, when Snow White arrives at the cabin, she pleads with the dwarfs to allow her to remain and promises that she will wash the dishes, mend their clothes, and clean the house. In Disney's film, she arrives and notices that the house is dirty. So, she convinces the animals to help her make the cottage tidy so that the dwarfs will perhaps let her stay there. Of course, the house for the Grimms and Disney was the place where good girls remained, and one shared aspect of the fairy tale and the film is about the domestication of women.

However, Disney went much further than the Grimms to make his film more memorable than the tale, for he does not celebrate the domestication of women so much as the triumph of the banished and the underdogs. That is, he celebrates his destiny, and insofar as he had shared marginal status with many Americans, he also celebrates an American myth of Horatio Alger: it is a male myth about perseverance, hard work, dedication, loyalty, and justice.

It may seem strange to argue that Disney perpetuated a male myth through his fairy-tale films when, with the exception of *Pinocchio* (1940), they all featured young women as "heroines": *Sleeping Beauty* (1959), *Cinderella* (1950), and *The Little Mermaid* (1989). However, despite their beauty and charm, these figures are pale and pathetic compared to the more active and demonic characters in the film. The witches are not only agents of evil but represent erotic and subversive forces that are more appealing both for the artists who drew them and the audiences.[6] The young women are helpless ornaments in need of protection, and when it comes to the action of the film, they are omitted. In *Snow White and the Seven Dwarfs*, the film does not really become lively until the dwarfs enter the narrative. They are the mysterious characters who inhabit a cottage, and it is through their hard work and solidarity that they are able to maintain a world of justice and restore harmony to the world. The dwarfs can be interpreted as the humble American workers, who pull together during a depression. They keep their spirits up by singing a song "Hi ho, it's home from work we go," or "Hi ho, it's off to work we go," and their determination is the determination of every worker, who will succeed just as long as he does his share while women stay at home and keep the house clean. Of course, it is also possible to see the workers as Disney's own employees, on whom he depended for the glorious outcome of his films. In this regard, the prince can be interpreted as Disney, who directed the love story from the beginning. If we recall, it is the prince who frames the narrative. He announces his great love at the beginning of the film, and Snow White cannot be fulfilled until he arrives to kiss her. During the major action of the film, he, like Disney, is lurking in the background and waiting for the proper time to make himself known. When he does arrive, he takes all the credit as champion of the disenfranchised, and he takes Snow White to his castle while the dwarfs are left as keepers of the forest.

But what has the prince actually done to deserve all the credit? What did Disney actually do to have his name flash on top of the title as "Walt Disney's Snow White and the Seven Dwarfs" in big letters and later credit his coworkers in small letters? As we know, Disney never liked to give credit to the animators who worked with him, and they had to fight for acknowledgment.[7] Disney always made it clear that he was the boss and owned total rights to his products. He had struggled for his independence against his greedy and unjust father and against fierce and ruthless competitors in the film industry. As producer of the fairy-tale films and major owner of the Disney studios, he wanted to figure in the films and sought, as Crafton has noted, to create a more indelible means of self-figuration. In *Snow White*, he accomplished this by stamping his signature as owner on the title frame of the film and then by having himself embodied in the figure of the prince. It is the prince Disney who made inanimate figures come to life through his animated films, and it is the prince who is to be glorified in *Snow White and the Seven Dwarfs* when he resuscitates Snow White with a magic kiss. Afterward he holds Snow White in his arms, and in the final frame, he leads her off on a white horse to his golden castle on a hill. His golden castle—every woman's dream—supersedes the dark, sinister castle of the queen. The prince becomes Snow White's reward, and his power and wealth are glorified in the end.

There are obviously mixed messages or multiple messages in *Snow White and the Seven Dwarfs*, but the overriding sign, in my estimation, is the signature of Disney's self-glorification in the name of justice. Disney wants the world *cleaned up*, and the pastel colors with their sharply drawn ink lines create images of cleanliness, just as each sequence reflects a clearly conceived and preordained destiny for all the characters in the film. For Disney, the Grimms' tale is not a vehicle to explore the deeper implications of the narrative and its history.[8] Rather, it is a vehicle to display what he can do as an animator with the latest technological and artistic developments in the industry. The story is secondary, and if there is a major change in the plot, it centers on the power of the prince, the only one who can save Snow White, and he becomes the focal point by the end of the story.

In Disney's early work with fairy tales in Kansas City, he had a wry and irreverent attitude toward the classical narratives. There was a strong suggestion, given the manner in which he and Iwerks rewrote and filmed the tales, that they were "revolutionaries," the new boys on the block, who were about to introduce innovative methods of animation into the film industry and speak for the outcasts. However, in 1934, Disney was already the kingpin of animation, and he used all that he had learned to reinforce his power and command of fairy-tale animation. The manner in which he copied the musical plays and films of his time, and his close adaptation of fairy tales with patriarchal codes, indicate that all the technical experiments would not be used to foster social change in America but to keep power in the hands of individuals like himself, who felt empowered to design and create new worlds. As Richard Schickel has perceptively remarked, Disney

> could make something his own, all right, but that process nearly always robbed the work at hand of its uniqueness, of its soul, if you will. In its place he put jokes and songs and fright effects, but he always seemed to diminish what he touched. He came always as a conqueror, never as a servant. It is a trait, as many have observed, that many Americans share when they venture into foreign lands hoping to do good but equipped only with knowhow instead of sympathy and respect for alien traditions. (1968,227)

Disney always wanted to do something new and unique just as long as he had absolute control. He also knew that novelty would depend on the collective skills of his employees, whom he had to keep happy or indebted to him in some way. Therefore, from 1934 onward, about the time that he conceived his first feature-length fairy-tale film, Disney became the orchestrator of a corporate network that changed the function of the fairy-tale genre in America. The power of Disney's fairy-tale films does not reside in the uniqueness or novelty of the productions, but in Disney's great talent for holding antiquated views of society *still* through animation and his use of the latest technological developments in cinema to his advantage. His adaptation of the literary fairy tale for the screen led to the following changes in the institution of the genre:

1. Technique takes precedence over the story, and the story is used to celebrate the technician and his means.

2. The carefully arranged images narrate through seduction and imposition of the animator's hand and the camera.

3. The images and sequences engender a sense of wholeness, seamless totality, and harmony that is orchestrated by a savior/technician on and off the screen.

4. Though the characters are fleshed out to become more realistic, they are also one-dimensional and are to serve functions in the film. There is no character development because the characters are stereotypes, arranged according to a credo of domestication of the imagination.

5. The domestication is related to colonization insofar as the ideas and types are portrayed as models of behavior to be emulated. Exported through the screen as models, the "American" fairy tale colonizes other national audiences. What is good for Disney is good for the world, and what is good in a Disney fairy tale is good in the rest of the world.

6. The thematic emphasis on cleanliness, control, and organized industry reinforces the technics of the film itself: the clean frames with attention paid to every detail; the precise drawing and manipulation of the characters as real people; the careful plotting of the events that focus on salvation through the male hero.

7. Private reading pleasure is replaced by pleasurable viewing in an impersonal cinema. Here one is brought together with other viewers not for the development of community but to be diverted in the French sense of *divertissement* and American sense of diversion.

8. The diversion of the Disney fairy tale is geared toward nonreflective viewing. Everything is on the surface, one-dimensional, and we are to delight in one-dimensional portrayal and thinking, for it is adorable, easy, and comforting in its simplicity.

Once Disney realized how successful he was with his formula for feature- length fairy tales, he never abandoned it, and in fact, if one regards the two most recent Disney Studio productions of *Beauty and the Beast* (1991) and *Aladdin* (1992), Disney's contemporary animators have continued in his footsteps. There is nothing but the "eternal return of the same" in *Beauty and the Beast* and *Aladdin* that makes for enjoyable viewing and delight in techniques of these films as commodities, but nothing new in the exploration of narration, animation, and signification.

There is something sad in the manner in which Disney "violated" the literary genre of the fairy tale and packaged his versions in his name through the merchandising of books, toys, clothing, and records. Instead of using technology to enhance the communal aspects of narrative and bring about major changes in viewing stories to stir and animate viewers, he employed animators and technology to stop thinking about change, to return to his films, and to long nostalgically for neatly ordered patriarchal realms. Fortunately, the animation of the literary fairy tale did not stop with Disney, but that is another tale to tell, a tale about breaking Disney's magic spell.

Notes

1. See Straparola's *Le piacevoli notti* (1550–53), translated as *The Facetious Nights* or *The Delectable Nights*, and Basile's *Lo Cunto de li Cunti {The Story of Stories,* 1634–36), better known as *The Pentamerone.* The

reason that the Italians did not "institutionalize" the genre is that the literary culture in Italy was not prepared to introduce the tales as part of the civilizing process, nor were there groups of writers who made the fairy-tale genre part of their discourse.

2. Cf. *Die Domestizierte Phantasie: Studien zur Kinderliteratur, Kinderlektüre und Literaturpädagogik des 18. und frühen 19—Jahrhunderts* (Heidelberg: Carl Winter, 1987).

3. This list would include the Grimms, Wilhelm Hauff, Ludwig Bechstein, Hans Christian Andersen, and Madame De Ségur. In addition, numerous collections of expurgated folk tales from different countries became popular in primers by the end of the nineteenth century. Here one would have to mention the series of color fairy books edited by Andrew Lang in Great Britain.

4. Cf. Russell Merrit and J. B. Kaufman, *Walt in Wonderland: The Silent Films of Walt Disney,* for the most complete coverage of Disney's early development.

5. I am purposely using the word designer instead of animator because Disney was always designing things, made designs, and had designs. A designer is someone who indicates with a distinctive mark, and Disney put his mark on everything in his studios. A designing person is often a crafty person who manages to put his schemes into effect by hook or by crook. Once Disney stopped animating, he became a designer.

6. Solomon cites the famous quotation by Woody Allen in *Annie Hall*: "You know, even as a kid I always went for the wrong women. When my mother took me to see 'Snow White,' everyone fell in love with Snow White; I immediately fell for the Wicked Queen" (1980, 28).

7. Bill Peet, for example, an "in-betweener" in the early Disney studio, worked for a year and a half on *Pinocchio* (1940). Peet relates that, after watching the film in his neighborhood theatre,"I was dumbfounded when the long list of screen credits didn't include my name" (1989, 108).

8. Karen Merritt makes the interesting point that "Disney's *Snow White* is an adaptation of a 1912 children's play (Disney saw it as a silent movie during his adolescence) still much performed today, written by a male Broadway producer under a female pseudonym; this play was an adaptation of a play for immigrant children from the tenements of lower East Side New York; and that play, in turn, was a translation and adaptation of a German play for children by a prolific writer of children's comedies and fairy-tale drama. Behind these plays was the popularity of nineteenth- and early twentieth-century fairy-tale pantomimes at Christmas in England and fairy-tale plays in Germany and America. The imposition of childish behavior on the dwarfs, Snow White's resulting mothering, the age ambiguities in both Snow White and the dwarfs, the 'Cinderella' elements, and the suppression of any form of sexuality were transmitted by that theatrical tradition, which embodied a thoroughly developed philosophy of moral education in representations for children. … By reading Disney's *Snow White* by the light of overt didacticism of his sources, he no longer appears the moral reactionary disdained by contemporary critics. Rather, he is the entertainer who elevates the subtext of play found in his sources and dares once again to frighten children" (1994, 106). Though it may be true that Disney was more influenced by an American theatrical and film tradition, the source of all these productions, one acknowledged by Disney, was the Grimms' tale. And, as I have argued, Disney was not particularly interested in experimenting with the narrative to shock children or provide a new perspective on the traditional story. For all intents and purposes his film reinforces the didactic messages of the Grimms' tale, and it is only in the technical innovations and designs that he did something startlingly new. It is not the object of critique to "disdain" or "condemn" Disney for reappropriating the Grimms' tradition to glorify the great designer, but to understand those cultural and psychological forces that led him to map out his narrative strategies in fairy-tale animation.

References

Armstrong, Nancy, and Leonard Tennenhouse, eds. 1989. *The Violence of Representation: Literature and the History of Violence.* New York: Routledge.

Benjamin, Walter. 1968. "The Work of Art in the Age of Mechanical Reproduction." In *Illuminations,* trans. Harry Zohn. New York: Harcourt, Brace & World.

Crafton, Donald. 1 9 8 2. *Before Mickey: The Animated Film 1898–1928,* Cambridge: MIT Press.

Gilbert, Sandra, and Susan Gubar. 1979. *The Madwoman in the Attic: The Woman Writer and the 'Nineteenth-Century Literary Imagination.* New Haven: Yale University Press.

Jacobs, Lewis. 1979. "George Méliès: Artificiality Arranged Scenes." *In The Emergence of Film Art: The Evolution and Development of the Motion Picture as an Art, from 1900 to the Present,* ed. Lewis Jacobs. 2 N D ed. New York: Norton.

Merritt, Karen. 1988. "The Little Girl/Little Mother Transformation: The American Evolution of 'Snow White and the Seven Dwarfs.' " In *Storytelling in Animation: The Art of the Animated Image,* ed. John Canemaker. Los Angeles: American Film Institute.

Merritt, Russell, and J. B. Kaufman. 1994 – *Walt in Wonderland: The Silent Films of Walt Disney.* Baltimore: Johns Hopkins University Press.

Mosley, Leonard. 1985. *Disney3s World.* New York: Stein and Day.

Peet, Bill. 1989. *Bill Feet: An Autobiography.* Boston: Houghton Mifflin.

Schickel, Richard. 1968. *The Disney Version.* New York: Simon and Schuster.

Solomon, Charles. *1980.* "Bad Girls Finish First in Memory of Disney Fans." *Milwaukee Journal,* 17 August.

Thomas, Bob. 1991. *Disney's Art of Animation: From Mickey Mouse to Beauty and the Beast.* New York: Hyperion.

Zipes, Jack. 1989. "The Rise of the French Fairy Tale and the Decline of France." In *Beauties, Beasts and Enchantment: Classic French Fairy Tales,* trans. Jack Zipes. New York: New American Library.